SIXTH EDITION

Language Awareness

SIXTH EDITION

Language
Awareness

EDITORS

Paul Eschholz

Alfred Rosa

Virginia Clark

University of Vermont

ST. MARTIN'S PRESS   New York

Senior editor: Catherine Pusateri
Development editor: Edward Hutchinson
Manager, publishing services: Emily Berleth
Project management: Denise Quirk
Art director: Sheree Goodman
Cover art: Marek Antoniak
Cartoonist: Jeff Danziger

For information, write:
St. Martin's Press, Inc.
175 Fifth Avenue
New York, NY 10010

ISBN: 0-312-08410-2

ACKNOWLEDGMENTS

Acknowledgments and copyrights are continued at the back of the book on pages 509–511, which constitute an extension of the copyright page.

It is a violation of the law to reproduce these selections by any means whatsoever without the written permission of the copyright holder.

Allport, Gordon. "The Language of Prejudice." From *The Nature of Prejudice*, © 1979 by Addison-Wesley Publishing Company, Inc. Reprinted with permission of the publisher.

AT&T. Ad. Reprinted by permission of AT&T.

Birk, Newman P., and Genevieve B. Birk. "Selection, Slanting, and Charged Language." Reprinted with the permission of Macmillan Publishing Company from *Understanding and Using English*, Fifth Edition, by Newman P. Birk and Genevieve B. Birk. Copyright © 1972 by Macmillan Publishing Company.

Borden, Inc. Ad. Reprinted by permission of Borden, Inc.

Bryson, Bill. "Order out of Chaos." From *The Mother Tongue: English and How It Got That Way* by Bill Bryson. Copyright © 1990 by Bill Bryson. By permission of William Morrow & Company, Inc.

Callen, Michael. "AIDS: The Linguistic Battlefield." By Michael Callen in Christopher Ricks and Leonard Michaels, *The State of the Language*, 1990 ed., pages 171–181. Copyright © 1989 The Regents of the University of California. Reprinted by permission. Founding Mission Statement of the National Association of People with AIDS. Reprinted by permission.

Chevron. Ad. Reprinted by permission of Chevron.

CIBA-GEIGY Corp. Ad. Reprinted by permission of CIBA-GEIGY Corp.

Consumers Union. "It's Natural! It's Organic! Or Is It?" Copyright © 1980 by Consumers Union of U.S., Inc. Yonkers, NY 10703–1057. Reprinted by permission from *Consumer Reports*, July 1980.

Cross, Donna Woolfolk. "Propaganda: How Not to Be Bamboozled." By Donna Woolfolk Cross. From *Speaking of Words: A Language Reader*. Reprinted by permission of Donna Woolfolk Cross.

PREFACE

Since the first edition of *Language Awareness* appeared in 1974, its purpose has been twofold: to foster an appreciation of the richness, flexibility, and vitality of the English language and to encourage and help students to use their language more responsibly and effectively in speech and particularly in writing. Because of these purposes, *Language Awareness* has been used in a variety of courses over the years. Its primary use, however, has been and continues to be in college composition courses. Clearly, many instructors believe as we do that the study of language and the study of writing go hand in hand.

The study of language has many facets; so, while covering a broad spectrum of topics (including the history of English, contemporary debates on cultural diversity and the use and misuse of Standard English, the language of prejudice and of euphemism, for example), we have tried to concentrate on those areas in which language use exerts the widest social effects—politics, advertising, media, and gender roles. Opening students' eyes to the power of language—its ability to shape and to manipulate one's understanding, perceptions, and cultural attitudes—is, we believe, one of the worthiest goals a writing class can pursue.

We also provide extensive material to help students improve their abilities as readers and writers. As in the fifth edition, the **general introduction** to *Language Awareness* provides a discussion of reading and writing that includes **guidelines and questions** students can use to increase their abilities as thoughtful, analytical readers, as well as explanations of how the various writing strategies can be put to work. At the end of the text an **alternate table of contents** classifies the reading selections in *Language Awareness* according to the rhetorical strategies they exemplify, and a **detailed glossary** defines rhetorical terms and concepts important to the study of writing.

The fifty-six readings in *Language Awareness* have been chosen not only for their subject matter but also to provide students of composition with practical illustrations of rhetorical principles and techniques. After each selection, in addition to **questions on the content of the essay**, we have provided **questions that address these rhetorical concerns**, adding cross-references to the glossary where useful. The **vocabulary list** after each selection calls attention to a few words that students will find worth adding to their own active vocabularies. Finally, two or more **writing topics** follow each reading, and each section concludes with **topics and guidelines** for writing essays that make connections among the readings in the section. In our own teaching we have found such topics helpful in promoting both writing and classroom discussion of language issues.

NEW TO THIS EDITION

As always, we have emphasized pieces written in nontechnical language on topics and issues of current interest. Guided by comments and advice from many colleagues across the country who have used the fifth edition, we have retained in this new edition those essays that teachers and students have valued most. But over half of the selections in *Language Awareness* are new to this edition. Among the **thirty-three new essays** are William Lutz's analysis of public doublespeak; Bill Bryson's popular discussion of three early dictionary makers and the "order" that they've brought to English; Peggy Noonan's examination of the process by which a political speech comes into being; Rosalie Maggio's timely discussion of ways to avoid the use of discriminatory language; and Deborah Tannen's exploration of the differences between the ways men and women talk.

In response to the many requests for actual political language for analysis, we have added a **casebook of texts and speeches** to Part 4. Included are Thomas Jefferson's Declaration of Independence, Elizabeth Cady Stanton's "Declaration of Sentiments and Resolutions," Abraham Lincoln's Gettysburg Address, John F. Kennedy's Inaugural Address, Martin Luther King, Jr.'s "I Have a Dream," and Bill Clinton's 1993 Inaugural Address. These eighteenth-, nineteenth-, and twentieth-century texts offer students a variety of styles, purposes, and language. Each selection is followed by a number of **questions for study and discussion** designed to help students identify the key points and rhetorical features of the text. **Writing assignments** at the end of Part 4 ask students to compare and contrast both the content and the rhetorical features of two or more of the texts.

Many instructors asked us to include more on **advertising**, so we have expanded that section, adding Gloria Steinem's provocative and candid look at the often shady relationship between advertisers and women's magazines, and five contemporary advertisements for students to analyze. Other users asked for several new articles in the **section on gender and languge**, so we have added Deborah Tannen's essay on gender-related differences in speech and Bernard R. Goldberg's essay on "male bashing" in television sitcoms and commercials.

Students and teachers asked us for more **essays about censorship**, so we have included a new section called "Censorship and the First Amendment." Free-speech advocate Nat Hentoff questions the rise of speech codes on college campuses, while Susan Jacoby rejects feminist arguments for the censorship of pornography. Censorship and the world of rock music is the subject of the essays by Caryl Rivers, Tipper Gore, and Frank Zappa. Other new sections created in response to reader demand include **"Usage, Words, and Standard English"**—essays that explore the varieties of English and their relation to Standard English—and **"Cul-**

tural Diversity: Searching for Common Ground"—essays that recount experiences when two cultures, and thus two languages, collide. Users of previous editions of *Language Awareness* will notice that we have retitled some sections in an effort to articulate more clearly the issues under discussion.

All of our aims in *Language Awareness* are serious ones, but a serious book need not be humorless or unnecessarily academic. William Lutz's "The World of Doublespeak" addresses the problem of using language to deceive or manipulate, but some of his examples are sure to bring a smile to your face. There's humor and wit also in Lance Morrow's "If Slang Is Not a Sin"; Peggy Noonan's "Speech! Speech!"; Barbara Ehrenreich's "Drawing the Line"; and Frank Zappa's "The Wives of Big Brother"—among others. Indeed, we like to think that readers of *Language Awareness* will have as much fun using this edition as we have had in preparing it.

ACKNOWLEDGMENTS

We are grateful to the following colleagues across the country who have sent helpful reactions and suggestions for this sixth edition: Janice Albert, Las Positas College; Lena Ampadu, Towson State University; Anne M. Boyle, Wake Forest University; Jo Ann Campbell, Indiana University; Ralph Carlson, Azusa Pacific University; Hal Colony, University of Nebraska at Kearney; Charles S. Didier, Housatonic Community College; Belden Durtschi, Shoreline Community College; Don Ellis, University of Hartford; Kenneth J. Ericksen, Linfield College; Barbara Fox, University of Colorado; Helen Frink, Keene State College; Cayo Gamber, George Washington University; Claudia Greenwood, Kent State University; Dorothy Margaret Guinn, Florida Atlantic University; Jorge Guitart, State University of New York at Buffalo; Sheila Gullickson, Moorhead State University; Alan C. Hardis, California State University at Northridge; Greg Jacob, Pacific University; Philip Kaltenbach, Guilford College; Patricia Killian, Salisbury State University; Paula Krebs, Wheaton College; Zhihua Long, University of Colorado; Carol R. Mehler, Kent State College; Tracy Montgomery, Idaho State University; Dallin Oaks, Brigham Young University; Shaun O'Connor, University of Arizona; Cornelia Paraskevas, Western Oregon State College; Doris M. Piatak, Kishwaukee College; Michael T. Siconolfi, Gonzaga University; Michele Geslin Small, Northland College; Sandra Stephan, Youngstown State University; Stephen H. Stremmel, American River College; Richard Sweterlitsch, University of Vermont.

We would like to express our appreciation to the staff at St. Martin's Press, especially Cathy Pusateri and Edward Hutchinson. Our special thanks go to Samuel Feitelberg and the faculty and staff of the race and culture program at the University of Vermont for their help in selecting articles on issues of cultural diversity and then testing the usefulness of these articles in their classes. Our thanks also go to Susan Palmer for her work on the *Instructor's Manual* that accompanies this edition. Finally, we are grateful to all our students at the University of Vermont for their enthusiasm for language study and writing and their invaluable responses to materials included in this book. They teach us something new every day.

PAUL ESCHHOLZ
ALFRED ROSA
VIRGINIA CLARK

CONTENTS

Introduction   1

I   DISCOVERING LANGUAGE   7

Malcolm X **Coming to an Awareness of Language   9**
"I saw that the best thing I could do was get hold of a dictionary—to study, to learn some words."

Helen Keller **The Day Language Came into My Life   13**
The celebrated deaf and blind writer recalls her discovery of language.

Peter Farb **The Story of Human Language   17**
"Not every human being can play the violin, do calculus, jump high hurdles, or sail a canoe, no matter how excellent his teachers or how arduous his training—but every person constantly creates utterances never before spoken on earth."

Victoria Fromkin and Robert Rodman **What Is Language?   25**
"To understand our humanity we must understand the language that makes us human."

Writing Assignments for "Discovering Language"   34

II   LANGUAGE USE AND MISUSE   37

S. I. Hayakawa and Alan R. Hayakawa **Giving Things Names   39**
Two semanticists believe that naming "is not a matter of identifying 'essences.' It is simply a reflection of social convenience or necessity."

Newman P. Birk and Genevieve B. Birk **Selection, Slanting, and Charged Language   47**
Two researchers describe some ways language can be manipulated to create particular impressions.

William Lutz **The World of Doublespeak   59**
An English professor exposes the disguises of doublespeak, "language which pretends to communicate but doesn't."

George Orwell **Politics and the English Language   70**
The English language is like the air we breathe. When it becomes polluted, we all suffer.

Writing Assignments for "Language Use and Misuse"   83

III   USAGE, WORDS, AND STANDARD ENGLISH   87

Paul Roberts   **A Brief History of English**   89

"In 1500 English was a minor language, spoken by a few people on a small island. Now it is perhaps the greatest language of the world."

David Crystal   **The Prescriptive Tradition**   101

A British linguist examines the prescriptivist attitudes that "motivate a widespread concern that linguistic standards should be maintained."

Bill Bryson   **Order out of Chaos**   108

"The English-speaking world has the finest dictionaries, a somewhat curious fact when you consider that we have never formalized the business of compiling them."

Dorothy Z. Seymour   **Black Children, Black Speech**   122

"Should children who speak Black English be excused from learning the Standard in school? Should they perhaps be given books in Black English to learn from?"

Rachel L. Jones   **What's Wrong with Black English**   131

A student's goal is to see more black people, like herself, "less dependent on a dialect that excludes them from full participation."

Lance Morrow   **If Slang Is Not a Sin**   135

A respected columnist explores the relative decline of slang in America.

Robert MacNeil   **English Belongs to Everybody**   140

A language enthusiast puts to rest the fear that English is on the skids as some pop-grammarians would have the public believe.

Writing Assignments for "Usage, Words, and Standard English"   145

IV   THE LANGUAGE OF POLITICS   147

Donna Woolfolk Cross   **Propaganda: How Not to Be Bamboozled**   149

"If we are to continue to be a government 'by the people,' let us become informed about the methods and purposes of propaganda, so we can be the masters, not the slaves of our destiny."

Peggy Noonan   **"Speech! Speech!"**   160

"Speeches are important because they are one of the great constants of our political history."

Casebook: A Selection of Political Texts for Analysis   176

Thomas Jefferson   **The Declaration of Independence**   176

No document in history offers a more logical or stirring argument for human rights than the Declaration of Independence.

Elizabeth Cady Stanton   **Declaration of Sentiments and Resolutions**   **181**
A nineteenth-century reformer presents a list of grievances against laws and customs that restrict the rights of all women.

Abraham Lincoln   **The Gettysburg Address**   **186**
The great emancipator renders a classic statement of American ideals and principles of government.

John F. Kennedy   **Inaugural Address**   **188**
A young president implores his fellow Americans to "ask not what your country can do for you; ask what you can do for your country."

Martin Luther King, Jr.   **I Have a Dream**   **192**
The great civil rights leader gives his vision of freedom and equality.

William Jefferson Clinton   **Inaugural Address**   **197**
The first American president born after World War II challenges Americans to "make change our friend and not our enemy."

Writing Assignments for "The Language of Politics"   201

V   THE LANGUAGE OF MEDIA AND ADVERTISING   203

Neil Postman   **"Now . . . This"**   **205**
A media watcher points out the frightening implications of television news programs that fail to see life as a complex series of interrelated events.

Gloria Steinem   **Sex, Lies, and Advertising**   **217**
"The magazines serving the female half of this country are still far below the journalistic and ethical standards of news and general interest publications."

Jib Fowles   **Advertising's Fifteen Basic Appeals**   **231**
A mass media professor examines the basic emotional appeals that advertising makes to each one of us.

Jeffrey Schrank   **The Language of Advertising Claims**   **249**
"Students, and many teachers, are notorious believers in their immunity to advertising."

Ron Rosenbaum   **The Hard Sell**   **257**
A New York writer believes that contemporary advertising has succeeded by boldly scaring and humiliating customers.

Consumers Union   **It's Natural! It's Organic! Or Is It?**   **268**
A nonprofit consumer group wants us to read labels carefully. Many products don't deliver what they seem to promise.

Writing Assignments for "The Language of Media and Advertising"   276

VI   PREJUDICE, DISCRIMINATION, AND LANGUAGE   285

Gordon Allport   **The Language of Prejudice**   287

A leading expert on prejudice discusses some of the ways in which language itself, very often subtly, expresses and even causes prejudice.

S. I. Hayakawa and Alan R. Hayakawa   **Words with Built-in Judgments**   298

The power of some words to hurt and victimize is made clear by these leading language experts.

Gloria Naylor   **The Meanings of a Word**   305

An African-American writer believes that "words themselves are innocuous; it is the consensus that gives them true power."

Rosalie Maggio   **A Guide to Nondiscriminatory Language**   309

"One of the most rewarding . . . side effects of breaking away from traditional, biased language is a dramatic improvement in writing style."

Writing Assignments for "Prejudice, Discrimination, and Language"   322

VII   CULTURAL DIVERSITY: SEARCHING FOR COMMON GROUND   325

Barbara Ehrenreich   **Drawing the Line**   327

A popular journalist spoofs the English-only movement and its motives.

Edite Cunha   **Talking in the New Land**   331

"Your name will be Mary Edith Cunha," she declared. "In America you only need two or three names. Mary Edith is a lovely name. And it will be easier to pronounce."

Roberto Santiago   **Black *and* Latino**   342

"'There is no way that you can be black and Puerto Rican at the same time.' What? Despite the many times I've heard this over the years, that statement still perplexes me."

Itabari Njeri   **What's in a Name?**   345

"'What's your *real* name?'
"'Itabari Njeri is my real, legal name,' I explain."

Amy Tan   **The Language of Discretion**   352

"To this day, I wonder which parts of my behavior were shaped by Chinese, which by English. I am tempted to think, for example, that if I am of two minds on some matter it is due to the richness of my linguistic experiences."

Writing Assignments for "Cultural Diversity: Searching for Common Ground"   361

VIII   GENDER AND LANGUAGE   363

Alleen Pace Nilsen   **Sexism in English: A 1990s Update   365**
A study of the dictionary provides some surprising linguistic evidence for
the view of gender in our society.

Casey Miller and Kate Swift   **One Small Step for Genkind   377**
Two pioneers in the study of sexism and language demonstrate the ways
in which language discriminates against women.

Deborah Tannen   **"I'll Explain It to You": Lecturing and
Listening   389**
"One situation that frustrates many women is a conversation that has
mysteriously turned into a lecture, with the man delivering the lecture to
the woman, who has become an appreciative audience."

Bernard R. Goldberg   **Television Insults Men, Too   404**
A CBS journalist wonders why nobody complains about the male-bashing
taking place on television.

Writing Assignments for "Gender and Language"   407

IX   EUPHEMISM AND TABOOS   411

Neil Postman   **Euphemism   413**
A professor of media ecology argues that while some euphemisms are
bad, others serve worthwhile social purposes.

S. I. Hayakawa and Alan R. Hayakawa   **Verbal Taboo   418**
"In every language, there seem to be 'unmentionables'—words of such
strong affective connotations that they cannot be used in polite discourse."

Barbara Lawrence   **Four-Letter Words Can Hurt You   422**
"Why should any words be called obscene? Don't they all describe natural human functions?"

Michael Callen   **AIDS: The Linguistic Battlefield   426**
"When I was diagnosed in 1982, I decided that I'd have to pay close attention to the language of AIDS—to keep my wits about me in order to
see beyond the obfuscating medical mumbo-jumbo meant to dazzle me
into a deadly passivity."

Writing Assignments for "Euphemism and Taboos"   433

X   CENSORSHIP AND THE FIRST AMENDMENT   437

Nat Hentoff   **"Speech Codes" on the Campus and Problems of Free
Speech   439**
A longtime First Amendment advocate reports on the rise of "speech
codes" on American college campuses.

Susan Jacoby   **Notes from a Free-Speech Junkie**   **447**

An essayist and *Times* columnist takes on feminists out to censor pornography.

Caryl Rivers   **What Should Be Done about Rock Lyrics?**   **451**

"Make no mistake, it is not sex we are talking about here, but violence. Violence against women."

Tipper Gore   **Curbing the Sexploitation Industry**   **455**

"I'm not advocating censorship but rather a candid and vigorous debate about the dangers posed for our children by what I call the 'sexploitation industry.'"

Frank Zappa   **The Wives of Big Brother**   **459**

A famous rock musician questions the motives of the Parents' Music Resource Center.

Writing Assignments for "Censorship and the First Amendment"   466

XI   WRITING WELL: FIVE WRITERS ON WRITING   469

Maxine Hairston   **What Happens When People Write?**   **471**

A respected teacher of writing offers an overview of how professional writers work and then examines two basic types of writing.

Jack Rawlins   **Five Principles for Getting Good Ideas**   **477**

Helpful advice on how to get not just ideas but good ideas.

Linda Flower   **Writing for an Audience**   **483**

"The goal of the writer is to create a momentary common ground between the reader and the writer."

William Zinsser   **Simplicity**   **486**

"If you find that writing is hard, it's because it *is* hard. It's one of the hardest things that people do."

Lewis Thomas   **Notes on Punctuation**   **492**

A leading scientist and writer offers a refreshingly entertaining view of punctuation.

Writing Assignments for "Writing Well: Five Writers on Writing"   495

Rhetorical Table of Contents   497
Glossary of Rhetorical Terms   500
Topics for Research Papers   507

SIXTH EDITION

Language Awareness

INTRODUCTION

Language Awareness is a collection of readings aimed at college writing students and designed to emphasize the crucial role language plays in virtually every aspect of our lives. For most of us language is like the air we breathe: we cannot survive without it, but we take it for granted nearly all of the time. Seldom are we conscious of language's real power to lead us (or mislead us) or of the effect our own use of language has on others. Even rarer is the recognition that our perceptions of the world are influenced, our very thoughts at least partially shaped, by language. It is also true that liberation begins with our awareness of that fact. To foster such an awareness is one of the goals of this book. We hope, therefore, that as you use this text you will gain a heightened appreciation of the richness, flexibility, and vitality of your language and be moved to explore its possibilities further.

THE STUDY OF LANGUAGE

Language is one of humankind's greatest achievements and one of its most important resources. *Language Awareness* represents the most immediate and interesting fields of language study with a diverse range of thought-provoking essays grouped into eleven broad sections. The first part, "Discovering Language," provides an overview of the central issues: the nature of language, the power of words to shape our thinking, and what it means to know a language. Part 2, "Language Use and Misuse," shows the importance of using language responsibly so as not to deceive or manipulate other people. The third part, "Usage, Words, and Standard English," starts with several articles that give an historical perspective on the evolution of the English language, usage standards, and dictionary-making and then moves on to consider the debate between standard and nonstandard English. "The Language of Politics," the fourth part, focuses on the ways leaders can use language to manipulate our thinking or to rouse our sense of purpose and includes a casebook of six political texts for analysis. Part 5, "The Language of Media and Advertising," raises critical questions about the objectivity of network news, the relationship between advertising and editorializing in popular magazines, and the ways advertisers use language to create a positive image for a product, to imply what they cannot say directly, and to exploit consumer vulnerability.

Part 6, "Prejudice, Discrimination, and Language," explores how we can become more sensitive to the ways words can lock us into particular one-dimensional categories, create powerfully discriminatory impres-

1

sions, and deeply affect our judgments of others. In Part 7, "Cultural Diversity: Searching for Common Ground," various writers recount their personal experiences of what happens when languages and cultures collide in the United States. Part 8, "Gender and Language," concentrates specifically on sexism in language, on stereotypical images of women and men implied in our language, and suggests some of the difficulties involved in overcoming linguistic prejudice. In "Euphemisms and Taboos," Part 9, the readings explore how we tend to cloak sensitive topics in "nice" language and confront some of our culture's "dirty words" to determine how and why these words may seem offensive. Part 10, "Censorship and the First Amendment," explores how and why we censor—or decline to censor—through examination of speech codes on college campuses, pornography, and rock music lyrics.

Finally—because our further purpose in this sixth edition of *Language Awareness*, as in earlier editions, is to encourage you to write responsibly and effectively—we have included in our final section, "Writing Well: Five Writers on Writing," essays in which professional writers reflect on their craft, on the way they write. Each writer offers practical advice on the qualities of good writing and the writing process—getting started, drafting, identifying an audience, being truthful to yourself and your audience, revising, and editing. Although this section is at the end of the book, you may find the readings useful as you start your writing course, because together they provide a detailed overview of the composing process. Or, as you work on particular assignments during the school term, you may want to look at one or more of these essays for direction and encouragement about specific aspects of your writing.

The common denominator of all good writing is the writer's conscious concern for language, and this concern is emphasized, in various ways, by every essay in *Language Awareness*. We have chosen them not only because they explore important issues of language and communication but also because they provide excellent models of how writers give effective expression to their thoughts. Thus, reading and studying the selections throughout the text, by making you more sensitive to how you use language yourself and to how the language of others affects you, can help you become a better reader and, perhaps most important, a better writer. The more aware you are of the many subtleties and complexities of language use, the greater your mastery and control of language will be. This sense of control will, in turn, allow you to read more thoughtfully and critically and to achieve greater competence and confidence in your own writing.

THE IMPORTANCE OF READING WELL

Reading is most rewarding when you do it actively, in a thoughtful spirit and with an alert and inquiring mind. For writers—and in one way or another we are all writers—there are special reasons to cultivate the habits and skills of careful, attentive reading. By analyzing the ideas and techniques of the writers you read, you can increase your mastery and refine your own personal style as a writer. Furthermore, for everything you write you will be your own first reader and critic. How well you are able to read your own drafts will powerfully affect how well you can revise them; and revising well is crucial to writing well. So, close, critical reading of what others have written is useful and important practice for anyone who wishes to improve his or her writing skills.

Your first important task as a reader sensitive to language is to read every essay assigned from this text at least twice. In your first reading you will be concerned primarily with understanding the points about language a writer is trying to make. In your second reading—and perhaps even a third—you can refine and develop your understanding of the content, working especially at the difficult passages and analyzing more carefully the author's purpose and his or her means of achieving that purpose. You should determine which features of the essay's organization and style seem particularly successful, so you can learn from them and, perhaps, adapt them to your own work. You may also begin to look for the general strategy or strategies a writer uses to develop the essay's ideas. For example, Malcom X uses *narration* to tell the story of his "Coming to an Awareness of Language." In "The Language of Advertising Claims," Jeffrey Shrank uses *classification* to explain the different strategies and techniques advertisers use to manipulate the public. In her essay "Black Children, Black Speech," Dorothy Z. Seymour uses *comparison and contrast* to detail the similarities and differences between Black English and Standard English. And in "What Should Be Done about Rock Lyrics?" Caryl Rivers uses *argumentation* to convince us that images of violence against women in rock lyrics are being met by public silence and that something needs to be done. These and the other rhetorical forms—*description, definition, analogy, cause and effect, process analysis*, and *example* (or *illustration*)—are important ways of structuring our thoughts and getting our point across to others. (The Glossary at the end of *Language Awareness* explains these and other rhetorical terms in detail. In developing your understanding of these rhetorical forms, you may find it helpful to consult the Glossary as well as the Rhetorical Table of Contents, which classifies the essays in the text according to the rhetorical patterns that they demonstrate.)

Expanding your awareness of how writers use language, then, will require you to pay careful attention not only to what an essay says but also to the way it has been put together. To do so most effectively, keep a pencil in your hand and use it as you read. Make note, first, of your own responses. If you disagree with a fact or a conclusion, object in the margin: "*NO!*" If you feel skeptical, indicate that response: "*Why?*" If you are impressed by an argument or a turn of phrase, compliment the writer: "*Good!*" Mark words or passages you don't understand at first reading. A question mark in the margin may do the job, or you may want to circle words or phrases in the text. During the second reading you can look up the words and puzzle out the difficult passages. Be sure, as well, to highlight key points. Mark off the essay into its main sections, such as the introduction, body, and conclusion.

Write in whatever marginal notes come naturally to you. These quick, brief responses will help you later when you begin asking and answering more specific analytical questions. When annotating a text, don't be timid. Mark up your book as much as you like. But don't let annotating become burdensome or meaningless. It should be an aid, not a chore, and a word or phrase is usually as good as a sentence. To avoid annotating or underlining more than necessary, always ask yourself why you believe the sentence or paragraph is important. You may, in fact, want to delay much of your annotating until a second reading, so that your first reading can be fast and free.

Once you've finished reading and annotating an essay, you'll want to make sure that you've gotten everything from it you can. One good way to complete your analysis is to answer some basic questions about the essay's content and form. Here are several such questions that you may find useful:

1. What does the author want to say about language? What is the essay's main idea or thesis?
2. What are the chief supporting ideas, and how do they relate to the main idea?
3. What is the author's general purpose? Is it to *persuade* you to a particular point of view? to *explain* a subject to you? to *entertain* you? to *tell* a story? or to *describe* a language phenomenon? Does the author state his or her purpose directly? If not, how do you know what the author's purpose is?
4. What strategy or rhetorical form—narration, comparison and contrast, definition, argument, etc.—does the author use as the principal form for the essay?
5. Why and how does the author's writing strategy suit both the subject and the purpose?
6. What other strategies or rhetorical forms does the author use? Where and for what reason(s)?
7. How is the essay structured? How does its organization relate to its main idea and to the author's purpose?
8. What is the author's attitude toward the essay's subject—enthusiastically positive, objective, ironic, hostile, etc.?
9. To whom is the essay addressed? What should the audience expect from this particular type of essay—to find out how something works, to discover what something means, to understand why something happened?
10. Does the author supply enough information to support the essay's ideas and enough details to make its descriptions precise? Is all of the information relevant and, as far as you can tell, accurate?
11. Has the author left out any information that you think might be relevant

to the thesis? Does he or she fail to consider any important views—including perhaps your own view?

12. Does the author assume anything without supporting the assumption or even stating it? Are these assumptions acceptable, or would you challenge them?

13. Overall, how effective is the essay? Has the writer accomplished his or her purpose?

Each of the essays in *Language Awareness* is followed by questions for analysis similar to the ones suggested above, but more specific to the text at hand. In addition to content questions on the language issues explored in each essay, we have provided questions that direct your attention to specific rhetorical principles and techniques illustrated by the selection. Each essay is also followed by a list of words that you will find worth adding to your active vocabulary, including paragraph references to help you see each word in its original context in the essay. The questions on content and rhetoric as well as the vocabulary items work best when you try to answer them as fully as you can, remembering and considering many details from the selection to support your answers.

LEARNING TO WRITE WELL

As we suggested before, one of our main purposes in encouraging you to give such thoughtful attention to the essays in *Language Awareness* is to help increase your own competence and confidence as a writer. By considering how a variety of writers have solved the problem of providing an opening and closing paragraph for their essays, you can achieve a fuller understanding of the possibilities available to you as you work on introductions and conclusions in essays of your own. Similarly, the essays you read in *Language Awareness* will show you how writers develop coherent paragraphs, how they use transitional words and phases to create clear connections among the parts of their essays, how they choose words carefully to bring about an appropriate response in their readers. Increasing your sensitivity to matters like these can have a big impact on your own writing.

Furthermore, recognizing how and why the writers in *Language Awareness* have used certain rhetorical strategies will help you put these powerful patterns of thought and organization into practice for yourself. You'll see, for example, that a writer who wants to explain the differences between the language of men and the language of women will naturally choose the strategy of *comparison and contrast* to provide her essay's structure. On the other hand, if a writer wants to explain *why* such differences exist, you'll see that no amount of comparing will do the job: it will be necessary to use the strategy of analyzing *cause and effect*. If a writer wants to communicate the meaning of a term like "jargon" or "euphemism," the strategy of *definition* suggests itself naturally. Every topic and purpose for writing will suggest one or another writing strategy. As you write, you may often wish to plan your strategy before you start, consciously deciding which one or which combination of strategies best fits what you have to say and what you want to accomplish. When you've completed a rough draft, you need to read what you've written, making sure that your choice of strategy was a good one and that it expresses your content accurately and effectively. The sort of reading *Language Awareness* encourages will help you become more skilled at making the decisions that lead to such improvement in your own writing.

Language Awareness will also provide you with many possibilities for practicing your writing skills. Each essay in the text is followed by two or more writing assignments based upon the essay's content and/or its rhetorical features. These assignments will give you a chance to use the essay as a model or as a starting point for an essay of your own. At the end of each section of the text, we have provided further topics and instructions for writing that bring together ideas from several different selections, allowing you to synthesize your thoughts about the overall subject of a section. Finally, at the end of the book there is a list of suggested topics for longer papers involving some library research. Each of the many suggestions is designed to help you think more closely about some particular aspect of language as you refine your ability to express your thoughts forcefully and coherently in writing.

PART I

Discovering Language

I know what he said, but who ever takes weatherpeople literally?

COMING TO AN AWARENESS OF LANGUAGE

Malcolm X

On February 21, 1965, Malcolm X, the Black Muslim leader, was shot to death as he addressed an afternoon rally in Harlem. He was thirty-nine years old. In the course of his brief life, he had risen from a world of thieving, pimping, and drug pushing to become one of the most articulate and powerful African Americans in the United States during the early 1960s. In 1992 the life of this influential African-American leader was reexamined in Spike Lee's film Malcolm X.*

With the assistance of the late Alex Haley, the author of Roots, *Malcolm X told his story in* The Autobiography of Malcolm X, *a moving account of his search for fulfillment. In the following selection taken from the* Autobiography, *Malcolm X narrates the story of how his frustration at not being able to express himself in the letters he wrote led to his discovery of the power of language.*

I've never been one for inaction. Everything I've ever felt strongly about, I've done something about. I guess that's why, unable to do anything else, I soon began writing to people I had known in the hustling world, such as Sammy the Pimp, John Hughes, the gambling house owner, the thief Jumpsteady, and several dope peddlers. I wrote them all about Allah and Islam and Mr. Elijah Muhammad. I had no idea where most of them lived. I addressed their letters in care of the Harlem or Roxbury bars and clubs where I'd known them.

I never got a single reply. The average hustler and criminal was too uneducated to write a letter. I have known many slick sharp-looking hustlers, who would have you think they had an interest in Wall Street; privately, they would get someone else to read a letter if they received one. Besides, neither would I have replied to anyone writing me something as wild as "the white man is the devil."

What certainly went on the Harlem and Roxbury wires was that Detroit Red was going crazy in stir, or else he was trying some hype to shake up the warden's office.

During the years that I stayed in the Norfolk Prison Colony, never did any official directly say anything to me about those letters, although, of course, they all passed through the prison censorship. I'm sure, however, they monitored what I wrote to add to the files which every state and federal prison keeps on the conversion of Negro inmates by the teachings of Mr. Elijah Muhammad.

But at that time, I felt that the real reason was that the white man   5
knew that he was the devil.

Later on, I even wrote to the Mayor of Boston, to the Governor of   6
Massachusetts, and to Harry S. Truman. They never answered; they probably never even saw my letters. I handscratched to them how the white man's society was responsible for the black man's condition in this wilderness of North America.

It was because of my letters that I happened to stumble upon starting   7
to acquire some kind of a homemade education.

I became increasingly frustrated at not being able to express what I   8
wanted to convey in letters that I wrote, especially those to Mr. Elijah Muhammad. In the street, I had been the most articulate hustler out there—I had commanded attention when I said something. But now, trying to write simple English, I not only wasn't articulate, I wasn't even functional. How would I sound writing in slang, the way I would *say* it, something such as, "Look, daddy, let me pull your coat about a cat. Elijah Muhammad—"

Many who today hear me somewhere in person, or on television, or   9
those who read something I've said, will think I went to school far beyond the eighth grade. This impression is due entirely to my prison studies.

It had really begun back in the Charlestown Prison, when Bimbi first   10
made me feel envy of his stock of knowledge. Bimbi had always taken charge of any conversation he was in, and I had tried to emulate him. But every book I picked up had few sentences which didn't contain anywhere from one to nearly all of the words that might as well have been in Chinese. When I just skipped those words, of course, I really ended up with little idea of what the book said. So I had come to the Norfolk Prison Colony still going through only book-reading motions. Pretty soon, I would have quit even these motions, unless I had received the motivation that I did.

I saw that the best thing I could do was get hold of a dictionary—to   11
study, to learn some words. I was lucky enough to reason also that I should try to improve my penmanship. It was sad. I couldn't even write in a straight line. It was both ideas together that moved me to request a dictionary along with some tablets and pencils from the Norfolk Prison Colony school.

I spent two days just riffling uncertainly through the dictionary's pages.   12
I'd never realized so many words existed! I didn't know *which* words I needed to learn. Finally, just to start some kind of action, I began copying.

In my slow, painstaking, ragged handwriting, I copied into my tablet   13
everything printed on that first page, down to the punctuation marks.

I believe it took me a day. Then, aloud, I read back, to myself, everything I'd written on the tablet. Over and over, aloud, to myself, I read my own handwriting.   14

I woke up the next morning, thinking about those words—immensely proud to realize that not only had I written so much at one time, but I'd written words that I never knew were in the world. Moreover, with a little effort, I also could remember what many of these words meant. I reviewed the words whose meanings I didn't remember. Funny thing, from the dictionary's first page right now, that "aardvark" springs to my mind. The dictionary had a picture of it, a long-tailed, long-eared, burrowing African mammal, which lives off termites caught by sticking out its tongue as an anteater does for ants.   15

I was so fascinated that I went on—I copied the dictionary's next page. And the same experience came when I studied that. With every succeeding page, I also learned of people and places and events from history. Actually the dictionary is like a miniature encyclopedia. Finally the dictionary's A section had filled a whole tablet—and I went on into the B's. That was the way I started copying what eventually became the entire dictionary. It went a lot faster after so much practice helped me pick up handwriting speed. Between what I wrote in my tablet, and writing letters, during the rest of my time in prison I would guess I wrote a million words.   16

I suppose it was inevitable that as my word-base broadened, I could for the first time pick up a book and read and now begin to understand what the book was saying. Anyone who has read a great deal can imagine the new world that opened. Let me tell you something: from then until I left that prison, in every free moment I had, if I was not reading in the library, I was reading on my bunk. You couldn't have gotten me out of books with a wedge. Between Mr. Muhammad's teachings, my correspondence, my visitors . . . and my reading of books, months passed without my even thinking about being imprisoned. In fact, up to then, I never had been so truly free in my life.   17

QUESTIONS ON CONTENT

1. What motivated Malcolm X "to acquire some kind of a homemade education" (7)?

2. What does Malcolm X mean when he says that he was "going through only book-reading motions" (10)? How did he decide to solve this problem?

3. In paragraph 8 Malcolm X points to the difference between being "articulate" and being "functional" in his speaking and writing. What exactly is the distinction that he makes?

4. Why did the word *aardvark* spring to mind when Malcolm X recalled his study of the first page of the dictionary?

5. In what ways is the dictionary like a "miniature encyclopedia"(16)? How are dictionaries and encyclopedias different?

6. What is the nature of the freedom that Malcolm X refers to in the final sentence?

QUESTIONS ON RHETORIC

1. Malcolm X narrates his experiences as a prisoner in the first person. Why is the first person particularly appropriate? (Glossary: *Point of View*).

2. How has Malcolm X organized his essay? (Glossary: *Organization*)

3. The first sentences of paragraphs 1 and 2 are both short declarative sentences. Why are they especially effective as introductory sentences?

4. Could paragraphs 12, 13, and 14 be combined into a single paragraph? What would be gained or lost if they were to be combined?

5. Why is Malcolm X's relatively simple vocabulary in this narrative appropriate? (Glossary: *Diction*)

VOCABULARY

frustrated (8)   functional (8)   inevitable (17)
articulate (8)   emulate (10)

WRITING TOPICS

1. All of us have been in situations in which our ability to use language seemed inadequate—for example, when taking an exam; being interviewed for a job; giving directions; or expressing sympathy, anger, or grief. Write a brief essay in which you recount one such frustrating incident in your life. In preparing to write your narrative, you may find it helpful to ask yourself such questions as: Why is the incident important to me? What details are necessary for me to re-create the incident in an interesting and engaging way? How can my narrative of the incident be most effectively organized? Compare your experiences with those of your classmates.

2. Malcolm X solved the problems of his own illiteracy by carefully studying the dictionary. Would this be a practical solution to the national problem of illiteracy? Are there any alternatives to Malcolm X's approach? What are they?

THE DAY LANGUAGE CAME INTO MY LIFE

Helen Keller

*Helen Keller (1880–1968) became blind and deaf at the
age of eighteen months as the result of a disease. It wasn't
until she was seven years old that her family hired Anne
Sullivan to be her teacher. As Keller learned to think and
communicate through language, the world opened up to her.
Thus, she is in a unique position to remind us of what it is
like to pass from the "fog" of prethought into the world
where "everything had a name, and each name gave birth to
a new thought."*

The most important day I remember in all my life is the one on which   1
my teacher, Anne Mansfield Sullivan, came to me. I am filled with
wonder when I consider the immeasurable contrast between the two lives
which it connects. It was the third of March 1887, three months before I
was seven years old.

On the afternoon of that eventful day, I stood on the porch, dumb,   2
expectant. I guessed vaguely from my mother's signs and from the hurry-
ing to and fro in the house that something unusual was about to happen,
so I went to the door and waited on the steps. The afternoon sun pene-
trated the mass of honeysuckle that covered the porch and fell on my
upturned face. My fingers lingered almost unconsciously on the familiar
leaves and blossoms which had just come forth to greet the sweet southern spring. I did not know what the future held of marvel or surprise for
me. Anger and bitterness had preyed upon me continually for weeks and
a deep languor had succeeded this passionate struggle.

Have you ever been at sea in a dense fog, when it seemed as if a   3
tangible white darkness shut you in, and the great ship, tense and anxious, groped her way toward the shore with plummet and sounding-line,
and you waited with beating heart for something to happen? I was like
that ship before my education began, only I was without compass or
sounding-line and had no way of knowing how near the harbor was.
"Light! give me light!" was the wordless cry of my soul, and the light of
love shone on me in that very hour.

I felt approaching footsteps. I stretched out my hand as I supposed to   4
my mother. Someone took it, and I was caught up and held close in the
arms of her who had come to reveal all things to me, and, more than all
things else, to love me.

The morning after my teacher came she led me into her room and   5

13

gave me a doll. The little blind children at the Perkins Institution had sent it and Laura Bridgman had dressed it; but I did not know this until afterward. When I had played with it a little while, Miss Sullivan slowly spelled into my hand the word "d-o-l-l." I was at once interested in this finger play and tried to imitate it. When I finally succeeded in making the letters correctly I was flushed with childish pleasure and pride. Running downstairs to my mother I held up my hand and made the letters for doll. I did not know that I was spelling a word or even that words existed; I was simply making my fingers go in monkeylike imitation. In the days that followed I learned to spell in this uncomprehending way a great many words, among them *pin, hat, cup* and a few verbs like *sit, stand* and *walk*. But my teacher had been with me several weeks before I understood that everything has a name.

One day, while I was playing with my new doll, Miss Sullivan put   6
my big rag doll into my lap also, spelled "d-o-l-l" and tried to make me understand that "d-o-l-l" applied to both. Earlier in the day we had had a tussle over the words "m-u-g" and "w-a-t-e-r." Miss Sullivan had tried to impress it upon me that "m-u-g" is *mug* and that "w-a-t-e-r" is *water*, but I persisted in confounding the two. In despair she had dropped the subject for the time, only to renew it at the first opportunity. I became impatient at her repeated attempts and, seizing the new doll, I dashed it upon the floor. I was keenly delighted when I felt the fragments of the broken doll at my feet. Neither sorrow nor regret followed my passionate outburst. I had not loved the doll. In the still, dark world in which I lived there was no strong sentiment or tenderness. I felt my teacher sweep the fragments to one side of the hearth, and I had a sense of satisfaction that the cause of my discomfort was removed. She brought me my hat, and I knew I was going out into the warm sunshine. This thought, if a wordless sensation may be called a thought, made me hop and skip with pleasure.

We walked down the path to the well-house, attracted by the fra-   7
grance of the honeysuckle with which it was covered. Some one was drawing water and my teacher placed my hand under the spout. As the cool stream gushed over one hand she spelled into the other the word *water*, first slowly, then rapidly. I stood still, my whole attention fixed upon the motions of her fingers. Suddenly I felt a misty consciousness as of something forgotten—a thrill of returning thought; and somehow the mystery of language was revealed to me. I knew then that "w-a-t-e-r" meant the wonderful cool something that was flowing over my hand. The living word awakened my soul, gave it light, hope, joy, set it free! There were barriers still, it is true, but barriers that could in time be swept away.

I left the well-house eager to learn. Everything had a name, and each   8
name gave birth to a new thought. As we returned to the house every object which I touched seemed to quiver with life. That was because I saw everything with the strange, new sight that had come to me. On entering the door I remembered the doll I had broken. I felt my way to

the hearth and picked up the pieces. I tried vainly to put them together. Then my eyes filled with tears; for I realized what I had done, and for the first time I felt repentance and sorrow.

I learned a great many new words that day. I do not remember what they all were; but I do know that *mother, father, sister, teacher* were among them—words that were to make the world blossom for me, "like Aaron's rod, with flowers." It would have been difficult to find a happier child than I was as I lay in my crib at the close of that eventful day and lived over the joys it had brought me, and for the first time longed for a new day to come.

QUESTIONS ON CONTENT

1. Keller defines her most important day as the day Anne Sullivan came into her life. Knowing the importance Keller places on language, why do you suppose she chose as her most important day the one on which she understood language for the first time?

2. Until she learned language, Keller could not express her feelings. Nevertheless, she experienced many emotions. What were some of these emotions? What usually precipitated them? When language came to Keller, she experienced a feeling she had never had before. What was that feeling?

3. In paragraphs 7 and 8, Keller explains how "the mystery of language" was revealed to her and how it affected her. In your own words, what was that mystery and what was its significance for Keller?

QUESTIONS ON RHETORIC

1. In her opening sentence, Keller says her meeting with Anne Sullivan was wonderful in that it brought together two lives of such contrast. Read over Keller's story and make a list of Keller's and Sullivan's personality traits. Then, using examples from the text, explain how Keller uses telling details to enhance this contrast.

2. Keller believed that over time words would make her world open up. Identify the parts of speech of her first words. In what way do these parts of speech open up one's world? Does this give you any insight into the nature of writing?

3. Keller uses a narrative (Glossary: *Narrative*) to make her point that language is the key to life and learning. Why do you suppose she chose this method? Could she have made her point as effectively using another writing strategy, cause and effect analysis for example? (Glossary: *Cause and Effect Analysis*)

VOCABULARY

languor (2)   plummet (3)   confounding (6)
tangible (3)

WRITING TOPICS

1. In paragraph 3, Keller uses the metaphor of being lost in a fog to explain her feeling of helplessness and her frustration at not being able to communicate. Perhaps you have had a similar feeling over an inability to communicate with parents or teachers or of not being able to realize some other longed-for goal. In an essay, describe these feelings using a metaphor or some other figure of speech of your own creation.

2. Keller explains that she felt no remorse when she shattered her doll. "In the still, dark world in which I lived there was no strong sentiment or tenderness." However, once she understood that things had names, Keller was able to feel repentance and sorrow. In your own words, try to describe why you think this is true. You may want to discuss this in class or do some research of your own into the ways language alters perception among people who are blind and deaf.

THE STORY OF
HUMAN LANGUAGE

Peter Farb

Although the ability to use language is perhaps the most distinguishing characteristic of human beings, most people underestimate the miracle of language, the linguistic creativity involved "in exploiting a language's total resources." This linguistic creativity is the birthright of every human being, as Peter Farb reminds us in this selection from his provocative book Word Play: What Happens When People Talk. *Farb uses striking examples to illustrate the complexity and the infinitely flexible nature of the English language, which he compares and contrasts to other human languages as well as to animal sounds.*

Some twenty-five hundred years ago, Psamtik, an Egyptian pharaoh, desired to discover man's primordial tongue. He entrusted two infants to an isolated shepherd and ordered that they should never hear a word spoken in any language. When the children were returned to the pharaoh several years later, he thought he heard them utter *bekos*, which means "bread" in Phrygian, a language of Asia Minor. And so he honored Phrygian as man's "natural" language. Linguists today know that the story of the pharaoh's experiment must be apocryphal. No child is capable of speech until he has heard other human beings speak, and even two infants reared together cannot develop a language from scratch. Nor does any single "natural" language exist. A child growing up anywhere on earth will speak the tongue he hears in his speech community, regardless of the race, nationality, or language of his parents. 1

Every native speaker is amazingly creative in the various strategies of speech interaction, in word play and verbal dueling, in exploiting a language's total resources to create poetry and literature. Even a monosyllabic *yes*—spoken in a particular speech situation, with a certain tone of voice, and accompanied by an appropriate gesture—might constitute an original use of English. This sort of linguistic creativity is the birthright of every human being on earth, no matter what language he speaks, the kind of community he lives in, or his degree of intelligence. As Edward Sapir pointed out, when it comes to language "Plato walks with the Macedonian swineherd, Confucius with the head-hunting savage of Assam." 2

And at a strictly grammatical level also, native speakers are unbelievably creative in language. Not every human being can play the violin, 3 do calculus, jump high hurdles, or sail a canoe, no matter how excellent his teachers or how arduous his training—but every person constantly creates utterances never before spoken on earth. Incredible as it may seem at first thought, the sentence you just read possibly appeared in exactly this form for the first time in the history of the English language—and the same thing might be said about the sentence you are reading now. In fact, if conventional remarks—such as greetings, farewells, stock phrases like *thank you*, proverbs, clichés, and so forth—are disregarded, in theory all of a person's speech consists of sentences never before uttered.

A moment's reflection reveals why that may be so. Every language   4
groups its vocabulary into a number of different classes such as nouns, verbs, adjectives, and so on. If English possessed a mere 1,000 nouns (such as *trees, children, horses*) and only 1,000 verbs (*grow, die, change*), the number of possible two-word sentences, therefore, would be 1,000 x 1,000, or one million. Of course, most of these sentences will be meaningless to a speaker today—yet at one time people thought *atoms split* was a meaningless utterance. The nouns, however, might also serve as the objects of these same verbs in three-word sentences. So with the same meager repertory of 1,000 nouns and 1,000 verbs capable of taking an object, the number of possible three-word sentences increases to 1,000 x 1,000 x 1,000 or one billion. These calculations, of course, are just for minimal sentences and an impoverished vocabulary. Most languages offer their speakers many times a thousand nouns and a thousand verbs, and in addition they possess other classes of words that function as adverbs, adjectives, articles, prepositions, and so on. Think, too, in terms of four-word, ten-word, even fifty-word sentences—and the number of possible grammatical combinations becomes astronomical. One linguist calculated that it would take ten trillion years (two thousand times the estimated age of the earth) to utter all the possible English sentences that use exactly twenty words. Therefore, it is improbable that any twenty-word sentence a person speaks was ever spoken previously—and the same thing would hold true, of course, for sentences of greater length, and for most shorter ones as well.

For a demonstration of just why the number of sentences that can be   5
constructed in a language is, at least in theory, infinite, show twenty-five speakers of English a cartoon and ask them to describe in a single sentence what they see. Each of the twenty-five speakers will come up with a different sentence, perhaps examples similar to these:

> I see a little boy entering a magic and practical-joke shop to buy something and not noticing that the owner, a practical joker himself, has laid a booby trap for him.

> The cartoon shows an innocent little kid, who I guess is entering a magic shop because he wants to buy something, about to be captured in a trap by the owner of the shop, who has a diabolical expression on his face.

It has been calculated that the vocabulary and the grammatical structures used in only twenty-five such sentences about this cartoon might provide the raw material for nearly twenty *billion* grammatical sentences—a number so great that about forty human life spans would be needed to speak to them, even at high speed. Obviously, no one could ever speak, read, or hear in his lifetime more than the tiniest fraction of the possible sentences in his language. That is why almost every sentence in this book— as well as in all the books ever written or to be written—is possibly expressed in its exact form for the first time.

This view of creativity in the grammatical aspects of language is a   6 very recent one. It is part of the revolution in ideas about the structure of language that has taken place since 1957, when Noam Chomsky, of the Massachusetts Institute of Technology, published his *Syntactic Structures*. Since then Chomsky and others have put forth a theory of language that bears little resemblance to the grammar most people learned in "grammar" school. Not all linguists accept Chomsky's theories. But his position, whether it is ultimately shown to be right or wrong, represents an influential school in theoretical linguistics today, one that other schools often measure themselves against.

Chomsky believes that all human beings possess at birth an innate   7 capacity to acquire language. Such a capacity is biologically determined—that is, it belongs to what is usually termed "human nature"— and it is passed from parents to children as part of the offspring's biological inheritance. The innate capacity endows speakers with the general shape of human language, but it is not detailed enough to dictate the precise tongue each child will speak—which accounts for why different languages are spoken in the world. Chomsky states that no one learns a language by learning all of its possible sentences, since obviously that would require countless lifetimes. For example, it is unlikely that any of the speakers who saw the cartoon of the child entering the magic store ever encountered such a bizarre situation before—yet none of the speakers had any difficulty in constructing sentences about it. Nor would a linguist who wrote down these twenty-five sentences ever have heard them previously—yet he had no difficulty understanding them. So, instead of learning billions of sentences, a person unconsciously acquires a grammar that can generate an infinite number of new sentences in his language.

Such a grammar is innately within the competence of any native   8 speaker of a language. However, no speaker—not even Shakespeare, Dante, Plato, or the David of the Psalms—lives up to his theoretical competence. His actual performance in speaking a language is considerably different, and it consists of numerous errors, hesitations, repetitions, and so forth. Despite these very uneven performances that a child hears all around him, in only a few years—and before he even receives instruction in reading and writing in "grammar" school—he puts together for himself the theoretical rules for the language spoken in his community. Since most sentences that a child hears are not only unique but also filled with errors, how can he ever learn the grammar of his language? Chomsky's answer is that children are born with the capacity to learn only grammars that accord with the innate human blueprint. Children disregard performance errors because such errors result in sentences that could not be described by such a grammar. Strong evidence exists that native speakers of a language know intuitively whether a sentence is grammatical or not. They usually cannot specify exactly what is wrong, and very possibly they make the same mistakes in their own speech, but they know—unconsciously, not as a set of rules they learned in school—when a sentence is incorrect.

The human speaker—born with a capacity for language, infinitely   9
creative in its use, capable of constructing novel utterances in unfamiliar speech situations—shares the globe with a variety of animals that whistle, shriek, squeak, bleat, hoot, coo, call, and howl. And so it has been assumed, ever since Aristotle first speculated about the matter, that human speech is only some superior kind of animal language. Alexander Graham Bell saw nothing odd about his attempts to teach a dog to speak by training it to growl at a steady rate while he manipulated its throat and jaws. The dog finally managed to produce a sequence of syllables which sounded somewhat like *ow ah oo gwah mah*—the closest it could come to "How are you, Grandma?" And Samuel Pepys, in his *Diary* entry for August 24, 1661, noted:

> by and by we are called to Sir W. Batten's to see the strange creature that Captain Holmes hath brought with him from Guiny; it is a great baboon [apparently not a baboon at all but rather a chimpanzee], but so much like a man in most things, that though they say there is a species of them, yet I cannot believe but that it is a monster got of a man and a she-baboon. I do believe that it already understands much English, and I am of the mind it might be taught to speak or make signs.

Other experimenters concluded that animals could not be taught hu-   10
man languages, but they saw no reason why they themselves should not learn to speak the way animals do. A few enthusiasts have even published dictionaries for various bird and animal languages—among them E. I. Du Pont de Nemours, the French-born founder of the American chemical firm, who in 1807 compiled dictionaries for the languages of such birds as crows and nightingales. These efforts are ludicrous because human speech is quite different from most animal communication. Between the bird's call to its mate and the human utterance *I love you* lie a few hundred million years of evolution, at least one whole day of Biblical Creation. St. Francis of Assisi, talking to the birds, may have had much to say to them, but they had nothing to discuss with him.

Human speech seemingly resembles animal calls in that it employs a   11
small number of sounds, often no more than the number emitted by many

species of birds and mammals. But, unlike animal calls, human sounds are combined to form a vast vocabulary, which in turn is structured into an infinite number of utterances. The number of different units of sound in each human language, such as the *m* in *man* or the *ou* in *house*, varies between about a dozen and a little more than five dozen. English recognizes about 45 units, Italian 27, Hawaiian 13. This range is not notably different from the separate units of sound emitted by many kinds of animals: prairie dog, 10; various species of monkeys, about 20; domestic chicken, 25; chimpanzee, 25; bottle-nosed dolphins, 28; fox, 36.

Chimpanzees, with their 25 units of sound, are incapable of speech, while Hawaiians, with only 13 units, possess a very expressive language. That is because the chimpanzee employs one unit of sound in social play, another when a juvenile is lost, a third when attacked, and so on—but two or more calls cannot be combined to generate additional messages. In contrast, the 13 sounds of Hawaiian can be combined to form 2,197 potential three-sound words, nearly five million six-sound words—and an astronomical number if the full repertory of 13 sounds is used to form longer words. In the same way, a speaker of English can select three units of sound out of his store of 45, such as the sounds represented in writing by *e, n*, and *d*—and then combine them into such meaningful words as *end, den*, and *Ned*. But the chimpanzee cannot combine the three units of sound that mean play, lost juvenile, and threat of attack to form some other message. Nor can the chimpanzee's call that means "Here is food" ever be changed to talk about the delicacies it consumed yesterday or its expectations about finding certain fruits tomorrow. Generation after generation, as far into the future as the chimpanzee survives as a species, it will use that call solely to indicate the immediate presence of food. | 12

Certain animals—most notably parrots, mynahs, and other mimicking birds—can emit a wide repertory of sounds, and they also have an uncanny ability to combine them into longer utterances. Nevertheless, they do not exploit their abilities the way human beings do. A trained mynah bird can so unerringly repeat an English sentence that it is scarcely distinguishable on a tape recording from the same sentence spoken by a human being. Parrots also can duplicate human speech with awesome fidelity, and they have been taught vocabularies of more than a hundred words. A parrot can easily enough be trained to mimic the utterance *a pail of water* and also to mimic a variety of nouns such as *sand* and *milk*. But, for all its skill, the parrot will never substitute nouns for each other and on its own say *a pail of sand* or *a pail of milk*. | 13

Even the most vocal animals are utterly monotonous in what they say in a given situation. The well-known nursery rhyme does not reveal what Jack said to Jill when they went up the hill to fetch a pail of water, and in fact no way exists to predict which of the tremendous strategies two people will select in such a speech situation. But everyone knows what a male songbird will say when another male enters its territory during the | 14

breeding season. It will emit a distinctive series of sounds that signify
"Go away!" It cannot negotiate with the intruder, nor can it say "I'm
sorry that I must ask you to depart now, but I will be happy to make your
acquaintance after the breeding season is concluded." The male defender
of the territory is simply responding to the stimulus of an intruder at a
certain time of the year by uttering a general statement about the existence of such a stimulus.

Specialists in animal behavior infer the "meaning" of animal sounds   15
from the behavior of the animals at the time they emit sounds, but it is
safe to conclude that the sounds express only indefinable emotions. Individuals belonging to the same animal species emit approximately the
same sounds to convey the same emotions. All expressions of pain uttered by any individuals of a monkey species are very much the same, but
in the human species the sounds that a speaker uses to communicate his
pain are quite arbitrary. A speaker of English says *ouch*, but a Spaniard
says *ay* and a Nootka Indian *ishka-takh*. Jill might have emitted an ani-
mal-like cry of pain as she came tumbling down the hill—but, as a
speaker of English, she also had the choice of saying *I hurt my head* or
Please take me to a doctor. Even if Jill merely uttered the conventional
word *ouch*, which signifies pain in English, this sound is nevertheless
considerably different from an animal's cry of pain. An animal's cry
cannot be removed from its immediate context, but Jill's *ouch* can. She
could, for example, tell someone the next day about her accident by
saying *When I fell down the hill, I cried "ouch."* Or she could utter *ouch*
in a completely different context, as when someone makes a feeble pun
and she wishes to convey that her sensibilities, not her bones, have been
wounded.

An animal, though, has no such choices. As Bertrand Russell re-   16
marked about a dog's ability to communicate, "No matter how eloquently
a dog may bark, he cannot tell you that his parents were poor but honest." Despite the variety of sounds in the babel of the animal world,
nonhuman calls are emotional responses to a very limited number of immediate stimuli. Every other kind of sound made by living things on the
planet belongs to human speech alone.

QUESTIONS ON CONTENT

1. What does Farb mean when he says that "native speakers are unbelievably creative in language" (3) and that "linguistic creativity is the
birthright of every human being on earth" (2)?

2. Who is Noam Chomsky? Why, according to Farb, is he important?

3. What, according to Farb, is the central tenet of Chomsky's theory of
language?

4. What evidence does Farb present to support Chomsky's claim that "no one learns a language by learning all of its possible sentences" (7)?

5. What distinctions, according to Farb, does Chomsky draw between *competence* and *performance*?

6. In paragraphs 11–16 Farb discusses the differences between human language and animal sounds. What are the essential differences that Farb sees?

7. Farb states that "strong evidence exists that native speakers of a language know intuitively whether a sentence is grammatical or not" (8). As an experiment, examine the following sentences. Which ones do you believe are grammatical; which are not? Try to explain what is wrong with the ones you believe are ungrammatical.

    a. That student continually sleeps in class.
    b. Student in class continually that sleeps.
    c. The basketball player were trying to stall at the end of the game.
    d. The chicken is too hot to eat.
    e. Colorless green ideas sleep furiously.
    f. The band marched smooth in the parade.

QUESTIONS ON RHETORIC

1. Farb opens his essay with the brief story of the Egyptian pharaoh and his search for man's earliest language. How is this story related to the subject of Farb's essay? Did you find his opening effective? Why, or why not? (Glossary: *Beginnings*)

2. What is the relationship between paragraph 4 and paragraph 3? between paragraph 5 and paragraph 4?

3. Writers use transitions to make natural and logical connections between sentences as well as between paragraphs. Such transitions are one way of giving an essay coherence. Discuss the kinds of transitions that Farb uses to link the paragraphs in his essay. (Glossary: *Transitions* and *Coherence*)

4. Farb's essay breaks nicely into three major sections: (1) a discussion of linguistic creativity, (2) a description of Noam Chomsky's theory of language, and (3) an explanation of the differences between human languages and animal "languages." Why are these sections presented in the order that they are? What would happen if they were to be rearranged? (Glossary: *Organization*)

5. How does Farb organize his discussion of the differences between human language and animal sounds in paragraphs 11-16? (Glossary: *Comparison* and *Contrast*)

VOCABULARY

primordial (1)	clichés (3)	innate (7)
apocryphal (1)	repertory (4)	ludicrous (10)
arduous (3)	grammar (6)	awesome (13)

WRITING TOPICS

1. As Peter Farb suggests, "show twenty-five speakers of English [e.g., the members of your class] a cartoon and ask them to describe in a single sentence what they see" (5). Compare and contrast the sentences produced. What conclusions can you draw?

2. As a native speaker of English, you have several basic language competencies. For example, you can determine whether or not an utterance is a grammatical sentence. Other competencies include the ability to tell when two or more sentences are synonymous, recognize ambiguity in a sentence, and interpret completely novel utterances. Discuss these competencies in a brief essay that uses examples to illustrate your points.

3. Pet lovers will tell you that their animals can communicate with them. Using your own personal experience or that of someone you know, describe how people and pets communicate with each other. Do you think that this communication fits Farb's definition of language?

WHAT IS LANGUAGE?

Victoria Fromkin and Robert Rodman

"The ability to carry out the simplest conversation requires profound knowledge of which speakers are unaware," write linguists Victoria Fromkin of the University of California at Los Angeles and Robert Rodman of North Carolina State University. Yes, language is something that most of us take for granted because we use it—almost without thinking—to communicate with the people in our lives each day. But what does it mean to know a language? In the following chapter from An Introduction to Language *Fromkin and Rodman discuss exactly what each of us does know when we use a language.*

When we study human language, we are approaching what some might call the "human essence," the distinctive qualities of mind that are, so far as we know, unique to man. —NOAM CHOMSKY, *Language and Mind*

Whatever else people do when they come together—whether they play, fight, make love, or make automobiles—they talk. We live in a world of language. We talk to our friends, our associates, our wives and husbands, our lovers, our teachers, our parents and in-laws. We talk to bus drivers and total strangers. We talk face to face and over the telephone, and everyone responds with more talk. Television and radio further swell this torrent of words. Hardly a moment of our waking lives is free from words, and even in our dreams we talk and are talked to. We also talk when there is no one to answer. Some of us talk aloud in our sleep. We talk to our pets and sometimes to ourselves. We are the only animals that do so—that talk.

The possession of language, more than any other attribute, distinguishes humans from other animals. To understand our humanity we must understand the language that makes us human. According to the philosophy expressed in the myths and religions of many peoples, it is language that is the source of human life and power. To some people of Africa, a newborn child is a *kuntu*, a "thing," not yet a *muntu*, a "person." Only by the act of learning does the child become a human being. According to this tradition, we all become "human" because we all come to know at least one language. But what does it mean to "know" a language?

LINGUISTIC KNOWLEDGE

When you know a language, you can speak and be understood by others 3
who know that language. This means you have the capacity to produce
sounds that signify certain meanings and to understand or interpret the
sounds produced by others. We are referring here to normal-hearing individuals. Deaf persons produce and understand sign languages just as
hearing persons produce and understand spoken languages.

Everyone knows a language. Why write an entire book on what ap- 4
pears to be so simple a phenomenon? After all, five-year-old children are
almost as proficient at speaking and understanding as their parents are.
Nevertheless the ability to carry out the simplest conversation requires
profound knowledge of which speakers are unaware. This fact is as true
for speakers of Japanese as for English speakers, for Eskimos as for Na-
vajos. A speaker of English can produce a sentence with two relative
clauses, like

> My goddaughter who was born in Sweden and who now lives in Vermont is
> named Disa, after a Viking queen.

without knowing what a relative clause is. In a parallel fashion a child
can walk without understanding or being able to explain the principles of
balance, support, and sequence that permit one to walk. The fact that we
know something unconsciously is not unique to language.

What, then, do speakers of English or Quechua or French or Mohawk 5
or Arabic know?

Knowledge of the Sound System

Knowing a language means knowing what sounds are in that language 6
and what sounds are not. This unconscious knowledge is revealed by the
way speakers of one language pronounce words from another language. If
you speak only English, for example, you may substitute an English
sound for a non-English sound when pronouncing "foreign" words. Most
English speakers pronounce the name *Bach* with a final *k* sound because
the sound represented by the letters *ch* in German is not an English
sound. If you pronounce it as the Germans do, you are using a sound
outside the English sound system. French people speaking English often
pronounce words like *this* and *that* as if they were spelled *zis* and *zat*. The
English sound represented by the initial letters *th* is not part of the French
sound system, and the French mispronunciation reveals the speakers' unconscious knowledge of this fact.

Even some involuntary cries are constrained by our own language 7
system, and the filled pauses that are sprinkled through conversational
speech—like *er* or *uh* or *you know* in English—contain only the sounds

found in the language. French speakers, for example, often fill their pauses with the vowel sound that starts their word for egg, *oeuf*—a sound that does not occur in English.

Knowing the sound system of a language includes more than knowing   8
the **inventory** of sounds: it includes knowing which sounds may start a word, end a word, and follow each other. The name of a former president of Ghana was *Nkrumah*, pronounced with an initial sound identical to the sound ending the English word *sing* (for most Americans). Most speakers of English mispronounce it (by Ghanaian standards) by inserting a short vowel before or after the *n* sound. Similarly, the first name of the Australian mystery writer Ngaio Marsh is usually mispronounced in this way. The reason for these "errors" is that no word in English begins with the *ng* sound. Children who learn English discover this fact about our language, just as Ghanaian and Australian children learn that words in their language may begin with the *ng* sound. . . .

Knowledge of the Meaning of Words

The minute I set eyes on an animal I know what it is. I don't have to reflect a moment; the right name comes out instantly. . . . I seem to know just by the shape of the creature and the way it acts what animal it is. When the dodo came along he [Adam] thought it was a wildcat. . . . But I saved him. . . . I just spoke up in a quite natural way . . . and said "Well, I do declare if there isn't the dodo!" —MARK TWAIN, *Eve's Diary*

Knowing the sounds and sound patterns in our language constitutes   9
only one part of our linguistic knowledge. In addition, knowing a language is knowing that certain sound sequences **signify** certain concepts or **meanings**. Speakers of English know what *boy* means and that it means something different from *toy* or *girl* or *pterodactyl*. Knowing a language is therefore knowing how to relate sounds and meanings.

If you do not know a language, the sounds spoken to you will be   10
mainly incomprehensible, because the relationship between speech sounds and the meanings they represent is, for the most part, an **arbitrary** one. You have to learn (when you are acquiring the language) that the sounds represented by the letters *house* (in the written form of the language)

signify the concept ⌂ ; if you know French, this same meaning is represented by *maison*; if you know Twi, it is represented by [ɔdaŋ]; if you know Russian, by *dom*; if you know Spanish, by *casa*. Similarly, the

concept ⟶ is represented by *hand* in English, *main* in French, *nsa* in Twi, and *ruka* in Russian.

The following are words in some different languages. How many of   11
them can you understand?

a. kyinii	d. asa	g. wartawan
b. doakam	e. toowq	h. inaminatu
c. odun	f. bolna	i. yawwa

Speakers of the languages from which these words are taken know that they have the following meanings:

a. a large parasol (in a Ghanaian language, Twi)
b. living creature (in the native American language, Papago)
c. wood (in Turkish)
d. morning (in Japanese)
e. is seeing (in a California Indian language. Luiseño)
f. to speak (in a Pakistani language, Urdu); ache (in Russian)
g. reporter (in Indonesian)
h. teacher (in a Venezuelan Indian language, Warao)
i. right on! (in a Nigerian language, Hausa)

These examples show that the sounds of words are only given meaning by the language in which they occur. Mark Twain satirizes the idea that something is called X because it looks like X or called Y because it sounds like Y in the quotation at the beginning of this section. Neither the shape nor the other physical attributes of objects determine their pronunciation in any language. . . . 12

This arbitrary relationship between the **form** (sounds) and **meaning** (concept) of a word in spoken language is also true of the sign languages used by the deaf. If you see someone using a sign language you do not know, it is doubtful that you will understand the message from the signs alone. A person who knows Chinese Sign Language would find it difficult to understand American Sign Language. Signs that may have originally been **mimetic** (similar to miming) or **iconic** (with a nonarbitrary relationship between form and meaning) change historically as do words, and the iconicity is lost. These signs become **conventional**, so knowing the shape or movement of the hands does not reveal the meaning of the gestures in sign languages. 13

There is, however, some "**sound symbolism**" in language—that is, words whose pronunciation suggests the meaning. A few words in most languages are **onomatopoeic**—the sounds of the words supposedly imitate the sounds of nature. Even here, the sounds differ from one language to another, reflecting the particular sound system of the language. In English we say *cockadoodledoo* to represent the rooster's crow, but in Russian they say *kukuriku*. 14

Sometimes particular sound sequences seem to relate to a particular concept. In English many words beginning with *gl* relate to sight, such as *glare, glint, gleam, glitter, glossy, glaze, glance, glimmer, glimpse*, and *glisten*. However, such words are a very small part of any language, and *gl* may have nothing to do with "sight" in another language, or even in 15 other words in English, such as *gladiator, glucose, glory, glycerine, globe*, and so on.

English speakers know the *gl* words that relate to sight and those that   16
do not; they know the onomatopoeic words, and all the words in the basic
vocabulary of the language. There are no speakers of English who know
all 450,000 words listed in Webster's *Third New International Dictionary*; but even if there were and that were all they knew, they would not
know English. Imagine trying to learn a foreign language by buying a
dictionary and memorizing words. No matter how many words you
learned, you would not be able to form the simplest phrases or sentences
in the language or understand a native speaker. No one speaks in isolated
words. (Of course, you could search in your traveler's dictionary for
individual words to find out how to say something like "car—gas—
where?" After many tries, a native might understand this question and
then point in the direction of a gas station. If you were answered with a
sentence, however, you probably would not understand what was said or
be able to look it up, because you would not know where one word ended
and another began.) . . .

The Creativity of Linguistic Knowledge

Knowledge of a language enables you to combine words to form phrases,   17
and phrases to form sentences. You cannot buy a dictionary of any language with all the sentences, because no dictionary can list all the possible sentences. Knowing a language means being able to produce new
sentences never spoken before and to understand sentences never heard
before. The linguist Noam Chomsky refers to this ability as part of the
"creative aspect" of language use. Not every speaker of a language can
create great literature, but you, and all persons who know a language, can
and do "create" new sentences when you speak and understand new sentences "created" by others.

This creativity shows that language use is not limited to stimulus-   18
response behavior. True, if someone steps on your toe, you will "automatically" respond with a scream or gasp or grunt, but these sounds are
really not part of language; they are involuntary reactions to stimuli. After you automatically cry out, you can say, "That was some clumsy act,
you big oaf!" or "Thank you very much for stepping on my toe; I was
afraid I had elephantiasis and now that I can feel it hurt I know it isn't
so," or any one of an infinite number of sentences, because the particular
sentence you produce is not controlled by any stimulus.

Knowing a language includes knowing what sentences are appropriate   19
in various situations. Saying "Hamburger costs $2.00 a pound" after
someone has just stepped on your toe would hardly be an appropriate
response, although it would be possible.

Consider the following sentence: 20

Daniel Boone decided to become a pioneer because he dreamed of pigeon-toed giraffes and cross-eyed elephants dancing in pink skirts and green berets on the wind-swept plains of the Midwest.

You may not believe the sentence; you may question its logic; but you can understand it, although you probably never heard or read it before now.

Knowledge of a language, then, makes it possible to understand and   21
produce new sentences. If you counted the number of sentences in this [chapter] that you have seen or heard before, the number would be small. Next time you write an essay or a letter, see how many of your sentences are new. Few sentences are stored in your brain, to be "pulled out" to fit some situation or matched with some sentence that you hear. Novel sentences never spoken or heard before cannot be in your memory.

Simple memorization of all the possible sentences in a language is   22
impossible in principle. If for every sentence in the language a longer sentence can be formed, then there is no limit to the length of any sentence and therefore no limit to the number of sentences. In English you can say:

This is the house.

or

This is the house that Jack built.

or

This is the malt that lay in the house that Jack built.

or

This is the dog that chased the cat that killed the rat that ate the malt that lay in the house that Jack built.

and you need not stop there. How long, then, is the longest sentence? A speaker of English can say:

The old man came.

or

The old, old, old, old, old man came.

How many "olds" are too many? Seven? Twenty-three?

It is true that the longer these sentences become, the less likely we   23 would be to hear or to say them. A sentence with 276 occurrences of "old" would be highly unlikely in either speech or writing, even to describe Methuselah; but such a sentence is theoretically possible. That is, if you know English, you have the knowledge to add any number of adjectives as modifiers to a noun.

All human languages permit their speakers to form indefinitely long sentences; "creativity" is a universal property of human language. 24

To memorize and store an infinite set of sentences would require an infinite storage capacity. However, the brain is finite, and even if it were not, we could not store novel sentences. 25

Knowledge of Sentences and Nonsentences

When you learn a language you must learn something finite. Your vocabulary is finite (however large it may be), and that can be stored. If sentences in a language were formed by putting one word after another in any order, then knowledge of a language could simply be a set of words. You can see that words are not enough by examining the following strings of words: 26

(1) a. John kissed the little old lady who owned the shaggy dog.
   b. Who owned the shaggy dog John kissed the little old lady.
   c. John is difficult to love.
   d. It is difficult to love John.
   e. John is anxious to go.
   f. It is anxious to go John.
   g. John, who was a student, flunked his exams.
   h. Exams his flunked student a was who John.

If you were asked to put a star or asterisk before the examples that seemed "funny" or "no good" to you, which ones would you star? Our "intuitive" knowledge about what is or is not an allowable sentence in English convinces us to star b, f, and h. Which ones did you star? 27

Would you agree with the following judgments? 28

(2) a. What he did was climb a tree.
   b. *What he thought was want a sports car.
   c. Drink your beer and go home!
   d. *What are drinking and go home?
   e. I expect them to arrive a week from next Thursday.
   f. *I expect a week from next Thursday to arrive them.
   g. Linus lost his security blanket.
   h. *Lost Linus security blanket his.

If you starred the same ones we did, then you agree that not all strings of words constitute sentences in a language, and knowledge of a language determines which are and which are not. Therefore, in addition to know- 29 ing the words of the language, linguistic knowledge must include "rules" for forming sentences and making judgments like those you made about the examples in (1) and (2). These rules must be finite in length and finite in number so that they can be stored in our finite brains; yet they must permit us to form and understand an infinite set of new sentences, as we discussed above. . . .

A language, then, consists of all the sounds, words, and possible   30
sentences. When you know a language, you know the sounds, the words, and the rules for their combination.

QUESTIONS ON CONTENT

1. What, according to Fromkin and Rodman, distinguishes humans from other animals? Why is "talk" so important?

2. Specifically, what does it mean to know a language?

3. In addition to a knowledge of the inventory of sounds, what does knowing the sound system of a language include? Explain your answer with several examples from English or another language that you are familiar with.

4. What do Fromkin and Rodman mean when they say that the relationship between speech sounds and meanings is "arbitrary"?

5. What is an onomatopoeic word? Give several examples.

6. In what ways is each one of us creative in our use of language? And what does this creativity reveal about language use?

7. In paragraph 29, the writers talk about but don't give any examples of the "rules" that we all know and use to distinguish sentences from non-sentences. What are some of the rules that you used to analyze the strings of words given in paragraphs 26 and 28?

QUESTIONS ON RHETORIC

1. What is Fromkin and Rodman's thesis, and where is it stated? (Glossary: *Thesis*)

2. What is the function of paragraph 5 in the context of the essay?

3. Fromkin and Rodman are careful to use examples to clarify and explain many of their points. Identify several of the examples that you found effective and explain why you found them so.

4. The writers claim that "simple memorization of all the possible sentences in a language is impossible in principle" (22). How do they convince you of the validity of their claim?

5. How have Fromkin and Rodman organized their essay? You may find it helpful to make a scratch outline in answering this question. (Glossary: *Organization*)

VOCABULARY

torrent (1)	parallel (4)	finite (25)
attribute (2)	incomprehensible (10)	constitute (29)
profound (4)	iconicity (13)	

WRITING TOPICS

1. Write an essay responding to Fromkin and Rodman's statement that "We live in a world of language." Be sure to illustrate your points with examples from your experiences.

2. Write an essay in which you agree or disagree with Fromkin and Rodman's claim that "to understand our humanity we must understand the language that makes us human."

3. Many people have argued that a limited or impoverished vocabulary restricts one's perceptions of and ability to deal with the world. Using examples from your own personal experiences, discuss how your vocabulary has affected you—has it ever made you feel restricted or at a disadvantage, or has it given you the feeling that you were in charge, in complete control of a situation? You may wish to consider your work in a particular job or area of academic study.

WRITING ASSIGNMENTS FOR "DISCOVERING LANGUAGE"

1. Like Malcom X, we can all tell of an experience that has been unusually significant for us. Think about your own experiences. Identify one incident that has been especially important for you and write an essay about it. In preparing to write, ask yourself such questions as these: Why is the incident important for me? What aspects of the incident might interest someone else? What details will help me re-create the incident in the most engaging way? How can my narrative of the incident be most effectively organized?

2. The writers in this section have at least one thing in common: they all agree that using language is an indispensable aspect of being human. "Everything had a name, and each name gave birth to a new thought," Helen Keller says at the end of her essay. "Whatever else people do when they come together—whether they play, fight, make love, or make automobiles—they talk," said Victoria Fromkin and Robert Rodman in the first paragraph of their essay. But much of modern psychology and many New Age practices encourage us to really "feel" our emotions and "experience" the truth of those feelings. Does this idea conflict with the ideas of thinkers such as Keller, Fromkin and Rodman, and the other writers in this section? In your own words, what is the role of language in humanity?

3. It has often been said that language reveals the character of the person using it. Write an essay in which you analyze the character of a particular writer or speaker with whom you are familiar, based on his or her use of language.

4. No two writers in this section "sound alike." Through choice of words and length and structure of sentences, each creates a "style" uniquely his or her own. Examine some of your own work: term papers and reports, letters to friends and relatives, or essays for college applications. Do you hear a distinct "voice" in your own writing? Do you notice a difference between the way you sound in letters to friends and in college papers? Does your writing tend to be more formal in some kinds of writing than in others? Does your vocabulary differ for different kinds of writing? Write an essay discussing your findings.

5. In order for communication to be clear and effective, people must define their words as precisely as possible. As a writer you will need to define, and the more precise your definitions, the more clearly you will communicate. One way of defining a term is to place it in a class of similar items and then to show how it is different from the other items in that class. For example:

Word	Class	Characteristics
a *watch*	is a *mechanical device*	*for telling time and is usually carried or worn*
semantics	is an *area of linguistics*	*concerned with the study of the meaning of words*

Certainly such definitions are not complete, and one could write an entire paragraph, essay, or book to define these terms more fully. This process, however, is useful in getting started in both thinking and writing.

Place each of the following terms in a class, and then write a statement of the characteristics that differentiate it from other members of its class:

paper clip	anger
pamphlet	love
anxiety	mountain bike
freedom	Post-it

Now write a brief essay in which you fully define one of the above terms or one of your own choosing.

6. Most of us while we were growing up heard from our parents and teachers that it was important to have a large vocabulary. Malcolm X, for example, tells of how his street vocabulary limited him in certain ways. Do you think it is important to have a large working vocabulary? Is it difficult to acquire a large vocabulary? What exactly is involved in increasing your vocabulary—memorizing, practice, writing, reading, speaking, all of these? Write an essay in which you discuss the benefits of having a large vocabulary at your command.

PART II

Language Use
and Misuse

Now, you probably remember the old term "bomb" . . .

GIVING THINGS NAMES

S. I. Hayakawa and Alan R. Hayakawa

S. I. Hayakawa, a former senator from California and honorary chairman of the "English Only" movement, authored the influential semantics text Language in Thought and Action, *which, with the help of his son, he brought out in a fifth edition just before his death. In the following selection taken from that book, the Hayakawas reveal for us the power words can have over our thoughts. The terms we use to classify things—whether people, objects, or concepts—can and do affect our reactions to them.*

The figure below shows eight objects, let us say animals, four large and four small, a different four with round heads with another four with square heads, and still another four with curly tails and another four with straight tails. These animals, let us say, are scampering about your village, but since at first they are of no importance to you, you ignore them. You do not even give them a name.

One day, however, you discover that the little ones eat up your grain, while the big ones do not. A differentiation sets itself up, and, abstracting the common characteristics of A, B, C, D, you decide to call these *gogo*; E, F, G, and H you decide to call *gigi*. You chase away the *gogo*, but leave the *gigi* alone. Your neighbor, however, has had a different experience; he finds that those with square heads bite, while those with round heads do not. Abstracting the common characteristics of B, D, F, and H, he calls them *daba*, and A, C, E, and G, he calls *dobo*. Still another neighbor discovers, on the other hand, that those with curly tails kill snakes, while those with straight tails do not. He differentiates them, abstracting still another set of common characteristics: A, B, E, and F are *busa*, while C, D, G, and H are *busana*.

Now imagine that the three of you are together when E runs by. You   3
. say, "There goes the *gigi*"; your first neighbor says, "There goes the
dobo"; your other neighbor says, "There goes the *busa*." Here, immediately, a great controversy arises. What is it *really*, a *gigi*, a *dobo*, or a
busa? What is its *right name*? You are quarreling violently when along
comes a fourth person from another village who calls it a *muglock*, an
edible animal, as opposed to *uglock*, an inedible animal—which doesn't
help matters a bit.

Of course, the question, "What is it *really*?" "What is its *right*   4
name?" is a nonsense question. By a nonsense question is meant one that
is not capable of being answered. Things can have "right names" only if
there is a necessary connection between symbols and things symbolized,
and we have seen that there is not. That is to say, in the light of your
interest in protecting your grain, it may be necessary for you to distinguish the animal E as a *gigi*; your neighbor, who doesn't like to be bitten,
finds it practical to distinguish it as a *dobo*: your other neighbor, who
likes to see snakes killed, distinguishes it as a *busa*. What we call things
and where we draw the line between one class of things and another
depend upon the interests we have and the purposes of the classification.
For example, animals are classified in one way by the meat industry, in a
different way by the leather industry, in another different way by the fur
industry, and in a still different way by the biologist. None of these
classifications is any more final than any of the others; each of them is
useful for its purpose.

This holds, of course, regarding everything we perceive. A table "is"   5
a table to us, because we can understand its relationship to our conduct
and interests; we eat at it, work on it, lay things on it. But to a person
living in a culture where no tables are used, it may be a very strong stool,
a small platform, or a meaningless structure. If our culture and upbringing were different, that is to say, our world would not even look the same
to us.

Many of us, for example, cannot distinguish between pickerel, pike,   6
salmon, smelt, perch, crappie, halibut, and mackerel; we say that they
are "just fish, and I don't like fish." To a seafood connoisseur, however,
these distinctions are real, since they mean the difference to him between
one kind of a good meal, a very different kind of good meal, or a poor
meal. To a zoologist, who has other and more general ends in view, even
finer distinctions assume great importance. When we hear the statement,
then, "This fish is a specimen of pompano, *Trachinotus carolinus*," we
accept this as being "true," even if we don't care, not because that is its
"right name," but because that is how it is *classified* in the most complete
and most general system of classification that people scientifically interested in fish have evolved.

When we name something, then, we are classifying. *The individual*   7
object or event we are naming, of course, has no name and belongs to no

class until we put it in one. To illustrate again, suppose that we were to give the extensional meaning of the word "Korean." We would have to point to all "Koreans" living at a particular moment and say, "The word 'Korean' denotes at the present moment these persons: A_1, A_2, A_3, . . . A_n." Now, let us say, a child, whom we shall designate as Z, is born among these "Koreans." *The extensional meaning of the word "Korean," determined prior to the existence of Z, does not include Z.* Z is a new individual belonging to no classification, since all classifications were made without taking Z into account. Why, then, is Z also a "Korean"? *Because we say so.* And, saying so—fixing the classification—we have determined to a considerable extent future attitudes toward Z. For example, Z will always have certain rights in Korea; in other nations he will be regarded as an "alien" and will be subject to laws applicable to "aliens."

In matters of "race" and "nationality," the way in which classifica-   8 tions work is especially apparent. For example, I am by birth a "Canadian," by "race" a "Japanese," and am now an "American." Although I was legally admitted to the United States on a Canadian passport as a "non-quota immigrant," I was unable to apply for American citizenship until after 1952. Until 1965, American immigration law used classifications based on "nationality" and on "race." A Canadian entering the United States as a permanent resident had no trouble getting in, unless he happened to be of Oriental extraction, in which case his "nationality" became irrelevant and he was classified by "race." If the quota for his "race"—for example, Japanese—was filled (and it often was), and if he could not get himself classified as a non-quota immigrant, he was not able to get in at all. (Since 1965, race and national origin have been replaced with an emphasis on "family reunification" as the basis for American immigration law, and race is no longer explicitly mentioned.) Are all these classifications "real"? Of course they are, *and the effect that each of them has upon what he may or may not do constitutes their "reality."*

I have spent my entire life, except for short visits abroad, in Canada   9 and the United States. I speak Japanese haltingly, with a child's vocabulary and an American accent; I do not read or write it. Nevertheless, because classifications seem to have a kind of hypnotic power over some people, I am occasionally credited with (or accused of) having an "Oriental mind." Since Buddha, Confucius, General Tojo, Mao Tse-tung, Pandit Nehru, Rajiv Gandhi, and the proprietor of the Golden Pheasant Chop Suey House all have "Oriental minds," it is difficult to know whether to feel complimented or insulted.

When is a person "black"? By the definition once widely accepted in   10 the United States, any person with even a small amount of "Negro blood"—that is, whose parents or ancestors were classified as "Negroes"—is "black." *It would be exactly as justifiable to say that any person with even a small amount of "white blood" is "white".* Why say one rather than the other? Because the former system of classification *suits the convenience of those making the classification.* (The classification of blacks and other minorities in this country has often suited the convenience of whites.) Classification is not a matter of identifying "essences." It is simply a reflection of social convenience or necessity—and different necessities are always producing different classifications.

There are few complexities about classifications at the level of dogs and cats, knives and forks, cigarettes and candy, but when it comes to classifications at high levels of abstraction, for example, those describing conduct, social institutions, philosophical and moral problems, serious difficulties occur. When one person kills another, is it an act of murder, an act of temporary insanity, an act of homicide, an accident, or an act of heroism? As soon as the process of classification is completed, our attitudes and our conduct are, to a considerable degree, determined. We hang the murderer, we treat the insane, we absolve the victim of circumstance, we pin a medal on the hero. 11

THE BLOCKED MIND

We need not concern ourselves here with the injustices done to "Jews," "Roman Catholics," "Republicans," "redheads," "chorus girls," "sailors," "Southerners," "Yankees," and so on, by snap judgments or, as it is better to call them, fixed reactions. "Snap judgments" suggests that such errors can be avoided by thinking more slowly; this, of course, is not the case, for some people think very slowly with no better results. What we are concerned with is the way in which we block the development of our own minds by automatic reactions. 12

In the grip of such reactions, some people may say, "A Jew's a Jew. There's no getting around that"—confusing the denoted, extensional Jew with the fictitious "Jew" inside their heads. Such persons, the reader will have observed, can usually be made to admit, on being reminded of certain "Jews" whom they admire—perhaps Albert Einstein, Sandy Koufax, Jascha Heifetz, Benny Goodman, Woody Allen, Henry Kissinger, or Kitty Dukakis—that "there are exceptions, of course." They have been compelled by experience, that is to say, to take cognizance of at least a few of the multitude of Jews who do not fit their preconceptions. At this point, however, they continue triumphantly, "But exceptions only prove the rule?"[1]—which is another way of saying, "Facts don't count." 13

People who "think" in this way may identify some of their best friends as "Jewish"; but to explain this they may say, "I don't think of them as Jews at all. They're just friends." In other words, the fictitious "Jew" inside their heads remains unchanged *in spite of their experience.* 14

---

[1]This extraordinarily fatuous saying originally meant, "The exception tests the rule"— *Exceptio probat regulum.* This older meaning of the word "prove" survives in such an expression as "automobile proving ground."

People like this may be said to be impervious to new information. 15
They continue to vote Republican or Democratic, no matter what the
Republicans or Democrats do. They continue to object to socialists, no
matter what the socialists propose. They continue to regard mothers as
sacred, no matter who the mother. A woman who had been given up on
both by physicians and psychiatrists as hopelessly insane was being considered by a committee whose task it was to decide whether or not she
should be committed to an asylum. One member of the committee doggedly refused to vote for commitment. "Gentlemen," he said in tones of
deepest reverence, "you must remember that this woman is, after all, a
mother." Similarly, some people continue to hate Protestants or Catholics, no matter which Protestant or Catholic. Ignoring characteristics left
out in the process of classification, they overlook—when the term Republican is applied to the party of Abraham Lincoln, the party of Warren
Harding, the party of Richard Nixon, and the party of Ronald Reagan—
the rather important differences among them.

COW₁ IS NOT COW₂

How do we prevent ourselves from getting into such intellectual blind 16
alleys, or, finding we are in one, how do we get out again? One way is to
remember that practically all statements in ordinary conversation, debate,
and public controversy taking the form "Republicans are Republicans,"
"Business is business," "Boys will be boys," "Woman drivers are woman
drivers," and so on, are *not true*. Let us put one of these blanket statements back into a context in life.

> "I don't think we should go through with this deal, Bill. Is it altogether
> fair to the railroad company?"
> "Aw, forget it! *Business is business*, after all."

Such an assertion, although it looks like a "simple statement of fact," 17
is not simple and is not a statement of fact. The first "business" *denotes*
the transaction under discussion; the second "business" invokes the *connotations* of the word. The sentence is a *directive*, saying, "Let us treat
this transaction with complete disregard for considerations other than
profit, as the word 'business' suggests." Similarly, when a father tries to
excuse the mischief done by his sons, he says, "Boys will be boys"; in
other words, "Let us regard the actions of my sons with that indulgent
amusement customarily extended toward those whom we call "boys,'"
though the angry neighbor will say, of course, "Boys, my eye! They're
little hoodlums; that's what they are!" Such assertions are not informative
statements but directives, directing us to classify the object or event under
discussion in given ways, in order that we may feel or act as suggested by
the terms of the classification.

There is a simple technique for preventing such directives from hav- 18
ing their harmful effect on our thinking. It is the suggestion made by
Korzybski that we add "index numbers" to our terms, thus: Englishman$_1$,
Englishman$_2$ . . . ; cow$_1$, cow$_2$, cow$_3$ . . . ; communist$_1$, communist$_2$,
communist$_3$. The terms of the classification tell us what the individuals in
that class have in common; *the index numbers remind us of the charac-*
teristics left out. A rule can then be formulated as a general guide in all
our thinking and reading: police officer$_1$ *is not* police officer$_2$; mother-in-
law$_1$ *is not* mother-in-law$_2$, and so on. This rule, if remembered, prevents
us from confusing levels of abstraction and forces us to consider the facts
on those occasions when we might otherwise find ourselves leaping to
conclusions which we may later have cause to regret.

"TRUTH"

Many semantic problems are, ultimately, problems of classification and 19
nomenclature. Take, for example, the extensive debate over abortion. To
opponents of legalized abortion, the unborn entity within a woman's
womb is a "baby." Because abortion foes *want* to end abortion, they
insist that the "baby" *is* a human being with its own legal rights and that
therefore "*abortion is murder.*" They call themselves "pro-life" to emphasize their position. Those who *want* individual women to be able to
choose whether or not to end a pregnancy call that same unborn entity a
"fetus" and insist that the "fetus" *is not* a viable human being capable of
living on its own, and claim that a woman has a "right" to make such a
choice. Partisans of either side have accused the other of "perverting the
meanings of words" and of "not being able to understand plain English."

The decision finally rests not upon appeals to past authority, but upon 20
what society wants. In the case *Roe v. Wade*, the Supreme Court found
that a "right"—specifically, a right to privacy—permits women to make
a private, medical decision before a certain stage of pregnancy. If society
again wants doctors prosecuted for performing abortions, as they often
were before 1973, it will obtain a new decision from Congress or the
Supreme Court that abortion "is" murder or that the unborn entity "is" a
human being. Either way, society will ultimately get the decision it col-
lectively wants, even if it must wait until the present members of the
Supreme Court are dead and an entirely new court is appointed. When the
desired decision is handed down, people will say, "Truth has triumphed."
Society, in short, regards as "true" those systems of classification that
produce the desired results.

The scientific test of "truth," like the social test, is strictly practical, 21
except for the fact that the "desired results" are more severely limited.
The results desired by society may be irrational, superstitious, selfish, or
humane, but the results desired by scientists are only that our systems of

classification produce predictable results. Classifications, as amply indicated already, determine our attitudes and behavior toward the object or event classified. When lightning was classified as "evidence of divine wrath," no courses of action other than prayer were suggested to prevent one's being struck by lightning. But after Benjamin Franklin classified it as "electricity," a measure of control over it was achieved by the invention of the lightning rod. Certain physical disorders were formerly classified as "demonic possession," and this suggested that we "drive the demons out" by whatever spells or incantations we could think of. The results were uncertain. But when those disorders were classified as "bacillus infections," courses of action were suggested that led to more predictable results. Science seeks only the *most generally useful* systems of classification; these it regards for the time being, until more useful classifications are invented, as "true."

QUESTIONS ON CONTENT

1. As the Hayakawas assert, "The question, 'What is it *really*?' 'What is its *right name*?' is a nonsense question" (4). Why do you think that people persist in asking this question? Have you ever witnessed people "quarrel violently" about what is the "correct term" for something? What do you suppose causes such arguments?

2. According to the authors, "What we call things and where we draw the line between one class of things and another depend upon the interests we have and the purposes of the classification" (4). They cite the different methods of animal classification by the meat, leather, and fur industries as one example of what they mean. Choose a popular song, motion picture, or book, and list four or five different terms one could use to classify it. Who would be likely to use each of these terms, and why?

3. The Hayakawas remind us that the United States once defined "any person with even a small amount of 'Negro blood' . . . [as] 'black'" (10). Why did this system of classification suit the convenience of American whites? What were some of the implications of this system for those individuals so classified?

4. Explain in your own words how labels of classification serve to perpetuate the "automatic reactions" of "the blocked mind" (12). Can you think of times when you have been the target of such classification? Explain.

5. According to the Hayakawas, is there any such thing as a "true" system of classification? Can language convey "truth"? Explain.

QUESTIONS ON RHETORIC

1. In their first three paragraphs, the Hayakawas tell a story about several types of animals and their various names. Explain how they use this narrative to introduce the concept of classification. (Glossary: *Beginnings*)

2. The authors use a personal anecdote to illustrate their statement, "In matters of 'race' and 'nationality,' the way in which classifications work is especially apparent" (8). Does this example strengthen their argument about the effect that classifications have upon individuals? Explain.

3. In a statement like "*business is business*," "the first 'business' *denotes* the transaction under discussion; the second 'business' invokes the *connotations* of the word" (17). When someone uses this sort of construction in speech or writing, how, according to the Hayakawas, does this difference turn the statement into a *directive*, telling the listener or reader to react in a given way? (Glossary: *Connotation/Denotation*)

4. The Hayakawas italicize words, phrases, and even entire sentences throughout the essay. What purpose(s) do these italics serve? Do you think they are used effectively? Why, or why not?

5. In paragraph 13 the Hayakawas provide a footnote to the saying, "But exceptions only prove the rule." What is the purpose of their footnote, and why do you suppose they chose not to include this material in the text itself?

VOCABULARY

connoisseur (6)	preconceptions (13)	semantic (19)
extensional (13)	impervious (15)	nomenclature (19)
cognizance (13)	directive (17)	

WRITING TOPICS

1. According to the Hayakawas, "If our culture and upbringing were different, our world would not even look the same to us" (5). Write an essay explaining specific ways you believe your culture, upbringing, and language may have affected your view of the world.

2. In their discussion of "truth," the Hayakawas conclude that "*Society, in short, regards as 'true' those systems of classification that produce the desired results.*" They use the notorious debate over abortion rights to illustrate what they mean. Think of other issues that either support or challenge the Hayakawas' position. Write an essay in which you discuss your own beliefs on the nature of "truth."

SELECTION, SLANTING, AND CHARGED LANGUAGE

Newman P. Birk and Genevieve B. Birk

The more we learn about language and how it works, the more abundantly clear it becomes that our language shapes our perceptions of the world. Because we all have the same set of physical organs for perceiving reality—eyes to see, ears to hear, noses to smell, tongues to taste, and skins to feel, it seems as though reality should be the same for all of us. But we know that it isn't; and language, it seems, is the big difference. Our language, in effect, acts as a filter, heightening certain perceptions, dimming others, and totally voiding still others. In the following selection from their book Understanding and Using English, *Newman and Genevieve Birk discuss how we learn new things, how we put our knowledge into words, and how language can be manipulated to create particular impressions.*

A. THE PRINCIPLE OF SELECTION

Before it is expressed in words, our knowledge, both inside and outside, 1
is influenced by the principle of selection. What we know or observe
depends on what we notice; that is, what we select, consciously or unconsciously, as worthy of notice or attention. As we observe, the principle of
selection determines which facts we take in.

Suppose, for example, that three people, a lumberjack, an artist, and 2
a tree surgeon, are examining a large tree in a forest. Since the tree itself
is a complicated object, the number of particulars or facts about it that
one could observe would be very great indeed. Which of these facts a
particular observer will notice will be a matter of selection, a selection
that is determined by his interests and purposes. A lumberjack might be
interested in the best way to cut the tree down, cut it up and transport it to
the lumber mill. His interest would then determine his principle of selection in observing and thinking about the tree. The artist might consider
painting a picture of the tree, and his purpose would furnish his principle
of selection. The tree surgeon's professional interest in the physical
health of the tree might establish a principle of selection for him. If each
man were now required to write an exhaustive, detailed report on every

thing he observed about the tree, the facts supplied by each would differ, for each would report those facts that his particular principle of selection led him to notice.[1]

The principle of selection holds not only for the specific facts that   3
people observe but also for the facts they remember. A student suddenly embarrassed may remember nothing of the next ten minutes of class discussion but may have a vivid recollection of the sensation of the blood mounting, as he blushed, up his face and into his ears. In both noticing and remembering, the principle of selection applies, and it is influenced not only by our special interest and point of view but by our whole mental state of the moment.

The principle of selection then serves as a kind of sieve or screen   4
through which our knowledge passes before it becomes our knowledge. Since we can't notice everything about a complicated object or situation or action or state of our own consciousness, what we do notice is determined by whatever principle of selection is operating for us at the time we gain the knowledge.

It is important to remember that what is true of the way the principle   5
of selection works for us is true also of the way it works for others. Even before we or other people put knowledge into words to express meaning, that knowledge has been screened or selected. Before an historian or an economist writes a book, or before a reporter writes a news article, the facts that each is to present have been sifted through the screen of a principle of selection. Before one person passes on knowledge to another, that knowledge has already been selected and shaped, intentionally or unintentionally, by the mind of the communicator.

B. THE PRINCIPLE OF SLANTING

When we put our knowledge into words, a second process of selection,   6
the process of slanting, takes place. Just as there is something, a rather mysterious principle of selection, which chooses for us what we will notice, and what will then become our knowledge, there is also a principle which operates, with or without our awareness, to select certain facts and feelings from our store of knowledge, and to choose the words and the emphasis that we shall use to communicate our meaning.[2] Slanting may be defined as the process of selecting (1) knowledge—factual and attitudinal; (2) words; and (3) emphasis, to achieve the intention of the communicator. Slanting is present in some degree in all communication:

[1]Of course, all three observers would probably report a good many facts in common— the height of the tree, for example, and the size of the trunk. The point we wish to make is that each observer would give us a different impression of the tree because of the different principle of selection that guided his observation.
 [2]Notice that the "principle of selection" is at work as *we take in* knowledge, and that slanting occurs as *we express* our knowledge in words.

one may *slant for* (favorable slanting), *slant against* (unfavorable slanting), or *slant both ways* (balanced slanting). . . .

C. SLANTING BY USE OF EMPHASIS

Slanting by use of the devices of emphasis is unavoidable,[3] for emphasis
is simply the giving of stress to subject matter, and so indicating what is
important and what is less important. In speech, for example, if we say
that Socrates was *a wise old man*, we can give several slightly different
meanings, one by stressing *wise*, another by stressing *old*, another by
giving equal stress to *wise* and *old*, and still another by giving chief stress
to *man*. Each different stress gives a different slant (favorable or unfavorable or balanced) to the statement because it conveys a different attitude
toward Socrates or a different judgment of him. Connectives and word
order also slant by the emphasis they give: consider the difference in
slanting or emphasis produced by *old but wise, old and wise, wise but
old*. In writing, we cannot indicate subtle stresses on words as clearly as
in speech, but we can achieve our emphasis and so can slant by the use of
more complex patterns of word order, by choice of connectives, by underlining heavily stressed words, and by marks of punctuation that indicate short or long pauses and so give light or heavy emphasis. Question
marks, quotation marks, and exclamation points can also contribute to
slanting.[4] It is impossible either in speech or in writing to put two facts
together without giving some slight emphasis or slant. For example, if we
have in mind only two facts about a man, his awkwardness and his
strength, we subtly slant those facts favorably or unfavorably in whatever
way we may choose to join them.

More Favorable Slanting	Less Favorable Slanting
He is awkward and strong.	He is strong and awkward.
He is awkward but strong.	He is strong but awkward.
Although he is somewhat	He may be strong, but
awkward, he is very strong.	he's very awkward.

With more facts and in longer passages it is possible to maintain a delicate
balance by alternating favorable emphasis and so producing a balanced effect.

    All communication, then, is in some degree slanted by the *emphasis*
of the communicator.

---

[3]When emphasis is present—and we can think of no instance in the use of language in
which it is not—it necessarily influences the meaning by playing a part in the favorable,
unfavorable, or balanced slant of the communicator. We are likely to emphasize by voice
stress, even when we answer *yes* or *no* to simple questions.

[4]Consider the slanting achieved by punctuation in the following sentences: He called the
Senator an honest man? *He* called the Senator an honest man? He called the Senator an
honest man! He said one more such "honest" senator would corrupt the state.

D. SLANTING BY SELECTION OF FACTS

To illustrate the technique of slanting by selection of facts, we shall ex-   9
amine three passages of informative writing which achieve different effects simply by the selection and emphasis of material. Each passage is
made up of true statements or facts about a dog, yet the reader is given
three different impressions. The first passage is an example of objective
writing or balanced slanting, the second is slanted unfavorably, and the
third is slanted favorably.

1. Balanced Presentation

Our dog, Toddy, sold to us a cocker, produces various reactions in various
people. Those who come to the back door she usually growls and barks at (a
milkman has said that he is afraid of her); those who come to the front door,
she whines at and paws; also she tries to lick people's faces unless we have
forestalled her by putting a newspaper in her mouth. (Some of our friends
encourage these actions; others discourage them. Mrs. Firmly, one friend,
slaps the dog with a newspaper and says, "I know how hard dogs are to
train.") Toddy knows and responds to a number of words and phrases, and
guests sometimes remark that she is a "very intelligent dog." She has fleas in
the summer, and she sheds, at times copiously, the year round. Her blonde
hairs are conspicuous when they are on people's clothing or on rugs or furniture. Her color and her large brown eyes frequently produce favorable comment. An expert on cockers would say that her ears are too short and set too
high and that she is at least six pounds too heavy.

The passage above is made up of facts, verifiable fact,[5] deliberately   10
selected and emphasized to produce a *balanced* impression. Of course not
all the facts about the dog have been given—to supply *all* the facts on
any subject, even such a comparatively simple one, would be an almost
impossible task. Both favorable and unfavorable facts are used, however,
and an effort has been made to alternate favorable and unfavorable details
so that neither will receive greater emphasis by position, proportion, or
grammatical structure.

2. Facts Slanted Against

That dog put her paws on my white dress as soon as I came in the door, and
she made so much noise that it was two minutes before she had quieted down
enough for us to talk and hear each other. Then the gas man came and she did

---

[5]*Verifiable facts* are facts that can be checked and agreed upon and proved to be true by
people who wish to verify them. That a particular theme received a failing grade is a
verifiable fact; one needs merely to see the theme with the grade on it. That the instructor
should have failed the theme is not, strictly speaking, a verifiable fact, but a matter of
opinion. That women on the average live longer than men is a verifiable fact; that they live
better is a matter of opinion, *a value judgment*.

a great deal of barking. And her hairs are on the rug and on the furniture. If you wear a dark dress they stick to it like lint. When Mrs. Firmly came in, she actually hit the dog with a newspaper to make it stay down, and she made some remark about training dogs. I wish the Birks would take the hint or get rid of that noisy, short-eared, overweight "cocker" of theirs.

This unfavorably slanted version is based on the same facts, but now   11 these facts have been selected and given a new emphasis. The speaker, using her selected facts to give her impression of the dog, is quite possibly unaware of her negative slanting.

Now for a favorably slanted version: 12

3. Facts Slanted For

What a lively and responsive dog! When I walked in the door, there she was with a newspaper in her mouth, whining and standing on her hind legs and wagging her tail all at the same time. And what an intelligent dog. If you suggest going for a walk, she will get her collar from the kitchen and hand it to you, and she brings Mrs. Birk's slippers whenever Mrs. Birk says she is "tired" or mentions slippers. At a command she catches balls, rolls over, "speaks," or stands on her hind feet and twirls around. She sits up and balances a piece of bread on her nose until she is told to take it; then she tosses it up and catches it. If you are eating something, she sits up in front of you and "begs" with those big dark brown eyes set in that light, buff-colored face of hers. When I got up to go and told her I was leaving, she rolled her eyes at me and sat up like a squirrel. She certainly is a lively and intelligent dog.

Speaker 3, like Speaker 2, is selecting from the "facts" summarized in   13 balanced version 1, and is emphasizing his facts to communicate his impression.

All three passages are examples of *reporting* (i.e., consist only of   14 verifiable facts), yet they give three very different impressions of the same dog because of the different ways the speakers slanted the facts. Some people say that figures don't lie, and many people believe that if they have the "facts," they have the "truth." Yet if we carefully examine the ways of thought and language, we see that any knowledge that comes to us through words has been subjected to the double screening of the principle of selection and the slanting of language. . . .

Wise listeners and readers realize that the double screening that is   15 produced by the principle of selection and by slanting takes place even when people honestly try to report the facts as they know them. (Speakers 2 and 3, for instance, probably thought of themselves as simply giving information about a dog and were not deliberately trying to mislead.) Wise listeners and readers know too that deliberate manipulators of language, by mere selection and emphasis, can make their slanted facts appear to support almost any cause.

In arriving at opinions and values we cannot always be sure that the   16 facts that sift into our minds through language are representative and relevant and true. We need to remember that much of our information about politics, governmental activities, business conditions, and foreign affairs comes to us selected and slanted. More than we realize, our opinions on these matters may depend on what newspaper we read or what news commentator we listen to. Worth-while opinions call for knowledge of reliable facts and reasonable arguments for and against—and such opinions include beliefs about morality and truth and religion as well as about public affairs. Because complex subjects involve knowing and dealing with many facts on both sides, reliable judgments are at best difficult to arrive at. If we want to be fairminded, we must be willing to subject our opinions to continual testing by new knowledge, and must realize that after all they *are* opinions, more or less trustworthy. Their trustworthiness will depend on the representativeness of our facts, on the quality of our reasoning, and on the standard of values that we choose to apply.

We shall not give here a passage illustrating the unscrupulous slanting   17 of facts. Such a passage would also include irrelevant facts and false statements presented as facts, along with various subtle distortions of fact. Yet to the uninformed reader the passage would be indistinguishable from a passage intended to give a fair account. If two passages (2 and 3) of casual and unintentional slanting of facts about a dog can give such contradictory impressions of a simple subject, the reader can imagine what a skilled and designing manipulation of facts and statistics could do to mislead an uninformed reader about a really complex subject. An example of such manipulation might be the account of the United States that Soviet propaganda has supplied to the average Russian. Such propaganda, however, would go beyond the mere slanting of the facts: it would clothe the selected facts in charged words and would make use of the many other devices of slanting that appear in charged language.

E. SLANTING BY USE OF CHARGED WORDS

In the passages describing the dog Toddy, we were illustrating the tech-   18 nique of slanting by the selection and emphasis of facts. Though the facts selected had to be expressed in words, the words chosen were as factual as possible, and it was the selection and emphasis of facts and not of words that was mainly responsible for the two distinctly different impressions of the dog. In the passages below we are demonstrating another way of slanting—by the use of charged words. This time the accounts are very similar in the facts they contain; the different impressions of the subject, Corlyn, are produced not by different facts but by the subtle selection of charged words.

The passages were written by a clever student who was told to choose   19 as his subject a person in action, and to write two descriptions, each using the "same facts." The instructions required that one description be slanted positively and the other negatively, so that the first would make the reader favorably inclined toward the person and the action, and the second would make him unfavorably inclined.

Here is the favorably charged description. Read it carefully and form   20
your opinion of the person before you go on to read the second description.

Corlyn

Corlyn paused at the entrance to the room and glanced about. A well-cut black dress draped subtly about her slender form. Her long blonde hair gave her chiseled features the simple frame they required. She smiled an engaging smile as she accepted a cigarette from her escort. As he lit it for her she looked over the flame and into his eyes. Corlyn had that rare talent of making every male feel that he was the one man in the world.

She took his arm and they descended the steps into the room. She walked with an effortless grace and spoke with equal ease. They each took a cup of coffee and joined a group of friends near the fire. The flickering light danced across her face and lent an ethereal quality to her beauty. The good conversation, the crackling logs, and the stimulating coffee gave her a feeling of internal warmth. Her eyes danced with each leap of the flames.

Taken by itself this passage might seem just a description of an attrac-   21
tive girl. The favorable slanting by use of charged words has been done so skillfully that it is inconspicuous. Now we turn to the unfavorable slanted description of the "same" girl in the "same" actions:

Corlyn

Corlyn halted at the entrance to the room and looked around. A plain black dress hung on her thin frame. Her stringy bleached hair accentuated her harsh features. She smiled an inane smile as she took a cigarette from her escort. As he lit it for her she stared over the lighter and into his eyes. Corlyn had a habit of making every male feel that he was the last man on earth.

She grasped his arm and they walked down the steps and into the room. Her pace was fast and ungainly, as was her speech. They walked down the steps and into the room. Her pace was fast and ungainly, as was her speech. They each reached for some coffee and broke into a group of acquaintances near the fire. The flickering light played across her face and revealed every flaw. The loud talk, the fire, and the coffee she had gulped down made her feel hot. Her eyes grew more red with each leap of the flames.

When the reader compares these two descriptions, he can see how   22
charged words influence the reader's attitude. One needs to read the two descriptions several times to appreciate all the subtle differences between them. Words, some rather heavily charged, others innocent-looking but

lightly charged, work together to carry to the reader a judgment of a person and a situation. If the reader had seen only the first description of Corlyn, he might well have thought that he had formed his "own judgment on the basis of the facts." And the examples just given only begin to suggest the techniques that may be used in heavily charged language. For one thing, the two descriptions of Corlyn contain no really good example of the use of charged abstractions; for another, the writer was obliged by the assignment to use the same set of facts and so could not slant by selecting his material.

F. SLANTING AND CHARGED LANGUAGE

. . . When slanting of facts, or words, or emphasis, or any combination   23
of the three *significantly influences* feelings toward, or judgments about, a subject, the language used is charged language. . . .

Of course communications vary in the amount of charge they carry   24
and in their effect on different people; what is very favorably charged for one person may have little or no charge, or may even be adversely charged, for others. It is sometimes hard to distinguish between charged and uncharged expression. But it is safe to say that whenever we wish to convey any kind of inner knowledge—feelings, attitudes, judgments, values—we are obliged to convey that attitudinal meaning through the medium of charged language; and when we wish to understand the inside knowledge of others, we have to interpret the charged language that they choose, or are obliged to use. Charged language, then, is the natural and necessary medium for the communication of charged or attitudinal meaning. At times we have difficulty in living with it, but we should have even greater difficulty in living without it.

Some of the difficulties in living with charged language are caused by   25
its use in dishonest propaganda, in some editorials, in many political speeches, in most advertising, in certain kinds of effusive salesmanship, and in blatantly insincere, or exaggerated, or sentimental expressions of emotion. Other difficulties are caused by the misunderstandings and misinterpretations that charged language produces. A charged phrase misinterpreted in a love letter; a charged word spoken in haste or in anger; an acrimonious argument about religion or politics or athletics or fraternities; the frustrating uncertainty produced by the effort to understand the complex attitudinal meaning in a poem or play or a short story—these troubles, all growing out of the use of charged language, may give us the feeling that Robert Louis Stevenson expressed when he said, "The battle goes sore against us to the going down of the sun."

But however charged language is abused and whatever misunder-   26
standings it may cause, we still have to live with it—and even by it. It

shapes our attitudes and values even without our conscious knowledge; it gives purpose to, and guides, our actions; through it we establish and maintain relations with other people and by means of it we exert our greatest influence on them. Without charged language, life would be but half life. The relatively uncharged language of bare factual statement, though it serves its informative purpose well and is much less open to abuse and to misunderstanding, can describe only the bare land of factual knowledge; to communicate knowledge of the turbulencies and the calms and the deep currents of the sea of inner experience we must use charged language.

QUESTIONS ON CONTENT

1. What is the "principle of selection," and how does it work?

2. How is "slanting" different from the "principle of selection"? What devices can a writer or speaker use to slant knowledge?

3. Paragraph 7 is full of examples of slanting by use of emphasis. Explain how each example works.

4. What exactly are "charged words"? Demonstrate your understanding of charged language by picking good examples from the two descriptions of Corlyn. What are some of the difficulties in living with charged language?

5. Why does a given word—like *lilac, religion*, or *lady*—mean different things to different people?

6. What do the Birks mean when they say, "Without charged language, life would be but half life" (26)?

QUESTIONS ON RHETORIC

1. Did you find the examples about Toddy the dog and Corlyn particularly helpful? What would have been lost had the examples not been included? (Glossary: *Examples*)

2. What is the relationship between paragraphs 1 and 2?

3. How have the Birks organized their essay? Is the organizational pattern appropriate for the subject matter? Explain. (Glossary: *Organization*)

4. What is the Birks' purpose in this essay? Do they seem more intent on explaining or arguing their position? (Glossary: *Purpose*)

VOCABULARY

exhaustive (2)	attitudinal (6)	abstractions (22)
blushed (3)	verifiable (10)	turbulencies (26)
sieve (4)	inconspicuous (21)	

WRITING TOPICS

1. Select an article about a current event from a newspaper or news magazine. Without changing the facts given, rewrite the article so that it makes a different impression on the reader. Hand in the original article, your rewritten version, and your comments about how each version should affect the reader.

2. Following the Birks' example of their dog Toddy, write three descriptions (one balanced, one slanted for, and one slanted against) of one of the following:

   a. your room
   b. your best friend
   c. your favorite coffee cup
   d. a rock star or other celebrity
   e. your school's dining hall
   f. a hamburger
   g. sunglasses
   h. your mother, your father, or a sibling
   i. a video game
   j. a book

3. The following news stories about a Little League World Series appeared in two very different newspapers. Carefully read each article, looking for slanting and charged language. Point out the "verifiable facts." How do you know?

LITTLE LEAGUE SERIES BARS FOREIGNERS

WILLIAMSPORT, PA., NOV. 11 (AP)—The Little League will confine future world series to teams from the continental United States.

This was announced today at the headquarters of the national baseball organization. The effect was to exclude Taiwan, which won the series for boys 8 to 12 years old in the last four years, causing protests in that country. Japan won the two previous years, and Monterrey, Mexico, took the series in 1957 and 1958. The last United States winner was Wayne, N.J., in 1970.

The league said its board of directors had acted after a review of the competition. It said the regional championship series would be continued in Canada, the Far East, Europe and Latin America, and the play-offs for senior (ages 13 to 15) or big league (16 to 18) programs would not be affected.

A spokesman cited travel costs for foreign entries and the nationalistic approach taken abroad as reasons for the change. He described the United States programs as regional in make-up.

Since the Little League expanded in 1957 to include teams outside the continental United States, 20 foreign teams have competed. There are 9,000 teams in the United States.

Robert H. Stirrat, vice president and public relations director, would only say: ↔

"We are standing by the board's resolution and will offer no further details."

The world series will be played next Aug. 19 to 23 at Williamsport, the birthplace of Little League baseball. Only four teams—the United States regional champions—will be entered. There were eight when foreign teams competed.

The ruling eliminates from world series competition children of American servicemen stationed in Europe because, a spokesman said, they are considered "foreign."

The first world series was played in 1947.

Last Aug. 24 Taiwan wrapped up its fourth straight world series with a 12-1 victory in the final over Red Bluff, Calif. The run was the first allowed by the Taiwanese in 46 innings, so complete did they dominate the series.

The team was led by Lin Wen-hsiung, a 12-year-old, right-handed pitcher, who hit two home runs and hurled a two-hitter in the final, striking out 15 of the 21 batters he faced.

The game was shown throughout Taiwan on television via satellite at 3 A.M., but many fans there considered the outcome such a foregone conclusion that they elected to go to sleep rather than watch.

Nevertheless, there were bursts of firecrackers before dawn to celebrate the victory.

So proficient have Taiwanese youngsters become at baseball that they have dominated not only Little League competition, but also divisions for older boys.

This year a Taiwanese team captured the Senior Little League world championship in Gary, Ind., for the third straight time, and the island's Big League team won the title at Fort Lauderdale, Fla., in its first attempt.

LITTLE LEAGUE BANS FOREIGNERS

No More Chinese HRs

Little League Shrinks Map
Limits World Series after Taiwan Romp

After watching Taiwan dominate the Little League World Series at Williamsport, Pa., for four years, the American sponsors found a way yesterday to end that victory streak: they banned foreign entries.

The ban, obviously, will do away with the so-called Chinese home run, a phrase New Yorkers learned about when the upper deck hung out over the playing field at the defunct Polo Grounds where the foul lines were short and homers were plentiful.

Peter J. McGovern, chief executive officer and board chairman of the Little League, said that the series would be restricted to the four regional U.S. champions from now on.

Robert H. Stirrat, vice president and public relations director for the league, said that the organization "is not nationalistic in its point of view." Stirrat said the group feels Little League is basically a community program and it intends returning to the original concept.

"The board took a long view of the international aspects of the program and decided a reassessment of the World Series competition for children aged 12 and under had to be regarded," Stirrat said. "It was their decision to limit the series from here on to the United States."

Stirrat also emphasized the ban on foreign clubs involves only the Little League series at Williamsport. He added that the senior league (13–15) and big league (16–18) are not affected. Those championships will still be waged on an international basis.

"The senior division is the world's largest baseball program," Stirrat said. "But they are unaffected by the decision." The seniors' finale will be played at Gary, Ind., with the big league finals at Fort Lauderdale, Fla.

Japanese Led the Parade

League officials deny the latest ruling was an effort to exclude Taiwan or any other non-U.S. Squad. There are 9,000 little leagues in this country and since the Williamsport brass broadened its program in 1957 to include "outside" teams, 20 foreign clubs have competed.

An American team hasn't been the Little League champ since Wayne, N.J., in 1970. Since then, Japanese representatives won in 1968 and 1969, followed by Taiwan the past four years.

Regional championships will continue to be held in Canada, Latin America, Europe and the Far East, but those winners will not compete in Williamsport.

"The Little League is taken pretty much as a summertime activity for kids in the United States," Stirrat said, "and the World Series is sort of a natural finish of the season for them."

Now, with only four clubs contesting for the 1975 title, which will be decided Aug. 19–23 at Williamsport, Little League brass were undecided as to its new format. They must determine whether sudden-death or a double elimination series will be played.

In any event, the Little League World Series will be an all-American affair.

What kind of newspaper do you think each article appeared in? On what stylistic evidence did you base your decision? Does a knowledge of the kind of newspaper it appeared in help to explain the way in which it was written? In an essay compare and contrast the two reports and your evaluations of their use of slanting and charged language.

THE WORLD OF DOUBLESPEAK

William Lutz

William Lutz, professor of English at Rutgers University and chair of the National Council of Teachers of English's Committee on Public Doublespeak, has been a watchdog of public officials who use language to "mislead, distort, deceive, inflate, circumvent, and obfuscate." Each year the committee presents the Orwell Awards, recognizing the most outrageous uses of public doublespeak in the world of government and business. In the following essay Lutz identifies the various types of doublespeak and cautions us about the possible serious effects that doublespeak can have on our thinking.

Farmers no longer have cows, pigs, chickens, or other animals on their farms; according to the U.S. Department of Agriculture farmers have "grain-consuming animal units" (which, according to the Tax Reform Act of 1986, are kept in "single-purpose agricultural structures," not pig pens and chicken coops). Attentive observers of the English language also learned recently that the multibillion dollar stock market crash of 1987 was simply a "fourth quarter equity retreat"; that airplanes don't crash, they just have "uncontrolled contact with the ground"; that janitors are really "environmental technicians"; that it was a "diagnostic misadventure of a high magnitude" which caused the death of a patient in a Philadelphia hospital, not medical malpractice; and that President Reagan wasn't really unconscious while he underwent minor surgery, he was just in a "non-decision-making form." In other words, doublespeak continues to spread as the official language of public discourse.

Doublespeak is a blanket term for language which pretends to communicate but doesn't, language which makes the bad seem good, the negative appear positive, the unpleasant attractive, or at least tolerable. It is language which avoids, shifts, or denies responsibility, language which is at variance with its real or its purported meaning. It is language which conceals or prevents thought. Basic to doublespeak is incongruity, the incongruity between what is said, or left unsaid, and what really is: between the word and the referent, between seem and be, between the essential function of language, communication, and what doublespeak does—mislead, distort, deceive, inflate, circumvent, obfuscate.

When shopping, we are asked to check our packages at the desk "for our convenience," when it's not for our convenience at all but for the store's "program to reduce inventory shrinkage." We see advertisements for "preowned," "experienced," or "previously distinguished" cars, for "genuine imitation leather," "virgin vinyl," or "real counterfeit diamonds." Television offers not reruns but "encore telecasts." There are no slums or ghettos, just the "inner city" or "substandard housing" where the "disadvantaged," "economically nonaffluent," or "fiscal underachievers" live. Nonprofit organizations don't make a profit, they have "negative deficits" or "revenue excesses." In the world of doublespeak dying is "terminal living."

We know that a toothbrush is still a toothbrush even if the advertisements on television call it a "home plaque removal instrument," and even that "nutritional avoidance therapy" means a diet. But who would guess that a "volume-related production schedule adjustment" means closing an entire factory in the doublespeak of General Motors, or that "advanced downward adjustments" means budget cuts in the doublespeak of Caspar Weinberger, or that "energetic disassembly" means an explosion in a nuclear power plant in the doublespeak of the nuclear power industry?

The euphemism, an inoffensive or positive word or phrase designed to avoid a harsh, unpleasant, or distasteful reality, can at times be doublespeak. But the euphemism can also be a tactful word or phrase; for example, "passed away" functions not just to protect the feelings of another person but also to express our concern for another's grief. This use of the euphemism is not doublespeak but the language of courtesy. A euphemism used to mislead or deceive, however, becomes doublespeak. In 1984, the U.S. State Department announced that in its annual reports on the status of human rights in countries around the world it would no longer use the word "killing." Instead, it would use the phrase "unlawful or arbitrary deprivation of life." Thus the State Department avoids discussing government-sanctioned killings in countries that the United States supports and has certified as respecting human rights.

The Pentagon also avoids unpleasant realities when it refers to bombs and artillery shells which fall on civilian targets as "incontinent ordnance" or killing the enemy as "servicing the target." In 1977 the Pentagon tried to slip funding for the neutron bomb unnoticed into an appropriations bill by calling it an "enhanced radiation device." And in 1971 the CIA gave us that most famous of examples of doublespeak when it used the phrase "eliminate with extreme prejudice" to refer to the execution of a suspected double agent in Vietnam.

Jargon, the specialized language of a trade or profession, allows colleagues to communicate with each other clearly, efficiently, and quickly. Indeed, it is a mark of membership to be able to use and understand the group's jargon. But it can also be doublespeak—pretentious, obscure, and esoteric terminology used to make the simple appear complex, and not to express but impress. In the doublespeak of jargon, smelling something becomes "organoleptic analysis," glass becomes "fused silicate," a crack in a metal support beam becomes a "discontinuity," conservative economic policies become "distributionally conservative notions."

Lawyers and tax accountants speak of an "involuntary conversion" of   8 property when discussing the loss or destruction of property through theft, accident, or condemnation. So if your house burns down, or your car is stolen or destroyed in an accident, you have, in legal jargon, suffered an "involuntary conversion" of your property. This is a legal term with a specific meaning in law and all lawyers can be expected to understand it. But when it is used to communicate with a person outside the group who does not understand such language, it is doublespeak. In 1978 a National Airlines 727 airplane crashed while attempting to land at the Pensacola, Florida, airport, killing three passengers, injuring twenty-one others, and destroying the airplane. Since the insured value of the airplane was greater than its book value, National made an after-tax insurance benefit of $1.7 million on the destroyed airplane, or an extra eighteen cents a share. In its annual report, National reported that this $1.7 million was due to "the involuntary conversion of a 727," thus explaining the profit without even hinting at the crash and the deaths of three passengers.

Gobbledygook or bureaucratese is another kind of doublespeak. Such   9 doublespeak is simply a matter of overwhelming the audience with technical, unfamiliar words. When asked why U.S. forces lacked intelligence information on Grenada before they invaded the island in 1983. Admiral Wesley L. McDonald told reporters that "We were not micromanaging Grenada intelligence-wise until about that time frame."

Some gobbledygook, however impressive it may sound, doesn't even   10 make sense. During the 1988 presidential campaign, vice presidential candidate Senator Dan Quayle explained the need for a strategic defense initiative by saying: "Why wouldn't an enhanced deterrent, a more stable peace, a better prospect to denying the ones who enter conflict in the first place to have a reduction of offensive systems and an introduction to defensive capability. I believe this is the route the country will eventually go."

In 1974, Alan Greenspan, then chairman of the President's Council of   11 Economic Advisors, was testifying before a Senate committee and was in the difficult position of trying to explain why President Nixon's economic policies weren't effective in fighting inflation: "It is a tricky problem to find the particular calibration in timing that would be appropriate to stem the acceleration in risk premiums created by falling incomes without prematurely aborting the decline in the inflation-generated risk premiums." In 1988, when speaking to a meeting of the Economic Club of New York, Mr. Greenspan, now Federal Reserve chairman, said, "I guess I should warn you, if I turn out to be particularly clear, you've probably misunderstood what I've said."

The investigation into the Challenger disaster in 1986 revealed the   12 gobbledygook and bureaucratese used by many involved in the shuttle program. When Jesse Moore, NASA's associate administrator, was asked if the performance of the shuttle program had improved with each launch or if it had remained the same, he answered, "I think our performance in terms of the liftoff performance and in terms of the orbital performance, we knew more about the envelope we were operating under, and we have been pretty accurately staying in that. And so I would say the performance has not by design drastically improved. I think we have been able to characterize the performance more as a function of our launch experience as opposed to it improving as a function of time."

A final kind of doublespeak is simply inflated language. Car me-   13
chanics may be called "automotive internists," elevator operators "members of the vertical transportation corps," and grocery store checkout clerks "career associate scanning professionals," while television sets are proclaimed to have "nonmulticolor capability." When a company "initiates a career alternative enhancement program" it is really laying off five thousand workers; "negative patient care outcome" means that the patient died; and "rapid oxidation" means a fire in a nuclear power plant.

The doublespeak of inflated language can have serious consequences.   14
The U.S. Navy didn't pay $2,043 a piece for steel nuts; it paid all that money for "hexiform rotatable surface compression units," which, by the way, "underwent catastrophic stress-related shaft detachment." Not to be outdone, the U.S. Air Force paid $214 a piece for Emergency Exit Lights, or flashlights. This doublespeak is in keeping with such military doublespeak as "preemptive counterattack" for first strike, "engage the enemy on all sides" for ambush, "tactical redeployment" for retreat, and "air support" for bombing. In the doublespeak of the military, the 1983 invasion of Grenada was conducted not by the U.S. Army, Navy, Air Force, and Marines but by the "Caribbean Peace Keeping Forces." But then according to the Pentagon it wasn't an invasion, it was a "predawn vertical insertion."

These last examples of doublespeak should make it clear that double-   15
speak is not the product of careless language or sloppy thinking. Indeed, serious doublespeak is the product of clear thinking and is carefully designed and constructed to appear to communicate but in fact to mislead. Thus, it's not a tax increase but "revenue enhancement," "tax base broadening," or "user fees," so how can you complain about higher taxes? It's not acid rain, it's just "poorly buffered precipitation," so don't worry about all those dead trees. That isn't the Mafia in Atlantic City, those are just "members of a career-offender cartel," so don't worry about the influence of organized crime in the city. The Supreme Court Justice wasn't addicted to the painkilling drug he was taking, it's just that the drug had simply "established an interrelationship with the body, such that if the drug is removed precipitously, there is a reaction," so don't worry that his decisions might have been influenced by his drug addiction. It's not a

Titan II nuclear-armed, intercontinental, ballistic missile 630 times more powerful than the atomic bomb dropped on Hiroshima, it's just a "very large, potentially disruptive reentry system," so don't worry about the threat of nuclear destruction. Serious doublespeak is highly strategic, and it breeds suspicion, cynicism, distrust, and, ultimately, hostility.

In his famous and now-classic essay "Politics and the English Language," which was published in 1946, George Orwell wrote that the "great enemy of clear language is insincerity. When there is a gap between one's real and one's declared aims, one turns as it were instinctively to long words and exhausted idioms, like a cuttlefish squirting out ink." For Orwell, language was an instrument for "expressing and not for concealing or preventing thought." In his most biting comment, Orwell observes that "in our time, political speech and writing are largely the defense of the indefensible. . . . Political Language has to consist largely of euphemism, question-begging and sheer cloudy vagueness. . . . Political language . . . is designed to make lies sound truthful and murder respectable, and to give an appearance of solidity to pure wind."

Orwell understood well the power of language as both a tool and a weapon. In the nightmare world of his novel *1984*, he depicted language as one of the most important tools of the totalitarian state. Newspeak, the official state language in *1984*, was designed not to extend but to *diminish* the range of human thought, to make only "correct" thought possible and all other modes of thought impossible. It was, in short, a language designed to create a reality which the state wanted.

Newspeak had another important function in Orwell's world of *1984*. It provided the means of expression for doublethink, which Orwell described in his novel as "the power of holding two contradictory beliefs in one's mind simultaneously, and accepting both of them." The classic example of doublethink in Orwell's novel is the slogan "War is Peace." And lest you think doublethink is confined only to Orwell's novel, you need only recall the words of Secretary of State Alexander Haig when he testified before a Congressional Committee in 1982 that a continued weapons build-up by the United States is "absolutely essential to our hopes for meaningful arms reduction." Or the words of Senator Orrin Hatch in 1988: "Capital punishment is our society's recognition of the sanctity of human life."

The more sophisticated and powerful uses of doublespeak can at times be difficult to identify. On 27 July 1981, President Ronald Reagan said in a television speech: "I will not stand by and see those of you who are dependent on Social Security deprived of the benefits you've worked so hard to earn. You will continue to receive your checks in the full amount due you." This speech had been billed as President Reagan's position on Social Security, a subject of much debate at the time. After the speech, public opinion polls recorded the great majority of the public as believing that President Reagan had affirmed his support for Social Security and that he would not support cuts in benefits. Five days after the speech, however, White House spokesperson David Gergen was quoted in the press as saying that President Reagan's words had been "carefully chosen." What President Reagan did mean, according to Gergen, was that he was reserving the right to decide who was "dependent" on those benefits, who had "earned" them, and who, therefore, was "due" them.

During the 1982 Congressional election campaign, the Republican   20
National Committee sponsored a television advertisement which pictured an elderly, folksy postman delivering Social Security checks "with the 7.4 percent cost-of-living raise that President Reagan promised." Looking directly at his audience, the postman then adds that Reagan "promised that raise and he kept his promise, in spite of those sticks-in-the-mud who tried to keep him from doing what we elected him to do."

The commercial was deliberately misleading. The cost-of-living in-   21
creases had been provided automatically by law since 1975, and President Reagan had tried three times to roll them back or delay them but was overruled by congressional opposition. When these discrepancies were pointed out to an official of the Republican National Committee, he called the commercial "inoffensive" and added, "Since when is a commercial supposed to be accurate? Do women really smile when they clean their ovens?"

In 1986, with the Challenger tragedy and subsequent investigation,   22
we discovered that doublespeak seemed to be the official language of NASA, the National Aeronautics and Space Administration, and of the contractors engaged in the space shuttle program. The first thing we learned is that the Challenger tragedy wasn't an accident. As Kay Parker of NASA said, experts were "working in the anomaly investigation." The "anomaly" was the explosion of the Challenger.

When NASA reported that it was having difficulty determining how   23
or exactly when the Challenger astronauts died, Rear Admiral Richard Truly reported that "whether or not a cabin rupture occurred prior to water impact has not yet been determined by a superficial examination of the recovered components." The "recovered components" were the bodies of the astronauts. Admiral Truly also said that "extremely large forces were imposed on the vehicle as evidenced by the immediate breakup into many pieces." He went on to say that "once these forces have been accurately determined, if in fact they can be, the structural analysts will attempt to estimate the effect on the structural and pressure integrity of the crew module." NASA referred to the coffins of the astronauts as "crew transfer containers."

Arnold Aldrich, manager of the national space transportation systems   24
program at Johnson Space Center, said that "the normal process during the countdown is that the countdown proceeds, assuming we are in a go posture, and at various points during the countdown we tag up on the operational loops and face to face in the firing room to ascertain the facts

that project elements that are monitoring the data and that are understanding the situation as we proceed are still in the go condition."

In testimony before the commission investigating the Challenger acci-   25
dent, Allen McDonald, an engineer for Morton Thiokol (the maker of the rocket), said he had expressed concern about the possible effect of cold weather on the booster rocket's O-ring seals the night before the launch: "I made the comment that lower temperatures are in the direction of badness for both O-rings, because it slows down the timing function."

Larry Mulloy, manager of the space shuttle solid rocket booster pro-   26
gram at Marshall Space Flight Center, responded to a question assessing whether problems with the O-rings or with the insulation of the liner of the nozzle posed a greater threat to the shuttle by saying, "The criticality in answering your question, sir, it would be a real foot race as to which one would be considered more critical, depending on the particular time that you looked at your experience with that."

After several executives of Rockwell International, the main contrac-   27
tor to build the shuttle, had testified that Rockwell had been opposed to launching the shuttle because of the danger posed by ice formation on the launch platform, Martin Cioffoletti, vice president for space transportation at Rockwell, said: "I felt that by telling them we did not have a sufficient data base and could not analyze the trajectory of the ice, I felt he understood that Rockwell was not giving a positive indication that we were for the launch."

Officials at Morton Thiokol, when asked why they reversed earlier   28
decisions not to launch the shuttle, said the reversal was "based on the reevaluation of those discussions." The Presidential commission investigating the accident suggested that this statement could be translated to mean there was pressure from NASA.

One of the most chilling uses of doublespeak occurred in 1981 when   29
then Secretary of State Alexander Haig was testifying before congressional committees about the murder of three American nuns and a Catholic lay worker in El Salvador. The four women had been raped and then shot at close range, and there was clear evidence that the crime had been committed by soldiers of the Salvadoran government. Before the House Foreign Affairs Committee, Secretary Haig said, "I'd like to suggest to you that some of the investigations would lead one to believe that perhaps the vehicle the nuns were riding in may have tried to run a roadblock, or may accidentally have been perceived to have been doing so, and there'd been an exchange of fire and then perhaps those who inflicted the casualties sought to cover it up. And this could have been at a very low level of both competence and motivation in the context of the issue itself. But the facts on this are not clear enough for anyone to draw a definitive conclusion."

The next day, before the Senate Foreign Relations Committee, Secre-   30
tary Haig claimed that press reports on his previous testimony were inac-

curate. When Senator Claiborne Pell asked whether Secretary Haig was suggesting the possibility that "the nuns may have run through a roadblock," Secretary Haig replied, "You mean that they tried to violate . . . ? Not at all, no, not at all. My heavens! The dear nuns who raised me in my parochial schooling would forever isolate me from their affections and respect." When Senator Pell asked Secretary Haig, "Did you mean that the nuns were firing at the people, or what did 'an exchange of fire' mean?" Secretary Haig replied, "I haven't met any pistol-packing nuns in my day, Senator. What I meant was that if one fellow starts shooting, then the next thing you know they all panic." Thus did the Secretary of State of the United States explain official government policy on the murder of four American citizens in a foreign land.

The congressional hearings for the Irancontra affair produced more doublespeak. During his second day of testimony before the Select Committee on Secret Military Assistance to Iran and the Nicaraguan Opposition, Oliver North admitted that he had on different occasions lied to the Iranians, his colleague Maj. Gen. Richard Secord, congressional investigators, and the Congress, and that he had destroyed evidence and created false documents. North then asserted to the committee that everything he was about to say would be the truth. 31

North used the words "residuals" and "diversions" to refer to the millions of dollars which were raised for the contras by overcharging Iran for arms. North also said that he "cleaned" and "fixed" things up, that he was "cleaning up the historical record," and that he "took steps to ensure" that things never "came out"—meaning he lied, destroyed official government documents, and created false documents. Some documents weren't destroyed; they were "non-log" or kept "out of the system so that outside knowledge would not necessarily be derived from having the documents themselves." 32

North was also careful not to "infect other people with unnecessary knowledge." He explained that the Nicaraguan Humanitarian Assistance Office provided humanitarian aid in "mixed loads," which, according to North, "meant . . . beans and Band-Aids and boots and bullets." For North, people in other countries who helped him were "assets." "Project Democracy" was a "euphemism" he used at the time to refer to the organization that was building an airfield for the contras. 33

In speaking of a false chronology of events which he helped construct, North said that he "was provided with additional input that was radically different from the truth. I assisted in furthering that version." He mentions "a different version from the facts" and calls the chronology "inaccurate." North also testified that he and William Casey, then head of the C.I.A., together falsified the testimony that Casey was to give to Congress. "Director Casey and I fixed that testimony and removed the offensive portions. We fixed it by omission. We left out—it wasn't made accurate, it wasn't made fulsome, it was fixed by omission." Official lies were "plausible deniability." 34

While North admitted that he had shredded documents after being   35
informed that officials from the Attorney General's office wanted to in-
spect some of the documents in his office, he said, "I would prefer to say
that I shredded documents that day like I did on all other days, but perhaps with increased intensity."

North also preferred to use the passive to avoid responsibility. When   36
asked, "Where are the non-logged documents?" he replied, "I think they
were shredded." Again, when asked on what authority he agreed to allow
Secord to make a personal profit off the arms sale to Iran, North replied
with a long, wordy response filled with such passive constructions as "it
was clearly indicated," "it was already known," and "it was recognized."
But he never answered the question.

For North, the whole investigation by Congress was just an attempt   37
"to criminalize policy differences between coequal branches of government and the Executive's conduct of foreign affairs." Lying to Congress,
shredding official documents, violating laws, conducting unauthorized
activities were all just "policy differences" to North. But North was generous with the committee: "I think there's fault to go on both sides. I've
said that repeatedly throughout my testimony. And I have accepted the
responsibility for my role in it." While North accepts responsibility, he
does not accept accountability.

This final statement of North's bears close reading for it reveals the   38
subtlety of his language. North states as fact that Congress was at fault,
but at fault for what he doesn't specify. Furthermore, he does not accept
responsibility for any specific action, only for his "role," whatever that
may have been, in "it." In short, while he may be "responsible" (not
guilty) for violating the law, Congress shares in that responsibility for
having passed the law.

In Oliver North's doublespeak, then, defying a law is complying with   39
it, noncompliance is compliance. North's doublespeak allowed him to
help draft a letter to Congress saying that "we are complying with the
letter and spirit" of the Boland Amendment, when what the letter really
meant, North later admitted, was that "Boland doesn't apply to us and so
we're complying with its letter and spirit."

Contrary to his claim that he was a "stand up guy" who would tell all   40
and take whatever was coming to him, North disclaimed all responsibility
for his actions: "I was authorized to do everything that I did." Yet when
he was asked who gave him authorization, North replied, "My supe-
riors." When asked which superior, he replied: "Well, who—look who
sign—I didn't sign those letters to the—to this body." And North's renowned steel-trap memory went vague or forgetful again.

After North had testified, Admiral John Poindexter, North's superior,   41
testified before the committee. Once again, doublespeak flourished. In
the world of Admiral John Poindexter, one does not lie but "misleads" or
"withholds information." Likewise, one engages in "secret activities"
which are not the same as covert actions. In Poindexter's world, one can

"acquiesce" in a shipment of weapons while at the same time not authorize the shipment. One can transfer millions of dollars of government money as a "technical implementation" without making a "substantive decision." One can also send subordinates to lie to congressional committees if one does not "micromanage" them. In Poindexter's world, "outside interference" occurs when Congress attempts to fulfill its constitutional function of passing legislation.

For Poindexter, withholding information was not lying. When asked about Col. North's testimony that he had lied to a congressional committee and that Poindexter had known that North intended to lie, Poindexter replied, "there was a general understanding that he [North] was to withhold information. . . . I . . . did not expect him to lie to the committee. I expected him to be evasive. . . . I'm sure they [North's answers] were very carefully crafted, nuanced. The total impact, I am sure, was one of withholding information from the Congress, but I'm still not convinced . . . that he lied."

Yet Poindexter protested that it is not "fair to say that I have misinformed Congress or other Cabinet officers. I haven't testified to that. I've testified that I withheld information from Congress. And with regard to the Cabinet officers, I didn't withhold anything from them that they didn't want withheld from them." Poindexter did not explain how it is possible to withhold information that a person wants withheld.

The doublespeak of Alexander Haig, Oliver North, and John Poindexter occurred during their testimony before congressional committees. Perhaps their doublespeak was not premeditated but just happened to be the way they spoke, and thought. President Jimmy Carter in 1980 could call the aborted raid to free the American hostages in Tehran an "incomplete success" and really believe that he had made a statement that clearly communicated with the American public. So too could President Ronald Reagan say in 1985 that "ultimately our security and our hopes for success at the arms reduction talks hinge on the determination that we show here to continue our program to rebuild and refortify our defenses" and really believe that greatly increasing the amount of money spent building new weapons will lead to a reduction in the number of weapons in the world. If we really believe that we understand such language and that such language communicates and promotes clear thought, then the world of *1984* with its control of reality through language is upon us.

QUESTIONS ON CONTENT

1. What, according to Lutz, is doublespeak? What are its essential characteristics?

2. What is a euphemism? Are all euphemisms examples of doublespeak? Explain.

3. What, according to Orwell, is *doublethink*? Provide several examples of doublethink to show how it works.

4. In his discussion of Oliver North's testimony during the Iran–contra hearings, Lutz states "While North accepts responsibility, he does not accept accountability" (37). Explain what Lutz means here.

5. Why, according to Lutz, does "doublespeak continue to spread as the official language of public discourse"? And why does he believe that we must recognize doublespeak for what it is and voice our dissatisfaction with those who use it?

QUESTIONS ON RHETORIC

1. In paragraph 2 Lutz provides his readers with a comprehensive definition of *doublespeak*. What does he achieve by clearly defining this term early in the essay?

2. Lutz is careful to illustrate each of his points with examples. Why is it important for him to use plenty of examples in an essay like this? What do his many examples reveal about Lutz's expertise on this subject?

3. In paragraphs 5 through 14 Lutz discusses various types of doublespeak. How does his classification help to clarify his discussion? Explain. (Glossary: *Classification*)

4. How does paragraph 15 function in the context of the entire essay? How are paragraphs 16 through 44 related to Lutz's statement that "serious doublespeak is highly strategic, and it breeds suspicion, cynicism, distrust, and, ultimately, hostility" (15)?

5. What is the "passive voice" and how does it work? Explain how Oliver North used the passive voice to avoid responsibility in his testimony.

VOCABULARY

variance (2)	obfuscate (2)	cynicism (15)
purported (2)	esoteric (7)	fulsome (34)
incongruity (2)	calibration (11)	nuanced (42)
referent (2)		

WRITING TOPICS

1. Using examples from Lutz's essay and other reading you have done, write an essay is which you discuss the differences among euphemisms, jargon, bureaucratese, and inflated language.

2. In his concluding paragraph Lutz states, "If we really believe that we understand such language [doublespeak] and that such language communicates and promotes clear thought, then the world of *1984* with its control of reality through language is upon us." Is Lutz overstating the case and being too pessimistic, or is the American public really unaware of— or apathetic about—how doublespeak manipulates and deceives? Write an essay in which you discuss the serious implications of doublespeak for the American public.

POLITICS AND THE ENGLISH LANGUAGE

George Orwell

An essay usually becomes a classic because it makes an important statement about a subject with unusual effectiveness. Such is the case with this essay, written in the 1940s. Here George Orwell (1903–1950), author of 1984, discusses the condition of the English language and the ways in which he believes it has seriously deteriorated. He attributes this decline to political and economic causes. Orwell concludes by suggesting a number of remedies to help restore the language to a healthier state.

Most people who bother with the matter at all would admit that the English language is in a bad way, but it is generally assumed that we cannot by conscious action do anything about it. Our civilization is decadent and our language—so the argument runs—must inevitably share in the general collapse. It follows that any struggle against the abuse of language is a sentimental archaism, like preferring candles to electric light or hansom cabs to aeroplanes. Underneath this lies the half-conscious belief that language is a natural growth and not an instrument which we shape for our own purposes.

Now, it is clear that the decline of a language must ultimately have political and economic causes: it is not due simply to the bad influence of this or that individual writer. But an effect can become a cause, reinforcing the original cause and producing the same effect in an intensified form, and so on indefinitely. A man may take to drink because he feels himself to be a failure, and then fail all the more completely because he drinks. It is rather the same thing that is happening to the English language. It becomes ugly and inaccurate because our thoughts are foolish, but the slovenliness of our language makes it easier for us to have foolish thoughts. The point is that the process is reversible. Modern English, especially written English, is full of bad habits which spread by imitation and which can be avoided if one is willing to take the necessary trouble. If one gets rid of these habits one can think more clearly, and to think clearly is a necessary first step towards political regeneration: so that the fight against bad English is not frivolous and is not the exclusive concern of professional writers. I will come back to this presently, and I hope that by that time the meaning of what I have said here will have become clearer. Meanwhile here are five specimens of the English language as it is now habitually written.

These five passages have not been picked out because they are espe-

70

cially bad—I could have quoted far worse if I had chosen—but because they illustrate various of the mental vices from which we now suffer. They are a little below the average, but are fairly representative samples. I number them so that I can refer back to them when necessary:

(1) I am not, indeed, sure whether it is not true to say that the Milton who once seemed not unlike a seventeenth-century Shelley had not become, out of an experience ever more bitter in each year, more alien [*sic*] to the founder of that Jesuit sect which nothing could induce him to tolerate.

> Professor Harold Laski (Essay in *Freedom of Expression*)

(2) Above all, we cannot play ducks and drakes with a native battery of idioms which prescribes such egregious collocations of vocables as the Basic *put up with* for *tolerate* or *put at a loss* for *bewilder*.

> Professor Lancelot Hogben (*Interglossa*)

(3) On the one side we have the free personality: by definition it is not neurotic, for it has neither conflict nor dream. Its desires, such as they are, are transparent, for they are just what institutional approval keeps in the forefront of consciousness; another institutional pattern would alter their number and intensity; there is little in them that is natural, irreducible, or culturally dangerous. But *on the other side*, the social bond itself is nothing but the mutual reflection of these self-secure integrities. Recall the definition of love. Is not this the very picture of a small academic? Where is there a place in this hall of mirrors for either personality or fraternity?

> Essay on psychology in *Politics* (New York)

(4) All the "best people" from the gentlemen's clubs, and all the frantic fascist captains, united in common hatred of Socialism and bestial horror of the rising tide of the mass revolutionary movement, have turned to acts of provocation, to foul incendiarism, to medieval legends of poisoned wells, to legalize their own destruction of proletarian organizations, and rouse the agitated petty-bourgeoisie to chauvinistic fervor on behalf of the fight against the revolutionary way out of the crisis.

> Communist pamphlet

(5) If a new spirit *is* to be infused into this old country, there is one thorny and contentious reform which must be tackled, and that is the humanization and galvanization of the B.B.C. Timidity here will bespeak canker and atrophy of the soul. The heart of Britain may be sound and of strong beat, for instance, but the British lion's roar at present is like that of Bottom in Shakespeare's *Midsummer Night's Dream*—as gentle as any sucking dove. A virile new Britain cannot continue indefinitely to be traduced in the eyes or rather ears, of the world by the effete languors of Langham Place, brazenly masquerading as "standard English." When the voice of Britain is heard at nine o'clock, better far and infinitely less ludicrous to hear aitches honestly dropped than the present priggish, inflated, inhibited, school-ma'amish arch braying of blameless bashful mewing maidens!

> Letter in *Tribune*

Each of these passages has faults of its own, but, quite apart from avoidable ugliness, two qualities are common to all of them. The first is 4 staleness of imagery; the other is lack of precision. The writer either has a meaning and cannot express it, or he inadvertently says something else, or he is almost indifferent as to whether his words mean anything or not. This mixture of vagueness and sheer incompetence is the most marked characteristic of modern English prose, and especially of any kind of political writing. As soon as certain topics are raised, the concrete melts into the abstract and no one seems able to think of turns of speech that are not hackneyed: prose consists less and less of *words* chosen for the sake of their meaning, and more and more of *phrases* tacked together like the sections of a prefabricated henhouse. I list below, with notes and examples, various of the tricks by means of which the work of prose-construction is habitually dodged:

DYING METAPHORS.   A newly invented metaphor assists thought by   5
evoking a visual image, while on the other hand a metaphor which is technically "dead" (e.g., *iron resolution*) has in effect reverted to being an ordinary word and can generally be used without loss of vividness. But in between these two classes there is a huge dump of worn-out metaphors which have lost all evocative power and are merely used because they save people the trouble of inventing phrases for themselves. Examples are: *Ring the changes on, take up the cudgels for, toe the line, ride roughshod over, stand shoulder to shoulder with, play into the hands of, no axe to grind, grist to the mill, fishing in troubled waters, on the order of the day, Achilles' heel, swan song, hotbed.* Many of these are used without knowledge of their meaning (what is a "rift," for instance?), and incompatible metaphors are frequently mixed, a sure sign that the writer is not interested in what he is saying. Some metaphors now current have been twisted out of their original meaning without those who use them even being aware of the fact. For example, *toe the line* is sometimes written *tow the line*. Another example is the *hammer and the anvil*, now always used with the implication that the anvil gets the worst of it. In real life it is always the anvil that breaks the hammer, never the other way about: a writer who stopped to think what he was saying would be aware of this, and would avoid perverting the original phrase.

OPERATORS OR VERBAL FALSE LIMBS.   These save the trouble of pick-   6
ing out appropriate verbs and nouns, and at the same time pad each sentence with extra syllables which give it an appearance of symmetry. Characteristic phrases are *render inoperative, militate against, make contact with, be subjected to, give rise to, give grounds for, have the effect of, play a leading part (role) in, make itself felt, take effect, exhibit a tendency to, serve the purpose of,* etc., etc. The keynote is the elimination of simple verbs. Instead of being a single word, such as *break, stop, spoil, mend, kill,* a verb becomes a *phrase,* made up of a noun or adjec-

tive tacked on to some general-purposes verb such as *prove, serve, form, play, render*. In addition, the passive voice is wherever possible used in preference to the active, and noun constructions are used instead of gerunds (*by examination of* instead of *by examining*). The range of verbs is further cut down by means of the *-ize* and *de-* formations, and the banal statements are given an appearance of profundity by means of the *not un-* formation. Simple conjunctions and prepositions are replaced by such phrases as *with respect to, having regard to, the fact that, by dint of, in view of, in the interests of, on the hypothesis that*; and the ends of sentences are saved from anticlimax by such resounding common-places as *greatly to be desired, cannot be left out of account, a development to be expected in the near future, deserving of serious consideration, brought to a satisfactory conclusion*, and so on and so forth.

PRETENTIOUS DICTION.   Words like *phenomenon, element, individual*   7 (as noun), *objective, categorical, effective, virtual, basic, primary, promote, constitute, exhibit, exploit, utilize, eliminate, liquidate*, are used to dress up simple statements and give an air of scientific impartiality to biased judgments. Adjectives like *epoch-making, epic, historic, unforgettable, triumphant, age-old, inevitable, inexorable, veritable*, are used to dignify the sordid processes of international politics, while writing that aims at glorifying war usually takes on an archaic color, its characteristic words being: *realm, throne, chariot, mailed fist, trident, sword, shield, buckler, banner, jackboot, clarion*. Foreign words and expressions such as *cul de sac, ancien régime, deus ex machina, mutatis mutandis, status quo, gleichschaltung, weltanschauung*, are used to give an air of culture and elegance. Except for the useful abbreviations *i.e., e.g.*, and *etc.*, there is no real need for any of the hundreds of foreign phrases now current in English. Bad writers, and especially scientific, political and sociological writers, are nearly always haunted by the notion that Latin or Greek words are grander than Saxon ones, and unnecessary words like *expedite, ameliorate, predict, extraneous, deracinated, clandestine, subaqueous* and hundreds of others constantly gain ground from their Anglo-Saxon opposite numbers.[1] The jargon peculiar to Marxist writing (*hyena, hangman, cannibal, petty bourgeois, these gentry, lacquey, flunkey, mad dog, White Guard*, etc.) consists largely of words and phrases translated from Russian, German or French; but the normal way of coining a new word is to use a Latin or Greek root with the appropriate affix and, where necessary, the *-ize* formation. It is often easier to make up words of this kind (*deregionalize, impermissible, extramarital, non-fragmentary* and so

[1]An interesting illustration of this is the way in which the English flower names which were in use till very recently are being ousted by Greek ones, *snapdragon* becoming *antirrhinum, forget-me-not* becoming *myosotis*, etc. It is hard to see any practical reason for this change of fashion: it is probably due to an instinctive turning-away from the more homely word and a vague feeling that the Greek word is scientific.

forth) than to think up the English words that will cover one's meaning. The result, in general, is an increase in slovenliness and vagueness.

MEANINGLESS WORDS.   In certain kinds of writing, particularly in art   8 criticism and literary criticism, it is normal to come across long passages which are almost completely lacking in meaning.[2] Words like *romantic, plastic, values, human, dead, sentimental, natural, vitality*, as used in art criticism, are strictly meaningless, in the sense that they not only do not point to any discoverable object, but are hardly ever expected to do so by the reader. When one critic writes, "The outstanding feature of Mr. X's work is its living quality," while another writes, "The immediately striking thing about Mr. X's work is its peculiar deadness," the reader accepts this as a simple difference of opinion. If words like *black* and *white* were involved, instead of the jargon words *dead* and *living*, he would see at once that language was being used in an improper way. Many political words are similarly abused. The word *Fascism* has now no meaning except in so far as it signifies "something not desirable." The words *democracy, freedom, patriotic, realistic, justice*, have each of them several different meanings which cannot be reconciled with one another. In the case of a word like *democracy*, not only is there no agreed definition, but the attempt to make one is resisted from all sides. It is almost universally felt that when we call a country democratic we are praising it: consequently the defenders of every kind of regime claim that it is a democracy, and fear that they might have to stop using the word if it were tied down to any one meaning. Words of this kind are often used in a consciously dishonest way. That is, the person who uses them has his own private definition, but allows his hearer to think he means something quite different. Statements like, *Marshal Pétain was a true patriot, The Soviet Press is the freest in the world, The Catholic Church is opposed to persecution*, are almost always made with intent to deceive. Other words used in variable meanings, in most cases more or less dishonestly, are: *class, totalitarian, science, progressive, reactionary, bourgeois, equality*.

Now that I have made this catalogue of swindles and perversions, let   9 me give another example of the kind of writing that they lead to. This time it must of its nature be an imaginary one. I am going to translate a passage of good English into modern English of the worst sort. Here is a well-known verse from *Ecclesiastes*:

> I returned and saw under the sun, that the race is not to the swift, nor the
> battle to the strong, neither yet bread to the wise, nor yet riches to men of

---

[2]Example: "Comfort's catholicity of perception and image, strangely Whitmanesque in range, almost the exact opposite in aesthetic compulsion, continues to evoke that trembling atmospheric accumulative hinting at a cruel, an inexorably serene timelessness. . . . Wrey Gardiner scores by aiming at simple bull's-eyes with precision. Only they are not so simple, and through this contented sadness runs more than the surface bittersweet of resignation." (*Poetry Quarterly*)

understanding, nor yet favour to men of skill; but time and chance happeneth to them all.

Here it is in modern English: 10

Objective consideration of contemporary phenomena compels the conclusion that success or failure in competitive activities exhibits no tendency to be commensurate with innate capacity, but that a considerable element of the unpredictable must invariably be taken into account.

This is a parody, but a very gross one. Exhibit (3), above, for in-   11
stance, contains several patches of the same kind of English. It will be seen that I have not made a full translation. The beginning and ending of the sentence follow the original meaning fairly closely, but in the middle the concrete illustrations—race, battle, bread—dissolve into the vague phrase "success or failure in competitive activities." This had to be so, because no modern writer of the kind I am discussing—no one capable of using phrases like "objective consideration of contemporary phenomena"—would ever tabulate his thoughts in that precise and detailed way. The whole tendency of modern prose is away from concreteness. Now analyse these two sentences a little more closely. The first contains forty-nine words but only sixty syllables, and all its words are those of everyday life. The second contains thirty-eight words of ninety syllables: eighteen of its words are from Latin roots, and one from Greek. The first sentence contains six vivid images, and only one phrase ("time and chance") that could be called vague. The second contains not a single fresh, arresting phrase, and in spite of its ninety syllables it gives only a shortened version of the meaning contained in the first. Yet without a doubt it is the second kind of sentence that is gaining ground in modern English. I do not want to exaggerate. This kind of writing is not yet universal, and outcrops of simplicity will occur here and there in the worst-written page. Still, if you or I were told to write a few lines on the uncertainty of human fortunes, we should probably come much nearer to my imaginary sentence than to the one from *Ecclesiastes*.

As I have tried to show, modern writing at its worst does not consist   12
in picking out words for the sake of their meaning and inventing images in order to make the meaning clearer. It consists in gumming together long strips of words which have already been set in order by someone else, and making the results presentable by sheer humbug. The attraction of this way of writing is that it is easy. It is easier—even quicker, once you have the habit—to say *In my opinion it is not an unjustifiable assumption that* than to say *I think*. If you use ready-made phrases, you not only don't have to hunt about for words; you also don't have to bother with the rhythms of your sentences, since these phrases are generally so arranged as to be more or less euphonious. When you are composing in a

hurry—when you are dictating to a stenographer, for instance, or making a public speech—it is natural to fall into a pretentious, Latinized style. Tags like *a consideration which we should do well to bear in mind* or *a conclusion to which all of us would readily assent* will save many a sentence from coming down with a bump. By using stale metaphors, similes and idioms, you save much mental effort, at the cost of leaving your meaning vague, not only for your reader but for yourself. This is the significance of mixed metaphors. The sole aim of a metaphor is to call up a visual image. When these images clash— as in *The Fascist octopus has sung its swan song, the jackboot is thrown into the melting pot*—it can be taken as certain that the writer is not seeing a mental image of the objects he is naming; in other words he is not really thinking. Look again at the examples I gave at the beginning of this essay. Professor Laski (1) uses five negatives in fifty-three words. One of these is superfluous, making nonsense of the whole passage, and in addition there is the slip *alien* for *akin*, making further nonsense, and several avoidable pieces of clumsiness which increase the general vagueness. Professor Hogben (2) plays ducks and drakes with a battery which is able to write prescriptions, and, while disapproving of the everyday phrase *put up with*, is unwilling to look *egregious* up in the dictionary and see what it means; (3), if one takes an uncharitable attitude towards it, is simply meaningless: probably one could work out its intended meaning by reading the whole of the article in which it occurs. In (4), the writer knows more or less what he wants to say, but an accumulation of stale phrases chokes him like tea leaves blocking a sink. In (5), words and meaning have almost parted company. People who write in this manner usually have a general emotional meaning—they dislike one thing and want to express solidarity with another—but they are not interested in the detail of what they are saying. A scrupulous writer, in every sentence that he writes, will ask himself at least four questions, thus: What am I trying to say? What words will express it? What image or idiom will make it clearer? Is this image fresh enough to have an effect? And he will probably ask himself two more: Could I put it more shortly? Have I said anything that is avoidably ugly? But you are not obliged to go to all this trouble. You can shirk it by simply throwing your mind open and letting the ready-made phrases come crowding in. They will construct your sentences for you—even think your thoughts for you, to a certain extent—and at need they will perform the important service of partially concealing your meaning even from yourself. It is at this point that the special connection between politics and the debasement of language becomes clear.

In our time it is broadly true that political writing is bad writing. Where it is not true, it will generally be found that the writer is some kind of rebel, expressing his private opinions and not a "party line." Orthodoxy, of whatever color, seems to demand a lifeless, imitative style. The political dialects to be found in pamphlets, leading articles, manifestos, 13

White Papers and the speeches of under-secretaries do, of course, vary from party to party, but they are all alike in that one almost never finds in them a fresh, vivid, homemade turn of speech. When one watches some tired hack on the platform mechanically repeating the familiar phrases— *bestial atrocities, iron heel, bloodstained tyranny, free peoples of the world, stand shoulder to shoulder*—one often has a curious feeling that one is not watching a live human being but some kind of dummy: a feeling which suddenly becomes stronger at moments when the light catches the speaker's spectacles and turns them into blank discs which seem to have no eyes behind them. And this is not altogether fanciful. A speaker who uses that kind of phraseology has gone some distance towards turning himself into a machine. The appropriate noises are coming out of his larynx, but his brain is not involved as it would be if he were choosing his words for himself. If the speech he is making is one that he is accustomed to make over and over again, he may be almost unconscious of what he is saying, as one is when one utters the responses in church. And this reduced state of consciousness, if not indispensable, is at any rate favorable to political conformity.

In our time, political speech and writing are largely the defence of the indefensible. Things like the continuance of British rule in India, the Russian purges and deportations, the dropping of the atom bombs on Japan, can indeed be defended, but only by arguments which are too brutal for most people to face, and which do not square with the professed aims of political parties. Thus political language has to consist largely of euphemism, question-begging and sheer cloudy vagueness. Defenceless villages are bombarded from the air, the inhabitants driven out into the countryside, the cattle machine-gunned, the huts set on fire with incendiary bullets: this is called *pacification*. Millions of peasants are robbed of their farms and sent trudging along the roads with no more than they can carry: this is called *transfer of population* or *rectification of frontiers*. People are imprisoned for years without trial, or shot in the back of the neck or sent to die of scurvy in Arctic lumber camps: this is called *elimination of unreliable elements*. Such phraseology is needed if one wants to name things without calling up mental pictures of them. Consider for instance some comfortable English professor defending Russian totalitarianism. He cannot say outright, "I believe in killing off your opponents when you can get good results by doing so." Probably, therefore, he will say something like this:

> While freely conceding that the Soviet régime exhibits certain features which the humanitarian may be inclined to deplore, we must, I think, agree that a certain curtailment of the right to political opposition is an unavoidable concomitant of transitional periods, and that the rigors which the Russian people have been called upon to undergo have been amply justified in the sphere of concrete achievement.

The inflated style is itself a kind of euphemism. A mass of Latin   15
words falls upon the facts like soft snow, blurring the outlines and covering up all the details. The great enemy of clear language is insincerity.
When there is a gap between one's real and one's declared aims, one
turns as it were instinctively to long words and exhausted idioms, like a
cuttlefish squirting out ink. In our age there is no such thing as "keeping
out of politics." All issues are political issues, and politics itself is a mass
of lies, evasions, folly, hatred and schizophrenia. When the general atmosphere is bad, language must suffer. I should expect to find—this is a
guess which I have not sufficient knowledge to verify—that the German,
Russian and Italian languages have all deteriorated in the last ten or fifteen years, as a result of dictatorship.

But if thought corrupts language, language can also corrupt thought.   16
A bad usage can spread by tradition and imitation, even among people
who should and do know better. The debased language that I have been
discussing is in some ways very convenient. Phrases like *a not unjustifiable assumption, leaves much to be desired, would serve no good purpose,
a consideration which we should do well to bear in mind*, are a continuous temptation, a packet of aspirins always at one's elbow. Look back
through this essay, and for certain you will find that I have again and
again committed the very faults I am protesting against. By this morning's post I have received a pamphlet dealing with conditions in Germany. The author tells me that he "felt impelled" to write it. I open it at
random, and here is almost the first sentence that I see: "[The Allies]
have an opportunity not only of achieving a radical transformation of
Germany's social and political structure in such a way as to avoid a
nationalistic reaction in Germany itself, but at the same time of laying the
foundations of a cooperative and unified Europe." You see, he "feels
impelled" to write—feels, presumably, that he has something new to
say—and yet his words, like cavalry horses answering the bugle, group
themselves automatically into the familiar dreary pattern. The invasion of
one's mind by ready-made phrases (*lay the foundations, achieve a radical
transformation*) can only be prevented if one is constantly on guard
against them, and every such phrase anaesthetizes a portion of one's
brain.

I said earlier that the decadence of our language is probably curable.   17
Those who deny this would argue, if they produced an argument at all,
that language merely reflects existing social conditions, and that we cannot influence its development by any direct tinkering with words and
constructions. So far as the general tone or spirit of a language goes, this
may be true, but it is not true in detail. Silly words and expressions have
often disappeared, not through any evolutionary process but owing to the
conscious action of a minority. Two recent examples were *explore every
avenue* and *leave no stone unturned*, which were killed by the jeers of a
few journalists. There is a long list of fly-blown metaphors which could

similarly be got rid of if enough people would interest themselves in the job; and it should also be possible to laugh the *not un-* formation out of existence,[3] to reduce the amount of Latin and Greek in the average sentence, to drive out foreign phrases and strayed scientific words, and, in general, to make pretentiousness unfashionable. But all these are minor points. The defence of the English language implies more than this, and perhaps it is best to start by saying what it does *not* imply.

To begin with, it has nothing to do with archaism, with the salvaging of obsolete words and turns of speech, or with the setting up of a "standard English" which must never be departed from. On the contrary, it is especially concerned with the scrapping of every word or idiom which has outworn its usefulness. It has nothing to do with correct grammar and syntax, which are of no importance so long as one makes one's meaning clear, or with the avoidance of Americanisms, or with having what is called a "good prose style." On the other hand it is not concerned with fake simplicity and the attempt to make written English colloquial. Nor does it even imply in every case preferring the Saxon word to the Latin one, though it does imply using the fewest and shortest words that will cover one's meaning. What is above all needed is to let the meaning choose the word, and not the other way about. In prose, the worst thing one can do with words is to surrender to them. When you think of a concrete object, you think wordlessly, and then, if you want to describe the thing you have been visualizing you probably hunt about till you find the exact words that seem to fit it. When you think of something abstract you are more inclined to use words from the start, and unless you make a conscious effort to prevent it, the existing dialect will come rushing in and do the job for you, at the expense of blurring or even changing your meaning. Probably it is better to put off using words as long as possible and get one's meaning as clear as one can through pictures or sensations. Afterwards one can choose—not simply *accept*—the phrases that will best cover the meaning, and then switch round and decide what impression one's words are likely to make on another person. This last effort of the mind cuts out all stale or mixed images, all prefabricated phrases, needless repetitions, and humbug and vagueness generally. But one can often be in doubt about the effect of a word or a phrase, and one needs rules that one can rely on when instinct fails. I think the following rules will cover most cases:

1. Never use a metaphor, simile, or other figure of speech which you are used to seeing in print.
2. Never use a long word where a short one will do.
3. If it is possible to cut a word out, always cut it out.

---

[3]One can cure oneself of the *not un-* formation by memorizing this sentence: *A not unblack dog was chasing a not unsmall rabbit across a not ungreen field.*

4. Never use the passive where you can use the active.
5. Never use a foreign phrase, a scientific word or a jargon word if you can think of an everyday English equivalent.
6. Break any of these rules sooner than say anything outright barbarous.

These rules sound elementary, and so they are, but they demand a deep change of attitude in anyone who has grown used to writing in the style now fashionable. One could keep all of them and still write bad English, but one could not write the kind of stuff that I quoted in those five specimens at the beginning of this article.

I have not here been considering the literary use of language, but   19
merely language as an instrument for expressing and not for concealing or preventing thought. Stuart Chase and others have come near to claiming that all abstract words are meaningless, and have used this as a pretext for advocating a kind of political quietism. Since you don't know what Fascism is, how can you struggle against Fascism? One need not swallow such absurdities as this, but one ought to recognize that the present political chaos is connected with the decay of language, and that one can probably bring about some improvement by starting at the verbal end. If you simplify your English, you are freed from the worst follies of orthodoxy. You cannot speak any of the necessary dialects, and when you make a stupid remark its stupidity will be obvious, even to yourself. Political language—and with variations this is true of all political parties, from Conservatives to Anarchists—is designed to make lies sound truthful and murder respectable, and to give an appearance of solidity to pure wind. One cannot change this all in a moment, but one can at least change one's own habits, and from time to time one can even, if one jeers loudly enough, send some worn-out and useless phrase—some *jackboot, Achilles' heel, hotbed, melting pot, acid test, veritable inferno* or other lump of verbal refuse—into the dustbin where it belongs.

QUESTIONS ON CONTENT

1. In your own words, summarize Orwell's argument in this essay.

2. It is often said that "mixed metaphors" (for example, "politicians who have their heads in the sand are leading the country over the precipice") are undesirable in either speech or writing because they are inaccurate. For Orwell, a mixed metaphor is symptomatic of a greater problem. What is that problem?

3. Reread paragraph 2 of the essay. What, according to Orwell, is the nature of cause-and-effect relationships?

4. Our world is becoming increasingly prefabricated. What does the concept of prefabrication have to do with Orwell's argument concerning the prevalance of the habitual and trite phrase?

5. Orwell states that he himself in this essay is guilty of some of the errors he is pointing out. Can you detect any of them?

6. According to Orwell, what are four important prewriting questions scrupulous writers ask themselves?

7. Orwell says that one of the evils of political language is "question-begging" (14). What does he mean? Why, according to Orwell, has political language deteriorated? Do you agree with him that "the decadence of our language is probably curable" (17)? Explain.

QUESTIONS ON RHETORIC

1. Why does Orwell present the "five specimens of the English language as it is now habitually written" (2)? What use does he make of these five passages later in his essay?

2. Following are some of the metaphors and similes that Orwell uses in his essay. (Glossary: *Figures of Speech*) Explain how each one works and comment on its effectiveness.

   a. . . . prose consists less . . . of *words* chosen for the sake of their meaning, and more . . . of *phrases* tacked together like the sections of a prefabricated hen-house (4).
   b. But in between these two classes there is a huge dump of worn-out metaphors which have lost all evocative power. . . . (5).
   c. . . . the writer knows . . . what he wants to say, but an accumulation of stale phrases chokes him like tea leaves blocking a sink (12).
   d. A mass of Latin words falls upon the facts like soft snow, blurring the outlines and covering up all the details (15).
   e. When there is a gap between one's real and one's declared aims, one turns . . . instinctively to long words and exhausted idioms, like a cuttlefish squirting out ink (15).
   f. . . . he . . . feels, presumably, that he has something new to say—and yet his words, like cavalry horses answering the bugle, group themselves automatically into the familiar dreary pattern (16).

3. At the end of paragraph 4 Orwell speaks of "the tricks by means of which the work of prose-construction is habitually dodged," and he then goes on to classify them. Why is classification a useful rhetorical strategy in this situation? (Glossary: *Division and Classification*)

4. Point out several terms and concepts that Orwell defines in this essay. What is his purpose in defining them? How does he go about it in each instance? (Glossary: *Definition*)

5. In this essay Orwell moves from negative arguments to positive ones. Where does he make the transition from criticisms to proposals? What is the effect of his organizing the argument in this way?

6. Orwell describes many of the language abuses that he is criticizing as "habits" or "mental vices." Are these terms consistent with his thesis? Explain. (Glossary: *Diction*)

7. Orwell suggests that you should never use the passive voice when you can use the active voice. Consider the following example:

Passive: The welfare budget was cut by Congress.
Active: Congress cut the welfare budget.

Not only is the active version shorter, but it is more precise in that it properly emphasizes "Congress" as the doer of the action. Rewrite each of the following sentences in the active voice.

   a. The line-drive single was hit by John.
   b. Two eggs and one stick of butter should be added to the other ingredients.
   c. Information of a confidential nature cannot be released by doctors.
   d. Figures showing that the cost of living rose sharply during the past twelve months were released by the administration today.
   e. It was decided that a meeting would be held on each Monday.

Are there any situations in which the passive voice is more appropriate than the active? Explain. What conclusions can you draw about the active and passive voices?

VOCABULARY

decadent (1)   impartiality (7)   scrupulous (12)
frivolous (2)   biased (7)   humanitarian (14)
inadvertently (4)   reconciled (8)   evolutionary (17)
implication (5)   pretentious (12)

WRITING TOPICS

1. Gather five examples of recent American political English that you consider, in Orwell's words, "ugly and inaccurate." You should be able to find more than enough material in current newspapers, magazines, and books. Are the "tricks" used by today's writers the same as those used in Orwell's day? If not, what terms would you invent to describe the "new" tricks?

2. As many of Orwell's examples suggest, language is sometimes used not to express but to conceal meaning. Is this true only of politics? Can you think of any situation in which you or others you know have been under pressure to say something, yet had nothing that you were ready or willing to say? What happened? Write an essay in which you first give some examples of the problem and then suggest ways of handling such situations honestly.

WRITING ASSIGNMENTS FOR "LANGUAGE USE AND MISUSE"

1. In his essay "The Marks of an Educated Man" (*Context*, Spring 1961), Alan Simpson presents the following example of inflated prose, or, as he aptly dubs it, "verbal smog."

> It is inherent to motivational phenomena that there is a drive for more gratification than is realistically possible, on any level or in any type of personality organization. Likewise it is inherent to the world of objects that not all potentially desirable opportunities can be realized within a human life span. Therefore, any personality must involve an organization that allocates opportunities for gratifications, that systematizes precedence relative to the limited possibilities. The possibilities of gratification, simultaneously or sequentially, of all need dispositions are severely limited by the structure of the object system and by the intrasystemic incompatibility of the consequences of gratifying them all.

What is the author of this passage trying to say? Rewrite the paragraph eliminating the unnecessary verbiage. Using materials from two or more of the articles in this section, write an essay in which you argue for the use of clear, unambiguous prose in public documents.

2. The following item appeared in the *San Francisco Chronicle*.

STATE MAKES IT PERFECTLY CLEAR

SACRAMENTO For some time the public has wondered what to make of most bureaucratic twaddle—but a new State law has set the record straight at last.

From the revised State code of the Division of Consumer Services, Department of Consumer Affairs, Title 4: subsection 2102, comes the official word:

"Tenses, Gender and Number: For the purpose of the rules and regulations contained in this chapter, the present tense includes the past and future tenses, and the future, the present; the masculine gender includes the feminine, and feminine, the masculine; and the singular includes the plural, and the plural the singular."

Our Correspondent

Comment on this example of gobbledygook. Why is bureaucratic and legal writing particularly prone to gobbledygook?

The academic world is not immune to bureaucratic language. Collect examples of such writing on your campus and write an essay in which you discuss your findings. Are administrators more prone to doublespeak than student government leaders or faculty on your campus? Use materials from the Birk and Birk, Lutz, and Orwell articles in analyzing the writing you collect.

3. Governments and the news media are prone to using euphemisms, misplaced technical jargon, stock phrases, and connotatively "loaded" words for propaganda purposes. Depending on your position, for example, a "terrorist" and a "freedom fighter" are two very different things. To

refer to a group as "self-styled" or as "calling themselves . . ." or to world leaders as "intransigent," "belligerent," "stern," and "forceful" is to use language that embodies strong value judgments. Examine a recent newspaper or news magazine article on a current event for examples of "loaded" words. Then write an analysis of how the writer of the article has attempted to alter your attitudes through biased language.

4. In his book *The Second Sin*, psychiatrist Thomas Szasz makes the following observations:

    a. The prevention of parenthood is called "planned parenthood."
    b. Policemen receive bribes; politicians receive campaign contributions.
    c. Homicide by physicians is called "euthanasia."
    d. Marijuana and heroin are sold by pushers; cigarettes and alcohol are sold by businessmen.
    e. Imprisonment by psychiatrists is called "mental hospitalization."

Using Szasz's observations or similar ones of your own, write an essay in which you discuss the way people manipulate words and meanings to suit their particular needs.

5. Using Orwell's standards of good writing, write an essay in which you analyze a newspaper editorial, a political speech, a public service advertisement, or a comparable example of contemporary political prose.

6. Orwell says, "As soon as certain topics are raised, the concrete melts into the abstract . . ." (4). One such topic has always been war. Compare the following two war prayers, the first from a Catholic missal and the second by Mark Twain:

> O Lord, graciously regard the sacrifice which we offer up: that it may deliver us from all the evil of war, and establish us under Thy sure protection. Through our Lord Jesus Christ, Thy Son, who liveth and reigneth with Thee in the unity of the Holy Ghost.

> Oh Lord our God, help us to tear their soldiers to bloody shreds with our shells; help us to cover their smiling fields with their patriot dead; help us to lay waste their humble homes with a hurricane of fire; help us to wring the hearts of their unoffending widows with unavailing grief; help us to turn them out roofless with their little children to wander unfriended the wastes of their desolated land in rags and hunger and thirst. Lord, blast their hopes, blight their lives, protract their bitter pilgrimage, make heavy their steps, water their way with their tears. We ask it, in the spirit of love, of Him Who is the Source of Love, and who is the ever-faithful refuge and friend of all that are sore beset and seek his aid.

How would you characterize the very different effects of these two war prayers? Specifically, how do you account for the differences in effect?

7. Write an essay in which you compare and contrast a national tabloid newspaper (such as the *National Enquirer*) with your local newspaper. You may wish to consider one or more of the following:

    a. intended audience
    b. types of stories covered
    c. placement of stories
    d. formality or informality of writing

   e. amount of visual material

   f. amount and type of advertising

8. Choose an editorial dealing with a controversial issue. Assume that you have been offered equal space in the newspaper in which to present the opposing viewpoint. Write a rebuttal. Hand in both your rebuttal and the original editorial that stimulated it.

9. Write three paragraphs in which you describe the same incident, person, scene, or thing. In the first paragraph, use language that will produce a neutral impression; in the second, language that will produce a favorable impression; and in the third, language that will produce an unfavorable impression. Keep the factual content of each of your paragraphs constant; vary only the language.

PART III

Usage, Words, and Standard English

Jill, fax Farble and ask her what our phone conversation just meant.

A BRIEF HISTORY OF ENGLISH

Paul Roberts

In the following selection from his book Understanding
English, *the late Professor Paul Roberts recounts the major
events in the history of England and discusses their
relationship to the development of the English language. He
shows us how the people who invaded England influenced the
language and how, in recent times, the rapid spread of
English has resulted in its becoming a major world language.*

HISTORICAL BACKGROUNDS

No understanding of the English language can be very satisfactory with-   1
out a notion of the history of the language. But we shall have to make do
with just a notion. The history of English is long and complicated, and
we can only hit the high spots.

The history of our language begins a little after A.D. 600. Everything   2
before that is pre-history, which means that we can guess at it but can't
prove much. For a thousand years or so before the birth of Christ our
linguistic ancestors were savages wandering through the forests of northern Europe. Their language was a part of the Germanic branch of the
Indo-European Family.

At the time of the Roman Empire—say, from the beginning of the   3
Christian Era to around A.D. 400—the speakers of what was to become
English were scattered along the northern coast of Europe. They spoke a
dialect of Low German. More exactly, they spoke several different dialects, since they were several different tribes. The names given to the
tribes who got to England are *Angles, Saxons*, and *Jutes*. For convenience, we can refer to them as Anglo-Saxons.

Their first contact with civilization was a rather thin acquaintance   4
with the Roman Empire on whose borders they lived. Probably some of
the Anglo-Saxons wandered into the Empire occasionally, and certainly
Roman merchants and traders traveled among the tribes. At any rate, this
period saw the first of our many borrowings from Latin. Such words as
kettle, wine, cheese, butter, cheap, plum, gem, bishop, church were borrowed at this time. They show something of the relationship of the Anglo-Saxons with the Romans. The Anglo-Saxons were learning, getting
their first taste of civilization.

They still had a long way to go, however, and their first step was to   5
help smash the civilization they were learning from. In the fourth century

89

the Roman power weakened badly. While the Goths were pounding away at the Romans in the Mediterranean countries, their relatives, the Anglo-Saxons, began to attack Britain.

The Romans had been the ruling power in Britain since A.D. 43. They   6 had subjugated the Celts whom they found living there and had succeeded in setting up a Roman administration. The Roman influence did not extend to the outlying parts of the British Isles. In Scotland, Wales, and Ireland the Celts remained free and wild, and they made periodic forays against the Romans in England. Among other defense measures, the Romans built the famous Roman Wall to ward off the tribes in the north.

Even in England the Roman power was thin. Latin did not become   7 the language of the country as it did in Gaul and Spain. The mass of people continued to speak Celtic, with Latin and the Roman civilization it contained in use as a top dressing.

In the fourth century, troubles multiplied for the Romans in Britain.   8 Not only did the untamed tribes of Scotland and Wales grow more and more restive, but the Anglo-Saxons began to make pirate raids on the eastern coast. Furthermore, there was growing difficulty everywhere in the Empire, and the legions in Britain were siphoned off to fight elsewhere. Finally, in A.D. 410, the last Roman ruler in England, bent on becoming emperor, left the islands and took the last of the legions with him. The Celts were left in possession of Britain but almost defenseless against the impending Anglo-Saxon attack.

Not much is surely known about the arrival of the Anglo-Saxons in   9 England. According to the best early source, the eighth-century historian Bede, the Jutes came in 449 in response to a plea from the Celtic king, Vortigern, who wanted their help against the Picts attacking from the north. The Jutes subdued the Picts but then quarreled and fought with Vortigern, and, with reinforcements from the Continent, settled permanently in Kent. Somewhat later the Angles established themselves in eastern England and the Saxons in the south and west. Bede's account is plausible enough, and these were probably the main lines of the invasion.

We do know, however, that the Angles, Saxons, and Jutes were a   10 long time securing themselves in England. Fighting went on for as long as a hundred years before the Celts in England were all killed, driven into Wales, or reduced to slavery. This is the period of King Arthur, who was not entirely mythological. He was a Romanized Celt, a general, though probably not a king. He had some success against the Anglo-Saxons, but it was only temporary. By 550 or so the Anglo-Saxons were firmly established. English was in England.

OLD ENGLISH

All this is pre-history, so far as the language is concerned. We have no   11 record of the English language until after 600, when the Anglo-Saxons were converted to Christianity and learned the Latin alphabet. The conversion began, to be precise, in the year 597 and was accomplished within thirty or forty years. The conversion was a great advance for the Anglo-Saxons, not only because of the spiritual benefits but because it reestablished contact with what remained of Roman civilization. This civilization didn't amount to much in the year 600, but it was certainly superior to anything in England up to that time.

It is customary to divide the history of the English language into three   12 periods: Old English, Middle English, and Modern English. Old English runs from the earliest records—i.e., seventh century—to about 1100; Middle English from 1100 to 1450 or 1500; Modern English from 1500 to the present day. Sometimes Modern English is further divided into Early Modern, 1500–1700, and Late Modern, 1700 to the present.

When England came into history, it was divided into several more or   13 less autonomous kingdoms, some of which at times exercised a certain amount of control over the others. In the century after the conversion the most advanced kingdom was Northumbria, the area between the Humber River and the Scottish border. By A.D. 700 the Northumbrians had developed a respectable civilization, the finest in Europe. It is sometimes called the Northumbrian Renaissance, and it was the first of the several renaissances through which Europe struggled upward out of the ruins of the Roman Empire. It was in this period that the best of the Old English literature was written, including the epic poem *Beowulf*.

In the eighth century, Northumbrian power declined, and the center of   14 influence moved southward to Mercia, the kingdom of the Midlands. A century later the center shifted again, and Wessex, the country of the West Saxons, became the leading power. The most famous king of the West Saxons was Alfred the Great, who reigned in the second half of the ninth century, dying in 901. He was famous not only as a military man and administrator but also as a champion of learning. He founded and supported schools and translated or caused to be translated many books from Latin into English. At this time also much of the Northumbrian literature of two centuries earlier was copied in West Saxon. Indeed, the great bulk of Old English writing which has come down to us in the West Saxon dialect of 900 or later.

In the military sphere, Alfred's great accomplishment was his suc-   15 cessful opposition to the Viking invasions. In the ninth and tenth centuries, the Norsemen emerged in their ships from their homelands in Denmark and the Scandinavian peninsula. They traveled far and attacked and plundered at will and almost with impunity. They ravaged Italy and Greece, settled in France, Russia, and Ireland, colonized Iceland and Greenland, and discovered America several centuries before Columbus. Nor did they overlook England.

After many years of hit-and-run raids, the Norsemen landed an army   16 on the east coast of England in the year 866. There was nothing much to oppose them except the Wessex power led by Alfred. The long struggle ended in 877 with a treaty by which a line was drawn roughly from the northwest of England to the southeast. On the eastern side of the line Norse rule was to prevail. This was called the Danelaw. The western side was to be governed by Wessex.

The linguistic result of all this was a considerable injection of Norse   17 into the English language. Norse was at this time not so different from English as Norwegian or Danish is now. Probably speakers of English could understand, more or less, the language of the newcomers who had moved into eastern England. At any rate, there was considerable interchange and word borrowing. Examples of Norse words in the English language are *sky, give, law, egg, outlaw, leg, ugly, scant, sly, crawl, scowl, take, thrust*. There are hundreds more. We have even borrowed some pronouns from Norse—*they, their*, and *them*. These words were borrowed first by the eastern and northern dialects and then in the course of hundreds of years made their way into English generally.

It is supposed also—indeed, it must be true—that the Norsemen in-   18 fluenced the sound structure and the grammar of English. But this is hard to demonstrate in detail.

A SPECIMEN OF OLD ENGLISH

We may now have an example of Old English. The favorite illustration is   19 the Lord's Prayer, since it needs no translation. This has come to us in several different versions. Here is one:

Fæder ure,
þu þe eart on heofonum,
si þin nama gehalgod.
Tobecume þin rice.
Gewurþe ðin willa on eor ðan swa swa on heofonum.
Urne gedæghwamlican hlaf syle us to dæg.
And forgyf us ure gyltas, swa swa we forgyfa ðurum gyltendum.
And ne gelæd þu us on costnunge,
ac alys us of yfele. Soþlice.

Some of the differences between this and Modern English are merely   20 differences in orthography. For instance, the sign æ is what Old English writers used for a vowel sound like that in modern *hat* or *and*. The *th* sounds of modern *thin* or *then* are represented in Old English by þ or ð. But of course there are many differences in sound too. *Ure* is the ancestor of modern *our*, but the first vowel was like that in *too* or *ooze*. *Hlaf* is modern *loaf*; we have dropped the *h* sound and changed the vowel, which in *hlaf* was pronounced something like the vowel in *father*. Old English had some sounds which we do not have. The sound represented by *y* does not occur in Modern English. If you pronounce the vowel in *bit* with your lips rounded, you may approach it.

In grammar, Old English was much more highly inflected than Mod-   21
ern English is. That is, there were more case endings for nouns, more
person and number endings for verbs, a more complicated pronoun system, various endings for adjectives, and so on. Old English nouns had
four cases—nominative, genitive, dative, accusative. Adjectives had
five—all these and an instrumental case besides. Present-day English has
only two cases for nouns—common case and possessive case. Adjectives
now have no case system at all. On the other hand, we now use a more
rigid word order and more structure words (prepositions, auxiliaries, and
the like) to express relationships than Old English did.

Some of this grammar we can see in the Lord's Prayer. *Heofonum*,   22
for instance, is a dative plural; the nominative singular was *heofon*. *Urne*
is an accusative singular; the nominative is *ure*. In *urum glytendum* both
words are dative plural. *Forgyfap* is the first person plural form of the
verb. Word order is different: "urne gedæghwamlican hlaf syle us" in
place of "Give us our daily bread." And so on.

In vocabulary Old English is quite different from Modern English.   23
Most of the Old English words arc what we may call native English: that
is, words which have not been borrowed from other languages but which
have been a part of English ever since English was a part of Indo-European. Old English did certainly contain borrowed words. We have seen
that many borrowings were coming in from Norse. Rather large numbers
had been borrowed from Latin, too. Some of these were taken while the
Anglo-Saxons were still on the Continent (*cheese, butter, bishop, kettle*,
etc.); a large number came into English after the conversion (*angel, can-
dle, priest, martyr, radish, oyster, purple, school, spend*, etc.). But the
great majority of Old English words were native English.

Now, on the contrary, the majority of words in English are borrowed,   24
taken mostly from Latin and French. Of the words in *The American College Dictionary* only about 14 percent are native. Most of these, to be
sure, are common, high-frequency words—*the, of, I, and, because, man,
mother, road*, etc.; of the thousand most common words in English,
some 62 percent are native English. Even so, the modern vocabulary is
very much Latinized and Frenchified. The Old English vocabulary was
not.

MIDDLE ENGLISH

Sometime between the years 1000 and 1200 various important changes   25
took place in the structure of English, and Old English became Middle
English. The political event which facilitated these changes was the Norman Conquest. The Normans, as the name shows, came originally from
Scandinavia. In the early tenth century they established themselves in
northern France, adopted the French language, and developed a vigorous

kingdom and a very passable civilization. In the year 1066, led by Duke William, they crossed the Channel and made themselves masters of England. For the next several hundred years, England was ruled by kings whose first language was French.

One might wonder why, after the Norman Conquest, French did not become the national language, replacing English entirely. The reason is that the Conquest was not a national migration, as the earlier Anglo-Saxon invasion had been. Great numbers of Normans came to England, but they came as rulers and landlords. French became the language of the court, the language of the nobility, the language of polite society, the language of literature. But it did not replace English as the language of the people. There must always have been hundreds of towns and villages in which French was never heard except when visitors of high station passed through. 26

But English, though it survived as the national language, was profoundly changed after the Norman Conquest. Some of the changes—in sound structure and grammar—would no doubt have taken place whether there had been a Conquest or not. Even before 1066 the case system of English nouns and adjectives was becoming simplified; people came to rely more on word order and prepositions than on inflectional endings to communicate their meanings. The process was speeded up by sound changes which caused many of the endings to sound alike. But no doubt the Conquest facilitated the change. German, which didn't experience a Norman Conquest, is today rather highly inflected compared to its cousin English. 27

But it is in vocabulary that the effects of the Conquest are most obvious. French ceased, after a hundred years or so, to be the native language of very many people in England, but it continued—and continues still—to be a zealously cultivated second language, the mirror of elegance and civilization. When one spoke English, one introduced not only French ideas and French things but also their French names. This was not only easy but socially useful. To pepper one's conversation with French expressions was to show that one was well-bred, elegant, *au courant*. The last sentence shows that the process is not yet dead. By using *au courant* instead of, say, *abreast of things*, the writer indicates that he is no dull clod who knows only English but an elegant person aware of how things are done in *le haut monde*. 28

Thus French words came into English, all sorts of them. There were words to do with government: *parliament, majesty, treaty, alliance, tax, government*; church words: *parson, sermon, baptism, incense, crucifix, religion*; words for foods: *veal, beef, mutton, bacon, jelly, peach, lemon, cream, biscuit*; colors: *blue, scarlet, vermilion*; household words: *curtain, chair, lamp, towel, blanket, parlor*; play words: *dance, chess, music, leisure, conversation*; literary words: *story, romance, poet, literary*; learned words: *study, logic, grammar, noun, surgeon, anatomy, stomach*; 29

just ordinary words of all sorts: *nice, second, very, age, bucket, gentle, final, fault, flower, cry, count, sure, move, surprise, plain.*

All these and thousands more poured into the English vocabulary be-   30
tween 1100 and 1500 until, at the end of that time, many people must
have had more French words than English at their command. This is not
to say that English became French. English remained English in sound
structure and in grammar, though these also felt the ripples of French
influence. The very heart of the vocabulary, too, remained English. Most
of the high-frequency words—the pronouns, the prepositions, the conjunctions, the auxiliaries, as well as a great many ordinary nouns and
verbs and adjectives—were not replaced by borrowings.

Middle English, then, was still a Germanic language, but it differed   31
from Old English in many ways. The sound system and the grammar
changed a good deal. Speakers made less use of case systems and other
inflectional devices and relied more on word order and structure words to
express their meanings. This is often said to be a simplification, but it
isn't really. Languages don't become simpler; they merely exchange one
kind of complexity for another. Modern English is not a simple language,
as any foreign speaker who tries to learn it will hasten to tell you.

For us Middle English is simpler than Old English just because it is   32
closer to Modern English. It takes three or four months at least to learn to
read Old English prose and more than that for poetry. But a week of good
study should put one in touch with the Middle English poet Chaucer.
Indeed, you may be able to make some sense of Chaucer straight off,
though you would need instruction in pronunciation to make it sound like
poetry. Here is a famous passage from the *General Prologue to the Canterbury Tales*, fourteenth century:

> *Ther was also a nonne, a Prioresse,*
> *That of hir smyling was ful symple and coy,*
> *Hir gretteste oath was but by Seinte Loy,*
> *And she was cleped° Madame Eglentyne.*   named
> *Ful wel she song the service dyvyne,*
> *Entuned in hir nose ful semely.*
> *And Frenshe she spak ful faire and fetisly,°*   elegantly
> *After the scole of Stratford-atte-Bowe,*
> *For Frenshe of Parys was to hir unknowe.*

EARLY MODERN ENGLISH

Sometime between 1400 and 1600 English underwent a couple of sound   33
changes which made the language of Shakespeare quite different from
that of Chaucer. Incidentally, these changes contributed much to the
chaos in which English spelling now finds itself.

One change was the elimination of a vowel sound in certain un-   34 stressed positions at the end of words. For instance, the words *name, stone, wine, dance* were pronounced as two syllables by Chaucer but as just one by Shakespeare. The *e* in these words became, as we say, "silent." But it wasn't silent for Chaucer; it represented a vowel sound. So also the words *laughed, seemed, stored* would have been pronounced by Chaucer as two-syllable words. The change was an important one because it affected thousands of words and gave a different aspect to the whole language.

The other change is what is called the Great Vowel Shift. This was a   35
systematic shifting of half a dozen vowels and diphthongs in stressed syllables. For instance, the word *name* had in Middle English a vowel something like that in the modern word *father*; *wine* had the vowel of modern *mean*; *he* was pronounced something like modern *hey*; *mouse* sounded like *moose*; *moon* had the vowel of *moan*. Again the shift was thoroughgoing and affected all the words in which these vowel sounds occurred. Since we still keep the Middle English system of spelling these words, the differences between Modern English and Middle English are often more real than apparent.

The vowel shift has meant also that we have come to use an entirely   36
different set of symbols for representing vowel sounds than is used by writers of such languages as French, Italian, or Spanish, in which no such vowel shift occurred. If you come across a strange word—say, *bine*—in an English book, you will pronounce it according to the English system, with the vowel of *wine* or *dine*. But if you read *bine* in a French, Italian, or Spanish book, you pronounce it with the vowel of *mean* or *seen*.

These two changes, then, produced the basic differences between   37
Middle English and Modern English. But there were several other developments that had an effect upon the language. One was the invention of printing, an invention introduced into England by William Caxton in the year 1475. Where before books had been rare and costly, they suddenly became cheap and common. More and more people learned to read and write. This was the first of many advances in communication which have worked to unify languages and to arrest the development of dialect differences, though of course printing affects writing principally rather than speech. Among other things it hastened the standardization of spelling.

The period of Early Modern English—that is, the sixteenth and sev-   38
enteenth centuries—was also the period of the English Renaissance, when people developed, on the one hand, a keen interest in the past and, on the other, a more daring and imaginative view of the future. New ideas multiplied, and new ideas meant new language. Englishmen had grown accustomed to borrowing words from French as a result of the Norman Conquest; now they borrowed from Latin and Greek. As we have seen, English had been raiding Latin from Old English times and before, but now the floodgates really opened, and thousands of words from the classical languages poured in. *Pedestrian, bonus, anatomy, con-*

tradict, climax, dictionary, benefit, multiply, exist, paragraph, initiate, scene, inspire are random examples. Probably the average educated American today has more words from French in his vocabulary than from native English sources, and more from Latin than from French.

The greatest writer of the Early Modern English period is of course   39
Shakespeare, and the best-known book is the King James Version of the Bible, published in 1611. The Bible (if not Shakespeare) has made many features of Early Modern English perfectly familiar to many people down to the present time, even though we do not use these features in present-day speech and writing. For instance, the old pronouns *thou* and *thee* have dropped out of use now, together with their verb forms, but they are still familiar to us in prayer and in Biblical quotations: "Whither thou goest, I will go." Such forms as *hath* and *doth* have been replaced by *has* and *does*; "Goes he hence tonight?" would now be "Is he going away tonight?"; Shakespeare's "Fie, on't, sirrah" would be "Nuts to that, Mac." Still, all these expressions linger with us because of the power of the works in which they occur.

It is not always realized, however, that considerable sound changes   40
have taken place between Early Modern English and the English of the present day. Shakespearian actors putting on a play speak the words, properly enough, in their modern pronunciation. But it is very doubtful that this pronunciation would be understood at all by Shakespeare. In Shakespeare's time, the word *reason* was pronounced like modern *raisin*; *face* had the sound of modern *glass*; the *l* in *would, should, palm* was pronounced. In these points and a great many others the English language has moved a long way from what it was in 1600.

RECENT DEVELOPMENTS

The history of English since 1700 is filled with many movements and   41
countermovements, of which we can notice only a couple. One of these is the vigorous attempt made in the eighteenth century, and the rather half-hearted attempts made since, to regulate and control the English language. Many people of the eighteenth century, not understanding very well the forces which govern language, proposed to polish and prune and restrict English, which they felt was proliferating too wildly. There was much talk of an academy which would rule on what people could and could not say and write. The academy never came into being, but the eighteenth century did succeed in establishing certain attitudes which, though they haven't had much effect on the development of the language itself, have certainly changed the native speaker's feeling about the language.

In part, a product of the wish to fix and establish the language was the   42
development of the dictionary. The first English dictionary was published

in 1603; it was a list of 2,500 words briefly defined. Many others were published with gradual improvements until Samuel Johnson published his *English Dictionary* in 1755. This, steadily revised, dominated the field in England for nearly a hundred years. Meanwhile in America, Noah Webster published his dictionary in 1828, and before long dictionary publishing was a big business in this country. The last century has seen the publication of one great dictionary: the twelve-volume *Oxford English Dictionary*, compiled in the course of seventy-five years through the labors of many scholars. We have also, of course, numerous commercial dictionaries which are as good as the public wants them to be if not, indeed, rather better.

Another product of the eighteenth century was the invention of "English grammar." As English came to replace Latin as the language of scholarship, it was felt that one should also be able to control and dissect it, parse and analyze it, as one could Latin. What happened in practice was that the grammatical description that applied to Latin was removed and superimposed on English. This was silly, because English is an entirely different kind of language, with its own forms and signals and ways of producing meaning. Nevertheless, English grammars on the Latin model were worked out and taught in the schools. In many schools they are still being taught. This activity is not often popular with school children, but it is sometimes an interesting and instructive exercise in logic. The principal harm in it is that it has tended to keep people from being interested in English and has obscured the real features of English structure. 43

But probably the most important force on the development of English in the modern period has been the tremendous expansion of English-speaking peoples. In 1500 English was a minor language, spoken by a few people on a small island. Now it is perhaps the greatest language of the world, spoken natively by over a quarter of a billion people and as a second language by many millions more. When we speak of English now, we must specify whether we mean American English, British English, Australian English, Indian English, or what, since the differences are considerable. The American cannot go to England or the Englishman to America confident that he will always understand and be understood. The Alabaman in Iowa or the Iowan in Alabama shows himself a foreigner every time he speaks. It is only because communication has become fast and easy that English in this period of its expansion has not broken into a dozen mutually unintelligible languages. 44

QUESTIONS ON CONTENT

1. What are the three major periods in the history of the English language? When did each occur?

2. Roberts is careful to describe the relationship between historical

events in England and the development of the English language. In what ways did historical events affect the English language?

3. When the Anglo-Saxons invaded England, their language, with some modifications, became the language of the land. How does Roberts explain the fact that French did not become the language of England after the invasion of William the Conqueror?

4. How would you characterize in social terms the French words that were brought into English by the Norman Conquest? In what areas of life did French have the greatest influence?

5. Explain what changes the English language underwent as a result of the Great Vowel Shift. What is the importance of this linguistic phenomenon for the history of English?

6. Why, according to Roberts, have school children tended not to be interested in the study of the English language?

QUESTIONS ON RHETORIC

1. What is Robert's thesis in this essay? (Glossary: *Thesis*) Where is it stated?

2. Why is a chronological organization appropriate for this essay? (Glossary: *Organization*)

3. Roberts makes extensive use of examples in his essay. Of what value are these examples for the reader? (Glossary: *Examples*)

4. How does Roberts use comparison and contrast to help him discuss Old English? (Glossary: *Comparison and Contrast*)

5. Roberts uses the pronouns *we, our*, and *us* throughout his essay. What effect does this have on you?

6. Roberts wrote this essay in the 1950s when people were not as sensitive to racial and ethnic prejudice as they are today. Reread the first ten paragraphs, paying particular attention to Roberts's use of such words as *savages, untamed tribes*, and *civilization*. Did you find any of his diction offensive or see how others might find it so? Suggest ways in which Roberts' diction could be changed to eliminate the invidious comparisons he makes.

VOCABULARY

forays (6)	impunity (15)	zealously (28)
siphoned (8)	facilitated (25)	linger (39)
conversion (11)		

WRITING TOPICS

1. Using your dictionary, identify the language from which each of the following words was borrowed:

barbecue	hustle
buffalo	marmalade
casino	orangutan
decoy	posse
ditto	raccoon
fruit	veranda

What other examples of borrowed words can you find in your dictionary? Write an essay in which you show with examples that today "the majority of words in English are borrowed" (24).

2. During its relatively brief 1400-year history, the English language has consistently been characterized by change. How is American English still changing today? What effects, if any, have the Vietnam War, the NASA space program, the drug culture, computers and other new technology, the women's movement, and/or recent waves of immigration had on American English?

THE PRESCRIPTIVE TRADITION

David Crystal

By the time most people graduate from high school they are familiar with the "rules" of English and the "exceptions" to those rules. These rules, it turns out, are the legacy of the prescriptive tradition in English that had its beginnings in the eighteenth century. In the following article from The Cambridge Encyclopedia of Language, *British linguist David Crystal traces the history of prescriptivism, an authoritarian tradition that sought to codify the principles of English and to preserve the language's purity. This background information provides us with an understanding of the current philosophical debate between linguists who want to* prescribe *and those who want to* describe *the language, a debate that Crystal does not see as resolvable by an either/or solution.*

PRESCRIPTIVISM

In its most general sense, prescriptivism is the view that one variety of language has an inherently higher value than others, and that this ought to be imposed on the whole of the speech community. The view is propounded especially in relation to grammar and vocabulary, and frequently with reference to pronunciation. The variety which is favoured, in this account, is usually a version of the "standard" written language, especially as encountered in literature, or in the formal spoken language which most closely reflects this style. Adherents to this variety are said to speak or write "correctly"; deviations from it are said to be "incorrect." 1

All the main European languages have been studied prescriptively, especially in the 18th century approach to the writing of grammars and dictionaries. The aims of these early grammarians were threefold: (a) they wanted to codify the principles of their languages, to show that there was a system beneath the apparent chaos of usage, (b) they wanted a means of settling disputes over usage, (c) they wanted to point out what they felt to be common errors, in order to "improve" the language. The authoritarian nature of the approach is best characterized by its reliance on "rules" of grammar. Some usages are "prescribed," to be learnt and followed accurately; others are "proscribed," to be avoided. In this early period, there were no half-measures: usage was either right or wrong, and it was the 2 task of the grammarian not simply to record alternatives, but to pronounce judgment upon them.

These attitudes are still with us, and they motivate a widespread concern that linguistic standards should be maintained. Nevertheless, there is an alternative point of view that is concerned less with "standards" than with the *facts* of linguistic usage. This approach is summarized in the statement that it is the task of the grammarian to *describe*, not *prescribe*—to record the facts of linguistic diversity, and not to attempt the impossible tasks of evaluating language variation or halting language change. In the second half of the 18th century, we already find advocates of this view, such as Joseph Priestly, whose *Rudiments of English Grammar* (1761) insists that "the custom of speaking is the original and only just standard of any language." Linguistic issues, it is argued, cannot be solved by logic and legislation. And this view has become the tenet of the modern linguistic approach to grammatical analysis.

In our own time, the opposition between "descriptivists" and "prescriptivists" has often become extreme, with both sides painting unreal pictures of the other. Descriptive grammarians have been presented as people who do not care about standards, because of the way they see all forms of usage as equally valid. Prescriptive grammarians have been presented as blind adherents to a historical tradition. The opposition has even been presented in quasi-political terms—of radical liberalism vs elitist conservatism.

If these stereotypes are abandoned, we can see that both approaches are important, and have more in common than is often realized—involving a mutual interest in such matters as acceptability, ambiguity, and intelligibility. The descriptive approach is essential because it is the only way in which the competing claims of different standards can be reconciled: when we know the facts of language use, we are in a better position to avoid the idiosyncrasies of private opinions, and to make realistic recommendations about teaching or style. The prescriptive approach provides a focus for the sense of linguistic values which everyone possesses, and which ultimately forms part of our view of social structure, and of our own place within it. After 200 years of dispute, it is perhaps sanguine to expect any immediate rapport to be achieved, but there are some grounds for optimism, now that sociolinguists are beginning to look more seriously at prescriptivism in the context of explaining linguistic attitudes, uses, and beliefs.

THE ACADEMIES

Some countries have felt that the best way to look after a language is to place it in the care of an academy. In Italy, the *Accademia della Crusca* was founded as early as 1582, with the object of purifying the Italian language. In France, in 1635, Cardinal Richelieu established the *Académie française*, which set the pattern for many subsequent bodies. The statues of the *Académie* define as its principal function:

> to labour with all possible care and diligence to give definite rules to our language, and to render it pure, eloquent, and capable of treating the arts and sciences.

The 40 academicians were drawn from the ranks of the church, nobility, and military—a bias which continues to the present day. The *Académie's* first dictionary appeared in 1694.

Several other academies were founded in the 18th and 19th centuries.   7
The Spanish Academy was founded in 1713 by Philip V, and within 200 years corresponding bodies had been set up in most South American Spanish countries. The Swedish Academy was founded in 1786; the Hungarian in 1830. There are three Arabic academies, in Syria, Iraq, and Egypt. The Hebrew Language Academy was set up more recently, in 1953.

In England, a proposal for an academy was made in the 17th century,   8
with the support of such men as John Dryden and Daniel Defoe. In Defoe's view, the reputation of the members of this academy

> would be enough to make them the allowed judges of style and language; and no author would have the impudence to coin without their authority . . . There should be no more occasion to search for derivations and constructions, and it would be as a criminal then to coin words as money.

In 1712, Jonathan Swift presented his *Proposal for Correcting, Improving and Ascertaining the English Tongue*, in which he complains to the Lord Treasurer of England, the Earl of Oxford, that

> our language is extremely imperfect; that its daily improvements are by no means in proportion to its daily corruptions; that the pretenders to polish and refine it have chiefly multiplied abuses and absurdities; and that in many instances it offends against every part of grammar.

His academy would "fix our language for ever," for,

> I am of the opinion, it is better a language should not be wholly perfect, than it should be perpetually changing.

The idea received a great deal of support at the time, but nothing was done. And in due course, opposition to the notion grew. It became evident that the French and Italian academies had been unsuccessful in stopping the course of language change. Dr. Johnson, in the Preface to his Dictionary, is under no illusion about the futility of an academy, especially in England, where he finds 'the spirit of English liberty' contrary to the whole idea:

> When we see men grow old and die at a certain time one after another, century after century, we laugh at the elixir that promises to prolong life to a thousand years; and with equal justice may the lexicographer be derided, who being able to produce no example of a nation that has preserved their words and phrases from mutability, shall imagine that his dictionary can embalm his language, and secure it from corruption, and decay, that it is in his power to change sublunary nature, or clear the world at once from folly, vanity, and affectation.

From time to time, the idea of an English Academy continues to be voiced, but the response has never been enthusiastic. A similar proposal in the USA was also rejected. By contrast, since the 18th century, there has been an increasing flow of individual grammars, dictionaries, and manuals of style in all parts of the English-speaking world.

LANGUAGE CHANGE

The phenomenon of language change probably attracts more public notice   9
and criticism than any other linguistic issue. There is a widely held belief that change must mean deterioration and decay. Older people observe the casual speech of the young, and conclude that standards have fallen markedly. They place the blame in various quarters—most often in the schools, where patterns of language education have changed a great deal in recent years, but also in state public broadcasting institutions, where any deviations from traditional norms provide an immediate focus of attack by conservative, linguistically sensitive listeners. The concern can even reach national proportions, as in the widespread reaction in Europe against what is thought of as the "American" English invasion.

Unfounded Pessimism

It is understandable that many people dislike change, but most of the   10
criticism of linguistic change is misconceived. It is widely felt that the contemporary language illustrates the problem at its worst, but this belief is shared by every generation. Moreover, many of the usage issues recur across generations: several of the English controversies which are the focus of current attention can be found in the books and magazines of the 18th and 19th centuries—the debate over *it's me* and *very unique*, for example. In *The Queen's English* (1863), Henry Alford, the Dean of Canterbury, lists a large number of usage issues which worried his contemporaries, and gave them cause to think that the language was rapidly decaying. Most are still with us, with the language not obviously affected. In the mid-19th century, it was predicted that British and American English would be mutually unintelligible within 100 years!
There are indeed cases where linguistic change can lead to problems   11

of unintelligibility, ambiguity, and social division. If change is too rapid, there can be major communication problems, as in contemporary Papua New Guinea—a point which needs to be considered in connection with the field of language planning. But as a rule, the parts of language which are changing at any given time are tiny, in comparison to the vast, unchanging areas of language. Indeed, it is because change is so infrequent that it is so distinctive and noticeable. Some degree of caution and concern is therefore always desirable, in the interests of maintaining precise and efficient communication; but there are no grounds for the extreme pessimism and conservatism which is so often encountered—and which in English is often summed up in such slogans as "Let us preserve the tongue that Shakespeare spoke."

The Inevitability of Change

For the most part, language changes because society changes. To stop or control the one requires that we stop or control the other—a task which can succeed to only a very limited extent. Language change is inevitable and rarely predictable, and those who try to plan a language's future waste their time if they think otherwise—time which would be better spent in devising fresh ways of enabling society to cope with the new linguistic forms that accompany each generation. These days, there is in fact a growing recognition of the need to develop a greater linguistic awareness and tolerance of change, especially in a multi-ethnic society. This requires, among other things, that schools have the knowledge and resources to teach a common standard, while recognizing the existence and value of linguistic diversity. Such policies provide a constructive alternative to the emotional attacks which are so commonly made against the development of new words, meanings, pronunciations, and grammatical constructions. But before these policies can be implemented, it is necessary to develop a proper understanding of the inevitability and consequences of linguistic change. 12

Some people go a stage further, and see change in language as a progression from a simple to a complex state—a view which was common as a consequence of 19th-century evolutionary thinking. But there is no evidence for this view. Languages do not develop, progress, decay, evolve, or act according to any of the metaphors which imply a specific endpoint and level of excellence. They simply change, as society changes. If a language dies out, it does so because its status alters in society, as other cultures and languages take over its role: it does not die because it has "got too old," or "becomes too complicated," as is sometimes maintained. Nor, when languages change, do they move in a predetermined direction. Some are losing inflections; some are gaining them. Some are moving to an order where the verb precedes the object; others to an order where the object precedes the verb. Some languages are los- 13 ing vowels and gaining consonants; others are doing the opposite. If metaphors must be used to talk about language change, one of the best is that of a system holding itself in a state of equilibrium, while changes take place within it; another is that of the tide, which always and inevitably changes, but never progresses, while it ebbs and flows.

QUESTIONS ON CONTENT

1. According to Crystal, what does it mean to be a language prescriptivist? How does a prescriptivist differ from a descriptivist?

2. What were the aims of eighteenth-century English grammarians? What is the legacy of their work with language?

3. Why does Crystal believe that both the prescriptive and descriptive approaches are important?

4. What was the purpose of language academies? How successful were they in fulfilling their objectives? Why was an English academy never formed?

5. According to Crystal, what linguistic issue attracts the most public notice and criticism? What are his views on the issue?

6. What are some of the commonly held misconceptions about language change? How does Crystal refute each? What metaphors does Crystal believe are best to use when discussing language change? Do they seem appropriate to you? Why, or why not?

QUESTIONS ON RHETORIC

1. What is Crystal's purpose in this selection? (Glossary: *Purpose*)

2. How would you describe Crystal's tone? (Glossary: *Tone*) Is his tone appropriate for his subject, audience, and purpose? Explain.

3. How has Crystal organized his essay? (Glossary: *Organization*) The heads in the text highlight the three main sections of his essay. Could these three sections be reordered without losing anything? Why, or why not?

4. Why do you think Crystal italicized *facts*, *describe*, and *prescribe* in paragraph 3?

5. In paragraph 8 Crystal quotes Dr. Samuel Johnson from the Preface to his *Dictionary*. What function does this extensive quotation serve in the context of the paragraph in which it appears?

6. What transitional devices does Crystal use between paragraphs? (Glossary: *Transitions*) Which ones seem to work best for you? Explain.

VOCABULARY

inherently (1)	ambiguity (5)	illusion (8)
codify (2)	sanguine (5)	norms (9)
advocates (3)	rapport (5)	slogans (11)
elitist (4)	academy (6)	

WRITING TOPICS

1. After doing some library research, write an essay in which you highlight the essentials in the debate between descriptivists and prescriptivists. From what you can gather, why has this debate become so emotionally charged?

2. Write an essay in which you recount your early school experiences with English. Did your teachers hold a prescriptive or descriptive attitude toward language? Do you remember being taught grammar, spelling, and penmanship in school? In what ways did these experiences help shape your current attitudes toward speaking, reading, and writing?

ORDER OUT OF CHAOS

Bill Bryson

*Today dictionaries are big business. Many different kinds of
dictionaries are published for many different audiences.
Whole sections of bookstores and reference rooms in libraries
are devoted to dictionaries. In the following essay Bill
Bryson, author of* A Dictionary of Troublesome Words, *
reveals the complex nature of attitudes toward dictionaries
and the considerable amount of misunderstanding about
dictionary making in general. In particular, Bryson discusses
the herculean efforts of three lexicographers who have given
English speakers the "finest dictionaries" in the world.*

How big is the English language? That's not an easy question. Samuel 1
Johnson's dictionary contained 43,000 words. The unabridged *Random
House* of 1987 has 315,000. *Webster's Third New International* of 1961
contained 450,000. And the revised *Oxford English Dictionary* of 1989
has 615,000 entries. But in fact this only begins to hint at the total.

For one thing, meanings in English are much more various than a 2
bald count of entry words would indicate. The mouse that scurries across
your kitchen floor and the mouse that activates your personal computer
clearly are two quite separate entities. Shouldn't they then be counted as
two words? And then what about related forms like *mousy, mouselike*,
and *mice*? Shouldn't they also count as separate words? Surely there is a
large difference between something that is a mouse and something that is
merely mousy.

And then of course there are all the names of flora and fauna, medical 3
conditions, chemical substances,[1] laws of physics, and all the other scientific
and technical terms that don't make it into ordinary dictionaries. Of insects
alone, there are 1.4 million named species. Total all these together and you
have—well, no one knows. But certainly not less than three million.

So how many of these words do we know? Again, there is no simple 4
answer. Many scholars have taken the trouble (or more probably compelled their graduate students to take the trouble) of counting the number
of words used by various authors, on the assumption, one supposes, that
that tells us something about human vocabulary. Mostly what it tells us is
that academics aren't very good at counting. Shakespeare, according to

---

[1]One of which, incidentally, is said to be the longest word in the English language. It
begins *methianylglutaminyl* and finishes 1,913 letters later as *alynalalanylthreonilarginyl-
serase*. I don't know what it is used for, though I daresay it would take some rubbing to get
it out of the carpet.

Pei and McCrum, had a vocabulary of 30,000 words, though Pei acknowledges seeing estimates putting the figure as low as 16,000. Lincoln Barnett puts it at 20,000 to 25,000. But most other authorities—Shipley, Baugh and Cable, Howard—put the number at a reassuringly precise 17,677. The King James Bible, according to Laird, contains 8,000 words, but Shipley puts the number at 7,000, while Barnett confidently zeroes in on a figure of 10,442. Who knows who's right?

One glaring problem with even the most scrupulous tabulation is that   5 the total number of words used by an author doesn't begin to tell us the true size of his vocabulary. I know the meanings of *frangible, spiffing*, and *cutesy-poo*, but have never had occasion to write them before now. A man of Shakespeare's linguistic versatility must have possessed thousands of words that he never used because he didn't like or require them. Not once in his plays can you find the words *Bible, Trinity*, or *Holy Ghost*, and yet that is not to suggest that he was not familiar with them.

Estimates of the size of the average person's vocabulary are even   6 more contentious. Max Müller, a leading German philologist at the turn of the century, thought the average farm laborer had an everyday vocabulary of no more than 300 words. Pei cites an English study of fruit pickers, which put the number at no more than 500, though he himself thought that the figure was probably closer to 30,000. Stuart Berg Flexner, the noted American lexicographer, suggests that the average well-read person has a vocabulary of about 20,000 words and probably uses about 1,500 to 2,000 in a normal week's conversation. McCrum puts an educated person's vocabulary at about 15,000.

There are endless difficulties attached to adjudging how many words   7 a person knows. Consider just one. If I ask you what *incongruent* means and you say, "It means not congruent," you are correct. That is the first definition given in most dictionaries, but that isn't to say that you have the faintest idea what the word means. Every page of the dictionary contains words we may not have encountered before—*inflationist, forbiddance, moosewood, pulsative*—and yet whose meanings we could very probably guess.

At the same time there are many words that we use every day and   8 clearly know and yet might have difficulty proving. How would you define *the* or *what* or *am* or *very*? Imagine trying to explain to a Martian in a concise way just what *is* is. And then what about all those words with a variety of meanings? Take *step. The American Heritage Dictionary* lists a dozen common meanings for the word, ranging from the act of putting one foot in front of the other to the name for part of a staircase. We all know all these meanings, yet if I gave you a pencil and a blank sheet of paper could you list them? Almost certainly not. The simple fact is that it is hard to remember what we remember, so to speak. Put another way, our memory is a highly fickle thing. Dr. Alan Baddeley, a British authority on memory, cites a study in which people were asked to name the capital cities of several countries. Most had trouble with the capitals of countries like Uruguay and Bulgaria, but when they were told the initial letter of the capital city, they often suddenly remembered and their success rate soared. In another study people were shown long lists of random words and then asked to write down as many of them as they could remember. A few hours later, without being shown the list again, they were asked to write down as many of the words as they could remember then. Almost always the number of words would be nearly identical, but the actual words recalled from one test to another would vary by 50 percent or more. In other words, there is vastly more verbal information locked away in our craniums than we can get out at any one time. So the problem of trying to assess accurately just how much verbal material we possess in total is fraught with difficulties.

For this reason educational psychologists have tended to shy away   9 from such studies, and such information as exists is often decades old. One of the most famous studies was conducted in 1940. In it, two American researchers, R. H. Seashore and L. D. Eckerson, selected a random word from each left-hand page of a Funk & Wagnalls standard desktop dictionary and asked a sampling of college students to define those words or use them in a sentence. By extrapolating those results onto the number of entries in the dictionary, they concluded that the average student had a vocabulary of about 150,000 words—obviously very much larger than previously supposed. A similar study carried out by K. C. Diller in 1978, cited by Aitchison in *Words in the Mind*, put the vocabulary level even higher—at about 250,000 words. On the other hand, Jespersen cites the case of a certain Professor E. S. Holden who early in the century laboriously tested himself on every single word in *Webster's Dictionary* and arrived at a total of just 33,456 known words. It is clearly unlikely that a university professor's vocabulary would be four to six times smaller than that of the average student. So such studies would seem to tell us more about the difficulties of framing tests than about the size of our vocabularies.

What is certain is that the number of words we use is very much   10 smaller than the number of words we know. In 1923 a lexicographer named G. H. McKnight did a comprehensive study of how words are used and found that just forty-three words account for fully half of all the words in common use, and that just nine account for fully one quarter of all the words in almost any sample of written English. Those nine are: *and, be, have, it, of, the, to, will,* and *you.*

By virtue of their brevity, dictionary definitions often fail to convey   11 the nuances of English. *Rank* and *rancid* mean roughly the same thing, but, as Aitchison notes, we would never talk about eating rank butter or wearing rancid socks. A dictionary will tell you that *tall* and *high* mean much the same thing, but it won't explain to you that while you can apply either term to a building you can apply only tall to a person. On the strength of dictionary definitions alone a foreign visitor to your home could be excused for telling you that you have an abnormal child, that your wife's cooking is exceedingly odorous, and that your speech at a recent sales conference was laughable, and intend nothing but the warmest praise.

The fact is that the real meanings are often far more complex than the simple dictionary definitions would lead us to suppose. In 1985, the department of English at the University of Birmingham in England ran a computer analysis of words as they are actually used in English and came up with some surprising results. The primary dictionary meaning of words was often far adrift from the sense in which they were actually used. *Keep*, for instance, is usually defined as to retain, but in fact the word is much more often employed in the sense of continuing, as in "keep cool" and "keep smiling." *See* is only rarely required in the sense of utilizing one's eyes, but much more often used to express the idea of knowing, as in "I see what you mean." *Give*, even more interestingly, is most often used, to quote the researchers, as "mere verbal padding," as in "give it a look" or "give a report." (London Sunday *Times*, March 31, 1985)

In short, dictionaries may be said to contain a certain number of definitions, but the true number of meanings contained in those definitions will always be much higher. As the lexicographer J. Ayto put it: "The world's largest data bank of examples in context is dwarfed by the collection we all carry around subconsciously in our heads."

English is changing all the time and at an increasingly dizzy pace. At the turn of the century words were being added at the rate of about 1,000 a year. Now, according to a report in *The New York Times* (April 3, 1989), the increase is closer to 15,000 to 20,000 a year. In 1987, when Random House produced the second edition of its masterly twelve-pound unabridged dictionary, it included over 50,000 words that had not existed twenty-one years earlier and 75,000 new definitions of old words. Of its 315,000 entries, 210,000 had to be revised. That is a phenomenal amount of change in just two decades. The new entries included *preppy, quark, flextime, chairperson, sunblocker,* and the names of 800 foods that had not existed or been generally heard of in 1966—*tofu piña colada, chapati, sushi,* and even *crêpes.*

Unabridged dictionaries have about them a stern, immutable air, as if here the language has been captured once and for all, and yet from the day of publication they are inescapably out of date. Samuel Johnson recognized this when he wrote: "No dictionary of a living tongue can ever be perfect, since while it is hastening to publication, some words are budding, and some are fading away." That, however, has never stopped anyone from trying, not least Johnson himself.

The English-speaking world has the finest dictionaries, a somewhat curious fact when you consider that we have never formalized the business of compiling them. From the seventeenth century when Cardinal Richelieu founded the Académie Française, dictionary making has been earnest work indeed. In the English-speaking world, the early dictionaries were almost always the work of one man rather than a ponderous committee of academics, as was the pattern on the Continent. In a kind of instinctive recognition of the mongrel, independent, idiosyncratic genius of the English tongue, these dictionaries were often entrusted to people bearing those very characteristics themselves. Nowhere was this more gloriously true than in the person of the greatest lexicographer of them all, Samuel Johnson.

Johnson, who lived from 1709 to 1784, was an odd candidate for   17
genius. Blind in one eye, corpulent, incompletely educated, by all accounts coarse in manner, he was an obscure scribbler from an impoverished provincial background when he was given a contract by the London publisher Robert Dodsley to compile a dictionary of English.

Johnson's was by no means the first dictionary in English. From   18
Cawdrey's Table Alphabeticall in 1604 to his opus a century and a half later there were at least a dozen popular dictionaries, though many of these were either highly specialized or slight (*Cawdrey's Table Alphabeticall* contained just 3,000 words and ran to barely a hundred pages). Many also had little claim to scholarship. *Cawdrey's*, for all the credit it gets as the first dictionary, was a fairly sloppy enterprise. It gave the definition of *aberration* twice and failed to alphabetize correctly on other words.

The first dictionary to aim for anything like comprehensiveness was   19
the *Universal Etymological Dictionary* by Nathaniel Bailey, published in 1721, which anticipated Johnson's classic volume by thirty-four years and actually defined more words. So why is it that Johnson's dictionary is the one we remember? That's harder to answer than you might think.

His dictionary was full of shortcomings. He allowed many spelling   20
inconsistencies to be perpetuated—*deceit* but *receipt*, *deign* but *disdain*, *hark* but *hearken*, *convey* but *inveigh*, *moveable* but *immovable*. He wrote *downhil* with one *l*, but *uphill* with two; *install* with two *l*'s, but *reinstal* with one; *fancy* with an *f*, but *phantom* with a *ph*. Generally he was aware of these inconsistencies, but felt that in many cases the inconsistent spellings were already too well established to tamper with. He did try to make spelling somewhat more sensible, institutionalizing the differences between *flower* and *flour* and between *metal* and *mettle*—but essentially he saw his job as recording English spelling as it stood in his day, not changing it. This was in sharp contrast to the attitude taken by the revisers of the Académie Française dictionary a decade or so later, who would revise almost a quarter of French spellings.

There were holes in Johnson's erudition. He professed a preference   21
for what he conceived to be Saxon spellings for words like *music, critic*, and *prosaic*, and thus spelled them with a final *k*, when in fact they were

all borrowed from Latin. He was given to flights of editorializing, as when he defined a *patron* as "one who supports with insolence, and is paid with flattery" or *oats* as a grain that sustained horses in England and people in Scotland. His etymologies, according to Baugh and Cable, were "often ludicrous" and his proofreading sometimes strikingly careless. He defined a *garret* as a "room on the highest floor in the house" and a *cockloft* as "the room over the garret." Elsewhere, he gave identical definitions to *leeward* and *windward*, even though they are quite obviously opposites.

Even allowing for the inflated prose of his day, he had a tendency to write passages of remarkable denseness, as here: "The proverbial oracles of our parsimonious ancestors have informed us, that the fatal waste of our fortune is by small expenses, by the profusion of sums too little singly to alarm our caution, and which we never suffer ourselves to consider together." *Too little singly?* I would wager good money that that sentence was as puzzling to his contemporaries as it is to us. And yet at least it has the virtue of relative brevity. Often Johnson constructed sentences that ran to 250 words or more, which sound today uncomfortably like the ramblings of a man who has sat up far too late and drunk rather too much port.   22

Yet for all that, his *Dictionary of the English Language*, published in two volumes in June 1755, is a masterpiece, one of the landmarks of English literature. Its definitions are supremely concise, its erudition magnificent, if not entirely flawless. Without a nearby library to draw on, and with appallingly little financial backing (his publisher paid him a grand total of just £1,575, less than £200 a year, from which he had to pay his assistants), Johnson worked from a garret room off Fleet Street, where he defined some 43,000 words, illustrated with more than 114,000 supporting quotations drawn from every area of literature. It is little wonder that he made some errors and occasionally indulged himself with barbed definitions.   23

He had achieved in under nine years what the forty members of the Académie Française could not do in less than forty. He captured the majesty of the English language and gave it a dignity that was long overdue. It was a monumental accomplishment and he well deserved his fame.   24

But its ambitious sweep was soon to be exceeded by a persnickety schoolteacher/lawyer half a world away in Connecticut. Noah Webster (1758–1843) was by all accounts a severe, correct, humorless, religious, temperate man who was not easy to like, even by other severe, religious, temperate, humorless people. A provincial schoolteacher and not-very-successful lawyer from Hartford, he was short, pale, smug, and boastful. (He held himself superior to Benjamin Franklin because he was a Yale man while Franklin was self-educated.) Where Samuel Johnson spent his free hours drinking and discoursing in the company of other great men,   25

Webster was a charmless loner who criticized almost everyone but was himself not above stealing material from others, most notably from a spelling book called *Abysel-pha* by an Englishman named Thomas Dilworth. In the marvelously deadpan phrase of H. L. Mencken, Webster was "sufficiently convinced of its merits to imitate it, even to the extent of lifting whole passages." He credited himself with coining many words, among them *demoralize, appreciation, accompaniment, ascertainable,* and *expenditure,* which in fact had been in the language for centuries. He was also inclined to boast of learning that he simply did not possess. He claimed to have mastered twenty-three languages, including Latin, Greek, all the Romance languages, Anglo-Saxon, Persian, Hebrew, Arabic, Syriac, and a dozen more. Yet, as Thomas Pyles witheringly puts it, he showed "an ignorance of German which would disgrace a freshman," and his grasp of other languages was equally tenuous. According to Charlton Laird, he knew far less Anglo-Saxon than Thomas Jefferson, who never pretended to be an expert at it. Pyles calls his *Dissertations on the English Language* "a fascinating farago of the soundest linguistic common sense and the most egregious poppycock." It is hard to find anyone saying a good word about him.

Webster's first work, *A Grammatical Institute of the English Language*—consisting of three books: a grammar, a reader, and a speller—appeared between 1783 and 1785, but he didn't capture the public's attention until the publication in 1788 of *The American Spelling Book.* This volume (later called the *Elementary Spelling Book*) went through so many editions and sold so many copies that historians appear to have lost track. But it seems safe to say that there were at least 300 editions between 1788 and 1829 and that by the end of the nineteenth century it had sold more than sixty million copies—though some sources put the figure as high as a hundred million. In either case, with the possible exception of the Bible, it is probably the best-selling book in American history. [26]

Webster is commonly credited with changing American spelling, but what is seldom realized is how wildly variable his own views on the matter were. Sometimes he was in favor of radical and far-reaching changes—insisting on such spellings as *soop, bred, wimmen, groop, definit, fether, fugitiv, tuf, thum, hed, bilt,* and *tung*—but at other times he acted the very soul of orthographic conservatism, going so far as to attack the useful American tendency to drop the *u* from *colour, humour,* and the like. The main book with which he is associated in the popular mind, his massive *American Dictionary of the English Language* of 1828, actually said in the preface that it was "desirable to perpetuate the sameness" of American and British spellings and usages. [27]

Many of the spellings that he insisted on in his *Compendious Dictionary of the English Language* (1806) and its later variants were simply ignored by his loyal readers. They overlooked them, as one might a tic or stammer, and continued to write *group* rather than *groop, crowd* rather [28] than *croud*, *medicine* rather than *medicin*, *phantom* for *fantom*, and many hundreds of others. Such changes as Webster did manage to establish were relatively straightforward and often already well underway—for instance, the American tendency to transpose the British *re* in *theatre*, *centre*, and other such words. Yet even here Webster was by no means consistent. His dictionaries retained many irregular spellings, some of which have stuck in English to this day (*acre*, *glamour*) and some of which were corrected by the readers themselves (*frolick*, *wimmen*). Other of his ideas are of questionable benefit. His insistence on dropping one of the *l*'s in words such as *traveller* and *jeweller* (which way they are still spelled in England) was a useful shortcut, but it has left many of us unsure whether we should write *excelling* or *exceling*, or *fulfilled*, *fullfilled*, or *fulfiled*.

Webster was responsible also for the American *aluminum* in favor of   29
the British *aluminium*. His choice has the fractional advantage of brevity, but defaults in terms of consistency. *Aluminium* at least follows the pattern set by other chemical elements—*potassium*, *radium*, and the like.

But for the most part the differences that distinguish American spell-   30
ing from British spelling became common either late in his life or after his death, and would probably have happened anyway.

In terms of pronunciation he appears to have left us with our pronun-   31
ciation of *schedule* rather than the English "shedjulle" and with our standard pronunciation of *lieutenant* which was then widely pronounced "lefftenant" in America, as it still is in England today. But just as he sometimes pressed for odd spellings, so he called for many irregular pronunciations: "deef" for *deaf*, "nater" for *nature*, "heerd" for *heard*, "booty" for *beauty*, "voloom" for *volume*, and others too numerous (and, I am tempted to add, too laughable) to dwell on. He insisted that *Greenwich* and *Thames* be pronounced as spelled and favored giving *quality* and *quantity* the short "aă" of *hat*, while giving *advance*, *clasp*, and *grant* the broad "ah" sound of southern England. No less remarkably, Webster accepted a number of clearly ungrammatical usages, among them "it is me," "we was," and "them horses." It is a wonder that anyone paid any attention to him at all. Often they didn't.

Nonetheless his dictionary was the most complete of its age, with   32
70,000 words—far more than Johnson had covered—and its definitions were models of clarity and conciseness. It was an enormous achievement.

All Webster's work was informed by a passionate patriotism and the   33
belief that American English was at least as good as British English. He worked tirelessly, churning out endless hectoring books and tracts, as well as working on the more or less constant revisions of his spellers and dictionaries. In between time he wrote impassioned letters to congressmen, dabbled in politics, proffered unwanted advice to presidents, led his church choir, lectured to large audiences, helped found Amherst College, and produced a sanitized version of the Bible, in which Onan doesn't

spill his seed but simply "frustrates his purpose," in which men don't have testicles but rather "peculiar members," and in which women don't have wombs (or evidently anything else with which to contribute to the reproductive process).

Like Samuel Johnson, he was a better lexicographer than a business- 34 man. Instead of insisting on royalties he sold the rights outright and never gained the sort of wealth that his tireless labors merited. After Webster's death in 1843, two businessmen from Springfield, Massachusetts, Charles and George Merriam, bought the rights to his dictionaries and employed his son-in-law, the rather jauntily named Chauncey A. Goodrich, to prepare a new volume (and, not incidentally, expunge many of the more ridiculous spellings and far-fetched etymologies). This volume, the first Merriam-Webster dictionary, appeared in 1847 and was an instant success. Soon almost every home had one. There is a certain neat irony in the thought that the book with which Noah Webster is now most closely associated wasn't really his work at all and certainly didn't adhere to many of his most cherished precepts.

In early February 1884, a slim paperback book bearing the title *The New* 35 *English Dictionary on Historical Principles*, containing all the words in the language (obscenities apart) between *A* and *ant* was published in Britain at the steepish price of twelve shillings and six pence. This was the first of twelve volumes of the most masterly and ambitious philological exercise ever undertaken, eventually redubbed the *Oxford English Dictionary*. The intention was to record every word used in English since 1150 and to trace it back through all its shifting meanings, spellings, and uses to its earliest recorded appearance. There was to be at least one citation for each century of its existence and at least one for each slight change of meaning. To achieve this, almost every significant piece of English literature from the last 7½ centuries would have to be not so much read as scoured.

The man chosen to guide this enterprise was James Augustus Henry 36 Murray (1837–1915), a Scottish-born bank clerk, schoolteacher, and self-taught philologist. He was an unlikely, and apparently somewhat reluctant, choice to take on such a daunting task. Murray, in the best tradition of British eccentrics, had a flowing white beard and liked to be photographed in a long black housecoat with a mortarboard on his head. He had eleven children, all of whom were, almost from the moment they learned the alphabet, roped into the endless business of helping to sift through and alphabetize the several million slips of paper on which were recorded every twitch and burble of the language over seven centuries.

The ambition of the project was so staggering that one can't help 37 wondering if Murray really knew what he was taking on. In point of fact, it appears he didn't. He thought the whole business would take a dozen years at most and that it would fill half a dozen volumes covering some

6,400 pages. In the event, the project took more than four decades and sprawled across 15,000 densely printed pages.

Hundreds of volunteers helped with the research, sending in citations   38 from all over the world. Many of them were, like Murray, amateur philologists and often they were as eccentric as he. One of the most prolific contributors was James Platt, who specialized in obscure words. He was said to speak a hundred languages and certainly knew as much about comparative linguistics as any man of his age, and yet he owned no books of his own. He worked for his father in the City of London and each lunchtime collected one book—never more—from the Reading Room of the British Museum, which he would take home, devour, and replace with another volume the next day. On weekends he haunted the opium dens and dockyards of Wapping and Whitechapel looking for native speakers of obscure tongues whom he would query on small points of semantics. He provided the histories of many thousands of words. But an even more prolific contributor was an American expatriate named Dr. W. C. Minor, a man of immense erudition who provided from his private library the etymologies of tens of thousands of words. When Murray invited him to a gathering of the dictionary's contributors, he learned, to his considerable surprise, that Dr. Minor could not attend for the unfortunate reason that he was an inmate at Broadmoor, a hospital for the criminally insane, and not sufficiently in possession of his faculties to be allowed out. It appears that during the U.S. Civil War, having suffered an attack of sunstroke, Dr. Minor developed a persecution mania, believing he was being pursued by Irishmen. After a stay in an asylum he was considered cured and undertook, in 1871, a visit to England. But one night while walking in London his mania returned and he shot dead an innocent stranger whose misfortune it was to have been walking behind the crazed American. Clearly Dr. Minor's madness was not incompatible with scholarship. In one year alone, he made 12,000 contributions to the *OED* from the private library he built up at Broadmoor.

Murray worked ceaselessly on his dictionary for thirty-six years, from   39 his appointment to the editorship in 1879 to his death at the age of seventy-eight in 1915. (He was knighted in 1908.) He was working on the letter *u* when he died, but his assistants carried on for another thirteen years until in 1928 the final volume, Wise to Wyzen, was issued. (For some reason, volume 12, XYZ, had appeared earlier.) Five years later, a corrected and slightly updated version of the entire set was reissued, under the name by which it has since been known: the *Oxford English Dictionary*. The completed dictionary contained 414,825 entries supported by 1,827,306 citations (out of 6 million collected) described in 44 million words of text spread over 15,487 pages. It is perhaps the greatest work of scholarship ever produced.

The *OED* confirmed a paradox that Webster had brought to light dec-   40 ades earlier—namely, that although readers will appear to treat a dictio-

language ('læŋgwɪdʒ), *sb.*¹ Forms: 3-6 langage, (3 langag, 4 longage, langwag, 5 langwache, langegage), 3, 5- language. [a. F. *langage* (recorded from 12th c.) = Pr. *leng(u)atge, lengage,* Sp. *lenguaje,* Pg. *linguagem, lt. linguaggio:*— pop.L. type *°linguāticum,* f. *lingua* tongue, language (F. *langue*: see LANGUE).

The form with u, due to assimilation with the F. *langue,* occurs in AF writings of the 12th c., and in Eng from about 1300.]

1. a. The whole body of words and of methods of combination of words used by a nation, people, or race; a 'tongue'. *dead language:* a language no longer in vernacular use. *first language:* one's native language. *second language:* a language spoken in addition to one's native language; the first foreign language one learns.

c 1290 *S E Leg* I. 108/55 With men pat onder-stoden hire langage. 1297 R. GLOUC. (Rolls) 1569 Vor in þe langage of rome rane a frogge is. *a* 1300 *Cursor M.* 247 (Gött.) Seldom was for ani chance Englis tong preched in france, Gif we raim ilkan pair language [MS. *Cott.* langage], And þan do we na vtetrage. *Ibid.,* 6384 (Gött.) þis mete.. þai called it in pair langag man. 1387 TREVISA *Higden* (Rolls) II. 157 Walsche men and Scottes, þat beeþ nouȝt i-medled wiþ oþer nacions, holdeþ wel nyȝh hir firste longage and speche. *c* 1400 *Apol. Loll.* 32 In a langwag vnknowun t:k man and womman mai rede. *c* 1449 PECOCK *Repr.* 1 xii. 66 Thei.. han vsid the hool Bible in her modris langage. *c* 1450 *Mirour Saluacioun* 3650 Wymmen spak these diuerse langegages. 1588 SHAKS. *L L L.* v. i 40 They haue beene at a great feast of Languages, and stolne the scraps. 1589 PUTTENHAM *Eng. Poesie* iii iv (Arb.) 156 After a speach is fully fashioned to the common vnderstanding, and accepted by consent of a whole countrey and nation, it is called a language. 1699 BENTLEY *Phal.* xiii. 392 Every living Language.. is in perpetua: motion and alteration. 1769 De Foe's *Tour Gt. Brit.* (ed. 7) IV. 392 It is called in the Irish Language, l-colm-kill; some call it Iona. 1779-81 JOHNSON *L.P., Addison* Wks. III 44 A dead language, in which nothing is mean because nothing is familiar. 1823 DE QUINCEY *Lett. Yng. Man* Wks. 1860 XIV. 37 On this Babel of an earth.. there are said to be about three thousand languages and jargons. 1845 M. PATTISON *Ess.* (1889) I. 13 In fact, Bede is writing in a dead language, Gregory in a living. 1875 STUBBS *Const. Hist.* II. 414 The use of the English language in the Courts of law was ordered in 1362. 1875 W. D. WHITNEY *Life & Growth of Language* ii 25 We realize better in the case of a second or 'foreign', than in that of a first or 'native' language, that the process of acquisition is a never-ending one. 1876 C. M. YONGE *Womankind* vi. 40 The second language has been really and grammatically learnt. 1943 I. A. RICHARDS *Basic Eng.* 8 iii *Uses* 14 The history of the nationalist movement in India is an instructive instance. Its leaders and its chief supporters are speakers of English and sometimes use it rather as their first than as their second language. 1962 R. QUIRK *Use of English* i. 6 Something like 250 million people for whom English is the mother-tongue or 'first language'. 1971 *Guardian* 23 June 7/3 Indians and Pakistanis.. using a second language at school and their first language for many home activities.

fig 1720 GAY *Prol. Dione* 4 Love, devoid of art, Spoke the consenting language of the heart. 1812 W. C. BRYANT *Thanatopsis* 3 To him who in the love of Nature holds Communion with her visible forms, she speaks A various language.

b. *transf.* Applied to methods of expressing the thoughts, feelings, wants, etc., otherwise than by words. *finger language =* DACTYLOLOGY. *language of flowers:* a method of expressing sentiments by means of flowers.

1606 SHAKS. *Tr. & Cr.* iv. v. 55 Ther's a language in her eye, her cheeke, her lip. 1697 COLLIER *Ess Mor Subj.* II. 120 As the language of the Face is universal so 'tis very comprehensive. 1711 STEELE *Spect.* No. 66 P 2 She is utterly a Foreigner to the Language of Looks and Glances 1827 WHATELY *Logic* (1850) Introd. §6 A Deaf-mute, before he has been taught a Language, either the Finger-language, or Reading, cannot carry on a train of Reasoning. 1834 tr. *C. de la Tour's Lang. Flowers* 95 It is more especially by.. modifications that the Language of Flowers becomes the

interpretation of our thoughts. 1837 *Penny Cycl.* VIII. 282 2 Dactylology must not be confounded with the natural language of the deaf and dumb, which is purely a language of mimic signs. 1847 THACKERAY *Van. Fair* (1848) iv. 31 Perhaps she just looked first into the bouquet, to see whether there was a *billet-doux* hidden.. 'Do they talk the language of flowers at Boggley Wollah, Sedley?' asked Osborne, laughing. 1876 MOZLEY *Univ. Serm.* vi. 134 All action is.. besides being action, language. 1880 *Times* 23 June 9 5 Teaching the deaf by signs and by finger language. 1894 H. DRUMMOND *Ascent Man* 212 A sign Language is of no use when one savage is at one end of a wood and his wife at the other. 1949 *Enquire within upon Everything* (ed. 122) 462 *Language of Flowers.* The symbolism of flowers has always possessed a certain fascination, especially for the young person of either sex.

c. *transf.* Applied to the inarticulate sounds used by the lower animals, birds, etc.

1601 SHAKS. *All's Well* iv. i. 22 Choughs language, gabble enough, and good enough. 1667 MILTON *P L.* viii. 373 Is not the Earth With various living creatures, and the Aire Replenisht,. know'st thou not Thir language and thir wayes? 1797 BEWICK *Brit. Birds* (1847) I p. xxvii, The notes, or as it may with more propriety be called, the language of birds.

d. *Computers.* Any of numerous systems of precisely defined symbols and rules for using them that have been devised for writing programs or representing instructions and data.

1959 E. M. GRABBE et al. *Handbk. Automation, Computation, & Control* II ii. 186 The purpose of these activities has been to.. set up a class of languages that will be easily translatable by machine from one to another, and also easily recognizable to the ordinary human user... Such languages form the input to a class of automatic computer programs called translators, which perform a translation into a second or target language. The latter may be either (1) an assembly language such as SOAP, SAP, or MAGIC., or (2) a straight machine language, in pure decimal, binary (or in some cases such as the Univac I and II), alphanumeric. 1961 LEEDS & WEINBERG *Computer Programming Fund.* ii. 46 The best way of writing down operations is to write them in alphabetical format. A format used for writing down these alphabetical instructions is called the programming language or paper language, to distinguish it from the machine language.. acceptable to the machine circuitry. 1964 F. L. WESTWATER *Electronic Computers* ix. 145 As the benefits of these codes were realised, each manufacturer produced different 'languages'. 1966 A. BATTERSBY *Math. in Managem.* viii. 206 If each manufacturer prepares a compiler routine which will translate instructions in some universal 'language' into a program in his own code, then programs written in the universal language can be run on any machine. 1967 A. HASSITT *Computer Programming* i. 1 An efficient way of learning to use a computing machine utilizes one of the problem oriented languages such as Fortran, Algol, or PL 1. 1970 A. CAMERON et al. *Computers & Old Eng. Concordances* 27 If we program in so-called higher-languages, like Fortran, conceivably PLI... I myself will be very surprised if the next generation of machines will not accept Fortran programming and probably Cobol, Algol, and PLI programming.

2. a. In generalized sense: Words and the methods of combining them for the expression of thought.

1599 SHAKS. *Much Ado* iv. i. 98 There is not chastitie enough in language, Without offence to vtter them 1644 MILTON *Educ.* Wks. (1847) 98/2 Language is but the instrument conveying to us things useful to be known. 1781 COWPER *Convers.* 15 So language in the mouths of the adult,. Too often proves an implement of play. 1841 TRENCH *Parables* ii. (1877) 25 Language is ever needing to be recalled, minted and issued anew. 1862 J. MARTINEAU *Ess.* (1891) IV. 104 Language, that wonderful crystallization of the very flow and spray of thought. 1892 WESTCOTT *Gospel of Life* 186 Language must be to the last inadequate to express the results of perfect observation.

b. Power or faculty of speech; ability to speak a foreign tongue. Now rare.

1526 WOLSEY *Let. to Tayler* in Strype *Eccl. Mem.* I. v. 66 A gentleman.. who had knowledge of the country and good language to pass 1601 SHAKS. *All's Well* iv. i. 77, I shall loose my life for want of language. If there be heere German or Dane, Low Dutch, Italian, or French, let him speake to me. **1610** —— *Temp* II. ii. 86 Here is that which will giue language to you Cat; open your mouth. **1790** COWPER *Receipt Mother's Pict.* 1 Oh that those lips had language!

3. a. The form of words in which a person expresses himself; manner or style of expression. *bad language*: coarse or vulgar expressions. *strong language*: expressions indicative of violent or excited feeling.

1809-10 COLERIDGE *Friend* (1865) 135 These pretended constitutionalists recurred to the language of insult. **1849** MACAULAY *Hist. Eng.* vi. II. 118 He lived and died, in the significant language of one of his countrymen, a bad Christian, but a good Protestant. **1855** MOTLEY *Dutch Rep.* II. ii (1856) 155 In all these interviews he had uniformly used one language his future wife was to 'live as a Catholic'. *c* **1863** T. TAYLOR in M. R. Booth *Eng. Plays of 19th Cent.* (1969) II. 109 Come, cheeky! Don't you use bad language. **1875** JOWETT *Plato* (ed. 2) V. 348 The language used to a servant ought always to be that of a command. *a* **1910** 'MARK TWAIN' *Autobiogr.* (1924) II. 88 She made a guarded remark which censured strong language. **1934** R. MACAULAY *Milton* II. 100 Milton's familiarity with the tradition [of scurrility] may account for much of his strong language, even when reviling in English.

b. The phraseology or terms of a science, art, profession, etc., or of a class of persons.

1502 *Ord. Crysten Men* (W. de W. 1506) Prol. 4 The swete and fayre langage of theyr phylosophy. **1596** SHAKS. *1 Hen. IV*, II. iv. 21, I can drinke with any Tinker in his owne Language. **1611** —— *Cymb.* III. iii. 74 This is not Hunters Language. **1651** HOBBES *Leviath.* III. xxxiv 207 The words Body, and Spirit, which in the language of the Schools are termed Substances, Corporeall and Incorporeall. **1747** SPENCE *Polymetis* VIII. xv. 243 Those attributes of the Sword, Victory, and Globe, say very plainly (in the language of the statuaries) that [etc.]. **1841** J. R. YOUNG *Math. Dissert.* I. 10 Thus can be expressed in the language of algebra, not only distance but position. **1891** *Speaker* 2 May 532 1 In its metaphysics have again condescended to speak the language of polite letters.

c. The style (of a literary composition); also, the wording (of a document, statute, etc.).

1712 ADDISON *Spect.* No. 285 ¶6 It is not therefore sufficient that the Language of an Epic Poem be Perspicuous, unless it be also Sublime. **1781** COWPER *Conversat.* 236 A tale should be judicious, clear, succinct. The language plain. **1886** SIR J. STIRLING in *Law Times Rep.* LV. 283 2 There are two remarks which I desire to make on the language of the Act.

d. *long language*: †(*a*) verbosity (tr. Gr. μακρολογία; (*b*) language composed of words written in full, as opposed to cipher.

e. † *vulgar*. Short for *bad language* (see above).

1860 DICKENS *Uncomm. Trav.* (1861) v. 65 Mr. Victualler's assurance that he 'never allowed any language, and never suffered any disturbance'. **1865** —— *Dr. Marigold's Prescriptions* 1, in *All Year Round* Extra Christmas No. 7 Dec 4 1 But have a temper in the cart, flinging language and the hardest goods in stock at you, and where are you then! **1886** BESANT *Childr. Gibeon* II xxv. That rude eloquence which is known in Ivy Lane as 'language'. **1863** SALOLS *Trav. S E Africa* 3 The sailor had never ceased to pour out a continuous flood of 'language' all the time. **1929** C C MARTINDALE *Risen Sun* 173, I have heard more 'language' in a 'gentleman's' club in ten minutes than in all that evening in the Melbourne Stadium. **1974** 'M. INNES' *Mysterious Commission* vii. 75 'You behave like bloody fools.' 'Language, now. Mr Honeybath, language.'

f. *Phr. to speak* (*talk*) *someone's language, to speak* (*talk*) *the same language*: to have an understanding with someone through similarity of outlook and expression, to get on well with someone; *to speak a different language* (*from someone*): to have little in common (with someone).

†4. a. The act of speaking or talking; the use of speech. *by language*: so to speak. *in language with*: in conversation with. *without language*: not to make many words. *Obs.*

a **1400** *Cov. Myst.* IV. *Noah's Flood* II. Affryr Adam withoutyn language, The secunde fadyr am I [Noe] in fay. *a* **1450** *Knt. de la Tour* (1868) 18 My fader sette me in langage with her. **1461** *Paston Lett.* No. 303 II. 17, I said I dwelled upon the cost of the see here, and be langage hit were more necessare to with hold men here than take from hit. **1477** EARL RIVERS (Caxton) *Dictes* 57 One was surer in keping his tunge, than in moche speking, for in moche langage one may lightly erre. **1490** CAXTON *Eneydos* xxviii. 107 Wythout eny more langage dydo. sessed thenne the swerde. **1514** BARCLAY *Cyt. & Uplondyshm.* (Percy Soc.) p. xviii, To morowe of court we may have more language.

†b. That which is said, words, talk, report; *esp.* words expressive of censure or opprobrium. Also *pl.* reports, sayings. *to say language against*: to talk against, speak opprobriously of. *Obs.*

a **1450** *Knt. de la Tour* (1868) 2 And so thei dede bothe deceiue ladies and gentilwomen, and bere forthe diuerse langages on hem. **1465** MARG. PASTON in *P. Lett.* No. 502 II. 188, I hyre moch langage of the demenyng betwene you and herte. **1467** *Mann. & Housh. Exp.* (Roxb.) 173 Ye haue mekel on setenge langwache ayenste me, were of I mervel gretely for I haue yeffen yowe no schwsche kawse **1470-85** MALORY *Arthur* II. xl, Euery daye syre Palomydes brauled and sayd langage ayeynst syr Tristram. **1485** CAXTON *Chas. Gt.* 225 Feragus said in this manere .. The valyaunt Rolland was contente ryght wel, & accepted hys langage. **1636** SIR H. BLUNT *Voy. Levant* 33 A Turke gave such a Language of our Nation, and threatning to all whom they should light upon, as made me upon all demands professe my selfe a Scotchman.

5. a. A community of people having the same form of speech, a nation. *arch.* [A literalism of translation.]

1388 WYCLIF *Dan.* v 19 Alle puplis, lynagis, and longagis [**1382** tungis]. **1611** BIBLE *Ibid* 1653 ¶ AQUHART *Rabelais* I. x, All people, and all languages and nations.

b. A national division or branch of a religious and military Order, *e.g.* of the Hospitallers.

1727-52 CHAMBERS *Cycl. Language* is also used, in the order of Malta, for nation. **1728** MORGAN *Algiers* I v. 314 Don Raimond Perellos de Riccapuul, of the Language of Aragon, was elected Grand Master. **1885** *Catholic Dict.* (ed. 3) 413 2 The order [of Hospitallers] was divided into eight 'languages', Provence, Auvergne, France, Aragon, Castile, England, Germany, and Italy.

6. *attrib.* and *Comb.* **a.** simple attributive, as *language acquisition*, *-capacity*, *change*, *course*, *description*, *engineering*, *event*, *-family*, *form*, *-group*, *-history*, *-pattern*, *sign*, *structure*, *-study*, *-system*, *-turn*, *-use*. **b.** objective, as *language-learner*, *-learning*, *-maker*, *-teacher*, *-teaching*, *-user*, *-using*. *language area*, (*a*) an area of the cerebral cortex regarded as especially concerned with the use of language; (*b*) a region where a particular language is spoken; *language barrier*, a barrier to communication between people which results from their speaking or writing different languages; *language-contact Linguistics* (see quot. 1964); *language-game Philos.*, a speech-activity or limited system of communication and action, complete in itself, which may or may not form a part of our existing use of language; *language laboratory* (*colloq.* language lab), a classroom, equipped with tape recorders, etc., where foreign languages are learnt by means of repeated oral practice; *language-master*, a teacher of language or languages; *language-particular a.*, = *language-specific* adj.; *language-specific a. Linguistics*, distinctive to a specified language.

nary with the utmost respect, they will generally ignore anything in it that doesn't suit their tastes. The *OED*, for instance, has always insisted on *-ize* spellings for words such as *characterize, itemize*, and the like, and yet almost nowhere in England, apart from the pages of *The Times* newspaper (and not always there) are they observed. The British still spell almost all such words with *-ise* endings and thus enjoy a consistency with words such as *advertise, merchandise*, and *surprise* that we in America fail to achieve. But perhaps the most notable of all the *OED*'s minor quirks is its insistence that Shakespeare should be spelled Shakspere. After explaining at some length why this is the only correct spelling, it grudgingly acknowledges that the commonest spelling "is perh. Shakespeare." (To which we might add, it cert. is.)

In the spring of 1989, a second edition of the dictionary was issued, 41 containing certain modifications, such as the use of the International Phonetic Alphabet instead of Murray's own quirky system. It comprised the original twelve volumes, plus four vast supplements issued between 1972 and 1989. Now sprawling over twenty volumes, the updated dictionary is a third bigger than its predecessor, with 615,000 entries, 2,412,000 supporting quotations, almost 60 million words of exposition, and about 350 million keystrokes of text (or one for each native speaker of English in the world). No other language has anything even remotely approaching it in scope. Because of its existence, more is known about the history of English than any other language in the world.

QUESTIONS ON CONTENT

1. Why, according to Bryson, is it so difficult to determine the number of words in the English language? What effect, if any, does this have on the job of the lexicographer? Explain.

2. Bryson discusses the work of Samuel Johnson, Noah Webster, and James Murray. What did each lexicographer contribute to the world of English dictionary making?

3. While Bryson does address the shortcomings of Johnson, Webster, and Murray, he is quick to praise each man's work as a monumental accomplishment. What is so monumental about the work of each man?

4. What was James Murray's intention in compiling his *Oxford English Dictionary*? How did his intention differ from that of Samuel Johnson in his *Dictionary of the English Language* (1755) and that of Noah Webster in his *American Dictionary of the English Language* (1828)?

5. What book is Noah Webster most closely associated with today? What, according to Bryson, is ironic about that association?

6. What truth is there in the assertion that a lexicographer's work is neverending? Explain.

QUESTIONS ON RHETORIC

1. How has Bryson organized his essay? (Glossary: *Organization*) How are the first sixteen paragraphs related to the remainder of the essay?

2. What is Bryson's purpose in this essay, and how successfully does achieve that purpose? (Glossary: *Purpose*)

3. Did you find Bryson's title appropriate for his essay? (Glossary: *Title*) Why, or why not?

4. Bryson makes the claim that "English is changing all the time and at an increasingly dizzy pace" (14). What evidence does he provide to substantiate this generalization?

5. What is Bryson's tone in this essay? Cite examples of his diction that led you to your conclusion. (Glossary: *Tone*)

VOCABULARY

unabridged (1)	fraught (8)	daunting (36)
assumption (4)	immutable (15)	sprawled (37)
scrupulous (5)	idiosyncratic (16)	paradox (40)
adjudging (7)	egregious (25)	

WRITING TOPICS

1. According to Bryson, Noah Webster's *The American Spelling Book* is the best-selling book in American history with the exception of the Bible. What does this tell you about the importance that Americans attach to spelling? What is your own attitude toward spelling? Do you have difficulty with spelling? Do you consider yourself a dictionary user, or it is "just too much trouble"? And do you use the spell-check on your personal computer? Write a brief essay in which you discuss the importance of spelling as you see it, exploring your attitude toward spelling and the reason(s) for that attitude.

2. Most Americans consider the dictionary—like the encyclopedia—the ultimate authority. Often arguments are settled by "consulting the dictionary." But paradoxically, as Bryson tells us, "although readers will appear to treat a dictionary with the utmost respect, they will generally ignore anything in it that doesn't suit their tastes" (40). Why do you suppose this is true? What is your own attitude toward dictionaries? Survey your friends on this issue and present your findings in an essay.

BLACK CHILDREN, BLACK SPEECH

Dorothy Z. Seymour

In this essay, linguist and former elementary-school reading teacher Dorothy Seymour discusses an important question facing present-day educators: On the basis of available evidence, how does one approach the conflict between the patterns of a nonstandard dialect, which the child learns either at home or from other children, and the equivalent patterns of Standard English? The issue, as you can well imagine, is highly controversial and emotional. Seymour first analyzes the distinguishing features of Black English and then considers the impact of Black English on schools in America, before making her case for a program of bidialectism. She believes that teachers and parents need to be informed about nonstandard language in order to implement such a program in our nation's schools.

"C'mon, man, les git goin'!" called the boy to his companion. "Dat 1
bell ringin'. It say, 'Git in rat now!'" He dashed into the school yard.

"Aw, f'get you," replied the other. "Whe' Richuh? Whe' da' muv- 2
vuh? He be goin' to schoo'."

"He in de' now, man!" was the answer as they went through the door. 3

In the classroom they made for their desks and opened their books. 4
The name of the story they tried to read was "Come." It went:

Come, Bill, come
Come with me.
Come and see this.
See what is here.

The first boy poked the second. "Wha' da' wor'?"

"Da' wor' *is*, you dope." 5

"*Is*? Ain't no wor' *is*. You jivin' me? Wha' da' wor' mean?" 6

"Ah dunno. Jus' *is*." 7

To a speaker of Standard English, this exchange is only vaguely com- 8
prehensible. But it's normal speech for thousands of American children.
In addition it demonstrates one of our biggest educational problems: children whose speech style is so different from the writing style of their
books that they have difficulty learning to read. These children speak
Black English, a dialect characteristic of many inner-city Negroes. Their

books are, of course, written in Standard English. To complicate matters, the speech they use is also socially stigmatized. Middle-class whites and Negroes alike scorn it as low-class poor people's talk.

Teachers sometimes make the situation worse with their attitudes to- 9 ward Black English. Typically, they view the children's speech as "bad English" characterized by "lazy pronunciation," "poor grammar," and "short, jagged words." One result of this attitude is poor mental health on the part of the pupils. A child is quick to grasp the feeling that while school speech is "good," his own speech is "bad," and that by extension he himself is somehow inadequate and without value. Some children re-act to this feeling by withdrawing; they stop talking entirely. Others de-velop the attitude of "F'get you, honky." In either case, the psychological results are devastating and lead straight to the dropout route.

It is hard for most teachers and middle-class Negro parents to accept 10 the idea that Black English is not just "sloppy talk" but a dialect with a form and structure of its own. Even some eminent black educators think of it as "bad English grammar" with "slurred consonants" (Professor Nick Aaron Ford of Morgan State College in Baltimore) and "ghettoese" (Dr. Kenneth B. Clark, the prominent educational psychologist).

Parents of Negro school children generally agree. Two researchers of 11 Columbia University report that the adults they worked with in Harlem almost unanimously preferred that their children be taught Standard En-glish in school.

But there is another point of view, one held in common by black 12 militants and some white liberals. They urge that middle-class Negroes stop thinking of the inner-city dialect as something to be ashamed of and repudiated. Black author Claude Brown, for example, pushes this view.

Some modern linguists take a similar stance. They begin with the 13 premise that no dialect is intrinsically "bad" or "good," and that a non-standard speech style is not defective speech but different speech. More important, they have been able to show that Black English is far from being a careless way of speaking the Standard; instead, it is a rather rigidly constructed set of speech patterns, with the same sort of specializ-ation in sounds, structure, and vocabulary as any other dialect.

THE SOUNDS OF BLACK ENGLISH

Middle-class listeners who hear black inner-city speakers say "dis" and 14 "tin" for "this" and "thin" assume that the black speakers are just being careless. Not at all; these differences are characteristic aspects of the dialect. The original cause of such substitutions is generally a carryover from one's original language or that of his immigrant parents. The inter-ference from that carryover probably caused the substitution of /d/ for the voiced *th* sound in *this*, and /t/ for the unvoiced *th* sound in *thin*. (Linguists represent language sounds by putting letters within slashes or brackets.) Most speakers of English don't realize that the two *th* sounds of English are lacking in many other languages and are difficult for most foreigners trying to learn English. Germans who study English, for example, are surprised and confused about these sounds because the only Germans who use them are the ones who lisp. These two sounds are almost nonexistent in the West African languages which most black immigrants brought with them to America.

Similar substitutions used in Black English are /f/, a sound similar to   15
the unvoiced *th*, in medial word-position, as in *birfday* for *birthday*, and in final word-position, as in *roof* for *Ruth* as well as /v/ for the voiced *th* in medial position, as in *bruvver* for *brother*. These sound substitutions are also typical of Gullah, the language of black speakers in the Carolina Sea Islands. Some of them are also heard in Caribbean Creole.

Another characteristic of the sounds of Black English is the lack of /l/   16
at the end of words, sometimes replaced by the sound /w/. This makes words like *tool* sound like *too*. If /l/ occurs in the middle of a Standard English word, in Black English it may be omitted entirely: "I can hep you." This difference is probably caused by the instability and sometimes interchangeability of /l/ and /r/ in West African languages.

One difference that is startling to middle-class speakers is the fact that   17
Black English words appear to leave off some consonant sounds at the end of words. Like Italian, Japanese and West African words, they are more likely to end in vowel sounds. Standard English *boot* is pronounced *boo* in Black English. *What* is *wha*. *Sure* is *sho*. *Your* is *yo*. This kind of difference can make for confusion in the classroom. Dr. Kenneth Goodman, a psycholinguist, tells of a black child whose white teacher asked him to use *so* in a sentence—not "sew a dress" but "the other *so*." The sentence the child used was "I got a *so* on my leg."

A related feature of Black English is the tendency in many cases not   18
to use sequences of more than one final consonant sound. For example, *just* is pronounced *jus'*, *past* is *pass*, *mend* sounds like *men* and *hold* like *hole*. *Six* and *box* are pronounced *sick* and *bock*. Why should this be? Perhaps because West African languages, like Japanese, have almost no clusters of consonants in their speech. The Japanese, when importing a foreign word, handle a similar problem by inserting vowel sounds between every consonant, making *baseball* sound like *besuboru*. West Africans probably made a simpler change, merely cutting a series of two consonant sounds down to one. Speakers of Gullah, one linguist found, have made the same kind of adaptation of Standard English.

Teachers of black children seldom understand the reason for these   19
differences in final sounds. They are apt to think that careless speech is the cause. Actually, black speakers aren't "leaving off" any sounds; how can you leave off something you never had in the first place?

Differences in vowel sounds are also characteristic of the nonstandard   20 language. Dr. Goodman reports that a black child asked his teacher how to spell rat. "R-a-t," she replied. But the boy responded "No ma'am, I don't mean rat mouse, I mean rat now." In Black English, *right* sounds like *rat*. A likely reason is that in West African languages, there are very few vowel sounds of the type heard in the word *right*. This type is common in English. It is called a glided or dipthongized vowel sound. A glided vowel sound is actually a close combination of two vowels; in the word *right* the two parts of the sound "eye" are actually "ah-ee." West African languages have no such long, two-part, changing vowel sounds; their vowels are generally shorter and more stable. This may be why in Black English, *time* sounds like *Tom*, *oil* like *all*, and *my* like *ma*.

LANGUAGE STRUCTURE

Black English differs from Standard English not only in its sounds but [21] also in its structure. The way the words are put together does not always fit the description in English grammar books. The method of expressing time, or tense, for example, differs in significant ways.

The verb *to be* is an important one in Standard English. It's used as [22] an auxiliary verb to indicate different tenses. But Black English speakers use it quite differently. Sometimes an inner-city Negro says "He coming"; other times he says "He be coming." These two sentences mean different things. To understand why, let's look at the tenses of West African languages; they correspond with those of Black English.

Many West African languages have a tense which is called the habit- [23] ual. This tense is used to express action which is always occurring and it is formed with a verb that is translated as *be*. "He be coming" means something like "He's always coming," "He usually comes," or "He's been coming."

In Standard English there is no regular grammatical construction for [24] such a tense. Black English speakers, in order to form the habitual tense in English, use the word *be* as an auxiliary: *He be doing it. My Momma be working. He be running.* The habitual tense is not the same as the present tense, which is constructed in Black English without any form of the verb *to be: He do it. My Momma working. He running.* (This means the action is occurring right now.)

There are other tense differences between Black English and Standard [25] English. For example, the nonstandard speech does not use changes in grammar to indicate the past tense. A white person will ask, "What did your brother say?" and the black person will answer, "He say he coming." (The verb *say* is not changed to *said*.) "How did you get here?" "I walk." This style of talking about the past is paralleled in the Yoruba, Fante, Hausa, and Ewe languages of West Africa.

Expression of plurality is another difference. The way a black child [26] will talk of "them boy" or "two dog" makes some white listeners think Negroes don't know how to turn a singular word into a plural word. As a matter of fact, it isn't necessary to use an *s* to express plurality. In Chinese and Japanese, singular and plural are not generally distinguished by such inflections; plurality is conveyed in other ways. For example, in Chinese it's correct to say "There are three book on the table." This sentence already has two signals of the plural, *three* and *are*; why require a third? This same logic is the basis of plurals in most West African languages, where nouns are often identical in the plural and the singular. For example, in Ibo, one correctly says *those man*, and in both Ewe and Yoruba one says *they house*. American speakers of Gullah retain this style; it is correct in Gullah to say *five dog*.

Gender is another aspect of language structure where differences can 27 be found. Speakers of Standard English are often confused to find that the nonstandard vernacular often uses just one gender of pronoun, the masculine, and refers to women as well as men as *he* or *him*. "He a nice girl," even "Him a nice girl" are common. This usage probably stems from West African origins, too, as does the use of multiple negatives, such as "Nobody don't know it."

Vocabulary is the third aspect of a person's native speech that could 28 affect his learning of a new language. The strikingly different vocabulary often used in Negro Nonstandard English is probably the most obvious aspect of it to a casual white observer. But its vocabulary differences don't obscure its meaning the way different sounds and different structure often do.

Recently there has been much interest in the African origins of words 29 like *goober* (peanut), *cooter* (turtle), and *tote* (carry), as well as others that are less certainly African, such as *to dig* (possibly from the Wolof *degan*, "to understand"). Such expressions seem colorful rather than low-class to many whites; they become assimilated faster than their black originators do. English professors now use *dig* in their scholarly articles, and current advertising has enthusiastically adopted *rap*.

Is it really possible for old differences in sound, structure, and vocab- 30 ulary to persist from the West African languages of slave days into present-day inner city Black English? Easily. Nothing else really explains such regularity of language habits, most of which persist among black people in various parts of the Western Hemisphere. For a long time scholars believed that certain speech forms used by Negroes were merely leftovers from archaic English preserved in the speech of early English settlers in America and copied by their slaves. But this theory has been greatly weakened, largely as the result of the work of a black linguist, Dr. Lorenzo Dow Turner of the University of Chicago. Dr. Turner studied the speech of Gullah Negroes in the Sea Islands off the Carolina coast and found so many traces of West African languages that he thoroughly discredited the archaic-English theory.

When anyone learns a new language, it's usual to try speaking the   31
new language with the sounds and structure of the old. If a person's first
language does not happen to have a particular sound needed in the language he is learning, he will tend to substitute a similar or related sound
from his native language and use it to speak the new one. When French-
man Charles Boyer said "Zees ees my heart," and when Latin American
Carmen Miranda sang "Souse American way," they were simply using
sounds of their native languages in trying to pronounce sounds of English. West Africans must have done the same thing when they first attempted English words. The tendency to retain the structure of the native
language is a strong one, too. That's why a German learning English is
likely to put his verb at the end: "May I a glass beer have?" The vocabulary of one's original language may also furnish some holdovers. Jewish
immigrants did not stop using the word *bagel* when they came to America; nor did Germans stop saying *sauerkraut*.

Social and geographical isolation reinforces the tendencies to retain   32
old language habits. When one group is considered inferior, the other
group avoids it. For many years it was illegal to give any sort of instruction to Negroes, and for slaves to try to speak like their masters would
have been unthinkable. Conflict of value systems doubtless retards
changes, too. As Frantz Fanon observed in *Black Skin, White Masks*,
those who take on white speech habits are suspect in the ghetto, because
others believe they are trying to "act white." Dr. Kenneth Johnson, a
black linguist, put it this way: "As long as disadvantaged black children
live in segregated communities and most of their relationships are confined to those within their own subculture, they will not replace their
functional nonstandard dialect with the nonfunctional standard dialect."

Linguists have made it clear that language systems that are different   33
are not necessarily deficient. A judgment of deficiency can be made only
in comparison with another language system. Let's turn the tables on
Standard English for a moment and look at it from the West African point
of view. From this angle, Standard English: (1) is lacking in certain language sounds, (2) has a couple of unnecessary language sounds for which
others may serve as good substitutes, (3) doubles and drawls some of its
vowel sounds in sequences that are unusual and difficult to imitate, (4)
lacks a method of forming an important tense, (5) requires an unnecessary number of ways to indicate tense, plurality and gender, and (6)
doesn't mark negatives sufficiently for the result to be a good strong
negative statement.

Now whose language is deficient?   34

How would the adoption of this point of view help us? Say we ac-   35
cepted the evidence that Black English is not just a sloppy Standard but
an organized language style which probably has developed many of its
features on the basis of its West African heritage. What would we gain?

The psychological climate of the classroom might improve if teachers   36 understood why many black students speak as they do. But we still have not reached a solution of the main problem. Does the discovery that Black English has pattern and structure mean that it should not be tampered with? Should children who speak Black English be excused from learning the Standard in school? Should they perhaps be given books in Black English to learn from?

Any such accommodation would surely result in a hardening of the 37 new separatism being urged by some black militants. It would probably be applauded by such people as Roy Innis, Director of C.O.R.E., who is currently recommending dual autonomous education systems for white and black. And it might facilitate learning to read, since some experiments have indicated that materials written in Black English syntax aid problem readers from the inner city.

But determined resistance to the introduction of such printed materials 38 into schools can be expected. To those who view inner-city speech as bad English, the appearance in print of sentences like "My mama, he work" can be as shocking and repellent as a four-letter word. Middle-class Negro parents would probably mobilize against the move. Any stratagem that does not take into account such practicalities of the matter is probably doomed to failure. And besides, where would such a permissive policy on language get these children in the larger society, and in the long run? If they want to enter an integrated America they must be able to deal with it on its own terms. Even Professor Toni Cade of Rutgers, who doesn't want "ghetto accents" tampered with, advocates mastery of Standard English because, as she puts it, "if you want to get ahead in this country, you must master the language of the ruling class." This has always been true, wherever there has been a minority group.

The problem then appears to be one of giving these children the abil- 39 ity to speak (and read) Standard English without denigrating the vernacular and those who use it, or even affecting the ability to use it. The only way to do this is to officially espouse bidialectism. The result would be the ability to use either dialect equally well—as Dr. Martin Luther King did—depending on the time, place, and circumstances. Pupils would have to learn enough about Standard English to use it when necessary, and teachers would have to learn enough about the inner-city dialect to understand and accept it for what it is—not just a "careless" version of Standard English but a different form of English that's appropriate in certain times and places.

Can we accomplish this? If we can't, the result will be continued 40 alienation of a large section of the population, continued dropout trouble with consequent loss of earning power and economic contribution to the nation, but most of all, loss of faith in America as a place where a minority people can at times continue to use those habits that remind them of their link with each other and with their past.

QUESTIONS ON CONTENT

1. How does Seymour define Black English?

2. What characteristics of Black English establish it as a distinct dialect rather than as improper usage of Standard English? How does Seymour account for the differences between Black English and Standard English?

3. Why does Seymour believe that African-American children need facility with Standard English as well?

4. What distinction does Seymour make between a person's language being "different" and its being "defective"? In what ways is this distinction important to her argument?

5. In what ways, according to Seymour, is Standard English "deficient" when looked at from the West African point of view?

6. Why does Seymour advocate a program of bidialectism? What does she believe such a program will require of teachers, parents, and students?

QUESTIONS ON RHETORIC

1. What is Seymour's purpose in this essay? Does she seem to be more interested in explaining the issues to her readers or in persuading them to her point of view? (Glossary: *Purpose*) Do you think that she accomplishes her purpose? Why, or why not?

2. In what ways do the first seven paragraphs form an appropriate introduction for Seymour's essay? (Glossary: *Beginnings*)

3. Seymour presents her argument inductively; that is, she first introduces the problem, then examines and analyzes the evidence, and finally draws a conclusion based on her considered analysis. Is this organization effective given the nature of her topic? Could she have, for example, introduced her solution early in the essay? Why, or why not?

4. Seymour frequently cites authorities to strengthen her argument. What exactly is gained with each of these citations?

5. Seymour's essay includes a great deal of technical linguistic information about the sounds, structure, and vocabulary of Black English. Did you have any difficulties understanding her descriptions and explanations? Has Seymour done anything to accommodate readers without a linguistics background? If so, what? (Glossary: *Technical Language*)

6. How would you characterize Seymour's tone in this essay? (Glossary: *Tone*) Did you find it appropriate for her argument? Why, or why not?

7. Do you think paragraph 34 could be joined to paragraph 33? Why do you suppose Seymour chooses to make a separate, one-sentence paragraph?

8. In paragraphs 34-36 Seymour presents a series of questions. How do these questions function in the context of the essay? (Glossary: *Rhetorical Questions*)

VOCABULARY

stigmatized (8)	intrinsically (13)	stratagem (38)
devastating (9)	assimilated (29)	denigrating (39)
eminent (10)	autonomous (37)	vernacular (39)
repudiated (12)		

WRITING TOPICS

1. According to Seymour, linguists believe that when children become ashamed of their language, they become ashamed of themselves. Write an essay in which you first discuss how your attitude toward other people is affected by the way they speak. Second, discuss the nature of the relationship between one's use of language and one's feelings of self-worth. Be sure to describe any specific experiences that have made these relationships clear for you.

2. How important do you believe it is for individuals to understand the characteristics of nonstandard dialects like Black English? Write an essay in which you evaluate the possible advantages for individuals and for American society as a whole.

3. Many critics of bidialectism argue that while materials written in Black English syntax may facilitate learning for many inner-city children, they also make these children dependent on a dialect that excludes them from full participation in the American way of life. Where do you stand on the issue of bidialectism? Cite reasons to support your position.

WHAT'S WRONG WITH BLACK ENGLISH

Rachel L. Jones

Rachel L. Jones was a sophomore at Southern Illinois University when she published the following essay in Newsweek *in December 1982. Jones argues against a belief she perceives in some of her fellow African-American students and African-American authorities that "talking white" is a betrayal of her racial heritage.*

William Labov, a noted linguist, once said about the use of black English, "It is the goal of most black Americans to acquire full control of the standard language without giving up their own culture." He also suggested that there are certain advantages to having two ways to express one's feelings. I wonder if the good doctor might also consider the goals of those black Americans who have full control of standard English but who are every now and then troubled by that colorful, grammar-to-the-winds patois that is black English. Case in point—me.

I'm a 21-year-old black born to a family that would probably be considered lower-middle class—which in my mind is a polite way of describing a condition only slightly better than poverty. Let's just say we rarely if ever did the winter-vacation thing in the Caribbean. I've often had to defend my humble beginnings to a most unlikely group of people for an even less likely reason. Because of the way I talk, some of my black peers look at me sideways and ask, "Why do you talk like you're white?"

The first time it happened to me I was nine years old. Cornered in the school bathroom by the class bully and her sidekick, I was offered the opportunity to swallow a few of my teeth unless I satisfactorily explained why I always got good grades, why I talked "proper" or "white." I had no ready answer for her, save the fact that my mother had from the time I was old enough to talk stressed the importance of reading and learning, or that L. Frank Baum and Ray Bradbury were my closest companions. I read all my older brothers' and sisters' literature textbooks more faithfully than they did, and even lightweights like the Bobbsey Twins and Trixie Belden were allowed into my bookish inner circle. I don't remember exactly what I told those girls, but I somehow talked my way out of a beating.

I was reminded once again of my "white pipes" problem while apartment hunting in Evanston, Ill., last winter. I doggedly made out lists of available places and called all around. I would immediately be invited over—and immediately be turned down. The thinly concealed looks of shock when the front door opened clued me in, along with the flustered instances of "just getting off the phone with the girl who was ahead of you and she wants the rooms." When I finally found a place to live, my roommate stirred up old memories when she remarked a few months later, "You know, I was surprised when I first saw you. You sounded white over the phone." Tell me another one, sister.

I should've asked her a question I've wanted an answer to for years: 5 how does one "talk white"? The silly side of me pictures a rabid white foam spewing forth when I speak. I don't use Valley Girl jargon, so that's not what's meant in my case. Actually, I've pretty much deduced what people mean when they say that to me, and the implications are really frightening.

It means that I'm articulate and well versed. It means that I can talk   6 as freely about John Steinbeck as I can about Rick James. It means that "ain't" and "he be" are not staples of my vocabulary and are only used around family and friends. (It is almost Jekyll and Hyde-ish the way I can slip out of academic abstractions into a long, lean, double-negative-filled dialogue, but I've come to terms with that aspect of my personality.) As a child, I found it hard to believe that's what people meant by "talking proper"; that would've meant that good grades and standard English were equated with white skin, and that went against everything I'd ever been taught. Running into the same type of mentality as an adult has confirmed the depressing reality that for many blacks, standard English is not only unfamiliar, it is socially unacceptable.

James Baldwin once defended black English by saying it had added   7 "vitality to the language," and even went so far as to label it a language in its own right, saying, "Language [i.e., black English] is a political instrument" and a "vivid and crucial key to identity." But did Malcolm X urge blacks to take power in this country "any way y'll can"? Did Martin Luther King Jr. say to blacks, "I has been to the mountaintop, and I done seed the Promised Land"? Toni Morrison, Alice Walker and James Baldwin did not achieve their eloquence, grace and stature by using only black English in their writing. Andrew Young, Tom Bradley and Barbara Jordan did not acquire political power by saying, "Y'all crazy if you ain't gon vote for me." They all have full command of standard English, and I don't think that knowledge takes away from their blackness or commitment to black people.

I know from experience that it's important for black people, stripped   8 of culture and heritage, to have something they can point to and say, "This is ours, *we* can comprehend it, *we* alone can speak it with a soulful flourish." I'd be lying if I said that the rhythms of my people caught up in "some serious rap" don't sound natural and right to me sometimes. But how heartwarming is it for those same brothers when they hit the pavement searching for employment? Studies have proven that the use of ethnic dialects decreases power in the marketplace. "I be" is acceptable on the corner, but not with the boss.

Am I letting capitalistic, European-oriented thinking fog the issue? 9 Am I selling out blacks to an ideal of assimilating, being as much like white as possible? I have not formed a personal political ideology, but I do know this: it hurts me to hear black children use black English, knowing that they will be at yet another disadvantage in an educational system already full of stumbling blocks. It hurts me to sit in lecture halls and hear fellow black students complain that the professor "be tripping dem out using big words dey can't understand." And what hurts most is to be stripped of my own blackness simply because I know my way around the English language.

I would have to disagree with Labov in one respect. My goal is not so 10 much to acquire full control of both standard and black English, but to one day see more black people less dependent on a dialect that excludes them from full participation in the world we live in. I don't think I talk white, I think I talk right.

QUESTIONS ON CONTENT

1. When did Jones first realize that she "talked white"?

2. After years of reflection, Jones figured out what people meant by the expression "talk white." What "frightening implications" did these words hold for her? What is the "depressing reality" they confirmed?

3. Jones insists that talking white does not detract from her "blackness." What kind of arguments does she use to persuade her readers? Which of her arguments do you find most convincing?

4. What is Black English? Where does Jones define the term?

5. Jones names five major concerns she has for African Americans who refuse to learn standard English. What are they and where are they stated? Can you think of any other concerns?

QUESTIONS ON RHETORIC

1. Jones begins her essay with a quote from a noted linguist. How does his point of view set the tone for Jones's essay? What is that tone? Give examples of Jones' diction to support your answer (Glossary: *Tone*).

2. Jones relies on a liberal use of examples to illustrate her main point. Choose several passages that show the variety of ways in which Jones uses examples and discuss how these examples help persuade her readers.

3. Jones says talking white means being "articulate and well versed." Is Jones herself articulate and well versed? Give examples of Jones's diction and presentation to support your answer.

4. Jones concludes with a reference to the quote she used in the begin-

ning of her essay. What purpose does this reiteration serve? Is it effective? Explain your answer.

5. In paragraph 7 Jones argues against James Baldwin's claim that Black English "is a political instrument." In the examples that she uses, do you think that Jones is being fair to Black English or merely caricaturing it? Explain.

VOCABULARY

linguist (1)	deduced (5)	staples (6)
patois (1)	articulate (6)	dialect (10)
doggedly (4)		

WRITING TOPICS

1. Many colleges across the country include an African-American studies program in the curriculum. How are issues of African-American history and culture being dealt with on your campus? What are some of the arguments students make for including African-American history in the school curriculum? What are some of the arguments against it? Is African-American history included in your school's curriculum? How do you feel about it? In light of what you have read in this section, write an essay exploring the issue.

2. Rachel Jones was just a sophomore in college when she wrote this essay, yet her writing and the expression of her ideas show remarkable sophistication and care. Reread Jones's essay with an eye to what her writing style says about her personality; then write an essay showing how Jones might argue that these qualities should be taken for granted in any definition of "blackness."

IF SLANG IS NOT A SIN

Lance Morrow

If a word "is the skin of a living thought," then, says Lance Morrow in this essay, "the flesh of slang is a little weaker than usual now." America has always had the richest slang in the world, reaching a zenith in the 1960s with the publication of Stuart Berg Flexner's Dictionary of American Slang. *What has happened in recent years? Morrow, an author and a staff writer for* Time, *offers some reasons for our slang slump and finds some hope in an unexpected place.*

The classic slang of the '60s is almost a dead language now. In un- 1
adulterated form it survives only under the protection of certain purists
with long memories, heirs to the medieval tradition of monastic scribes.
Their honorary abbot is Phil Donahue.

The '60s-bred clergyman, especially the Episcopalian, is for some 2
reason a wondrous curator of the lingo. He ascends his pulpit. "God
doesn't want you on a *guilt trip*," he begins, inspired. "God's not *into*
guilt. *Bad vibes*! He knows *where you're coming from*. God says, 'Guilt,
that's a *bummer*.' The Lord can be pretty *far out* about these things, you
know." He goes into a wild fugue of nostalgia: "*Sock it to me! Outasight!
Right on*!"

But slang cannot live forever on the past, no matter how magnificent 3
it may have been. Slang needs to be new. Its life is brief, intense and
slightly disreputable, like adolescence. Soon it either settles down and
goes into the family business of the language (like *taxi* and *cello* and *hi*),
or, more likely, slips off into oblivion, dead as Oscan and Manx. The
evening news should probably broadcast brief obituaries of slang words
that have passed on. The practice would prevent people from embarrassing themselves by saying things like *swell* or *super*. "*Groovy*, descendant
of *cool* and *hip*, vanished from the language today."

Where is the next generation of slang to come from? Not from Valley 4
Girl, the argot made famous lately by singer Frank Zappa and his daughter, who is named Moon Unit Zappa. "Val" is really a sort of satire of
slang, a goof on language and on the dreamily dumb and self-regarding
suburban kids who may actually talk like that. It would come out all
wrong if a minister were to compose his sermon in Val. "The Lord is
awesome," he would have to begin. "He knows that life can sometimes
be, like, *grody—grody to the max! Fer shirr*!"

Still, slang has deep resources. The French resist barbaric intrusions 5
into the language of Voltaire and Descartes. But American English has
traditionally welcomed any bright word that sailed in, no matter how

ragged it may have looked on arrival. That Whitmanesque hospitality has given America the richest slang in the world.

An inventory of American slang now, however, can be somewhat   6
disappointing. Slang today seems to lack the playful energy and defiant self-confidence that can send language darting out to make raffish back-alley metaphorical connections and shrewdly teasing inductive games of synonym.

Examine one fairly new item: *airhead*. It means, of course, a brain-   7
less person, someone given to stupid behavior and opinions. But it is a vacuous, dispiriting little effort. The word has no invective force or meta-phorical charm. When slang settles for the wearily literal (*airhead* equals empty head), it is too tired to keep up with the good stuff.

Much new slang originates with people who have to be in by 8. Ju-   8
nior high and even grade school are unexpectedly productive sources. Sometimes children simply take ordinary words and hold them up to the light at a slightly different angle, an old trick of slang. The ten-year-old will pronounce something *"excellent"* in the brisk, earnest manner of an Army colonel who has just inspected his regiment. (*Primo* means the same thing.) The movie *E.T.* has contributed *penis breath*, an aggres-sively weird phrase in perfect harmony with the aggressively weird psyche of the eight-year-old. In Minnesota, they say, *for weird*. *Bogus* is an ordinary, though slightly out-of-the-way word that has been recommis-sioned as youth slang that means fraudulent or simply second-rate or silly. *Bogus* is a different shading of *lame*. Something that is easy is *cinchy*. Overexcited? One is *blowing a hype*.

The young, as always, use slang as an instrument to define status, to   9
wave to peers and even to discipline reality. A real jerk may be a *nerkey*, a combination of *nerd* and *turkey*. Is something *gnarly*? That may be good or bad. But if it is *mega-gnarly*, that is excellent. One may leave a sorority house at U.C.L.A. to *mow a burger*. Slang has less ideological content now than it had in the '60s. Still, it sometimes arises, like humor, from apprehension. High school students say, "That English test really nuked me." On the other hand, in black neighborhoods of Washington, D.C., if you had a good time at a party, you *dropped the bomb*.

The old '50s frat-house leer is evident in today's collegiate slang. To   10
get naked means to have a good time, whether or not sex is involved. (That is a new shortened form of the *get-drunk-and-get-naked-party*, which collegians fantasized about 20 years ago.) At Michigan State Univer-sity, one who is vomiting is *driving the bus*, a reference to the toilet seat and the wretch's need to hang on to it. *Sckacks* means ugly. A *two-bagger* is a girl who requires exactly that to cover her ugliness. Young women, of course, retaliate. At breakfast in Bates Hall at Wellesley, they wonder, "Why bother with a guy if he doesn't *make your teeth fall out?*" *Time to book* means time to leave, which can also be *time to bail*. None of this is exactly brilliant. Slang is sometimes merely a conspiracy of airheads.

American slang is fed by many tributaries. Feminists are busy *net-*   11
working—the liberated version of using the old-boy network. Cops, as
sardonic with language as criminals are, refer to a gunshot wound in the
head as a *serious headache*. Drug users have their codes, but they seem
to have lost some of their glamour. Certain drugs have a fatality about
them that cannot be concealed in jaunty language. The comedian Richard
Pryor introduced the outer world to *freebasing* a couple of years ago, and
John Belushi died after he *speed-balled* (mixed heroin and cocaine). Punk
language has made a couple of its disarmingly nasty contributions: *sleaze*
(as in, "There was a lot of sleaze at the party," meaning much of the
transcendentally rotten) has passed from the homosexual vocabulary into
punk, and is headed for mainstream English.

The Pentagon speaks of *the power curve*, meaning the direction in   12
which things are tending. Employees at McDonald's describe their specialized burnout as being *burgered-out*. Homosexuals possess a deca-
dently rich special vocabulary that is on the whole inaccessible to
breeders (heterosexuals).

Television has developed an elaborate jargon that has possibilities as   13
slang. *Voice-over, segue, intro* and *out of sync* have been part of the
more general language for a long time. Now there is the *out-tro*, the
stand-up spiel at the end of a news reporter's segment. A vividly cynical
new item of TV news jargon is *bang-bang*, meaning the kind of film
coverage that TV reporters must have in order to get their reports from El
Salvador or the Middle East onto the evening news.

Black slang may not be quite as strong as it was in the '60s. That may   14
mean either that black slang is less productive than before or that it is
more successful at remaining exclusive and secret. Two expressions that
have popped up . . . (recently): *serious as a heart attack* and *that's Kool
and the Gang*. The second is a reference to a popular musical group and a
little flourish added to the ancient *that's cool*.

The richest new territory for slang is computer technology. That is   15
unexpected. Slang is usually thought of as a kind of casual conversation
in the street, not as a dialogue between the human brain and a machine.
Those who go mountaineering up the interface, however, are developing
a wonderfully recondite vocabulary. *Hackers* (computer fanatics) at
M.I.T. and Stanford maintain a Hacker's Dictionary to keep their common working language accessible to one another. *Input* and *output* have
long since entered the wider language. So have *software* and *hardware*.
The human brain in some circles is now referred to as *wetware*. When a
computer *goes down*, of course, it *crashes*. *Menu*, meaning a computer's
directory of functions, is turning up now as noun and verb, as in "Let me
menu my schedule and I'll get back to you about lunch."

In the Hacker's Dictionary, one finds *gronk* (a verb that means to   16
become unusable, as in "the monitor *gronked*"), *gweep* (one who spends
unusually long periods of time hacking), *cuspy* (anything that is excep-

tionally good or performs its functions exceptionally well), *dink* (to modify in some small way so as to produce large or catastrophic results), *bagbiter* (equipment or program that fails, usually intermittently) and *deadlock* (a situation wherein two or more processes are unable to proceed because each is waiting for the other to do something. This is the electronic equivalent of *gridlock*, a lovely, virtually perfect word that describes automobile traffic paralyzed both ways through an intersection). The hacker's lexicon is endless and weirdly witty, and inspiring in a peculiar way; the human language is caught there precisely in the act of improvisation as it moves through a strange new country. The mind is making itself at home in the mysteries and possibilities of the machines.

A word, Justice Oliver Wendell Holmes wrote, "is the skin of a living thought." The flesh of slang is a little weaker than usual now. Why? For several reasons. Perhaps slang follows the economy and now finds itself a bit recessed.   17

Tribes make slang, and the old tribes are dissolving. Slang has always been the decoration and camouflage of nervous subgroups: youth, blacks, homosexuals, minorities, pickpockets, small tribes using language as solidarity against the big tribes. Slang proclaims one's specialness and conceals one's secrets. Perhaps the slang of today seems a bid faded because we still live in an aftermath of the '60s, the great revolt of the tribes. The special-interest slangs generated then were interminably publicized. Like the beads and the Afros and gestures and costumes and theatrical rages, slang became an ingredient of the national mixed-media pageant. Now, with more depressingly important things to do (earn a living, for example), Americans may feel a sense of cultural lull.   18

As the University of Cincinnati's William Lasher remarks, "Slang doesn't get written down, so it doesn't endure. If you do write it down, it gets into the language, and stops being slang." In a maniacally open electronic society, the news and entertainment industries sift hungrily through the culture searching for color, anecdote, personality, uniqueness and, of course, slang. All these items instantly become part of the show. Slang is wonderful entertainment. But its half-life is shorter now. Good slang gets commercial in a hurry, like certain country-music singers.   19

There may be a deeper reason for the relative decline of slang. Standard English is losing prestige and even legitimacy. Therefore, deviations from the "correct" also lose some of their force. Slang forfeits a little of its renegade quality, its outlaw savor. If slang is no longer a kind of sin, it cannot be as much fun as it once was.   20

QUESTIONS ON CONTENT

1. How does Morrow define slang, and what is its chief characteristic?

2. What does Morrow say is wrong with slang today? Do you agree? Give examples of good or weak slang that you hear.

3. Why do we use slang? Cite specific examples of slang that you use to support your answer.

4. Name some groups that Morrow identifies as good originators of slang. Can you add additional ones? Give examples of slang that groups you belong to use. Do others in your family use different slang?

5. What subgroup is producing the most inventive slang today? Why do you suppose that is true? How do the "decoration and camouflage" functions of slang serve this subgroup?

6. What reasons does Morrow give for today's disappointing slang?

QUESTIONS ON RHETORIC

1. What is Morrow's thesis, and how does he develop it? (Glossary: *Thesis*)

2. What kind of figure of speech is Morrow's comparison between slang and adolescence? On what three ideas does the comparison turn? Are these appropriate points of comparison?

3. What image does Morrow create when he says slang "has deep resources" (5), "bright words regularly sail into our language" (5), and "American slang is fed by many tributaries" (11)? To what is slang being compared? What is his purpose in creating this image? (Glossary: *Analogy*)

4. Why does Morrow give his reasons for the anemia or decline of slang at the end of the essay instead of at the beginning?

VOCABULARY

lingo (2)	vacuous (7)	lexicon (16)
argot (4)	invective (7)	maniacally (19)
raffish (6)	recondite (15)	savor (20)

WRITING TOPICS

1. This essay first appeared in *Time* in 1982. Do you think today, over ten years later, the situation Morrow describes has become better or worse? Support your opinion with specific examples of slang and at least one reason for the change(s) you perceive.

2. Choose a paragraph from a newspaper or a magazine article and rewrite it in slang. How would the intended audience of the original piece react to your version?

3. Morrow says the entertainment industries are always searching for color and uniqueness and, therefore, slang is wonderful entertainment. As you listen to the radio or watch television, jot down the slang you hear. Who uses it, and in what situations? For what purpose? Write an essay in which you present your observations and conclusions.

ENGLISH BELONGS
TO EVERYBODY

Robert MacNeil

"The genius of English," for Robert MacNeil, "is that it has always been the tongue of the common people, literate or not." In the following selection from his book Wordstruck, *MacNeil, popular public television newscaster and author of* The Story of English, *celebrates the richness and diversity of present-day English. For him, English "has prospered and grown because it was able to accept and absorb change."*

This is a time of widespread anxiety about the language. Some Americans fear that English will be engulfed or diluted by Spanish and want to make it the official language. There is anxiety about a crisis of illiteracy, or a crisis of semiliteracy among high school, even college, graduates.

Anxiety, however, may have a perverse side effect: experts who wish to "save" the language may only discourage pleasure in it. Some are good-humored and tolerant of change, others intolerant and snobbish. Language reinforces feelings of social superiority or inferiority; it creates insiders and outsiders; it is a prop to vanity or a source of anxiety, and on both emotions the language snobs play. Yet the changes and the errors that irritate them are no different in kind from those which have shaped our language for centuries. As Hugh Kenner wrote of certain British critics in *The Sinking Island*, "They took note of language only when it annoyed them." Such people are killjoys: they turn others away from an interest in the language, inhibit their use of it, and turn pleasure off.

Change is inevitable in a living language and is responsible for much of the vitality of English; it has prospered and grown because it was able to accept and absorb change.

As people evolve and do new things, their language will evolve too. They will find ways to describe the new things and their changed perspective will give them new ways of talking about the old things. For example, electric light switches created a brilliant metaphor for the oldest of human experiences, being *turned on* or *turned off*. To language conservatives those expressions still have a slangy, low ring to them; to others they are vivid, fresh-minted currency, very spendable, very "with it."

That tolerance for change represents not only the dynamism of the English-speaking peoples since the Elizabethans, but their deeply rooted ideas of freedom as well. This was the idea of the Danish scholar Otto

Jespersen, one of the great authorities on English. Writing in 1905, Jespersen said in his *Growth and Structure of the English Language*:

> The French language is like the stiff French garden of Louis XIV, while the English is like an English park, which is laid out seemingly without any definite plan, and in which you are allowed to walk everywhere according to your own fancy without having to fear a stern keeper enforcing rigorous regulations. The English language would not have been what it is if the English had not been for centuries great respecters of the liberties of each individual and if everybody had not been free to strike out new paths for himself.

I like that idea and do not think it just coincidence. Consider that the   6
same cultural soil, the Celtic-Roman-Saxon-Danish-Norman amalgam, which produced the English language also nourished the great principles of freedom and rights of man in the modern world. The first shoots sprang up in England and they grew stronger in America. Churchill called them "the joint inheritance of the English-speaking world." At the very core of those principles are popular consent and resistance to arbitrary authority; both are fundamental characteristics of our language. The English-speaking peoples have defeated all efforts to build fences around their language, to defer to an academy on what was permissible English and what not. They'll decide for themselves, thanks just the same.

Nothing better expresses resistance to arbitrary authority than the per-   7
sistence of what grammarians have denounced for centuries as "errors." In the common speech of English-speaking peoples—Americans, Englishmen, Canadians, Australians, New Zealanders, and others—these usages persist, despite rising literacy and wider education. We hear them every day:

> Double negative: "I don't want none of that."
> Double comparative: "Don't make that any more heavier!"
> Wrong verb: "Will you learn me to read?"

These "errors" have been with us for at least four hundred years,   8
because you can find each of them in Shakespeare.

> Double negative: In *Hamlet*, the King says:

> Nor what he spake, though it lack'd form a little,
> Was not like madness.

> Double comparative: In *Othello*, the Duke says:

> Yet opinion . . . throws a more safer voice on you.

> Wrong verb: In *Othello*, Desdemona says:

> My life and education both do learn me how to respect you.

I find it very interesting that these forms will not go away and lie   9
down. They were vigorous and acceptable in Shakespeare's time; they are
far more vigorous today, although not acceptable as standard English.
Regarded as error by grammarians, they are nevertheless in daily use all
over the world by a hundred times the number of people who lived in
Shakespeare's England.

It fascinates me that *axe*, meaning "ask," so common in black Ameri-   10
can English, is standard in Chaucer in all forms—*axe, axen, axed*: "and
axed him if Troilus were there." Was that transmitted across six hundred
years or simply reinvented?

English grew without a formal grammar. After the enormous cre-   11
ativity of Shakespeare and the other Elizabethans, seventeenth- and eighteenth-century critics thought the language was a mess, like an overgrown
garden. They weeded it by imposing grammatical rules derived from ti-
dier languages, chiefly Latin, whose precision and predictability they
trusted. For three centuries, with some slippage here and there, their rules
have held. Educators taught them and written English conformed. Today,
English-language newspapers, magazines, and books everywhere broadly
agree that correct English obeys these rules. Yet the wild varieties continue to threaten the garden of cultivated English and, by their numbers,
actually dominate everyday usage.

Nonstandard English formerly knew its place in the social order.   12
Characters in fiction were allowed to speak it occasionally. Hemingway
believed that American literature really did not begin until Mark Twain,
who outraged critics by reproducing the vernacular of characters like
Huck Finn. Newspapers still clean up the grammar when they quote the
ungrammatical, including politicians. The printed word, like Victorian
morality, has often constituted a conspiracy of respectability.

People who spoke grammatically could be excused the illusion that   13
their writ held sway, perhaps the way the Normans thought that French
had conquered the language of the vanquished Anglo-Saxons. A generation ago, people who considered themselves educated and well-spoken
might have had only glancing contact with nonstandard English, usually
in a well-understood class, regional, or rural context.

It fascinates me how differently we all speak in different circum-   14
stances. We have levels of formality, as in our clothing. There are very
formal occasions, often requiring written English: the job application or
the letter to the editor—the dark-suit, serious-tie language, with everything pressed and the lint brushed off. There is our less formal out-in-the-
world language—a more comfortable suit, but still respectable. There is
language for close friends in the evenings, on weekends—blue-jeans-and-
sweat-shirt language, when it's good to get the tie off. There is family
language, even more relaxed, full of grammatical short cuts, family
slang, echoes of old jokes that have become intimate shorthand—the lan-

guage of pajamas and uncombed hair. Finally, there is the language with no clothes on; the talk of couples—murmurs, sighs, grunts—language at its least self-conscious, open, vulnerable, and primitive.

Broadcasting has democratized the publication of language, often at   15 its most informal, even undressed. Now the ears of the educated cannot escape the language of the masses. It surrounds them on the news, weather, sports, commercials, and the ever-proliferating talk and call-in shows.

This wider dissemination of popular speech may easily give purists   16 the idea that the language is suddenly going to hell in this generation, and may explain the new paranoia about it.

It might also be argued that more Americans hear more correct, even   17 beautiful, English on television than was ever heard before. Through television more models of good usage reach more American homes than was ever possible in other times. Television gives them lots of colloquial English, too, some awful, some creative, but that is not new.

Hidden in this is a simple fact: our language is not the special private   18 property of the language police, or grammarians, or teachers, or even great writers. The genius of English is that it has always been the tongue of the common people, literate or not.

English belongs to everybody: the funny turn of phrase that pops into   19 the mind of a farmer telling a story; or the traveling salesman's dirty joke; or the teenager saying, "Gag me with a spoon"; or the pop lyric—all contribute, are all as valid as the tortured image of the academic, or the line the poet sweats over for a week.

Through our collective language sense, some may be thought beauti-   20 ful and some ugly, some may live and some may die; but it is all English and it belongs to everyone—to those of us who wish to be careful with it and those who don't care.

QUESTIONS ON CONTENT

1. Why, according to MacNeil, is there widespread anxiety about the language? And what does he see as one side effect of this anxiety?

2. What for MacNeil does change bring to a language? Why does change occur in a language in the first place?

3. In what sense does MacNeil see "popular consent" and "resistance to arbitrary authority" as "fundamental characteristics of our language" (6)?

4. When was a formal grammar imposed on English? Where, according to MacNeil, is "correct English" used?

5. What reasons does MacNeil give to dismiss the purist's notion that English is "suddenly going to hell in this generation." Do you find his reasoning acceptable? Why, or why not?

QUESTIONS ON RHETORIC

1. What is MacNeil's thesis, and where does he state it? (Glossary: *Thesis*)

2. In paragraph 5 MacNeil quotes the Danish linguist Otto Jespersen. What function does the rather extended quotation serve?

3. In paragraphs 7 and 8 MacNeil gives examples of common usages that have been labeled "errors" by prescriptive grammarians. What point does MacNeil make with these examples?

4. What devices does MacNeil use to make transitions between paragraphs? (Glossary: *Transitions*) Which transitions seem to work best for you? Explain why.

5. Identify the analogy MacNeil uses to explain the various levels of formality with language (14). (Glossary: *Analogy*) Does the analogy, in fact, help to clarify the levels of formality for you? Explain.

6. Would you describe MacNeil's tone in this essay as academic, objective, sarcastic, conversational, or ironic? (Glossary: *Tone*) Cite examples of his diction that led you to your response.

VOCABULARY

engulfed (1)	persistence (7)	colloquial (17)
illiteracy (1)	conspiracy (12)	
perverse (2)	paranoia (16)	

WRITING TOPICS

1. Where does MacNeil stand in debate between standard and nonstandard English? What is the place of standard English? nonstandard English? Write an essay in which you discuss the importance of knowing standard English and when to use it.

2. MacNeil sees it as a strength of English that it has resisted arbitrary authority, that "our language is not the special private property of the language police, or grammarians, or teachers, or even great writers." Based on your own experiences and observations, write an essay in which you agree or disagree with MacNeil's position.

WRITING ASSIGNMENTS FOR "USAGE, WORDS, AND STANDARD ENGLISH"

1. Using examples and ideas from two or three of the essays in this section, write an essay in which you describe the state of American English today. Is there a language crisis as some critics would have us believe, or is the language simply continuing to change as it has for the last 250 years in this country? Be sure to use examples from your experiences and observations to illustrate your essay.

2. Paul Roberts argues that "no understanding of the English language can be very satisfactory without a notion of the history of the language." What exactly does Roberts mean by "understanding"? Write an essay in which you substantiate or dispute his claim.

3. The concept of "Standard English" has caused much misunderstanding and debate. For many Americans, "standard" implies that one variety of English is more correct or more functional than other varieties. Write an essay in which you attempt to define "Standard English" and explain its power or mystique.

4. While you were in high school you may have been exposed to the "back to basics" movement, educational reform that stressed the fundamentals of reading, writing, and mathematics. What exactly did "back to basics" or "fundamentals" mean in your area of the country? How did it affect the curriculum? In your opinion, did this approach adequately address students' language problems in writing, reading, and speaking? In an essay, discuss the advantages and disadvantages of the "back to basics" movement.

5. Noted linguist Harvey Daniels believes that by insisting upon correctness, prescriptivists, or pop grammarians as they are widely known, "encourage us to continue using minor differences in language as ways of identifying, classifying, avoiding, or punishing anyone whom we choose to consider our social or intellectual inferior." Have you ever reacted to anyone negatively or positively on the basis of the English that he or she used, or have you ever been judged on that same basis? Using several articles in this section as resources, write an essay in which you recount one such incident and discuss how language can prejudice opinion.

6. Each of the following items is normally discussed as a question of usage by usage guides and dictionaries. Consult three or four usage guides in the reference room of your library for information about each item. What advice does each guide offer? How does the advice given by one guide compare with that given by another? What conclusions can you draw about the usefulness of such usage guides?

   a. hopefully
   b. nauseous
   c. imply/infer

    d. contact (as a verb)
    e. ain't
    f. among/between
    g. enthuse
    h. irregardless
    i. lay/lie
    j. uninterested/disinterested

7. In her essay "Black Children, Black Speech," Dorothy Z. Seymour suggests that African-American children shouldn't have to choose between "black" and "white" English. Instead, she believes a way must be found for these children to learn to speak the basics of Standard English without compromising the vernacular. One solution to the problem, Seymour suggests, is the official adoption of bidialectism. In her words, "The result would be the ability to use either dialect equally well . . . depending on the time, place, and circumstances." With this in mind, reread Jones's essay and in a short paper of your own discuss how you think Jones would react to Seymour's proposition. Give examples from both essays to support your position.

8. Bidialectism and bilingualism are highly controversial subjects. Pick one and then prepare a report that (a) presents the opposing views objectively, or (b) supports one particular view over the other. What sociologic and economic factors are important? What issues do not seem to be relevant? From an educational point of view, which argument do you think is strongest? Defend whatever position you take.

PART IV

The Language of Politics

PROPAGANDA: HOW NOT TO BE BAMBOOZLED

Donna Woolfolk Cross

While most people are against propaganda in principle, few people know exactly what it is and how it works. In the following essay, Donna Woolfolk Cross, who teaches at Onondaga Community College in New York, takes the mystery out of propaganda. Cross starts by providing a definition of propaganda. She then classifies the tricks of the propagandist into thirteen major categories and discusses each thoroughly. Her essay is chock-full of useful advice on how not to be manipulated by propaganda.

Propaganda. If an opinion poll were taken tomorrow, we can be sure that nearly everyone would be against it because it *sounds* so bad. When we say, "Oh, that's just propaganda," it means, to most people, "That's a pack of lies." But really, propaganda is simply a means of persuasion and so it can be put to work for good causes as well as bad—to persuade people to give to charity, for example, or to love their neighbors, or to stop polluting the environment.

For good or evil, propaganda pervades our daily lives, helping to shape our attitudes on a thousand subjects. Propaganda probably determines the brand of toothpaste you use, the movies you see, the candidates you elect when you get to the polls. Propaganda works by tricking us, by momentarily distracting the eye while the rabbit pops out from beneath the cloth. Propaganda works best with an uncritical audience. Joseph Goebbels, Propaganda Minister in Nazi Germany, once defined his work as "the conquest of the masses." The masses would not have been conquered, however, if they had known how to challenge and to question, how to make distinctions between propaganda and reasonable argument.

People are bamboozled mainly because they don't recognize propaganda when they see it. They need to be informed about the various devices that can be used to mislead and deceive—about the propagandist's overflowing bag of tricks. The following, then, are some common pitfalls for the unwary.

1. NAME-CALLING

As its title suggests, this device consists of labeling people or ideas with words of bad connotation, literally, "calling them names." Here the propagandist tries to arouse our contempt so we will dismiss the "bad name" person or idea without examining its merits.

149

Bad names have played a tremendously important role in the history   5
of the world. They have ruined reputations and ended lives, sent people
to prison and to war, and just generally made us mad at each other for
centuries.

Name-calling can be used against policies, practices, beliefs and ide-   6
als, as well as against individuals, groups, races, nations. Name-calling is
at work when we hear a candidate for office described as a "foolish ideal-
ist" or a "two-faced liar" or when an incumbent's policies are denounced
as "reckless," "reactionary," or just plain "stupid." Some of the most
effective names a public figure can be called are ones that may not denote
anything specific: "Congresswoman Jane Doe is a *bleeding heart!*" (Did
she vote for funds to help paraplegics?) or "The Senator is a *tool of
Washington!*" (Did he happen to agree with the President?) Senator
Yakalot uses name-calling when he denounces his opponent's "radical
policies" and calls them (and him) "socialist," "pinko," and part of a
"heartless plot." He also uses it when he calls cars "puddle-jumpers,"
"can openers," and "motorized baby buggies."

The point here is that when the propagandist uses name-calling, he   7
doesn't want us to think—merely to react, blindly unquestioningly. So
the best defense against taken in by name-calling is to stop and ask,
"Forgetting the bad name attached to it, what are the merits of the idea
itself? What does this name really mean, anyway?"

2. GLITTERING GENERALITIES

Glittering generalities are really name-calling in reverse. Name-calling   8
use words with bad connotations; glittering generalities are words with
good connotations—"virtue words," as the Institute for Propaganda Analysis has called them. The Institute explains that while name-calling tries
to get us to *reject* and *condemn* someone or something without examining
the evidence, glittering generalities try to get us to *accept* and *agree*
without examining the evidence.

We believe in, fight for, live by "virtue words" which we feel deeply   9
about: "justice," "motherhood," "the American way," "our Constitutional
rights," "our Christian heritage." These sound good, but when we examine them closely, they turn out to have no specific, definable meaning.
They just make us feel good. Senator Yakalot uses glittering generalities
when he says, "I stand for all that is good in America, for our American
way and our American birthright." But what exactly *is* "good for America"? How can we define our "American birthright"? Just what parts of
the American society and culture does "our American way" refer to?

We often make the mistake of assuming we are personally unaffected   10
by glittering generalities. The next time you find yourself assuming that,
listen to a political candidate's speech on TV and see how often the use

of glittering generalities elicits cheers and applause. That's the danger of propaganda; it *works*. Once again, our defense against it is to ask questions: Forgetting the virtue words attached to it, what are the merits of the idea itself? What does "Americanism" (or "freedom" or "truth") really *mean* here? . . .

Both name-calling and glittering generalities work by stirring our   11
emotions in the hope that this will cloud our thinking. Another approach that propaganda uses is to create a distraction, a "red herring," that will make people forget or ignore the real issues. There are several different kinds of "red herrings" that can be used to distract attention.

3. PLAIN FOLKS APPEAL

"Plain folks" is the device by which a speaker tries to win our confidence   12
and support by appearing to be a person like ourselves—"just one of the plain folks." The plain-folks appeal is at work when candidates go around shaking hands with factory workers, kissing babies in supermarkets, and sampling pasta with Italians, fried chicken with Southerners, bagels and blintzes with Jews. "Now I'm a businessman like yourselves" is a plain-folks appeal, as is "I've been a farm boy all my life." Senator Yakalot tries the plain-folks appeal when he says, "I'm just a small-town boy like you fine people." The use of such expressions once prompted Lyndon Johnson to quip, "Whenever I hear someone say, 'I'm just an old country lawyer,' the first thing I reach for is my wallet to make sure it's still there."

The irrelevancy of the plain-folks appeal is obvious: even if the man   13
is "one of us" (which may not be true at all), that doesn't mean that his ideas and programs are sound—or even that he honestly has our best interests at heart. As with glittering generalities, the danger here is that we may mistakenly assume we are immune to this appeal. But propagandists wouldn't use it unless it had been proved to work. You can protect yourself by asking, "Aside from his 'nice guy next door' image, what does this man stand for? Are his ideas and his past record really supportive of my best interests?"

4. *ARGUMENTUM AD POPULUM* (STROKING)

Argumentum ad populum means "argument to the people" or "telling the   14
people what they want to hear." The colloquial term from the Watergate era is "stroking," which conjures up pictures of small animals or children being stroked or soothed with compliments until they come to like the person doing the complimenting—and, by extension, his or her ideas.

We all like to hear nice things about ourselves and the group we   15 belong to—we like to be liked—so it stands to reason that we will respond warmly to a person who tells us we are "hard-working taxpayers" or "the most generous, free-spirited nation in the world." Politicians tell farmers they are the "backbone of the American economy" and college students that they are the "leaders and policy makers of tomorrow." Commercial advertisers use stroking more insidiously by asking a question which invites a flattering answer: "What kind of a man reads *Playboy?*" (Does he really drive a Porsche and own $10,000 worth of sound equipment?) Senator Yakalot is stroking his audience when he calls them the "decent law-abiding citizens that are the great pulsing heart and the life blood of this, our beloved country," and when he repeatedly refers to them as "you fine people," "you wonderful folks."

Obviously, the intent here is to sidetrack us from thinking critically   16
about the man and his ideas. Our own good qualities have nothing to do with the issue at hand. Ask yourself, "Apart from the nice things he has to say about me (and my church, my nation, my ethnic group, my neighbors), what does the candidate stand for? Are his or her ideas in my best interests?"

5. ARGUMENTUM AD HOMINEM

Argumentum ad hominem means "argument to the man" and that's exactly what it is. When a propagandist uses *argumentum ad hominem*, he   17
wants to distract our attention from the issue under consideration with personal attacks on the people involved. For example, when Lincoln issued the Emancipation Proclamation, some people responded by calling him the "baboon." But Lincoln's long arms and awkward carriage had nothing to do with the merits of the Proclamation or the question of whether or not slavery should be abolished.

Today *argumentum ad hominem* is still widely used and very effec-   18
tive. You may or may not support the Equal Rights Amendment, but you should be sure your judgment is based on the merits of the idea itself, and not the result of someone's denunciation of the people who support the ERA as "fanatics" or "lesbians" or "frustrated old maids." Senator Yakalot is using *argumentum ad hominem* when he dismisses the idea of using smaller automobiles with a reference to the personal appearance of one of its supporters, Congresswoman Doris Schlepp. Refuse to be waylaid by *argumentum ad hominem* and ask, "Do the personal qualities of the person being discussed have anything to do with the issue at hand? Leaving him or her aside, how good is the idea itself?"

6. TRANSFER (GUILT OR GLORY BY ASSOCIATION)

In *argumentum ad hominem*, an attempt is made to associate negative   19
aspects of a person's character or personal appearance with an issue or idea he supports. The transfer device uses this same process of association to make us accept or condemn a given person or idea.

A better name for the transfer device is guilt (or glory) by association.   20
In glory by association, the propagandist tries to transfer the positive
feelings of something we love and respect to the group or idea he wants
us to accept. "This bill for a new dam is in the best tradition of this
country, the land of Lincoln, Jefferson, and Washington," is glory by
association at work. Lincoln, Jefferson, and Washington were great
leaders that most of us revere and respect, but they have no logical connection to the proposal under consideration—the bill to build a new dam.
Senator Yakalot uses glory by association when he says full-sized cars
"have always been as American as Mom's apple pie or a Sunday drive in
the country."

The process works equally well in reverse, when guilt by association   21
is used to transfer our dislike or disapproval of one idea or group to some
other idea or group that the propagandist wants us to reject and condemn.
"John Doe says we need to make some changes in the way our government operates; well, that's exactly what the Ku Klux Klan has said, so
there's a meeting of great minds!" That's guilt by association for you;
there's no logical connection between John Doe and the Ku Klux Klan
apart from the one the propagandist is trying to create in our minds. He
wants to distract our attention from John Doe and get us thinking (and
worrying) about the Ku Klux Klan and its politics of violence. (Of
course, there are sometimes legitimate associations between the two
things; if John Doe had been a *member* of the Ku Klux Klan, it would be
reasonable and fair to draw a connection between the man and his group.)
Senator Yakalot tries to trick his audience with guilt by association when
he remarks that "the words 'Community' and 'Communism' look an awful lot alike!" He does it again when he mentions that Mr. Stu Pott
"sports a Fidel Castro beard."

How can we learn to spot the transfer device and distinguish between   22
fair and unfair associations? We can teach ourselves to *suspend judgment*
until we have answered these questions: "Is there any legitimate connection between the idea under discussion and the thing it is associated with?
Leaving the transfer device out of the picture, what are the merits of the
idea by itself?"

7. BANDWAGON

Ever hear of the small, ratlike animal called the lemming? Lemmings are   23
arctic rodents with a very odd habit: periodically, for reasons no one
entirely knows, they mass together in a large herd and commit suicide by
rushing into deep water and drowning themselves. They all run in together, blindly, and not one of them ever seems to stop and ask, *"Why
am I doing this? Is this really what I want to do?"* and thus save itself
from destruction. Obviously, lemmings are driven to perform their
strange mass suicide rites by common instinct. People choose to "follow

the herd" for more complex reasons, yet we are still all too often the unwitting victims of the bandwagon appeal.

Essentially, the bandwagon urges us to support an action or an opinion because it is popular—because "everyone else is doing it." This call to "get on the bandwagon" appeals to the strong desire in most of us to be one of the crowd, not to be left out or alone. Advertising makes extensive use of the bandwagon appeal ("join the Pepsi people"), but so do politicians ("Let us join together in this great cause"). Senator Yakalot uses the bandwagon appeal when he says that "More and more citizens are rallying to my cause every day," and asks his audience to "join them—and me—in our fight for America."

One of the ways we can see the bandwagon appeal at work is in the overwhelming success of various fashions and trends which capture the interest (and the money) of thousands of people for a short time, then disappear suddenly and completely. For a year or two in the fifties, every child in North America wanted a coonskin cap so they could be like Davy Crockett; no one wanted to be left out. After that there was the hula-hoop craze that helped to dislocate the hips of thousands of Americans. More recently, what made millions of people rush out to buy their very own "pet rocks"?

The problem here is obvious: just because everyone's doing it doesn't mean that *we* should too. Group approval does not prove that something is true or is worth doing. Large numbers of people have supported actions we now condemn. Just a generation ago, Hitler and Mussolini rose to absolute and catastrophically repressive rule in two of the most sophisticated and cultured countries of Europe. When they came into power they were welled up by massive popular support from millions of people who didn't want to be "left out" at a great historical moment.

Once the mass begins to move—on the bandwagon—it becomes harder and harder to perceive the leader *riding* the bandwagon. So don't be a lemming, rushing blindly on to destruction because "everyone else is doing it." Stop and ask, "Where is this bandwagon headed? Never mind about everybody else, is this what is best for *me*?" . . .

As we have seen, propaganda can appeal to us by arousing our emotions or distracting our attention from the real issues at hand. But there's a third way that propaganda can be put to work against us—by the use of faulty logic. This approach is really more insidious than the other two because it gives the appearance of reasonable, fair argument. It is only when we look more closely that the holes in the logical fiber show up. The following are some of the devices that make use of faulty logic to distort and mislead.

8. FAULTY CAUSE AND EFFECT

As the name suggests, this device sets up a cause-and-effect relationship that may not be true. The Latin name for this logical fallacy is *post hoc ergo propter hoc*, which means "after this, therefore because of this." But just because one thing happened after another doesn't mean that one *caused* the other.

An example of false cause-and-effect reasoning is offered by the story (probably invented) of the woman aboard the ship *Titanic*. She woke up from a nap and, feeling seasick, looked around for a call button to summon the steward to bring her some medication. She finally located a small button on one of the walls of her cabin and pushed it. A split second later, the *Titanic* grazed an iceberg in the terrible crash that was to send the entire ship to its destruction. The woman screamed and said, "Oh, God, what have I done? What have I done?" The humor of that anecdote comes from the absurdity of the woman's assumption that pushing the small red button resulted in the destruction of a ship weighing several hundred tons: "It happened after I pushed it, therefore it must be *because* I pushed it"—*post hoc ergo propter hoc* reasoning. There is, of course, no cause-and-effect relationship there. 30

The false cause-and-effect fallacy is used very often by political candidates. "After I came to office, the rate of inflation dropped to 6 percent." But did the person do anything to cause the lower rate of inflation or was it the result of other conditions? Would the rate of inflation have dropped anyway, even if he hadn't come to office? Senator Yakalot uses false cause and effect when he says "our forefathers who made this country great never had free hot meal handouts! And look what they did for our country!" He does it again when he concludes that "driving full-sized cars means a better car safety record on our American roads today." 31

False cause-and-effect reasoning is terribly persuasive because it seems so logical. Its appeal is apparently to experience. We swallowed X product—and the headache went away. We elected Y official and unemployment went down. Many people think, "There *must* be a connection." But causality is an immensely complex phenomenon; you need a good deal of evidence to prove that an event that follows another in time was "therefore" caused by the first event. 32

Don't be taken in by false cause and effect; be sure to ask, "Is there enough evidence to prove that this cause led to that effect? Could there have been any *other* causes?" 33

9. FALSE ANALOGY

An analogy is a comparison between two ideas, events, or things. But comparisons can be fairly made only when the things being compared are alike in significant ways. When they are not, false analogy is the result. 34

A famous example of this is the old proverb "Don't change horses in the middle of a stream," often used as an analogy to convince voters not to change administrations in the middle of a war or other crisis. But the analogy is misleading because there are so many differences between the things compared. In what ways is a war or political crisis like a stream? 35

Is the President or head of state really very much like a horse? And is a nation of millions of people comparable to a man trying to get across a stream? Analogy is false and unfair when it compares two things that have little in common and assumes that they are identical. Senator Yakalot tries to hoodwink his listeners with false analogy when he says, "Trying to take Americans out of the kind of cars they love is as undemocratic as trying to deprive them of the right to vote."

Of course, analogies can be drawn that are reasonable and fair. It 36 would be reasonable, for example, to compare the results of busing in one small Southern city with the possible results in another, *if* the towns have the same kind of history, population, and school policy. We can decide for ourselves whether an analogy is false or fair by asking, "Are the things being compared truly alike in significant ways? Do the differences between them affect the comparison?"

10. BEGGING THE QUESTION

Actually, the name of this device is rather misleading, because it does not 37 appear in the form of a question. Begging the question occurs when, in discussing a questionable or debatable point, a person assumes as already established the very point that he is trying to prove. For example, "No thinking citizen could approve such a completely unacceptable policy as this one." But isn't the question of whether or not the policy *is* acceptable the very point to be established? Senator Yakalot begs the question when he announces that his opponent's plan won't work "because it is unworkable."

We can protect ourselves against this kind of faulty logic by asking, 38 "What is assumed in this statement? Is the assumption reasonable, or does it need more proof?"

11. THE TWO EXTREMES FALLACY (FALSE DILEMMA)

Linguists have long noted that the English language tends to view reality 39 in sets of two extremes or polar opposites. In English, things are either black or white, tall or short, up or down, front or back, left or right, good or bad, guilty or not guilty. We can ask for a "straightforward yes-or-no answer" to a question, the understanding being that we will not accept or consider anything in between. In fact, reality cannot always be dissected along such strict lines. There may be (usually are) *more* than just two possibilities or extremes to consider. We are often told to "listen to both sides of the argument." But who's to say that every argument has only two sides? Can't there be a third—even a fourth or fifth—point of view?

The two-extremes fallacy is at work in this statement by Lenin, the 40 great Marxist leader: "You cannot eliminate *one* basic assumption, one substantial part of this philosophy of Marxism (it is as if it were a block of steel), without abandoning truth, without falling into the arms of bourgeois-reactionary falsehood." In other words, if we don't agree 100 percent with every premise of Marxism, we must be placed at the opposite end of the political-economic spectrum—for Lenin, "bourgeois-reactionary falsehood." If we are not entirely *with* him, we must be against him; those are the only two possibilities open to us. Of course, this is a logical fallacy; in real life there are any number of political positions one can maintain *between* the two extremes of Marxism and capitalism. Senator Yakalot uses the two-extremes fallacy in the same way as Lenin when he tells his audience that "in this world a man's either for private enterprise or he's for socialism."

One of the most famous examples of the two-extremes fallacy in recent history is the slogan, "America: Love it or leave it," with its implicit suggestion that we either accept everything just as it is in America today without complaint—or get out. Again, it should be obvious that there is a whole range of action and belief between those two extremes.   41

Don't be duped; stop and ask, "Are those really the only two options I can choose from? Are there other alternatives not mentioned that deserve consideration?"   42

12. CARD STACKING

Some questions are so multifaceted and complex that no one can make an intelligent decision about them without considering a wide variety of evidence. One selection of facts could make us feel one way and another selection could make us feel just the opposite. Card stacking is a device of propaganda which selects only the facts that support the propagandist's point of view, and ignores all the others. For example, a candidate could be made to look like a legislative dynamo if you say, "Representative McNerd introduced more new bills than any other member of the Congress," and neglect to mention that most of them were so preposterous that they were laughed off the floor.   43

Senator Yakalot engages in card stacking when he talks about the proposal to use smaller cars. He talks only about jobs without mentioning the cost to the taxpayers or the very real—though still denied—threat of depletion of resources. He says he wants to help his countrymen keep their jobs, but doesn't mention that the corporations that offer the jobs will also make large profits. He praises the "American chrome industry," overlooking the fact that most chrome is imported. And so on.   44

The best protection against card stacking is to take the "Yes, but . . ." attitude. This device of propaganda is not untrue, but then again it is not the *whole* truth. So ask yourself, "Is this person leaving something out   45 that I should know about? Is there some other information that should be brought to bear on this question?" . . .

So far, we have considered three approaches that the propagandist can   46
use to influence our thinking: appealing to our emotions, distracting our attention, and misleading us with logic that may appear to be reasonable but is in fact faulty and deceiving. But there is a fourth approach that is probably the most common propaganda trick of them all.

13. TESTIMONIAL

The testimonial device consists in having some loved or respected person   47
give a statement of support (testimonial) for a given product or idea. The problem is that the person being quoted may *not* be an expert in the field; in fact, he may know nothing at all about it. Using the name of a man who is skilled and famous in one field to give a testimonial for something in another field is unfair and unreasonable.

Senator Yakalot tries to mislead his audience with testimonial when   48
he tells them that "full-sized cars have been praised by great Americans like John Wayne and Jack Jones, as well as by leading experts on car safety and comfort."

Testimonial is used extensively in TV ads, where it often appears in   49
such bizarre forms as Joe Namath's endorsement of a pantyhose brand. Here, of course, the "authority" giving the testimonial not only is no expert about pantyhose, but obviously stands to gain something (money!) by making the testimonial.

When celebrities endorse a political candidate, they may not be mak-   50
ing money by doing so, but we should still question whether they are in any better position to judge than we ourselves. Too often we are willing to let others we like or respect make our decisions *for us*, while we follow along acquiescently. And this is the purpose of testimonial—to get us to agree and accept *without* stopping to think. Be sure to ask, "Is there any reason to believe that this person (or organization or publication or whatever) has any more knowledge or information than I do on this subject? What does the idea amount to on is own merits, without the benefit of testimonial?"

The cornerstone of democratic society is reliance upon an informed   51
and educated electorate. To be fully effective citizens we need to be able to challenge and to question wisely. A dangerous feeling of indifference toward our political processes exists today. We often abandon our right, our duty, to criticize and evaluate by dismissing *all* politicians as "crooked," *all* new bills and proposals as "just more government bureaucracy." But there are important distinctions to be made, and this kind of apathy can be fatal to democracy.

If we are to be led, let us not be led blindly, but critically, intel-   52
ligently, with our eyes open. If we are to continue to be a government

"by the people," let us become informed about the methods and purposes of propaganda, so we can be the masters, not the slaves of our destiny.

QUESTIONS ON CONTENT

1. What is propaganda? Who uses propaganda? Why is it used?

2. Why does Cross think that people should be informed about propaganda? What is her advice for dealing with it?

3. What is "begging the question"?

4. What, according to Cross, is the most common propaganda trick of them all? Provide some examples of it from your own experience.

5. Why does Cross believe that it is necessary for people in a democratic society to become informed about the methods and practices of propaganda?

QUESTIONS ON RHETORIC

1. Why is classification an appropriate organizational strategy for Cross to use in this essay? (Glossary: *Division and Classification*)

2. How does Cross organize the discussion of each propaganda device she includes in her essay?

3. What use does Cross make of examples in her essay? How effective do you find them? Explain. (Glossary: *Examples*)

4. In her discussion of the bandwagon appeal, Cross uses the analogy of the lemmings. How does this analogy work? Why is it not a "false analogy"? (Glossary: *Analogy*)

VOCABULARY

connotations (8)	colloquial (14)	spectrum (40)
elicits (10)	insidiously (15)	

WRITING TOPICS

1. As Cross says in the beginning of her essay, propaganda "can be put to work for good causes as well as bad" (1). Using materials from the Red Cross, United Way, or some other public service organization, write an essay in which you discuss the propaganda used by such organizations. How would you characterize their appeals? Do you ever find such propaganda objectionable? Does the end always justify the means?

2. Using the devices described by Cross, try to write a piece of propaganda yourself. You can attempt to persuade your classmates to (a) join a particular campus organization, (b) support, either spiritually or financially, a controversial movement or issue on campus, or (c) vote for one candidate and not another in a campus election.

"SPEECH! SPEECH!"

Peggy Noonan

Political speeches are everyday fare in the United States. On the evening news any given night Americans can watch their president or other government officials delivering speeches to one group or another. Too often one speech seems to blur into others, resulting in Americans' failure to see that these speeches actually do count. While it's no secret that some anonymous speechwriter actually penned the words, most people have no idea of the complicated process involved in developing a major political speech. In the following selection from her book What I Saw at the Revolution, *Peggy Noonan, presidental speechwriter for the Reagan administration, shares her thoughts on the importance of political speeches in our history. And she offers an insider's view of the speechwriting process and the frustrations she felt when her writing was compromised by political policy matters.*

A speech is a soliloquy—one man[1] on a bare stage with a big spotlight. He will tell us who he is and what he wants and how he will get it and what it means that he wants it and what it will mean when he does or does not get it, and . . .

And he looks up at us in the balconies and clears his throat. "Ladies and gentlemen . . ." We lean forward, hungry to hear. Now it will be said, now we will hear the thing we long for.

A speech is part theater and part political declaration; it is a personal communication between a leader and his people; it is art, and all art is a paradox, being at once a thing of great power and great delicacy.

A speech is poetry: cadence, rhythm, imagery, sweep! A speech reminds us that words, like children, have the power to make dance the dullest beanbag of a heart.

Speeches are not significant because we have the technological ability to make them heard by every member of our huge nation simultaneously. Speeches are important because they are one of the great constants of our political history. For two hundred years, from "Give me liberty or give me death" to "Ask not what your country can do for you," they have been not only the way we measure public men, they have been how we tell each other who we are. For two hundred years they have been changing—making, forcing—history: Lincoln, Bryan and the cross of gold,

[1](The use of man, here, is generic; I mean man and woman; he also means she.)

FDR's first inaugural, Kennedy's, Martin Luther King in '63, Reagan and the Speech in '64. They count. They more than count, they shape what happens. (An irony: You know who doesn't really know this? Political professionals. The men who do politics as a business in America are bored by speeches. They call them "the rah rah." They prefer commercials.)

Another reason speeches are important: because the biggest problem in America, the biggest problem in any modern industrialized society, is loneliness. A great speech from a leader to the people eases our isolation, breaks down the walls, includes people: It takes them inside a spinning thing and makes them part of the gravity.

All speechwriters have things they think of when they write. I think of being a child in my family at the dinner table, with seven kids and hubbub and parents distracted by worries and responsibilities. Before I would say anything at the table, before I would approach my parents, I would plan what I would say. I would map out the narrative, sharpen the details, add color, plan momentum. This way I could hold their attention. This way I became a writer.

The American people too are distracted by worries and responsibilities and the demands of daily life, and you have to know that and respect it—and plan the narrative, sharpen the details, add color and momentum.

I work with an image: the child in the mall. When candidates for president are on the campaign trail they always go by a mall and walk through followed by a pack of minicams and reporters. They go by Colonel Sanders and have their picture taken eating a piece of chicken, they josh around with the lady in the mall information booth, they shake hands with the shoppers. But watch: Always there is a child, a ten-year-old girl, perhaps, in an inexpensive, tired-looking jacket. Perhaps she is by herself, perhaps with a friend. But she stands back, afraid of the lights, and as the candidate comes she runs away. She is afraid of his fame, afraid of the way the lights make his wire-rim glasses shine, afraid of dramatic moments, dense moments. When you are a speechwriter you should think of her when you write, and of her parents. They are Americans. They are good people for whom life has not been easy. Show them respect and be honest and logical in your approach and they will understand every word you say and hear—and know—that you thought of them.

The irony of modern speeches is that as our ability to disseminate them has exploded (an American president can speak live not only to America but to Europe, to most of the world), their quality has declined.

Why? Lots of reasons, including that we as a nation no longer learn the rhythms of public utterance from Shakespeare and the Bible. When young Lincoln was sprawled in front of the fireplace reading *Julius Caesar*—"Th' abuse of greatness is, when it disjoins remorse from power"—he was, unconsciously, learning to be a poet. You say, "That was Lincoln, not the common man." But the common man was flocking to the docks to get the latest installment of Dickens off the ship from England.

The modern egalitarian impulse has made politicians leery of flaunt-   12
ing high rhetoric; attempts to reach, to find the right if sometimes esoteric quote or allusion seem pretentious. They don't really know what "the common man" knows anymore; they forget that we've all had at least some education and a number of us read on our own and read certain classics in junior high and high school. The guy at the gas station read *Call of the Wild* when he was fourteen, and sometimes thinks about it. Moreover, he has imagination. Politicians forget. They go in lowest common denominator—like a newscaster.

People say the problem is soundbites. But no it isn't.   13

A word on the history: "Soundbite" is what television producers have   14
long called the short tape of a politician talking, which is inserted into a longer piece voiced by a reporter. Imagine a speech as a long string of licorice; the mouth-sized bite the reporter takes as it goes by is the sound-bite.

The cliché is to say, "It all has to be reduced to a tidy little thirty-   15
second soundbite." But soundbites don't go thirty seconds, they go seven seconds. Or four seconds. When I got to the White House I never met anyone who had heard of soundbites or thought of them, and the press never wrote of them. I used to tell Ben, "What we're going to see of this speech on TV is five seconds that a producer in New York thinks is the best or most interesting moment." Then I'd tell him what they were going to pick. I knew because I used to pick them. Now people who don't understand soundbites talk about them all the time.

Soundbites in themselves are not bad. "We have nothing to fear . . ."   16
is a soundbite. "Ask not . . ." is a soundbite. So are "You shall not crucify mankind upon a cross of gold," and "With malice toward none; With charity for all . . ."

Great speeches have always had great soundbites. The problem now   17
is that the young technicians who put together speeches are paying atten-tion only to the soundbite, not to the text as a whole, not realizing that all great soundbites happen by accident, which is to say, all great soundbites are yielded up inevitably, as part of the natural expression of the text. They are part of the tapestry, they aren't a little flower somebody sewed on.

They sum up a point, or make a point in language that is pithy or   18
profound. They are what the politician is saying! They are not separate and discrete little one-liners that a bright young speechwriter just pro-moted out of the press office and two years out of business school slaps on.

But that is what they've become. Young speechwriters forget the   19
speech and write the soundbite, plop down a hunk of porridge and stick on what they think is a raisin. (In the Dukakis campaign they underlined them in the text.)

The problem is not the soundbitization of rhetoric, it's the Where's-   20 the-beef-ization. The good news: Everyone in America is catching on to the game, and it's beginning not to work anymore. A modest hope: Politicians will stop hiring communications majors to write their speeches and go to history majors, literature majors, writers—people who can translate the candidate's impulses into literature that is alive, and true.

A speech is also a statement of policy. Sometimes it is This Is What   21
We Must Do about the Budget and sometimes it is Why We Must Go to War, but always it is about plans and their effect on people: policy. It is impossible to separate speechwriting from policy because a policy is made of words, and the speechwriter makes the words. A speechwriter is obviously not free to invent out of whole cloth, but—by articulating a policy he invents it.

An example: If an American president goes to Berlin and stands next   22
to the Berlin Wall, it is one thing (and one kind of policy) if he says, "The American people support the German people." It's quite another if he says, "I am a Berliner." The first means, "We support you," the second means, "We really mean it, we're really here, and if we ever abandon you it will forever be a stain on our honor." Sorensen knew it, Kennedy knew it, and the crowd knew it.

In the Reagan administration there was an unending attempt to sepa-   23
rate the words from the policy. A bureaucrat from State who was assigned to work with the NSC on the annual economic summits used to come into speechwriting and refer to himself and his colleagues as "we substantive types" and to the speechwriters as "you wordsmiths." He was saying, We do policy and you dance around with the words. We would smile back. Our smiles said, The dancer is the dance.

It was a constant struggle over speeches, a constant struggle over who   24
was in charge and what view would prevail and which group would triumph. Each speech was a battle in a never-ending war; when the smoke cleared there was Reagan, holding the speech and saying the words as the mist curled about his feet. I would watch and think, That's not a speech it's a truce. A temporary truce.

How were speeches made in the Reagan administration? Here's an   25
image: Think of a bunch of wonderful, clean, shining, perfectly shaped and delicious vegetables. Then think of one of those old-fashioned metal meat grinders. Imagine the beautiful vegetables being forced through the grinder and being rendered into a smooth, dull, textureless purée.

Here's another image: The speech is a fondue pot, and everyone has a   26
fork. And I mean everyone.

This is how a speech came about: 27

First, the president's top advisers would agree for him to accept an   28
invitation to speak at a certain time or a certain place. If NYU invites the president to deliver a commencement address, someone on the president's staff might note that this would be a perfect spot to unveil the administration's new urban enterprise-zone policy. The invitation is accepted.

The speech is then included on the weekly and monthly schedule of   29
presidential appearances. The writers would get the schedule, read it,
complain about the work load and lobby for various speeches. When
more than one writer wanted a speech, the decision was made by the head
of the speechwriting staff—Ben Elliott, who also functioned as chief
speechwriter. Ben made his decisions based on merit. I say that because
he gave me a lot of good speeches.

Each speech was also assigned a researcher. There were five young   30
researchers when I got there, and they were usually assigned more
speeches than they could do well. I learned to rely on the research people
not for creative input—ideas, inspiration, connections one wouldn't have
thought of—but for fact-checking, at which they were uniformly reliable
and sometimes spectacularly diligent.

A writer usually had a week or two to work on a big speech, or a few   31
days to write a small one. I'd ask research to gather pertinent books from
the White House library and to go through Nexis and pull out whatever
there was on the subject at hand. They'd also get me the president's
previous speeches on that subject or in that place. Research would get
precise and up-to-date information from the advance office on the who-
what-when-where-why of the event. And then I'd begin, haltingly, to
write.

You may be thinking, How did she know what to say? At first I   32
didn't, but after a while I figured it out. As for point of view, the president's stand on any given issue was usually a matter of record. He'd been
in politics twenty years, and his basic philosophy wasn't exactly a secret.
As for new initiatives, various agencies would phone in directives. Ben
would get a call from the Department of Energy, for instance, asking that
we mention some new energy initiative in the speech in Boston on Sunday. Ben would pass the word to the writer and a paragraph would be
inserted.

In the research phase I'd read a lot and take notes and think of phrases   33
and snatches of thought and type them out, and then take them home and
stare at them. When I was in the writing part on an important speech I
never read pertinent reference books. I would read poetry and biographies, the former because the rush of words would help loosen the rocks
that clogged the words in my head, the latter because biographies are
about the great, and the great lead lives of struggle, and reading about
their epic pain put the small discomforts of a speech in nice perspective.

I always kept Walter Jackson Bate's biography of Samuel Johnson   34
nearby, and Stephen Vincent Benét's *John Brown's Body*, and the Bible
(especially the Psalms), and Ezra Pound's *Cantos*, though I don't think I
ever understood a one. It didn't matter, the anarchy of the language and
the sweeping away of syntax had force.

Also, Pound helped me with the State Department. I used to be vis-   35 ited by people from State who wanted to help me write. I always thought of this as the descent of the Harvardheads. They all had thick, neat, straight-back hair and little bitty wire-rim glasses and wives named Sydney, and there was only one way to handle them in my view and that was to out-Sydney them. So a man from State would come in and see the books on the coffee table and the first thing he'd do is signify:

"Oh, Pound," he'd say.   36

"Yes," I'd breathe, with the gravity of a Radcliffe beatnik who'd just   37
met Lenny Bruce in a basement in the Village.

"Took a gut on Pound at Yale. Of course that was before the Decon-   38
structionists."

"Don't laugh. They might have helped." Snap snap.   39

"So." He seats himself on the couch, readjusts the pillows. "Beijing.   40
How go our efforts."

With State guys you had to remember that if you dropped the right   41
cultural references they'd realize it might not work if they patronized you, and if they couldn't patronize you they didn't have a style to fall back on to shape the meeting so they were a little less sure, which is precisely the way you wanted them.

I'd write and rewrite. I'm about a fifth-draft speechwriter. When I   42
was new in the White House it helped me, I think, that I was changing from writing on an electric typewriter to writing on a word processor. On a word processor you have to exert so little pressure on the keys that it didn't really seem like official writing, it felt like playing on a children's typewriter. That helped free things up.

I'd also walk around and talk to people. I'd turn to someone in the   43
mess and say, "I'm writing a speech on Nicaragua. If there was one sentence on that subject you could communicate to the American people, what would it be?" I got some interesting and helpful answers, but I can't remember any of them.

I chain-smoked when I wrote in those days. I'd be dizzy from the   44
chemicals. I'd do anything to avoid writing, and then I'd force myself to sit down at the computer—Edna Ferber wrote in her diary, "I could not lie down to my work today," an assertion whose implications I do not choose to ponder except to say I know what she means—and I would write very badly at first, very clunkily and awkwardly. It wasn't even grammatical. When people would come by and say, "Let me see," I'd shield the screen with my hands.

The whole speechwriting department was computerized, so I'd write   45
my first draft on a floppy disk, and my secretary would print it out. Then I'd rewrite it from there, and ask her to run it out again. Then she'd give it to me, and I'd rewrite again. Each draft would get a little better as I relaxed and got tired. I was relaxing because I wasn't desperate because: at least I had something on paper. Then, on about the fourth draft, I'd see

that I'd written three or four sentences that I liked, and that would relax me further: At least there's something of worth here! That would get my shoulders down. Then I'd really barrel.

I'd read over the final product and realize that once again I'd failed, what I thought was witty was only cute, what I thought was elegant would seem so only to the ill-read, and that imagery didn't come close. I'd hand it in, having reached the deadline. I would tell Ben, "It isn't up to snuff and I'm sorry." He would say calmly that he was sure it would be fine. I would go for a long walk and rationalize my failure: I was tired, they were working me too hard, you can't get blood from a turnip or juice from a stone or whatever the hell.

I would get it back from Ben. He would not have changed it much, but he would have written little exclamation points along the margins, and sometimes on some sections he would write, "Excellent!" And I would be shocked that Ben's critical faculties had failed him. Then I would read over the speech and realize for the first time that it was actually pretty brilliant, so delicate and yet so vital, so vital and yet so tender.

My secretary would incorporate Ben's changes. Then the speech would go out into the world for review. This is where my heart was plucked from my breast and dragged along West Exec, hauled along every pebble and pothole. This was my Heartbreak Hill, my Hanoi Hilton, this was . . . the staffing process.

In staffing, a speech was sent out to all of the pertinent federal agencies and all the important members of the White House staff and the pertinent White House offices. If the speech was relatively unimportant perhaps twenty people in all would see it and comment on it. An important speech would be gone over by fifty or so. The way the system was supposed to work was that the reviewers were to suggest changes, additions, and deletions. The key word here is suggest. They were also supposed to scrutinize all factual assertions and make corrections where necessary.

In the first administration Dick Darman received, along with the speechwriter, a copy of each suggestion, and it was Dick who had the final say on which suggestions must be included and which could be ignored. I didn't always agree with Dick's decisions, but he was open to appeal. More important, I could see his logic. He also didn't mind offending people if it meant preserving a script. I doubt anyone ever pressured him into accepting a change that was frivolous or unhelpful. He didn't care who got mad.

In the second administration a young Regan aide was given control, for a time, of the staffing process. He incorporated many more suggestions than Darman, which was in the short run bureaucratically wise because it made the twenty people who wanted changes think he was smart and easy to work with, and alienated only the speechwriter. But in the long run it proved unwise because it contributed to the diminution in the grace and effectiveness of the president's rhetoric that marked the second administration. It was the first administration that was the fondue pot, it was the second that was the meat grinder.

(The aide's problem was not that he wished to be perverse. It was that 52 he simply could not tell the difference between good writing and bad. It was said of Donald Regan that he did not know what he did not know. His aides were oblivious to what they were oblivious to.)

Speeches in the staffing process were always in danger of becoming 53 lowest-common-denominator art. There were so many people with so many questions, so many changes. I sometimes thought it was like sending a beautiful newborn fawn out into the jagged wilderness where the grosser animals would pierce its tender flesh and render mortal wounds; but perhaps I understate.

There were at any rate two battlefields, art and policy, and sometimes 54 they intersected.

The art problem was . . . delicate. Most of the people in the staffing 55 process thought of themselves as writers, which is understandable because everyone is. Everyone writes letters home to Mom or keeps a diary in weight-loss class on What Food Means to Me. Not everyone plays the piano so most people don't claim to be pianists, but everyone is a writer, and if you're a writer why can't you write the president's speeches?

Complicating this is the fact that there's an odd thing about writing as 56 an art: The critical faculty often fails. When people who can't paint try to paint they can usually step back when they're done, smile a rueful smile, and admit that painting's not their talent. But when people who can't write try to write they often can't tell they're not good. In fact, they often think they're pretty close to wonderful, and they're genuinely hurt—and often suspicious—when told otherwise.

I always wanted to handle these people with a lovely finesse, a mar- 57 velous grace. I wanted to do it the way Gerald Murphy did when he told the off-key singer, "Ah yes, and now you must rest your lovely vocal chords." But because I always felt threatened—the people most insistent about changes were always more powerful than I—I would sputter. "I'm sorry," I'd say, "but that doesn't work. It's not quite right. Well, it just doesn't. It's just not—oh look, it's just dumb, I'm sorry it's dumb but it is, it's shit." It's a wonderful look an undersecretary gets when you tell him this. His eyebrows jump up right over his hairline, and that's only the beginning.

The policy problem was . . . well, the policy problem was the reason 58 we were all there every day. The policy problem was government. Government is words on paper—the communiqué after the summit, the top-secret cable to the embassy, the memo to the secretary outlining a strategy, the president's speech—it's all words on paper. Government draws aggressive people who feel that if government is words on paper then they will damn well affect the words. After all, this is why they came to Washington: to change things, to make a difference. . . .

What I learned from the Pointe du Hoc speech was that to the men of   59
the Reagan White House, a good speech is really a sausage skin, the
stronger it is the more you shove in.

The Pointe du Hoc speech was scheduled for . . . June 6, 1984, the   60
fortieth anniversary of D-Day. It was to be the central speech of the
spring European trip. The setting was the windswept cliffs of Pointe du
Hoc, where forty years before a group of American Rangers had climbed
into France in one of the bravest hours of the longest days.

When I was assigned the speech I was overjoyed. Ben was surprised.   61
"I hired you to write this speech."

The subject matter was one of those moments that really captures the   62
romance of history. I thought that if I could get at what impelled the
Rangers to do what they did, I could use it to suggest what impels us
each day as we live as a nation in the world. This would remind both us
and our allies of what it is that holds us together. . . .

The head of advance came to my office. "Look, I want this to be like   63
the Gettysburg Address. . . ."

I threw my hands up. "What do you guys mean when you say that?   64
What did the Gettysburg Address do?"

He threw a hand in front of his face and moved his fingers up and   65
down. He was saying, The Gettysburg Address made people cry.

I shook my head. "The Gettysburg Address wasn't a tearjerker. What   66
happened at Gettysburg was in itself so moving and dramatic that Lincoln
knew he had no choice but to use cool words to convey the meaning.
'Fourscore and seven years ago our fathers brought forth upon this continent a new nation, conceived in liberty, and dedicated to the proposition
that all men are created equal. Now we are engaged in a great civil war,
testing whether that nation or any other nation so conceived and so dedicated, can long endure. We are met on a great battlefield of that war.'"

I hoped to impress with my mastery of my discipline. He stared at the   67
pleat on his knee.

"People didn't cry to it, they thought to it, it was a new kind of   68
poem."

He fingered the pleat. "Well, I'm not going to argue," he said.   69

I drifted around waiting for the speech to come; sometimes they do. I   70
don't mean they come complete, I mean the basic shape and bits of the
literature of the speech start to present themselves. But the only thing that
came was a phrase: *Here the West stood.* I tried writing on weekends,
writing at odd hours. I tried writing a letter to my aunt. "Dear Aunt Peg,
They died for a cause and the cause was just," it says in my notes. I ran
out of time; the work got done.

I had decided on a plan. The first paragraph would be full of big,   71
emotional words and images so advance and Mike Deaver would be
happy. And so it began:

"We are here to mark that day in history when the Allied Armies   72 joined in battle to reclaim this continent to liberty. For four long years much of Europe had been under a terrible shadow. Free nations had fallen, Jews cried out in the camps, millions cried out for liberation from the conquerers. Europe was enslaved, and the world waited for its rescue. Here in Normandy the rescue began. Here on a lonely windswept point on the western shore of France."

Then: 73

"As we stand here today the air is soft and full of sunlight, and if we 74 pause and listen we will hear the snap of flags and the click of cameras and the gentle murmur of people come to visit a place of great sanctity and meaning.

"But forty years ago at this moment the air was dense with smoke and 75 the cries of men, the air was filled with the crack of rifle fire and the boom of cannons . . ."

What I was doing here was placing it all in time and space for myself 76 and, by extension, for the audience. If we really listen to and hear the snap of the flags, the reality of that sound—snap . . . suhnapp—will help us imagine what it sounded like on D-Day. And that would help us imagine what D-Day itself was like. Then your head snaps back with remembered information: History is real.

Then move on to what happened. This part was a little for the average 77 viewer but mostly for kids watching TV at home in the kitchen at breakfast:

"Before dawn on the morning of the sixth of June, 1944, two hundred 78 American Rangers jumped off a British landing craft and ran to the bottom of these cliffs. Their mission was one of the most difficult and daring of the invasion: to climb these sheer and desolate cliffs and take out the enemy guns. The Allies had been told that here were concentrated the mightiest of those guns, which would be trained on the beaches to stop the Allied advance. Removing the guns was pivotal to the Normandy invasion, which itself was pivotal to the reclaiming of Europe and the end of the war."

I wanted American teenagers to stop chewing their Rice Krispies for a 79 minute and hear about the greatness of those tough kids who are now their grandfathers:

"The Rangers looked up and saw the big casements. . . . And the 80 American Rangers began to climb. They shot their rope ladders into the face of these cliffs and they pulled themselves up. And when one Ranger would fall another would take his place, and when one rope was cut and a Ranger would hurtle to the bottom he would find another rope and begin his climb again. They climbed and shot back and held their footing—"

I wanted this to have the rhythm of a rough advance: 81

"—and in time the enemy guns were quieted, in time the Rangers 82 held the cliffs, in time the enemy pulled back and one by one the Rangers pulled themselves over the top—and in seizing the firm land at the top of these cliffs they seized back the continent of Europe."

Pause, sink in, bring it back to now, history is real.   83

"Forty years ago as I speak they were fighting to hold these cliffs.   84
They had radioed back and asked for reinforcements and they were told:
There aren't any. But they did not give up. It was not in them to give up.
They would not be turned back; they held the cliffs.

"Two hundred twenty-five came here. After a day of fighting only   85
ninety could still bear arms.

"Behind me is a memorial that symbolizes the Ranger daggers that   86
were thrust into the top of these cliffs. And before me are the men who
put them there.

"These are the boys of Pointe du Hoc. These are the men who took   87
the cliffs. These are the champions who helped free a continent. These
are the heroes who helped end a war."

The day he gave the speech it was at this point that the cameras cut to   88
the Rangers, all of them sitting there on their folding chairs, middle-aged,
heavy, and gray. One of them began to weep. But maybe that's just the
way I remember it because that's the way Deaver used it in the convention film.

"These are the boys of Pointe du Hoc" came out of another conversa-   89
tion with the head of advance. He was still disappointed in the speech
because it wasn't moving enough. He told me that the other speech of the
day, by the speechwriter Tony Dolan, which consisted of a sweet and
emotional letter from a young woman named Lisa Zanata to her father,
who had fought at Normandy but hadn't lived to see this anniversary, had
made him cry. I said wonderful, that speech will make 'em cry and this
one will make 'em think and the day will be a hit. He kept saying, "But
they'll be there, they'll be there," and suddenly I realized, He means the
Rangers.

But they would be scattered throughout the crowd. No, he said, the   90
Rangers were going to be sitting all together in the front rows, sitting
right there five feet from the president.

Oh, I didn't know. Oh. Well then he should refer directly to them. He   91
should talk to them. He should describe what they did and then say—

The phrase came with ease because I had just finished Roger Kahn's   92
lovely memoir of his beloved Brooklyn Dodgers, *The Boys of Summer*. O
happy steal: "These are the boys of Pointe du Hoc . . ."

The speech went on to talk about the rebuilding and reconciliation at   93
the end of the war. The State/NSC draft that I'd been given weeks before
wanted the president to go off on this little tangent about arms control,
and as I read it I thought, in the language of the day, Oh gag me with a
spoon. This isn't a speech about arms negotiations you jackasses, this is a
speech about splendor. But of course I did have to mention the Soviets,
because a subtext of the speech was, The things that held the Allies
together then hold us together now, even if we forget to know. Our alliance was always a successful effort to stop totalitarians.

"Why did you do it? What impelled you to put all thought of self-   94
preservation behind you and risk your lives to take these cliffs? What
inspired all of the men of the armies that met here?

". . . It was faith and belief; it was loyalty and love.   95

"The men of Normandy had faith that what they were doing was   96
right, faith that they fought for all humanity, faith that a just God would
grant them mercy on this beachhead—or the next. It was the deep knowledge . . . that there is a profound moral difference between the use of
force for liberation and the use of force for conquest. They were here to
liberate, not to conquer, and so they did not doubt their cause . . .

"They knew that some things are worth dying for, that one's country   97
is worth dying for and that democracy is worth dying for because it is the
most deeply honorable form of government ever devised by man. They
loved liberty and they were happy to fight tyranny . . .

"In spite of our great efforts and our great successes, not all of what   98
followed the end of the war was happy or planned. Some of the countries
that had been liberated were lost. The great sadness of that fact echoes
down to our own time in the streets of Warsaw, Prague and East Berlin.
The Soviet troops that came to the center of this continent did not leave
when peace came. They are there to this day, uninvited, unwanted, and
unyielding almost forty years after the war.

"Because of this, Allied forces still stand on this continent . . ."   99

All of this for the purposes of history but also for that young man   100
with the soggy Rice Krispies in his mouth.

"Today, as forty years ago, our armies are here for only one pur-   101
pose—to protect and defend democracy. The only territories we hold are
the graveyards where our heroes rest.

"We in America have learned the bitter lessons of two world wars: 102
that it is better to be here and ready to preserve and protect the peace,
than to take blind shelter in our homes across the sea, rushing to respond
only after freedom has been threatened. We have learned that isolation-
ism never was and never will be an acceptable response to tyrannical
governments with expansionist intent."

Then a plea for peace with the Soviets, a reiteration of fealty to the   103
alliance, a vow to the dead: "Let our actions say to them the words for
which Matthew Ridgway listened: 'I will not fail thee nor forsake thee.'
Strengthened by their courage, heartened by their valor and borne by their
memory, let us continue to stand for the ideals for which they lived and
died."

The speech got stripped down by advance and by Deaver's office. For   104
some reason they thought the networks were going to pull the plug after
eight minutes. I don't know why they thought this since the networks had
allotted more time than that, and after they aired the cut-down version of
Pointe du Hoc they had to fill for a long time. About half the cuts made
me bleed.

At the beginning, the part about hearing the snap of the flags and the [105] click of the cameras was cut here and there to save time, and what remained was of diminished power. There were some good catches: NSC changed the "boom" of the cannon to the more elegant "roar," and "rushing to respond only after freedom is threatened" to "rushing to respond only after freedom has been lost."

But after they cut the speech down they kept shoving stuff in. [106] Deaver's office kept telling us to put in the phrase "pride and purpose." Deaver liked it. He also wanted us to use "prepared for peace." Deaver apparently liked *P*-words.

Advance kept telling us to put in "selfless effort" and "impossible [107] odds" and "indomitable will" and "courage" and "bravery." NSC wanted, "It is fitting here to remember also the great sacrifices made by the Russian people during World War II. Their terrible loss of twenty million lives testifies to all the world the necessity of avoiding another war."

That started a nice little war. I was upset because the speech was [108] losing part of its literature to save time and they kept shoving in last-minute policy and I had to keep cutting lines to make room. But it was more. The insert on the Soviets had that egregious special-pleading ring that certain bureaucrats get when they deal with totalitarians, and it was going to rob the speech of some of its authenticity. And the Soviets didn't take part in Normandy; they weren't at that party, why stop the speech dead to throw a fish to the bear? For what? So the Soviets could say thanks, we're so moved we'll change our behavior? There was a secondary reason for fighting it: If I held them off till they left and they fought for it on the plane or on the helicopter on the way to Pointe du Hoc, they'd have to scribble it in and they wouldn't have time to take something out. So at least I wouldn't lose more of the text.

That's what happened. The insertion did no harm except for slowing [109] the speech with buzz sounds that everyone knows are buzz sounds. It was the first time a dispute over a speech I'd been involved in got leaked to the press. *Newsweek*, the following week, reported, "In Normandy, his elegant speech on the cliff had gone through several drafts to pencil out anti-Soviet rhetoric. Pentagon hard-liners at first opposed any reference to Soviet losses in the war. Secretary of State Shultz insisted on a compromise: In the end, Reagan noted that Soviet troops are still there (in Central Europe), 'uninvited, unwanted, unyielding almost forty years after the war'—but then he did recall the 'terrible' loss of twenty million Soviet lives and called for East-West reconciliation."

You could hardly be wronger than that report was. The reporter was a [110] professional (Eleanor Clift, who did a candid and unusual thing recently when, as a guest yeller on *The McLaughlin Group*, she frankly and happily identified herself as a liberal) whose primary source, I believe, was a gentleman of similar ideological views who had worked, as a Carter appointee, at the NSC and who, brought in to help on European trips, was an active participant in the battle for the Soviet reference and who tended to reduce these things to a fight between the forces of light and rampant Reaganism. He was also the guy who said, "We substantive types, you wordsmiths."

Other odd things happened. Bud McFarlane kept rewriting the end. 111 Where I had "borne by their memory," he'd put "sustained by their sacrifice." I'd say to Ben and Darman, "I'm the writer, right, and he's the policy maven, I mean that's what he's always saying, right? So you'll tell him to stop writing 'sustained by their sacrifice,' right?" Right, they'd say. Then we'd get another draft from NSC: "Bud wants 'sustained by their sacrifice." He'd X my phrase out, I'd X his phrase out.

I told Ben: Look, this guy who talks like a computer, who in fact 112 probably *is* a computer—I'm going to interface with him and tell him to leave my work alone.

Ben told me: He's a computer with more power than you and he's the 113 computer who'll be on the plane, and we'll all try very hard to preserve the integrity of your work.

My version prevailed. I don't know why, since McFarlane was on the 114 trip and at the speech site and I wasn't. He must have forgotten. Or maybe Darman thought it was my turn to win one.

I wondered, Did the president know of the controversies and disagree- 115 ments that raged about him? Did he write, at night, alone, in his diary, like Claudius: "They all think I am unaware, but I know of their m-m-m-machinations, I am not as d-dull as they imagine, or as removed."

I don't know. I think the fellas just . . . handled it. "Aw, something 116 in speechwriting's holding it up, but we took care of it and the draft'll be here in what, Dick, by lunch? You can read it over lunch, Mr. President."

A year later, when speechwriting was beginning to fall apart, I had a 117 fantasy. Someday the president would look up from an inadequate or less than striking piece of work and a look the fellas had never seen would cross his face. "There's something curiously lifeless about this thing. Let me see the earlier draft."

He'd get it and see all the changes. 118

"Listen," he'd say, snapping the draft impatiently on his knee, "this 119 started as something good and now it's common, boneless and banal. Who had the temerity to change this speech? Who made these changes in my name without my authority? This early version is clearly superior— can't you knuckleheads see that? From now on I want to run the staffing process, or there'll be hell to pay."

Sometimes he'd fire people. Sometimes he'd say, "Get me Noonan. 120

Hello, Peg? Your long national nightmare is over. If anyone tries to tamper with your work again you just tell them to dial G for Gippuh, got it?"

QUESTIONS ON CONTENT

1. What, for Noonan, is a speech? Why are speeches important?

2. What image does Noonan keep in mind while working on a speech? Why? What important lesson did Noonan learn at her family's dinner table that she has taken to heart as a writer?

3. Noonan believes that "the irony of modern speeches is that as our ability to disseminate them has exploded . . . , their quality has declined" (10). How does she account for this state of affairs?

4. What is a soundbite? According to Noonan, how are soundbites being misused by today's speechwriters? If Noonan had her preference, whom would she hire as presidential speechwriters? Do you agree with her thinking? Why, or why not?

5. What, according to Noonan, is the biggest difference between the speeches of Reagan's first term and those of his second? What images does she use to capture this difference?

6. Why did Noonan fear the staffing process? What is the nature of the battle between "art and policy" that sometimes occurred? How did Noonan resolve this conflict between literature and policy for herself?

7. In paragraphs 59 through 114 Noonan describes her writing of the Pointe du Hoc speech. What did she learn from this experience? What did you learn about political speechwriting? Explain.

QUESTIONS ON RHETORIC

1. How has Noonan organized her essay? (Glossary: *Organization*) What are the major sections of the essay, and how are they related to each other?

2. In paragraphs 28 through 58, Noonan uses process analysis to describe how a speech comes about. (Glossary: *Process Analysis*) List the discrete steps in the speechwriting process. Why does Noonan give more details for some steps in the process? Explain.

3. Identify several of the metaphors and similes that Noonan uses, and explain how each one works in the context of her essay. (Glossay: *Figures of Speech*)

4. What transitional devices does Noonan use in moving from one paragraph to the next? (Glossary: *Transitions*) Identify several that you think work particularly well for Noonan.

5. How would you describe Noonan's tone in this essay? (Glossary: *Tone*) Is her tone appropriate for both her subject and her audience? Explain.

VOCABULARY

soliloquy (1)	tapestry (17)	reconciliation (93)
josh (9)	patronize (41)	fealty (103)
leery (12)	rationalize (46)	ideological (110)
esoteric (12)	diminuation (51)	maven (111)
pretentious (12)	sheer (78)	temerity (119)
inevitably (17)	pivotal (78)	

WRITING TOPICS

1. Using Noonan's description of her own writing process as a model, write an essay in which you describe your writing process. How do you choose topics, or do you rely on your teachers giving you assignments? What parts of the process are easiest for you? most difficult? How many drafts does it take to get a piece of writing the way you want it to be?

2. During the 1992 presidential campaign, soundbites, catchy phrases designed to be slotted easily into evening newscasts, were once again the order of the day. Noonan claims that "great speeches have always had great soundbites." Were there any great speeches given during the 1992 campaign? If so, what soundbites do you remember? If not, is this evidence supporting Noonan's belief that "the young technicians who put together speeches are paying attention only to the soundbite, not to the text as a whole, not realizing that all great soundbites happen by accident" (17). Write an essay in which you discuss the use of soundbites in current political speeches.

Casebook: A Selection of Political Texts for Analysis

THE DECLARATION OF INDEPENDENCE

Thomas Jefferson

President, governor, statesman, diplomat, lawyer, architect, philosopher, thinker, and writer, Thomas Jefferson (1743–1826) was one of the most important figures in the early history of our country. In 1776 Jefferson, a man with political insight, vision, and the rhetorical skill to speak for the fledgling nation, drafted the Declaration of Independence, America's justification of it's revolution to the world. Although it was revised by Benjamin Franklin and his colleagues in the Continental Congress, the document retains, in its sound logic and forceful and direct style, the unmistakable qualities of Jefferson's prose.

When in the course of human events, it becomes necessary for one 1 people to dissolve the political bands which have connected them with another, and to assume among the Powers of the earth, the separate and equal station to which the Laws of Nature and of Nature's God entitle them, a decent respect to the opinions of mankind requires that they should declare the causes which impel them to the separation.

We hold these truths to be self-evident, that all men are created equal, 2 that they are endowed by their Creator with certain unalienable Rights, that among these are Life, Liberty and the pursuit of Happiness. That to secure these rights, Governments are instituted among Men deriving their just powers from the consent of the governed. That whenever any Form of Government becomes destructive of these ends, it is the Right of the People to alter or to abolish it, and to institute new Government, laying its foundation on such principles and organizing its powers in such form, as to them shall seem most likely to effect their Safety and Happiness. Prudence, indeed, will dictate that Governments long established should not be changed for light and transient causes; and accordingly all experience hath shown, that mankind are more disposed to suffer, while evils are sufferable, than to right themselves by abolishing the forms to which they are accustomed. But when a long train of abuses and usurpations pursuing invariably the same Object evinces a design to reduce them under absolute Despotism, it is their right, it is their duty, to throw off such government, and to provide new Guards for their future security. Such has been the patient sufferance of these Colonies; and such is now the necessity which constrains them to alter their former Systems of Government. The history of the present King of Great Britain is a history of repeated injuries and usurpations, all having in direct object the establishment of an absolute Tyranny over these States. To prove this, let Facts be submitted to a candid world.

He has refused his Assent to Laws, the most wholesome and necessary for the public good. 3

He has forbidden his Governors to pass Laws of immediate and pressing importance, unless suspended in their operation till his Assent should be obtained; and when so suspended, he has utterly neglected to attend to them. 4

He has refused to pass other Laws for the accommodation of large districts of people, unless those people would relinquish the right of Representation in the Legislature, a right inestimable to them and formidable to tyrants only. 5

He has called together legislative bodies at places unusual, uncomfortable, and distant from the depository of their Public Records, for the sole purpose of fatiguing them into compliance with his measures. 6

He has dissolved Representative Houses repeatedly, for opposing with manly firmness his invasions on the rights of the people. 7

He has refused for a long time, after such dissolutions, to cause others to be elected; whereby the Legislative Powers, incapable of Annihilation, have returned to the People at large for their exercise; the State remaining in the mean time exposed to all the dangers of invasion from without, and convulsions within. 8

He has endeavoured to prevent the population of these States; for that purpose obstructing the Laws of Naturalization of Foreigners; refusing to pass others to encourage their migration hither, and raising the conditions of new Appropriations of Lands. 9

He has obstructed the Administration of Justice, by refusing his Assent to Laws for establishing Judiciary Powers. 10

He has made Judges dependent on his Will alone, for the tenure of   11
their offices, and the amount and payment of their salaries.

He has erected a multitude of New Offices, and sent hither swarms of   12
Officers to harass our People, and eat out their substance.

He has kept among us, in time of peace, Standing Armies without the   13
Consent of our Legislature.

He has affected to render the Military independent of and superior to   14
the Civil Power.

He has combined with others to subject us to jurisdictions foreign to   15
our constitution, and unacknowledged by our laws; giving his Assent to
their acts of pretended Legislation:

For quartering large bodies of armed troops among us: 16

For protecting them, by a mock Trial, from Punishment for any Mur-   17
ders which they should commit on the Inhabitants of these States:

For cutting off our Trade with all parts of the world: 18

For imposing Taxes on us without our Consent: 19

For depriving us in many cases, of the benefits of Trial by Jury: 20

For transporting us beyond Seas to be tried for pretended offenses: 21

For abolishing the free System of English Laws in a Neighbouring   22
Province, establishing therein an Arbitrary government, and enlarging its
boundaries so as to render it at once an example and fit instrument for
introducing the same absolute rule into these Colonies:

For taking away our Charters, abolishing our most valuable Laws,   23
and altering fundamentally the Forms of our Governments:

For suspending our own Legislatures, and declaring themselves in-   24
vested with Power to legislate for us in all cases whatsoever.

He has abdicated Government here, by declaring us out of his Protec-   25
tion and waging War against us.

He has plundered our seas, ravaged our Coasts, burnt our towns and   26
destroyed the Lives of our people.

He is at this time transporting large Armies of foreign Mercenaries to   27
compleat works of death, desolation and tyranny, already begun with
circumstances of Cruelty & perfidy scarcely paralleled in the most barbarous ages, and totally unworthy the Head of a civilized nation.

He has constrained our fellow Citizens taken Captive on the high Seas   28
to bear Arms against their Country, to become the executioners of their
friends and Brethren, or to fall themselves by their Hands.

He has excited domestic insurrections amongst us, and has endeav-   29
oured to bring on the inhabitants of our frontiers, the merciless Indian
Savages, whose known rule of warfare, is an undistinguished destruction
of all ages, sexes and conditions.

In every stage of these Oppressions We Have Petitioned for Redress   30
in the most humble terms: Our repeated petitions have been answered
only by repeated injury. A Prince, whose character is thus marked by
every act which may define a Tyrant, is unfit to be the ruler of a free
People.

Nor have We been wanting in attention to our British brethren. We have warned them from time to time of attempts by their legislature to extend an unwarrantable jurisdiction over us. We have reminded them of the circumstances of our emigration and settlement here. We have appealed to their native justice and magnanimity and we have conjured them by the ties of our common kindred to disavow these usurpations, which would inevitably interrupt our connections and correspondence. They too have been deaf to the voice of justice and of consanguinity. We must, therefore acquiesce in the necessity, which denounces our Separation, and hold them, as we hold the rest of mankind, Enemies in War, in Peace Friends. 31

We, therefore, the Representatives of the United States of America, in General Congress, Assembled, appealing to the Supreme Judge of the world for the rectitude of our intentions, do, in the Name, and by Authority of the good People of these Colonies, solemnly publish and declare, That these United Colonies are, and of Right ought to be Free and Independent States; that they are Absolved from all Allegiance to the British Crown, and that all political connection between them and the State of Great Britain, is and ought to be totally dissolved; and that as Free and Independent States, they have full power to levy War, conclude Peace, contract Alliances, establish Commerce, and to do all other Acts and Things which Independent States may of right do. And for the support of this Declaration, with a firm reliance on the protection of Divine Providence, we mutually pledge to each other our lives, our Fortunes and our sacred Honor. 32

QUESTIONS FOR STUDY AND DISCUSSION

1. What, according to the Declaration of Independence, is the purpose of government? Are there other legitimate purposes that governments serve? If so, what are they?

2. Where, according to Jefferson, do rulers get their authority?

3. In paragraph 2, Jefferson presents certain "self-evident" truths. What are these truths, and how are they related to the intent of his argument?

4. What is the chief argument offered by the Declaration for "abolishing" English rule over the American colonies? How is that argument supported?

5. What argument does the Declaration make for overthrowing any unacceptable government? What assumptions underlie this argument? Where does sovereignty lie, according to the Declaration?

6. According to the Declaration, how did the colonists try to persuade the English king to rule more justly?

7. The Declaration of Independence is a deductive argument; it is, therefore, possible to present it in the form of a syllogism. What are the major

premise, the minor premise, and the conclusion of Jefferson's argument? (Glossary: *Syllogism*)

8. What purpose does a document like the Declaration of Independence serve? Who is meant to read it, and how are the readers expected to respond?

9. The list of charges against the king is given as evidence in support of Jefferson's minor premise. Does he offer any evidence in support of his major premise? Why, or why not? (Glossary: *Supporting Evidence*)

10. Is the language of the Declaration of Independence coolly reasonable or emotional, or does it change from one to the other? Give examples from the text to support your answer.

DECLARATION OF SENTIMENTS AND RESOLUTIONS

Elizabeth Cady Stanton

Elizabeth Cady Stanton (1815–1902) was an American reformer and leader of the women's rights movement. Influenced by the legal restrictions placed upon women and the discrimination shown against them, Stanton also showed early interest in the temperance and antislavery movements. Together with fellow reformer Lucretia Mott, she organized the first women's rights convention, held in Seneca Falls, New York, in 1848. And it was at this convention, generally regarded as the beginning of the women's rights movement, that Stanton read her "Declaration of Sentiments and Resolutions," a compelling list of women's grievances against restrictive laws and customs and an argument for woman suffrage. In recognition of her pioneering work and tireless efforts on behalf of women, Stanton was elected president of the National American Woman Suffrage Association in 1890.

ADOPTED BY THE SENECA FALLS CONVENTION, JULY 19–20, 1848

When, in the course of human events, it becomes necessary for one portion of the family of man to assume among the people of the earth a position different from that which they have hitherto occupied, but one to which the laws of nature and of nature's God entitle them, a decent respect to the opinions of mankind requires that they should declare the causes that impel them to such a course. 1

We hold these truths to be self-evident: that all men and women are created equal; that they are endowed by their Creator with certain inalienable rights; that among these are life, liberty, and the pursuit of happiness; that to secure these rights governments are instituted, deriving their just powers from the consent of the governed. Whenever any form of government becomes destructive of these ends, it is the right of those who suffer from it to refuse allegiance to it, and to insist upon the institution of a new government, laying its foundation on such principles, and organizing its powers in such form, as to them shall seem most likely to 2 effect their safety and happiness. Prudence, indeed, will dictate that governments long established should not be changed for light and transient causes; and accordingly all experience hath shown that mankind are more disposed to suffer, while evils are sufferable, than to right themselves by abolishing the forms to which they were accustomed. But when a long train of abuses and usurpations, pursuing invariably the same object, evinces a design to reduce them under absolute despotism, it is their duty to throw off such government, and to provide new guards for their future security. Such has been the patient sufferance of the women under this government, and such is now the necessity which constrains them to demand the equal station to which they are entitled.

The history of mankind is a history of repeated injuries and usurpa-   3
tions on the part of man toward woman, having in direct object the establishment of an absolute tyranny over her. To prove this, let facts be submitted to a candid world.

He has never permitted her to exercise her inalienable right to the   4
elective franchise.

He has compelled her to submit to laws, in the formation of which   5
she had no voice.

He has withheld from her rights which are given to the most ignorant   6
and degraded men—both natives and foreigners.

Having deprived her of this first right of a citizen, the elective fran-   7
chise, thereby leaving her without representation in the halls of legislation, he has oppressed her on all sides.

He has made her, if married, in the eye of the law, civilly dead.   8

He has taken from her all right in property, even to the wages she earns.   9

He has made her, morally, an irresponsible being, as she can commit   10
many crimes with impunity, provided they be done in the presence of her husband. In the covenant of marriage, she is compelled to promise obedience to her husband, he becoming to all intents and purposes, her master—the law giving him power to deprive her of her liberty, and to administer chastisement.

He has so framed the laws of divorce, as to what shall be the proper   11
causes, and in case of separation, to whom the guardianship of the children shall be given, as to be wholly regardless of the happiness of women—the law, in all cases, going upon a false supposition of the supremacy of man, and giving all power into his hands.

After depriving her of all rights as a married woman, if single, and   12
the owner of property, he has taxed her to support a government which recognizes her only when her property can be made profitable to it.

He has monopolized nearly all the profitable employments, and from   13
those she is permitted to follow, she receives but a scanty remuneration. He closes against her all the avenues to wealth and distinction which he considers most honorable to himself. As a teacher of theology, medicine, or law, she is not known.

He has denied her the facilities for obtaining a thorough education, all   14
colleges being closed against her.

He allows her in Church, as well as State, but a subordinate position,   15
claiming Apostolic authority for her exclusion from the ministry, and, with
some exceptions, from any public participation in the affairs of the Church.

He has created a false public sentiment by giving to the world a dif-   16
ferent code of morals for men and women, by which moral delinquencies
which exclude women from society, are not only tolerated, but deemed of
little account in man.

He has usurped the prerogative of Jehovah himself, claiming it as his   17
right to assign for her a sphere of action, when that belongs to her conscience and to her God.

He has endeavored, in every way that he could, to destroy her confi-   18
dence in her own powers, to lessen her self-respect, and to make her
willing to lead a dependent and abject life.

Now, in view of this entire disfranchisement of one-half the people of   19
this country, their social and religious degradation—in view of the unjust
laws above mentioned, and because women do feel themselves ag-
grieved, oppressed, and fraudulently deprived of their most sacred rights,
we insist that they have immediate admission to all the rights and privileges which belong to them as citizens of the United States.

In entering upon the great work before us, we anticipate no small   20
amount of misconception, misrepresentation, and ridicule; but we shall
use every instrumentality within our power to effect our object. We shall
employ agents, circulate tracts, petition the State and National legislatures, and endeavor to enlist the pulpit and the press in our behalf. We
hope this Convention will be followed by a series of Conventions em-
bracing every part of the country.

[The following resolutions were discussed by Lucretia Mott, Thomas   21
and Mary Ann McClintock, Amy Post, Catharine A. F. Stebbins, and
others, and were adopted:]

Whereas, the great precept of nature is conceded to be, that "man   22
shall pursue his own true and substantial happiness." Blackstone [1] in his
Commentaries remarks, that this law of Nature being coeval[2] with mankind, and dictated by God himself, is of course superior in obligation to
any other. It is binding over all the globe, in all countries and at all times;
no human laws are of any validity if contrary to this, and such of them as
are valid, derive all their force, and all their validity, and all their authority, mediately and immediately, from this original; therefore,

Resolved, That such laws as conflict, in any way, with the true and   23

---

[1] Sir William Blackstone (1723–1780): The most influential of English scholars of the
law. His *Commentaries of the Laws of England* (4 vols. 1765–1769) form the basis of the
study of law in England.
[2] coeval: Existing simultaneously.

substantial happiness of woman, are contrary to the great precept of nature and of no validity, for this is "superior in obligation to any other."

Resolved, That all laws which prevent woman from occupying such a   24
station in society as her conscience shall dictate, or which place her in a
position inferior to that of man, are contrary to the great precept of nature, and therefore of no force or authority.

Resolved, That woman is man's equal—was intended to be so by the   25
Creator, and the highest good of the race demands that she should be
recognized as such.

Resolved, That the women of this country ought to be enlightened in   26
regard to the laws under which they live, that they may no longer publish
their degradation by declaring themselves satisfied with their present position, nor their ignorance, by asserting that they have all the rights they
want.

Resolved, That inasmuch as man, while claiming for himself intellec-   27
tual superiority, does accord to woman moral superiority, it is preeminently his duty to encourage her to speak and teach, as she has an opportunity, in all religious assemblies.

Resolved, That the same amount of virtue, delicacy, and refinement   28
of behavior that is required of woman in the social state, should also be
required of man, and the same transgressions should be visited with equal
severity on both man and woman.

Resolved, That the objection of indelicacy and impropriety, which is   29
so often brought against woman when she addresses a public audience,
comes with a very ill-grace from those who encourage, by their attendance, her appearance on the stage, in the concert, or in feats of the
circus.

Resolved, That woman has too long rested satisfied in the circum-   30
scribed limits which corrupt customs and a perverted application of the
Scriptures have marked out for her, and that it is time she should move in
the enlarged sphere which her great Creator has assigned her.   .

Resolved, That it is the duty of the women of this country to secure to   31
themselves their sacred right to the elective franchise.

Resolved, That the equality of human rights results necessarily from   32
the fact of the identity of the race in capabilities and responsibilities.

Resolved, therefore, That, being invested by the Creator with the   33
same capabilities, and the same consciousness of responsibility for their
exercise, it is demonstrably the right and duty of woman, equally with
man, to promote every righteous cause by every righteous means; and
especially in regard to the great subjects of morals and religion, it is self-
evidently her right to participate with her brother in teaching them, both
in private and in public, by writing and by speaking, by any instrumen-
talities proper to be used, and in any assemblies proper to be held; and
this being a self-evident truth growing out of the divinely implanted principles of human nature, any custom or authority adverse to it, whether

modern or wearing the hoary sanction of antiquity, is to be regarded as a self-evident falsehood, and at war with mankind.

[At the last session Lucretia Mott[3] offered and spoke to the following   34
resolution:]

Resolved, That the speedy success of our cause depends upon the   35
zealous and untiring efforts of both men and women, for the overthrow of
the monopoly of the pulpit, and for the securing to woman an equal
participation with men in the various trades, professions, and commerce.

QUESTIONS FOR STUDY AND DISCUSSION

1. What is it that Stanton and her associates at the Seneca Falls Convention wanted to accomplish? What specific demands were they making?

2. The opening paragraphs of the Seneca Falls declaration closely parallel those of the Declaration of Independence. Why do you suppose Stanton chose to associate her movement and its ideas with that document?

3. What is the "elective franchise"? Why is it so fundamental to Stanton's argument?

4. What is a parody? Is Stanton's essay a parody of the Declaration of
Independence? Why, or why not?

5. In paragraphs 4 through 18 Stanton catalogs the abuses women suffer.
Who is the "he" referred to in each of the statements? What is the rhetorical effect of listing these abuses and starting each one with similar phrasing? (Glossary: *Parallelism*)

6. At what audience is Stanton's declaration aimed? (Glossary: *Audience*) What in the declaration itself led you to this conclusion?

7. What is the function of the resolutions that conclude the declaration?
What would have been gained or lost if Stanton had concluded the declaration with paragraph 20?

8. Is there anything in the style, tone, or voice of this document that
would lead you to call it "feminine" or "female"? Explain by citing particular words or phrases.

9. What progress has been made in the area of women's rights since
Stanton first made her declaration? What grievances have been resolved?
Which still need to be redressed? What new issues have been raised by
women in the last few decades?

---

[3]Lucretia Mott (1793–1880): One of the founders of the 1848 convention at which these
resolutions were presented. She is one of the earliest and most important of the feminists
who struggled to proclaim their rights. She was also a prominent abolitionist.

THE GETTYSBURG ADDRESS

Abraham Lincoln

With the possible exception of the Declaration of Independence, no document of American history is as famous as Lincoln's speech dedicating the national cemetery at Gettysburg. The Battle of Gettysburg was fought in the rolling countryside of southeastern Pennsylvania during the first three days of July 1863. We now know that it was the turning point of the American Civil War. Abraham Lincoln (1809–1865), one of the most beloved of all presidents, delivered his now-famous speech at the Gettysburg battlefield on November 19, 1863. Since then millions of Americans have memorized it, and countless others have quoted it or imitated its rhetoric for their own various purposes. It is illuminating to look again at the familiar words with their original context in mind to see how they served Lincoln's purpose, his sense of the occasion, and his larger sense of the nation's history and destiny.

Four score and seven years ago our fathers brought forth on this continent, a new nation, conceived in Liberty, and dedicated to the proposition that all men are created equal.

Now we are engaged in a great civil war, testing whether that nation, or any nation so conceived and so dedicated, can long endure. We are met on a great battle-field of that war. We have come to dedicate a portion of that field, as a final resting place for those who here gave their lives that that nation might live. It is altogether fitting and proper that we should do this.

But, in a larger sense, we can not dedicate—we can not consecrate—we can not hallow—this ground. The brave men, living and dead, who struggled here, have consecrated it, far above our poor power to add or detract. The world will little note, nor long remember what we say here, but it can never forget what they did here. It is for us the living, rather, to be dedicated here to the unfinished work which they who fought here have thus far so nobly advanced. It is rather for us to be here dedicated to the great task remaining before us—that from these honored dead we take increased devotion to that cause for which they gave the last full measure of devotion—that we here highly resolve that these dead shall not have died in vain—that this nation, under God, shall have a new birth of freedom—and that government of the people, by the people, for the people, shall not perish from the earth.

QUESTIONS FOR STUDY AND DISCUSSION

1. To what issue of the Civil War is Lincoln referring in his two opening sentences?

2. What specifically did our country's founders do eighty-seven years before the Gettysburg Address? What purpose is served by linking the Civil War with the acts and intentions of the founders of the United States?

3. Lincoln's diction in the opening paragraph is calculated to achieve a certain effect on listeners and readers. (Glossary: *Diction*) Discuss the nature of this effect by comparing the opening paragraph to the following one:

> Eighty-seven years ago our ancestors formed a new North American nation based on liberty and the idea that all men are created equal.

4. In an early draft of the address, the last sentence in paragraph 2 reads: "This we may, in all propriety, do." Why do you suppose Lincoln rewrote this sentence?

5. In the first sentence of paragraph 3, Lincoln uses the words *dedicate, consecrate*, and *hallow*. Do these words have the same denotative meaning? Why do you think Lincoln placed them in this particular order?

6. The tone of the Gettysburg Address can be described as reverential, a tone that is appropriate both for the subject and the occasion. (Glossary: *Tone*) Cite specific examples of Lincoln's diction that help to create this tone. (Glossary: *Diction*)

7. In your opinion, why has the Gettysburg Address endured? What about this speech makes it live on in the collective American memory? What relevance does it have for us in the 1990s?

INAUGURAL ADDRESS

John F. Kennedy

John Fitzgerald Kennedy (1917–1963), the thirty-fifth president of the United States, was assassinated in Dallas, Texas, on November 22, 1963. Kennedy, the youngest man ever elected president, was known both for the youthful and hopeful image he brought to the White House and for the eloquence of his speeches. In his inaugural address Kennedy used powerful rhetoric to urge people both to become involved in their country's affairs and to join the fight against the spread of communism.

We observe today not a victory of party but a celebration of freedom, symbolizing an end as well as a beginning, signifying renewal as well as change. For I have sworn before you and Almighty God the same solemn oath our forebears prescribed nearly a century and three-quarters ago.   1

The world is very different now. For man holds in his mortal hands the power to abolish all forms of human poverty and all forms of human life. And yet the same revolutionary belief for which our forebears fought is still at issue around the globe, the belief that the rights of man come not from the generosity of the state but from the hand of God.   2

We dare not forget today that we are the heirs of that first revolution. Let the word go forth from this time and place, to friend and foe alike, that the torch has been passed to a new generation of Americans, born in this century, tempered by war, disciplined by a hard and bitter peace, proud of our ancient heritage, and unwilling to witness or permit the slow undoing of those human rights to which this nation has always been committed, and to which we are committed today at home and around the world.   3

Let every nation know, whether it wishes us well or ill, that we shall pay any price, bear any burden, meet and hardship, support any friend, oppose any foe to assure the survival and the success of liberty.   4

This much we pledge—and more.   5

To those old allies whose cultural and spiritual origins we share, we pledge the loyalty of faithful friends. United, there is little we cannot do in a host of co-operative ventures. Divided, there is little we can do, for we dare not meet a powerful challenge at odds and split asunder.   6

To those new states whom we welcome to the ranks of the free, we pledge our word that one form of colonial control shall not have passed away merely to be replaced by a far more iron tyranny. We shall not always expect to find them supporting our view. But we shall always hope to find them strongly supporting their own freedom, and to remem-   7 ber that, in the past, those who foolishly sought power by riding the back of the tiger ended up inside.

To those peoples in the huts and villages of half the globe struggling   8
to break the bonds of mass misery, we pledge our best efforts to help them help themselves, for whatever period is required, not because the Communists may be doing it, not because we seek their votes, but because it is right. If a free society cannot help the many who are poor, it cannot save the few who are rich.

To our sister republics south of our border, we offer a special pledge: 9
to convert our good words into good deeds, in a new alliance for progress, to assist free men and free governments in casting off the chains of poverty. But this peaceful revolution of hope cannot become the prey of hostile powers. Let all our neighbors know that we shall join with them to oppose aggression or subversion anywhere in the Americas. And let every other power know that this hemisphere intends to remain the master of its own house.

To that world assembly of sovereign states, the United Nations, our   10
last best hope in an age where the instruments of war have far outpaced the instruments of peace, we renew our pledge of support: to prevent it from becoming merely a forum for invective, to strengthen its shield of the new and the weak, and to enlarge the area in which its writ may run.

Finally, to those nations who would make themselves our adversary,   11
we offer not a pledge but a request: that both sides begin anew the quest for peace, before the dark powers of destruction unleashed by science engulf all humanity in planned or accidental self-destruction.

We dare not tempt them with weakness. For only when our arms are   12
sufficient beyond doubt can we be certain beyond doubt that they will never be employed.

But neither can two great and powerful groups of nations take comfort   13
from our present course—both sides over-burdened by the cost of modern weapons, both rightly alarmed by the steady spread of the deadly atom, yet both racing to alter that uncertain balance of terror that stays the hand of mankind's final war.

So let us begin anew, remembering on both sides that civility is not a   14
sign of weakness, and sincerity is always subject to proof. Let us never negotiate out of fear, but let us never fear to negotiate.

Let both sides explore what problems unite us instead of belaboring   15
those problems which divide us.

Let both sides, for the first time, formulate serious and precise pro-   16
posals for the inspection and control of arms, and bring the absolute power to destroy other nations under the absolute control of all nations.

Let both sides seek to invoke the wonders of science instead of its   17
terrors. Together let us explore the stars, conquer the deserts, eradicate disease, tap the ocean depths and encourage the arts and commerce.

Let both sides unite to heed in all corners of the earth the command of   18
Isaiah to "undo the heavy burdens . . . [and] let the oppressed go free."

And if a beachhead of co-operation may push back the jungle of sus-   19
picion, let both sides join in creating a new endeavor, not a new balance
of power, but a new world of law, where the strong are just and the weak
secure and the peace preserved.

All this will not be finished in the first one hundred days. Nor will it   20
be finished in the first one thousand days, nor in the life of this Administration, nor even perhaps in our lifetime on this planet. But let us begin.

In your hands, my fellow citizens, more than mine, will rest the final   21
success or failure of our course. Since this country was founded, each
generation of Americans has been summoned to give testimony to its
national loyalty. The graves of young Americans who answered the call
to service surround the globe.

Now the trumpet summons us again—not as a call to bear arms,   22
though arms we need; not as a call to battle, though embattled we are; but
a call to bear the burden of a long twilight struggle, year in and year out,
"rejoicing in hope, patient in tribulation," a struggle against the common
enemies of men: tyranny, poverty, disease and war itself.

Can we forge against these enemies a grand and global alliance,   23
North and South, East and West, that can assure a more fruitful life for
all mankind? Will you join in that historic effort?

In the long history of the world, only a few generations have been   24
granted the role of defending freedom in its hour of maximum danger. I
do not shrink from this responsibility; I welcome it. I do not believe that
any of us would exchange places with any other people or any other
generation. The energy, the faith, the devotion which we bring to this
endeavor will light our country and all who serve it, and the glow from
that fire can truly light the world.

And so, my fellow Americans, ask not what your country can do for   25
you; ask what you can do for your country.

My fellow citizens of the world, ask not what America will do for   26
you, but what together we can do for the freedom of man.

Finally, whether you are citizens of America or citizens of the world,   27
ask of us here the same high standards of strength and sacrifice which we
ask of you. With a good conscience our only sure reward, with history
that final judge of our deeds, let us go forth to lead the land we love,
asking His blessing and His help, but knowing that here on earth God's
work must truly be our own.

QUESTIONS FOR STUDY AND DISCUSSION

1. Kennedy's second paragraph begins with the statement, "The world is
very different now." How does Kennedy intend this remark?

2. The president's speech makes promises to several groups, not only to the citizens of the United States, but to groups outside the country as well. Is it clear which groups Kennedy means? See if you can identify a few of these groups; then explain what Kennedy gains by not "naming names."

3. Give several examples of Kennedy's use of parallelism. (Glossary: *Parallelism*) Does this rhetorical device add to the strength of his speech?

4. In paragraph 23, Kennedy asks two rhetorical questions. What is his purpose in asking these questions? (Glossary: *Rhetorical Questions*)

5. In his speech, Kennedy addresses other nations as well as the citizens of the United States. How would you characterize his tone in addressing each group? Why do you suppose Kennedy changes his tone in this way?

6. How has Kennedy organized his speech to stress the shift in emphasis from one group to the other? Prepare a scratch outline of his speech to help you answer this question. (Glossary: *Organization*)

7. In paragraph 7, what figure of speech does Kennedy use? What does it mean? Why do you suppose he uses it? (Glossary: *Figures of Speech*)

8. Kennedy makes clear what he wants to accomplish in his tenure as president; however, he doesn't say how he will achieve these goals. Do you find this problematic, or do you feel this inexplicitness is appropriate in a speech of this kind?

I HAVE A DREAM

Martin Luther King, Jr.

*Martin Luther King, Jr. (1929–1968) first came to
prominence in 1955, in Montgomery, Alabama, when he led
a successful boycott against the city's segregated bus system.
As the first president of the Southern Christian Leadership
Conference, King promoted a policy of massive but
nonviolent resistance to racial injustice. In 1964 his efforts
won him the Nobel Peace Prize. "I Have a Dream" was
delivered by King in 1963 from the steps of the Lincoln
Memorial to more than 200,000 people who had come to
Washington, D.C., to demonstrate for civil rights. In this
mighty sermon—replete with allusions to the Bible, the Negro
spiritual tradition, and great documents and speeches of the
past—King presented his indictment of the present and his
vision of the future.*

I am happy to join with you today in what will go down in history as the 1
greatest demonstration for freedom in the history of our nation.

Five score years ago, a great American, in whose symbolic shadow 2
we stand today, signed the Emancipation Proclamation. This momentous
decree came as a great beacon light of hope to millions of Negro slaves
who had been seared in the flames of withering injustice. It came as a
joyous daybreak to end the long night of their captivity. But one hundred
years later, the Negro still is not free. One hundred years later, the life of
the Negro is still sadly crippled by the manacles of segregation and the
chains of discrimination. One hundred years later, the Negro lives on a
lonely island of poverty in the midst of a vast ocean of material prosperity. One hundred years later, the Negro is still anguished in the corners of
American society and finds himself in exile in his own land. And so we
have come here today to dramatize a shameful condition.

In a sense we have come to our nation's capital to cash a check. 3
When the architects of our republic wrote the magnificent words of the
Constitution and the Declaration of Independence, they were signing a
promissory note to which every American was to fall heir. This note was
the promise that all men—yes, Black men as well as white men—would
be guaranteed the inalienable rights of life, liberty, and the pursuit of
happiness.

It is obvious today that America has defaulted on this promissory note 4
insofar as her citizens of color are concerned. Instead of honoring this
sacred obligation, America has given the Negro people a bad check, a

check which has come back marked "insufficient funds." But we refuse to believe that the bank of justice is bankrupt. We refuse to believe that there are insufficient funds in the great vaults of opportunity of this nation; and so we have come to cash this check, a check that will give us upon demand the riches of freedom and the security of justice.

We have also come to this hallowed spot to remind America of the fierce urgency of *now*. This is no time to engage in the luxury of cooling off or to take the tranquilizing drug of gradualism. *Now* is the time to make real the promises of democracy. *Now* is the time to rise from the dark and desolate valley of segregation to the sunlit path of racial justice. *Now* is the time to lift our nation from the quicksands of racial injustice to the solid rock of brotherhood. *Now* is the time to make justice a reality for all of God's children.

It would be fatal for the nation to overlook the urgency of the moment. This sweltering summer of the Negro's legitimate discontent will not pass until there is an invigorating autumn of freedom and equality. Nineteen Sixty-three is not an end, but a beginning. And those who hope that the Negro needed to blow off steam and will now be content will have a rude awakening if the nation returns to business as usual. There will be neither rest nor tranquility in America until the Negro is granted his citizenship rights. The whirlwinds of revolt will continue to shake the foundations of our nation until the bright day of justice emerges.

But there is something that I must say to my people who stand on the warm threshold which leads into the palace of justice. In the process of gaining our rightful place, we must not be guilty of wrongful deeds. Let us not seek to satisfy our thirst for freedom by drinking from the cup of bitterness and hatred. We must forever conduct our struggle on the high plane of dignity and discipline. We must not allow our creative protest to degenerate into physical violence. Again and again we must rise to the majestic heights of meeting physical force with soul force. And the marvelous new militancy which has engulfed the Negro community must not lead us to a distrust of all white people; for many of our white brothers, as evidenced by their presence here today, have come to realize that their destiny is tied up with our destiny, and they have come to realize that their freedom is inextricably bound to our freedom.

We cannot walk alone. And as we walk we must make the pledge that we shall always march ahead. We cannot turn back. There are those who are asking the devotees of civil rights, "When will you be satisfied?" We can never be satisfied as long as the Negro is the victim of the unspeakable horrors of police brutality. We can never be satisfied as long as our bodies, heavy with the fatigue of travel, cannot gain lodging in the motels of the highways and the hotels of the cities. We cannot be satisfied as long as the Negro's basic mobility is from a smaller ghetto to a larger one. We can never be satisfied as long as our children are stripped of their selfhood and robbed of their dignity by signs stating "For Whites

Only." We cannot be satisfied as long as the Negro in Mississippi cannot vote and a Negro in New York believes he has nothing for which to vote. No, no, we are not satisfied, and we will not be satisfied until justice rolls down like waters and righteousness like a mighty stream.

I am not unmindful that some of you have come here out of great   9
trials and tribulations. Some of you have come fresh from narrow jail cells. Some of you have come from areas where your quest for freedom left you battered by the storms of persecution and staggered by the winds of police brutality. You have been the veterans of creative suffering. Continue to work with the faith that unearned suffering is redemptive.

Go back to Mississippi, and go back to Alabama. Go back to South   10
Carolina. Go back to Georgia. Go back to Louisiana. Go back to the slums and ghettos of our Northern cities, knowing that somehow this situation can and will be changed. Let us not wallow in the valley of despair.

I say to you today, my friends, even though we face the difficulties of   11
today and tomorrow, I still have a dream. It is a dream deeply rooted in the American dream. I have a dream that one day this nation will rise up and live out the true meaning of its creed: "We hold these truths to be self-evident, that all men are created equal." I have a dream that one day, on the red hills of Georgia, sons of former slaves and the sons of former slave owners will be able to sit down together at the table of brotherhood. I have a dream that one day even the state of Mississippi, a state swelter-ing with the heat of injustice, sweltering with the heat of oppression, will be transformed into an oasis of freedom and justice. I have a dream that my four little children will one day live in a nation where they will not be judged by the color of their skin, but by the content of their character.

I have a dream today. I have a dream that one day down in Ala-   12
bama—with its vicious racists, with its governor's lips dripping with the words of interposition and nullification—one day right there in Alabama, little Black boys and Black girls will be able to join hands with little white boys and white girls as sisters and brothers.

I have a dream today. I have a dream that one day every valley shall be   13
exalted and every hill and mountain shall be made low, the rough places will be made plain and the crooked places will be made straight, and the glory of the Lord shall be revealed, and all flesh shall see it together.

This is our hope. This is the faith that I go back to the South with.   14
And with this faith we will be able to hew out of the mountain of despair a stone of hope. With this faith we will be able to transform the jangling discords of our nation into a beautiful symphony of brotherhood. With this faith we will be able to work together, to play together, to struggle together, to go to jail together, to stand up for freedom together, knowing that we will be free one day.

And this will be the day—this will be the day when all of God's   15
children will be able to sing with new meaning:

My country, 'tis of thee,
Sweet land of liberty,
   Of thee I sing;
Land where my fathers died,
Land of the Pilgrims' pride,
From every mountainside
   Let freedom ring.

And if America is to be a great nation, this must become true.

And so let freedom ring from the prodigious hilltops of New Hampshire. Let freedom ring from the mighty mountains of New York. Let freedom ring from the heightening Alleghenies of Pennsylvania. Let freedom ring from the snow-capped Rockies of Colorado. Let freedom ring from the curvaceous slopes of California.   16

But not only that. Let freedom ring from Stone Mountain of Georgia. Let freedom ring from Lookout Mountain of Tennessee. Let freedom ring from every hill and molehill of Mississippi. "From every mountainside let freedom ring."   17

And when this happens—when we allow freedom to ring, when we let it ring from every village and every hamlet, from every state and every city—we will be able to speed up that day when all of God's children, Black men and white men, Jews and Gentiles, Protestants and Catholics, will be able to join hands and sing in the words of the old Negro spiritual: "Free at last! Free at last! Thank God Almighty. We are free at last!"   18

QUESTIONS FOR STUDY AND DISCUSSION

1. What does King find wrong with America? What is his vision for the future? To what extent is King setting the agenda for the civil rights movement in 1963 in this speech?

2. How does King organize his speech? (Glossary: *Organization*) How many major sections can you identify? What is the purpose of each section?

3. How appropriate and effective is King's analogy of the bad check? (Glossary: *Analogy*) Why do you think so?

4. To whom does King address his speech? (Glossary: *Audience*) What references in the text reveal King's sensitivity to the occasion and the immediate experiences of his audience? Why do you think King chose to give his speech on the steps of the Lincoln Memorial?

5. In his speech, King's range of reference is wide and varied. Which allusions do you recognize? (Glossary: *Allusion*) What effect would you expect these references to have had on King's audience? How did they affect you? Explain.

6. King's speech, like Lincoln's Gettysburg Address, has outlasted the occasion for which it was written. In your opinion, why is this so? What qualities of language and thought are the source of its power? What phrase or phrases do you consider most memorable? Why?

7. What is your attitude toward America and its culturally diverse population? Do you see America as a nation that perpetuates injustice or as a nation struggling to realize an ideal of justice, King's dream? Explain.

8. Each year as our country celebrates King's birthday, we reflect on just how much of his dream for America has come true and what still needs to be done. Are we any closer to realizing King's powerful dream? What are the prospects for the future?

INAUGURAL ADDRESS

William Jefferson Clinton

On January 20, 1993, William Jefferson Clinton, former governor of the state of Arkansas, took the oath of office as the forty-second president of the United States. The transition of power from George Bush to Bill Clinton marked a transition from one generation to another. Clinton is the first of the post–World War II generation—the so-called baby boomers—to hold our nation's highest office. Moments after being sworn-in by Chief Justice William Rehnquist, Clinton delivered the following inaugural address to an audience estimated at over 40 million people.

$\mathbf{M}$y fellow citizens, today we celebrate the mystery of American renewal. This ceremony is held in the depth of winter, but by the words we speak and the faces we show the world, we force the spring. A spring reborn in the world's oldest democracy that brings forth the vision and courage to reinvent America.

When our founders boldly declared America's independence to the world and our purposes to the Almighty, they knew that America to endure would have to change. Not change for change's sake but change to preserve America's ideals—life, liberty, the pursuit of happiness. Though we march to the music of our time, our mission is timeless. Each generation of Americans must define what it means to be an American.

On behalf of our nation, I salute my predecessor, President Bush, for his half-century of service to America.

And I thank the millions of men and women whose steadfastness and sacrifice triumphed over depression, fascism and communism. Today, a generation raised in the shadows of the cold war assumes new responsibilities in a world warmed by the sunshine of freedom but threatened still by ancient hatreds and new plagues.

Raised in unrivaled prosperity, we inherit an economy that is still the world's strongest but is weakened by business failures, stagnant wages, increasing inequality and deep divisions among our own people.

When George Washington first took the oath I have just sworn to uphold, news traveled slowly across the land by horseback and across the ocean by boat. Now the sights and sounds of this ceremony are broadcast instantaneously to billions around the world. Communications and commerce are global, investment is mobile, technology is almost magical, and ambition for a better life is now universal. We earn our livelihood in America today in peaceful competition with people all across the earth. Profound and powerful forces are shaking and remaking our world. And the urgent question of our time is whether we can make change our friend and not our enemy.

This new world has already enriched the lives of millions of Americans who are able to compete and win in it. But when most people are working harder for less, when others cannot work at all, when the cost of health care devastates families and threatens to bankrupt our enterprises great and small, when the fear of crime robs law-abiding citizens of their freedom, and when millions of poor children cannot even imagine the lives we are calling them to lead, we have not made change our friend. We know we have to face hard truths and take strong steps, but we have not done so. Instead, we have drifted, and that drifting has eroded our resources, fractured our economy and shaken our confidence.   7

Though our challenges are fearsome, so are our strengths. Americans have ever been a restless, questing, hopeful people, and we must bring to our task today the vision and will of those who came before us. From our Revolution to the Civil War, to the Great Depression, to the civil rights movement, our people have always mustered the determination to construct from these crises the pillars of our history.   8

Thomas Jefferson believed that to preserve the very foundations of our nation we would need dramatic change from time to time. Well my fellow Americans, this is our time. Let us embrace it.   9

Our democracy must be not only the envy of the world but the engine of our own renewal. There is nothing wrong with America that cannot be cured by what is right with America. And so today we pledge an end to the era of deadlock and drift, and a new season of American renewal has begun.   10

To renew America we must be bold. We must do what no generation has had to do before. We must invest more in our own people—in their jobs and in their future—and at the same time cut our massive debt. And we must do so in a world in which we must compete for every opportunity. It will not be easy. It will require sacrifice. But it can be done and done fairly. Not choosing sacrifice for its own sake, but for our own sake. We must provide for our nation the way a family provides for its children.   11

Our founders saw themselves in the light of posterity. We can do no less. Anyone who has ever watched a child's eyes wander into sleep knows what posterity is. Posterity is the world to come. The world for whom we hold our ideals, from whom we have borrowed our planet and to whom we bear sacred responsibility. We must do what America does best: offer more opportunity to all and demand more responsibility from all.   12

It is time to break the bad habit of expecting something for nothing from our Government or from each other. Let us all take more responsibility not only for ourselves and our families but for our communities and our country.   13

To renew America we must revitalize our democracy. This beautiful capital, like every capital since the dawn of civilization, is often a place of intrigue and calculation. Powerful people maneuver for position and   14 worry endlessly about who is in and who is out, who is up and who is down, forgetting those people whose toil and sweat sends us here and pays our way.

Americans deserve better, and in this city today there are people who   15
want to do better. And so I say to all of you here, let us resolve to reform
our politics so that power and privilege no longer shout down the voice of
the people. Let us put aside personal advantage so that we can feel the
pain and see the promise of America. Let us resolve to make our Government a place for what Franklin Roosevelt called bold, persistent experi-
mentation, a Government for our tomorrows, not our yesterdays. Let us
give this capital back to the people to whom it belongs.

To renew America, we must meet challenges abroad as well as at   16
home. There is no longer a clear division between what is foreign and
what is domestic. The world economy, the world environment, the world
AIDS crisis, the world arms race—they affect us all.

Today, as an old order passes, the new world is more free but less   17
stable. Communism's collapse has called forth old animosities and new
dangers. Clearly, America must continue to lead the world we did so
much to make.

While America rebuilds at home, we will not shrink from the chal-   18
lenges nor fail to seize the opportunities of this new world. Together with
our friends and allies we will work to shape change lest it engulf us.
When our vital interests are challenged or the will and conscience of the
international community is defied, we will act, with peaceful diplomacy
whenever possible, with force when necessary.

The brave Americans serving our nation today in the Persian Gulf and   19
Somalia, and wherever else they stand, are testament to our resolve.

But our greatest strength is the power of our ideas, which are still new   20
in many lands. Across the world we see them embraced and we rejoice.
Our hopes, our hearts, our hands are with those on every continent who
are building democracy and freedom. Their cause is America's cause.

The American people have summoned the change we celebrate today.   21
You have raised your voices in an unmistakable chorus, you have cast
your votes in historic numbers, and you have changed the face of Congress, the Presidency and the political process itself. Yes, you, my fellow
Americans, have forced the spring.

Now we must do the work the season demands. To that work I now turn   22
with all the authority of my office. I ask the Congress to join with me. But
no President, no Congress, no government can undertake this mission alone.
My fellow Americans, you, too, must play your part in our renewal.

I challenge a new generation of young Americans to a season of ser-   23
vice; to act on your idealism by helping troubled children, keeping company with those in need, reconnecting our torn communities. There is so
much to be done. Enough, indeed, for millions of others who are still
young in spirit to give of themselves in service, too.

In serving, we recognize a simple but powerful truth: We need each   24 other and we must care for one another. Today we do more than celebrate America, we rededicate ourselves to the very idea of America: An idea born in revolution and renewed through two centuries of challenge; an idea tempered by the knowledge that but for fate we, the fortunate and the unfortunate, might have been each other; an idea ennobled by the faith that our nation can summon from its myriad diversity the deepest measure of unity; an idea infused with the conviction that America's long, heroic journey must go forever upward.

And so, my fellow Americans, as we stand at the edge of the 21st century, let us begin anew with energy and hope, with faith and discipline. And let us work until our work is done. The Scripture says, "And let us not be weary in well-doing, for in due season we shall reap if we faint not."   25

From this joyful mountaintop of celebration we hear a call to service in the valley. We have heard the trumpets, we have changed the guard. And now each in our own way, and with God's help, we must answer the call.   26

Thank you, and God bless you all.   27

QUESTIONS FOR STUDY AND DISCUSSION

1. What are the key points of Clinton's speech? How has he organized these points? (Glossary: *Organization*)

2. In what sense is the inauguration of the U.S. president a celebration of "the mystery of American renewal"? In this context, how does Clinton's image of spring work? Explain.

3. Clinton says that "each generation of Americans must define what it means to be an American." How does Clinton define what it means to be American? Do you find yourself agreeing or disagreeing with his definition? Why, or why not?

4. Clinton believes that "there is nothing wrong with America that cannot be cured by what is right with America." What, to Clinton, is right with America? What do you see as America's strengths? What needs to be done to renew America?

5. What parallels, if any, do you find between Clinton's speech and Kennedy's Inaugural Address?

6. The idea of change played a large role in Clinton's successful campaign for the presidency. Judging by what he says in his speech, what does *change* mean to Clinton? Does it mean the same thing to you? Explain.

7. How would you characterize Clinton's tone in this speech? What in his diction led you to this conclusion?

8. How would you assess Clinton's speech? How does it compare to the other speeches included in this casebook? What in this speech do you find particularly noteworthy or memorable? Explain.

WRITING ASSIGNMENTS FOR "THE LANGUAGE OF POLITICS"

1. In "Politics and the English Language" (pp. 70–82), George Orwell claims political speech is filled with "meaningless words" such as *patriotism, democracy*, and *freedom*. Why does Orwell consider these words "meaningless"? Choose two of the words Orwell mentions, or two of your own, and then review the speeches by Lincoln, Kennedy, King, and Clinton with these words in mind. Does each man define the same words in the same way? If not, does that render the words meaningless? In an essay, discuss any differences you find in their use of certain words and what you think each leader hoped to gain in using these words in the way he did. Or, assess Orwell's claim in light of the use these speakers make of such words.

2. The adoption of the Declaration of Independence was, among other things, a matter of practical politics. Using library sources, research the deliberations of the Continental Congress and explain how and why the final version of the Declaration differs from Jefferson's first draft. In light of what Peggy Noonan says, has the process of political speech writing changed in the last two-hundred years?

3. To many people the Declaration of Independence still accurately reflects America's political philosophy and way of life; to others it does not. What is your position? Discuss your view of the Declaration's contemporary relevance or lack of it.

4. Write an essay in which you compare and contrast the Declaration of Independence with Stanton's declaration. You should consider such things as purpose, audience, evidence, and style in your essay.

5. Using the six speeches in this section, write an essay in which you support Peggy Noonan's claim that "Speeches are important because they are one of the great constants of our political history. . . . They count. They more than count, they shape what happens."

6. Both Lincoln and Kennedy were presidents renowned for the eloquence, simplicity, and brevity of their speeches. Write an essay in which you compare and contrast Lincoln's Gettysburg Address with Kennedy's Inaugural Address.

7. Using Cross's list of propaganda devices, write an essay in which you analyze a newspaper editorial, a political speech, a public-service advertisement, or a comparable example of contemporary political prose. Submit the original editorial, speech, or ad with your essay.

8. Columnist and political commentator Garry Wills has written that "Hemingway claimed that all modern American novels are the offspring of *Huckleberry Finn*. It is no greater exaggeration to say that all modern political prose descends from the Gettysburg Address." Using the five

other speeches in this section, test Wills's claim. What are the major differences between the speeches of Jefferson and Stanton and those of Kennedy, King, and Clinton? What does Lincoln's address have in common with Kennedy's, King's, and Clinton's speeches?

9. In the 1988 presidential campaign, candidate George Bush effectively made the word *liberal* a dirty word. By referring to his opponent Michael Dukakis as a "card-carrying member of the American Civil Liberties Union," he made Dukakis "un-American" by association. A similar strategy backfired on Bush during the 1992 campaign when he tried to link candidate Clinton with the antiwar movement and communism during the 1960s and 1970s. What era in our history was Bush evoking when he employed these strategies? Why do you suppose it was effective in 1988 and not in 1992? In an essay, compare and contrast Bush's use of "charged language" in the two presidential campaigns. You may find it helpful to read "Selection, Slanting, and Charged Language" (pp. 47–58) while working on your paper.

10. Martin Luther King, Jr., says that his dream is "deeply rooted in the American dream." What is the American dream as you understand it? Can that dream be realized in the 1990s? If so, how? If not, why does the dream persist? In an essay discuss your thoughts on the American dream and its viability today.

11. Imagine that you have been elected president of the United States and that your inauguration is a week away. Using either Kennedy's or Clinton's speech as a model, write an inaugural address in which you identify the chief problems and issues of today and set forth your program for dealing with them. Consider first what approach to take—for example, you might write an inspirational address to the nation, or you may instead choose to describe in everyday language the problems that confront the nation and the actions you believe will solve these problems.

12. During the 1992 presidential campaign, Bill Clinton asked Americans to have the "courage to change." In this and many other campaign slogans he capitalized on the magic of the word *change* to propel himself into the presidency. Why do you think Americans were so in favor of "change"? Do you think that *change* meant the same thing to all Americans? What does *change* mean to you? Is *change* simply another example of what Orwell would call an empty or meaningless word? Why, or why not? Collect your thoughts on Clinton's use of the word *change* and Americans' response to it in an essay.

PART V

The Language of Media and Advertising

And here's that cozy eat-in kitchen, with that lovely view of water!

"NOW . . . THIS"

Neil Postman

In the following essay from his book Amusing Ourselves to
Death, *Neil Postman examines the ways in which the format
for broadcast news has trivialized the news itself. Postman, a
professor of media ecology at New York University, warns
that the effort to keep the news hour entertaining not only
keeps the public ignorant, it ultimately puts the entire culture
at risk of extinction.*

The American humorist H. Allen Smith once suggested that of all the
worrisome words in the English language, the scariest is "uh oh," as
when a physician looks at your X rays and with knitted brow says, "Uh
oh." I should like to suggest that the words which are the title of this
chapter are as ominous as any, all the more so because they are spoken
without knitted brow—indeed, with a kind of idiot's delight. The phrase,
if that's what it may be called, adds to our grammar a new part of speech,
a conjunction that does not connect anything to anything but does the
opposite: separates everything from everything. As such, it serves as a
compact metaphor for the discontinuities in so much that passes for public discourse in present-day America.

"Now . . . this" is commonly used on radio and television newscasts
to indicate that what one has just heard or seen has no relevance to what
one is about to hear or see, or possibly to anything one is ever likely to
hear or see. The phrase is a means of acknowledging the fact that the
world as mapped by the speeded-up electronic media has no order or
meaning and is not to be taken seriously. There is no murder so brutal, no
earthquake so devastating, no political blunder so costly—for that matter,
no ball score so tantalizing or weather report so threatening—that it cannot be erased from our minds by a newscaster saying, "Now . . . this."
The newscaster means that you have thought long enough on the previous
matter (approximately forty-five seconds), that you must not be morbidly
preoccupied with it (let us say, for ninety seconds), and that you must
now give your attention to another fragment of news or a commercial.

Television did not invent the "Now . . . this" worldview. . . . It is the
offspring of the intercourse between telegraphy and photography. But it is
through television that it has been nurtured and brought to a perverse
maturity. For on television, nearly every half hour is a discrete event,
separated in content, context, and emotional texture from what precedes
and follows it. In part because television sells its time in seconds and
minutes, in part because television must use images rather than words, in
part because its audience can move freely to and from the television set,

programs are structured so that almost each eight-minute segment may stand as a complete event in itself. Viewers are rarely required to carry over any thought or feeling from one parcel of time to another.

Of course, in television's presentation of the "news of the day," we may   4
see the "Now . . . this" mode of discourse in its boldest and most embarrassing form. For there, we are presented not only with fragmented news but news without context, without consequences, without value, and therefore without essential seriousness; that is to say, news as pure entertainment.

Consider, for example, how you would proceed if you were given the   5
opportunity to produce a television news show for any station concerned to attract the largest possible audience. You would, first, choose a cast of players, each of whom has a face that is both "likable" and "credible." Those who apply would, in fact, submit to you their eight-by-ten glossies, from which you would eliminate those whose countenances are not suitable for nightly display. This means that you will exclude women who are not beautiful or who are over the age of fifty, men who are bald, all people who are overweight or whose noses are too long or whose eyes are too close together. You will try, in other words, to assemble a cast of talking hair-do's. At the very least, you will want those whose faces would not be unwelcome on a magazine cover.

Christine Craft has just such a face, and so she applied for a co-   6
anchor position on KMBC-TV in Kansas City. According to a lawyer who represented her in a sexism suit she later brought against the station, the management of KMBC-TV "loved Christine's look." She was accordingly hired in January 1981. She was fired in August 1981 because research indicated that her appearance "hampered viewer acceptance." What exactly does "hampered viewer acceptance" mean? And what does it have to do with the news? Hampered viewer acceptance means the same thing for television news as it does for any television show: Viewers do not like looking at the performer. It also means that viewers do not believe the performer, that she lacks credibility. In the case of a theatrical performance, we have a sense of what that implies: The actor does not persuade the audience that he or she is the character being portrayed. But what does lack of credibility imply in the case of a news show? What character is a co-anchor playing? And how do we decide that the performance lacks verisimilitude? Does the audience believe that the newscaster is lying, that what is reported did not in fact happen, that something important is being concealed?

It is frightening to think that this may be so, that the perception of the   7
truth of a report rests heavily on the acceptability of the newscaster. In the ancient world, there was a tradition of banishing or killing the bearer of bad tidings. Does the television news show restore, in a curious form, this tradition? Do we banish those who tell us the news when we do not care for the face of the teller? Does television countermand the warnings we once received about the fallacy of the ad hominem argument?

If the answer to any of these questions is even a qualified "Yes," then   8
here is an issue worthy of the attention of epistemologists. Stated in its
simplest form, it is that television provides a new (or, possibly, restores
an old) definition of truth: The credibility of the teller is the ultimate test
of the truth of a proposition. "Credibility" here does not refer to the past
record of the teller for making statements that have survived the rigors of
reality-testing. It refers only to the impression of sincerity, authenticity,
vulnerability or attractiveness (choose one or more) conveyed by the ac-
tor/reporter.

This is a matter of considerable importance, for it goes beyond the   9
question of how truth is perceived on television news shows. If on television, credibility replaces reality as the decisive test of truth-telling, political leaders need not trouble themselves very much with reality provided
that their performances consistently generate a sense of verisimilitude. I
suspect, for example, that the dishonor that now shrouds Richard Nixon
results not from the fact that he lied but that on television he looks like a
liar. Which, if true, should bring no comfort to anyone, not even veteran
Nixon-haters. For the alternative possibilities are that one may look like a
liar but be telling the truth; or even worse, look like a truth-teller but in
fact be lying.

As a producer of a television news show, you would be well aware of   10
these matters and would be careful to choose your cast on the basis of
criteria used by David Merrick and other successful impresarios. Like
them, you would then turn your attention to staging the show on principles that maximize entertainment value. You would, for example, select a
musical theme for the show. All television news programs begin, end,
and are somewhere in between punctuated with music. I have found very
few Americans who regard this custom as peculiar, which fact I have
taken as evidence for the dissolution of lines of demarcation between
serious public discourse and entertainment. What has music to do with
the news? Why is it there? It is there, I assume, for the same reason
music is used in the theater and films—to create a mood and provide a
leitmotif for the entertainment. If there were no music—as is the case
when any television program is interrupted for a news flash—viewers
would expect something truly alarming, possibly life-altering. But as long
as the music is there as a frame for the program, the viewer is comforted
to believe that there is nothing to be greatly alarmed about; that, in fact,
the events that are reported have as much relation to reality as do scenes
in a play.

This perception of a news show as a stylized dramatic performance   11
whose content has been staged largely to entertain is reinforced by several
other features, including the fact that the average length of any story is
forty-five seconds. While brevity does not always suggest triviality, in
this case it clearly does. It is simply not possible to convey a sense of
seriousness about any event if its implications are exhausted in less than

one minute's time. In fact, it is quite obvious that TV news has no intention of suggesting that any story *has* any implications, for that would require viewers to continue to think about it when it is done and therefore obstruct their attending to the next story that waits panting in the wings. In any case, viewers are not provided with much opportunity to be distracted from the next story since in all likelihood it will consist of some film footage. Pictures have little difficulty in overwhelming words and short-circuiting introspection. As a television producer, you would be certain to give both prominence and precedence to any event for which there is some sort of visual documentation. A suspected killer being brought into a police station, the angry face of a cheated consumer, a barrel going over Niagara Falls (with a person alleged to be in it), the President disembarking from a helicopter on the White House lawn— these are always fascinating or amusing and easily satisfy the requirements of an entertaining show. It is, of course, not necessary that the visuals actually document the point of a story. Neither is it necessary to explain why such images are intruding themselves on public consciousness. Film footage justifies itself, as every television producer well knows.

It is also of considerable help in maintaining a high level of unreality 12 that the newscasters do not pause to grimace or shiver when they speak their prefaces or epilogs to the film clips. Indeed, many newscasters do not appear to grasp the meaning of what they are saying, and some hold to a fixed and ingratiating enthusiasm as they report on earthquakes, mass killings and other disasters. Viewers would be quite disconcerted by any show of concern or terror on the part of newscasters. Viewers, after all, are partners with the newscasters in the "Now . . . this" culture, and they expect the newscaster to play out his or her role as a character who is marginally serious but who stays well clear of authentic understanding. The viewers, for their part, will not be caught contaminating their responses with a sense of reality, any more than an audience at a play would go scurrying to call home because a character on stage has said that a murderer is loose in the neighborhood.

The viewers also know that no matter how grave any fragment of 13 news may appear (for example, on the day I write a Marine Corps general has declared that nuclear war between the United States and Russia is inevitable), it will shortly be followed by a series of commercials that will, in an instant, defuse the import of the news, in fact render it largely banal. This is a key element in the structure of a news program and all by itself refutes any claim that television news is designed as a serious form of public discourse. Imagine what you would think of me, and this book, if I were to pause here, tell you that I will return to my discussion in a moment, and then proceed to write a few words in behalf of United Airlines or the Chase Manhattan Bank. You would rightly think that I had no respect for you and, certainly, no respect for the subject. And if I did this not once but several times in each chapter, you would think the whole enterprise unworthy of your attention. Why, then, do we not think a news show similarly unworthy? The reason, I believe, is that whereas we expect books and even other media (such as film) to maintain a consistency of tone and a continuity of content, we have no such expectation of television, and especially television news. We have become so accustomed to its discontinuities that we are no longer struck dumb, as any sane person would be, by a newscaster who having just reported that a nuclear war is inevitable goes on to say that he will be right back after this word from Burger King; who says, in other words, "Now . . . this." One can hardly overestimate the damage that such juxtapositions do to our sense of the world as a serious place. The damage is especially massive to youthful viewers who depend so much on television for their clues as to how to respond to the world. In watching television news, they, more than any other segment of the audience, are drawn into an epistemology based on the assumption that all reports of cruelty and death are greatly exaggerated and, in any case, not to be taken seriously or responded to sanely.

I should go so far as to say that embedded in the surrealistic frame of   14
a television news show is a theory of anticommunication, featuring a type of discourse that abandons logic, reason, sequence and rules of contradiction. In aesthetics, I believe the name given to this theory is Dadaism; in philosophy, nihilism; in psychiatry, schizophrenia. In the parlance of the theater, it is known as vaudeville.

For those who think I am here guilty of hyperbole, I offer the follow-   15
ing description of television news by Robert MacNeil, executive editor and co-anchor of the "MacNeil-Lehrer Newshour." The idea, he writes, "is to keep everything brief, not to strain the attention of anyone but instead to provide constant stimulation through variety, novelty, action, and movement. You are required . . . to pay attention to no concept, no character, and no problem for more than a few seconds at a time." He goes on to say that the assumptions controlling a news show are "that bite-sized is best, that complexity must be avoided, that nuances are dispensible, that qualifications impede the simple message, that visual stimulation is a substitute for thought, and that verbal precision is an anachronism."

Robert MacNeil has more reason than most to give testimony about   16
the television news show as vaudeville act. The "MacNeil-Lehrer Newshour" is an unusual and gracious attempt to bring to television some of the elements of typographic discourse. The program abjures visual stimulation, consists largely of extended explanations of events and in-depth interviews (which even there means only five to ten minutes), limits the number of stories covered, and emphasizes background and coherence. But television has exacted its price for MacNeil's rejection of a show business format. By television's standards, the audience is minuscule, the

program is confined to public-television stations, and it is a good guess that the combined salary of MacNeil and Lehrer is one-fifth of Dan Rather's or Tom Brokaw's.

If you were a producer of a television news show for a commercial   17
station, you would not have the option of defying television's requirements. It would be demanded of you that you strive for the largest possible audience, and, as a consequence and in spite of your best intentions, you would arrive at a production very nearly resembling MacNeil's description. Moreover, you would include some things MacNeil does not mention. You would try to make celebrities of your newscasters. You would advertise the show, both in the press and on television itself. You would do "news briefs," to serve as an inducement to viewers. You would have a weatherman as comic relief, and a sportscaster whose language is a touch uncouth (as a way of his relating to the beer-drinking common man). You would, in short, package the whole event as any producer might who is in the entertainment business.

The result of all this is that Americans are the best entertained and   18
quite likely the least well-informed people in the Western world. I say this in the face of the popular conceit that television, as a window to the world, has made Americans exceedingly well informed. Much depends here, of course, on what is meant by being informed. I will pass over the now tiresome polls that tell us that, at any given moment, 70 percent of our citizens do not know who is the Secretary of State or the Chief Justice of the Supreme Court. Let us consider, instead, the case of Iran during the drama that was called the "Iranian Hostage Crisis."* I don't suppose there has been a story in years that received more continuous attention from television. We may assume, then, the Americans know most of what there is to know about this unhappy event. And now, I put these questions to you: Would it be an exaggeration to say that not one American in a hundred knows what language the Iranians speak? Or what the word "Ayatollah" means or implies? Or knows any details of the tenets of Iranian religious beliefs? Or the main outlines of their political history? Or knows who the Shah was, and where he came from?

Nonetheless, everyone had an opinion about this event, for in Amer-   19
ica everyone is entitled to an opinion, and it is certainly useful to have a few when a pollster shows up. But these are opinions of a quite different order from eighteenth- or nineteenth-century opinions. It is probably more accurate to call them emotions rather than opinions, which would account for the fact that they change from week to week, as the pollsters tell us. What is happening here is that television is altering the meaning of "being informed" by creating a species of information that might prop-

---

Ed. note: In 1979, American Embassy personnel were taken hostage by anti-American militants and kept captive in Iran for 444 days. The seeming inability of President Jimmy Carter to develop an effective response frustrated many Americans, who felt that the United States was being subjected to an intolerable humiliation in the world's eyes.

erly be called *disinformation*. I am using this word almost in the precise sense in which it is used by spies in the CIA or KGB. Disinformation does not mean false information. It means misleading information—misplaced, irrelevant, fragmented or superficial information—information that creates the illusion of knowing something but which in fact leads one away from knowing. In saying this, I do not mean to imply that television news deliberately aims to deprive Americans of a coherent, contextual understanding of their world. I mean to say that when news is packaged as entertainment, that is the inevitable result. And in saying that the television news show entertains but does not inform, I am saying something far more serious than that we are being deprived of authentic information. I am saying we are losing our sense of what it means to be well informed. Ignorance is always correctable. But what shall we do if we take ignorance to be knowledge?

Here is a startling example of how this process bedevils us. A *New* 20
York Times article is headlined on February 15, 1983:

REAGAN MISSTATEMENTS GETTING LESS ATTENTION

The article begins in the following way:

> President Reagan's aides used to become visibly alarmed at suggestions that he had given mangled and perhaps misleading accounts of his policies or of current events in general. That doesn't seem to happen much anymore.
>
> Indeed, the President continues to make debatable assertions of fact but news accounts do not deal with them as extensively as they once did. In the view of White House officials, the declining news coverage mirrors a *decline in interest by the general public*. (my italics)

This report is not so much a news story as a story about the news, and 21
our recent history suggests that it is not about Ronald Reagan's charm. It is about how news is defined, and I believe the story would be quite astonishing to both civil libertarians and tyrants of an earlier time. Walter Lippmann, for example, wrote in 1920: "There can be no liberty for a community which lacks the means by which to detect lies." For all of his pessimism about the possibilities of restoring an eighteenth- and nineteenth-century level of public discourse, Lippmann assumed, as did Thomas Jefferson before him, that with a well-trained press functioning as a lie-detector, the public's interest in a President's mangling of the truth would be piqued, in both senses of that word. Given the means to detect lies, he believed, the public could not be indifferent to their consequences.

But this case refutes his assumption. The reporters who cover the 22
White House are ready and able to expose lies, and thus create the grounds for informed and indignant opinion. But apparently the public declines to take an interest. To press reports of White House dissembling, the public has replied with Queen Victoria's famous line: "We are not

amused." However, here the words mean something the Queen did not have in mind. They mean that what is not amusing does not compel their attention. Perhaps if the President's lies could be demonstrated by pictures and accompanied by music the public would raise a curious eyebrow. If a movie, like *All the President's Men*, could be made from his misleading accounts of government policy, if there were a break-in of some sort or sinister characters laundering money, attention would quite likely be paid. We do well to remember that President Nixon did not begin to come undone until his lies were given a theatrical setting at the Watergate hearings. But we do not have anything like that here. Apparently, all President Reagan does is *say* things that are not entirely true. And there is nothing entertaining in that.

But there is a subtler point to be made here. Many of the President's   23 "misstatements" fall in the category of contradictions—mutually exclusive assertions that cannot possibly both, in the same context, be true. "In the same context" is the key phrase here, for it is context that defines contradiction. There is no problem in someone's remarking that he prefers oranges to apples, and also remarking that he prefers apples to oranges—not if one statement is made in the context of choosing a wallpaper design and the other in the context of selecting fruit for dessert. In such a case, we have statements that are opposites, but not contradictory. But if the statements are made in a single, continuous, and coherent context, then they are contradictions, and cannot both be true. Contradiction, in short, requires that statements and events be perceived as interrelated aspects of a continuous and coherent context. Disappear the context, or fragment it, and contradiction disappears. This point is nowhere made more clear to me than in conferences with my younger students about their writing. "Look here," I say. "In this paragraph you have said one thing. And in that you have said the opposite. Which is it to be?" They are polite, and wish to please, but they are as baffled by the question as I am by the response. "I know," they will say, "but that is *there* and this is *here*." The difference between us is that I assume "there" and "here," "now" and "then," one paragraph and the next to be connected, to be continuous, to be part of the same coherent world of thought. That is the way of typographic discourse, and typography is the universe I'm "coming from," as they say. But they are coming from a different universe of discourse altogether: the "Now . . . this" world of television. The fundamental assumption of that world is not coherence but discontinuity. And in a world of discontinuities, contradiction is useless as a test of truth or merit, because contradiction does not exist.

My point is that we are by now so thoroughly adjusted to the "Now   24 . . . this" world of news—a world of fragments, where events stand alone, stripped of any connection to the past, or to the future, or to other events—that all assumptions of coherence have vanished. And so, perforce, has contradiction. In the context of *no context*, so to speak, it simply disappears. And in its absence, what possible interest could there be in a list of what the President says *now* and what he said *then*? It is merely a rehash of old news, and there is nothing interesting or entertaining in that. The only thing to be amused about is the bafflement of reporters at the public's indifference. There is an irony in the fact that the very group that has taken the world apart should, on trying to piece it together again, be surprised that no one notices much, or cares.

For all his perspicacity, George Orwell would have been stymied by this situation; there is nothing "Orwellian" about it. The President does not have the press under the thumb. *The New York Times* and *The Washington Post* are not *Pravda*; the Associated Press is not Tass. And there is no Newspeak here. Lies have not been defined as truth nor truth as lies. All that has happened is that the public has adjusted to incoherence and been amused into indifference. Which is why Aldous Huxley would not in the least be surprised by the story. Indeed, he prophesied its coming. He believed that it is far more likely that the Western democracies will dance and dream themselves into oblivion than march into it, single file and manacled. Huxley grasped, as Orwell did not, that it is not necessary to conceal anything from a public insensible to contradiction and narcoticized by technological diversions. Although Huxley did not specify that television would be our main line to the drug, he would have no difficulty accepting Robert MacNeil's observation that "Television is the *soma* of Aldous Huxley's *Brave New World*." Big Brother turns out to be Howdy Doody.

I do not mean that the trivialization of public information is all accomplished *on* television. I mean that television is the paradigm for our conception of public information. As the printing press did in an earlier time, television has achieved the power to define the form in which news must come, and it has also defined how we shall respond to it. In presenting news to us packaged as vaudeville, television induces other media to do the same, so that the total information environment begins to mirror television.

For example, America's newest and highly successful national newspaper, *USA Today*, is modeled precisely on the format of television. It is sold on the street in receptacles that look like television sets. Its stories are uncommonly short, its design leans heavily on pictures, charts and other graphics, some of them printed in various colors. Its weather maps are a visual delight; its sports section includes enough pointless statistics to distract a computer. As a consequence, *USA Today*, which began publication in September 1982, has become the third largest daily in the United States (as of July 1984, according to the Audit Bureau of Circulations), moving quickly to overtake the *Daily News* and the *Wall Street Journal*. Journalists of a more traditional bent have criticized it for its superficiality and theatrics, but the paper's editors remain steadfast in their disregard of typographic standards. The paper's Editor-in-Chief,

John Quinn, has said: "We are not up to undertaking projects of the dimensions needed to win prizes. They don't give awards for the best investigative paragraph." Here is an astonishing tribute to the resonance of television's epistemology: In the age of television, the paragraph is becoming the basic unit of news in print media. Moreover, Mr. Quinn need not fret too long about being deprived of awards. As other newspapers join in the transformation, the time cannot be far off when awards will be given for the best investigative sentence.

It needs also to be noted here that new and successful magazines such 28 as *People* and *Us* are not only examples of television-oriented print media but have had an extraordinary "ricochet" effect on television itself. Whereas television taught the magazines that news is nothing but entertainment, the magazines have taught television that nothing but entertainment is news. Television programs, such as "Entertainment Tonight," turn information about entertainers and celebrities into "serious" cultural content, so that the circle begins to close: Both the form and content of news become entertainment.

Radio, of course, is the least likely medium to join in the descent into 29 Huxleyan world of technological narcotics. It is, after all, particularly well suited to the transmission of rational, complex language. Nonetheless, and even if we disregard radio's captivation by the music industry, we appear to be left with the chilling fact that such language as radio allows us to hear is increasingly primitive, fragmented, and largely aimed at invoking visceral response; which is to say, it is the linguistic analogue to the ubiquitous rock music that is radio's principal source of income. As I write, the trend in call-in shows is for the "host" to insult callers whose language does not, in itself, go much beyond humanoid grunting. Such programs have little content, as this word used to be defined, and are merely of archeological interest in that they give us a sense of what a dialogue among Neanderthals might have been like. More to the point, the language of radio newscasts has become, under the influence of television, increasingly decontextualized and discontinuous, so that the possibility of anyone's knowing about the world, as against merely knowing *of* it, is effectively blocked. In New York City, radio station WINS entreats its listeners to "Give us twenty-two minutes and we'll give you the world." This is said without irony, and its audience, we may assume, does not regard the slogan as the conception of a disordered mind.

And so, we move rapidly into an information environment which may 30 rightly be called trivial pursuit. As the game of that name uses facts as a source of amusement, so do our sources of news. It has been demonstrated many times that a culture can survive misinformation and false opinion. It has not yet been demonstrated whether a culture can survive if it takes the measure of the world in twenty-two minutes. Or if the value of its news is determined by the number of laughs it provides.

QUESTIONS ON CONTENT

1. Postman assigns great importance to the words "Now . . . this" not for themselves alone but for what they represent. What for Postman makes these two little words so frightening? What concept of the world does he suggest they imply?

2. In your own words, how does the division of time on television provide a nurturing atmosphere for what Postman calls the "Now . . . this" worldview?

3. What do the words "hampered viewer acceptance" mean? How does Postman relate this phrase to a theatrical performance?

4. How does Postman distinguish between the two kinds of truth he mentions in paragraph 8?

5. What are some of the features of a news show that contribute to its dramatic performance?

6. In your own words, define the term *contradiction*. How does the "Now . . . this" worldview make the concept of contradiction extinct?

QUESTIONS ON RHETORIC

1. In paragraph 13, Postman illustrates his point that commercial breaks "defuse the import of the news." Did you find his illustration convincing? Why or why not?

2. Postman asks several questions in his essay. Locate a few of the questions he poses, and explain the different ways Postman uses questions to engage the reader.

3. In paragraph 14, Postman uses comparison to support his idea that "embedded in the surrealistic frame of a television news show is a theory of anticommunication." What effect did these illustrations have on you? Do you think Postman has placed them in any particular order? Explain your answer. (Glossary: *Illustration*)

4. What do you think is Postman's attitude toward television news and the public that tolerates it? (Glossary: *Attitude*) Choose examples of Postman's diction to support your answer. (Glossary: *Diction*)

5. In the final paragraph, Postman makes a subtle prediction. What is it, and how well do you think it works as a conclusion to Postman's essay? (Glossary: *Beginnings and Endings*)

VOCABULARY

tantalizing (2)	leitmotif (10)	conceit (18)
perverse (3)	juxtapositions (13)	perspicacity (25)
discrete (3)	nuances (15)	paradigm (26)
epistemologists (8)	anachronism (15)	analogue (29)
verisimilitude (9)	abjures (16)	ubiquitous (29)

WRITING TOPICS

1. Postman says "Americans are the best entertained and quite likely the least well-informed people in the Western world." What evidence does he give to support his statement? In a brief essay, use examples from your own observations to argue for or against Postman's point of view.

2. Postman expresses his dread over the growing popularity of call-in shows. What is his fear? Listen to some of these shows in your area. Do you think his fear is valid? Why or why not? In a brief essay, discuss your conclusions.

3. In paragraph 18, Postman discusses the public's lack of knowledge about Iran and Islam despite there not having "been a story in years that received more attention from television" than the Iran hostage crisis. What are some of the "facts" we never got from watching that news story on television? Choose several other significant news events of more recent times. In an essay, discuss any points you know of relevant to those events that the television news never mentioned. Would you have been interested in knowing more than the television news provided?

SEX, LIES, AND ADVERTISING

Gloria Steinem

Gloria Steinem is a political activist, editor, lecturer, writer, and one of the country's leading supporters of the women's movement. After graduating from Smith College in 1956, she helped found two important magazines, New York *and* Ms. *A founding editor and writer for* Ms., *Steinem's autobiographical book,* Revolution from Within, *offers her personal insights into the women's movement. In the following article, from the first issue of* Ms. *to be published without advertising, Steinem openly discusses the often questionable demands that advertising places on editorial content, demands that she feels are the equivalent of blackmail threats. She is particularly incensed by advertisers' low estimate of women's magazines and general disrespect for women.*

About three years ago, as *glasnost* was beginning and *Ms.* seemed to be ending, I was invited to a press lunch for a Soviet official. He entertained us with anecdotes about new problems of democracy in his country. Local Communist leaders were being criticized in their media for the first time, he explained, and they were angry.

"So I'll have to ask my American friends," he finished pointedly, "how more *subtly* to control the press." In the silence that followed, I said, "Advertising."

The reporters laughed, but later, one of them took me aside: How *dare* I suggest that freedom of the press was limited? How dare I imply that his newsweekly could be influenced by ads?

I explained that I was thinking of advertising's media-wide influence on most of what we read. Even newsmagazines use "soft" cover stories to sell ads, confuse readers with "advertorials," and occasionally self-censor on subjects known to be a problem with big advertisers.

But, I also explained, I was thinking especially of women's magazines. There, it isn't just a little content that's devoted to attracting ads, it's almost all of it. That's why advertisers—not readers—have always been the problem for *Ms.* As the only women's magazine that didn't supply what the ad world euphemistically describes as "supportive editorial atmosphere" or "complementary copy" (for instance, articles that praise food/fashion/beauty subjects to "support" and "complement" food/fashion/beauty ads), *Ms.* could never attract enough advertising to break even.

"Oh, *women's* magazines," the journalist said with contempt. "Every-   6
body knows they're catalogs—but who cares? They have nothing to do
with journalism."

I can't tell you how many times I've had this argument in 25 years of   7
working for many kinds of publications. Except as moneymaking machines—"cash cows" as they are so elegantly called in the trade—
women's magazines are rarely taken seriously. Though changes being
made by women have been called more far-reaching than the industrial
revolution—and though many editors try hard to reflect some of them in
the few pages left to them after all the ad-related subjects have been
covered—the magazines serving the female half of this country are still
far below the journalistic and ethical standards of news and general interest publications. Most depressing of all, this doesn't even rate an exposé.

If *Time* and *Newsweek* had to lavish praise on cars in general and   8
credit General Motors in particular to get GM ads, there would be a
scandal—maybe a criminal investigation. When women's magazines
from *Seventeen* to *Lear's* praise beauty products in general and credit
Revlon in particular to get ads, it's just business as usual.

I.

When *Ms.* began, we didn't consider *not* taking ads. The most important   9
reason was keeping the price of a feminist magazine low enough for most
women to afford. But the second and almost equal reason was providing
a forum where women and advertisers could talk to each other and improve advertising itself. After all, it was (and still is) as potent a source of
information in this country as news or TV and movie dramas.

We decided to proceed in two stages. First, we would convince   10
makers of "people products" used by both men and women but advertised
mostly to men—cars, credit cards, insurance, sound equipment, financial
services, and the like—that their ads should be placed in a women's
magazine. Since they were accustomed to the division between editorial
and advertising in news and general interest magazines, this would allow
our editorial content to be free and diverse. Second, we would add the
best ads for whatever traditional "women's products" (clothes, shampoo,
fragrance, food, and so on) that surveys showed *Ms.* readers used. But
we would ask them to come in *without* the usual quid pro quo of "complementary copy."

We knew the second step might be harder. Food advertisers have   11
always demanded that women's magazines publish recipes and articles on
entertaining (preferably ones that name their products) in return for their
ads; clothing advertisers expect to be surrounded by fashion spreads (especially ones that credit their designers); and shampoo, fragrance, and

beauty products in general usually insist on positive editorial coverage of beauty subjects, plus photo credits besides. That's why women's magazines look the way they do. But if we could break this link between ads and editorial content, then we wanted good ads for "women's products," too.

By playing their part in this unprecedented mix of *all* the things our readers need and use, advertisers also would be rewarded: ads for products like cars and mutual funds would find a new growth market; the best ads for women's products would no longer be lost in oceans of ads for the same category; and both would have access to a laboratory of smart and caring readers whose response would help create effective ads for other media as well.

I thought then that our main problem would be the imagery in ads themselves. Carmakers were still draping blondes in evening gowns over the hoods like ornaments. Authority figures were almost always male, even in ads for products that only women used. Sadistic, he-man campaigns even won industry praise. (For instance, *Advertising Age* had hailed the infamous Silva Thin cigarette theme, "How to Get a Woman's Attention: Ignore Her," as "brilliant.") Even in medical journals, tranquilizer ads showed depressed housewives standing beside piles of dirty dishes and promised to get them back to work.

Obviously, *Ms.* would have to avoid such ads and seek out the best ones—but this didn't seem impossible. *The New Yorker* had been selecting ads for aesthetic reasons for years, a practice that only seemed to make advertisers more eager to be in its pages. *Ebony* and *Essence* were asking for ads with positive black images, and though their struggle was hard, they weren't being called unreasonable.

Clearly, what *Ms.* needed was a very special publisher and ad sales staff. I could think of only one woman with experience on the business side of magazines—Patricia Carbine, who recently had become a vice president of *McCall's* as well as its editor in chief—and the reason I knew her name was a good omen. She had been managing editor at *Look* (really *the* editor, but its owner refused to put a female name at the top of his masthead) when I was writing a column there. After I did an early interview with Cesar Chavez, then just emerging as a leader of migrant labor, and the publisher turned it down because he was worried about ads from Sunkist, Pat was the one who intervened. As I learned later, she had told the publisher she would resign if the interview wasn't published. Mainly because *Look* couldn't afford to lose Pat, it *was* published (and the ads from Sunkist never arrived).

Though I barely knew this woman, she had done two things I always remembered: put her job on the line in a way that editors often talk about but rarely do, and been so loyal to her colleagues that she never told me or anyone outside *Look* that she had done so.

Fortunately, Pat did agree to leave *McCall's* and take a huge cut in salary to become publisher of *Ms.* She became responsible for training and inspiring generations of young women who joined the *Ms.* ad sales force, many of whom went on to become "firsts" at the top of publishing. When *Ms.* first started, however, there were so few women with experience selling space that Pat and I made the rounds of ad agencies ourselves. Later, the fact that *Ms.* was asking companies to do business in a different way meant our saleswomen had to make many times the usual number of calls—first to convince agencies and then client companies besides—and to present endless amounts of research. I was often asked to do a final ad presentation, or see some higher decision-maker, or speak to women employees so executives could see the interest of women they worked with. That's why I spent more time persuading advertisers than editing or writing for *Ms.* and why I ended up with an unsentimental education in the seamy underside of publishing that few writers see (and even fewer magazines can publish).

Let me take you with us through some experiences, just as they happened: 18

· Cheered on by early support from Volkswagen and one or two other   19
car companies, we scrape together time and money to put on a major reception in Detroit. We know U.S. carmakers firmly believe that women choose the upholstery, not the car, but we are armed with statistics and reader mail to prove the contrary: a car is an important purchase for women, one that symbolizes mobility and freedom.

But almost nobody comes. We are left with many pounds of shrimp   20
on the table, and quite a lot of egg on our face. We blame ourselves for not guessing that there would be a baseball pennant play-off on the same day, but executives go out of their way to explain they wouldn't have come anyway. Thus begins ten years of knocking on hostile doors, presenting endless documentation, and hiring a full-time saleswoman in Detroit; all necessary before *Ms.* gets any real results.

This long saga has a semihappy ending: foreign and, later, domestic   21
carmakers eventually provided *Ms.* with enough advertising to make cars one of our top sources of ad revenue. Slowly, Detroit began to take the women's market seriously enough to put car ads in other women's magazines, too, thus freeing a few pages from the hothouse of fashion-beauty-food ads.

But long after figures showed a third, even a half, of many car models   22
being bought by women, U.S. makers continued to be uncomfortable addressing women. Unlike foreign carmakers, Detroit never quite learned the secret of creating intelligent ads that exclude no one, and then placing them in women's magazines to overcome past exclusion. (*Ms.* readers were so grateful for a routine Honda ad featuring rack and pinion steering, for instance, that they sent fan mail.) Even now, Detroit continues to ask, "Should we make special ads for women?" Perhaps that's why some foreign cars still have a disproportionate share of the U.S. women's market.

· In the *Ms.* Gazette, we do a brief report on a congressional hearing   23 into chemicals used in hair dyes that are absorbed through the skin and may be carcinogenic. Newspapers report this too, but Clairol, a Bristol-Myers subsidiary that makes dozens of products—a few of which have just begun to advertise in *Ms.*—is outraged. Not at newspapers or news-magazines, just at us. It's bad enough that *Ms.* is the only women's magazine refusing to provide the usual "complementary" articles and beauty photos, but to criticize one of their categories—*that* is going too far.

We offer to publish a letter from Clairol telling its side of the story. In   24
an excess of solicitousness, we even put this letter in the Gazette, not in Letters to the Editors where it belongs. Nonetheless—and in spite of surveys that show *Ms.* readers are active women who use more of almost everything Clairol makes than do the readers of any other women's maga-zine—*Ms.* gets almost none of these ads for the rest of its natural life.

Meanwhile, Clairol changes its hair coloring formula, apparently in   25
response to the hearings we reported.

• Our saleswomen set out early to attract ads for consumer electronics: 26
sound equipment, calculators, computers, VCRs, and the like. We know that our readers are determined to be included in the technological revolu-tion. We know from reader surveys that *Ms.* readers are buying this stuff in numbers as high as those of magazines like *Playboy*; or "men 18 to 34," the prime targets of the consumer electronics industry. Moreover, unlike traditional women's products that our readers buy but don't need to read articles about, these are subjects they want covered in our pages. There actually *is* a supportive editorial atmosphere.

"But women don't understand technology," say executives at the end   27
of ad presentations. "Maybe not," we respond, "but neither do men—and we all buy it."

"If women *do* buy it," say the decision-makers, "they're asking their   28
husbands and boyfriends what to buy first." We produce letters from *Ms.* readers saying how turned off they are when salesmen say things like "Let me know when your husband can come in."

After several years of this, we get a few ads for compact sound sys-   29
tems. Some of them come from JVC, whose vice president, Harry Elias, is trying to convince his Japanese bosses that there is something called a women's market. At his invitation, I find myself speaking at huge trade shows in Chicago and Las Vegas, trying to persuade JVC dealers that showrooms don't have to be locker rooms where women are made to feel unwelcome. But as it turns out, the shows themselves are part of the problem. In Las Vegas, the only women around the technology displays are seminude models serving champagne. In Chicago, the big attraction is Marilyn Chambers, who followed Linda Lovelace of *Deep Throat* fame as Chuck Traynor's captive and/or employee. VCRs are being demon-strated with her porn videos.

In the end, we get ads for a car stereo now and then, but no VCRs;   30
some IBM personal computers, but no Apple or Japanese ones. We no-

tice that office magazines like *Working Woman* and *Savvy* don't benefit as much as they should from office equipment ads either. In the electronics world, women and technology seem mutually exclusive. It remains a decade behind even Detroit.

• Because we get letters from little girls who love toy trains, and who   31 ask our help in changing ads and box-top photos that feature little boys only, we try to get toy-train ads from Lionel. It turns out that Lionel executives *have* been concerned about little girls. They made a pink train, and were surprised when it didn't sell.

Lionel bows to consumer pressure with a photograph of a boy *and* a   32 girl—but only on some of their boxes. They fear that, if trains are associated with girls, they will be devalued in the minds of boys. Needless to say, *Ms.* gets no train ads, and little girls remain a mostly unexplored market. By 1986, Lionel is put up for sale.

But for different reasons, we haven't had much luck with other kinds   33 of toys either. In spite of many articles on child-rearing; an annual listing of nonsexist, multiracial toys by Letty Cottin Pogrebin; Stories for Free Children, a regular feature also edited by Letty; and other prizewinning features for or about children, we get virtually no toy ads. Generations of *Ms.* saleswomen explain to toy manufacturers that a larger proportion of *Ms.* readers have preschool children than do the readers of other women's magazines, but this industry can't believe feminists have or care about children.

• When *Ms.* begins, the staff decides not to accept ads for feminine   34 hygiene sprays or cigarettes: they are damaging and carry no appropriate health warnings. Though we don't think we should tell our readers what to do, we do think we should provide facts so they can decide for themselves. Since the antismoking lobby has been pressing for health warnings on cigarette ads, we decide to take them only as they comply.

Philip Morris is among the first to do so. One of its brands, Virginia   35 Slims, is also sponsoring women's tennis and the first national polls of women's opinions. On the other hand, the Virginia Slims theme, "You've come a long way, baby," has more than a "baby" problem. It makes smoking a symbol of progress for women.

We explain to Philip Morris that this slogan won't do well in our   36 pages, but they are convinced its success with some women means it will work with *all* women. Finally, we agree to publish an ad for a Virginia Slims calendar as a test. The letters from readers are critical—and smart. For instance: Would you show a black man picking cotton, the same man in a Cardin suit, and symbolize the antislavery and civil rights movements by smoking? Of course not. But instead of honoring the test results, the Philip Morris people seem angry to be proven wrong. They take away ads for *all* their many brands.

This costs *Ms.* about $250,000 the first year. After five years, we can   37 no longer keep track. Occasionally, a new set of executives listens to *Ms.*

saleswomen, but because we won't take Virginia Slims, not one Philip Morris product returns to our pages for the next 16 years.

Gradually, we also realize our naiveté in thinking we *could* decide   38 against taking cigarette ads. They became a disproportionate support of magazines the moment they were banned on television, and few magazines could compete and survive without them; certainly not *Ms.*, which lacks so many other categories. By the time statistics in the 1980s showed that women's rate of lung cancer was approaching men's, the necessity of taking cigarette ads has become a kind of prison.

• General Mills, Pillsbury, Carnation, DelMonte, Dole, Kraft,   39 Stouffer, Hormel, Nabisco: you name the food giant, we try it. But no matter how desirable the *Ms.* readership, our lack of recipes is lethal.

We explain to them that placing food ads *only* next to recipes associ-   40 ates food with work. For many women, it is a negative that works *against* the ads. Why not place food ads in diverse media without recipes (thus reaching more men, who are now a third of the shoppers in supermarkets anyway), and leave the recipes to specialty magazines like *Gourmet* (a third of whose readers are also men)?

These arguments elicit interest, but except for an occasional ad for a   41 convenience food, instant coffee, diet drinks, yogurt, or such extras as avocados and almonds, this mainstay of the publishing industry stays closed to us. Period.

• Traditionally, wines and liquors didn't advertise to women: men   42 were thought to make the brand decisions, even if women did the buying. But after endless presentations, we begin to make a dent in this category. Thanks to the unconventional Michel Roux of Carillon Importers (distributors of Grand Marnier, Absolut Vodka, and others), who assumes that food and drink have no gender, some ads are leaving their men's club.

Beermakers are still selling masculinity. It takes *Ms.* fully eight years   43 to get its first beer ad (Michelob). In general, however, liquor ads are less stereotyped in their imagery—and far less controlling of the editorial content around them—than are women's products. But given the underrepresentation of other categories, these very facts tend to create a disproportionate number of alcohol ads in the pages of *Ms.* This in turn dismays readers worried about women and alcoholism.

• We hear in 1980 that women in the Soviet Union have been produc-   44 ing feminist *samizdat* (underground, self-published books) and circulating them throughout the country. As punishment, four of the leaders have been exiled. Though we are operating on our usual shoestring, we solicit individual contributions to send Robin Morgan to interview these women in Vienna.

The result is an exclusive cover story that includes the first news of a   45 populist peace movement against the Afghanistan occupation, a prediction of *glasnost* to come, and a grass-roots, intimate view of Soviet women's lives. From the popular press to women's studies courses, the response is great. The story wins a Front Page award.

Nonetheless, this journalistic coup undoes years of efforts to get an ad   46
schedule from Revlon. Why? Because the Soviet women on our cover *are not wearing makeup*. . . .

• Four years of research and presentations go into convincing airlines   47
that women now make travel choices and business trips. United, the first airline to advertise in *Ms*., is so impressed with the response from our readers that one of its executives appears in a film for our ad presentations. As usual, good ads get great results.

But we have problems unrelated to such results. For instance: because   48
American Airlines flight attendants include among their labor demands the stipulation that they could choose to have their last names preceded by "Ms." on their name tags—in a long-delayed revolt against the standard, "I am your pilot, Captain Rothgart, and this is your flight attendant, Cindy Sue"—American officials seem to hold the magazine responsible. We get no ads.

There is still a different problem at Eastern. A vice president cancels   49
subscriptions for thousands of copies on Eastern flights. Why? Because he is offended by ads for lesbian poetry journals in the *Ms*. Classified. A "family airline," as he explains to me coldly on the phone, has to "draw the line somewhere."

It's obvious that *Ms*. can't exclude lesbians and serve women. We've   50
been trying to make that point ever since our first issue included an article by and about lesbians, and both Suzanne Levine, our managing editor, and I were lectured by such heavy hitters as Ed Kosner, then editor of *Newsweek* (and now of *New York Magazine*), who insisted that *Ms*. should "position" itself *against* lesbians. But our advertisers have paid to reach a guaranteed number of readers, and soliciting new subscriptions to compensate for Eastern would cost $150,000, plus rebating money in the meantime.

Like almost everything ad-related, this presents an elaborate organiz-   51
ing problem. After days of searching for sympathetic members of the Eastern board, Frank Thomas, president of the Ford Foundation, kindly offers to call Roswell Gilpatrick, a director of Eastern. I talk with Mr. Gilpatrick, who calls Frank Borman, then the president of Eastern. Frank Borman calls me to say that his airline is not in the business of censoring magazines: *Ms*. will be returned to Eastern flights. . . .

• Women's access to insurance and credit is vital, but with the excep-   52
tion of Equitable and a few other ad pioneers, such financial services address men. For almost a decade after the Equal Credit Opportunity Act passes in 1974, we try to convince American Express that women are a growth market—but nothing works.

Finally, a former professor of Russian named Jerry Welsh becomes   53
head of marketing. He assumes that women should be cardholders, and

persuades his colleagues to feature women in a campaign. Thanks to this 1980s series, the growth rate for female cardholders surpasses that for men.

For this article, I asked Jerry Welsh if he would explain why American Express waited so long. "Sure," he said, "they were afraid of having a 'pink' card." 54

• Women of color read *Ms.* in disproportionate numbers. This is a source of pride to *Ms.* staffers, who are also more racially representative than the editors of other women's magazines. But this reality is obscured by ads filled with enough white women to make a reader snowblind. 55

Pat Carbine remembers mostly "astonishment" when she requested African American, Hispanic, Asian, and other diverse images. Marcia Ann Gillespie, a *Ms.* editor who was previously the editor in chief of *Essence*, witnesses ad bias a second time: having tried for *Essence* to get white advertisers to use black images (Revlon did so eventually, but L'Oréal, Lauder, Chanel, and other companies never did), she sees similar problems getting integrated ads for an integrated magazine. Indeed, the ad world often creates black and Hispanic ads only for black and Hispanic media. In an exact parallel of the fear that marketing a product to women will endanger its appeal to men, the response is usually, "But your [white] readers won't identify." 56

In fact, those we are able to get—for instance, a Max Factor ad made for *Essence* that Linda Wachner gives us after she becomes president—are praised by white readers, too. But there are pathetically few such images. 57

• By the end of 1986, production and mailing costs have risen astronomically, ad income is flat, and competition for ads is stiffer than ever. The 60/40 preponderance of edit over ads that we promised to readers becomes 50/50; children's stories, most poetry, and some fiction are causalities of less space, in order to get variety into limited pages, the length (and sometimes the depth) of articles suffers; and, though we do refuse most of the ads that would look like a parody in our pages, we get so worn down that some slip through. . . . Still, readers perform miracles. Though we haven't been able to afford a subscription mailing in two years, they maintain our guaranteed circulation of 450,000. . . . 58

In November 1987, by vote of the Ms. Foundation for Education and Communication (*Ms.*'s owner and publisher, the media subsidiary of the Ms. Foundation for Women), *Ms.* was sold to a company whose officers, Australian feminists Sandra Yates and Anne Summers, raised the investment money in their country that *Ms.* couldn't find in its own. They also started *Sassy* for teenage women. 59

In their two-year tenure, circulation was raised to 550,000 by investment in circulation mailings, and, to the dismay of some readers, editorial features on clothes and new products made a more traditional bid 60 for ads. Nonetheless, ad pages fell below previous levels. In addition, *Sassy*, whose fresh voice and sexual frankness were an unprecedented success with young readers, was targeted by two mothers from Indiana who began, as one of them put it, "calling every Christian organization I could think of." In response to this controversy, several crucial advertisers pulled out.

Such links between ads and editorial content was a problem in Australia, too, but to a lesser degree. "Our readers pay two times more for their magazines," Anne explained, "so advertisers have less power to threaten a magazine's viability."   61

"I was shocked," said Sandra Yates with characteristic directness. "In Australia, we think you have freedom of the press—but you don't."   62

Since Anne and Sandra had not met their budget's projections for ad revenue, their investors forced a sale. In October 1989, *Ms.* and *Sassy* were bought by Dale Lang, owner of *Working Mother, Working Woman*, and one of the few independent publishing companies left among the conglomerates. In response to a request from the original *Ms.* staff—as well as to reader letters urging that *Ms.* continue, plus his own belief that *Ms.* would benefit his other magazines by blazing a trail—he agreed to try the ad-free, reader-supported *Ms.* you hold now and to give us complete editorial control. . . .   63

II.

In recent years, advertisers' control over the editorial content of women's magazines has become so institutionalized that it is written into "insertion orders" or dictated to ad salespeople as official policy. The following are recent typical orders to women's magazines: 64

• Dow's Cleaning Products stipulates that ads for its Vivid and Spray 'n Wash products should be adjacent to "children or fashion editorial"; ads for Bathroom Cleaner should be next to "home furnishing/family" features; and so on for other brands. "If a magazine fails for 1/2 the brands or more," the Dow order warns, "it will be omitted from further consideration."   65

• Bristol-Myers, the parent of Clairol, Windex, Drano, Bufferin, and much more, stipulates that ads be placed next to "a full page of compatible editorial."   66

• S.C. Johnson & Son, makers of Johnson Wax, lawn and laundry products, insect sprays, hair sprays, and so on, orders that its ads *"should not be opposite extremely controversial features or material antithetical to the nature/copy of the advertised product."* (Italics theirs.)   67

• Maidenform, manufacturer of bras and other apparel, leaves a blank for the particular product and states: "The creative concept of the _____ campaign, and the very nature of the product itself appeal to the positive   68 emotions of the reader/consumer. Therefore, it is imperative that all editorial adjacencies reflect that same positive tone. The editorial must not be negative in content or lend itself contrary to the _____ product imagery/message (e.g., *editorial relating to illness, disillusionment, large size fashion, etc.*)." (Italics mine.)

• The De Beers diamond company, a big seller of engagement rings, prohibits magazines from placing its ads with "adjacencies to hard news or anti/love-romance themed editorial."   69

• Procter & Gamble, one of this country's most powerful and diversified advertisers, stands out in the memory of Anne Summers and Sandra Yates (no mean feat in this context): its products were not to be placed in *any* issue that included *any* material on gun control, abortion, the occult, cults, or the disparagement of religion. Caution was also demanded in any issue covering sex or drugs, even for educational purposes.   70

Those are the most obvious chains around women's magazines. There are also rules so clear they needn't be written down: for instance, an overall "look" compatible with beauty and fashion ads. Even "real" non-model women photographed for a woman's magazine are usually made up, dressed in credited clothes, and retouched out of all reality. When editors do include articles on less-than-cheerful subjects (for instance, domestic violence), they tend to keep them short and unillustrated. The point is to be "upbeat." Just as women in the street are asked, "Why don't you smile, honey?" women's magazines acquire an institutional smile.   71

Within the text itself, praise for advertisers' products has become so ritualized that fields like "beauty writing" have been invented. One of its frequent practitioners explained seriously that "It's a difficult art. How many new adjectives can you find? How much greater can you make a lipstick sound? The FDA restricts what companies can say on labels, but we create illusion. And ad agencies are on the phone all the time pushing you to get their product in. A lot of them keep the business based on how many editorial clippings they produce every month. The worst are products," like Lauder's as the writer confirmed, "with their own name involved. It's all ego."   72

Often, editorial becomes one giant ad. Last November, for instance, *Lear's* featured an elegant woman executive on the cover. On the contents page, we learned she was wearing Guerlain makeup and Samsara, a new fragrance by Guerlain. Inside were full-page ads for Samsara and Guerlain antiwrinkle cream. In the cover profile, we learned that this executive was responsible for launching Samsara and is Guerlain's director of public relations. When the *Columbia Journalism Review* did one of the few articles to include women's magazines in coverage of the influence of ads, editor Frances Lear was quoted as defending her magazine because "this kind of thing is done all the time."   73

Often, advertisers also plunge odd-shaped ads into the text, no matter   74
what the cost to the readers. At *Woman's Day*, a magazine originally
founded by a supermarket chain, editor in chief Ellen Levine said, "The
day the copy had to rag around a chicken leg was not a happy one."

Advertisers are also adamant about where in a magazine their ads   75
appear. When Revlon was not placed as the first beauty ad in one Hearst
magazine, for instance, Revlon pulled its ads from *all* Hearst magazines.
Ruth Whitney, editor in chief of *Glamour*, attributes some of these demands to "ad agencies wanting to prove to a client that they've squeezed
the last drop of blood out of a magazine." She also is, she says, "sick and
tired of hearing that women's magazines are controlled by cigarette ads."
Relatively speaking, she's right. To be as censoring as are many advertisers for women's products, tobacco companies would have to demand
articles in praise of smoking and expect glamorous photos of beautiful
women smoking their brands.

I don't mean to imply that the editors I quote here share my objec-   76
tions to ads: most assume that women's magazines have to be the way
they are. But it's also true that only former editors can be completely
honest. "Most of the pressure came in the form of direct product mentions," explains Sey Chassler, who was editor in chief of *Redbook* from
the sixties to the eighties. "We got threats from the big guys, the Re-
vlons, blackmail threats. They wouldn't run ads unless we credited them.

"But it's not fair to single out the beauty advertisers because these   77
pressures came from everybody. Advertisers want to know two things:
What are you going to charge me? What *else* are you going to do for me?
It's a holdup. For instance, management felt that fiction took up too
much space. They couldn't put any advertising in that. For the last ten
years, the number of fiction entries into the National Magazine Awards
has declined.

"And pressures are getting worse. More magazines are more bottom-   78
line oriented because they have been taken over by companies with no
interest in publishing.

"I also think advertisers do this to women's magazines especially," he   79
concluded, "because of the general disrespect they have for women." . . .

III.

It's almost three years away from life between the grindstones of adver-   80
tising pressures and readers' needs. I'm just beginning to realize how
edges got smoothed down—in spite of all our resistance.

I remember feeling put upon when I changed "Porsche" to "car" in a   81
piece about Nazi imagery in German pornography by Andrea Dworkin—
feeling sure Andrea would understand that Volkswagen, the distributor of
Porsche and one of our few supportive advertisers, asked only to be far

away from Nazi subjects. It's taken me all this time to realize that Andrea was the one with a right to feel put upon.

Even as I write this, I get a call from a writer for *Elle*, who is doing a whole article on where women part their hair. Why, she wants to know, do I part mine in the middle?   82

It's all so familiar. A writer trying to make something of a nothing assignment; an editor laboring to think of new ways to attract ads; readers assuming that other women must want this ridiculous stuff; more women suffering for lack of information, insight, creativity, and laughter that could be on these same pages.   83

I ask you: Can't we do better than this?   84

QUESTIONS ON CONTENT

1. How, according to Steinem, does advertising control the press in America?

2. Why did *Ms.* take ads when first starting out? In retrospect, do you think Steinem would agree that they were perhaps a bit idealistic? Explain.

3. Steinem thinks very highly of Patricia Carbine. What was it that Carbine did that first impressed Steinem? What did Carbine's actions say about her character? Explain.

4. Why do advertisers insist on determining where their ads appear within a magazine? Why are some positions more favorable or desirable than others? Explain.

5. What does Steinem mean when she says that women's magazines acquired "an institutional smile"? Why does she object to this state of affairs?

QUESTIONS ON RHETORIC

1. What is Steinem's thesis, and where is it stated? (Glossary: *Thesis*)

2. How effective is Steinem's title as a title? (Glossary: *Title*) How is her title related, if at all, to her thesis?

3. Steinem's first six paragraphs serve as the introduction to her essay. Specifically, how do these paragraphs "introduce" the essay? (Glossary: *Beginnings*)

4. How has Steinem organized her essay? (Glossary: *Organization*) Identify the major sections of the essay, and explain how they are related to each other. You may find it helpful to make a scratch outline in answering this question.

5. How does Steinem support her claim that "advertisers' control over editorial content of women's magazines has become so institutionalized that it is written into 'insertion orders' or dictated to ad salespeople as official policy" (64)? (Glossary: *Examples*)

6. How would you describe Steinem's tone in this essay? (Glossary: *Tone*) Is her tone appropriate for both her subject and her audience? Is it true that "only former editors can be completely honest" (76)? Explain.

VOCABULARY

glasnost (1)	documentation (20)	integrated (56)
anecdotes (1)	saga (21)	preponderance (58)
euphemistically (5)	naiveté (38)	parody (58)
aesthetic (14)	lethal (39)	tenure (60)
omen (15)	elicit (41)	ritualized (72)
unsentimental (17)	solicit (44)	adamant (75)

WRITING TOPICS

1. Select a popular women's magazine (*Redbook, Cosmopolitan, Vogue, Better Homes and Gardens, Ebony, Glamour*) from your newsstand and analyze the advertisements that it contains. What kinds of products are being advertised? Are the ads themselves primarily visual, or is there a large print component in many? Is there any relationship between advertising and editorial content? How does your analysis compare with that of Steinem? Were there any surprises in your study? Write an essay in which you present the findings of your analysis.

2. Write an essay in which you compare and contrast the advertisements appearing in a popular news magazine with those in a leading women's magazine. What are the most striking similarities? differences? What conclusions about magazine advertising in America can you draw from your comparison?

ADVERTISING'S FIFTEEN BASIC APPEALS

Jib Fowles

Jib Fowles, instructor of advertising and mass media at the University of Houston, discusses the basic emotions appealed to in advertisements. Fowles suggests it is no accident that the list parallels a "hierarchy of needs" described by several leading psychologists. The following article was published in Etc. *a magazine of general semantics, focusing on how words and their meanings influence the behavior of society.*

EMOTIONAL APPEALS

The nature of effective advertisements was recognized full well by the late media philosopher Marshall McLuhan. In his *Understanding Media*, the first sentence of the section on advertising reads, "The continuous pressure is to create ads more and more in the image of audience motives and desires." 1

By giving form to people's deep-lying desires, and picturing states of being that individuals privately yearn for, advertisers have the best chance of arresting attention and affecting communication. And that is the immediate goal of advertising: to tug at our psychological shirt sleeves and slow us down long enough for a word or two about whatever is being sold. We glance at a picture of a solitary rancher at work, and "Marlboro" slips into our minds. 2

Advertisers (I'm using the term as a shorthand for both the products' manufacturers, who bring the ambition and money to the process, and the advertising agencies, who supply the know-how) are ever more compelled to invoke consumers' drives and longings; this is the "continuous pressure" McLuhan refers to. Over the past century, the American marketplace has grown increasingly congested as more and more products have entered into the frenzied competition after the public's dollars. The economies of other nations are quieter than ours since the volume of goods being hawked does not so greatly exceed demand. In some economies, consumer wares are scarce enough that no advertising at all is necessary. But in the United States, we go to the other extreme. In order to stay in business, and advertiser must strive to cut through the considerable commercial hub-bub by any means available—including the emotional appeals that some observers have held to be abhorrent and underhanded. 3

The use of subconscious appeals is a comment not only on conditions 4

231

among sellers. As time has gone by, buyers have become stoutly resistant to advertisements. We live in a blizzard of these messages and have learned to turn up our collars and ward off most of them. A study done a few years ago at Harvard University's Graduate School of Business Administration ventured that the average American is exposed to some 500 ads daily from television, newspapers, magazines, radio, billboards, direct mail, and so on. If for no other reason than to preserve one's sanity, a filter must be developed in every mind to lower the number of ads a person is actually aware of—a number this particular study estimated at about seventy-five ads per day. (Of these, only twelve typically produced a reaction—nine positive and three negative, on the average.) To be among the few messages that do manage to gain access to minds, advertisers must be strategic, perhaps even a little underhanded at times.

There are assumptions about personality underlying advertisers' efforts to communicate via emotional appeals, and while these assumptions have stood the test of time, they still deserve to be aired. Human beings, it is presumed, walk around with a variety of unfulfilled urges and motives swirling in the bottom half of their minds. Lusts, ambitions, tendernesses, vulnerabilities—they are constantly bubbling up, seeking resolution. These mental forces energize people, but they are too crude and irregular to be given excessive play in the real world. They must be capped with the competent, sensible behavior that permits individuals to get along well in society. However, this upper layer of mental activity, shot through with caution and rationality, is not receptive to advertising's pitches. Advertisers want to circumvent this shell of consciousness if they can, and latch on to one of the lurching, subconscious drives.

In effect, advertisers over the years have blindly felt their way around the underside of the American psyche, and by trial and error have discovered the softest points of entree, the places where their messages have the greatest likelihood of getting by consumers' defenses. As McLuhan says elsewhere, "Gouging away at the surface of public sales resistance, the ad men are constantly breaking through into the *Alice in Wonderland* territory behind the looking glass, which is the world of subrational impulses and appetites."

An advertisement communicates by making use of a specially selected image (of a supine female, say, or a curly-headed child, or a celebrity) which is designed to stimulate "subrational impulses and desires" even when they are at ebb, even if they are unacknowledged by their possessor. Some few ads have their emotional appeal in the text, but for the greater number by far the appeal is contained in the artwork. This makes sense, since visual communication better suits more primal levels of the brain. If the viewer of an advertisement actually has the importuned motive, and if the appeal is sufficiently well-fashioned to call it up, then the person can be hooked. The product in the ad may then appear to take on the semblance of gratification for the summoned motive. Many ads seem to be saying, "If you have this need, then this product will help satisfy it." It is a primitive equation, but not an ineffective one for selling.

Thus, most advertisements appearing in national media can be understood as having two orders of content. The first is the appeal to deep-running drives in the minds of consumers. The second is information regarding the good[s] or service being sold: its name, its manufacturer, its picture, its packaging, its objective attributes, its functions. For example, the reader of a brassiere advertisement sees a partially undraped but blandly unperturbed woman standing in an otherwise commonplace public setting, and may experience certain sensations; the reader also sees the name "Maidenform," a particular brassiere style, and, in tiny print, words about the material, colors, price. Or, the viewer of a television commercial sees a demonstration with four small boxes labelled 650, 650, 650, and 800; something in the viewer's mind catches hold of this, as trivial as thoughtful consideration might reveal it to be. The viewer is also exposed to the name "Anacin," its bottle, and its purpose.

Sometimes there is an apparently logical link between an ad's emotional appeal and its product information. It does not violate common sense that Cadillac automobiles be photographed at country clubs, or that Japan Air Lines be associated with Orientalia. But there is no real need for the linkage to have a bit of reason behind it. Is there anything inherent to the connection between Salem cigarettes and mountains, Coke and a smile, Miller Beer and comradeship? The link being forged in minds between product and appeal is a pre-logical one.

People involved in the advertising industry do not necessarily talk in the terms being used here. They are stationed at the sending end of this communications channel, and may think they are up to any number of things—Unique Selling Propositions, explosive copywriting, the optimal use of demographics or psychographics, ideal media buys, high recall ratings, or whatever. But when attention shifts to the receiving end of the channel, and focuses on the instant of reception, then commentary becomes much more elemental: an advertising message contains something primary and primitive, an emotional appeal, that in effect is the thin end of the wedge, trying to find its way into a mind. Should this occur, the product information comes along behind.

When enough advertisements are examined in this light, it becomes clear that the emotional appeals fall into several distinguishable categories, and that every ad is a variation on one of a limited number of basic appeals. While there may be several ways of classifying these appeals, one particular list of fifteen has proven to be especially valuable.

Advertisements can appeal to:

1. The need for sex
2. The need for affiliation
3. The need to nurture
4. The need for guidance
5. The need to aggress
6. The need to achieve
7. The need to dominate
8. The need for prominence
9. The need for attention
10. The need for autonomy
11. The need to escape
12. The need to feel safe
13. The need for aesthetic sensations
14. The need to satisfy curiosity
15. Physiological needs: food, drink, sleep, etc.

MURRAY'S LIST

Where does this list of advertising's fifteen basic appeals come from? 12
Several years ago, I was involved in a research project which was to have
as one segment an objective analysis of the changing appeals made in
post–World War II American advertising. A sample of magazine ads
would have their appeals coded into the categories of psychological needs
they seemed aimed at. For this content analysis to happen, a complete
roster of human motives would have to be found.

The first thing that came to mind was Abraham Maslow's famous 13
four-part hierarchy of needs. But the briefest look at the range of appeals
made in advertising was enough to reveal that they are more varied, and
more profane, than Maslow had cared to account for. The search led on
to the work of psychologist Henry A. Murray, who together with his
colleagues at the Harvard Psychological Clinic had constructed a full tax-
onomy of needs. As described in *Explorations in Personality*, Murray's
team had conducted a lengthy series of in-depth interviews with a number
of subjects in order to derive from scratch what they felt to be the essential variables of personality. Forty-four variables were distinguished by
the Harvard group, of which twenty were motives. The need for achievement ("to overcome obstacles and obtain a high standard") was one, for
instance; the need to defer was another; the need to aggress was a third;
and so forth.

Murray's list had served as the groundwork for a number of subse- 14
quent projects. Perhaps the best-known of these was David C. McClelland's extensive study of the need for achievement, reported in his *The*

Achieving Society. In the process of demonstrating that a people's high need for achievement is predictive of later economic growth, McClelland coded achievement imagery and references out of a nation's folklore, songs, legends, and children's tales.

Following McClelland, I too wanted to cull the motivational appeals   15
from a culture's imaginative product—in this case, advertising. To develop categories expressly for this purpose, I took Murray's twenty motives and added to them others he had mentioned in passing in *Explorations in Personality* but not included on the final list. The extended list was tried out on a sample of advertisements, and motives which never seemed to be invoked were dropped. I ended up with eighteen of Murray's motives, into which 770 print ads were coded. The resulting distribution is included in the 1976 book *Mass Advertising as Social Forecast.*

Since that time, the list of appeals has undergone refinements as a   16
result of using it to analyze television commercials. A few more adjustments have stemmed from the efforts of students in my advertising classes to decode appeals; tens of term papers surveying thousands of advertisements have caused some inconsistencies in the list to be hammered out. Fundamentally, though, the list remains the creation of Henry Murray. In developing a comprehensive, parsimonious inventory of human motives, he pinpointed the subsurface mental forces that are the least quiescent and the most susceptible to advertising's entreaties.

FIFTEEN APPEALS

1. *Need for sex.* Let's start with sex, because this is the appeal which   17
seems to pop up first whenever the topic of advertising is raised. Whole books have been written about this one alone, to find a large audience of mildly titillated readers. Lately, due to campaigns to sell blue jeans, concern with sex in ads has redoubled.

The fascinating thing is not how much sex there is in advertising, but   18
how little. Contrary to impressions, unambiguous sex is rare in these messages. Some of this surprising observation may be a matter of definition: the Jordache ads with the lithe, blouse-less female astride a similarly clad male is clearly an appeal to the audience's sexual drives, but the same cannot be said about Brooke Shields in the Calvin Klein commercials. Directed at young women and their credit-card carrying mothers, the image of Miss Shields instead invokes the need to be looked at. Buy Calvins and you'll be the center of much attention, just as Brooke is, the ads imply; they do not primarily inveigle their target audience's need for sexual intercourse.

In the content analysis reported in *Mass Advertising as Social Fore-*   19
cast, only two percent of ads were found to pander to this motive. Even *Playboy* ads shy away from sexual appeals: a recent issue contained

eighty-three full-page ads, and just four of them (or less than five percent) could be said to have sex on their minds.

The reason this appeal is so little used is that it is too blaring and   20
tends to obliterate the product information. Nudity in advertising has the
effect of reducing brand recall. The people who do remember the product
may do so because they have been made indignant by the ad; this is not
the response most advertisers seek.

To the extent that sexual imagery is used, it conventionally works   21
better on men than women; typically a female figure is offered up to the
male reader. A Black Velvet liquor advertisement displays an attractive
woman wearing a tight black outfit, recumbent under the legend, "Feel
the Velvet." The figure does not have to be horizontal, however, for the
appeal to be present, as National Airlines revealed in its "Fly me" campaign. Indeed, there does not even have to be a female in the ad: "Flick
my Bic" was sufficient to convey the idea to many.

As a rule, though, advertisers have found sex to be a tricky appeal, to   22
be used sparingly. Less controversial and equally fetching are the appeals
to our need for affectionate human contact.

2. *Need for affiliation.* American mythology upholds autonomous in-   23
dividuals, and social statistics suggest that people are ever more going it
alone in their lives, yet the high frequency of affiliative appeals in ads
belies this. Or maybe it does not: maybe all the images of companionship
are compensation for what Americans privately lack. In any case, the
need to associate with others is widely invoked in advertising and is probably the most prevalent appeal. All sorts of goods and services are sold
by linking them to our unfulfilled desires to be in good company.

According to Henry Murray, the need for affiliation consists of de-   24
sires "to draw near and enjoyably cooperate or reciprocate with another;
to please and win affection of another; to adhere and remain loyal to a
friend." The manifestations of this motive can be segmented into several
different types of affiliation, beginning with romance.

Courtship may be swifter nowadays, but the desire for pair-bonding is   25
far from satiated. Ads reaching for this need commonly depict a youngish
male and female engrossed in each other. The head of the male is usually
higher than the female's, even at this late date; she may be sitting or
leaning while he is standing. They are not touching in the Smirnoff vodka
ads, but obviously there is an intimacy, sometimes frolicsome, between
them. The couple does touch for Martell Cognac when "The moment was
Martell." For Wind Song perfume they have touched, and "Your Wind
Song stays on his mind."

Depending on the audience, the pair does not absolutely have to be   26
young—just together. He gives her a DeBeers diamond, and there is a
tear in her laugh lines. She takes Geritol and preserves herself for him.
And numbers of consumers, wanting affection too, follow suit.

Warm family feelings are fanned in ads when another generation is   27 added to the pair. Hallmark Cards brings grandparents into the picture, and Johnson and Johnson Baby Powder has Dad, Mom, and baby, all fresh from the bath, encircled in arms and emblazoned with "Share the Feeling." A talc has been fused to familial love.

Friendship is yet another form of affiliation pursued by advertisers. Two women confide and drink Maxwell House coffee together; two men walk through the woods smoking Salem cigarettes. Miller Beer promises that afternoon "Miller Time" will be staffed with three or four good buddies. Drink Dr. Pepper, as Mickey Rooney is coaxed to do, and join in with all the other Peppers. Coca-Cola does not even need to portray the friendliness; it has reduced this appeal to "a Coke and a smile." 28

The warmth can be toned down and disguised, but it is the same affiliative need that is being fished for. The blonde has a direct gaze and her friends are firm businessmen in appearance, but with a glass of Old Bushmill you can sit down and fit right in. Or, for something more upbeat, sing along with the Pontiac choirboys. 29

As well as presenting positive images, advertisers can play to the need for affiliation in negative ways, by invoking the fear of rejection. If we don't use Scope, we'll have the "Ugh! Morning Breath" that causes the male and female models to avert their faces. Unless we apply Ultra-Brite or Close-Up to our teeth, it's good-bye romance. Our family will be cursed with "House-a-tosis" if we don't take care. Without Dr. Scholl's antiperspirant foot spray, the bowling team will keel over. There go all the guests when the supply of Dorito's nacho cheese chips is exhausted. Still more rejection if our shirts have ring-around-the-collar, if our car needs to be Midasized. But make a few purchases, and we are back in the bosom of human contact. 30

As self-directed as Americans pretend to be, in the last analysis we remain social animals, hungering for the positive, endorsing feelings that only those around us can supply. Advertisers respond, urging us to "Reach out and touch someone," in the hopes our monthly bills will rise. 31

3. *Need to nurture*. Akin to affiliative needs is the need to take care of small, defenseless creatures—children and pets, largely. Reciprocity is of less consequence here, though; it is the giving that counts. Murray uses synonyms like "to feed, help, support, console, protect, comfort, nurse, heal." A strong need it is, woven deep into our genetic fabric, for if it did not exist we could not successfully raise up our replacements. When advertisers put forth the image of something diminutive and furry, something that elicits the word "cute" or "precious," then they are trying to trigger this motive. We listen to the childish voice singing the Oscar Mayer weiner song, and our next hot-dog purchase is prescribed. Aren't those darling kittens something, and how did this Meow Mix get into our shopping cart? 32

This pitch is often directed at women, as Mother Nature's chief nurturers. "Make me some Kraft macaroni and cheese, please," says the 33 elfin preschooler just in from the snowstorm, and mothers' hearts go out, and Kraft's sales go up. "We're cold, wet, and hungry," whine the husband and kids, and the little woman gets the Manwiches ready. A facsimile of this need can be hit without children or pets: the husband is ill and sleepless in the television commercial, and the wife grudgingly fetches the NyQuil.

But it is not women alone who can be touched by this appeal. The   34
father nurses his son Eddie through adolescence while the John Deere lawn tractor survives the years. Another father counts pennies with his young son as the subject of New York Life Insurance comes up. And all over America are businessmen who don't know why they dial Qantas Airlines when they have to take a trans-Pacific trip; the koala bear knows.

4. *Need for guidance.* The opposite of the need to nurture is the need   35
to be nurtured: to be protected, shielded, guided. We may be loath to admit it, but the child lingers on inside every adult—and a good thing it does, or we would not be instructable in our advancing years. Who wants a nation of nothing but flinty personalities?

Parent-like figures can successfully call up this need. Robert Young   36
recommends Sanka coffee, and since we have experienced him for twenty-five years as television father and doctor, we take his word for it. Florence Henderson as the expert mom knows a lot about the advantages of Wesson oil.

The parent-ness of the spokesperson need not be so salient; sometimes   37
pure authoritativeness is better. When Orson Welles scowls and intones, "Paul Masson will sell no wine before its time," we may not know exactly what he means, but we still take direction from him. There is little maternal about Brenda Vaccaro when she speaks up for Tampax, but there is a certainty to her that many accept.

A celebrity is not a necessity in making a pitch to the need for guid-   38
ance, since a fantasy figure can serve just as well. People accede to the Green Giant, or Betty Crocker, or Mr. Goodwrench. Some advertisers can get by with no figure at all: "When E.F. Hutton talks, people listen."

Often it is tradition or custom that advertisers point to and consumers   39
take guidance from. Bits and pieces of American history are used to sell whiskeys like Old Crow, Southern Comfort, Jack Daniels. We conform to traditional male/female roles and age-old social norms when we purchase Barclay cigarettes, which informs us "The pleasure is back."

The product itself, if it has been around for a long time, can constitute   40
a tradition. All those old labels in the ad for Morton salt convince us that we should continue to buy it. Kool-Aid says, "You loved it as a kid. You trust it as a mother," hoping to get yet more consumers to go along.

Even when the product has no history at all, our need to conform to   41
tradition and to be guided are strong enough that they can be invoked through bogus nostalgia and older actors. Country-Time lemonade sells because consumers want to believe it has a past they can defer to.

So far the needs and the ways they can be invoked which have been   42
looked at are largely warm and affiliative; they stand in contrast to the
next set of needs, which are much more egoistic and assertive.

5. *Need to aggress.* The pressures of the real world create strong   43
retaliatory feelings in every functioning human being. Since these impulses can come forth as bursts of anger and violence, their display is
normally tabooed. Existing as harbored energy, aggressive drives present
a large, tempting target for advertisers. It is not a target to be aimed at
thoughtlessly, though, for few manufacturers want their products associated with destructive motives. There is always the danger that, as in the
case of sex, if the appeal is too blatant, public opinion will turn against
what is being sold.

Jack-in-the-Box sought to abruptly alter its marketing by going after   44
older customers and forgetting the younger ones. Their television commercials had a seventy-ish lady command, "Waste him," and the Jack-in-
the-Box clown exploded before our eyes. So did public reaction, until the
commercials were toned down. Print ads for Club cocktails carried the
faces of octogenarians under the headline, "Hit me with a Club"; response was contrary enough to bring the campaign to a stop.

Better disguised aggressive appeals are less likely to backfire: Tri-   45
umph cigarettes has models making a lewd gesture with their uplifted
cigarettes, but the individuals are often laughing and usually in the close
company of others. When Exxon said, "There's a Tiger in your tank," the
implausibility of it concealed the invocation of aggressive feelings.

Depicted arguments are a common way for advertisers to tap the audi-   46
ence's needs to aggress. Don Rickles and Lynda Carter trade gibes, and
consumers take sides as the name of Seven-Up is stitched on minds. The
Parkay tub has a difference of opinion with the user; who can forget it, or
who (or what) got the last word in?

6. *Need to achieve.* This is the drive that energizes people, causing   47
them to strive in their lives and careers. According to Murray, the need
for achievement is signalled by the desires "to accomplish something difficult. To overcome obstacles and attain a high standard. To excel one's
self. To rival and surpass others." A prominent American trait, it is one
that advertisers like to hook on to because it identifies their product with
winning and success.

The Cutty Sark ad does not disclose that Ted Turner failed at his   48
latest attempt at yachting's America Cup; here he is represented as a
champion on the water as well as off in his television enterprises. If we
drink this whiskey, we will be victorious alongside Turner. We can also
succeed with O.J. Simpson by renting Hertz cars, or with Reggie Jackson
by bringing home some Panasonic equipment. Cathy Rigby and Stayfree
Maxipads will put people out front.

Sports heroes are the most convenient means to snare consumers'   49
needs to achieve, but they are not the only one. Role models can be

established, ones which invite emulation, as with the profiles put forth by
Dewar's scotch. Successful, tweedy individuals relate they have "graduated to the flavor of Myer's rum." Or the advertiser can establish a prize:
two neighbors play one-on-one basketball for a Michelob beer in a television commercial, while in a print ad a bottle of Johnnie Walker Black
Label has been gilded like a trophy.

Any product that advertises itself in superlatives—the best, the first,   50
the finest—is trying to make contact with our needs to succeed. For
many consumers, sales and bargains belong in this category of appeals,
too; the person who manages to buy something at fifty percent off is
seizing an opportunity and coming out ahead of others.

7. *Need to dominate.* This fundamental need is the craving to be   51
powerful—perhaps omnipotent, as in the Xerox ad where Brother
Dominic exhibits heavenly powers and creates miraculous copies. Most
of us will settle for being just a regular potentate, though. We drink
Budweiser because it is the King of Beers, and here come the powerful
Clydesdales to prove it. A taste of Wolfschmidt vodka and "The spirit of
the Czar lives on."

The need to dominate and control one's environment is often thought   52
of as being masculine, but as close students of human nature advertisers
know, it is not so circumscribed. Women's aspirations for control are
suggested in the campaign theme, "I like my men in English Leather, or
nothing at all." The females in the Chanel No. 19 ads are "outspoken"
and wrestle their men around.

Male and female, what we long for is clout; what we get in its place   53
is Mastercard.

8. *Need for prominence.* Here comes the need to be admired and   54
respected, to enjoy prestige and high social status. These times, it appears, are not so egalitarian after all. Many ads picture the trappings of
high position; the Oldsmobile stands before a manorial doorway, the
Volvo is parked beside a steeplechase. A book-lined study is the setting
for Dewar's 12, and Lenox China is displayed in a dining room chock
full of antiques.

Beefeater gin represents itself as "The Crown Jewel of England" and   55
uses no illustrations of jewels or things British, for the words are sufficient indicators of distinction. Buy that gin and you will rise up the prestige hierarchy, or achieve the same effect on yourself with Seagram's 7
Crown, which unambiguously describes itself as "classy."

Being respected does not have to entail the usual accoutrements of   56
wealth: "Do you know who I am?" the commercials ask, and we learn
that the prominent person is not so prominent without his American Express card.

9. *Need for attention.* The previous need involved being *looked up to*,   57
while this is the need to be *looked at.* The desire to exhibit ourselves in
such a way as to make others look at us is a primitive, insuppressible

instinct. The clothing and cosmetic industries exist just to serve this need, and this is the way they pitch their wares. Some of this effort is aimed at males, as the ads for Hathaway shirts and Jockey underclothes. But the greater bulk of such appeals is targeted singlemindedly at women.

To come back to Brooke Shields: this is where she fits into American marketing. If I buy Calvin Klein jeans, consumers infer, I'll be the object of fascination. The desire for exhibition has been most strikingly played to in a print campaign of many years duration, that of Maidenform lingerie. The woman exposes herself, and sales surge. "Gentlemen prefer Hanes" the ads dissemble, and women who want eyes upon them know what they should do. Peggy Fleming flutters her legs for L'eggs, encouraging females who want to be the star in their own lives to purchase this product.

The same appeal works for cosmetics and lotions. For years, the little girl with the exposed backside sold gobs of Coppertone, but now the company has picked up the pace a little: as a female, you are supposed to "Flash 'em a Coppertone tan." Food can be sold the same way, especially to the diet-conscious; Angie Dickinson poses for California avocadoes and says, "Would this body lie to you?" Our eyes are too fixed on her for us to think to ask if she got that way by eating mounds of guacamole.

10. *Need for autonomy.* There are several ways to sell credit card services, as has been noted: Mastercard appeals to the need to dominate, and American Express to the need for prominence. When Visa claims, "You can have it the way you want it," yet another primary motive is being beckoned forward—the need to endorse the self. The focus here is upon the independence and integrity of the individual; this need is the antithesis of the need for guidance and is unlike any of the social needs. "If running with the herd isn't your style, try ours," says Rotan-Mosle, and many Americans feel they have finally found the right brokerage firm.

The photo is of a red-coated Mountie on his horse, posed on a snow-covered ledge; the copy reads, "Windsor—One Canadian stands alone." This epitome of the solitary and proud individual may work best with male customers, as may Winston's man in the red cap. But one-figure advertisements also strike the strong need for autonomy among American women. As Shelly Hack strides for Charlie perfume, females respond to her obvious pride and flair; she is her own person. The Virginia Slims' tale is of people who have come a long way from subservience to independence. Cachet perfume feels it does not need a solo figure to work this appeal, and uses three different faces in its ads; it insists, though, "It's different on every woman who wears it."

Like many psychological needs, this one can also be appealed to in a negative fashion, by invoking the loss of independence or self-regard. Guilt and regrets can be stimulated: "Gee, I could have had a V-8." Next time, get one and be good to yourself.

11. *Need to escape.* An appeal to the need for autonomy often co-   63
occurs with one for the need to escape, since the desire to duck out of our
social obligations, to seek rest or adventure, frequently takes the form of
one-person flight. The dashing image of a pilot, in fact, is a standard way
of quickening this need to get away from it all.

Freedom is the pitch here, the freedom that every individual yearns   64
for whenever life becomes too oppressive. Many advertisers like appealing to the need for escape because the sensation of pleasure often accompanies escape, and what nicer emotional nimbus could there be for a
product? "You deserve a break today," says McDonald's, and Stouffer's
frozen foods chime in, "Set yourself free."

For decades men have imaginatively bonded themselves to the Marl-   65
boro cowboy who dwells untarnished and unencumbered in Marlboro
Country some distance from modern life; smokers' aching needs for autonomy and escape are personified by that cowpoke. Many women can
identify with the lady ambling through the woods behind the words,
"Benson and Hedges and mornings and me."

But escape does not have to be solitary. Other Benson and Hedges   66
ads, part of the same campaign, contain two strolling figures. In Salem
cigarette advertisements, it can be several people who escape together
into the mountaintops. A commercial for Levi's pictured a cloudbank
above a city through which ran a whole chain of young people.

There are varieties of escape, some wistful like the Boeing "Some-   67
day" campaign of dream vacations, some kinetic like the play and parties
in soft drink ads. But in every instance, the consumer exposed to the
advertisement is invited to momentarily depart his everyday life for a
more carefree experience, preferably with the product in hand.

12. *Need to feel safe.* Nobody in their right mind wants to be intimi-   68
dated, menaced, battered, poisoned. We naturally want to do whatever it
takes to stave off threats to our well-being, and to our families'. It is the
instinct of self-preservation that makes us responsive to the ad of the St.
Bernard with the keg of Chivas Regal. We pay attention to the stern talk of
Karl Malden and the plight of the vacationing couples who have lost all their
funds in the American Express travelers cheques commercials. We want the
omnipresent stag from Hartford Insurance to watch over us too.

In the interest of keeping failure and calamity from our lives, we like   69
to see the durability of products demonstrated. Can we ever forget that
Timex takes a licking and keeps on ticking? When the American Tour-
ister suitcase bounces all over the highway and the egg inside doesn't
break, the need to feel safe has been adroitly plucked.

We take precautions to diminish future threats. We buy Volkswagen   70
Rabbits for the extraordinary mileage, and MONY insurance policies to
avoid the tragedies depicted in their black-and-white ads of widows and
orphans.

We are careful about our health. We consume Mazola margarine be-   71
cause it has "corn goodness" backed by the natural food traditions of the

American Indians. In the medicine cabinet is Alka-Seltzer, the "home remedy"; having it, we are snug in our little cottage.

We want to be safe and secure; buy these products, advertisers are saying, and you'll be safer than you are without them. 72

13. *Need for aesthetic sensations.* There is an undeniable aesthetic 73 component to virtually every ad run in the national media: the photography or filming or drawing is near-perfect, the type style is well chosen, the layout could scarcely be improved upon. Advertisers know there is little chance of good communication occurring if an ad is not visually pleasing. Consumers may not be aware of the extent of their own sensitivity to artwork, but it is undeniably large.

Sometimes the aesthetic element is expanded and made into an ad's 74 primary appeal. Charles Jordan shoes may or may not appear in the accompanying avant-garde photographs; Kohler plumbing fixtures catch attention through the high style of their desert settings. Beneath the slightly out of focus photograph, languid and sensuous in tone, General Electric feels called upon to explain, "This is an ad for the hair dryer."

This appeal is not limited to female consumers: J and B scotch says 75 "It whispers" and shows a bucolic scene of lake and castle.

14. *Need to satisfy curiosity.* It may seem odd to list a need for infor- 76 mation among basic motives, but this need can be as primal and compelling as any of the others. Human beings are curious by nature, interested in the world around them, and intrigued by tidbits of knowledge and new developments. Trivia, percentages, observations counter to conventional wisdom—these items all help sell products. Any advertisement in a question-and-answer format is strumming this need.

A dog groomer has a question about long distance rates, and Bell 77 Telephone has a chart with all the figures. An ad for Porsche 911 is replete with diagrams and schematics, numbers and arrows. Lo and behold, Anacin pills have 150 more milligrams than its competitors; should we wonder if this is better or worse for us?

15. *Physiological needs.* To the extent that sex is solely a biological 78 need, we are now coming around full circle, back toward the start of the list. In this final category are clustered appeals to sleeping, eating, drinking. The art of photographing food and drink is so advanced, sometimes these temptations are wondrously caught in the camera's lens: the crab meat in the Red Lobster restaurant ads can start us salivating, the Quarterpounder can almost be smelled, the liquor in the glass glows invitingly. Imbibe, these ads scream.

STYLES

Some common ingredients of advertisements were not singled out for 79 separate mention in the list of fifteen because they are not appeals in and of themselves. They are stylistic features, influencing the way a basic appeal is presented. The use of humor is one, and the use of celebrities is another. A third is time imagery, past and future, which goes to several purposes.

For all of its employment in advertising, humor can be treacherous,   80
because it can get out of hand and smother the product information. Supposedly, this is what Alka-Seltzer discovered with its comic commercials of the late sixties; "I can't believe I ate the whole thing," the sad-faced husband lamented, and the audience cackled so much it forgot the antacid. Or, did not take it seriously.

But used carefully, humor can punctuate some of the softer appeals   81
and soften some of the harsher ones. When Emma says to the Fruit-of-the-Loom fruits, "Hi, cuties. Whatcha doing in my laundry basket?" we smile as our curiosity is assuaged along with hers. Bill Cosby gets consumers tickled about the children in his Jell-O commercials, and strokes the need to nurture.

An insurance company wants to invoke the need to feel safe, but does   82
not want to leave readers with an unpleasant aftertaste; cartoonist Rowland Wilson creates an avalanche about to crush a gentleman who is saying to another, "My insurance company? New England Life, of course. Why?" The same tactic of humor undercutting threat is used in the cartoon commercials for Safeco when the Pink Panther wanders from one disaster to another. Often humor masks aggression: comedian Bob Hope in the outfit of a boxer promises to knock out the knock-knocks with Texaco; Rodney Dangerfield, who "can't get no respect," invites aggression as the comic relief in Miller Lite commercials.

Roughly fifteen percent of all advertisements incorporate a celebrity,   83
almost always from the fields of entertainment or sports. This approach can also prove troublesome for advertisers, for celebrities are human beings too, and fully capable of the most remarkable behavior; if anything distasteful about them emerges, it is likely to reflect on the product. The advertisers making use of Anita Bryant and Billy Jean King suffered several anxious moments. An untimely death can also reflect poorly on a product. But advertisers are willing to take risks because celebrities can be such a good link between producers and consumers, performing the social role of introducer.

There are several psychological needs these middlemen can play upon.   84
Let's take the product class of cameras and see how different celebrities can hit different needs. The need for guidance can be invoked by Michael Landon, who plays such a wonderful dad on "Little House on the Prairie"; when he says to buy Kodak equipment, many people listen. James Garner for Polaroid cameras is put in a similar authoritative role, so defined by a mocking spouse. The need to achieve is summoned up by Tracy Austin and other tennis stars for Canon AE-1; the advertiser first makes sure we see these athletes playing to win. When Cheryl Tiegs speaks up for Olympus cameras, it is the need for attention that is being targeted.

The past and future, being outside our grasp, are exploited by adver-   85
tisers as locales for the projection of needs. History can offer up heroes
(and call up the need to achieve) or traditions (need for guidance) as well
as art objects (need for aesthetic sensations). Nostalgia is a kindly version
of personal history and is deployed by advertisers to rouse needs for
affiliation and for guidance; the need to escape can come in here, too.
The same need to escape is sometimes the point of futuristic appeals, but
picturing the avant-garde can also be a way to get at the need to achieve.

ANALYZING ADVERTISEMENTS

When analyzing ads yourself for their emotional appeals, it takes a bit of   86
practice to learn to ignore the product information (as well as one's own
experience and feelings about the product). But that skill comes soon
enough, as does the ability to quickly sort out from all the non-product
aspects of an ad the chief element which is the most striking, the most
likely to snag attention first and penetrate brains farthest. The key to the
appeal, this element usually presents itself centrally and forwardly to the
reader or viewer.

Another clue: the viewing angle which the audience has on the ad's   87
subjects is informative. If the subjects are photographed or filmed from
below and thus are looking down at you much as the Green Giant does,
then the need to be guided is a good candidate for the ad's emotional
appeal. If, on the other hand, the subjects are shot from above and appear
deferential, as is often the case with children or female models, then
other needs are being appealed to.

To figure out an ad's emotional appeal, it is wise to know (or have a   88
good hunch about) who the targeted consumers are; this can often be
inferred from the magazine or television show it appears in. This piece of
information is a great help in determining the appeal and in deciding
between two different interpretations. For example, if an ad features a
partially undressed female, this would typically signal one appeal for
readers of *Penthouse* (need for sex) and another for readers of *Cosmopolitan* (need for attention).

It would be convenient if every ad made just one appeal, were aimed   89
at just one need. Unfortunately, things are often not that simple. A cigarette ad with a couple at the edge of a polo field is trying to hit both the
need for affiliation and the need for prominence; depending on the attitude of the male, dominance could also be an ingredient in this. An ad for
Chimere perfume incorporates two photos: in the top one the lady is
being commanding at a business luncheon (need to dominate), but in the
lower one she is being bussed (need for affiliation). Better ads, however,
seem to avoid being too diffused; in the study of post–World War II
advertising described earlier, appeals grew more focused as the decades

passed. As a rule of thumb, about sixty percent have two conspicuous appeals; the last twenty percent have three or more. Rather than looking for the greatest number of appeals, decoding ads is most productive when the loudest one or two appeals are discerned, since those are the appeals with the best chance of grabbing people's attention.

Finally, analyzing ads does not have to be a solo activity and proba- 90 bly should not be. The greater number of people there are involved, the better chance there is of transcending individual biases and discovering the essential emotional lure built into an advertisement.

DO THEY OR DON'T THEY?

Do the emotional appeals made in advertisements add up to the sinister 91 manipulation of consumers?

It is clear that these ads work. Attention is caught, communication 92 occurs between producers and consumers, and sales result. It turns out to be difficult to detail the exact relationship between a specific ad and a specific purchase, or even between a campaign and subsequent sales figures, because advertising is only one of a host of influences upon consumption. Yet no one is fooled by this lack of perfect proof; everyone knows that advertising sells. If this were not the case, then tight-fisted American businesses would not spend a total of fifty billion dollars annually on these messages.

But before anyone despairs that advertisers have our number to the 93 extent that they can marshall us at will and march us like automatons to the check-out counters, we should recall the resiliency and obduracy of the American consumer. Advertisers may have uncovered the softest spots in minds, but that does not mean they have found truly gaping apertures. There is no evidence that advertising can get people to do things contrary to their self-interests. Despite all the finesse of advertisements, and all the subtle emotional tugs, the public resists the vast majority of the petitions. According to the marketing division of the A.C. Nielsen Company, a whopping seventy-five percent of all new products die within a year in the marketplace, the victims of consumer disinterest which no amount of advertising could overcome. The appeals in advertising may be the most captivating there are to be had, but they are not enough to entrap the wiley consumer.

The key to understanding the discrepancy between, on the one hand, 94 the fact that advertising truly works, and, on the other, the fact that it hardly works, is to take into account the enormous numbers of people exposed to an ad. Modern-day communications permit an ad to be displayed to millions upon millions of individuals; if the smallest fraction of that audience can be moved to buy the product, then the ad has been successful. When one percent of the people exposed to a television advertising campaign reach for their wallets, that could be one million sales, which may be enough to keep the product in production and the advertisements coming.

In arriving at an evenhanded judgment about advertisements and their emotional appeals, it is good to keep in mind that many of the purchases which might be credited to these ads are experienced as genuinely gratifying to the consumer. We sincerely like the goods or service we have bought, and we may even like some of the emotional drapery that an ad suggests comes with it. It has sometimes been noted that the most avid students of advertisements are the people who have just bought the product; they want to steep themselves in the associated imagery. This may be the reason that Americans, when polled, are not negative about advertising and do not disclose any sense of being misused. The volume of advertising may be an irritant, but the product information as well as the imaginative material in ads are partial compensation.

A productive understanding is that advertising messages involve costs and benefits at both ends of the communications channel. For those few ads which do make contact, the consumer surrenders a moment of time, has the lower brain curried, and receives notice of a product; the advertiser has given up money and has increased the chance of sales. In this sort of communications activity, neither party can be said to be the loser.

QUESTIONS ON CONTENT

1. In his essay, Fowles states that "As time has gone by, buyers have become stoutly resistant to advertisements. We live in a blizzard of these messages and have learned to turn up our collars and ward off most of them." Do you agree with this statement? Give examples from your own experiences to support your answer.

2. Unlike the other authors in this section, Fowles suggests that "emotional appeal is contained in the artwork" of an ad. Choose a familiar ad from among those Fowles mentions in his essay. What emotion(s) is the artwork appealing to in your opinion? What makes you think so?

3. Fowles says that the endorsement of Wesson Oil by Florence Henderson satisfies our need for guidance. He also states that consumers buy Country-Time lemonade because they want to believe the drink "has a past they can defer to." How do you feel about Fowles's assessment of these ads? Does it offend you? Why or why not?

4. "Response was contrary enough to bring the [Club Cocktails'] campaign to a stop," writes Fowles, with respect to their "Hit me with a Club" commercials featuring elderly people. What type of opposition do you think it would take to halt an ad campaign?

QUESTIONS ON RHETORIC

1. What is the thesis advanced by Fowles in his essay? Is it implied or directly stated?

2. Fowles is making a very different statement from that of the other writers in this section. He claims that in addition to their use of unsubstantiated facts and their misleading claims, advertisers also appeal to the emotions of the viewer. What kinds of evidence does Fowles offer to support his argument? Is he convincing? Explain your answer.

3. Is the tone of Fowles's essay angry, supportive, or objective in your opinion? Use examples of Fowles's diction and attitude to support your answer. Compare the tone of this essay with Rosenbaum's tone. In what way is the tone of the two essays similar? (Glossary: *Diction, Tone*)

VOCABULARY

hawked (3)	titillated (17)	aesthetic (73)
abhorrent (3)	inveigle (18)	avant-garde (85)
circumvent (5)	facsimile (33)	avid (95)
importuned (7)	gibes (46)	curried (96)
profane (13)	nimbus (64)	

WRITING TOPICS

1. Fowles suggests that an advertiser can be successful by using psychology in writing ads. One topic Fowles does not discuss however, is *subliminal advertising*, the technique that attempts to convince the public to buy by "hiding" a message in an ad. For example, in a hypothetical ad for Krunchy Kookie Cereal one frame, moving too fast for the viewer to notice it consciously, will flash the message "Buy Krunchy Kookie Cereal." The viewer won't remember seeing the message, but the mind will get it. In an essay, discuss your position on the use of subliminal advertising. You may want to research this topic in some detail.

2. Evaluate the following syllogism:

> Advertising leads to adequate consumer information.
> Adequate consumer information leads to an informed buying decision.
> An informed buying decision leads to a personal buying preference.
> Therefore, advertising leads to a personal buying preference.

Does this kind of logic negate Fowles's ideas?

3. Using Fowles's "fifteen basic appeals," analyze one or more of the ads that appear on pages 279–283. Find examples of the advertiser's appeals in each ad, and describe your findings in a brief essay.

THE LANGUAGE OF ADVERTISING CLAIMS

Jeffrey Schrank

In this essay, Jeffrey Schrank explores the world of advertising claims. He has classified the most common techniques that adwriters use to sell products into ten categories. Schrank, a teacher by profession, challenges each of us to analyze and evaluate the fairness of the promises and claims in many ads.

S tudents, and many teachers, are notorious believers in their immunity to advertising. These naive inhabitants of consumerland believe that advertising is childish, dumb, a bunch of lies, and influences only the vast hordes of the less sophisticated. Their own purchases are made purely on the basis of value and desire, with advertising playing only a minor supporting role. They know about Vance Packard and his "hidden persuaders" and the adwriter's psychosell and bag of persuasive magic. They are not impressed.

Advertisers know better. Although few people admit to being greatly influenced by ads, surveys and sales figures show that a well-designed advertising campaign has dramatic effects. A logical conclusion is that advertising works below the level of conscious awareness and it works even on those who claim immunity to its message. Ads are designed to have an effect while being laughed at, belittled, and all but ignored.

A person unaware of advertising's claim on him or her is precisely the one most defenseless against the adwriter's attack. Advertisers delight in an audience which believes ads to be harmless nonsense, for such an audience is rendered defenseless by its belief that there is no attack taking place. The purpose of a classroom study of advertising is to raise the level of awareness about the persuasive techniques used in ads. One way to do this is to analyze ads in microscopic detail. Ads can be studied to detect their psychological hooks, they can be used to gauge values and desires of the common person, they can be studied for their use of symbols, color, and imagery. But perhaps the simplest and most direct way to study ads is through an analysis of the language of the advertising claim. The "claim" is the verbal or print part of an ad that makes some claim of superiority for the product being advertised. After studying claims, students should be able to recognize those that are misleading and accept as useful information those that are true. A few of these claims are downright lies, some are honest statements about a truly superior product, but most fit into the category of neither bold lies nor helpful consumer information. They balance on the narrow line between truth and falsehood by a careful choice of words.

The reason so many ad claims fall into this category of pseudoinfor- 4 mation is that they are applied to parity products, products in which all or most of the brands available are nearly identical. Since no one superior product exists, advertising is used to create the illusion of superiority. The largest advertising budgets are devoted to parity products such as gasoline, cigarettes, beer and soft drinks, soaps, and various headache and cold remedies.

The first rule of parity involves the Alice in Wonderlandish use of the 5 words "better" and "best." In parity claims, "better" means "best" and "best" means "equal to." If all brands are identical, they must all be equally good, the legal minds have decided. So "best" means that the product is as good as the other superior products in its category. When Bing Crosby declares Minute Maid Orange Juice "the best there is" he means it is as good as the other orange juices you can buy.

The word "better" has been legally interpreted to be a comparative 6 and therefore becomes a clear claim of superiority. Bing could not have said that Minute Maid is "better than any other orange juice." "Better" is a claim of superiority. The only time "better" can be used is when a product does indeed have superiority over other products in its category or when the better is used to compare the product with something other than competing brands. An orange juice therefore claim to be "better than a vitamin pill," or even "the better breakfast drink."

The second rule of advertising claim analysis is simply that if any 7 product is truly superior, the ad will say so very clearly and will offer some kind of convincing evidence of the superiority. If an ad hedges the least bit about a product's advantage over the competition you can strongly suspect it is not superior—maybe equal to but not better. You will never hear a gasoline company say "we will give you four miles per gallon more in your car than any other brand." They would love to make such a claim, but it would not be true. Gasoline is a parity product, and, in spite of some very clever and deceptive ads of a few years ago, no one has yet claimed one brand of gasoline better than any other brand.

To create the necessary illusion of superiority, advertisers usually re- 8 sort to one or more of the following ten basic techniques. Each is common and easy to identify.

1. THE WEASEL CLAIM

A weasel word is a modifier that practically negates the claim that fol- 9 lows. The expression "weasel word" is aptly named after the egg-eating habits of weasels. A weasel will suck out the inside of an egg, leaving it appear intact to the casual observer. Upon examination, the egg is discovered to be hollow. Words or claims that appear substantial upon first look but disintegrate into hollow meaninglessness on analysis are weasels. Commonly used weasel words include "helps" (the champion weasel); "like" (used in a comparative sense); "virtual" or "virtually"; "acts" or "works"; "can be"; "up to"; "as much as"; "refreshes"; "comforts"; "tackles"; "fights"; "come on"; "the feel of"; "the look of"; "looks like"; "fortified"; "enriched"; and "strengthened."

Samples of Weasel Claims

"*Helps control* dandruff *symptoms* with *regular use.*" The weasels include "helps control," and possibly even "symptoms" and "regular use." The claim is not "stops dandruff."

"Leaves dishes *virtually* spotless." We have seen so many ad claims that we have learned to tune out weasels. You are supposed to think "spotless," rather than "virtually" spotless.

"Only half the price of *many* color sets." "Many" is the weasel. The claim is supposed to give the impression that the set is inexpensive.

"Tests confirm one mouthwash *best* against mouth odor."

"Hot Nestlés' cocoa is the very *best.*" Remember the "best" and "better" routine.

"Listerine *fights* bad breath." "Fights" not "stops."

"Lots of things have changed, but Hershey's *goodness* hasn't." This claim does not say that Hershey's chocolate hasn't changed.

"Bacos, the crispy garnish that tastes just *like* its name."

2. THE UNFINISHED CLAIM

The unfinished claim is one in which the ad claims the product is better, or has more of something, but does not finish the comparison.   10

Samples of Unfinished Claims

"Magnavox gives you more." More what?

"Anacin: Twice as much of the pain reliever doctors recommend most." This claim fits in a number of categories but it does not say twice as much of what pain reliever.

"Supergloss does it with more color, more shine, more sizzle, more!"

"Coffee-mate gives coffee more body, more flavor." Also note that "body" and "flavor" are weasels.

"You can be sure if it's Westinghouse." Sure of what?

"Scott makes it better for you."

"Ford LTD—700% quieter."

When the FTC asked Ford to substantiate this claim, Ford revealed that they meant the inside of the Ford was 700% quieter than the outside.

3. THE "WE'RE DIFFERENT AND UNIQUE" CLAIM

This kind of claim states that there is nothing else quite like the product   11
advertised. For example, if Schlitz would add pink food coloring to its
beer they could say, "There's nothing like new pink Schlitz." The
uniqueness claim is supposed to be interpreted by readers as a claim to
superiority.

Samples of the "We're Different and Unique" Claim

"There's no other mascara like it."

"Only Doral has this unique filter system."

"Cougar is like nobody else's car."

"Either way, liquid or spray, there's nothing else like it."

"If it doesn't say Goodyear, it can't be polyglas." "Polyglas" is a trade name
copyrighted by Goodyear. Goodrich or Firestone could make a tire exactly
identical to the Goodyear one and yet couldn't call it "polyglas"—a name for
fiberglass belts.

"Only Zenith has chromacolor." Same as the "polyglas" gambit. Admiral has
solarcolor and RCA has accucolor.

4. THE "WATER IS WET" CLAIM

"Water is wet" claims say something about the product that is true for any   12
brand in that product category (for example, "Schrank's water is really
wet"). The claim is usually a statement of fact, but not a real advantage
over the competition.

Samples of the "Water Is Wet" Claim

"Mobil: the Detergent Gasoline." Any gasoline acts as a cleaning agent.

"Great Lash greatly increases the diameter of every lash."

"Rheingold, the natural beer." Made from grains and water as are other beers.

"SKIN smells differently on everyone." As do many perfumes.

5. THE "SO WHAT" CLAIM

This is the kind of claim to which the careful reader will react by saying   13
"So What?" A claim is made which is true but which gives no real advantage to the product. This is similar to the "water is wet" claim except that
it claims an advantage which is not shared by most of the other brands in
the product category.

Samples of the "So What" Claim

"Geritol has more than twice the iron of ordinary supplements." But is twice
as much beneficial to the body?

"Campbell's gives you tasty pieces of chicken and not one but two chicken
stocks." Does the presence of two stocks improve the taste?

"Strong enough for man but made for a woman." This deodorant claim says
only that the product is aimed at the female market.

6. THE VAGUE CLAIM

The vague claim is simply not clear. This category often overlaps with   14
others. The key to the vague claim is the use of words that are colorful
but meaningless, as well as the use of subjective and emotional opinions
that defy verification. Most contain weasels.

Samples of the Vague Claim

"Lips have never looked so luscious." Can you imagine trying to either prove
or disprove such a claim?

"Lipsavers are fun—they taste good, smell good and feel good."

"Its deep rich lather makes hair feel good again."

"For skin like peaches and cream."

"The end of meatloaf boredom."

"Take a bite and you'll think you're eating on the Champs Elysées."

"Winston tastes good like a cigarette should."

"The perfect little portable for all around viewing with all the features of
higher priced sets."

"Fleishman's makes sensible eating delicious."

7. THE ENDORSEMENT OR TESTIMONIAL

A celebrity or authority appears in an ad to lend his or her stellar qualities   15
to the product. Sometimes the people will actually claim to use the prod-

uct, but very often they don't. There are agencies surviving on providing products with testimonials.

Samples of Endorsements or Testimonials

"Joan Fontaine throws a shot-in-the-dark party and her friends learn a thing or two."

"Darling, have you discovered Masterpiece? The most exciting men I know are smoking it." (Eva Gabor)

"Vega is the best handling car in the U.S." This claim was challenged by the FTC, but GM answered that the claim is only a direct quote from *Road and Track* magazine.

8. THE SCIENTIFIC OR STATISTICAL CLAIM

This kind of ad uses some sort of scientific proof or experiment, very specific numbers, or an impressive sounding mystery ingredient.   16

Samples of Scientific or Statistical Claims

"Wonder Bread helps build strong bodies 12 ways." Even the weasel "helps" did not prevent the FTC from demanding this ad be withdrawn. But note that the use of the number 12 makes the claim far more believable than if it were taken out.

"Easy-Off has 33% more cleaning power than another popular brand." "Another popular brand" often translates as some other kind of oven cleaner sold somewhere. Also the claim does not say Easy-Off works 33% better.

"Special Morning—33% more nutrition." Also an unfinished claim.

"Certs contain a sparkling drop of Retsyn."

"ESSO with HTA."

"Sinarest. Created by a research scientist who actually gets sinus headaches."

9. THE "COMPLIMENT THE CONSUMER" CLAIM

This kind of claim butters up the consumer by some form of flattery.   17

Samples of the "Compliment the Consumer" Claim

"We think a cigar smoker is someone special."

"If what you do is right for you, no matter what others do, then RC Cola is right for you."

"You pride yourself on your good home cooking. . . ."

"The lady has taste."

"You've come a long way, baby."

10. THE RHETORICAL QUESTION

This technique demands a response from the audience. A question is   18
asked and the viewer or listener is supposed to answer in such a way as to
affirm the product's goodness.

Samples of the Rhetorical Question

"Plymouth—isn't that the kind of car America wants?"

"Shouldn't your family be drinking Hawaiian Punch?"

"What do you want most from coffee? That's what you get most from Hills."

"Touch of Sweden: Could your hands use a small miracle?"

QUESTIONS ON CONTENT

1. Schrank introduces the concept "immunity to advertising" in his first
paragraph. What does he mean by this phrase? Before reading Schrank's
essay, did you feel that you were immune to advertising? Explain.

2. In his essay, Schrank quotes the claim that "Only Zenith has chromacolor." Although this statement is true, it is also deceitful. Explain in
what way this and other such claims are deceitful. Give examples.

3. "Parity products" are those in which most of the available brands are
nearly identical. Do you agree with Schrank that claims of "superiority"
among parity products are invalid? Explain using examples from
Schrank's essay or your own observations.

4. Schrank says the words *better* and *best* have been redefined for advertisers. What does he claim these words mean when they are used in an ad?

QUESTIONS ON RHETORIC

1. In paragraphs 1 through 3, Schrank introduces his topic. In paragraphs
4 through 7, he discusses parity products. His discussion of ad claims is
preceded by a two-sentence transition, after which he uses a brief introduction, followed by a list of examples for each claim. Discuss this
change from paragraph form to listing examples.

2. Schrank does not use a concluding paragraph in this essay. Why do
you suppose he doesn't? Do you think Schrank's essay would be more
effective if he had used a conclusion? Explain your answer.

3. To define the "We're Different and Unique" claim, Schrank uses the analogy "If Schlitz would add pink food coloring to its beer they could say, 'There's nothing like new pink Schlitz.'" Find another analogy in the essay. Do you find these analogies helpful?

4. Schrank has used techniques of division and classification to identify ten advertising plays that he claims are "common and easy to identify." One of these, the vague claim, Schrank says often overlaps with others, but he never explains how or with which other categories vague claims overlap. Would you have benefitted from having this information? Explain.

VOCABULARY

notorious (1)   pseudoinformation (4)   gambit (11)
psychosell (1)   parity (4)   subjective (14)

WRITING TOPICS

1. Schrank describes ten types of claims commonly used by advertisers. Choose five of these claims and in your own words discuss how they work. Develop an ad of your own for each type of claim you describe. Make sure each ad is an example of just one category.

2. Pay attention to the ads for companies that offer rival products or services (for example, AT&T and MCI, Burger King and McDonald's, Coke and Pepsi). Make note of the ad techniques mentioned in Schrank's essay you see different companies using to compare their product or service to that of their competition. In an essay, discuss what effect you feel these techniques have on each company's intended audience.

3. Ads "can be studied for their use of symbols, color, and imagery," and for their use of unsubstantial claims. Choose three advertisements from your favorite magazine and, in an essay, discuss the visual effects used by the advertisers that support their claims or that detract the reader's attention from recognizing how misleading the claims being made really are.

4. Analyze one or more of the ads appearing on pages 279–283 for the claims being made by advertisers. How many of the claims described by Schrank can you find? Evaluate the fairness of the promises and claims found in your ad(s) in an essay.

THE HARD SELL

Ron Rosenbaum

In the following article Ron Rosenbaum, a New York *writer, discusses the way advertising agencies sell a company's products by "humiliating" the consumer. This piece was published in* Mother Jones, *a consumer advocate magazine that exposes the unfair practices of business, industry, and government.*

Too many viewers, I'm afraid, miss out on the most exciting intellec- 1
tual challenge offered by television: the commercials. That's right. I said the intellectual challenge of TV commercials and I don't mean just the task of choosing between Stove Top stuffing and potatoes. I mean the pleasure to be found in pitting your intellect against some of the cleverest minds in the country, the Masterminds of Madison Avenue, and trying to figure out how they've figured *you* out.

Too many TV watchers still leave the room during TV commercials 2
for some trivial reason. As a result, they miss some of the best-produced, most skillfully scripted and edited dramas on TV: more thought, more research into human nature and, in some cases, more dollars go into creating those 30- and 60-second ads than into the development of most 30- and 60-minute prime-time programs.

I never leave the room during the commercials. I sit spellbound 3
watching them. I take notes. The highpoint of an evening before the set for me can be discovering a new wrinkle in Mr. Whipple's war on secretive Charmin squeezers, or catching the debut of one of the grand, soaring production numbers the airline or beer people put on to get us in the mood for getting high. I find more intrigue in trying to figure out the mysterious appeal of Mrs. Olsen and Robert Young, those continuing characters in coffee commercials, than in the predictable puzzles of *Masterpiece Theatre*. And I'm convinced that future archaeologists will find more concentrated and reliable clues to the patterns of our culture in one Clorox ad than they could ever find in a week's worth of sit-coms.

Take a look at some of the key trends in TV ads of the 1980s, the 4
changes in tone and technique, and you can see what they tell us about ourselves and consciousness of the new decade.

NO MORE NICE GUYS

The early '80s have witnessed the return of the Hard Sell, or what might 5
be called the "no more Mr. Nice Guy" school of commercial strategy. If

you had been watching closely you could have picked up an advance warning, a seismic tremor of the shift to come, in the Buick slogan change. In the fall of 1979 Buick abruptly yanked its confident slogan, the one that told us "Make it Buick. After all, life is to enjoy." Then, after that, everything changed.

The Buick ads of the '80s no longer take a firm position on the mean-   6
ing of life. Instead they give us hard numbers and initials: EPA est. MPG. Which leaves us to wonder; if life is no longer "to enjoy," what is life to? In the world of the new no-nonsense ads, life is to *struggle*, life is to fight for survival in a nasty brutish world. "Life got tougher," the makers of Excedrin tell us, so "we got stronger." And the airways are filled with new, tougher, hard-edged combative spirit. Little old ladies are seen savagely socking gas pumps in the midsections. Vicious tempers flare into public displays of anger in Sanka commercials. For years, tough guy Robert Conrad postured pugnaciously and challenged the un-suspecting viewer: "I dare you to call this an ordinary battery," threat-ening by implication to step right out of the tube and commit some as-sault and battery right there in our living rooms.

This aggressive stance is echoed by the take-it-or-leave-it approach of   7
the Italian food canner who declares, "Make it Progresso, or make it yourself," and was heralded by the Japanese car maker who told us, "If you can find a better-built small car than Toyota, buy it." This dismissive imperative tone of voice is the new keynote of ads in the 1980s.

You could see the philosophy of the new no-nonsense school being   8
formulated by the deep-thinkers of Madison Avenue in the first year of the new decade. The pages of *Advertising Age* were filled with specula-tions by ad people about what to name the period. "The Aching '80s" was one suggestion. "The Decade of Difficult Decisions," "The Era of Uncertainty," "The Return to Reality" were others. Each sage of the new era wanted to distinguish the '80s from the previous decade, from what one advertising agency commentator called "the self-centered, the self-indulgent, self-gratifying of the Me Decade."

The battle between the old and the new is not confined to the pages of   9
Ad Age. If you want a quick tour of the combat zone, the best place to start is with the big-money brokerage battle. You can usually catch the clash on the Sunday interview shows (*Meet the Press* and the others). Here you can see four brokerage houses go after their potential client targets with two totally different advertising strategies. While Paine Web-ber and Dean Witter try to win hearts and minds with the Late-'70s-Wish-Fulfillment approach, Merrill Lynch and Smith Barney assault the viewer with the blasted landscape of Early '80s Angst.

To shift back and forth between the two worlds invites severe disori-   10
entation. Start with Dean Witter's world, where ecstatic customers are always getting calls and letters from their broker that cause them to burst with joyful financial fulfillment as a heavenly-sounding choir croons:

"You look like you just heard from Dean Witter." 11

Contrast that with the lead character from another brokerage ad. He's 12
alone. He's lost. There is pain in his big sad eyes; he's cutting his hooves
on icy rocks and crusts of snow as he slowly picks his way in search of
shelter. This harsh winter scene is "today's investment climate," a voice-
over tells us, a time to "protect your assets." We watch the bull finally
find a dark cave in which to shelter his assets (a parable about tax shel-
ters, it seems) just as a terrifying crack of thunder bursts over the frozen
wasteland outside. There hasn't been a storm more fraught with the sheer
terror of existence since the third act of *King Lear*. This is no mere
investment climate; this is all the cold and terror and loneliness of modern
life.

In his most recent appearances, we see the solitary bull wandering a 13
barren desert wasteland beset by the tormenting trickery of a mirage; in
another we see him stepping into a bewildering hedge maze, which conjures up the horror of the hedge maze chase in Stanley Kubrick's *The
Shining* as much as it does the subtle securities offered by hedge funds on
the financial scene. Finally—it was inevitable—the poor beast becomes
the proverbial "bull in the china shop," making his way through a maze
of crystal and making us feel the frightening fragility of the most clois-
tered of civilized interiors.

A BULL APART

That lonely bull. He's lonelier than ever now, farther off than ever from 14
any hope of reunion with his herd. Faithful bull-watchers realize that the
'80s have introduced the third major phase in the bull's relation to the
herd. In the original Merrill Lynch ads of the early '70s, when Merrill
Lynch was still unabashedly "bullish on America," he was joyfully romp-
ing with the whole happy herd. In fact, we didn't even single out any
particular bull, such was the togetherness of the big beasts. A late '70s
series of Merrill Lynch ads would open on a lone bull majestically pa-
trolling scenic outposts on his own but rejoining the herd in the final shot
because, in the modified slogan, Merrill Lynch was "*still* bullish on
America."

Then at the very beginning of the new decade the herd disappeared 15
from the ads completely. (What has become of the other bulls? PBB
poisoning? Cattle mutilations?) Gone too is any attempt to further refur-
bish the "bullish on America" slogan. (What could they say—"We're
really, truly, still bullish on America"?)

The new slogan, "Merrill Lynch—a breed apart," tells us there's no 16
time to worry about the herd; you have to look after your own assets in
today's cold and nasty economic climate, in which the market falls more
every day.

But wait—ten minutes later, on a break in *Issues and Answers*, for 17 instance, we're suddenly in a whole other America, the kind of place where everything goes right. We're back not just in civilization but at the summit of civilized achievements, where we hear the rattle of fine china teacups and the clink of crystal champagne glasses set to delicate waltz music. We're in the world of Paine Webber. Grateful clients are acquiring Renoirs, eating paté or otherwise comforting themselves with the satisfied obliviousness of the courtiers of Louis XVI. The ad includes a sort of disclaimer to the effect that while Paine Webber cannot guarantee you wealth, if you bring your money to them, maybe someday "you might say, 'Thank you, Paine Webber' too."

Ah, yes . . . *maybe someday* . . . It's that old wish-fulfillment witch- 18 craft working.

Another quick flick of the remote control button and the spell of such 19 summery sophistries shatters under the frosty glare with which John Houseman fixes us in the Smith Barney ads. It is a shock, the shift from the plush carpeted Paine Webber world to the trashy, torn-ticket-tape litter on the floor of the stock exchange, from the soaring choirs of Dean Witter to the bare ruined choirs of the Big Board.

Houseman puts on a great performance. Smith Barney has invested 20 wisely in him. "The New York Stock Exchange. The day's trading is over," he intones ominously in his classic debut spot. "Some tally their profits," he says with a wintry, dismissive smile that implies: "Fat chance that's you, fella." "Some," he concludes, impaling us with a veritable icicle of a glance, "lick their wounds."

Wounds. Suffering. Pain. Insecurity. The tragic view of life. House- 21 man's debut for Smith Barney was the perfect harbinger of the New Hard Sell. Unlike the old hard sell, with a fast-and-loud-talking salesperson pitching a product, the new sell portrays the world as cold, brutally tough. The product isn't pushed so much as the audience is impelled to reach—reach *hard*—for the hope of security the product offers. The *hope* of security—that is what the '80s hard sell offers to those of us frozen out by this brutal era.

THE TOUGH LIFE

A recent editorial in *Ad Age* denounced the new Excedrin "Life got 22 tougher" ads for "overkill," for giving the impression that "life is now akin to a forced march to the Gulag Archipelago . . . a kind of doomsday feeling."

Even if life is not getting *that* tough, *tough* is definitely the key word 23 in the world of today's TV commercials. Dodge trucks are "ram tough," and the Dodge ads feature hormone-crazed rams smashing horns against each other. Ford trucks are "built tough," and their promo featured a grueling tug of war with Toyota.

Then, too, the old-fashioned work ethic has returned to prominence.   24
"They make money the old-fashioned way. They earn it," John Houseman says in a Smith Barney ad. Back to basics. Don't express yourself,
protect yourself. Life is no longer to enjoy. Life is to avoid. The essence
of this new technique is to arouse anxiety and offer relief. It means something, I think, that dollar for dollar Tylenol is the single most frequently
purchased drugstore item in the United States today.

Certainly the older-type commercials, the softer, happier advertising   25
pitches, continue to be the most popular with TV viewers. A look at two
years of polls by Video Storyboards Test Inc. (a market research outfit
that asks a cross section of people what they think is the most outstanding
TV commercial they have seen recently) consistently registers the popularity of the spiritual, emotional, celebratory ad campaigns. The warmth
and emotion of the "Mean Joe Green and the Kid" Coke commercial
made it the most popular in recent years. The stirring musical Americana
of the soft drink spirituals, the lyrical beauty and hearty comaraderie of
the beer ads and the blood-curdling cuteness of cat food commercials
consistently push these upbeat celebrations of humanity, warmth and
friendship into the Top 10 of such ad polls.

Whether or not they will continue to be popular with ad people as   26
selling tools is another question. There have been some interesting
changes in the spiritual genre in the new season's ads.

Consider first the very popularity of the word. After a brief appear-   27
ance and quick death in 1976, the word *spirit* has arisen again. We have
the "catch that Pepsi spirit" campaign; we have the cloud-level soaring
"spirit of Hyatt" and the plucky American Motors gas-saving model,
Spirit.

But, hovering over the grand, "Main Street parade" Pepsi spirit spot   28
is an aura of anxiety. We watch the little drum majorette drop her baton
in practice at home. Now it's the Fourth of July parade, and we
are treated to the anxious glances of the parents and friends as they wait
to see if their child will suffer public humiliation. Of course, she catches
it; but anxiety and suspense giving way to relief, and people gulping
Pepsi to soothe throats dry from tension are not the unambiguous hall-
marks of joy that once reigned in soft drink ads. Even they now bode
harder times . . .

SOMETHING MORE THAN FEELINGS

Another technique of the late '70s school is the emphasis on feeling.   29
While this has been a good year for product feelings ("Feelin' 7-Up,"
"Oh, what a feeling . . . Toyota"), it has not been a particularly good
season for feelings of love.

Why is love slighted? Why did AT&T cancel its love song theme,   30

"Feelings," and switch to the California hot-tub gestalt "Reach Out and Touch Someone" theme? What was the flaw for the ad people in "Feelings"?

Many to be sure would call it a criminally sentimental piece of trash, but that never stopped other songs from making it. No, it is the fact that the Morris Albert classic is specifically a song about feelings of love. And with love there are always mixed feelings, touchy feelings, fiery feelings, not the comfortable nonthreatening warmth of reach-out-and-touch feelings. California closeness is a safer-selling feeling than those volatile feelings of love. 31

Increasingly, this year we find the notion of love ridiculed and scorned. In one of those male-bonding, beer-bar get-togethers, a starry-eyed man bursts in to announce, "I've found *the* woman." 32

"*Again*," some wise guy cracks scornfully to the roar of ridicule from a crowd clearly disillusioned with the Western Romantic tradition. 33

While some wine commercials celebrate passion and *amore* between men and women, the most conspicuous instance of love at first sight on screen these days is between man and car (Mazda's "Just one look . . ." theme), and the most conspicuous instance of erotic love is between a woman and herself (the Rive Gauche hard-driving, dawn-watching woman who "goes it alone," whose "auto-eroticism" as Jeff Greenfield called it before I got a chance to, is only thinly veiled—we even see the earth move as she watches the sun also rise). 34

In fact, the one new ad that treated love uncynically celebrated what is actually pubescent puppy love—the two shy kids in the 1980 "Love's Baby Soft" teenybopper fragrance ad. It's a brilliant and beguiling piece of work, but nowhere do you find the equivalent for post-teenagers. 35

The only innovative use of love in the past few years is in the less-than-romantic name of a cleansing product—"Love My Carpet." (The most interesting new-product name on the market in recent years has got to be "Gee, Your Hair Smells Terrific!" Look for more of these exclamatory-sentence brand names in future TV commercials.) 36

REALM OF NIGHTMARE

In fact, there have been some vicious anti-Romance ads running recently. The most insidious of the genre was the Longines spot that aired last Christmastime. A cozy marital scene; the man has just given his wife a watch he worked his heart out to afford. He's gazing at her, brimming over with loving generosity as she announces, "I love it." 37

She pauses. Only a microsecond, but one of the most deadly microseconds ever aired. "But?" he asks. "No, really," she replies with just a fleeting smile. 38

The guy's heart is breaking. She's not even faking enthusiasm. "C'mon, tell me," he pleads weakly. 39

"I guess I was hoping for a Longines," she says wistfully. 40

This is not Romance but a nasty little murder of it committed right 41 before our eyes.

Here, we have entered the realm of nightmare. Here, other kinds of 42 feelings reign. We are working not with human potential but with human paranoia. Anxiety. Loss. Fear of loss. Remember that nightmarish classic, the American Express Lost Traveler's Cheques series. Who can forget the smug sneer of the French concierge when the frantic young American couple confess that the traveler's checks they have lost were not American Express? "Ah," he says, as if gazing down from the frosty remoteness of Mont Blanc at a particularly distasteful specimen of grape blight. "Most people carry American Express."

What's shocking here is not the Gallic scorn but the supine response 43 of the American couple. Instead of grabbing the concierge by his starched, stuffed shirt and reminding him that his mother hadn't asked the Americans who liberated Paris what kind of bank checks they brought, the couple turns away in humiliation and self-abasement: We *are* such worms, we Americans, only good for our virtually worthless dollars, and here we are too stupid even to do what Most People do and at least avoid inconveniencing the concierge with our petty failures.

Certainly this abasement before foreigners must reflect more than the 44 lingering cringe of the colonials before continental civilization. It suggests a kind of sickening national self-image that masochistically relishes affronts to our representatives abroad.

Consider the slogan for the ad: "American Express Traveler's 45 Cheques—don't leave home without them." Isn't the net effect of that slogan—which follows portrait after panicked portrait of Americans robbed, humiliated, traumatized, everything but taken hostage, generally in foreign lands—isn't the net effect to feed the voice inside our national psyche, that fearful voice that simply says, "Don't leave home"?

THE HUMILIATION SELL

Humiliation, embarrassment and slovenliness seem to be at the core of 46 not just Miller but Schlitz and other "lite" beer commercials. Ads for full-bodied beers are still some of the most beautiful, most lyrical, glowingly lit tributes to the romance of workingpeople, the dignity of the work ethic and the nobility of adventure and athletic endeavor. But the Lite ads give us symbols of humiliation, such as comedians Rodney Dangerfield and malaprop-man Norm Crosby.

And there's Marv Throneberry, who has built a career out of two 47 humiliating seasons as last-place first baseman for the worst team in baseball. It's marvelous that Miller beer has made him a national celebrity—anybody's better than Bruce Jenner—but what does his popular following suggest about our new notion of the heroic figure? Rodney Dangerfield, of course, is famous for "I don't get no respect," but the "lite" beer ethos seems to play upon our feelings that we don't *deserve* respect.

There are also the repeated small moments of defeat for the noncel-   48
ebrity: the natural cereal eater who is constantly crestfallen at how many bowls of his brand it would take to equal the vitamins in Total; the shame-faced jerks ridiculed by their friends for forgetting Prestone, fail-ing to keep their guard up and stranding them all in the cold; the over-achieving, overtime-working eager beavers who are constantly being whispered about because they "need a deodorant that works overtime"; the guy in the Yellow Pages ad who rips the bottom of his pants so embarrassingly that he has to wait in a telephone booth for a tailor to make him fit to appear in public again.

The Humiliation Sell goes hand in hand with what's happening in the   49
"real people" genre of TV commercials. The real people being selected to appear in recent ads are, to put it bluntly, a much stupider, uglier breed than those of the late '70s. This is not the cute, stupid and ugly urban look of the late '60s "New York School" of filmic ad realists (the Alka-Seltzer "No Matter What Shape Your Stomach's In" campaign, for in-stance). No, this is a new kind of subhuman suburban subspecies. It is as if the ad people were saying to the public and the FTC: "You want hon-esty? You want truth and reality in ads? O.K. We'll rub your nose in realism! We'll show you 'real.'"

Someday, bits of this verité material will be recognized as some of   50
the most accurate journalism of our time. Nothing captures the bleak reality of the suburban teenager better than the picture of the "real kid" in a laundry detergent ad, staring vacantly with what looks like angel-dust-blasted eyes at two piles of white linen and grunting, "I'm not into wash, but like, that one's cleaner."

Not only do these real people look vacant, they seem totally cut off   51
from the people closest to them; they exhibit not merely mistaken product identification responses but an almost pathological failure to know the world around them.

After all these years, how is it possible for a real person in a super-   52
market aisle, approached by a man with a microphone, not to know that he or she ought to pick Stove Top stuffing instead of potatoes? And how could all those mothers in the Procter & Gamble ads fail to know their sons and husbands prefer clean clothes to dingy? Are ad people trying to rub the noses of real people in their nitty-gritty griminess?

And talk about rubbing it in: have you seen the latest Charmin toilet   53
paper ad with Mr. Whipple? It's a remarkable example of ad people boasting shamelessly about their manipulative trickery to the very people they have successfully hoodwinked.

This crown jewel of the epic Charmin campaign (first begun a decade   54
ago, it transformed Charmin from a minor regional brand into the No. 1 product of its kind) takes place outside Whipple's supermarket. He has

taken down his old Don't Squeeze the Charmin signs and is ushering in a new era, during which there will be no more silly prohibitions on squeezing. As he does so, he reflects on the whole "Don't Squeeze" theme of the campaign and confides at last the true motive behind the gimmick. "Squeezing the Charmin wasn't so bad after all," Whipple confesses. His "Don't Squeeze" prissiness was just a trick to provoke and then co-opt your rebelliousness. Hence, the brand-new Charmin slogan: "The squeezing gets you. The softness keeps you."

In other words, Whipple is virtually coming out and saying, "We   55 tricked you into buying it." You can almost hear the triumphant crowing of the ad people—you laughed at us for putting on such a ridiculous campaign, but, Mr. and Mrs. America, the joke's on you: you bought it anyway.

Perhaps the final, most insulting touch to top off this trend was the   56 reappearance of ventriloquists' dummies in place of real people in some campaigns. We have had one ventriloquists's dummy mouthing "ring around the collar" in a Wisk ad and another saying "butter" in the Parkay margarine spots. Real people are so malleable, so willing to say whatever the ad people want them to, they might as well be ventriloquists' dummies as far as the ad people are concerned. This explains, perhaps, the birth of the dummy trend and the displacement of their flesh-and-blood counterparts.

One gets the feeling that these commercials are expressing a certain   57 impatience with the consumer on the part of ad people, perhaps even a subconscious hostility. Industry has become tired of trying to persuade us, seduce us, flatter us, indulge our fantasies. The Me Decade is over on Madison Avenue, and from now on it's no more Mr. Nice Guy. Tough times are here, even for advertising.

Advertising is going through a period during which precipitous agency-   58 client shifts have raised cries of disloyalty and betrayal in some quarters. Product "positioning" wars and head-to-head comparison ad conflicts grow more fierce, even vicious. "ANOTHER ROUND IN COLA WARS"; "GF SENDS 'MASTER BLEND' INTO BATTLE"—the images in the trade paper headlines are grimly warlike. Even in the sweet little candy world, big battles are erupting: "LIFE-SAVERS, CHICLE READY FOR CANDY ROLL MARKET CLASH" proclaimed one front page battle dispatch in *Ad Age*.

There are signs of even tougher times to come, both on the screen and   59 in the offices of Madison Avenue. The trade papers are reporting with increasing frequency the problems ad agencies are having with slow-paying buyers. Credit problems are cropping up and forcing the creation of a new get-tough policy toward debtors.

It was around the turn of the decade that I first spotted a notice in *Ad*   60 *Age* for an outfit that said it specialized in "advertising debt-collection problems." Their slogan: "We're gentlemen."

Were they hinting with that line that there are nongentlemen working   61 the suites of Madison Avenue, tough guys who specialize in more forceful, no-nonsense ways of dealing with advertising debt collection? One cannot help but imagine a *Rocky* type in a gray flannel suit visiting a Creative Director and delivering the ultimatum, "Pay up or we'll mangle the syntax of your slogan." Perhaps the only satisfaction we can get from all this is that if ads are getting tougher on life, life is certainly getting tougher on advertising.

QUESTIONS ON CONTENT

1. Rosenbaum states that, initially, there was the Hard Sell era of the fast-talking salesman. This, he says, turned into the Hard Life era of bitter reality. Rosenbaum then discusses the Humiliation Sell and Love in advertising. What does Rosenbaum say about these topics? Why does he make repeated comparisons to sincere emotional ads such as the "Mean Joe Greene and the Kid" Coke commercial, while only devoting one paragraph to a discussion of these ads?

2. Adwriters for Excedrin explain that "Life got tough, so we got stronger." Why do you think advertisers exploit the idea that life is tough? Is life, in your opinion, really as tough as advertisements would lead us to believe?

3. What are the different ways in which love is portrayed in ads, according to Rosenbaum?

4. Rosenbaum's attitude toward advertisements is generally negative. Which types of ads does Rosenbaum dislike most? Are there any ads Rosenbaum likes? Based on the attitudes Jeffrey Schrank expresses in the previous reading, how do you think he would respond to these ads?

QUESTIONS ON RHETORIC

1. Rosenbaum's word choice is generally more sophisticated than Jeffrey Schrank's. Because diction should be suited to the author's audience, who do you think Rosenbaum intended his audience to be?

2. Rosenbaum discusses the effects of ads on "us" as "we" watch "our" television sets. Why do you think he uses first person plural rather than second person (you) or third person (they)?

3. Rosenbaum places a good deal of emphasis on the style of the advertisements of brokerage firms. What is the significance of this? What else does Rosenbaum emphasize to make his point?

4. What do you believe is Rosenbaum's purpose in writing this essay: to teach, to inform, to persuade, or to entertain? Explain your answer.

VOCABULARY

pugnaciously (6)	bode (28)	crestfallen (48)
cloistered (13)	gestalt (30)	hoodwinked (53)
sophistries (19)	malaprop (46)	malleable (56)
intones (20)	ethos (47)	precipitous (58)
harbinger (21)		

WRITING TOPICS

1. Society has tended to give nicknames to decades, the way people do to friends, to describe the characteristics and tendencies that distinguish them. For instance, the Roaring Twenties were so called for their wild impetuosity, while the seventies were called the "Me Decade." Judging by the social tendencies you see around you, what names do you think society might bestow on the nineties? In an essay, discuss the ways you think advertising might reflect and play up to these priorities.

2. Over the course of a week, pay close attention to the television commercials aired in a variety of different time slots. How many of the selling tactics Rosenbaum describes do you see used in any one evening? In an essay, describe the commercials and label them according to the selling tactic each employs.

IT'S NATURAL! IT'S ORGANIC! OR IS IT?

Consumers Union

"Natural" and "organic" are two advertising buzz words of the 1980s, products of the health and fitness movement that is sweeping the country. But these two words have the Consumers Union worried because products labeled "natural" and/or "organic" often don't deliver what customers expect. In the following essay, the Consumers Union, a nonprofit organization that provides "consumers with information and counsel on consumer goods and services," examines the words "natural" and "organic" and how they are being used by advertisers. To educate consumers, the Union classifies a number of the deceptive advertising techniques used by manufacturers and advertising agencies.

"No artificial flavors or colors!" reads the Nabisco advertisement in *Progressive Grocer*, a grocery trade magazine. "And research shows that's exactly what consumers are eager to buy." 1

The ad, promoting Nabisco's *Sesame Wheats* as "a natural whole wheat cracker," might raise a few eyebrows among thoughtful consumers of Nabisco's *Wheat Thins* and *Cheese Nips*, which contain artificial colors, or of its *Ginger Snaps* and *Oreo Cookies*, which have artificial flavors. But Nabisco has not suddenly become a champion of "natural" foods. Like other giants of the food industry, the company is merely keeping its eye on what will produce a profit. 2

Nabisco's trade ad, which was headlined "A Natural for Profits," is simply a routine effort by a food processor to capitalize on the concerns that consumers have about the safety of the food they buy. 3

Supermarket shelves are being flooded with "natural" products, some of them containing a long list of chemical additives. And some products that never did contain additives have suddenly sprouted "natural" or "no preservative" labels. Along with the new formulations and labels have come higher prices, since the food industry has realized that consumers are willing to pay more for products they think are especially healthful. 4

The mass merchandising of "natural" foods is a spillover onto supermarket shelves of a phenomenon once confined to health-food stores, as 5 major food manufacturers enter what was once the exclusive territory of small entrepreneurs. Health-food stores were the first to foster and capitalize on the growing consumer interest in nutrition and are still thriving. Along with honey-sweetened snacks, "natural" vitamins, and other "natural" food products, the health-food stores frequently feature "organic" foods.

Like the new merchandise in supermarkets, the products sold at health-food stores carry the implication that they're somehow better for you—safer or more nutritious. In this report, we'll examine that premise, looking at both "natural" foods, which are widely sold, and "organic" foods, which are sold primarily at health-food stores. While the terms "natural" and "organic" are often used loosely, "organic" generally refers to the way food is grown (without pesticides or chemical fertilizers) and "natural" to the character of the ingredients (no preservatives or artificial additives) and to the fact that the food product has undergone minimal processing.

Langendorf Natural Lemon Flavored Creme Pie contains no cream. It does contain sodium propionate, certified food colors, sodium benzoate, and vegetable gum.

That's natural?

Yes indeed, says L.A. Cushman, Jr., chairman of American Bakeries Co., the Chicago firm that owns Langendorf. The word "natural," he explains, modifies "lemon flavored," and the pie contains oil from lemon rinds. "The lemon flavor," Cushman states "comes from the natural lemon flavor as opposed to artificial lemon flavor, assuming there is such a thing as artificial lemon flavor."

Welcome to the world of natural foods.

You can eat your "natural" way from one end of the supermarket to the other. Make yourself a sandwich of *Kraft Cracker Barrel Natural Cheddar Cheese* on *Better Way Natural Whole Grain Wheat Nugget Bread* spread with *Autumn Natural Margarine*. Wash it down with *Anheuser-Busch Natural Light Beer* or *Rich-Life Natural Orange Nutri-Pop*. Snack on any number of brands of "natural" potato chips and "natural" candy bars. And don't exclude your pet: Feed your dog *Gravy Train Dog Food With Natural Beef Flavor* or, if it's a puppy, try *Blue Mountain Natural Style Puppy Food*.

The "natural" bandwagon doesn't end at the kitchen. You can bathe in *Batherapy Natural Mineral Bath* (sodium sesquicarbonate, isopropyl myristate, fragrance, D & C Green No. 5, D & C Yellow No. 10 among its ingredients), using *Queen Helene "All-Natural" Amino Peptide Shampoo* (propylene glycol, hydroxyethyl cellulose, methylparaben, D & C Red No. 3, D & C Brown No. 1) and *Organic Aid Natural Clear Soaps*. Then, if you're so inclined, you can apply *Naturade Conditioning Mascara with Natural Protein* (stearic acid, PVP, butylene glycol, sorbitan sesquioleate, triethanolamine, imidazolidinyl urea, methylparaben, propylparaben).

At its ridiculous extreme, the "natural" ploy extends to furniture, cig-   13
arettes, denture adhesives, and shoes.

The word "natural" does not have to be synonymous with "ripoff."   14
Over the years, the safety of many food additives has been questioned.
And a consumer who reads labels carefully can in fact find some foods in
supermarkets that have been processed without additives.

But the word "natural" does not guarantee that. All too often, as the   15
above examples indicate, the word is used more as a key to higher
profits. Often, it implies a health benefit that does not really exist.

Co-op News, the publication of the Berkeley Co-op, the nation's larg-   16
est consumer-cooperative store chain, reported on "two fifteen-ounce
cans of tomato sauce, available side-by-side" at one of its stores. One
sauce, called *Health Valley*, claimed on its label to have "no citric acid,
no sugars, no preservatives, no artificial colors or flavors." There were
none of those ingredients in the Co-op's house brand, either, but their
absence was hardly worth noting on the label, since canned tomato sauce
almost never contains artificial colors or flavors and doesn't need preservatives after being heated in the canning process. The visible difference
between the two products was price, not ingredients. The *Health Valley*
tomato sauce was selling for 85 cents; the Co-op house brand, for only 29
cents.

One supermarket industry consultant estimates that 7 percent of all   17
processed food products now sold are touted as "natural." And that could
be just the beginning. A Federal Trade Commission report noted that 63
percent of people polled in a survey agreed with the statement, "Natural
foods are more nutritious than other foods." Thirty-nine percent said they
regularly buy food because it is "natural," and 47 percent said they were
willing to pay 10 percent more for a food that is "natural."

According to those who have studied the trend, the consumer's desire   18
for "natural" foods goes beyond the fear of specific chemicals. "There is
a mistrust of technology," says Howard Moskowitz, a taste researcher
and consultant to the food industry. "There is a movement afoot to return
to simplicity in all aspects of life." A spokeswoman for Lever Bros., one
of the nation's major food merchandisers, adds: "'Natural' is a psychological thing of everyone wanting to get out of the industrial world."

Because consumers are acting out of such vague, undefined feelings,   19
they aren't sure what they should be getting when they buy a product
labeled "natural." William Wittenberg, president of Grandma's Food
Inc., comments: "Manufacturers and marketers are making an attempt to
appeal to a consumer who feels he should be eating something natural,
but doesn't know why. I think the marketers of the country in effect
mirror back to the people what they want to hear. People have to look to
themselves for their own protection." Grandma's makes a *Whole Grain
Date Filled Fruit 'n' Oatmeal Bar* labeled "naturally Good Flavor." The
ingredients include "artificial flavor."

"Natural" foods are not necessarily preferable nor, as we have seen,   20
necessarily natural.

Consider "natural" potato chips. They are often cut thick from un-   21
peeled potatoes, packaged without preservatives in heavy foil bags with
fancy lettering, and sold at a premium price. Sometimes, such chips include "sea salt," a product whose advantage over conventional "land" salt
has not been demonstrated. The packaging is intended to give the impression that "natural" potato chips are less of a junk food than regular chips.
But nutritionally there is no difference. Both are made from the same
food, the potato, and both have been processed so that they are high in
salt and in calories.

Sometimes the "natural" products may have ingredients you'd prefer   22
to avoid. *Quaker 100% Natural* cereal, for example, contains 24 percent
sugars, a high percentage, considering it's not promoted as a sugared
cereal. (*Kellog's Corn Flakes* has 7.8 percent sugar.) Many similar "natural" granola-type cereals have oil added, giving them a much higher fat
content than conventional cereals.

Taste researcher Moskowitz notes that food processors are "trying to   23
signal to the consumer a sensory impact that can be called natural." Two
of the most popular signals, says Moskowitz, are honey and coconut. But
honey is just another sugar, with no significant nutrients other than calories, and coconut is especially high in saturated fats.

While many processed foods are less nutritious than their fresh coun-   24
terparts, processing can sometimes help foods: Freezing preserves nutrients that could be lost if fresh foods are not consumed quickly; pasteuriz-
ation kills potentially dangerous bacteria in milk. Some additives are also
both safe and useful. Sorbic acid, for instance, prevents the growth of
potentially harmful molds in cheese and other products, and sodium benzoate has been used for more than 70 years to prevent the growth of
microorganisms in acidic foods.

"Preservative" has become a dirty word, to judge from the number of   25
"no preservative" labels on food products. Calcium propionate might
sound terrible on a bread label, but this mildew-retarding substance occurs naturally in both raisins and Swiss cheese. "Bread without preservatives could well cost you more than bread with them," says Vernal S.
Packard Jr., a University of Minnesota nutrition professor. "Without preservatives, the bread gets stale faster; it may go moldy with the production of hazardous aflatoxin. And already we in the United States return
[to producers] 100 million pounds of bread each year—this in a world
nagged by hunger and malnutrition."

Nor are all "natural" substances safe. Sassafras tea was banned by the   26
U.S. Food and Drug Administration several years ago because it contains
safrole, which has produced liver cancer in laboratory animals. Kelp, a
seaweed that is becoming increasingly fashionable as a dietary supple-
ment, can have a high arsenic content. Aflatoxin, produced by a mold

that can grow on improperly stored peanuts, corn, and grains, is a known carcinogen.

To complicate matters, our palates have become attuned to many un-   27 natural tastes. "We don't have receptors on our tongues that signal "natural," says taste researcher Moskowitz. He points out, for instance, that a panel of consumers would almost certainly reject a natural lemonade "in favor of a lemonade scientifically designed to taste natural. If you put real lemon, sugar, and water together, people would reject it as harsh. They are used to flavors developed by flavor houses." Similarly, Moskowitz points out, many consumers say that for health reasons they prefer less salty food—but the results of various taste tests have contradicted this, too.

In the midst of all this confusion, it's not surprising that the food   28 industry is having a promotional field day. Companies are using various tactics to convince the consumer that a food product is "natural"—and hence preferable. Here are some of the most common:

THE INDETERMINATE MODIFIER.   Use a string of adjectives and claim   29 that "natural" modifies only the next adjective in line, not the product itself. Take *Pillsbury Natural Chocolate Flavored Chocolate Chip Cookies*. Many a buyer might be surprised to learn from the fine print that these cookies contain artificial flavor, as well as the chemical antioxidant BHA. But Pillsbury doesn't bat an eyelash at this. "We're not trying to mislead anybody," says a company representative, explaining that the word "natural" modifies only "chocolate flavored," while the artificial flavoring is vanilla. Then why not call the product "Chocolate Chip Cookies with Natural Chocolate Flavoring"? "From a labeling point of view, we're trying to use a limited amount of space" was the answer.

INNOCENCE BY ASSOCIATION.   Put nature on your side. *Life Cinnamon*   30 *Flavor High Protein Cereal*, a Quaker Oats Co. product, contains BHA and artificial color, among other things. How could the company imply the cereal was "natural" and still be truthful? One series of *Life* boxes solves the problem neatly. The back panel has an instructional lesson for children entitled "Nature." The box uses the word "Nature" four times and "natural" once—but never actually to describe the cereal inside. Other products surround themselves with a "natural" aura by picturing outdoor or farm scenes on their packages.

THE "PRINTER'S ERROR."   From time to time, readers send us food   31 wrappers making a "natural" claim directly contradicted by the ingredients list. We have, for example, received a batch of individually wrapped *Devonsheer* crackers with a big red label saying: "A Natural Product, no preservatives." The ingredients list includes "calcium propionate (to retard spoilage)."

How could a manufacturer defend that? "At a given printing, the   32 printer was instructed to remove 'no preservatives, natural product' when we changed ingredients, but he didn't do it," says Curtis Marshall, vice president for operations at Devonsheer Melba Corp.

THE BEST DEFENSE. Don't defend yourself; attack the competition. 33 Sometimes the use of the word "natural" is, well, just plain unnatural. Take the battle that has been brewing between the nation's two largest beer makers, Miller Brewing Co. and Anheuser-Busch. The latter's product, *Anheuser-Busch Natural Light Beer*, has been the object of considerable derision by Miller.

Miller wants the word "natural" dropped from Anheuser-Busch's ad- 34 vertisements because beers are "highly processed, complex products, made with chemical additives and other components not in their natural form."

Anheuser-Busch has responded only with some digs at Miller, charg- 35 ing Miller with using artificial foam stabilizer and adding an industrial enzyme instead of natural malt to reduce the caloric content of its *Miller Lite* beer.

No victor has yet emerged from the great beer war, but the industry is 36 obviously getting edgy.

"Other brewers say it's time for the two companies to shut up," the 37 *Wall Street Journal* reported. "One thing they [the other brewers] are worried about, says William T. Elliot, president of C. Schmidt & Sons, a Philadelphia brewery, is all the fuss over ingredients. Publicity about that issue is disclosing to beer drinkers that their suds include sulfuric acid, calcium sulfate, alginic acid, or amyloglucosidase."

THE NEGATIVE PITCH. Point out in big letters on the label that the 38 product doesn't contain something it wouldn't contain anyway. The "no artificial preservatives" label stuck on a jar of jam or jelly is true and always has been—since sugar is all the preservative jams and jellies need. Canned goods, likewise, are preserved in their manufacture—by the heat of the canning process. Then there is the "no cholesterol" claim of vegetable oils, margarines, and even (in a radio commercial) canned pineapple. Those are also true, but beside the point, since cholesterol is found only in animal products.

What can be done about such all-but-deceptive practices? One might 39 suggest that the word "natural" is so vague as to be inherently deceptive, and therefore should not be available for promotional use. Indeed, the FTC staff suggested precisely that a few years ago but later backed away from the idea. The California legislature last year passed a weak bill defining the word "organic," but decided that political realities argued against tackling the word "natural."

"If we had included the word 'natural' in the bill, it most likely would 40 not have gotten out of the legislature," says one legislative staff member. "When you've got large economic interests in certain areas, the tendency is to guard those interests very carefully."

3. The writers use examples both to illustrate and to support their generalizations about the use of the words *natural* and *organic* in the advertisements. How effective did you find these examples? Which ones seemed to work best? Why?

4. How is this essay organized? You may find it helpful to make a scratch outline of the essay so that you can see the overall structure.

VOCABULARY

trade (1)	bandwagon (12)	palates (27)
foster (5)	ploy (13)	derision (33)
implication (6)	touted (17)	
premise (6)	carcinogen (26)	

WRITING TOPICS

1. What, for you, are the connotations of the words *natural* and *organic*? Do you believe, as some have claimed, that these words are inherently deceptive? Write an essay in which you argue for or against the banning of these words from advertising.

2. Collect five or six print advertisements that use the word *natural*, and analyze each one carefully. Which of the Consumers Union's "tactics of deception" do they employ? What benefits are implied in each ad? Do you think the advertisers are trying to deceive you? Write an essay in which you present your analysis and state your conclusions.

3. Spend some time in your local supermarket looking at the messages printed on a variety of products. Do you find other words that manufacturers and advertisers are using in much the same way they use *natural* and *organic*? Write an essay in which you discuss your findings.

WRITING ASSIGNMENTS FOR "THE LANGUAGE OF MEDIA AND ADVERTISING"

1. In "Now . . . This" Neil Postman compares the predictions of George Orwell, author of *1984*, to those of Aldous Huxley, author of *Brave New World*. Reread Postman's description of the two men's fears for the future of society, and then in your own words discuss why Postman agrees with Huxley's worldview. Do you agree with it? Why, or why not? In an essay describe your own vision of the future as you see it reflected in the attitudes those around you have toward the news.

2. Think of a product that you have used but that has failed to live up to advertising claims. Write and send a letter to the company explaining why you feel its advertisements have been misleading.

3. Many advertisers seem to believe that by manipulating language they can make any product appeal to consumers. Here is how a very common item might be made to appear desirable by means of advertising:

NEW! CONVENIENT!

Strike-Ups

The latest scientific advance for smokers since the cigarette lighter. Inexpensive and lightweight, you'll never want to be caught without Strike-Ups.

Why tolerate heavy, expensive cigarette lighters? Why run the risk of soiling your clothes with dangerous lighter fluid? Why be hassled by the technicalities of replacing flints? Why be embarrassed by a lighter that fails when it means everything to you?

Strike-Ups Has a Better Way

Lightweight, 100% reliable, Strike-Ups gives 20, that's right 20, or more lights. Each booklet has its own handy striking surface, right where you need it—up front. A striking surface so large ·you'll be able to get quick and easy lights even in the darkest places. Strike-Ups comes with a handsome decorator cover. An added feature, at no extra cost, is the plain white surface inside the cover, useful for phone numbers or doodling.

Once you use Strike-Ups, you'll agree, as many Americans have, that you simply can't do without them.

Ask for Strike-Ups at All Stores Where
Quality Smoking Accessories Are Sold.

Write an advertisement for any one of the items listed below; use as many of the advertising tricks or persuasive techniques as you can in order to sell your product.

paper clips
dental floss
toothpicks
rubber bands
salt shakers
staples
bottle caps

4. As more and more of our basic material needs are satisfied, the advertisers must create and push new "needs" so the buying process on which our consumer culture is based can continue. Many of these new "needs" are created by exploitative appeals to values we all cherish or even hold sacred. For example, the Gino's fast-food chain used the word *freedom* to sell its food: "Freedom of Choice—French Fries or Onion Rings." The word *love* is another highly exploited device of advertisers.

Jerry Rubin once said, "How can I say 'I love you' when 'Cars love Shell'?" Here are some other examples:

> "Canada Dry tastes like love."
>
> "Hello. I'm Catherine Denueve. When somebody loves me, I'm always surprised. But I don't want to be told. I prefer gestures. Like—Chanel No. 5."
>
> Olympic Gold Medal winner Mark Spitz: "You know what's a great feeling? Giving someone you love a gift. The Schick Flexamatic is a great gift."
>
> A beautiful woman in a trench coat stands alone in the fog on a waterfront. She says, "I like men. Even when they're unkind to me. But men are men. They need love. They need understanding. And they need English Leather."
>
> A good-looking man says, "I know what girls need. They need love. And love's a little color." A girl appears and the man starts applying makeup to her face. The announcer says, "Love's a Little Color isn't makeup. It's only a little color."
>
> "Love is being a nurse. Learn all about professional nursing by writing to. . . ."

In each of these ads, a product is being sold by using the affective connotations of the word *love*—in other words, the word *love* (which ought to be sacred) is being exploited for profits.

Collect examples of other words like *health, success,* or *power* being used for commercial or promotional purposes. Write an essay in which you discuss the ways the word is being used as well as the possible effects on its meaning that this widespread usage may have.

5. Some people believe that advertising performs a useful service to consumers, and that most consumers know enough not to be taken in by half-truths and exaggerations. Do you agree? Why, or why not? If you agree, what benefits do we receive either directly or indirectly from advertising? Write an essay in which you clearly support your position on this issue.

6. Many product names are chosen because of their connotative or suggestive values. For example, the name *Tide* for the detergent suggests the power of the ocean tides and the rhythmic surge of cleansing waters, the name *Pride* for the wax suggests how the user will feel after using the product. Write an essay in which you discuss how the connotations of the brand names in one of the following categories enhance the appeal of the various products: cosmetics, deodorants, candy, paint, car batteries, motorcycles, fast-food sandwiches, and so on.

7. The advertising industry is governed by the Federal Trade Commission, specifically the Wheeler-Lea amendment to the FTC act. Check your encyclopedia for what this amendment says. Discuss the roles of the FTC and its implications on the ad industry.

8. *Adweek*, an advertising trade journal, annually accepts nominations for the year's worst ads. Contributors to the "BADvertising" feature select ads they dislike for one reason or another. Nominate five ads that "irritate" you and another five you consider to be ineffective. Then in an essay, explain how each ad is qualified for an award in its category.

9. John Kenneth Galbraith, a prominent economist, has stated that ads result in "a control of consumer reactions which, though imperfect and greatly complicated by the rivalry, is still far more secure than would be the ungoverned responses of consumers in the absence of such effort." What do you think Galbraith means by this statement? Do you agree? In an essay, compare and contrast Galbraith's point of view to that of the other authors in this section.

10. In order to be effective, advertising must define social values; it must tell the public what the public wants and needs. But in doing so is advertising, in your opinion, merely reflecting values already current in society or is it setting standards to which the public is expected to live up? In an essay, discuss your point of view based on your own observations and experiences.

11. Watch television one evening with the sound turned down. Look for (1) ads whose true meaning comes through with the sound off; (2) ads that mean something very different with the sound off; and (3) ads whose visual presentation is so blatant that sound and text are not necessary. In an essay, discuss which kind of ad you find most persuasive, and explain why you feel this way.

12. Real estate advertisements are designed to manipulate buyers. For example, one language analyst noted that in his hometown, "adorable" meant "small," "eat-in kitchen" meant "no dining room," "handyman's special" meant "portion of building still standing," "by appointment only" meant "expensive," and "starter home" meant "cheap." Analyze the language used in the real estate advertisements in your local newspaper. Does the real estate that one company offers sound better to you than that offered by another company? While working on this project, you may want to read "Selection, Slanting, and Charged Language" by Newman P. and Genevieve B. Birk on page 47. Present your findings about the language of real estate in an essay.

13. Using several of the articles in this section, analyze one of the ads appearing on pages 279–283 (or an ad of your choice, if your instructor wishes). What is being "sold" in the ad? Who is the intended audience? Is the ad's appeal mainly logical or emotional? What is the relationship between the text of the ad and any visuals? Summarize your analysis in an essay.

WE WANT YOU BACK.

NOW SMALL BUSINESSES THAT SWITCH TO AT&T GET ONE MONTH OF LONG DISTANCE SERVICE.

You couldn't pick a better time to come back to AT&T. Because small businesses that switch by Dec. 18 will get credit for one month of AT&T long distance service—up to $2,000.*

So if your business left AT&T but didn't save what you'd hoped, or if you miss AT&T's fast connections for calls and faxes, or if you simply think AT&T quality is better, now is the perfect time to come back.

You'll find that AT&T has calling plans to fit the needs of most every small business. Like AT&T *PRO*® WATS, a discount calling plan that gives you AT&T quality at very competitive prices—4% to 18% off our regular rates.** And you can even save on AT&T Corporate Calling Card calls, plus most international calls.

> Call to switch now and we'll guarantee your satisfaction. If you're not happy for any reason within the first 90 days, we'll pay to switch you back to your old carrier†

We can also help you with your phone equipment. In fact, if you trade in your non-AT&T phone system, we'll give you credit toward a new AT&T small business phone system.

At AT&T, we're giving you more reasons than ever to return. We want you back. Call **1 800 835-3933** today.

AT&T
The right choice.

AFTER ALL THE SHOUTING, FLAG WAVING, AND PARADES, ONE FACT REMAINS: WE AMERICANS ARE AN HONEST, DECENT LOT. **B**ELIEVING VOLUNTEERISM IS THE WAY TO HELP OTHERS TO A BETTER LIFE. **T**O THOSE FOR WHOM SERVICE IS A CAREER, WE ARE COMMITTED TO PROTECTING THEIR FUTURES WITH PENSION RETIREMENT PROGRAMS BACKED BY NO-NONSENSE PORTFOLIOS MANAGED FOR GROWTH, NOT RISK. **A**ND INGENIOUS TOOLS LIKE "HOTLINE," OUR OWN COMPUTER NETWORK. **W**ITH IT THE EMPLOYER HAS INSTANT ACCESS TO OUR DATA BASE — AND YOUR MUTUAL OF AMERICA RECORDS — RIGHT IN YOUR OWN OFFICE. **S**IGN UP FOR "HOTLINE," AND YOU HAVE THE POWER TO ADD OR DELETE INFORMATION, EVEN ENROLL NEW PEOPLE, WHEN IT'S TIMELY AND CONVENIENT FOR YOU. **T**ODAY ORGANIZATIONS LIKE YOURS, AND THE MEN AND WOMEN WHO WORK FOR THEM, TRUST IN THE SPIRIT OF AMERICA— MUTUAL OF AMERICA.

THE INTEGRITY. THE INGENUITY. THE SPIRIT OF AMERICA...

MUTUAL OF AMERICA
666 Fifth Ave. New York, NY 10103

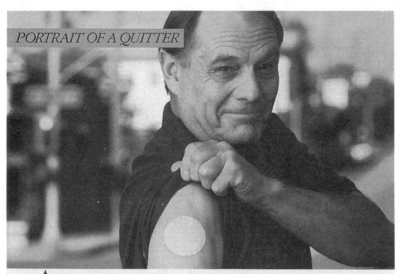

PORTRAIT OF A QUITTER

About six years ago, I decided to stop smoking. So I tried cold turkey. But soon, my wife caught me sneaking cigarettes out the bathroom window.

QUITE FRANKLY, I NEVER THOUGHT I COULD REALLY QUIT SMOKING.

Then my doctor suggested Habitrol™. Habitrol is a skin patch, available only by prescription to help relieve nicotine cravings. When used as part of a comprehensive behavioral smoking cessation program, it's been clinically proven to increase the chances of quitting in the critical first three months. That's when nicotine withdrawal symptoms force many people back to smoking.

As part of my smoking cessation program, I attended a support group my doctor recommended. He also gave me a free support kit with tips on getting through the rough times. And an audio tape for relaxation and motivation.

Since Habitrol contains nicotine, do NOT smoke or use other nicotine containing products while receiving Habitrol treatment. If you're pregnant or nursing, or have heart disease, be sure to first find out from your doctor all the ways you can stop smoking. If you're taking a prescription medicine or are under a doctor's care, talk with your doctor about the potential risks of Habitrol. Habitrol shouldn't be used for more than three months.

If you're really determined to quit, ask your doctor if Habitrol as part of a comprehensive smoking cessation program is right for you. Or call 1-800-YES-U-CAN, for a brochure today.

If you're tired of quitting and failing, Habitrol can help you with the nicotine craving and this can help you in your program to quit smoking. After that, it's up to you.

IF YOU'VE GOT THE WILL, NOW YOU CAN HAVE THE POWER. **Habitrol**™ (nicotine transdermal system)

BASEL Pharmaceuticals
Division of CIBA-GEIGY Corporation
Summit, New Jersey 07901
© 1992 CIBA-GEIGY Corporation

273-22860-A

See next page for additional important information.

Introducing Soup Starter® Quick Cook.™

New Soup Starter Quick Cook is the perfect answer to a busy life because all the hard work is done for you. We've already chopped up a delicious blend of garden vegetables, then combined them with just the right amount of herbs and spices. You simply add the meat, water–and thirty minutes later–delicious homemade soup that tastes like you spent the whole day making it.

IF IT'S BORDEN-ITS GOT TO BE GOOD

P A R T V I

Prejudice, Discrimination, and Language

Jerry, this is Winthrop Dumble III, my accountant

THE LANGUAGE
OF PREJUDICE

Gordon Allport

In this selection from The Nature of Prejudice, *Gordon
Allport examines the connection between language and
prejudice. Language plays a major role in the development
and continuation of prejudice because human thinking is
intimately linked to language. Allport identifies and explains
some of the specific ways in which language, often very
subtly and inadvertently, induces and shapes prejudice. Of
particular interest to Allport are the labels—Jew,
reactionary, jock, cripple—that we use to categorize people.
Unfortunately, such labels tend to magnify one attribute while
masking many other perhaps equally important ones.*

W ithout words we should scarcely be able to form categories at all. A   1
dog perhaps forms rudimentary generalizations, such as small-boys-are-
to-be avoided—but this concept runs its course on the conditioned reflex
level, and does not become the object of thought as such. In order to hold
a generalization in mind for reflection and recall, for identification and
for action, we need to fix it in words. Without words our world would
be, as William James said, an "empirical sand-heap."

NOUNS THAT CUT SLICES

In the empirical world of human beings there are some two and a half   2
billion grains of sand corresponding to our category "the human race."
We cannot possibly deal with so many separate entities in our thought,
nor can we individualize even among the hundreds whom we encounter
in our daily round. We must group them, form clusters. We welcome,
therefore, the names that help us to perform the clustering.

The most important property of a noun is that it brings many grains of   3
sand into a single pail, disregarding the fact that the same grains might
have fitted just as appropriately into another pail. To state the matter
technically, a noun *abstracts* from a concrete reality some one feature and
assembles different concrete realities only with respect to this one feature.
The very act of classifying forces us to overlook all other features, many
of which might offer a sounder basis than the rubric we select. Irving Lee
gives the following example:

I knew a man who had lost the use of both eyes. He was called a "blind man." He could also be called an expert typist, a conscientious worker, a good student, a careful listener, a man who wanted a job. But he couldn't get a job in the department store order room where employees sat and typed orders which came over the telephone. The personnel man was impatient to get the interview over. "But you're a blind man," he kept saying, and one could almost feel his silent assumption that somehow the incapacity in one aspect made the man incapable in every other. So blinded by the label was the interviewer that he could not be persuaded to look beyond it.

Some labels, such as "blind man," are exceedingly salient and power-   4
ful. They tend to prevent alternative classification, or even cross-classi-
fication. Ethnic labels are often of this type, particularly if they refer to
some highly visible feature, e.g., Negro, Oriental. They resemble the
labels that point to some outstanding incapacity—*feeble-minded, cripple,
blind man*. Let us call such symbols "labels of primary potency." These
symbols act like shrieking sirens, deafening us to all finer discriminations
that we might otherwise perceive. Even though the blindness of one man
and the darkness of pigmentation of another may be defining attributes
for some purposes, they are irrelevant and "noisy" for others.

Most people are unaware of this basic law of language—that every   5
label applied to a given person refers properly only to one aspect of his
nature. You may correctly say that a certain man is *human, a philanthro-
pist, a Chinese, a physician, an athlete*. A given person may be all of
these; but the chances are that *Chinese* stands out in your mind as the
symbol of primary potency. Yet neither this nor any other classificatory
label can refer to the whole of a man's nature. (Only his proper name can
do so.)

Thus each label we use, especially those of primary potency, distracts   6
our attention from concrete reality. The living, breathing, complex individual—the ultimate unit of human nature—is lost to sight. As in the
figure, the label magnifies one attribute out of all proportion to its true
significance, and masks other important attributes of the individual. . . .

A category, once formed with the aid of a symbol of primary po-   7
tency, tends to attract more attributes than it should. The category labeled
Chinese comes to signify not only ethnic membership but also reticence,

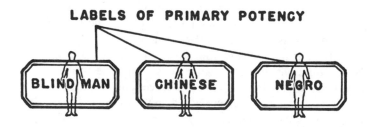

LABELS OF PRIMARY POTENCY

impassivity, poverty, treachery. To be sure, . . . there may be genuine ethnic-linked traits, making for a certain *probability* that the member of an ethnic stock may have these attributes. But our cognitive process is not cautious. The labeled category, as we have seen, includes indiscriminately the defining attribute, probable attributes, and wholly fanciful, nonexistent attributes.

Even proper names—which ought to invite us to look at the individual person—may act like symbols of primary potency, especially if they arouse ethnic associations. Mr. Greenberg is a person, but since his name is Jewish, it activates in the hearer his entire category of Jews-as-a-whole. An ingenious experiment performed by Razran shows this point clearly, and at the same time demonstrates how a proper name, acting like an ethnic symbol, may bring with it an avalanche of stereotypes. 8

> Thirty photographs of college girls were shown on a screen to 150 students. The subjects rated the girls on a scale from one to five for *beauty, intelligence, character, ambition, general likability*. Two months later the same subjects were asked to rate the same photographs (and fifteen additional ones introduced to complicate the memory factor). This time five of the original photographs were given Jewish surnames (Cohen, Kantor, etc.), five Italian (Valenti, etc.), and five Irish (O'Brien, etc); and the remaining girls were given names chosen from the signers of the Declaration of Independence and from the Social Register (Davis, Adams, Clark, etc.).
>
> When Jewish names were attached to photographs there occurred the following changes in ratings:
>
> decrease in liking
> decrease in character
> decrease in beauty
> increase in intelligence
> increase in ambition
>
> For those photographs given Italian names there occurred:
>
> decrease in liking
> decrease in character
> decrease in beauty
> decrease in intelligence

Thus a mere proper name leads to prejudgments of personal attributes. The individual is fitted to the prejudice ethnic category, and not judged in his own right.

While the Irish names also brought about depreciated judgment, the depreciation was not as great as in the case of the Jews and Italians. The falling of likability of the "Jewish girls" was twice as great as for "Italians" and five times as great as for "Irish." We note, however, that the "Jewish" photographs caused higher ratings in *intelligence* and in *ambition*. Not all stereotypes of out-groups are unfavorable.

The anthropologist, Margaret Mead, has suggested that labels of primary potency lose some of their force when they are changed from nouns into adjectives. To speak of a Negro soldier, a Catholic teacher, or a 9

Jewish artist calls attention to the fact that some other group classifications are just as legitimate as the racial or religious. If George Johnson is spoken of not only as a Negro but also as a *soldier*, we have at least two attributes to know him by, and two are more accurate than one. To depict him truly as an individual, of course, we should have to name many more attributes. It is a useful suggestion that we designate ethnic and religious membership where possible with *adjectives* rather than *nouns*.

EMOTIONALLY TONED LABELS

Many categories have two kinds of labels—one less emotional and one more emotional. Ask yourself how you feel, and what thoughts you have, when you read the words *school teacher*, and then *school marm*. Certainly the second phrase calls up something more strict, more ridiculous, more disagreeable than the former. Here are four innocent letters: m-a-r-m. But they make us shudder a bit, laugh a bit, and scorn a bit. They call up an image of a spare, humorless, irritable old maid. They do not tell us that she is an individual human being with sorrows and troubles of her own. They force her instantly into a rejective category.   10

In the ethnic sphere even plain labels such as Negro, Italian, Jew, Catholic, Irish-American, French-Canadian may have emotional tone for a reason that we shall soon explain. But they all have their higher key equivalents: nigger, wop, kike, papist, harp, canuck. When these labels are employed we can be almost certain that the speaker *intends* not only to characterize the person's membership, but also to disparage and reject him.   11

Quite apart from the insulting intent that lies behind the use of certain labels, there is also an inherent ("physiognomic") handicap in many terms designating ethnic membership. For example, the proper names characteristic of certain ethnic memberships strike us as absurd. (We compare them, of course, with what is familiar and therefore "right.") Chinese names are short and silly; Polish names intrinsically difficult and outlandish. Unfamiliar dialects strike us as ludicrous. Foreign dress (which, of course, is a visual ethnic symbol) seems unnecessarily queer.   12

But of all of these "physiognomic" handicaps the reference to color, clearly implied in certain symbols, is the greatest. The word Negro comes from the Latin *niger* meaning black. In point of fact, no Negro has a black complexion, but by comparison with other blonder stocks, he has come to be known as a "black man." Unfortunately *black* in the English language is a word having a preponderance of sinister connotations: the outlook is black, blackball, blackguard, black-hearted, black death, blacklist, blackmail, Black Hand. In his novel *Moby Dick*, Herman Melville considers at length the remarkably morbid connotations of black and the remarkably virtuous connotations of white.   13

Nor is the ominous flavor of black confined to the English language.   14
A cross-cultural study reveals that the semantic significance of black is
more or less universally the same. Among certain Siberian tribes, members of a privileged clan call themselves "white bones," and refer to all
others as "black bones." Even among Uganda Negroes there is some
evidence for a white god at the apex of the theocratic hierarchy; certain it
is that a white cloth, signifying purity, is used to ward off evil spirits and
disease.

There is thus an implied value-judgment in the very concept of *white*   15
race and *black race*. One might also study the numerous unpleasant connotations of *yellow*, and their possible bearing on our conception of the
people of the Orient.

Such reasoning should not be carried too far, since there are undoubt-   16
edly, in various contexts, pleasant associations with both black and yellow. Black velvet is agreeable, so too are chocolate and coffee. Yellow
tulips arc well liked; the sun and moon are radiantly yellow. Yet it is true
that "color" words are used with chauvinistic overtones more than most
people realize. There is certainly condescension indicated in many familiar phrases: dark as a nigger's pocket, darktown strutters, white hope (a
term originated when a white contender was sought against the Negro
heavyweight champion, Jack Johnson), the white man's burden, the yellow peril, black boy. Scores of everyday phrases are stamped with the
flavor of prejudice, whether the user knows it or not.

We spoke of the fact that even the most proper and sedate labels for   17
minority groups sometimes seem to exude a negative flavor. In many
contexts and situations the very terms *French-Canadian, Mexican*, or
Jew, correct and nonmalicious though thcy arc, sound a bit opprobrious.
The reason is that they are labels of social deviants. Especially in a culture where uniformity is prized, the name of *any* deviant carries with it
ipso facto a negative value-judgment. Words like *insane, alcoholic, pervert* are presumably neutral designations of a human condition, but they
are more: they are finger-pointing at a deviance. Minority groups are
deviants, and for this reason, from the very outset, the most innocent
labels in many situations imply a shading of disrepute. When we wish to
highlight the deviance and denigrate it still further we use words of a
higher emotional key: crackpot, soak, pansy, greaser, Okie, nigger, harp,
kike.

Members of minority groups are often understandably sensitive to   18
names given them. Not only do they object to deliberately insulting
epithets, but sometimes see evil intent where none exists. Often the word
Negro is spelled with a small *n*, occasionally as a studied insult, more
often from ignorance. (The term is not cognate with white, which is not
capitalized, but rather with Caucasian, which is.) Terms like "mulatto,"
or "octoroon" cause hard feeling because of the condescension with
which they have often been used in the past. Sex differentiations are

objectionable, since they seem doubly to emphasize ethnic difference: why speak of Jewess and not of Protestantess, or of Negress and not of whitess? Similar overemphasis is implied in the terms like Chinamen or Scotchman; why not American man? Grounds for misunderstanding lie in the fact that minority group members are sensitive to such shadings, while majority members may employ them unthinkingly.

THE COMMUNIST LABEL

Until we label an out-group it does not clearly exist in our minds. Take   19
the curiously vague situation that we often meet when a person wishes to locate responsibility on the shoulders of some out-group whose nature he cannot specify. In such a case he usually employs the pronoun "they" without an antecedent. "Why don't they make these sidewalks wider?" "I hear they are going to build a factory in this town and hire a lot of foreigners." "I won't pay this tax bill; they can just whistle for their money." If asked "who?" the speaker is likely to grow confused and embarrassed. The common use of the orphaned pronoun *they* teaches us that people often want and need to designate out-groups (usually for the purpose of venting hostility) even when they have no clear conception of the out-group in question. And so long as the target of wrath remains vague and ill-defined specific prejudice cannot crystallize around it. To have enemies we need labels.

Until relatively recently—strange as it may seem—there was no   20
agreed-upon symbol for *communist*. The word, of course, existed but it had no special emotional connotation, and did not designate a public enemy. Even when, after World War I, there was a growing feeling of economic and social menace in this country, there was no agreement as to the actual source of the menace.

A content analysis of the Boston *Herald* for the year 1920 turned up   21
the following list of labels. Each was used in a content implying some threat. Hysteria had overspread the country, as it did after World War II. Someone must be responsible for the postwar malaise, rising prices, uncertainty. There must be a villain. But in 1920 the villain was impartially designated by reporters and editorial writers with the following symbols:

alien, agitator, anarchist, apostle of bomb and torch, Bolshevik, communist, communist laborite, conspirator, emissary of false promise, extremist, foreigner, hyphenated-American, incendiary, IWW, parlor anarchist, parlor pink, parlor socialist, plotter, radical, red, revolutionary, Russian agitator, socialist, Soviet, syndicalist, traitor, undesirable.

From this excited array we note that the *need* for an enemy (someone   22
to serve as a focus for discontent and jitters) was considerably more apparent than the precise *identity* of the enemy. At any rate, there was no

clearly agreed upon label. Perhaps partly for this reason the hysteria abated. Since no clear category of "communism" existed there was no true focus for the hostility.

But following World War II this collection of vaguely interchangeable   23
labels became fewer in number and more commonly agreed upon. The out-group menace came to be designated almost always as *communist* or *red*. In 1920 the threat, lacking a clear label, was vague; after 1945 both symbol and thing became more definite. Not that people knew precisely what they meant when they said "communist," but with the aid of the term they were at least able to point consistently to *something* that inspired fear. The term developed the power of signifying menace and led to various repressive measures against anyone to whom the label was rightly or wrongly attached.

Logically, the label should apply to specifiable defining attributes,   24
such as members of the Communist Party, or people whose allegiance is with the Russian system, or followers, historically, of Karl Marx. But the label came in for far more extensive use.

What seems to have happened is approximately as follows. Having   25
suffered through a period of war and being acutely aware of devastating revolutions abroad, it is natural that most people should be upset, dreading to lose their possessions, annoyed by high taxes, seeing customary moral and religious values threatened, and dreading worse disasters to come. Seeking an explanation for this unrest, a single identifiable enemy is wanted. It is not enough to designate "Russia" or some other distant land. Nor is it satisfactory to fix blame on "changing social conditions." What is needed is a human agent near at hand: someone in Washington, someone in our schools, in our factories, in our neighborhood. If we *feel* an immediate threat, we reason, there must be a near-lying danger. It is, we conclude, communism, not only in Russia but also in America, at our doorstep, in our government, in our churches, in our colleges, in our neighborhood.

Are we saying that hostility toward communism is prejudice? Not   26
necessarily. There are certainly phases of the dispute wherein realistic social conflict is involved. American values (e.g., respect for the person) and totalitarian values as represented in Soviet practice are intrinsically at odds. A realistic opposition in some form will occur. Prejudice enters only when the defining attributes of *communist* grow imprecise, when anyone who favors any form of social change is called a communist. People who fear social change are the ones most likely to affix the label to any persons or practices that seem to them threatening.

For them the category is undifferentiated. It includes books, movies,   27
preachers, teachers who utter what for them are uncongenial thoughts. If evil befalls—perhaps forest fires or a factory explosion—it is due to communist saboteurs. The category becomes monopolistic, covering almost anything that is uncongenial. On the floor of the House of Rep-

resentatives in 1946, Representative Rankin called James Roosevelt a communist. Congressman Outland replied with psychological acumen, "Apparently everyone who disagrees with Mr. Rankin is a communist."

When differentiated thinking is at a low ebb—as it is in times of   28
social crises—there is a magnification of two-valued logic. Things are perceived as either inside or outside a moral order. What is outside is likely to be called communist. Correspondingly—and here is where damage is done—whatever is called communist (however erroneously) is immediately cast outside the moral order.

This associative mechanism places enormous power in the hands of a   29
demagogue. For several years Senator McCarthy managed to discredit many citizens who thought differently from himself by the simple device of calling them communist. Few people were able to see through this trick and many reputations were ruined. But the famous senator has no monopoly on the device. As reported in the Boston *Herald* on November 1, 1946, Representative Joseph Martin, Republican leader in the House, ended his election campaign against his Democratic opponent by saying, "The people will vote tomorrow between chaos, confusion, bankruptcy, state socialism or communism, and the preservation of our American life, with all its freedom and its opportunities." Such an array of emotional labels placed his opponent outside the accepted moral order. Martin was re-elected. . . .

Not everyone, of course, is taken in. Demagogy, when it goes too   30
far, meets with ridicule. Elizabeth Dilling's book, *The Red Network*, was so exaggerated in its two-valued logic that it was shrugged off by many people with a smile. One reader remarked, "Apparently if you step off the sidewalk with your left foot you're a communist." But it is not easy in times of social strain and hysteria to keep one's balance, and to resist the tendency of a verbal symbol to manufacture large and fanciful categories of prejudiced thinking.

VERBAL REALISM AND SYMBOL PHOBIA

Most individuals rebel at being labeled, especially if the label is uncom-   31
plimentary. Very few are willing to be called *fascistic, socialistic,* or *anti-Semitic*. Unsavory labels may apply to others; but not to us.

An illustration of the craving that people have to attach favorable   32
symbols to themselves is seen in the community where white people banded together to force out a Negro family that had moved in. They called themselves "Neighborly Endeavor" and chose as their motto the Golden Rule. One of the first acts of this symbol-sanctified band was to sue the man who sold property to Negroes. They then flooded the house which another Negro couple planned to occupy. Such were the acts performed under the banner of the Golden Rule.

Studies made by Stagner and Hartmann show that a person's political   33
attitudes may in fact entitle him to be called a fascist or a socialist, and
yet he will emphatically repudiate the unsavory label, and fail to endorse
any movement or candidate that overtly accepts them. In short, there is a
symbol phobia that corresponds to *symbol realism*. We are more inclined
to the former when we ourselves are concerned, though we are much less
critical when epithets of "fascist," "communist," "blind man," "school
marm" are applied to others.

When symbols provoke strong emotions they are sometimes regarded   34
no longer as symbols, but as actual things. The expressions "son of a
bitch" and "liar" are in our culture frequently regarded as "fighting
words." Softer and more subtle expressions of contempt may be accepted. But in these particular cases, the epithet itself must be "taken
back." We certainly do not change our opponent's attitude by making
him take back a word, but it seems somehow important that the word
itself be eradicated.

Such verbal realism may reach extreme length.   35

> The City Council of Cambridge, Massachusetts, unanimously passed a reso-
> lution (December, 1939) making it illegal "to possess, harbor, sequester,
> introduce or transport, within the city limits, any book, map, magazine,
> newspaper, pamphlet, handbill or circular containing the words Lenin or
> Leningrad."

Such naiveté in confusing language with reality is hard to comprehend
unless we recall that word-magic plays an appreciable part in human
thinking. The following examples, like the one preceding, are taken from
Hayakawa.

> The Malagasy soldier must eschew kidneys, because in the Malagasy lan-
> guage the word for kidney is the same as that for "shot"; so shot he would
> certainly be if he ate a kidney.

> In May, 1937, a state senator of New York bitterly opposed a bill for the
> control of syphilis because "the innocence of children might be corrupted by a
> widespread use of the term. . . . This particular word creates a shudder in
> every decent woman and decent man."

This tendency to reify words underscores the close cohesion that ex-   36
ists between category and symbol. Just the mention of "communist,"
"Negro," "Jew," "England," "Democrats," will send some people into a
panic of fear or a frenzy of anger. Who can say whether it is the word or
the thing that annoys them? The label is an intrinsic part of any monopolistic category. Hence to liberate a person from ethnic or political prejudice it is necessary at the same time to liberate him from *word fetishism*.
This fact is well known to students of general semantics who tell us that

prejudice is due in large part to verbal realism and to symbol phobia. Therefore any program for the reduction of prejudice must include a large measure of semantic therapy.

QUESTIONS ON CONTENT

1. Allport quotes William James's statement that without words our lives would be an "empirical sand-heap" (1). What did James mean by the phrase? What are the implications of a world in which we could not determine categories?

2. Nouns or names provide an essential service in making categorization possible. Yet, according to Allport, nouns are also words that "cut slices." What does he mean by "cut slices"? What is inherently unfair about nouns?

3. What does Allport mean by the "orphaned pronoun *they*" (19)? Why is it used so often?

4. What are "labels of primary potency" (4)? Why are they so important? Can and should we avoid the use of such labels?

5. Why may "labels of primary potency lose some of their force when they are changed from nouns into adjectives" (9)? Do you agree that "it is a useful suggestion that we designate ethnic and religious membership where possible with *adjectives* rather than with *nouns*" (9)? Why, or why not?

6. Allport wrote "The Language of Prejudice" in the early 1950s. Does this help explain why he devotes paragraphs 19 through 30 to a discussion of the label *communist*? How do Americans react to the label *communist* today?

7. What do the terms *reify* (36), *verbal realism* (35), *symbol phobia* (33), *word fetishism* (36), and *symbol realism* (33) mean? Why does Allport believe that "any program for the reduction of prejudice must include a large measure of semantic therapy" (36)?

QUESTIONS ON RHETORIC

1. What is Allport's thesis, and where is it stated? (Glossary: *Thesis*)

2. The first three paragraphs of Allport's essay become progressively concrete. Explain how these paragraphs logically narrow our focus to the noun and how it functions. (Glossary: *Concrete/Abstract*)

3. Allport includes six fairly lengthy quotations in his essay. What is the function of each one? Do you think each quotation is effective? Why, or why not? (Glossary: *Examples*)

4. In paragraph 17, identify the topic sentence. What method is used to develop the paragraph? (Glossary: *Topic Sentence* and *Examples*)

VOCABULARY

rudimentary (1)	sinister (13)	array (29)
ethnic (4)	morbid (13)	cohesion (36)
inherent (12)	sedate (17)	intrinsic (36)
ludicrous (12)		

WRITING TOPICS

1. Read the following newspaper article. Write an essay in which you attack or defend the UN recommendations.

UN GROUP URGES DROPPING OF WORDS WITH RACIST TINGE

In an effort to combat racial prejudice, a group of United Nations experts is urging sweeping revision of the terminology used by teachers, mass media and others dealing with race.

Words such as *Negro, primitive, savage, backward, colored, bushman* and *uncivilized* would be banned as either "contemptuous, unjust or inadequate." They were described as aftereffects of colonialism.

The report said that the terms were "so charged with emotive potential that their use, with or without conscious pejorative intent, to describe or characterize certain ethnic, social or religious groups, generally provoked an adverse reaction on the part of these groups."

The report said further that even the term *race* should be used with particular care since its scientific validity was debatable and that it "often served to perpetuate prejudice." The experts suggested that the word *tribe* should be used as sparingly as possible, since most of the "population groups" referred to by this term have long since ceased to be tribes or are losing their tribal character. A *native* should be called *inhabitant*, the group advised, and instead of *paganism* the words *animists, Moslems, Brahmans* and other precise words should be used. The word *savanna* is preferable to *jungle*, and the new countries should be described as *developing* rather than *underdeveloped*, the experts said.

2. Make an extensive list of the labels that have been or could be applied to you. Write an essay in which you discuss the labels that you find "truly offensive," those you can "live with," and those that you "like to be associated with." Explain your reasons for putting labels in each of these categories.

WORDS WITH BUILT-IN JUDGMENTS

S. I. Hayakawa and
Alan R. Hayakawa

In Language in Thought and Action, *from which the
following selection is taken, general semanticist and former
United States Senator S. I. Hayakawa and his son Alan
explore the complex relationships that exist between reality
and the language we use to describe it. They explain the
power that some words—especially those associated with
"race, religion, political heresy, and economic dissent"—
have to evoke strong emotional responses and how an
awareness of this power can help one both avoid stirring up
traditional prejudices and unintentionally giving offense.*

The fact that some words simultaneously arouse both informative and   1
affective connotations gives a special complexity to discussions involving
religious, racial, national, and political groups. To many people, the
word "communist" has both the informative connotation of "one who
believes in communism" and the affective connotation of "one whose
ideals and purposes are altogether repellent." Words applying to occupations of which one disapproves ("pickpocket," "racketeer," "prostitute")
and those applying to believers in philosophies of which one disapproves
("atheist," "radical," "heretic," "materialist," "fundamentalist") likewise
often communicate *simultaneously* a fact and a judgment on that fact.
Such words may be called "loaded"—that is, their affective connotations
may strongly shape people's thoughts.

In some parts of the United States, there is a strong prejudice against   2
certain ethnic groups, such as Mexican-Americans, whether immigrant or
American-born. The strength of this prejudice is revealed by the fact that
polite people and the press have stopped using the word "Mexican,"
using the term "Hispanic" instead to avoid any negative connotations.
There are also terms such as "Chicano" and "Latino" that Mexican-Amer-
ican and Spanish-speaking groups have chosen to describe themselves.

Names that are "loaded" tend to influence behavior toward those to   3
whom they are applied. Currently, the shop doorways and freeway under-
passes of American cities are sheltering tens of thousands of people who
have no work and no homes. These people used to be referred to as
"bums"—a word that suggests not only a lack of employment but a lack

of desire to work, people who are lazy, satisfied with little, and who have no desire to enter the mainstream of the American middle class or subscribe to its values. Thus, to think of these people as "bums" is to think that they are only getting what they deserve. With the search for new names for such people—"street people," "homeless," "displaced persons"—we may find new ways of thinking about their situation that may in turn suggest new ways of helping deal with it. Similarly, "problem drinker" has replaced "drunkard" and "substance abuser" has replaced "junkie." "Developmentally disabled" has replaced "retarded," which in turn replaced "idiot."

The negative connotations of words sometimes change because of deliberate changes in the way they are used. Michael Harrington, the American socialist, has said that "socialist" became a political dirty word in the 1930s and 1940s in the United States when opposing politicians and editorialists repeatedly linked "socialism" and "communism," obscuring what adherents to the two philosophies saw as distinctions between them. In the 1964 presidential campaign, it was said by his opponents that Senator Barry Goldwater was "too conservative" to be made president. The negative connotations of "conservative" had receded by 1988; in that presidential campaign, then Vice President George Bush repeatedly amplified the negative connotations of the word "liberal" and then accused his opponent, Michael Dukakis, of being one.

The meaning of words also changes from speaker to speaker, from hearer to hearer, and from decade to decade. An elderly Japanese woman of my acquaintance used to squirm at the mention of the word "Jap." "Whenever I hear that word," she used to say, "I feel dirty all over." She was reacting to the negative connotations as it was used during the Second World War and earlier. More recently, "JAP" is an acronym for "Jewish-American princess," heard as an insult by an entirely different ethnic group.

A black friend of mine recalls hitchhiking as a young man in the 1930s through an area of the country where very few blacks lived. He was given a ride by a white couple, who fed him and gave him a place to sleep in their home. However, they kept referring to him as "little nigger," which upset him profoundly. He finally asked them not to call him by that "insulting term," a request they had difficulty understanding, as they had not meant to offend him. One way my friend might have explained his point further would have been to say, "Excuse me, but in the part of the country I come from, white people who wish to show contempt for my race call us 'niggers.' I assume this is not your intention."

In recent times, the negative connotations of the word "nigger" are more widely understood. This is partly the result of efforts by black Americans and others to educate the public. Early in 1942, when I was living in Chicago and teaching at the Illinois Institute of Technology, I was invited to become a columnist for the *Chicago Defender*—at that time the most militant of Negro newspapers. I say "Negro" rather than "black" because this was 1942 and it was the mission of that newspaper to make people proud of being "Negro." The word "Negro" at that time was used with dignity and pride. In its editorial policy, the *Defender* saw to it that the word was used in that way. It was always capitalized. Later, during the civil rights movement of the 1950s and 1960s, a wider effort was made to make just this point in the mind of the American public as a whole, first substituting "Negro" for "colored," "nigger," "nigrah," and, later, substituting "black" for "Negro." "Black" is now the word most frequently chosen by people of African origin in the United States to describe themselves, and the word "Negro" is considered by many to be old-fashioned and condescending. Most recently, it has been proposed that "African-American" be substituted for "black." *Those who believe that the meaning of a word is innately part of the word risk offending or being offended because of having ignored differences in context or current usage.*

The conflicts that erupt over words are invariably an index to social   8
concerns over the reality that the words refer to. Much debate has arisen over the issue of sexual discrimination in language. Is it fair, many people ask, that the word "man" should stand for all human beings, male and female? Should we say, "Everyone should cast his vote," when half the voters are women? Are there biases that are unfair to women—and to men—built into the English language? If so, what can or should be done about it?

The problem can be better understood if we look at the disputed   9
words in the contexts in which they appear. In some contexts, the extensional meaning of "man" as a synonym for the species *Homo sapiens* covers both sexes, without any discrimination implied: men, women and children; Englishmen, Chinese, Eskimos, Aborigines, next-door neighbors, and so forth. In other contexts, "man" refers only to the male: "There is a man at the door." The problems with connotation occur in a context such as: "The work team is short ten men." In such a case the employer may be inclined to look for ten more males to hire, even when the work can be done equally well by women.

The Chinese ideograph [人], also used in Japanese, stands for "man"   10
in the generic sense: "person," "human being." A different ideograph [男] is used for "man" in the sense of "male human being." Since women traditionally have been assigned subordinate roles in both Chinese and Japanese cultures, discrimination against women cannot be said to be due solely to the peculiarities of language.

For those who have no difficulty with the different meanings of   11
"man," or who like the maleness they find in the generic term, the language needs no modification. But what about those who are dissatisfied with the masculine connotations of "man"? What about the woman on the softball team who insists on being called "first baseperson" or the com-

mittee leader who styles herself "chairperson"? What about the woman named "Cooperman" who wanted to change her name to "Cooperperson" and petitioned a court to legalize the change? (Her petition was denied.) Can the language accommodate them?

Fortunately, the language is flexible enough for people to make personal adjustments to meet their own standards. "Human beings" or "humans" or "people" are acceptable substitutes for the generic "man," though rhetorically they may not always sound as good. Instead of saying "Man is a tool-using animal," we can say, "Human beings are tool-using animals." 12

Once it becomes apparent that we can construct any sentence we please without incurring possible sexual stereotypes, a further question remains: Should we demand that all writers adopt a "nonsexist" vocabulary and always use it—for example, the neutral plural? On this point history offers some guidance. 13

Most of the attempts made to force living language into a doctrinaire program have failed resoundingly. Jonathan Swift once spoke out acidly against the use of the word "mob" as a corrupt shortening of the Latin term *mobile vulgus*. Dr. Samuel Johnson resisted, to no avail, the admission of the word "civilization" into his dictionary because it seemed to him a barbarism, despite its respectable Latin root. In this century, Mussolini tried to eliminate the informal *tu* in Italian (the second person singular pronoun, whose English counterpart, "thou," has disappeared in ordinary English usage). He covered Italy with posters commanding Italians to use the *voi* form instead. His campaign failed. The social forces that created the words in the first place could not be changed by logic, fiat, or program. Language has usually proven stronger than the individual. 14

It must not be forgotten that language, created over centuries and inherited with our culture, does not exert its tyranny uniformly over all who use it. In the novel *Kingsblood Royal* by Sinclair Lewis, actually a tract against racial prejudice, the central character is a vicious racial bigot—but he is careful never to use the word "nigger." 15

Similarly, an individual who uses "sexist" terms uncritically may have all kinds of discriminatory attitudes towards women, or he—or she—may be entirely free of them. The presence or absence of such terms has no necessary connection with the presence or absence of the corresponding attitudes. 16

This does not mean that writers who are sensitive to sexual bias in language should resign themselves to what they consider a sorry state of affairs. They can carry out their own programs within their own speech and writing. These efforts are not without risk of accidentally engendering new, unintended meanings. For example, in revising the words of hymns, the Episcopal Church changed "Christian Men, Rejoice!" to "Christian Friends, Rejoice!" However, as Sara Mosle pointed out in *The* 17

New Republic, the theological implications of extending joy only to friends—what about Christian enemies, or even strangers?—were entirely inappropriate to the message of the hymn. "How long would it be before Christmas cards read 'Peace on Earth, good will towards friends?' A different proposition altogether from the brotherly (or sisterly) benediction to all mankind."

The calling of attention to sex discrimination contained within language, a campaign conducted in a similar way to that by which "Negro" and then "black" were successfully substituted for "colored," has served to raise society's awareness of the problem of built-in bias in language, even though it has not yet transformed the language. Even if such efforts fail to dislodge all forms of gender bias in the language, the effort to correct the problem is, in itself, worthwhile. As the poet John Ciardi has observed: 18

> In the long run the usage of those who do not think about the language will prevail. Usages I resist will become acceptable. It will not do to resist uncompromisingly. Yet those who care have a duty to resist. Changes that occur against such resistance are tested changes. The language is better for them— and for the resistance.

One other curious fact needs to be recorded about the words we apply to such hotly debated issues as race, religion, political heresy, and economic dissent. Every reader is acquainted with people who, according to their own flattering descriptions of themselves, "believe in being frank" and like to "tell it like it is." By "telling it like it is," such people usually mean calling anything or anyone by the term which has the strongest and most disagreeable affective connotations. Why people should pin medals on themselves for "candor" for performing this nasty feat has often puzzled me. Sometimes it is necessary to violate verbal taboos as an aid to clearer thinking, but, more often, to insist upon "telling it like it is" is to provide our minds with a greased runway down which we may slide back into unexamined and reactive patterns of evaluation and behavior.   19

QUESTIONS ON CONTENT

1. What is the distinction the Hayakawas draw between "informative connotations" and "affective connotations"?

2. Why, according to the authors, have many people in the American Southwest stopped using the term "Mexican"?

3. How can names, as the Hayakawas assert, "influence behavior toward those to whom they are applied" (3)? What happened when Americans stopped calling people with no work and no homes "bums"?

4. Why is it important to realize that the meanings of words may change "from speaker to speaker, from hearer to hearer, and from decade to

decade" (5)? Explain how the African-American friend's story in paragraph 6 serves to illustrate this point.

5. What do the Hayakawas mean when they say, *"Those who believe that the meaning of a word is innately part of the word risk offending or being offended because of having ignored differences in context or current usage"* (7)?

6. What, according to the Hayakawas, does history tell us about attempts to force changes on a living language? Is a person who uses sexist terms necessarily sexist? Explain.

7. In what ways are the Hayakawas' "words with built-in judgments" similar to Allport's "labels of primary potency" (p. 288)?

QUESTIONS ON RHETORIC

1. Most of the paragraphs in this essay are organized in the same way. Explain how they are organized, paying particular attention to the topic sentences. (Glossary: *Topic Sentence* and *Examples*)

2. What technique do the Hayakawas use to define both informative and affective connotations? (Glossary: *Definition*) Did you find their definitions clear and easy to understand? Why, or why not?

3. Discuss the writers' use of transitions between paragraphs. What transitions do they use? What effect does each transition have? (Glossary: *Transitions*)

4. How effective is the metaphor of the "greased runway" in the final paragraph? Explain. (Glossary: *Figures of Speech*)

VOCABULARY

simultaneously (1)	synonym (9)	dissent (19)
repellent (1)	barbarism (14)	candor (19)
adherents (4)	tyranny (15)	
squirm (5)	bigot (15)	

WRITING TOPICS

1. Hayakawa lists a number of terms (*pickpocket, racketeer, prostitute, atheist, heretic, materialist, radical, liberal, Mexican, drunkard, bum, retarded, Jap, nigger*) that evoke simultaneously both affective connotations and informative connotations. Think of at least three other terms that also do this. Write an essay in which you explain the affective and informative connotations of each term.

2. Write an essay in which you examine the idea that by finding new names for people who are outside the American middle-class mainstream, "we may find new ways of thinking about their situations[s] that may in turn suggest new ways in helping deal with [them]" (3).

3. The Hayakawas claim that "sometimes it is necessary to violate verbal taboos as an aid to clearer thinking, but, more often, to insist upon 'tell-

ing it like it is' is to provide our minds with a greased runway down which we may slide back into unexamined and reactive patterns of evaluation and behavior" (19). What do they mean here? Are you in favor of "telling it like it is," or can you see the dangers inherent in such usage? Using examples from your own experience or this article, write an essay in which you agree or disagree with the Hayakawas' position.

THE MEANINGS OF A WORD

Gloria Naylor

More than any other form of prejudiced language, racial slurs are intended to wound and to shame. In the following essay, which first appeared in the New York Times *in 1986, novelist and essayist Gloria Naylor remembers a time when a third-grade classmate called her "nigger." By examining the ways in which words can take on meaning depending on who uses them and to what purpose, Naylor concludes that "words themselves are innocuous; it is the consensus that gives them true power."*

Language is the subject. It is the written form with which I've managed to keep the wolf away from the door and, in diaries, to keep my sanity. In spite of this, I consider the written word inferior to the spoken, and much of the frustration experienced by novelists is the awareness that whatever we manage to capture in even the most transcendent passages falls far short of the richness of life. Dialogue achieves its power in the dynamics of a fleeting moment of sight, sound, smell, and touch.

I'm not going to enter the debate here about whether it is language that shapes reality or vice versa. That battle is doomed to be waged whenever we seek intermittent reprieve from the chicken and egg dispute. I will simply take the position that the spoken word, like the written word, amounts to a nonsensical arrangement of sounds or letters without a consensus that assigns "meaning." And building from the meanings of what we hear, we order reality. Words themselves are innocuous; it is the consensus that gives them true power.

I remember the first time I heard the word *nigger*. In my third-grade class, our math tests were being passed down the rows, and as I handed the papers to a little boy in back of me, I remarked that once again he had received a much lower mark than I did. He snatched his test from me and spit out that word. Had he called me a nymphomaniac or a necrophiliac, I couldn't have been more puzzled. I didn't know what a nigger was, but I knew that whatever it meant, it was something he shouldn't have called me. This was verified when I raised my hand, and in a loud voice repeated what he had said and watched the teacher scold him for using a "bad" word. I was later to go home and ask the inevitable question that every black parent must face—"Mommy, what does *nigger* mean?"

And what exactly did it mean? Thinking back, I realize that this could not have been the first time the word was used in my presence. I was part of a large extended family that had migrated from the rural South after World War II and formed a close-knit network that gravitated around my maternal grandparents. Their ground-floor apartment in one of the buildings they owned in Harlem was a weekend mecca for my immediate family, along with countless aunts, uncles, and cousins who brought along assorted friends. It was a bustling and open house with assorted neighbors and tenants popping in and out to exchange bits of gossip, pick up an old quarrel, or referee the ongoing checkers game in which my grandmother cheated shamelessly. They were all there to let down their hair and put up their feet after a week of labor in the factories, laundries, and shipyards of New York.

Amid the clamor, which could reach deafening proportions—two or three conversations going on simultaneously, punctuated by the sound of a baby's crying somewhere in the back rooms or out on the street—there was still a rigid set of rules about what was said and how. Older children were sent out of the living room when it was time to get into the juicy details about "you-know-who" up on the third floor who had gone and gotten herself "p-r-e-g-n-a-n-t!" But my parents, knowing that I could spell well beyond my years, always demanded that I follow the others out to play. Beyond sexual misconduct and death, everything else was considered harmless for our young ears. And so among the anecdotes of the triumphs and disappointments in the various workings of their lives, the word *nigger* was used in my presence, but it was set within contexts and inflections that caused it to register in my mind as something else.

In the singular, the word was always applied to a man who had distinguished himself in some situation that brought their approval for his strength, intelligence, or drive:

"Did Johnny *really* do that?"

"I'm telling you, that nigger pulled in $6,000 of overtime last year. Said he got enough for a down payment on a house."

When used with a possessive adjective by a woman—"my nigger"— it became a term of endearment for her husband or boyfriend. But it could be more than just a term applied to a man. In their mouths it became the pure essence of manhood—a disembodied force that channeled their past history of struggle and present survival against the odds into a victorious statement of being: "Yeah, that old foreman found out quick enough—you don't mess with a nigger."

In the plural, it became a description of some group within the community that had overstepped the bounds of decency as my family defined it. Parents who neglected their children, a drunken couple who fought in public, people who simply refused to look for work, those with excessively dirty mouths or unkempt households were all "trifling niggers." This particular circle could forgive hard times, unemployment, the occasional bout of depression—they had gone through all of that themselves—but the unforgivable sin was a lack of self-respect.

A woman could never be a "nigger" in the singular, with its connotation of confirming worth. The noun *girl* was its closest equivalent in that sense, but only when used in direct address and regardless of the gender doing the addressing. *Girl* was a token of respect for a woman. The one-syllable word was drawn out to sound like three in recognition of the extra ounce of wit, nerve, or daring that the woman had shown in the situation under discussion.

"G-i-r-l, stop. You mean you said that to his face?"   12

But if the word was used in a third-person reference or shortened so   13 that it almost snapped out of the mouth, it always involved some element of communal disapproval. And age became an important factor in these exchanges. It was only between individuals of the same generation, or from any older person to a younger (but never the other way around), that *girl* would be considered a compliment.

I don't agree with the argument that use of the word *nigger* at this   14 social stratum of the black community was an internalization of racism. The dynamics were the exact opposite: the people in my grandmother's living room took a word that whites used to signify worthlessness or degradation and rendered it impotent. Gathering there together, they transformed *nigger* to signify the varied and complex human beings they knew themselves to be. If the word was to disappear totally from the mouths of even the most liberal of white society, no one in that room was naive enough to believe it would disappear from white minds. Meeting the word head-on, they proved it had absolutely nothing to do with the way they were determined to live their lives.

So there must have been dozens of times that *nigger* was spoken in   15 front of me before I reached the third grade. But I didn't "hear" it until it was said by a small pair of lips that had already learned it could be a way to humiliate me. That was the word I went home and asked my mother about. And since she knew that I had to grow up in America, she took me in her lap and explained.

QUESTIONS ON CONTENT

1. How does Naylor explain her preference for the spoken word over the written word? What does she mean by "context"?

2. How, according to Naylor, do words get meanings?

3. Naylor says she must have heard the word "nigger" many times while she was growing up; yet she "heard" it for the first time when she was in the third grade. How does she explain this seeming contradiction?

4. In the context of her family, what does the word *nigger* mean to Naylor? Why do you suppose she offers so little in the way of definition of her classmate's use of the word? What is the effect on you as a reader? Explain.

5. In what context is *girl* "a token of respect for a woman"? How do you think women in general would—or should—react to being called "girls"? Explain.

QUESTIONS ON RHETORIC

1. What is Naylor's thesis, and where is it stated? (Glossary: *Thesis*)

2. Naylor gives a detailed description of her family and its lifestyle in paragraphs 4 and 5. What kinds of detail does she include in her brief story? How do these paragraphs contribute to your understanding of the word "nigger" as used by her family?

3. Would you characterize Naylor's tone in this essay as angry, objective, cynical, or something else? (Glossary: *Tone*) Cite examples of her diction to support your answer. (Glossary: *Diction*)

4. What is the meaning of Naylor's last sentence? How well does it work as an ending for her essay? (Glossary: *Endings*)

VOCABULARY

transcendent (1)	mecca (4)	unkempt (10)
consensus (2)	clamor (5)	trifling (10)
innocuous (2)	anecdotes (5)	internalization (14)
nymphomaniac (3)	inflections (5)	impotent (14)
necrophiliac (3)		

WRITING TOPICS

1. Naylor disagrees with the notion that use of the word *nigger* in the African-American community can be taken as an "internalization of racism." Reexamine her essay and discuss in what ways her definition of the word *nigger* affirms or denies her position. Draw on your own experiences, observations, and reading to add support to your answer.

2. Look up the words *black* and *white* in your dictionary. What are the connotations of most phrases and metaphors that include the word *black*? the word *white*? Why do you suppose the word *black* has more negative connotations? Is it for racist reasons? Discuss your opinion and your reasons for having it in an essay.

3. Write a short essay in which you discuss a word that has more than one meaning depending on one's point of view. For example, consider *wife, macho, chick, liberal, radical, homosexual.*

A GUIDE TO NONDISCRIMINATORY LANGUAGE

Rosalie Maggio

Language carries certain biases within it because of the historical circumstances surrounding its development and the ways people have used it. Dominant groups within cultures have often used language to maintain their superior positions and to disempower others. Not only can language deny equality, it can deny individuality by reinforcing stereotypes. In the following selection from The Dictionary of Bias-Free Usage, *Rosalie Maggio discusses the power of biased language and examines linguistic situations with a high incidence of such language. Common sense says that the best way to avoid bias in language is to cultivate a sense of the equality of all people regardless of their age, gender, race, religion, country of origin, or sexual orientation and to make an effort not to intentionally or even subconsciously reinforce stereotypes.*

Language both reflects and shapes society. The textbook on American government that consistently uses male pronouns for the president, even when not referring to a specific individual (e.g., "a president may cast his veto"), reflects the fact that all our presidents have so far been men. But it also shapes a society in which the idea of a female president somehow "doesn't sound right."

Culture shapes language and then language shapes culture. "Contrary to the assumption that language merely reflects social patterns such as sex-role stereotypes, research in linguistics and social psychology has shown that these are in fact facilitated and reinforced by language" (Marlis Hellinger, in *Language and Power*, ed., Cheris Kramarae et al.).

Biased language can also, says Sanford Berman, "powerfully harm people, as amply demonstrated by bigots' and tyrants' deliberate attempts to linguistically dehumanize and demean groups they intend to exploit, oppress, or exterminate. Calling Asians 'gooks' made it easier to kill them. Calling blacks 'niggers' made it simpler to enslave and brutalize them. Calling Native Americans 'primitives' and 'savages' made it okay to conquer and despoil them. And to talk of 'fishermen,' 'councilmen,'

309

and 'longshoremen' is to clearly exclude and discourage women from those pursuits, to diminish and degrade them."

The question is asked: Isn't it silly to get upset about language when there are so many more important issues that need our attention?   4

First, it's to be hoped that there are enough of us working on issues large and small that the work will all get done—someday. Second, the interconnections between the way we think, speak, and act are beyond dispute. Language goes hand-in-hand with social change—both shaping it and reflecting it. Sexual harassment was not a term anyone used twenty years ago; today we have laws against it. How could we have the law without the language; how could we have the language without the law? In fact, the judicial system is a good argument for the importance of "mere words"; the legal profession devotes great energy to the precise interpretation of words—often with far-reaching and significant consequences.   5

On August 21, 1990, in the midst of the Iraqi offensive, front-page headlines told the big story: President Bush had used the word *hostages* for the first time. Up to that time, *detainee* had been used. The difference between two very similar words was of possible life-and-death proportions. In another situation—also said to be life-and-death by some people—the difference between *fetal tissue* and *unborn baby* (in referring to the very same thing) is arguably the most debated issue in the country. So, yes, words have power and deserve our attention.   6

Some people are like George Crabbe's friend: "Habit with him was all the test of truth, / it must be right: I've done it from my youth." They have come of age using *handicapped, black-and-white, leper, mankind*, and pseudogeneric *he*; these terms must therefore be correct. And yet if there's one thing consistent about language it is that language is constantly changing; when the *Random House Dictionary of the English Language: 2nd Edition* was published in 1988, it contained 50,000 new entries, most of them words that had come into use since 1966. There were also 75,000 new definitions. (Incidentally, *RHD-II* asks its readers to "use gender-neutral terms wherever possible" and it never uses *mankind* in definitions where *people* is meant, nor does it ever refer to anyone of unknown gender as *he*.) However, few supporters of bias-free language are asking for changes; it is rather a matter of choice—which of the many acceptable words available to us will we use?   7

A high school student who felt that nonsexist language did demand some changes said, "But you don't understand! You're trying to change the English language, which has been around a lot longer than women have!"   8

One reviewer of the first edition commented, "There's no fun in limiting how you say a thing." Perhaps not. Yet few people complain about looking up a point of grammar or usage or checking the dictionary for a correct spelling. Most writers are very fussy about finding the precise   9 best word, the exact rhythmic vehicle for their ideas. Whether or not these limits "spoil their fun" is an individual judgment. However, most of us accept that saying or writing the first thing that comes to mind is not often the way we want to be remembered. So if we have to think a little, if we have to search for the unbiased word, the inclusive phrase, it is not any more effort than we expend on proper grammar, spelling, and style.

Other people fear "losing" words, as though there weren't more 10 where those came from. We are limited only by our imaginations; vague, inaccurate, and disrespectful words can be thrown overboard with no loss to society and no impoverishment of the language.

Others are tired of having to "watch what they say." But what they 11 perhaps mean is that they're tired of being sensitive to others' requests. From childhood onward, we all learn to "watch what we say": we don't swear around our parents; we don't bring up certain topics around certain people; we speak differently to friend, boss, cleric, English teacher, lover, radio interviewer, child. Most of us are actually quite skilled at picking and choosing appropriate words; it seems odd that we are too "tired" to call people what they want to be called.

The greatest objection to bias-free language is that it will lead us to 12 absurdities. Critics have posited something utterly ridiculous, cleverly demonstrated how silly it is, and then accounted themselves victorious in the battle against linguistic massacre. For example: "So I suppose now we're going to say: He/she ain't heavy, Father/Sister; he/she's my brother/sister." "I suppose next it will be 'ottoperson'." Cases have been built up against the mythic "woperson," "personipulate," and "personhole cover" (none of which has ever been advocated by any reputable sociolinguist). No grist appears too ridiculous for these mills. And, yes, they grind exceedingly small. Using a particular to condemn a universal is a fault in logic. But then ridicule, it is said, is the first and last argument of fools.

One of the most rewarding—and, for many people, the most unex- 13 pected—side effects of breaking away from traditional, biased language is a dramatic improvement in writing style. By replacing fuzzy, overgeneralized, cliché-ridden words with explicit, active words and by giving concrete examples and anecdotes instead of one-word-fits-all descriptions you can express yourself more dynamically, convincingly, and memorably.

"If those who have studied the art of writing are in accord on any one 14 point, it is on this: the surest way to arouse and hold the attention of the reader is by being specific, definite, and concrete" (Strunk and White, *The Elements of Style*). Writers who talk about *brotherhood* or *spinsters* or *right-hand men* miss a chance to spark their writing with fresh descriptions; they leave their readers as uninspired as they are. Unthinking writing is also less informative. Why use the unrevealing *adman* when we could choose instead a precise, descriptive, inclusive word like *adver-*

tising executive, copywriter, account executive, ad writer, or *media buyer*?

The word *manmade*, which seems so indispensable to us, doesn't   15
actually say very much. Does it mean artificial? handmade? synthetic?
fabricated? machine-made? custom-made? simulated? plastic? imitation?
contrived?

Communication is—or ought to be—a two-way street. A speaker   16
who uses *man* to mean *human being* while the audience hears it as *adult
male* is an example of communication gone awry.

Bias-free language is logical, accurate, and realistic. Biased language   17
is not. How logical is it to speak of the "discovery" of America, a land
already inhabited by millions of people? Where is the accuracy in writing
"Dear Sir" to a woman? Where is the realism in the full-page automobile
advertisement that says in bold letters, "A good driver is a product of his
environment," when more women than men influence car-buying decisions? Or how successful is the ad for a dot-matrix printer that says, "In
3,000 years, man's need to present his ideas hasn't changed. But his tools
have," when many of these printers are bought and used by women, who
also have ideas they need to present? And when we use stereotypes to
talk about people ("isn't that just like a welfare mother/Indian/girl/old
man"), our speech and writing will be inaccurate and unrealistic most of
the time.

DEFINITION OF TERMS

Bias/Bias-Free

Biased language communicates inaccurately about what it means to be   18
male or female; black or white; young or old; straight, gay, or bi; rich or
poor; from one ethnic group or another; disabled or temporarily able-
bodied; or to hold a particular belief system. It reflects the same bias
found in racism, sexism, ageism, handicappism, classism, ethnocentrism,
anti-Semitism, homophobia, and other forms of discrimination.

Bias occurs in the language in several ways.   19

1. Leaving out individuals or groups. "Employees are welcome to bring their
   wives and children" leaves out those employees who might want to bring
   husbands, friends, or same-sex partners. "We are all immigrants in this
   country" leaves out Native Americans, who were here well before the first
   immigrants.
2. Making unwarranted assumptions. To address a sales letter about a new
   diaper to the mother assumes that the father won't be diapering the baby.
   To write "Anyone can use this fire safety ladder" assumes that all members of the household are able-bodied.
3. Calling individuals and groups by names or labels that they do not choose
   for themselves (e.g., *Gypsy, office girl, Eskimo, pygmy, Bushman, the*

elderly, colored man) or terms that are derogatory (*fairy, libber, savage, bum, old goat*).

4. Stereotypical treatment that implies that all lesbians/Chinese/women/people with disabilities/teenagers are alike.
5. Unequal treatment of various groups in the same material.
6. Unnecessary mention of membership in a particular group. In a land of supposedly equal opportunity, of what importance is a person's race, sex, age, sexual orientation, disability, or creed? As soon as we mention one of these characteristics—without a good reason for doing so—we enter an area mined by potential linguistic disasters. Although there may be instances in which a person's sex, for example, is germane ("A recent study showed that female patients do not object to being cared for by male nurses"), most of the time it is not. Nor is mentioning a person's race, sexual orientation, disability, age, or belief system usually germane.

Bias can be overt or subtle. Jean Gaddy Wilson (in Brooks and Pinson, *Working with Words*) says, "Following one simple rule of writing or speaking will eliminate most biases. Ask yourself: Would you say the same thing about an affluent, white man?"   20

Inclusive/Exclusive

Inclusive language includes everyone; exclusive language excludes some people. The following quotation is inclusive: "The greatest revolution of our generation is the discovery that human beings, by changing the inner attitudes of their minds, can change the outer aspects of their lives" (William James). It is clear that James is speaking of all of us.   21

Examples of sex-exclusive writing fill most quotation books: "Man is the measure of all things" (Protagoras). "The People, though we think of a great entity when we use the word, means nothing more than so many millions of individual men" (James Bryce). "Man is nature's sole mistake" (W.S. Gilbert).   22

Sexist/Nonsexist

Sexist language promotes and maintains attitudes that stereotype people according to gender while assuming that the male is the norm—the significant gender. Nonsexist language treats all people equally and either does not refer to a person's sex at all when it is irrelevant or refers to men and women in symmetrical ways.   23

"A society in which women are taught anything but the management of a family, the care of men, and the creation of the future generation is a society which is on the way out" (L. Ron Hubbard). "Behind every successful man is a woman—with nothing to wear" (L. Grant Glickman). "Nothing makes a man and wife feel closer, these days, than a joint tax return" (Gil Stern). These quotations display various characteristics of sexist writing: (1) stereotyping an entire sex by what might be appropriate for some of it; (2) assuming male superiority; (3) using unparallel terms   24 (*man and wife* should be either *wife and husband/husband and wife* or *woman and man/man and woman*).

The following quotations clearly refer to all people: "It's really hard   25
to be roommates with people if your suitcases are much better than
theirs" (J.D. Salinger). "If people don't want to come out to the ball
park, nobody's going to stop them" (Yogi Berra). "If men and women of
capacity refuse to take part in politics and government, they condemn
themselves, as well as the people, to the punishment of living under bad
government" (Senator Sam J. Ervin). "I studied the lives of great men
and famous women, and I found that the men and women who got to the
top were those who did the jobs they had in hand, with everything they
had of energy and enthusiasm and hard work" (Harry S. Truman).

Gender-Free/Gender-Fair/Gender-Specific

Gender-free terms do not indicate sex and can be used for either women/   26
girls or men/boys (e.g., *teacher, bureaucrat, employee, hiker, operations
manager, child, clerk, sales rep, hospital patient, student, grandparent,
chief executive officer*).

Writing or speech that is gender-fair involves the symmetrical use of   27
gender-specific words (e.g., *Ms. Leinwohl/Mr.Kelly, councilwoman/
councilman, young man/young woman*) and promotes fairness to both
sexes in the larger context. To ensure gender-fairness, ask yourself often:
Would I write the same thing in the same way about a person of the
opposite sex? Would I mind if this were said of me?

If you are describing the behavior of children on the playground, to   28
be gender-fair you will refer to girls and boys an approximately equal
number of times, and you will carefully observe what the children do,
and not just assume that only the boys will climb to the top of the jungle
gym and that only the girls will play quiet games.

Researchers studying the same baby described its cries as "anger"   29
when they were told it was a boy and as "fear" when they were told it
was a girl (cited in Cheris Kramarae, *The Voices and Words of Women
and Men*). We are all victims of our unconscious and most deeply held
biases.

Gender-specific words (for example, *alderwoman, businessman, altar   30
girl*) are neither good nor bad in themselves. However, they need to be
used gender-fairly; terms for women and terms for men should be used an
approximately equal number of times in contexts that do not discriminate
against either of them. One problem with gender-specific words is that
they identify and even emphasize a person's sex when it is not necessary
(and is sometimes even objectionable) to do so. Another problem is that
they are so seldom used gender-fairly.

Although gender-free terms are generally preferable, sometimes gen-   31
der-neutral language obscures the reality of women's or men's oppres-

sion. *Battered spouse* implies that men and women are equally battered; this is far from true. *Parent* is too often taken to mean *mother* and obscures the fact that more and more fathers are very much involved in parenting; it is better here to use the gender-specific *fathers and mothers* or *mothers and fathers* than the gender-neutral *parents*. . . .

SEX AND GENDER

An understanding of the difference between sex and gender is critical to the use of bias-free language.   32

Sex is biological: people with male genitals are male, and people with female genitals are female.   33

Gender is cultural: our notions of "masculine" tell us how we expect men to behave and our notions of "feminine" tell us how we expect women to behave. Words like *womanly/manly, tomboy/sissy, unfeminine/unmasculine* have nothing to do with the person's sex; they are culturally acquired, subjective concepts about character traits and expected behaviors that vary from one place to another, from one individual to another.   34

It is biologically impossible for a woman to be a sperm donor. It may be culturally unusual for a man to be a secretary, but it is not biologically impossible. To say "the secretary . . . she" assumes all secretaries are women and is sexist because the issue is gender, not sex. Gender describes an individual's personal, legal, and social status without reference to genetic sex; gender is a subjective cultural attitude. Sex is an objective biological fact. Gender varies according to the culture. Sex is a constant.   35

The difference between sex and gender is important because much sexist language arises from cultural determinations of what a woman or man "ought" to be. Once a society decides, for example, that to be a man means to hide one's emotions, bring home a paycheck, and be able to discuss football standings while to be a woman means to be soft-spoken, love shopping, babies, and recipes, and "never have anything to wear," much of the population becomes a contradiction in terms—unmanly men and unwomanly women. Crying, nagging, gossiping, and shrieking are assumed to be women's lot; roughhousing, drinking beer, telling dirty jokes, and being unable to find one's socks and keys are laid at men's collective door. Lists of stereotypes appear silly because very few people fit them. The best way to ensure unbiased writing and speaking is to describe people as individuals, not as members of a set.   36

Gender Role Words

Certain sex-linked words depend for their meanings on cultural stereotypes: *feminine/masculine, manly/womanly, boyish/girlish, husbandly/wifely, fatherly/motherly, unfeminine/unmasculine, unmanly/unwomanly,*   37 etc. What a person understands by these words will vary from culture to culture and even within a culture. Because the words depend for their meanings on interpretations of stereotypical behavior or characteristics, they may be grossly inaccurate when applied to individuals. Somewhere, sometime, men and women have said, thought, or done everything the other sex has said, thought, or done except for a very few sex-linked biological activities (e.g., only women can give birth or nurse a baby, only a man can donate sperm or impregnate a woman). To describe a woman as unwomanly is a contradiction in terms; if a woman is doing it, saying it, wearing it, thinking it, it must be—by definition—womanly.

F. Scott Fitzgerald did not use "feminine" to describe the unforgetta-   38
ble Daisy in *The Great Gatsby*. He wrote instead, "She laughed again, as if she said something very witty, and held my hand for a moment, looking up into my face, promising that there was no one in the world she so much wanted to see. That was a way she had." Daisy's charm did not belong to Woman; it was uniquely hers. Replacing vague sex-linked descriptors with thoughtful words that describe an individual instead of a member of a set can lead to language that touches people's minds and hearts.

NAMING

Naming is power, which is why the issue of naming is one of the most   39
important in bias-free language.

Self-Definition

People decide what they want to be called. The correct names for individ-   40
uals and groups are always those by which they refer to themselves. This "tradition" is not always unchallenged. Haig Bosmajian (*The Language of Oppression*) says, "It isn't strange that those persons who insist on defining themselves, who insist on this elemental privilege of self-naming, self-definition, and self-identity encounter vigorous resistance. Predictably, the resistance usually comes from the oppressor or would-be oppressor and is a result of the fact that he or she does not want to relinquish the power which comes from the ability to define others."

Dr. Ian Hancock uses the term *exonym* for a name applied to a group   41
by outsiders. For example, Romani peoples object to being called by the exonym *Gypsies*. They do not call themselves Gypsies. Among the many other exonyms are: the elderly, colored people, homosexuals, pagans, adolescents, Eskimos, pygmies, savages. The test for an exonym is whether people describe themselves as "redmen," "illegal aliens," "holy rollers," etc., or whether only outsiders describe them that way.

There is a very small but visible element today demanding that gay   42
men "give back" the word *gay*—a good example of denying people the
right to name themselves. A late-night radio caller said several times that
gay men had "stolen" this word from "our" language. It was not clear
what language gay men spoke.

A woman nicknamed "Betty" early in life had always preferred her   43
full name, "Elizabeth." On her fortieth birthday, she reverted to Elizabeth. An acquaintance who heard about the change said sharply, "I'll call
her Betty if I like!"

We can call them Betty if we like, but it's arrogant, insensitive, and   44
uninformed: the only rule we have in this area says we call people what
they want to be called.

"Insider/Outsider" Rule

A related rule says that insiders may describe themselves in ways that   45
outsiders may not. "Crip" appears in *The Disability Rag*; this does not
mean that the word is available to anyone who wants to use it. "Big Fag"
is printed on a gay man's T-shirt. He may use that expression; a non-gay
may not so label him. One junior-high student yells to another, "Hey,
nigger!" This would be highly offensive and inflammatory if the speaker
were not African American. A group of women talk about "going out
with the girls," but a coworker should not refer to them as "girls." When
questioned about just such a situation, Miss Manners replied that "people
are allowed more leeway in what they call themselves than in what they
call others."

"People First" Rule

Haim Ginott taught us that labels are disabling; intuitively most of us   46
recognize this and resist being labeled. The disability movement originated the "people first" rule, which says we don't call someone a "dia-
betic" but rather "a person with diabetes." Saying someone is "an AIDS
victim" reduces the person to a disease, a label, a statistic; use instead "a
person with/who has/living with AIDS." The 1990 Americans with Disabilities Act is a good example of correct wording. Name the person as a
person first, and let qualifiers (age, sex, disability, race) follow, but (and
this is crucial) only if they are relevant. Readers of a magazine aimed at
an older audience were asked what they wanted to be called (elderly?
senior citizens? seniors? golden agers?). They rejected all the terms; one
said, "How about 'people'?" When high school students rejected labels
like kids, teens, teenagers, youth, adolescents, and juveniles, and were
asked in exasperation just what they would like to be called, they said,
"Could we just be people?"

Women as Separate People

One of the most sexist maneuvers in the language has been the identifica-   47
tion of women by their connections to husband, son, or father—often
even after he is dead. Women are commonly identified as someone's
widow while men are never referred to as anyone's widower. Marie Mar-
vingt, a Frenchwoman who lived around the turn of the century, was an
inventor, adventurer, stunt woman, superathlete, aviator, and all-around
scholar. She chose to be affianced to neither man (as a wife) nor God (as
a religious), but it was not long before an uneasy male press found her a
fit partner. She is still known today by the revealing label "the Fiancée of
Danger." If a connection is relevant, make it mutual. Instead of "Frieda,
his wife of seventeen years," write "Frieda and Eric, married for seventeen years."

It is difficult for some people to watch women doing unconventional   48
things with their names. For years the etiquette books were able to tell us
precisely how to address a single woman, a married woman, a divorced
woman, or a widowed woman (there was no similar etiquette on men
because they have always been just men and we have never had a code to
signal their marital status). But now some women are Ms. and some are
Mrs., some are married but keeping their birth names, others are hyphen-
ating their last name with their husband's, and still others have constructed new names for themselves. Some women—including African
American women who were denied this right earlier in our history—take
great pride in using their husband's name. All these forms are correct.
The same rule of self-definition applies here: call the woman what she
wants to be called. . . .

GENERAL RULES

Parallel Treatment

Parallel treatment is essential when discussing different groups (e.g., per-   49
sons with and without disabilities, Christians and Jews, or heterosexual,
bisexual, and homosexual groups). Beware false parallels: "white" and
"nonwhite" are not parallel. "White" is specific while "nonwhite" simply
lumps together everyone else. The problems with nonparallel treatment
are most easily seen in gender asymmetries.

If you refer to a woman as Margaret Schlegel, refer to a man in the   50
same material as Gavan Huntley. If he is Huntley, she will be Schlegel,
or if she is Margaret, he will be Gavan, and if she is Ms. Schlegel, he is
Mr. Huntley.

Half the time use "girls and boys," half the time "boys and girls."   51
Because of a grammatical "convention" based on the belief that the masculine was the more worthy gender, the male word has always had the

right to be placed first. Thus we have Mr. and Mrs., husband and wife, male and female, etc. Vary this half the time (although be prepared for odd looks if you try Mrs. and Mr.).

Do not make of one sex a parenthetical expression: "hats off to the postal employees who manned (and womanned) the Olympic stamp cancellation booths"; "male (and female) students"; "his (or her)." 52

When sex-specific words are used, maintain sexual symmetry. Male-female word pairs are troublesome in three ways. (1) Certain words are used as parallel pairs, but are in fact asymmetrical, for example, cameragirl/cameraman, man Friday/girl Friday, mermaid/merman, makeup girl/makeup man. The worst offender in this category is man/wife; the correct pairs are man/woman and wife/husband. (2) Other words are so unequivalent that few people confuse them as pairs, but it is revealing to study them, knowing that they were once equals: governor/governess, patron/matron, courtier/courtesan, master/mistress, buddy/sissy, hubby/hussy, dog/bitch, patrimony/matrimony, call boy/call girl, showman/showgirl, Romeo/Juliet. We all know what a Romeo is, but if we didn't we could look it up in the dictionary; this is not true of a Juliet. A call boy is a page; a call girl is a prostitute. Buddy is affectionate; sissy is derogatory. A study of word pairs shows that words associated primarily with women ultimately become discounted and devalued. Muriel Schulz (*Language and Power*) calls it "semantic derogation." (3) Acceptable words and constructions become unacceptable sometimes because of the nonparallel way they are used. For example, *a male and three women*, *aldermen and women*, and *two girls and a man* should read: *a man and three women, aldermen and alderwomen*, and *two women and a man* (or *two girls and a boy*). . . . 53

Hidden Bias/Context

Writing may be completely free of biased terms yet still carry a biased message. According to a radio news item, "More women than ever before are living with men without being married to them. And more unmarried women than ever before are having babies." An accurate, unbiased report would have said: "More men and women than ever before are living together without being married. And more unmarried couples than ever before are having babies." 54

Too often language makes assumptions about people—that everyone is male, heterosexual, able-bodied, white, married, between the ages of twenty-six and fifty-four, of European extraction, etc. Until it becomes second nature to write without bias, re-read your material as though you were: a gay man, someone who uses a wheelchair, a Japanese American woman, an eighty-year-old man, or other "individuals" of your own creation. If you do not feel left out, discounted, and ignored but instead can read without being stopped by some incongruence, you have probably 55 avoided hidden bias. It is also wonderfully helpful to ask people from a group with which you aren't familiar to read your work; they can quickly spot any insensitivity.

QUESTIONS ON CONTENT

1. What does Maggio mean when she says, "language both reflects and shapes society" (1)? Using examples from your own experience, illustrate the truth in her statement.

2. According to Maggio, "few supporters of bias-free language are asking for changes" (7). If not changes in the language, what do these people want? Explain.

3. What are some of the reasons that people give for resisting unbiased language? How does Maggio counter each of these arguments?

4. According to Maggio, what is one of the most rewarding "side effects" of using unbiased language? Why do you suppose this is true?

5. Describe the ways in which bias occurs in language. Provide an example for each way from your own experience.

6. What, according to Maggio, are three key characteristics of sexist writing? Give an example of your own for each characteristic.

7. Maggio believes that it is important to know the difference between *sex* and *gender*. What exactly is the difference, and why do you suppose confusion surrounds these two terms? Where do our ideas of what is masculine or feminine come from? Explain.

QUESTIONS ON RHETORIC

1. Maggio's essay is chock full of examples. Why do you suppose she felt the need to present as many as she does? Which examples work best for you? Explain.

2. Explain how Maggio uses division and classification to develop her essay. (Glossary: *Division and Classification*) Is this strategy appropriate for her subject matter? Why, or why not?

3. How has Maggio organized her essay? (Glossary: *Organization*) How do the heads in her essay work within the framework of this organization?

4. How are paragraphs 28 and 29 related to paragraph 27?

5. How would you describe Maggio's tone in this essay? (Glossary: *Tone*). Cite examples of her diction that led you to your conclusion.

VOCABULARY

facilitated (2)	grist (12)	symmetrical (23)
demean (3)	simulated (15)	status (35)
harassment (5)	homophobia (18)	inflammatory (45)
posited (12)	affluent (20)	incongruence (55)

WRITING TOPICS

1. How do you react to the question: "Isn't it silly to get upset about language when there are so many more important issues that need our attention?" How would you answer this question? What would happen if no one got upset about biased language? Write a response to the above question in which you explain your beliefs and feelings about biased language.

2. For Maggio, "naming is power." Think of a situation in which you were not free to decide what you wanted to be called. How did you feel? Write an essay in which you explore the importance of names and why people feel empowered when they have control over what they want to be called. Draw examples from your own experiences, observations, or reading of articles in this text.

3. What is the relationship between good writing and unbiased language? In a brief essay, explain what each of us can do to become more sensitive to the biases in our own writing and to eliminate discriminatory language when it occurs.

WRITING ASSIGNMENTS FOR "PREJUDICE, DISCRIMINATION, AND LANGUAGE"

1. Members of a group often have different perceptions of the characteristics of that group from those held by outsiders. What is your own image of the racial, national, religious, and social groups to which you belong? How do nonmembers view these groups? Write an essay in which you compare the two images and attempt to account for the differences.

2. Write an essay in which you compare and/or contrast the discussions of prejudice and language by Allport and the Hayakawas.

3. Since the early 1960s African Americans have sought a self-identifying label for themselves. After suffering for years under the labels *nigger*, *colored*, and *Negro* imposed by the dominant white society, they have experimented with such labels as *Afro-American, black*, and *people of color*. Write an essay in which you trace the shifts that have taken place and construct a reasonable linguistic explanation for these shifts.

4. Write an essay in which you discuss what your name means to you. Some questions you might consider include: How did your parents decide on your name? How do you like your name? What does your name mean? How do others respond to your name? Are there any stereotypes associated with your first name? Are there any racial or ethnic stereotypes associated with your last name?

5. Show-business people often change their names. Here are the professional names and the original names of a number of celebrities.

Professional Name	Original Name
Tony Curtis	Bernard Schwartz
Mick Jagger	Michael Philip
Simone Signoret	Simone Kaminker
Roy Rogers	Leonard Slye
Raquel Welch	Raquel Tejada
James Garner	James Bumgarner
Bob Dylan	Robert Zimmerman
Doris Day	Doris von Kappelhoff
Fred Astaire	Frederick Austerlitz
John Wayne	Marion Michael Morrison
Cyd Charisse	Tula Finklea
Anne Bancroft	Annemaria Italiano
Michael Caine	Maurice J. Micklewhite
David Bowie	David Jones
Redd Foxx	John Elroy Sanford
Ringo Starr	Richard Starkey
Elizabeth Arden	Florence Nightingale Graham

Write an essay in which you speculate about the reasons for these name changes. Why, do you think, such changes are less common among younger performers?

6. CBS news commentator Charles Osgood once wrote, "To hate somebody, to hate them enough to kill them, you must first dehumanize them in your mind. . . . That is why racial and religious epithets are so evil. To call somebody a nigger or a kike or a spic or wop is to rob a human being of his humanity. It is a form of hate, a form of murder." Write an essay in which you discuss the dehumanizing effects of racial, ethnic, and religious labels.

7. The following news item appeared in the Burlington (Vt.) *Free Press* on June 4, 1977:

'NIGGER' CAN BE ERASED IN MAINE

AUGUSTA, Maine (AP)—Names such as Nigger Hill and Nigger Island could be erased from the Maine map under a new law approved Friday by Gov. James B. Longley.

Longley signed a measure into law which allows people to complain to the Maine Human Rights Commission when they feel that the use of the term "nigger" in the name of a geographic site is offensive.

About 10 geographic features in Maine—hills, brooks and islands—include the term.

Rep. Gerald Talbot, D-Portland, the state's only black lawmaker, introduced the bill after he said he tried in vain to have the names changed by other means.

His measure originally called for banning the use of any name which is offensive to a nationality or racial group, but lawmakers amended the bill when they said it was too broad.

They said the original plan could have been extended to include terms such as "squaw."

The law will take effect in the fall.

In an essay discuss whether this is an example of censorship or a sincere attempt to eradicate prejudice. In your opinion, was the law as originally proposed "too broad"? Why, or why not?

8. Almost every area of the country has its share of racial or ethnic slurs. What slurs are used in your area? Have you ever been the object of a racial, ethnic, or religious slur? How did it feel? In an essay, discuss how a group (of which you are a member) perceives itself in a way that differs from how outsiders perceive it.

9. Make a list of racial slurs you are familiar with. Research their meanings and write an essay about your findings. Include in your essay answers to the following: What is the origin of the word? Was the word originally intended to insult? How does the word relate to that people's image of themselves? In summary, were you surprised at your findings? How did your research add to your perception of racial understanding?

10. The linguist Charles F. Berlitz once wrote that "ancient customs, sanctified by time, of considering people who differ in color, customs, physical characteristics and habits—and by enlargement all strangers—as potential enemies is something mankind can no longer afford, even lin-

guistically." Write an essay in which you agree or disagree with Berlitz's position.

11. The newspaper columnist William Raspberry believes that African Americans "have to make our children understand that they are intelligent, competent people, capable of doing whatever they put their minds to and making it in the American mainstream, not just in a black subculture." Based on your own studies of history, consider the ways in which a culture develops positive ethnic traditions and fosters a people's good opinion of itself. To what degree would you say a minority group is at the mercy of the majority's opinion? In an essay offer some of your own insights into this issue.

PART VII

Cultural Diversity: Searching for Common Ground

DRAWING THE LINE

Barbara Ehrenreich

Barbara Ehrenreich is a columnist for Mother Jones *and the author of several books, including* Fear of Falling: The Inner Life of the Middle Class *and* The Worst Years of Our Lives: Irreverent Notes from a Decade of Greed. *Here, she delves into the possible reasons why some people argue that English should be the only publicly recognized language in the United States. Using very heavy doses of irony, Ehrenreich reveals her belief that such a movement is not only illogical but if successful would, as she concludes, make her feel "dumb."*

Those English-only types have finally gone too far. It all started with the commendable impulse to keep public-health doctors from communicating with immigrants in a language they can understand. At least this was the original modest intent of the Suffolk County, New York, English-only bill. And since even us real Americans can't always grasp the complex vocabulary of medical science (you know, "deductible," "unreimbursable procedure," "coinsurance," and so forth), why should a bunch of foreigners have the advantage?

But then the English-only people got carried away. First they took away the *au pairs, divas*, and *masseurs*. Then they moved in on the states and California street names. La Ciénaga Boulevard became Swamp Street, Colorado became Colored (until, of course, an emergency referendum renamed it Greater Denver). Next, it was the turn of the legal profession, which—without its *amicuses* and *de jures*—was left speechless for upward of 20 minutes. After that, a hush fell over the literati, deprived as they were of the delicate *frissons, scandales*, and *folies* with which they had for so long maintained their *esprit*. I didn't utter a word of protest, I blush to admit, not even when quiche turned into egg pie.

I used to be gung ho for English-only myself, on the grounds that my ancestors had spoken English-only for at least 20 generations, and not much of it at that—idle chitchat being considered a sign of insecurity or ill intent. The less sophisticated of my forebears avoided foreigners at all costs, for the very good reason that, in their circles, speaking in tongues was commonly a prelude to snake handling. The more tolerant amongst us regarded foreign languages as a kind of speech impediment that could be overcome by willpower. When confronted by one of the afflicted, we would speak very s-l-o-w-l-y and loudly, repeating ourselves until the poor soul caught on, or—as was more often the case—ran off in search of more quick-witted company.

Of course, people are drawn to English-only for all kinds of good

327

reasons. Some of them, for example, have been to Paris, where they strayed from the Holiday Inn and were spat upon by waiters for ordering "un-coffee" or "croy-sints." Others of them are driven by the fear, mounting to panic in the border states, that the United States will experience the same fate as Canada. And we all know what happened to Canada, which was once a semitropical paradise—famed for its tempestuous rhythms and piquant cuisine—until the tragic imposition of bilingualism rendered it large, cold, and boring.

Then there is the fear, common to all English-only speakers, that the chief purpose of foreign languages is to make fun of us. Otherwise, you know, why not just come out and *say* it? NO FUMAR, for example. I used to see it all over the place, and who knows what that means—CHILL OUT, GRINGO FOOL, maybe? Or that inscrutable message inscribed in so many airplane restrooms: POR FAVOR, NO TIRAR EL PAPEL DENTRO DEL INODORO. What is that supposed to mean? DO YOURSELF A FAVOR AND SOAK YOUR UGLY ANGLO HEAD IN THE TOILET? And if that isn't what it means, why do I see so many foreigners—no doubt bilingualists—winking and smirking as if they knew something we didn't?

But the real motive is patriotism. Look, we can't keep out foreign *people*, without whom we'd have to bus our own dishes, clean our own houses, and manage our own factories. And we can't keep out foreign *things*, without which there'd be no color TVs, calculators, or Nintendo. So we can at least draw the line at *words*; and words are important because they are so often the unwitting carriers of *ideas*. Think of the foreign ideas that have leaked in over the last two hundred years and the trouble that could have been saved by stopping them dead at the border: communism, Catholicism, calculus, and cubism—not to mention Freudianism, existentialism, fascism, and french fries.

For there can be no more ancient and traditional American value than ignorance. English-only speakers brought it with them to this country three centuries ago, and they quickly imposed it on the Africans—who were not allowed to learn to read and write—and on the Native Americans, who were simply not allowed. Today, our presidents and vice presidents proudly stand ready to prove in a court of law that they don't know anything and have forgotten what they did know. In fact, the original anti-immigrant movement of the 19th century, the forerunner of English-only, called itself, appropriately, the "Know-Nothings." They believed, as many patriots still do, that the mind of America should remain a—how do you put it in English?—*blank slate*?

But the movement has finally gone too far. It was a professor at Dartmouth, I believe, who first pointed out that English itself is a mongrel language—a corruption of the pure Saxon spoken by my ancestors before the disastrous events of 1066. Then a team of linguists at the Heritage Foundation issued the first "Saxon-only" manifesto, listing the many social problems that could be eliminated immediately by expunging all traces of foreign (i.e., Romance-language) influence: homosexuality, pornography, pederasty, feminism, and democracy—and that's just for starters!

There are advantages, I mean, good things, about this Saxon-only thing. Like it's nice I can carry the *Oxford Unabridged Dictionary* in my hip pocket now. And I don't need a lot of big words to *express*—I mean, say, what I gotta say. And we're all Americans now, no "bi" or "multi" nothing. But there's something about this language—you know, *talking*—thing that makes me feel sort of well—how do you say it in Saxon? *Dumb*, you know what I'm trying to say? Real dumb.

QUESTIONS ON CONTENT

1. What is the connection between Ehrenreich's first sentence and the rest of her first paragraph?

2. What is amusing about Ehrenreich's attitude toward what she calls "the complex vocabulary of medical science" (1)? What do you think of the examples that she gives to illustrate her point?

3. What point does Ehrenreich make by referring to the fact that English itself is a "mongrel language" (8)? What were "the disastrous events of 1066"?

4. Ehrenreich says the real motive of the English-only movement is "patriotism." How do you think she would define patriotism as far as English-only is concerned?

5. What does Ehrenreich mean by her last two sentences?

QUESTIONS ON RHETORIC

1. What is the figure of speech used in the title of this essay? (Glossary: *Figure of Speech*) How does it relate to the author's argument?

2. What is Ehrenreich's purpose in this essay? (Glossary: *Purpose*)

3. Define irony in your own words. (Glossary: *Irony*) Identify the point in the essay when you first realized that the author was using irony. In your view, has the irony Ehrenreich used been effective?

4. For what kind of audience do you think Ehrenreich wrote this essay? (Glossary: *Audience*) Explain.

5. Ehrenreich uses foreign words, phrases, and even sentences in her essay. Do you know the meanings of all these expressions? Do you have to know them to understand the essay? Explain.

VOCABULARY

commendable (1)	afflicted (3)	unwitting (6)
literati (2)	tempestuous (4)	manifesto (8)
gung ho (3)	inscrutable (5)	expunging (8)
impediment (3)	smirking (5)	

WRITING TOPICS

1. If you find Ehrenreich's ironic point unconvincing, you might write an essay in defense of the English-only movement. You may want to do some preliminary research on the movement and its beliefs in your school library before starting to write your essay.

2. The English-only movement has inspired many writers to take sides on this issue. One such writer, Edwin M. Yoder, wrote an essay in 1986 for the *Akron Beacon Journal* titled "The Alarmist Proponents of English." In it Yoder disputes the theory that English-only is an attempt to control the present influx of immigrants. However, he also concedes only one virtue on behalf of English-only proponents: that our present culture is drifting away from standards of civilization contained in such works as the King James Bible, Shakespeare's plays, Bunyan's *Pilgrim's Progress*, and books of common law brought here by early settlers. "Perhaps if we used the language of Shakespeare and the King James Bible as tenderly as our ancestors did, legal measures to assure its primacy would not be needed. Its appeal to new arrivals would be irresistible," Yoder writes. In a short essay, discuss your reaction to this point of view.

TALKING IN THE NEW LAND

Edite Cunha

*Shortly after moving from her native Portugal to Peabody,
Massachusetts, when she was seven years old, Edite Cunha's
name was changed by a teacher. Far from being a helpful
gesture, allowing her to fit into a new culture, the name
change left Cunha bereft of her personal identity, which only
added to her difficulties in learning a new language. In
addition, Cunha faced the difficulties of becoming bilingual.
As her family's translator, she had to be her father's
"voice," a responsibility she dreaded. In 1991 Cunha
graduated from Smith College where she was an Ada
Comstock Scholar.*

Before I started school in America I was Edite. Maria Edite dos Anjos   1
Cunha. Maria, in honor of the Virgin Mary. In Portugal it was customary
to use Maria as a religious and legal prefix to every girl's name. Virtually
every girl was so named. It had something to do with the apparition of
the Virgin to three shepherd children at Fatima. In naming their daughters
Maria, my people were expressing their love and reverence for their Lady
of Fatima.

Edite came from my godmother, Dona Edite Baetas Ruivo. The par-   2
ish priest argued that I could not be named Edite because in Portugal the
name was not considered Christian. But Dona Edite defended my right to
bear her name. No one had argued with her family when they had chris-
tened her Edite. Her family had power and wealth. The priest considered
privileges endangered by his stand, and I became Maria Edite.

The dos Anjos was for my mother's side of the family. Like her   3
mother before her, she had been named Maria dos Anjos. And Cunha
was for my father's side. Carlos dos Santos Cunha, son of Abilio dos
Santos Cunha, the tailor from Saíl.

I loved my name. "Maria Edite dos Anjos Cunha," I'd recite at the   4
least provocation. It was melodious and beautiful. And through it I knew
exactly who I was.

At the age of seven I was taken from our little house in Sobreira, São   5
Martinho da Cortiça, Portugal, and brought to Peabody, Massachusetts.
We moved into the house of Senhor João, who was our sponsor in the big
land. I was in America for about a week when someone took me to
school one morning and handed me over to the teacher, Mrs. Donahue.

Mrs. Donahue spoke Portuguese, a wondrous thing for a woman with   6
a funny, unpronounceable name.

"*Como é que te chamas*?" she asked as she led me to a desk by big   7
windows.

"Maria Edite dos Anjos Cunha," I recited, all the while scanning Mrs.   8
Donahue for clues. How could a woman with such a name speak my
language?

In fact, Mrs. Donahue was Portuguese. She was a Silva. But she had   9
married an Irishman and changed her name. She changed my name, too,
on the first day of school.

"Your name will be Mary Edith Cunha," she declared. "In America   10
you only need two or three names. Mary Edith is a lovely name. And it
will be easier to pronounce."

My name was Edite. Maria Edite. Maria Edite dos Anjos Cunha. I   11
had no trouble pronouncing it.

"Mary Edith, Edithhh, Mary Edithhh," Mrs. Donahue exaggerated it.   12
She wrinkled up her nose and raised her upper lip to show me the proper
positioning of the tongue for the *th* sound. She looked hideous. There
was a big pain in my head. I wanted to scream out my name. But you
could never argue with a teacher.

At home I cried and cried. *Mãe* and *Pai* wanted to know about the   13
day. I couldn't pronounce the new name for them. Senhor João's red face
wrinkled in laughter.

Day after day Mrs. Donahue made me practice pronouncing that   14
name that wasn't mine. Mary Edithhhhh. Mary Edithhh. Mary Edithhh.
But weeks later I still wouldn't respond when she called it out in class.
Mrs. Donahue became cross when I didn't answer. Later my other
teachers shortened it to Mary. And I never knew quite who I was. . . .

Mrs. Donahue was a small woman, not much bigger than my seven-year-   15
old self. Her graying hair was cut into a neat, curly bob. There was a
smile that she wore almost every day. Not broad. Barely perceptible. But
it was there, in her eyes, and at the corners of her mouth. She often wore
gray suits with jackets neatly fitted about the waist. On her feet she wore
matching black leather shoes, tightly laced. Matching, but not identical.
One of them had an extra-thick sole, because like all of her pupils, Mrs.
Donahue had an oddity. We, the children, were odd because we were of
different colors and sizes, and did not speak in the accepted tongue. Mrs.
Donahue was odd because she had legs of different lengths.

I grew to love Mrs. Donahue. She danced with us. She was the only   16
teacher in all of Carroll School who thought it was important to dance.
Every day after recess she took us all to the big open space at the back of
the room. We stood in a circle and joined hands. Mrs. Donahue would
blow a quivering note from the little round pitch pipe she kept in her
pocket, and we became a twirling, singing wheel. Mrs. Donahue hobbled
on her short leg and sang in a high trembly voice, "Here we go, loop-de-
loop." We took three steps, then a pause. Her last "loop" was always

very high. It seemed to squeak above our heads, bouncing on the ceiling. "Here we go, loop-de-lie." Three more steps, another pause, and on we whirled. "Here we go, loop-de-loop." Pause. "All on a Saturday night." To anyone looking in from the corridor we were surely an irregular sight, a circle of children of odd sizes and colors singing and twirling with our tiny hobbling teacher.

I'd been in Room Three with Mrs. Donahue for over a year when she 17 decided that I could join the children in the regular elementary classes at Thomas Carroll School. I embraced the news with some ambivalence. By then the oddity of Mrs. Donahue's classroom had draped itself over me like a warm safe cloak. Now I was to join the second-grade class of Miss Laitinen. In preparation, Mrs. Donahue began a phase of relentless drilling. She talked to me about what I could expect in second grade. Miss Laitinen's class was well on its way with cursive writing, so we practiced that every day. We intensified our efforts with multiplication. And we practiced pronouncing the new teacher's name.

"Lay-te-nun." Mrs. Donahue spewed the *t* out with excessive force to 18 demonstrate its importance. I had a tendency to forget it.

"Lay-nun." 19

"Mary Edith, don't be lazy. Use that tongue. It's Lay te"—she bared 20 her teeth for the *t* part—"nun."

One morning, with no warning, Mrs. Donahue walked me to the end 21 of the hall and knocked on the door to Room Six. Miss Laitinen opened the door. She looked severe, carrying a long rubber-tipped pointer which she held horizontally before her with both hands. Miss Laitinen was a big, masculine woman. Her light, coarse hair was straight and cut short. She wore dark cardigans and very long, pleated plaid kilts that looked big enough to cover my bed.

"This is Mary Edith," Mrs. Donahue said. Meanwhile I looked at 22 their shoes. Miss Laitinen wore flat, brown leather shoes that laced up and squeaked on the wooden floor when she walked. They matched each other perfectly, but they were twice as big as Mrs. Donahue's.

"Mary Edith, say hello to Miss Laitinen." Mrs. Donahue stressed the 23 *t*—a last-minute reminder.

"Hello, Miss Lay-te-nun," I said, leaning my head back to see her 24 face. Miss Laitinen was tall. Mrs. Donahue's head came just to her chest. They both nodded approvingly before I was led to my seat.

Peabody, Massachusetts. "The Leather City." It is stamped on the city 25 seal, along with the image of a tanned animal hide. And Peabody, an industrial city of less than fifty thousand people, has the smokestacks to prove it. They rise up all over town from sprawling, dilapidated factories. Ugly, leaning, wooden buildings that often stretch over a city block. Strauss Tanning Co. A. C. Lawrence Leather Co. Gnecco & Grilk Tanning Corp. In the early sixties, the tanneries were in full swing. The jobs were arduous and health-threatening, but it was the best-paying work around for unskilled laborers who spoke no English. The huge, firetrap factories were filled with men and women from Greece, Portugal, Ireland, and Poland.

In one of these factories, João Nunes, who lived on the floor above 26 us, fed animal skins into a ravenous metal monster all day, every day. The pace was fast. One day the monster got his right arm and wouldn't let go. When the machine was turned off João had a little bit of arm left below his elbow. His daughter Teresa and I were friends. She didn't come out of her house for many days. When she returned to school, she was very quiet and cried a lot.

"*Rosa Veludo's been hurt.*" News of such tragedies spread through 27 the community fast and often. People would tell what they had seen, or what they had heard from those who had seen. "*She was taken to the hospital by ambulance. Someone wrapped her fingers in a paper bag. The doctors may be able to sew them back on.*"

A few days after our arrival in the United States, my father went to 28 work at the Gnecco & Grilk leather tannery, on the corner of Howley and Walnut streets. Senhor João had worked there for many years. He helped *Pai* get the job. Gnecco & Grilk was a long, rambling, four-story factory that stretched from the corner halfway down the street to the railroad tracks. The roof was flat and slouched in the middle like the back of an old workhorse. There were hundreds of windows. The ones on the ground floor were covered with a thick wire mesh.

Pai worked there for many months. He was stationed on the ground 29 floor, where workers often had to stand ankle-deep in water laden with chemicals. One day he had a disagreement with his foreman. He left his machine and went home vowing never to return. . . .

Pai and I stood on a sidewalk in Salem facing a clear glass doorway. The 30 words on the door were big. DIVISION OF EMPLOYMENT SECURITY. There was a growing coldness deep inside me. At Thomas Carroll School, Miss Laitinen was probably standing at the side blackboard, writing perfect alphabet letters on straight chalk lines. My seat was empty. I was on a sidewalk with *Pai* trying to understand a baffling string of words. DIVISION had something to do with math, which I didn't particularly like. EMPLOYMENT I had never seen or heard before. SECURITY I knew. But not at that moment.

Pai reached for the door. It swung open into a little square of tiled 31 floor. We stepped in to be confronted by the highest, steepest staircase I had ever seen. At the top, we emerged into a huge, fluorescently lit room. It was too bright and open after the dim, narrow stairs. *Pai* took off his hat. We stood together in a vast empty space. The light, polished tiles reflected the fluorescent glow. There were no windows.

Far across the room, a row of metal desks lined the wall. Each had a 32 green vinyl-covered chair beside it. Off to our left, facing the empty space before us, was a very high green metal desk. It was easily twice as high as a normal-size desk. Its odd size and placement in the middle of the room gave it the appearance of a kind of altar that divided the room in half. There were many people working at desks or walking about, but the room was so big that it still seemed empty.

The head and shoulders of a white-haired woman appeared to rest on   33
the big desk like a sculptured bust. She sat very still. Above her head the word CLAIMS dangled from two pieces of chain attached to the ceiling. As I watched the woman she beckoned to us. *Pai* and I walked toward her.

The desk was so high that *Pai*'s shoulders barely cleared the top.   34
Even when I stood on tiptoe I couldn't see over it. I had to stretch and lean my head way back to see the woman's round face. I thought that she must have very long legs to need a desk that high. The coldness in me grew. My neck hurt.

"My father can't speak English. He has no work and we need money."   35

She reached for some papers from a wire basket. One of her fingers   36
was encased in a piece of orange rubber.

"Come around over here so I can see you." She motioned to the side   37
of the desk. I went reluctantly. Rounding the desk I saw with relief that she was a small woman perched on a stool so high it seemed she would need a ladder to get up there.

"How old are you?" She leaned down toward me.   38

"Eight."   39

"My, aren't you a brave girl. Only eight years old and helping daddy   40
like that. And what lovely earrings you have."

She liked my earrings. I went a little closer to let her touch them.   41
Maybe she would give us money.

"What language does your father speak?" She was straightening up,   42
reaching for a pencil.

"Portuguese."   43

"What is she saying?" Pai wanted to know.   44

"Wait," I told him. The lady hadn't yet said anything about money.   45

"Why isn't your father working?"   46

"His factory burned down."   47

"What is she saying?" Pai repeated.   48

"She wants to know why you aren't working."   49

"Tell her the factory burned down."   50

"I know. I did." The lady was looking at me. I hoped she wouldn't   51
ask me what my father had just said.

"What is your father's name?"   52

"Carlos S. Cunha. C-u-n-h-a." No one could ever spell *Cunha. Pai*   53
nodded at the woman when he heard his name.

"Where do you live?"   54

"Thirty-three Tracey Street, Peabody, Massachusetts." *Pai* nodded   55
again when he heard the address.

"When was your father born?"   56

"*Quando é que tu naçestes?*"   57

"When was the last day your father worked?"   58

"*Qual foi o último dia que trabalhastes?*"   59

"What was the name of the factory?"   60

"*Qual éra o nome da fábrica?*"   61

"How long did he work there?"   62

"*Quanto tempo trabalhastes lá?*"   63

"What is his Social Security number?"   64

I looked at her blankly, not knowing what to say. What was a Social   65
Security number?

"*What did she say?*" *Pai* prompted me out of silence.   66

"*I don't know. She wants a kind of number.*" I was feeling very tired   67
and worried. But *Pai* took a small card from his wallet and gave it to the
lady. She copied something from it onto her papers and returned it to
him. I felt a great sense of relief. She wrote silently for a while as we
stood and waited. Then she handed some papers to *Pai* and looked at me.

"Tell your father that he must have these forms filled out by his em-   68
ployer before he can receive unemployment benefits."

I stared at her. What was she saying? Employer? Unemployment ben-   69
efits? I was afraid she was saying we couldn't have any money. Maybe
not, though. Maybe we could have money if I could understand her
words.

"*What did she say? Can we have some money?*"   70

"*I don't know. I can't understand the words.*"   71

"*Ask her again if we can have money,*" *Pai* insisted. "*Tell her we*   72
have to pay the rent."

"We need money for the rent," I told the lady, trying to hold back   73
tears.

"You can't have money today. You must take the forms to your fa-   74
ther's employer and bring them back completed next week. Then your
father must sign another form which we will keep here to process his
claim. When he comes back in two weeks there may be a check for him."
The cold in me was so big now. I was trying not to shiver.

"Do you understand?" The lady was looking at me.   75

I wanted to say, "No, I don't," but I was afraid we would never get   76
money and *Pai* would be angry.

"Tell your father to take the papers to his boss and come back next   77
week."

Boss. I could understand boss.   78

"*She said you have to take these papers to your 'bossa' and come*   79
back next week."

"*We can't have money today?*"   80

"No. She said maybe we can have money in two weeks."   81
"Did you tell her we have to pay the rent?"   82
"Yes, but she said we can't have money yet."   83

The lady was saying good-bye and beckoning the next person from   84
the line that had formed behind us.

I was relieved to move on, but I think *Pai* wanted to stay and argue   85
with her. I knew that if he could speak English, he would have. I knew
that he thought it was my fault we couldn't have money. And I myself
wasn't so sure that wasn't true.

That night I sat at the kitchen table with a fat pencil and a piece of   86
paper. In my second-grade scrawl I wrote: Dear Miss Laitinen, Mary
Edith was sick.

I gave the paper to *Pai* and told him to sign his name.   87
"What does it say?"   88
"It says that I was sick today. I need to give it to my teacher."   89
"You weren't sick today."   90
"Ya, but it would take too many words to tell her the truth."   91

Pai signed the paper. The next morning in school, Miss Laitinen read   92
it and said that she hoped I was feeling better.

When I was nine, *Pai* went to an auction and bought a big house on   93
Tremont Street. We moved in the spring. The yard at the side of the
house dipped downward in a gentle slope that was covered with a dense
row of tall lilac bushes. I soon discovered that I could crawl in among the
twisted trunks to hide from my brothers in the fragrant shade. It was
paradise. . . .

I was mostly wild and joyful on Tremont Street. But there was a shadow   94
that fell across my days now and again.

"Ó Ediiiite." *Pai* would call me without the least bit of warning, to be   95
his voice. He expected me to drop whatever I was doing to attend him.
Of late, I'd had to struggle on the telephone with the voice of a woman
who wanted some old dishes. The dishes, along with lots of old furniture
and junk, had been in the house when we moved in. They were in the
cellar, stacked in cardboard boxes and covered with dust. The woman
called many times wanting to speak with *Pai*.

"My father can't speak English," I would say. "He says to tell you   96
that the dishes are in our house and they belong to us." But she did not
seem to understand. Every few days she would call.

"Ó Ediiiite." *Pai*'s voice echoed through the empty rooms. Hearing it   97
brought on a chill. It had that tone. As always, my first impulse was to
pretend I had not heard, but there was no escape. I couldn't disappear
into thin air as I wished to do at such calls. We were up in the third-floor
apartment of our new house. *Pai* was working in the kitchen. Carlos and
I had made a cavern of old cushions and were sitting together deep in its

bowels when he called. It was so dark and comfortable there I decided not to answer until the third call, though that risked *Pai*'s wrath.

"*Ó Ediiite*." Yes, that tone was certainly there. *Pai* was calling me to   98
do something only I could do. Something that always awakened a cold beast deep in my gut. He wanted me to be his bridge. What was it now? Did he have to talk to someone at City Hall again? Or was it the insurance company? They were always using words I couldn't understand: liability, and premium, and dividend. It made me frustrated and scared.

"You wait. My dotta come." *Pai* was talking to someone. Who could   99
it be? That was some relief. At least I didn't have to call someone on the phone. It was always harder to understand when I couldn't see people's mouths.

"*Ó Ediiiiite*." I hated Carlos. *Pai* never called his name like that. He   100
never had to do anything but play.

"*Que ééé?*"   101

"*Come over here and talk to this lady.*"   102

Reluctantly I crawled out from the soft darkness and walked through   103
the empty rooms toward the kitchen. Through the kitchen door I could see a slim lady dressed in brown standing at the top of the stairs in the windowed porch. She had on very skinny high-heeled shoes and a brown purse to match. As soon as *Pai* saw me he said to the lady, "Dis my dotta." To me he said, "*See what she wants.*"

The lady had dark hair that was very smooth and puffed away from   104
her head. The ends of it flipped up in a way that I liked.

"Hello. I'm the lady who called about the dishes."   105

I stared at her without a word. My stomach lurched.   106

"*What did she say?*" *Pai* wanted to know.   107

"*She says she's the lady who wants the dishes.*"   108

Pai's face hardened some.   109

"*Tell her she's wasting her time. We're not giving them to her. Didn't*   110
you already tell her that on the telephone?"

I nodded, standing helplessly between them.   111

"*Well, tell her again.*" *Pai* was getting angry. I wanted to disappear.   112

"My father says he can't give you the dishes," I said to the lady. She   113
clutched her purse and leaned a little forward.

"Yes, you told me that on the phone. But I wanted to come in person   114
and speak with your father because it's very important to me that—"

"My father can't speak English," I interrupted her. Why didn't she   115
just go away? She was still standing in the doorway with her back to the stairwell. I wanted to push her down.

"Yes, I understand that. But I wanted to see him." She looked at *Pai*,   116
who was standing in the doorway to the kitchen holding his hammer. The kitchen was up one step from the porch. *Pai* was a small man, but he looked kind of scary staring down at us like that.

"*What is she saying?*"   117

"*She says she wanted to talk to you about getting her dishes.*"   118

"*Tell her the dishes are ours. They were in the house. We bought the*   119
house and everything in it. Tell her the lawyer said so."

The brown lady was looking at me expectantly.   120

"My father says the dishes are ours because we bought the house and   121
the lawyer said everything in the house is ours now."

"Yes, I know that, but I was away when the house was being sold. I   122
didn't know . . ."

"*Eeii.*" There were footsteps on the stairs behind her. It was *Mãe*   123
coming up from the second floor to find out what was going on. The lady
moved away from the door to let *Mãe* in.

"Dis my wife," *Pai* said to the lady. The lady said hello to *Mãe*, who   124
smiled and nodded her head. She looked at me, then at *Pai* in a questioning way.

"*It's the lady who wants our dishes,*" *Pai* explained.   125

"*Ó.*" *Mãe* looked at her again and smiled, but I could tell she was a   126
little worried.

We stood there in kind of a funny circle; the lady looked at each of us   127
in turn and took a deep breath.

"I didn't know," she continued, "that the dishes were in the house. I   128
was away. They are very important to me. They belonged to my grandmother. I'd really like to get them back." She spoke this while looking
back and forth between *Mãe* and *Pai*. Then she looked down at me,
leaning forward again. "Will you tell your parents, please?"

The cold beast inside me had begun to rise up toward my throat as the   129
lady spoke. I knew that soon it would try to choke out my words. I spoke
in a hurry to get them out.

"*She said she didn't know the dishes were in the house she was away*   130
they were her grandmother's dishes she wants them back." I felt a deep
sadness at the thought of the lady returning home to find her grandmother's dishes sold.

"*We don't need all those dishes. Let's give them to her,*" *Mãe* said in 131
her calm way. I felt relieved. We could give the lady the dishes and she
would go away. But *Pai* got angry.

"*I already said what I had to say. The dishes are ours. That is all.*"   132

"*Pai, she said she didn't know. They were her grandmother's dishes.*   133
She needs to have them." I was speaking wildly and loud now. The lady
looked at me questioningly, but I didn't want to speak to her again.

"*She's only saying that to trick us. If she wanted those dishes she*   134
should have taken them out before the house was sold. Tell her we are
not fools. Tell her to forget it. She can go away. Tell her not to call or
come here again."

"What is he saying?" The lady was looking at me again.   135

I ignored her. I felt sorry for *Pai* for always feeling that people were 136 trying to trick him. I wanted him to trust people. I wanted the lady to have her grandmother's dishes. I closed my eyes and willed myself away.

"*Tell her what I said!*" *Pai* yelled.   137

"*Pai, just give her the dishes! They were her grandmother's dishes!*" 138 My voice cracked as I yelled back at him. Tears were rising.

I hated *Pai* for being so stubborn. I hated the lady for not taking the 139 dishes before the house was sold. I hated myself for having learned to speak English.

QUESTIONS ON CONTENT

1. Where did each part of Cunha's name come from? What, then, was the significance of her name?

2. Why did Mrs. Donahue change Cunha's name? Do you think that Mrs. Donahue's own ethnic heritage may have motivated her in making the change? Would you mind if someone wanted to change your name? Explain.

3. Did Cunha dislike Mrs. Donahue? Why, or why not? What irony do you see in paragraph 6?

4. Explain the irony in Mrs. Donahue's efforts to get Cunha to pronounce Mrs. Laitinen's name correctly.

5. Cunha says in her final sentence: "I hated myself for having learned to speak English." Why?

QUESTIONS ON RHETORIC

1. Cunha refers to a "coldness" (34) or "cold" (74) or "the cold beast" (129) that comes over her. What does she mean by these references to coldness? What circumstance brings about the feeling?

2. Why does Cunha re-create the scene in which she and her father visit the Division of Employment Security and the one in which they try to respond to the woman who wants the dishes? How do these two scenes help Cunha achieve her purpose in writing the essay (Glossary: *Purpose*)?

3. Why is it important for Cunha to describe Mrs. Donahue? What important and ironic information do we get from that description (Glossary: *Description*)?

4. Do you find Cunha's ending effective (Glossary: *Beginnings and Endings*)? Explain.

VOCABULARY

reverence (1)	ambivalence (17)	liability (98)
sponsor (5)	dilapidated (25)	premium (98)
bob (15)	arduous (25)	dividend (98)
quivering (16)	ravenous (26)	

WRITING TOPICS

1. Think back to your early experiences with language. Did you have problems learning English? What were they? Do you now find that you have greater facility with language? How do you account for any changes?

2. Discuss your own experience learning a foreign language. What are the greatest stumbling blocks, and what are the most effective ways of overcoming them? Were your experiences at all like Cunha's? Write an essay about the difficulties of learning another language.

3. Even though we may not have a second language spoken in the home like the Cunha family, we are all aware of the differences between the way we talk and write in public or at school and the way we talk at home or among close friends. Write an essay in which you analyze these differences and attempt to explain the reasons for them.

BLACK *AND* LATINO

Roberto Santiago

Being both African American and Latino, journalist Roberto Santiago is perplexed by those in each group who wish either to claim him or reject him as one of their own. Santiago has written for Omni, Village Voice, *and* Hispanic, *and currently works for* Emerge *magazine in New York City. His essay was first published in* Essence *in 1989.*

"There is no way that you can be black and Puerto Rican at the same time." What? Despite the many times I've heard this over the years, that statement still perplexes me. I *am* both and always have been. My color is a blend of my mother's rich, dark skin tone and my father's white complexion. As they were both Puerto Rican, I spoke Spanish before English, but I am totally bilingual. My life has been shaped by my black and Latino heritages, and despite other people's confusion, I don't feel I have to choose one or the other. To do so would be to deny a part of myself.

There has not been a moment in my life when I did not know that I looked black—and I never thought that others did not see it, too. But growing up in East Harlem, I was also aware that I did not "act black," according to the African-American boys on the block.

My lighter-skinned Puerto Rican friends were less of a help in this department. "You're not black," they would whine, shaking their heads. "You're a *boriqua* [slang for Puerto Rican], you ain't no *moreno* [black]." If that was true, why did my mirror defy the rules of logic? And most of all, why did I feel that there was some serious unknown force trying to make me choose sides?

Acting black. Looking black. Being a real black. This debate among us is almost a parody. The fact is that I am black, so why do I need to prove it?

The island of Puerto Rico is only a stone's throw away from Haiti, and, no fooling, if you climb a palm tree, you can see Jamaica bobbing on the Atlantic. The slave trade ran through the Caribbean basin, and virtually all Puerto Rican citizens have some African blood in their veins. My grandparents on my mother's side were the classic *negro como carbón* (black as carbon) people, but despite the fact that they were as dark as can be, they are officially not considered black.

There is an explanation for this, but not one that makes much sense, or difference, to a working-class kid from Harlem. Puerto Ricans identify themselves as Hispanics—part of a worldwide race that originated from eons of white Spanish conquests—a mixture of white, African, and *Indio* blood, which, categorically, is apart from black. In other words, the culture is the predominant and determinant factor. But there are frustrations in being caught in a duo-culture, where your skin color does not necessarily dictate what you are. When I read Piri Thomas's searing autobiography, *Down These Mean Streets*, in my early teens, I saw that he couldn't figure out other people's attitudes toward his blackness, either.

My first encounter with this attitude about the race thing rode on   7
horseback. I had just turned six years old and ran toward the bridle path in Central Park as I saw two horses about to trot past. "Yea! Horsie! Yea!" I yelled. Then I noticed one figure on horseback. She was white, and she shouted, "Shut up, you f———g nigger! Shut up!" She pulled back on the reins and twisted the horse in my direction. I can still feel the spray of gravel that the horse kicked at my chest. And suddenly she was gone. I looked back and, in the distance, saw my parents playing Whiffle Ball with my sister. They seemed miles away.

They still don't know about this incident. But I told my Aunt Aurelia   8
almost immediately. She explained what the words meant and why they were said. Ever since then I have been able to express my anger appropriately through words or action in similar situations. Self-preservation, ego, and pride forbid men from ever ignoring, much less forgetting, a slur.

Aunt Aurelia became, unintentionally, my source for answers I needed   9
about color and race. I never sought her out. She just seemed to appear at my home during the points in my childhood when I most needed her for solace. "Puerto Ricans are different from American blacks," she told me once. "There is no racism between what you call white and black. Nobody even considers the marriages interracial." She then pointed out the difference in color between my father and mother. "You never noticed that," she said, "because you were not raised with that hang-up."

Aunt Aurelia passed away before I could follow up on her observa-   10
tion. But she had made an important point. It's why I never liked the attitude that says I should be exclusive to one race.

My behavior toward this race thing pegged me as an iconoclast of   11
sorts. Children from mixed marriages, from my experience, also share this attitude. If I have to bear the label of iconoclast because the world wants people to be in set categories and I don't want to, then I will.

A month before Aunt Aurelia died, she saw I was a little down about   12
the whole race thing, and she said, "Roberto, don't worry. Even if—no matter what you do—black people in this country don't, you can always depend on white people to treat you like a black."

QUESTIONS ON CONTENT

1. Why do people want Santiago to declare himself either black or Latino? Why does he refuse to do so?

2. What does Santiago mean when he writes, "I was also aware that I did not act 'black'" (2)? He says, *"Acting black. Looking black. Being a real*

black. This debate among us is almost a parody." What does he mean by "parody" in this instance?

3. Santiago says that he felt a "serious unknown force trying to make me choose sides" (3). What do you think he is referring to?

4. Why didn't Santiago want to tell his mother and father what happened to him in Central Park (7)?

5. What did Santiago's aunt mean when she said, "you can always depend on white people to treat you like a black" (12)?

QUESTIONS ON RHETORIC

1. Santiago writes in an informal tone using words and phrases that would more readily be found in everyday speech than in a formal essay. (Glossary: *Tone*) Point out several examples of the diction that he uses to establish this informal tone. Why do you suppose Santiago has chosen to use such language?

2. Examine each instance in which Santiago uses dialogue in his essay. How does Santiago's use of dialogue help him make his point?

3. Santiago uses italics at several points in his essay. Locate the italicized words and phrases and explain why he uses italics in each instance.

VOCABULARY

perplexes (1)   eons (6)   iconoclast (11)
parody (4)   slur (8)

WRITING TOPICS

1. Write an essay in which you discuss your national identity or cultural heritage and the degree to which you feel comfortable in American society. Some of the questions you may want to consider are the following: Where were your parents born? Where were you born? Are they American citizens? Are you? Do you feel a part of more than one cultural heritage? If yes, how so? Are you bothered, as is Santiago, by forces working on you to act or look in certain ways?

2. Santiago writes that the "world wants people to be in set categories" with regard "to this race thing." Write an essay in which you explore your own attitudes toward people of racial backgrounds different than your own. Do you, too, tend to see people in "set categories"?

WHAT'S IN A NAME?

Itabari Njeri

Since the time that she legalized her traditional African name, Itabari Njeri has drawn unusual responses from strangers. The following encounter is typical:
    "'Oh, what an unusual and beautiful name. Where are you from?'
    "'Brooklyn,' I say. I can see the disappointment in their eyes. Just another home-grown Negro."
    In the following essay, Itabari Njeri, a Los Angeles Times *journalist and the author of* Every Good-bye Ain't Gone, *reflects on the importance of one's name and investigates the consequences of changing it, of changing the way one views and is viewed by society.*

The decade was about to end when I started my first newspaper job.   1
The seventies might have been the disco generation for some, but it was a continuation of the Black Power, post–civil rights era for me. Of course in some parts of America it was still the pre–civil rights era. And that was the part of America I wanted to explore. As a good reporter I needed a sense of the whole country, not just the provincial Northeast Corridor in which I was raised.

I headed for Greenville ("Pearl of the Piedmont"), South Carolina.   2

"*Wheeere*," some people snarled, their nostrils twitching, their   3
mouths twisted so their top lips went slightly to the right, the bottom ones way down and to the left, "did you get *that* name from?"

Itabiddy, Etabeedy. Etabeeree. Eat a berry. Mata Hari. Theda Bara.   4
And one secretary in the office of the Greenville Urban League told her employer: "It's Ms. Idi Amin."

Then, and now, there are a whole bunch of people who greet me   5
with: "Hi, Ita." They think "Bari" is my last name. Even when they don't, they still want to call me "Ita." When I tell them my first name is Itabari, they say, "Well, what do people call you for short?"

"They don't call me anything for short," I say. "The name is Itabari."   6

Sophisticated white people, upon hearing my name, approach me as   7
would a cultural anthropologist finding a piece of exotica right in his own living room. This happens a lot, still, at cocktail parties.

"Oh, what an unusual and beautiful name. Where are you from?"   8

"Brooklyn," I say. I can see the disappointment in their eyes. Just   9
another home-grown Negro.

Then there are other white people who, having heard my decidedly   10 northeastern accent, will simply say, "What a lovely name," and smile knowingly, indicating that they saw *Roots* and understand.

Then there are others, black and white, who for different reasons take   11
me through this number:

"What's your *real* name?"   12

"Itabari Njeri is my real, legal name," I explain.   13

"Okay, what's your original name?" they ask, often with eyes rolling,   14
exasperation in their voices.

After Malcolm X, Muhammad Ali, Kareem Abdul-Jabbar, Ntozake   15
Shange, and Kunta Kinte, who, I ask, should be exasperated by this question-and-answer game?

Nevertheless, I explain, "Because of slavery, black people in the   16
Western world don't usually know their original names. What you really want to know is what my slave name was."

Now this is where things get tense. Four hundred years of bitter his-   17
tory, culture, and politics between blacks and whites in America is evoked by this one term, "slave name."

Some white people wince when they hear the phrase, pained and em-   18
barrassed by this reminder of their ancestors' inhumanity. Further, they quickly scrutinize me and conclude that mine was a post–Emancipation Proclamation birth. "You were never a slave."

I used to be reluctant to tell people my slave name unless I surmised   19
that they wouldn't impose their cultural values on me and refuse to use my African name. I don't care anymore. When I changed my name, I changed my life, and I've been Itabari for more years now than I was Jill. Nonetheless, people will say: "Well, that's your *real* name, you were born in America and that's what I am going to call you." My mother tried a variation of this on me when I legalized my traditional African name. I respectfully made it clear to her that I would not tolerate it. Her behavior, and subsequently her attitude, changed.

But many black folks remain just as skeptical of my name as my   20
mother was.

"You're one of those black people who changed their name, huh,"   21
they are likely to begin. "Well, I still got the old slave master's Irish name," said one man named O'Hare at a party. This man's defensive tone was a reaction to what I call the "blacker than thou" syndrome per-petrated by many black nationalists in the sixties and seventies. Those who reclaimed their African names made blacks who didn't do the same thing feel like Uncle Toms.

These so-called Uncle Toms couldn't figure out why they should use   22
an African name when they didn't know a thing about Africa. Besides, many of them were proud of their names, no matter how they had come by them. And it should be noted that after the Emancipation Proclamation in 1863, four million black people changed their names, adopting sur-

names such as Freeman, Freedman, and Liberty. They eagerly gave up names that slave masters had imposed upon them as a way of identifying their human chattel.

Besides names that indicated their newly won freedom, blacks chose   23
common English names such as Jones, Scott, and Johnson. English was their language. America was their home, and they wanted names that would allow them to assimilate as easily as possible.

Of course, many of our European surnames belong to us by birth-   24
right. We are the legal as well as "illegitimate" heirs to the names Jefferson, Franklin, Washington, et al., and in my own family, Lord.

Still, I consider most of these names to be by-products of slavery, if   25
not actual slave names. Had we not been enslaved, we would not have been cut off from our culture, lost our indigenous languages, and been compelled to use European names.

The loss of our African culture is a tragic fact of history, and the   26
conflict it poses is a profound one that has divided blacks many times since Emancipation: do we accept the loss and assimilate totally or do we try to reclaim our culture and synthesize it with our present reality?

A new generation of black people in America is reexamining the is-   27
sues raised by the cultural nationalists and Pan-Africanists of the sixties and seventies: what are the cultural images that appropriately convey the "new" black aesthetic in literature and art?

The young Afro-American novelist Trey Ellis has asserted that the   28
"New Black Aesthetic shamelessly borrows and reassembles across both race and class lines." It is not afraid to embrace the full implications of our hundreds of years in the New World. We are a new people who need not be tied to externally imposed or self-inflicted cultural parochialism. Had I understood that as a teenager, I might still be singing today.

Even the fundamental issue of identity and nomenclature, raised by   29
Baraka and others twenty years ago, is back on the agenda: are we to call ourselves blacks or African-Americans?

In reality, it's an old debate. "Only with the founding of the Ameri-   30
can Colonization Society in 1816 did blacks recoil from using the term African in referring to themselves and their institutions," the noted historian and author Sterling Stuckey pointed out in an interview with me. They feared that using the term "African" would fuel white efforts to send them back to Africa. But they felt no white person had the right to send them back when they had slaved to build America.

Many black institutions retained their African identification, most no-   31
tably the African Methodist Episcopal Church. Changes in black self-identification in America have come in cycles, usually reflecting the larger dynamics of domestic and international politics.

The period after World War II, said Stuckey, "culminating in the   32
Cold War years of Roy Wilkins's leadership of the NAACP," was a time

of "frenzied integrationism." And there was "no respectable black leader on the scene evincing any sort of interest in Africa—neither the NAACP or the Urban League."

This, he said, "was an example of historical discontinuity, the likes of   33
which we, as a people, had not seen before." Prior to that, for more than a century and a half, black leaders were Pan-Africanists, including Frederick Douglass. "He recognized," said Stuckey, "that Africa was important and that somehow one had to redeem the motherland in order to be genuinely respected in the New World."

The Reverend Jesse Jackson has, of course, placed on the national   34
agenda the importance of blacks in America restoring their cultural, historical, and political links with Africa.

But what does it really mean to be called an African-American?   35

"Black" can be viewed as a more encompassing term, referring to all   36
people of African descent. "Afro-American" and "African-American" refer to a specific ethnic group. I use the terms interchangeably, depending on the context and the point I want to emphasize.

But I wonder: as the twenty-first century breathes down our necks—   37
prodding us to wake up to the expanding mélange of ethnic groups immigrating in record numbers to the United States, inevitably intermarrying, and to realize the eventual reshaping of the nation's political imperatives in a newly multicultural society—will the term "African-American" be as much of a racial and cultural obfuscation as the term "black"? In other words, will we be the only people, in a society moving toward cultural pluralism, viewed to have no history and no culture? Will we just be a color with a new name: African-American?

Or will the term be—as I think it should—an ethnic label describing   38
people with a shared culture who descended from Africans, were transformed in (as well as transformed) America, and are genetically intertwined with myriad other groups in the United States?

Such a definition reflects the historical reality and distances us from   39
the fallacious, unscientific concept of separate races when there is only one: *Homo sapiens*.

But to comprehend what should be an obvious definition requires   40
knowledge and a willingness to accept history.

When James Baldwin wrote *Nobody Knows My Name*, the title was a   41
metaphor—at the deepest level of the collective African-American psyche—for the blighting of black history and culture before the nadir of slavery and since.

The eradication or distortion of our place in world history and culture is   42
most obvious in the popular media. Liz Taylor—and, for an earlier generation, Claudette Colbert—still represent what Cleopatra—a woman of color in a multiethnic society, dominated at various times by blacks—looks like.

And in American homes, thanks to reruns and cable, a new genera-   43
tion of black kids grow up believing that a simpleton shouting "Dy-no-

mite!" is a genuine reflection of Afro-American culture, rather than a white Hollywood writer's stereotype.

More recently, *Coming to America*, starring Eddie Murphy as an African prince seeking a bride in the United States, depicted traditional African dancers in what amounted to a Las Vegas stage show, totally distorting the nature and beauty of real African dance. But with every burlesque-style pelvic thrust on the screen, I saw blacks in the audience burst into applause. They think that's African culture, too. 44

And what do Africans know of us, since blacks don't control the organs of communication that disseminate information about us? 45

"No!" screamed the mother of a Kenyan man when he announced his engagement to an African-American woman who was a friend of mine. The mother said marry a European, marry a white American. But please, not one of those low-down, ignorant, drug-dealing, murderous black people she had seen in American movies. Ultimately, the mother prevailed. 46

In Tanzania, the travel agent looked at me indignantly. "Njeri, that's Kikuyu. What are you doing with an African name?" he demanded. 47

I'd been in Dar es Salaam about a month and had learned that Africans assess in a glance the ethnic origins of the people they meet. 48

Without a greeting, strangers on the street in Tanzania's capital would comment, "Oh, you're an Afro-American or West Indian." 49

"Both." 50

"I knew it," they'd respond, sometimes politely, sometimes not. 51

Or, people I got to know while in Africa would mention, "I know another half-caste like you." Then they would call in the "mixed-race" person and say, "Please meet Itabari Njeri." The darker-complected African, presumably of unmixed ancestry, would then smile and stare at us like we were animals in the zoo. 52

Of course, this "half-caste" (which I suppose is a term preferable to "mulatto," which I hate, and which every person who understands its derogatory meaning— "mule"—should never use) was usually the product of a mixed marriage, not generations of ethnic intermingling. And it was clear from most "half-castes" I met that they did not like being compared to so mongrelized and stigmatized a group as Afro-Americans. 53

I had minored in African studies in college, worked for years with Africans in the United States, and had no romantic illusions as to how I would be received in the motherland. I wasn't going back to find my roots. The only thing that shocked me in Tanzania was being called, with great disdain, a "white woman" by an African waiter. Even if the rest of the world didn't follow the practice, I then assumed everyone understood that any known or perceptible degree of African ancestry made one "black" in America by law and social custom. 54

But I was pleasantly surprised by the telephone call I received two minutes after I walked into my Dar es Salaam hotel room. It was the hotel operator. "Sister, welcome to Tanzania. . . . Please tell everyone in 55

Harlem hello for us." The year was 1978, and people in Tanzania were wearing half-foot-high platform shoes and dancing to James Brown wherever I went.

Shortly before I left, I stood on a hill surrounded by a field of endless   56
flowers in Arusha, near the border of Tanzania and Kenya. A toothless woman with a wide smile, a staff in her hand, and two young girls at her side, came toward me on a winding path. I spoke to her in fractured Swahili and she to me in broken English.

"I know you," she said smiling. "Wa-Negro." "Wa" is a prefix in   57
Bantu languages meaning people. "You are from the lost tribe," she told me. "Welcome," she said, touching me, then walked down a hill that lay in the shadow of Mount Kilimanjaro.

I never told her my name, but when I told other Africans, they'd say: 58
"*Emmmm*, Itabari. Too long. How about I just call you Ita."

QUESTIONS ON CONTENT

1. How do whites react to Njeri's name? How do African Americans?

2. Why did four million black people change their names after the Emancipation Proclamation (22)?

3. What was Njeri's name before she changed it? Why do you suppose she does not inform her readers more directly about her former name? Is her former name important to you? to her? Explain.

4. What does Njeri say is the difference between the terms "black," "Afro-American," and "African-American"?

5. What are some examples of the distortion of blacks in world history and culture that Njeri cites? What does she say is at least one reason for such distortions?

6. What is your understanding of Njeri's last paragraph?

QUESTIONS ON RHETORIC

1. What is Njeri's thesis in this essay? (Glossary: *Thesis*) Where is the thesis located?

2. What is the function of the many examples and quotations that Njeri uses? Why are they important? (Glossary: *Examples*)

3. Njeri originally wrote "What's in a Name?" as an article for the *Los Angeles Times*. Because newspaper columns are narrow, journalists use short paragraphs in their writing. Do Njeri's paragraphs seem undeveloped to you? Why, or why not?

4. Njeri not only relies on her own experiences in this article but also makes use of research. Where does her research enter into her writing? How does that research serve her purpose?

VOCABULARY

provincial (1)	chattel (22)	evincing (32)
anthropologist (7)	assimilate (23)	pluralism (37)
exotica (7)	indigenous (25)	nadir (41)
evoked (17)	aesthetic (27)	disseminate (45)
syndrome (21)	parochialism (28)	fractured (56)

WRITING TOPICS

1. What thoughts and feelings do you have about your own name? Do you like it, dislike it, think it suits you? Do you think that your name has an influence on the way you regard yourself; in other words, do you think that your name has shaped who you are to some extent? Write an essay in which you reflect on what your name signifies for you and how you think it might influence the way others regard you.

2. Have you ever thought about changing your name? What new name might you consider? Write an essay in which you consider what the advantages and disadvantages of such a name change might be.

THE LANGUAGE
OF DISCRETION

Amy Tan

Having grown up in a bilingual and bicultural family, Amy Tan, author of the best-selling The Joy Luck Club, *questions just how seriously we are to take the so-called Sapir-Whorf hypothesis that the language one uses shapes reality and is, in turn, shaped by reality. Isn't it too easy and aren't we too prone to error if we associate particular worldviews to particular languages and, thus, cultures? Are two languages ever translatable, she asks? Can cultures be reliably compared? The answers, of course, are not easy to determine.*

At a recent family dinner in San Francisco, my mother whispered to 1
me: "Sau-sau [Brother's Wife] pretends too hard to be polite! Why bother? In the end, she always takes everything."

My mother thinks like a *waixiao*, an expatriate, temporarily away 2
from China since 1949, no longer patient with ritual courtesies. As if to prove her point, she reached across the table to offer my elderly aunt from Beijing the last scallop from the Happy Family seafood dish.

Sau-sau scowled. "*B'yao, zhen b'yao!*" (I don't want it, really I 3
don't!) she cried, patting her plump stomach.

"Take it! Take it!" scolded my mother in Chinese. 4

"Full, I'm already full," Sau-sau protested weakly, eyeing the be- 5
loved scallop.

"Ai!" exclaimed my mother, completely exasperated. "Nobody else 6
wants it. If you don't take it, it will only rot!"

At this point, Sau-sau sighed, acting as if she were doing my mother 7
a big favor by taking the wretched scrap off her hands.

My mother turned to her brother, a high-ranking communist official 8
who was visiting her in California for the first time: "In America a Chinese person could starve to death. If you say you don't want it, they won't ask you again forever."

My uncle nodded and said he understood fully: Americans take things 9
quickly because they have no time to be polite. I thought about this misunderstanding again—of social contexts failing in translation—when a friend sent me an article from the *New York Times Magazine* (24 April 1988). The article, on changes in New York's Chinatown, made passing reference to the inherent ambivalence of the Chinese language.

Chinese people are so "discreet and modest," the article stated, there   10
aren't even words for "yes" and "no."

That's not true, I thought, although I can see why an outsider might   11
think that. I continued reading.

If one is Chinese, the article went on to say, "One compromises, one   12
doesn't hazard a loss of face by an overemphatic response."

My throat seized. Why do people keep saying these things? As if we   13
truly were those little dolls sold in Chinatown tourist shops, heads bobbing up and down in complacent agreement to anything said!

I worry about the effect of one-dimensional statements on the unwary   14
and guileless. When they read about this so-called vocabulary deficit, do
they also conclude that Chinese people evolved into a mild-mannered lot
because the language only allowed them to hobble forth with minced
words?

Something enormous is always lost in translation. Something insid-   15
ious seeps into the gaps, especially when amateur linguists continue to
compare, one-for-one, language differences and then put forth notions
wide open to misinterpretation: that Chinese people have no direct linguistic means to make decisions, assert or deny, affirm or negate, just say
no to drug dealers, or behave properly on the witness stand when told,
"Please answer yes or no."

Yet one can argue, with the help of renowned linguists, that the Chi-   16
nese are indeed up a creek without "yes" and "no." Take any number of
variations on the old language-and-reality theory stated years ago by Edward Sapir: "Human beings . . . are very much at the mercy of the
particular language which has become the medium for their society. . . .
The fact of the matter is that the 'real world' is to a large extent built up
on the language habits of the group."[1]

This notion was further bolstered by the famous Sapir-Whorf hypoth-   17
esis, which roughly states that one's perception of the world and how one
functions in it depends a great deal on the language used. As Sapir,
Whorf, and new carriers of the banner would have us believe, language
shapes our thinking, channels us along certain patterns embedded in
words, syntactic structures, and intonation patterns. Language has become the peg and the shelf that enables us to sort out and categorize the
world. In English, we see "cats" and "dogs"; what if the language had
also specified *glatz*, meaning "animals that leave fur on the sofa," and
glotz, meaning "animals that leave fur and drool on the sofa"? How
would language, the enabler, have changed our perceptions with slight
vocabulary variations?

And if this were the case—of language being the master of destined   18
thought—think of the opportunities lost from failure to evolve two little

---

[1]Edward Sapir, *Selected Writings*, ed. D. G. Mandelbaum (Berkeley and Los Angeles,
1949).

words, *yes* and *no*, the simplest of opposites! Ghenghis Khan could have been sent back to Mongolia. Opium wars might have been averted. The Cultural Revolution could have been sidestepped.

There are still many, from serious linguists to pop psychology cultists, who view language and reality as inextricably tied, one being the consequence of the other. We have traversed the range from the Sapir-Whorf hypothesis to est and neurolinguistic programming, which tell us "you are what you say."   19

I too have been intrigued by the theories. I can summarize, albeit   20
badly, ages-old empirical evidence: of Eskimos and their infinite ways to say "snow," their ability to *see* the differences in snowflake configurations, thanks to the richness of their vocabulary, while non-Eskimo speakers like myself founder in "snow," "more snow," and "lots more where that came from."

I too have experienced dramatic cognitive awakenings via the word.   21
Once I added "mauve" to my vocabulary I began to see it everywhere. When I learned how to pronounce *prix fixe*, I ate French food at prices better than the easier-to-say *à la carte* choices.

But just how seriously are we supposed to take this?   22

Sapir said something else about language and reality. It is the part that   23
often gets left behind in the dot-dot-dots of quotes: ". . . No two languages are ever sufficiently similar to be considered as representing the same social reality. The worlds in which different societies live are distinct worlds, not merely the same world with different labels attached."

When I first read this, I thought, Here at last is validity for the di-   24
lemmas I felt growing up in a bicultural, bilingual family! As any child of immigrant parents knows, there's a special kind of double bind attached to knowing two languages. My parents, for example, spoke to me in both Chinese and English; I spoke back to them in English.

"Amy-ah!" they'd call to me.   25

"What?" I'd mumble back.   26

"Do not question us when we call," they scolded me in Chinese. "It is   27
not respectful."

"What do you mean?"   28

"Ai! Didn't we just tell you not to question?"   29

To this day, I wonder which parts of my behavior were shaped by   30
Chinese, which by English. I am tempted to think, for example, that if I am of two minds on some matter it is due to the richness of my linguistic experiences, not to any personal tendencies toward wishy-washiness. But which mind says what?

Was it perhaps patience—developed through years of deciphering my   31
mother's fractured English—that had me listening politely while a woman announced over the phone that I had won one of five valuable prizes? Was it respect—pounded in by the Chinese imperative to accept convoluted explanations—that had me agreeing that I might find it worth-

while to drive seventy-five miles to view a time-share resort? Could I have been at a loss for words when asked, "Wouldn't you like to win a Hawaiian cruise or perhaps a fabulous Star of India designed exclusively by Carter and Van Arpels?"

And when this same woman called back a week later, this time com- 32 plaining that I had missed my appointment, obviously it was my type A language that kicked into gear and interrupted her. Certainly, my blunt denial—"Frankly I'm not interested"—was as American as apple pie. And when she said, "But it's in Morgan Hill," and I shouted, "Read my lips. I don't care if it's Timbuktu," you can be sure I said it with the precise intonation expressing both cynicism and disgust.

It's dangerous business, this sorting out of language and behavior. 33 Which one is English? Which is Chinese? The categories manifest them-selves: passive and aggressive, tentative and assertive, indirect and direct. And I realize they are just variations of the same theme: that Chinese people are discreet and modest.

Reject them all! 34

If my reaction is overly strident, it is because I cannot come across as 35 too emphatic. I grew up listening to the same lines over and over again, like so many rote expressions repeated in an English phrasebook. And I too almost came to believe them.

Yet if I consider my upbringing more carefully, I find there was noth- 36 ing discreet about the Chinese language I grew up with. My parents made everything abundantly clear. Nothing wishy-washy in their demands, no compromises accepted: "Of course you will become a famous neuro-surgeon," they told me. "And yes, a concert pianist on the side."

In fact, now that I remember, it seems that the more emphatic out- 37 bursts always spilled over into Chinese: "Not that way! You must wash rice so not a single grain spills out."

I do not believe that my parents—both immigrants from mainland 38 China—are an exception to the modest-and-discreet rule. I have only to look at the number of Chinese engineering students skewing minority ratios at Berkeley, MIT, and Yale. Certainly they were not raised by passive mothers and fathers who said, "It is up to you, my daughter. Writer, welfare recipient, masseuse, or molecular engineer—you de-cide."

And my American mind says, See, those engineering students weren't 39 able to say no to their parents' demands. But then my Chinese mind remembers: Ah, but those parents all wanted their sons and daughters to be *pre-med*.

Having listened to both Chinese and English, I also tend to be sus- 40 picious of any comparisons between the two languages. Typically, one language—that of the person doing the comparing—is often used as the standard, the benchmark for a logical form of expression. And so the language being compared is always in danger of being judged deficient or superfluous, simplistic or unnecessarily complex, melodious or cacophonous. English speakers point out that Chinese is extremely difficult because it relies on variations in tone barely discernible to the human ear. By the same token, Chinese speakers tell me English is extremely difficult because it is inconsistent, a language of too many broken rules, of Mickey Mice and Donald Ducks.

Even more dangerous to my mind is the temptation to compare both   41
language and behavior *in translation*. To listen to my mother speak English, one might think she has no concept of past or future tense, that she doesn't see the difference between singular and plural, that she is gender blind because she calls my husband "she." If one were not careful, one might also generalize that, based on the way my mother talks, all Chinese people take a circumlocutory route to get to the point. It is, in fact, my mother's idiosyncratic behavior to ramble a bit.

Sapir was right about differences between two languages and their real-   42
ities. I can illustrate why word-for-word translation is not enough to translate meaning and intent. I once received a letter from China which I read to non-Chinese speaking friends. The letter, originally written in Chinese, had been translated by my brother-in law in Beijing. One portion described the time when my uncle at age ten discovered his widowed mother (my grandmother) had remarried—as a number three concubine, the ultimate disgrace for an honorable family. The translated version of my uncle's letter read in part:

> In 1925, I met my mother in Shanghai. When she came to me, I didn't have greeting to her as if seeing nothing. She pull me to a corner secretly and asked me why didn't have greeting to her. I couldn't control myself and cried, "Ma! Why did you leave us? People told me: one day you ate a beancake yourself. Your sister in-law found it and sweared at you, called your names. So . . . is it true?" She clasped my hand and answered immediately. "It's not true, don't say what like this." After this time, there was a few chance to meet her.

"What!" cried my friends. "Was eating a beancake so terrible?"   43

Of course not. The beancake was simply a euphemism; a ten-year-old   44
boy did not dare question his mother on something as shocking as concubinage. Eating a beancake was his equivalent for committing this selfish act, something inconsiderate of all family members, hence, my grandmother's despairing response to what seemed like a ludicrous charge of gluttony. And sure enough, she was banished from the family, and my uncle saw her only a few times before her death.

While the above may fuel people's argument that Chinese is indeed a   45
language of extreme discretion, it does not mean that Chinese people speak in secrets and riddles. The contexts are fully understood. It is only to those on the *outside* that the language seems cryptic, the behavior inscrutable.

I am, evidently, one of the outsiders. My nephew in Shanghai, who   46
recently started taking English lessons, has been writing me letters in
English. I had told him I was a fiction writer, and so in one letter he
wrote, "Congratulate to you on your writing. Perhaps one day I should
like to read it." I took it in the same vein as "Perhaps one day we can get
together for lunch." I sent back a cheery note. A month went by and
another letter arrived from Shanghai. "Last one perhaps I hadn't writing
distinctly," he said. "In the future, you'll send a copy of your works for
me."

I try to explain to my English-speaking friends that Chinese language   47
use is more *strategic* in manner, whereas English tends to be more direct;
an American business executive may say, "Let's make a deal," and the
Chinese manager may reply, "Is your son interested in learning about
your widget business?" Each to his or her own purpose, each with his or
her own linguistic path. But I hesitate to add more to the pile of generalizations, because no matter how many examples I provide and explain, I
fear that it appears defensive and only reinforces the image: that Chinese
people are "discreet and modest"—and it takes an American to explain
what they really mean.

Why am I complaining? The description seems harmless enough (after   48
all, the *New York Times Magazine* writer did not say "slippery and evasive"). It is precisely the bland, easy acceptability of the phrase that worries me.

I worry that the dominant society may see Chinese people from a   49
limited—and limiting—perspective. I worry that seemingly benign stereotypes may be part of the reason there are few Chinese in top management positions, in mainstream political roles. I worry about the power of
language: that if one says anything enough times—in *any* language—it
might become true.

Could this be why Chinese friends of my parents' generation are will-   50
ing to accept the generalization?

"Why are you complaining?" one of them said to me. "If people think   51
we are modest and polite, let them think that. Wouldn't Americans be
pleased to admit they are thought of as polite?"

And I do believe anyone would take the description as a compli-   52
ment—at first. But after a while, it annoys, as if the only things that
people heard one say were phatic remarks: "I'm so pleased to meet you.
I've heard many wonderful things about you. For me? You shouldn't
have!"

These remarks are not representative of new ideas, honest emotions,   53
or considered thought. They are what is said from the polite distance of
social contexts: of greetings, farewells, wedding thank-you notes, convenient excuses, and the like.

It makes me wonder though. How many anthropologists, how many   54 sociologists, how many travel journalists have documented so-called "natural interactions" in foreign lands, all observed with spiral notebook in hand? How many other cases are there of the long-lost primitive tribe, people who turned out to be sophisticated enough to put on the stone-age show that ethnologists had come to see?

And how many tourists fresh off the bus have wandered into China- 55
town expecting the self-effacing shopkeeper to admit under duress that the goods are not worth the price asked? I have witnessed it.

"I don't know," the tourist said to the shopkeeper, a Cantonese 56
woman in her fifties. "It doesn't look genuine to me. I'll give you three dollars."

"You don't like my price, go somewhere else," said the shopkeeper. 57

"You are not a nice person," cried the shocked tourist, "not a nice 58
person at all!"

"Who say I have to be nice," snapped the shopkeeper. 59

"So how does one say 'yes' and 'no' in Chinese?" ask my friends a bit 60
warily.

And here I do agree in part with the *New York Times Magazine* arti- 61
cle. There is no one word for "yes" or "no"—but not out of necessity to be discreet. If anything, I would say the Chinese equivalent of answering "yes" or "no" is dis*crete*, that is, specific to what is asked.

Ask a Chinese person if he or she has eaten, and he or she might say 62
chrle (eaten already) or perhaps *meiyou* (have not).

Ask, "So you had insurance at the time of the accident?" and the 63
response would be *dwei* (correct) or *meiyou* (did not have).

Ask, "Have you stopped beating your wife?" and the answer refers 64
directly to the proposition being asserted or denied: stopped already, still have not, never beat, have no wife.

What could be clearer? 65

As for those who are still wondering how to translate the language of 66
discretion, I offer this personal example.

My aunt and uncle were about to return to Beijing after a three-month 67
visit to the United States. On their last night I announced I wanted to take them out to dinner.

"Are you hungry?" I asked in Chinese. 68

"Not hungry," said my uncle promptly, the same response he once 69
gave me ten minutes before he suffered a low-blood-sugar attack.

"Not too hungry," said my aunt. "Perhaps you're hungry?" 70

"A little," I admitted. 71

"We can eat, we can eat," they both consented. 72

"What kind of food?" I asked. 73

"Oh, doesn't matter. Anything will do. Nothing fancy, just some sim- 74
ple food is fine."

"Do you like Japanese food? We haven't had that yet," I suggested. 75

They looked at each other. 76

"We can eat it," said my uncle bravely, this survivor of the Long 77
March.

"We have eaten it before," added my aunt. "Raw fish." 78

"Oh, you don't like it?" I said. "Don't be polite. We can go some- 79
where else."

"We are not being polite. We can eat it," my aunt insisted. 80

So I drove them to Japantown and we walked past several restaurants 81
featuring colorful plastic displays of sushi.

"Not this one, not this one either," I continued to say, as if searching for 82
a Japanese restaurant similar to the last. "Here it is," I finally said, turning into a restaurant famous for its Chinese fish dishes from Shandong.

"Oh, Chinese food!" cried my aunt, obviously relieved. 83

My uncle patted my arm. "You think Chinese." 84

"It's your last night here in America," I said. "So don't be polite. Act 85
like an American."

And that night we ate a banquet. 86

QUESTIONS ON CONTENT

1. What upsets Tan about the *New York Times Magazine* article that was
sent to her by a friend?

2. Tan writes that she has herself at times come under the influence of
the Sapir-Whorf hypothesis. Does she, then, disagree with the conclusion
that the writer of the *New York Times Magazine* reaches? How do you
know? Where does she make her response perfectly clear? Where does
she qualify her response?

3. "Chinese speakers," writes Tan, "tell me English is extremely difficult
because it is inconsistent, a language of too many broken rules, of
Mickey Mice and Donald Ducks" (40). What does she mean? Of what
broken rules are you aware?

4. In paragraph 84, Tan's uncle pays her a compliment. What does he
mean when he says, "You think Chinese"?

5. Tan's last sentence reads: "And that night we ate a banquet." What
connection does Tan make in that statement to the opening anecdote?

QUESTIONS ON RHETORIC

1. Comment on Tan's title. To what does it relate? Is it an effective title
for the essay? (Glossary: *Title*)

2. Tan begins and ends her essay with anecdotes. How effective do you
find these anecdotes as ways of beginning and concluding an essay?
(Glossary: *Beginnings and Endings*)

3. How does Tan illustrate Sapir's statement, "No two languages are ever sufficiently similar to be considered as representing the same reality. The worlds in which different societies live are distinct worlds, not merely the same world with different labels attached" (23)? (Glossary: *Example*)

4. In paragraph 61, Tan uses a pair of homonyms, words that sound alike but whose meanings are different: *discreet* and *discrete*. What does each of these words mean? What is Tan's point in using them?

5. Paragraphs 62 through 64 each begin with "ask." Is the repetition of this key word effective? Would the three sentences be better placed in a single paragraph? Why, or why not?

VOCABULARY

wretched (7)	averted (18)	cacophonous (40)
complacent (13)	cognitive (21)	idiosyncratic (41)
guileless (14)	fractured (31)	cryptic (45)
syntactic (17)	strident (35)	inscrutable (45)
intonation (17)	skewing (38)	self-effacing (55)

WRITING TOPICS

1. Tan's uncle agrees with the idea that "Americans take things quickly because they have no time to be polite" (9). Write an essay in which you consider the way you think foreigners see Americans. Are we impolite? cordial? abrupt? impatient? considerate? self-important? deferential? Under what circumstances? Is it easy to characterize a people?

2. In part, Tan's essay concerns how well one language can be translated into another. "*Traddutore, tradditore*" is an old Italian adage that means "translator, traitor." If you know another language well, write an essay in which you assess the extent to which the adage is accurate. Give as many examples as you can to substantiate your argument.

WRITING ASSIGNMENTS FOR "CULTURAL DIVERSITY: SEARCHING FOR COMMON GROUND"

1. Cultural diversity is a popular term today, but what does it mean? Write an essay in which you attempt to define the term. Does it mean the same thing for all people? Does the term have special significance on your campus?

2. Americans are lucky in that they speak English, which is increasingly becoming a world language. Many Americans, however, are smug in believing that people everywhere should either know or learn English. Write an essay putting forth some arguments for why we should all learn at least one foreign language. What are the advantages to knowing another language? Can a person really know another culture without knowing its language?

3. It is not always possible to know a person's cultural background from a surname. Edite Cunha was surprised to learn that Mrs. Donahue was, in fact, Portuguese. Women who marry men from cultural backgrounds different than their own and take their names are themselves sometimes surprised that they are regarded differently because of their surnames. If you know someone for whom this is true, interview her about her change of name. Did she find that she had a new identity? Was she regarded differently? What revealing stories, if any, can she tell? Write an essay discussing what you learned from the person you interviewed that you think might be interesting for your readers.

4. Roberto Santiago writes that his Aunt Aurelia was his source for information about race and color. Write an essay in which you explain where your ideas about race and color come from. Were your parents your main source of knowledge and attitudes? What role did your schooling have in forming your outlook? How instrumental were your friends?

5. What do you imagine would be the special problems that children of mixed races face? the special benefits that they enjoy? Are there any particular language considerations that come into play? Check into the research that has been done on children of mixed marriages and then write a report on your findings.

6. What should our schools do about educating children with different language backgrounds? Should all, none, or only some of their classes be taught in their native tongue? How should classes in which a number of languages are represented be taught? What are the advantages and disadvantages of bilingual teaching? What are the logistical problems? What were your experiences with bilingualism in the schools you attended? As a parent, what would be your preference? Write an essay in which you argue for your point of view.

7. Write an essay in which you argue that to deny someone's language is to deny that person his or her culture and self-identity.

8. Write an essay in which you discuss the various problems you have had in learning a second language. Do your experiences make you more or less sympathetic to immigrants who settle in America and must learn a new language?

PART VIII

Gender and Language

SEXISM IN ENGLISH:
A 1990s UPDATE

Alleen Pace Nilsen

*More than twenty years ago, Alleen Pace Nilsen, an English
professor and assistant vice-president for academic affairs at
Arizona State University, began a card catalog of sexist
language. What began as a study of language grew into a
commitment to social change. Nilsen concludes that sexism
will not disappear from our language until it is erased from
our minds.*

Twenty years ago I embarked on a study of the sexism inherent in
American English. I had just returned to Ann Arbor, Michigan, after
living for two years (1967-69) in Kabul, Afghanistan, where I had begun
to look critically at the role society assigned to women. The Afghan
version of the *chaderi* prescribed for Moslem women was particularly
confining. Afghan jokes and folklore were blatantly sexist, such as this
proverb: "If you see an old man, sit down and take a lesson; if you see an
old woman, throw a stone."

But it wasn't only the native culture that made me question women's
roles, it was also the American community.

Most of the American women were like myself—wives and mothers
whose husbands were either career diplomats, employees of USAID, or
college professors who had been recruited to work on various contract
teams. We were suddenly bereft of our traditional roles: some of us
became alcoholics, others got very good at bridge, while still others
searched desperately for ways to contribute either to our families or to the
Afghans. The local economy provided few jobs for women and certainly
none for foreigners; we were isolated from former friends and the social
goals we had grown up with.

When I returned in the fall of 1969 to the University of Michigan in
Ann Arbor, I was surprised to find that many other women were also
questioning the expectations they had grown up with. In the spring of
1970, a women's conference was announced. I hired a babysitter and
attended, but I returned home more troubled than ever. The militancy of
these women frightened me. Since I wasn't ready for a revolution, I
decided I would have my own feminist movement. I would study the
English language and see what it could tell me about sexism. I started
reading a desk dictionary and making notecards on every entry that
seemed to tell something about male and female. I soon had a dog-eared
dictionary, along with a collection of notecards filling two shoe boxes.

Ironically, I started reading the dictionary because I wanted to avoid   5
getting involved in social issues, but what happened was that my notecards brought me right back to looking at society. Language and society
are as intertwined as a chicken and an egg. The language a culture uses is
telltale evidence of the values and beliefs of that culture. And because
there is a lag in how fast a language changes—new words can easily be
introduced, but it takes a long time for old words and usages to disappear—a careful look at English will reveal the attitudes that our ancestors
held and that we as a culture are therefore predisposed to hold. My notecards revealed three main points. Friends have offered the opinion that I
didn't need to read the dictionary to learn such obvious facts. Nevertheless, it was interesting to have linguistic evidence of sociological observations.

WOMEN ARE SEXY; MEN ARE SUCCESSFUL

First, in American culture a woman is valued for the attractiveness and   6
sexiness of her body, while a man is valued for his physical strength and
accomplishments. A woman is sexy. A man is successful.

A persuasive piece of evidence supporting this view are the epo-   7
nyms—words that have come from someone's name—found in English.
I had a two-and-a-half-inch stack of cards taken from men's names but
less than a half-inch stack from women's names, and most of those came
from Greek mythology. In the words that came into American English
since we separated from Britain, there are many eponyms based on the
names of famous American men: *Bartlett pear, boysenberry, diesel engine, Franklin stove, Ferris wheel, Gatling gun, mason jar, sideburns,
sousaphone, Schick test,* and *Winchester rifle.* The only common eponyms taken from American women's names are *Alice blue* (after Alice
Roosevelt Longworth), *bloomers* (after Amelia Jenks Bloomer), and *Mae
West jacket* (after the buxom actress). Two out of the three feminine
eponyms relate closely to a woman's physical anatomy, while the masculine eponyms (except for *sideburns* after General Burnsides) have nothing to do with the namesake's body but, instead, honor the man for an
accomplishment of some kind.

Although in Greek mythology women played a bigger role than they   8
did in the biblical stories of the Judeo-Christian cultures and so the names
of goddesses are accepted parts of the language in such place names as
Pomona from the goddess of fruit and Athens from Athena and in such
common words as *cereal* from Ceres, *psychology* from Psyche, and
arachnoid from Arachne, the same tendency to think of women in relation to sexuality is seen in the eponyms *aphrodisiac* from Aphrodite, the
Greek name for the goddess of love and beauty, and *veneral disease* from
Venus, the Roman name for Aphrodite.

Another interesting word from Greek mythology is *Amazon*. According to Greek folk etymology, the *a* means "without" as in *atypical* or *amoral*, while *mazon* comes from *mazos* meaning "breast" as still seen in *mastectomy*. In the Greek legend, Amazon women cut off their right breasts so that they could better shoot their bows. Apparently, the storytellers had a feeling that for women to play the active, "masculine" role the Amazons adopted for themselves, they had to trade in part of their femininity.

This preoccupation with women's breasts is not limited to ancient stories. As a volunteer for the University of Wisconsin's *Dictionary of American Regional English (DARE)*, I read a western trapper's diary from the 1930s. I was to make notes of any unusual usages or language patterns. My most interesting finding was that the trapper referred to a range of mountains as *The Teats*, a metaphor based on the similarity between the shapes of the mountains and women's breasts. Because today we use the French wording, *The Grand Tetons*, the metaphor isn't as obvious, but I wrote to mapmakers and found the following listings: *Nippletop* and *Little Nipple Top* near Mount Marcy in the Adirondacks; *Nipple Mountain* in Archuleta County, Colorado; *Nipple Peak* in Coke County, Texas; *Nipple Butte* in Pennington, South Dakota; *Squaw Peak* in Placer County, California (and many other locations); *Maiden's Peak* and *Squaw Tit* (they're the same mountain) in the Cascade Range in Oregon; *Mary's Nipple* near Salt Lake City, Utah; and *Jane Russell Peaks* near Stark, New Hampshire.

Except for the movie star Jane Russell, the women being referred to are anonymous—it's only a sexual part of their body that is mentioned. When topographical features are named after men, it's probably not going to be to draw attention to a sexual part of their bodies but instead to honor individuals for an accomplishment. For example, no one thinks of a part of the male body when hearing a reference to Pike's Peak, Colorado, or Jackson Hole, Wyoming.

Going back to what I learned from my dictionary cards, I was surprised to realize how many pairs of words we have in which the feminine word has acquired sexual connotations while the masculine word retains a serious businesslike aura. For example, a *callboy* is the person who calls actors when it is time for them to go on stage, but a *callgirl* is a prostitute. Compare *sir* and *madam*. *Sir* is a term of respect, while *madam* has acquired the specialized meaning of a brothel manager. Something similar has happened to *master* and *mistress*. Would you rather have a painting by an *old master* or an *old mistress*?

It's because the word *woman* had sexual connotations, as in "She's his woman," that people began avoiding its use, hence such terminology as *ladies' room, lady of the house*, and *girls' school* or *school for young ladies*. Feminists, who ask that people use the term *woman* rather than *girl* or *lady*, are rejecting the idea that *woman* is primarily a sexual term.

They have been at least partially successful in that today *woman* is commonly used to communicate gender without intending implications about sexuality.

I found two hundred pairs of words with masculine and feminine   14
forms, e.g., *heir-heiress, hero-heroine, steward-stewardess, usher-usherette*. In nearly all such pairs, the masculine word is considered the base, with some kind of a feminine suffix being added. The masculine form is the one from which compounds are made, e.g., from *king-queen* comes *kingdom* but not *queendom*, from *sportsman-sportslady* comes *sportsmanship* but not *sportsladyship*. There is one—and only one—semantic area in which the masculine word is not the base or more powerful word. This is in the area dealing with sex and marriage. When someone refers to a *virgin*, a listener will probably think of a female, unless the speaker specifies *male* or uses a masculine pronoun. The same is true for *prostitute*.

In relation to marriage, there is much linguistic evidence showing that   15
weddings are more important to women than to men. A woman cherishes the wedding and is considered a bride for a whole year, but a man is referred to as a groom only on the day of the wedding. The word *bride* appears in *bridal attendant, bridal gown, bridesmaid, bridal shower*, and even *bridegroom*. *Groom* comes from the Middle English *grom*, meaning "man," and in the sense is seldom used outside of the wedding. With most pairs of male/female words, people habitually put the masculine word first, *Mr. and Mrs., his and hers, boys and girls, men and women, kings and queens, brothers and sisters, guys and dolls*, and *host and hostess*, but it is the *bride and groom* who are talked about, not the *groom and bride*.

The importance of marriage to a woman is also shown by the fact that   16
when a marriage ends in death, the woman gets the title of *widow*. A man gets the derived title of *widower*. This term is not used in other phrases or contexts, but *widow* is seen in *widowhood, widow's peak*, and *widow's walk*. A *widow* in a card game is an extra hand of cards, while in typesetting it is an extra line of type.

How changing cultural ideas bring changes to language is clearly visi-   17
ble in this semantic area. The feminist movement has caused the differences between the sexes to be downplayed, and since I did my dictionary study two decades ago, the word *singles* has largely replaced such sex specific and value-laden terms as *bachelor, old maid, spinster, divorcee, widow*, and *widower*. And in 1970 I wrote that when a man is called *a professional* he is thought to be a doctor or a lawyer, but when people hear a woman referred to as *a professional* they are likely to think of a prostitute. That's not as true today because so many women have become doctors and lawyers that it's no longer incongruous to think of women in those professional roles.

Another change that has taken place is in wedding announcements.   18

They used to be sent out from the bride's parents and did not even give the name of the groom's parents. Today, most couples choose to list either all or none of the parents' names. Also it is now much more likely that both the bride and groom's picture will be in the newspaper, while a decade ago only the bride's picture was published on the "Women's" or the "Society" page. Even the traditional wording of the wedding ceremony is being changed. Many officials now pronounce the couple "husband and wife" instead of the old "man and wife," and they ask the bride if she promises "to love, honor, and cherish," instead of "to love, honor, and obey."

WOMEN ARE PASSIVE; MEN ARE ACTIVE

The wording of the wedding ceremony also relates to the second point   19
that my cards showed, which is that women are expected to play a passive or weak role while men play an active or strong role. In the traditional ceremony, the official asks, "Who gives the bride away?" and the father answers, "I do." Some fathers answer, "Her mother and I do," but that doesn't solve the problem inherent in the question. The idea that a bride is something to be handed over from one man to another bothers people because it goes back to the days when a man's servants, his children, and his wife were all considered to be his property. They were known by his name because they belonged to him, and he was responsible for their actions and their debts.

The grammar used in talking or writing about weddings as well as   20
other sexual relationships shows the expectation of men playing the active role. Men *wed* women while women *become* brides of men. A man *possesses* a woman; he *deflowers* her; he *performs*; he *scores*; he *takes away* her virginity. Although a woman can *seduce* a man, she cannot offer him her virginity. When talking about virginity, the only way to make the woman the actor in the sentence is to say that "She lost her virginity," but people lose things by accident rather than by purposeful actions, and so she's only the grammatical, not the real-life, actor.

The reason that women tried to bring the term *Ms.* into the language   21
to replace *Miss* and *Mrs.* relates to this point. Married women resent being identified only under their husband's names. For example, when Susan Glascoe did something newsworthy, she would be identified in the newspaper only as Mrs. John Glascoe. The dictionary cards showed what appeared to be an attitude on the part of the editors that it was almost indecent to let a respectable woman's name march unaccompanied across the pages of a dictionary. Women were listed with male names whether or not the male contributed to the woman's reason for being in the dictionary or in his own right was as famous as the woman. For example, Charlotte Brontë was identified as Mrs. Arthur B. Nicholls, Amelia Ear-

hart as Mrs. George Palmer Putnam, Helen Hayes as Mrs. Charles Mac-
Arthur, Jenny Lind as Mme. Otto Goldschmit, Cornelia Otis Skinner as
the daughter of Otis, Harriet Beecher Stowe as the sister of Henry Ward
Beecher, and Edith Sitwell as the sister of Osbert and Sacheverell. A very
small number of women got into the dictionary without the benefit of a
masculine escort. They were rebels and crusaders: temperance leaders
Frances Elizabeth Caroline Willard and Carry Nation, women's rights
leaders Carrie Chapman Catt and Elizabeth Cady Stanton, birth control
educator Margaret Sanger, religious leader Mary Baker Eddy, and slaves
Harriet Tubman and Phillis Wheatley.

Etiquette books used to teach that if a woman had *Mrs.* in front of her 22
name, then the husband's name should follow because *Mrs.* is an abbreviated form of *Mistress* and a woman couldn't be a mistress of herself.
As with many arguments about "correct" language usage, this isn't very
logical because *Miss* is also an abbreviation of *Mistress*. Feminists hoped
to simplify matters by introducing *Ms.* as an alternative to both *Mrs.* and
Miss, but what happened is that *Ms.* largely replaced *Miss*, to become a
catch-all business title for women. Many married women still prefer the
title *Mrs.*, and some resent being addressed with the term *Ms.* As one
frustrated newspaper reporter complained, "Before I can write about a
woman, I have to know not only her marital status but also her political
philosophy." The result of such complications may contribute to the demise of titles, which are already being ignored by many computer pro-
grammers who find it more efficient to simply use names, for example in
a business letter: "Dear Joan Garcia," instead of "Dear Mrs. Joan Garcia," "Dear Ms. Garcia," or "Dear Mrs. Louis Garcia."

The titles given to royalty provide an example of how males can be 23
disadvantaged by the assumption that they are always to play the more
powerful role. In British royalty, when a male holds a title, his wife is
automatically given the feminine equivalent. But the reverse is not true.
For example, a *count* is a high political officer with a *countess* being his
wife. The same is true for a *duke* and a *duchess* and a *king* and a *queen*.
But when a female holds the royal title, the man she marries does not
automatically acquire the matching title. For example, Queen Elizabeth's
husband has the title of *prince* rather than *king*, but if Prince Charles
should become king while he is still married to Lady or Princess Diana,
she will be known as the queen. The reasoning appears to be that since
masculine words are stronger, they are reserved for true heirs and withheld from males coming into the royal family by marriage. If Prince
Phillip were called *King Phillip*, it would be much easier for British subjects to forget where the true power lies.

The names that people give their children show the hopes and dreams 24
they have for them, and when we look at the differences between male
and female names in a culture, we can see the cumulative expectations of
that culture. In our culture girls often have names taken from small, aes-

thetically pleasing items, e.g., *Ruby, Jewel*, and *Pearl*. *Esther* and *Stella* mean "star," *Ada* means "ornament," and *Vanessa* means "butterfly." Boys are more likely to be given names with meanings of power and strength, e.g., *Neil* means "champion," *Martin* is from Mars, the God of War, *Raymond* means "wise protection," *Harold* means "chief of the army," *Ira* means "vigilant," *Rex* means "king," and *Richard* means "strong king."

We see similar differences in food metaphors. Food is a passive sub-   25
stance just sitting there waiting to be eaten. Many people have recognized this and so no longer feel comfortable describing women as "delectable morsels." However, when I was a teenager, it was considered a compliment to refer to a girl (we didn't call anyone a *woman* until she was middle-aged) as a *cute tomato*, a *peach*, a *dish*, a *cookie, honey, sugar*, or *sweetie-pie*. When being affectionate, women will occasionally call a man *honey* or *sweetie*, but in general, food metaphors are used much less often with men than with women. If a man is called a *fruit*, his masculinity is being questioned. But it's perfectly acceptable to use a food metaphor if the food is heavier and more substantive than that used for women. For example pin-up pictures of women have long been known as *cheesecake*, but when Burt Reynolds posed for a nude centerfold the picture was immediately dubbed *beefcake*, c.f., *a hunk of meat*. That such sexual references to men have come into the language is another reflection of how society is beginning to lessen the differences between their attitudes toward men and women.

Something similar to the *fruit* metaphor happens with references to   26
plants. We insult a man by calling him a *pansy*, but it wasn't considered particularly insulting to talk about a girl being a *wallflower*, a *clinging vine*, or a *shrinking violent*, or to give girls such names as *Ivy, Rose, Lily, Iris, Daisy, Camellia, Heather*, and *Flora*. A plant metaphor can be used with a man if the plant is big and strong, for example, Andrew Jackson's nickname of *Old Hickory*. Also, the phrases *blooming idiots* and *budding geniuses* can be used with either sex, but notice how they are based on the most active thing a plant can do which is to bloom or bud.

Animal metaphors also illustrate the different expectations for males   27
and females. Men are referred to as *studs, bucks*, and *wolves* while women are referred to with such metaphors as *kitten, bunny, beaver, bird, chick*, and *lamb*. In the 1950s we said that boys went *tomcatting*, but today it's just *catting around* and both boys and girls do it. When the term *foxy*, meaning that someone was sexy, first became popular it was used only for girls, but now someone of either sex can be described as *a fox*. Some animal metaphors that are used predominantly with men have negative connotations based on the size and/or strength of the animals, e.g., *beast, bullheaded, jackass, rat, loanshark*, and *vulture*. Negative metaphors used with women are based on smaller animals, e.g., *social*

butterfly, mousy, catty, and *vixen*. The feminine terms connote action, but not the same kind of large scale action as with the masculine terms.

WOMEN ARE CONNECTED WITH NEGATIVE CONNOTATIONS; MEN WITH POSITIVE CONNOTATIONS

The final point that my notecards illustrated was how many positive con-   28
notations are associated with the concept of masculine, while there are either trivial or negative connotations connected with the corresponding feminine concept. An example from the animal metaphors makes a good illustration. The word *shrew* taken from the name of a small but especially vicious animal was defined in my dictionary as "an ill-tempered scolding woman," but the word *shrewd* taken from the same root was defined as "marked by clever, discerning awareness" and was illustrated with the phrase "a shrewd businessman."

Early in life, children are conditioned to the superiority of the mas-   29
culine role. As child psychologists point out, little girls have much more freedom to experiment with sex roles than do little boys. If a little girl acts like a *tomboy*, most parents have mixed feelings, being at least partially proud. But if their little boy acts like a *sissy* (derived from *sister*), they call a psychologist. It's perfectly acceptable for a little girl to sleep in the crib that was purchased for her brother, to wear his hand-me-down jeans and shirts, and to ride the bicycle that he has outgrown. But few parents would put a boy baby in a white and gold crib decorated with frills and lace, and virtually no parents would have their little boys wear his sister's hand-me-down dresses, nor would they have their son ride a girl's pink bicycle with a flower-bedecked basket. The proper names given to girls and boys show this same attitude. Girls can have "boy" names—*Cris, Craig, Jo, Kelly, Shawn, Teri, Toni*, and *Sam*—but it doesn't work the other way around. A couple of generations ago, *Beverley, Frances, Hazel, Marion*, and *Shirley* were common boys' names. As parents gave these names to more and more girls, they fell into disuse for males, and some older men who have these names prefer to go by their initials or by such abbreviated forms as *Haze* or *Shirl*.

When a little girl is told to *be a lady*, she is being told to sit with her   30
knees together and to be quiet and dainty. But when a little boy is told to *be a man* he is being told to be noble, strong, and virtuous—to have all the qualities that the speaker looks on as desirable. The concept of manliness has such positive connotations that it used to be a compliment to call someone a *he-man*, to say that he was doubly a man. Today many people are more ambivalent about this term and respond to it much as they do to the word *macho*. But calling someone a *manly man* or a *virile man* is nearly always meant as a compliment. *Virile* comes from the Indo-European *vir* meaning "man," which is also the basis of *virtuous*. Contrast the

positive connotations of both *virile* and *virtuous* with the negative connotations of *hysterical*. The Greeks took this latter word from their name for
uterus (as still seen in *hysterectomy*). They thought that women were the
only ones who experienced uncontrolled emotional outbursts, and so the
condition must have something to do with a part of the body that only
women have.

Differences in the connotations between positive male and negative   31
female connotations can be seen in several pairs of words that differ
denotatively only in the matter of sex. *Bachelor* as compared to *spinster*
or *old maid* has such positive connotations that women try to adopt them
by using the term *bachelor-girl* or *bachelorette*. *Old maid* is so negative
that it's the basis for metaphors: pretentious and fussy old men are called
old maids, as are the leftover kernels of unpopped popcorn, and the last
card in a popular children's game.

Patron and *matron* (Middle English for *father* and *mother*) have such   32
different levels of prestige that women try to borrow the more positive
masculine connotations with the word *patroness*, literally "female father." Such a peculiar term came about because of the high prestige attached to *patron* in such phrases as *a patron of the arts* or *a patron saint*.
Matron is more apt to be used in talking about a woman in charge of a
jail or a public restroom.

When men are doing jobs that women often do, we apparently try to   33
pay the men extra by giving them fancy titles, for example, a male cook
is more likely to be called a *chef* while a male seamstress will get the title
of *tailor*. The armed forces have a special problem in that they recruit
under such slogans as "The Marine Corps builds men!" and "Join the
Army! Become a Man." Once the recruits are enlisted, they find themselves doing much of the work that has been traditionally thought of as
"women's work." The solution to getting the work done and not insulting
anyone's masculinity was to change the titles as shown below:

waitress	orderly
nurse	medic or corpsman
secretary	clerk-typist
assistant	adjutant
dishwasher or	KP (kitchen police)
kitchen helper	

Compare *brave* and *squaw*. Early settlers in America truly admired   34
Indian men and hence named them with a word that carried connotations
of youth, vigor, and courage. But they used the Algonquin's name for
"woman" and over the years it developed almost opposite connotations to
those of *brave*. *Wizard* and *witch* contrast almost as much. The masculine
wizard implies skill and wisdom combined with magic, while the feminine *witch* implies evil intentions combined with magic. Part of the unat-
tractiveness of both *witch* and *squaw* is that they have been used so often

to refer to old women, something with which our culture is particularly uncomfortable, just as the Afghans were. Imagine my surprise when I ran across the phrases *grandfatherly advice* and *old wives' tales* and realized that the underlying implication is the same as the Afghan proverb about old men being worth listening to while old women talk only foolishness.

Other terms that show how negative we view old women as compared to young women are *old nag* as compared to *filly, old crow* or *old bat* as compared to *bird*, and of being *catty* as compared to being *kittenish*. There is no matching set of metaphors for men. The chicken metaphor tells the whole story of a woman's life. In her youth she is a *chick*. Then she marries and begins *feathering her nest*. Soon she begins feeling *cooped up*, so she goes to *hen parties* where she *cackles* with her friends. Then she has her *brood*, begins to *henpeck* her husband, and finally turns into an *old biddy*. 35

I embarked on my study of the dictionary not with the intention of prescribing language change but simply to see what the language would tell me about sexism. Nevertheless I have been both surprised and pleased as I've watched the changes that have occurred over the past two decades. I'm one of those linguists who believes that new language customs will cause a new generation of speakers to grow up with different expectations. This is why I'm happy about people's efforts to use inclusive language, to say *he or she* or *they* when speaking about individuals whose names they do not know. I'm glad that leading publishers have developed guidelines to help writers use language that is fair to both sexes, and I'm glad that most newspapers and magazines list women by their own names instead of only by their husbands' names and that educated and thoughtful people no longer begin their business letters with "Dear Sir" or "Gentlemen," but instead use a memo form or begin with such salutations as "Dear Colleagues," "Dear Reader," or "Dear Committee Members." I'm also glad that such words as *poetess, authoress, conductress*, and *aviatrix* now sound quaint and old-fashioned and that *chairman* is giving way to *chair* or *head, mailman* to *mail carrier, clergyman* to *clergy*, and *stewardess* to *flight attendant*. I was also pleased when the National Oceanic and Atmospheric Administration bowed to feminist complaints and in the late 1970s began to alternate men's and women's names for hurricanes. However, I wasn't so pleased to discover that the change did not immediately erase sexist thoughts from everyone's mind, as shown by a headline about Hurricane David in a 1979 New York tabloid, "David Rapes Virgin Islands." More recently a similar metaphor appeared in a headline in the *Arizona Republic* about Hurricane Charlie, "Charlie Quits Carolinas, Flirts with Virginia." 36

What these incidents show is that sexism is not something existing independently in American English or in the particular dictionary that I happened to read. Rather, it exists in people's minds. Language is like an X ray in providing visible evidence of invisible thoughts. The best thing 37 about people being interested in and discussing sexist language is that as they make conscious decisions about what pronouns they will use, what jokes they will tell or laugh at, how they will write their names, or how they will begin their letters, they are forced to think about the underlying issue of sexism. This is good because as a problem that begins in people's assumptions and expectations, it's a problem that will be solved only when a great many people have given it a great deal of thought.

QUESTIONS ON CONTENT

1. What precipitated Nilsen's investigation of sexism in the English language? How did her private "feminist movement" differ from the feminist movement of others? Why was she unable to avoid facing social issues head on?

2. What point does Nilsen make about each of the following:

   a. English words derived from the name of a person
   b. geographical names
   c. pairs of words, one masculine and the other feminine
   d. the use of words referring to foods, plants, and animals in connection with women
   e. the first names given to male and female infants
   f. the use of *Ms.*
   g. dictionary entries concerning famous women
   h. positive and negative connotations connected with the concepts "masculine" and "feminine."

3. Most dictionary makers try to describe accurately the ways in which speakers of English use the language. Can we, therefore, reasonably fault them for reflecting cultural attitudes in word definitions?

4. According to Nilsen, in what two areas does the English language reveal the importance of women?

5. Nilsen states she has seen many changes in the language since she began her study twenty years ago. List these changes and discuss what Nilsen says they reveal to her about the nature of sexist language. In what ways, for example, has the pronoun *Ms.* proven unsatisfactory?

QUESTIONS ON RHETORIC

1. What techniques does Nilsen use to support her conclusions? Is her evidence convincing? Why, or why not? (Glossary: *Examples*)

2. How has Nilsen organized her essay? (Glossary: *Organization*) You may find it helpful to make a scratch outline of her main ideas.

3. What is the tone of this essay? How does Nilsen maintain this tone? Is her tone appropriate for her subject and audience? (Glossary: *Tone*)

4. In essays of substantial length such as this one, short transitional paragraphs are often used to link the main sections of the essay. Identify two

such paragraphs in Nilsen's article. Are they effective? When would you use a transitional paragraph? When would you avoid doing so? (Glossary: *Transition*)

5. Nilsen uses a simile in her concluding paragraph. (Glossary: *Figures of Speech*) Identify the simile and explain how it works to make Nilsen's point. Did you like it? Why, or why not?

VOCABULARY

inherent (1)	semantic (14)	ambivalent (30)
eponyms (7)	temperance (21)	quaint (36)
gender (13)	trivial (28)	

WRITING TOPICS

1. Nilsen provides us with an extensive catalog of words that reveal a disparaging attitude toward women. It is not her purpose, however, to offer any solutions to the problem of bias in the language. Write an essay in which you discuss the possible improvements that you as a user of the language, lexicographers as makers of dictionaries, and women and men as leaders of the equal rights movement can bring about.

2. Like any attempt to change the status quo, women's attempts to change language have aroused a great deal of opposition. Who is the opposition? To what do they seem to be reacting? Does the opposition seem justified in any of its objections? What techniques does the opposition employ?

ONE SMALL STEP
FOR GENKIND

Casey Miller and Kate Swift

Casey Miller and Kate Swift's articles on language and sexism have appeared nationwide in magazines and newspapers. In this 1972 essay they examine the ways that sexist attitudes reveal themselves, not only in our everyday speech, but in the language of textbooks, dictionaries, religion, and the media.

A riddle is making the rounds that goes like this: A man and his young son were in an automobile accident. The father was killed and the son, who was critically injured, was rushed to a hospital. As attendants wheeled the unconscious boy into the emergency room, the doctor on duty looked down at him and said, "My God, it's my son!" What was the relationship of the doctor to the injured boy?

If the answer doesn't jump to your mind, another riddle that has been around a lot longer might help: The blind beggar had a brother. The blind beggar's brother died. The brother who died had no brother. What relation was the blind beggar to the blind beggar's brother?

As with all riddles, the answers are obvious once you see them: The doctor was the boy's mother and the beggar was her brother's sister. Then why doesn't everyone solve them immediately? Mainly because our language, like the culture it reflects, is male oriented. To say that a woman in medicine is an exception is simply to confirm that statement. Thousands of doctors are women, but in order to be seen in the mind's eye, they must be called women doctors.

Except for words that refer to females by definition (mother, actress, Congresswoman), and words for occupations traditionally held by females (nurse, secretary, prostitute), the English language defines everyone as male. The hypothetical person ("If a man can walk 10 miles in two hours . . ."), the average person ("the man in the street") and the active person ("the man on the move") are male. The assumption is that unless otherwise identified, people in general—including doctors and beggars—are men. It is a semantic mechanism that operates to keep women invisible: *man* and *mankind* represent everyone; *he* in generalized use refers to either sex; the "land where our fathers died" is also the land of our mothers—although they go unsung. As the beetle-browed and mustachioed man in a Steig cartoon says to his two male drinking companions, "When I speak of mankind, one thing I *don't* mean is womankind."

Semantically speaking, woman is not one with the species of man,   5
but a distinct subspecies. "Man," says the 1971 edition of the Britannica
Junior Encyclopedia, "is the highest form of life on earth. His superior
intelligence, combined with certain physical characteristics, have enabled
man to achieve things that are impossible for other animals." (The prose
style has something in common with the report of a research team describing its studies on "the development of the uterus in rats, guinea pigs
and men.") As though quoting the Steig character, still speaking to his
friends in McSorley's, the Junior Encyclopedia continues: "Man must
invent most of his behavior, because he lacks the instincts of lower animals. . . . Most of the things he learns have been handed down from his
ancestors by language and symbols rather than by biological inheritance."

Considering that for the last 5,000 years society has been patriarchal,   6
that statement explains a lot. It explains why Eve was made from Adam's
rib instead of the other way around, and who invented all those Adam-rib
words like *fe*male and *wo*man in the first place. It also explains why,
when it is necessary to mention woman, the language makes her a lower
caste, a class separate from the rest of man; why it works to "keep her in
her place."

This inheritance through language and other symbols begins in the   7
home (also called a man's castle) where man and wife (not husband and
wife, or man and woman) live for a while with their children. It is reinforced by religious training, the educational system, the press, government, commerce and the law. As Andrew Greeley wrote not long ago in
his magazine, "Man is a symbol-creating animal. He orders and interprets
his reality by his symbols, and he uses the symbols to reconstruct their
reality."

Consider some of the reconstructed realities of American history.   8
When schoolchildren learn from their textbooks that the early colonists
gained valuable experience in governing themselves, they are not told
that the early colonists who were women were denied the privilege of
self-government; when they learn that in the 18th century the average
man had to manufacture many of the things he and his family needed,
they are not told that this "average man" was often a woman who manu-
factured much of what she and her family needed. Young people learn
that intrepid pioneers crossed the country in covered wagons with their
wives, children and cattle; they do not learn that women themselves were
intrepid pioneers rather than part of the baggage.

In a paper published this year in Los Angeles as a guide for authors   9
and editors of social-studies textbooks, Elizabeth Burr, Susan Dunn and
Norma Farquhar document unintentional skewings of this kind that occur
either because women are not specifically mentioned as affecting or being
affected by historical events, or because they are discussed in terms of
outdated assumptions. "One never sees a picture of women captioned
simply 'farmers' or 'pioneers,'" they point out. The subspecies nomen-

clature that requires a caption to read "women farmers" or "women pioneers" is extended to impose certain jobs on women by definition. The textbook guide gives as an example the word *housewife*, which it says not only "suggests that domestic chores are the exclusive burden of females," but gives "female students the idea that they were born to keep house and teaches male students that they are automatically entitled to laundry, cooking and housecleaning services from the women in their families."

Sexist language is any language that expresses such stereotyped attitudes and expectations, or that assumes the inherent superiority of one sex over the other. When a woman says of her husband, who had drawn up plans for a new bedroom wing and left out closets, "Just like a man," her language is as sexist as the man's who says, after his wife has changed her mind about needing the new wing after all, "Just like a woman."

Male and female are not sexist words, but masculine and feminine almost always are. Male and female can be applied objectively to individual people and animals and, by extension, to things. When electricians and plumbers talk about male and female couplings, everyone knows or can figure out what they mean. The terms are graphic and culture free.

Masculine and feminine, however, are as sexist as any words can be, since it is almost impossible to use them without invoking cultural stereotypes. When people construct lists of "masculine" and "feminine" traits they almost always end up making assumptions that have nothing to do with innate differences between the sexes. We have a friend who happens to be going through the process of pinning down this very phenomenon. He is 7 years old and his question concerns why his coats and shirts button left over right while his sister's button the other way. He assumes it must have something to do with the differences between boys and girls, but he can't see how.

What our friend has yet to grasp is that the way you button your coat, like most sex-differentiated customs, has nothing to do with real differences but much to do with what society wants you to feel about yourself as a male or a female person. Society decrees that it is appropriate for girls to dress differently from boys, to act differently, and to think differently. Boys must be masculine, whatever that means, and girls must be feminine.

Unabridged dictionaries are a good source for finding out what society decrees to be appropriate, though less by definition than by their choice of associations and illustrations. Words associated with males—*manly, virile* and *masculine,* for example—are defined through a broad range of positive attributes like strength, courage, directness and independence, and they are illustrated through such examples of contemporary usage as "a manly determination to face what comes," "a virile literary style," "a masculine love of sports." Corresponding words associated with females are defined with fewer attributes (though weakness is often one of them) and the examples given are generally negative if not clearly pejorative: "feminine wiles," "womanish tears," "a womanlike lack of promptness," "convinced that drawing was a waste of time, if not downright womanly."

Male-associated words are frequently applied to females to describe   15 something that is either incongruous ("a mannish voice") or presumably commendable ("a masculine mind," "she took it like a man"), but female-associated words are unreservedly derogatory when applied to males, and are sometimes abusive to females as well. The opposite of "masculine" is "effeminate," although the opposite of "feminine" is simply "unfeminine."

One dictionary, after defining the word *womanish* as "suitable to or   16 resembling a woman," further defines it as "unsuitable to a man or to a strong character of either sex." Words derived from "sister" and "brother" provide another apt example, for whereas "sissy," applied either to a male or female, conveys the message that sisters are expected to be timid and cowardly, "buddy" makes clear that brothers are friends.

The subtle disparagement of females and corresponding approbation   17 of males wrapped up in many English words is painfully illustrated by "tomboy." Here is an instance where a girl who likes sports and the out-of-doors, who is curious about how things work, who is adventurous and bold instead of passive, is defined in terms of something she is not—a boy. By denying that she can be the person she is and still be a girl, the word surreptitiously undermines her sense of identity: it says she is unnatural. A "tomboy," as defined by one dictionary, is a "girl, especially a young girl, who behaves like a spirited boy." But who makes the judgment that she is acting like a spirited boy, not a spirited girl? Can it be a coincidence that in the case of the dictionary just quoted the editor, executive editor, managing editor, general manager, all six members of the Board of Linguists, the usage editor, science editor, all six general editors of definitions, and 94 out of the 104 distinguished experts consulted on usage—are men?

It isn't enough to say that any invidious comparisons and stereotypes   18 lexicographers perpetuate are already present in the culture. There are ways to define words like womanly and tomboy that don't put women down, though the tradition has been otherwise. Samuel Johnson, the lexicographer, was the same Dr. Johnson who said, "A woman preaching is like a dog's walking on his hind legs. It is not done well; but you are surprised to find it done at all."

Possibly because of the negative images associated with womanish   19 and womanlike, and with expressions like "woman driver" and "woman of the street," the word *woman* dropped out of fashion for a time. The women at the office and the women on the assembly line and the women one first knew in school all became ladies or girls or gals. Now a counter-movement, supported by the very term *women's liberation*, is putting back into words like *woman* and *sister* and *sisterhood* the meaning they were losing by default. It is as though, in the nick of time, women had seen that the language itself could destroy them.

Some long-standing conventions of the news media add insult to in-   20
jury. When a woman or girl makes news, her sex is identified at the beginning of a story, if possible in the headline or its equivalent. The assumption, apparently is that whatever event or action is being reported, a woman's involvement is less common and therefore more newsworthy than a man's. If the story is about achievement, the implication is: "pretty good for a woman." And because people are assumed to be male unless otherwise identified, the media have developed a special and extensive vocabulary to avoid the constant repetition of "woman." The results, "Grandmother Wins Nobel Prize," "Blonde Hijacks Airliner," "House-wife to Run for Congress," convey the kind of information that would be ludicrous in comparable headlines if the subjects were men. Why, if "Un-salaried Husband to Run for Congress," is unacceptable to editors, do women have to keep explaining that to describe them through external or superficial concerns reflects a sexist view of women as decorative ob-jects, breeding machines and extensions of men, not real people?

Members of the Chicago chapter of the National Organization for   21
Women recently studied the newspapers in their area and drew up a set of guidelines for the press. These include cutting out descriptions of the "clothes, physical features, dating life and marital status of women where such references would be considered inappropriate if about men": using language in such a way as to include women in copy that refers to home-owners, scientists and business people where "newspaper descriptions of-ten convey the idea that all such persons are male"; and displaying the same discretion in printing generalizations about women as would be shown toward racial, religious and ethnic groups. "Our concern with what we are called may seem trivial to some people," the women said, "but we regard the old usages as symbolic of women's position within this society."

The assumption that an adult woman is flattered by being called a girl   22
is matched by the notion that a woman in a menial or poorly paid job finds compensation in being called a lady. Ethel Strainchamps has pointed out that since *lady* is used as an adjective with nouns designating both high and low occupations (lady wrestler, lady barber, lady doctor, lady judge), some writers assume they can use the noun form without betraying value judgments. Not so, Strainchamps says, rolling the issue into a spitball: "You may write, 'He addressed the Republican ladies,' or 'The Democratic ladies convened' . . . but I have never seen 'the Com-munist ladies' or 'the Black Panther ladies' in print."

Thoughtful writers and editors have begun to repudiate some of the   23
old usages. "Divorcée," "grandmother" and "blonde," along with "viva-
cious," "pert," "dimpled" and "cute," were dumped by the *Washington
Post* in the spring of 1970 by the executive editor, Benjamin Bradlee. In
a memo to his staff, Bradlee wrote, "The meaningful equality and dignity
of women is properly under scrutiny today . . . because this equality has
been less than meaningful and the dignity not always free of stereotype
and condescension."

What women have been called in the press—or at least the part that   24
operates above ground—is only a fraction of the infinite variety of alternatives to "women" used in the subcultures of the English-speaking
world. Beyond "chicks," "dolls," "dames," "babes," "skirts" and
"broads" are the words and phrases in which women are reduced to their
sexuality and nothing more. It would be hard to think of another area of
language in which the human mind has been so fertile in devising and
borrowing abusive terms. In *The Female Eunuch*, Germaine Greer devotes four pages to anatomical terms and words for animals, vegetables,
fruits, baked goods, implements and receptacles, all of which are used to
dehumanize the female person. Jean Faust, in an article aptly called
"Words That Oppress," suggests that the effort to diminish women
through language is rooted in a male fear of sexual inadequacy. "Woman
is made to feel guilty for and akin to natural disasters," she writes; "hurricanes and typhoons are named after her. Any negative or threatening
force is given a feminine name. If a man runs into bad luck climbing up
the ladder of success (a male-invented game), he refers to the 'bitch goddess' success."

The sexual overtones in the ancient and no doubt honorable custom of   25
calling ships "she" have become more explicit and less honorable in an
age of air travel: "I'm Karen. Fly me." Attitudes of ridicule, contempt
and disgust toward female sexuality have spawned a rich glossary of insults and epithets not found in dictionaries. And the usage in which four-
letter words meaning copulate are interchangeable with *cheat, attack* and
destroy can scarcely be unrelated to the savagery of rape.

In her updating of Ibsen's *A Doll's House*, Clare Booth Luce has   26
Nora tell her husband she is pregnant—"In the way only men are supposed to get pregnant." "Men, pregnant?" he says, and she nods; "With
ideas. Pregnancies there [*she taps his head*] are masculine. And a very
superior form of labor. Pregnancies here [*taps her tummy*] are feminine—
a very inferior form of labor."

Public outcry followed a revised translation of the New Testament   27
describing Mary as "pregnant" instead of "great with child." The objections were made in part on esthetic grounds: there is no attractive adjective in modern English for a woman who is about to give birth. A less
obvious reason was that replacing the euphemism with a biological term

undermined religious teaching. The initiative and generative power in the conception of Jesus are understood to be God's; Mary, the mother, was a vessel only.

Whether influenced by this teaching or not, the language of human reproduction lags several centuries behind scientific understanding. The male's contribution to procreation is still described as though it were the entire seed from which a new life grows: the initiative and generative power involved in the process are thought of as masculine, receptivity and nurturance as feminine. "Seminal" remains a synonym for "highly original," and there is no comparable word to describe the female's equivalent contribution.   28

An entire mythology has grown from this biological misunderstanding and its semantic legacy; its embodiment in laws that for centuries made women nonpersons was a key target of the 19th-century feminist movement. Today, more than 50 years after women finally won the basic democratic right to vote, the word "liberation" itself, when applied to women, means something less than when used of other groups of people. An advertisement for the N.B.C. news department listed Women's Liberation along with crime in the streets and the Vietnam War as "bad news." Asked for his views on Women's Liberation, a highly placed politician was quoted as saying, "Let me make one thing perfectly clear. I wouldn't want to wake up next to a lady pipe-fitter."   29

One of the most surprising challenges to our male-dominated culture is coming from within organized religion, where the issues are being stated, in part, by confronting the implications of traditional language. What a growing number of theologians and scholars are saying is that the myths of the Judeo-Christian tradition, being the products of patriarchy, must be reexamined, and that the concept of an exclusively male ministry and the image of a male god have become idolatrous.   30

Women are naturally in the forefront of this movement, both in their efforts to gain ordination and full equality and through their contributions to theological reform, although both these efforts are often subtly diminished. When the Rev. Barbara Anderson was ordained by the American Lutheran Church, one newspaper printed her picture over a caption headed "Happy Girl." *Newsweek's* report of a protest staged last December by women divinity students at Harvard was jocular ("another tilt at the windmill") and sarcastic: "Every time anyone in the room lapsed into what [the students] regarded as male chauvinism—such as using the word 'mankind' to describe the human race in general—the outraged women . . . drowned out the offender with earpiercing blasts from party-favor kazoos . . . What annoyed the women most was the universal custom of referring to God as 'He.'"   31

The tone of the report was not merely unfunny; it missed the connection between increasingly outmoded theological language and the acceler-   32 ating number of women (and men) who are dropping out of organized religion, both Jewish and Christian. For language, including pronouns, can be used to construct a reality that simply mirrors society's assumptions. To women who are committed to the reality of religious faith, the effect is doubly painful. Professor Harvey Cox, in whose classroom the protest took place, stated the issue directly: The women, he said, were raising the "basic theological question of whether God is more adequately thought of in personal or suprapersonal terms."

Toward the end of Don McLean's remarkable ballad "American Pie," 33 a song filled with the imagery of abandonment and disillusion, there is a stanza that must strike many women to the quick. The church bells are broken, the music has died; then:

> *And the three men I admire most,*
> *The Father, Son and the Holy Ghost,*
> *They caught the last train for the Coast—*
> *The day the music died.*

Three men I admired most. There they go, briefcases in hand and 34 topcoats buttoned left over right, walking down the long gold platform under the city, past the baggage wagons and the hissing steam onto the Pullman. Bye, bye God—all three of you—made in the image of male supremacy. Maybe out there in L.A. where the weather is warmer, someone can believe in you again.

The Roman Catholic theologian Elizabeth Farian says "the bad theol- 35 ogy of an overmasculinized church continues to be one of the root causes of women's oppression." The definition of oppression is "to crush or burden by abuse of power or authority; burden spiritually or mentally as if by pressure."

When language oppresses, it does so by any means that disparage and 36 belittle. Until well into the 20th century, one of the ways English was manipulated to disparage women was through the addition of feminine endings to nonsexual words. Thus a woman who aspired to be a poet was excluded from the company of real poets by the label poetess, and a woman who piloted an airplane was denied full status as an aviator by being called an aviatrix. At about the time poetess, aviatrix, and similar Adam-ribbisms were dropping out of use, H. W. Fowler was urging that they be revived. "With the coming expansion of women's vocations," he wrote in the first edition (1926) of *Modern English Usage*, "feminines for vocation-words are a special need of the future." There can be no doubt he subconsciously recognized the relative status implied in the -*ess* designations. His criticism of a woman who wished to be known as an author rather than an authoress was that she had no need "to raise herself to the level of the male author by asserting her right to his name."

Who has the prior right to a name? The question has an interesting 37 bearing on words that were once applied to men alone, or to both men and women, but now, having acquired abusive associations, are assigned to women exclusively. Spinster is a gentle case in point. Prostitute and many of its synonyms illustrate the phenomenon better. If Fowler had chosen to record the changing usage of harlot from hired man (in Chaucer's time) through rascal and entertainer to its present definition, would he have maintained that the female harlot is trying to raise herself to the level of the male harlot by asserting her right to his name? Or would he have plugged for harlotress?

The demise of most -*ess* endings came about before the start of the 38 new feminist movement. In the second edition of *Modern English Usage*, published in 1965, Sir Ernest Gowers frankly admitted what his predecessors had been up to. "Feminine designations," he wrote, "seem now to be falling into disuse. Perhaps the explanation of this paradox is that it symbolizes the victory of women in their struggle for equal rights; it reflects the abandonment by men of those ideas about women in the professions that moved Dr. Johnson to his rude remark about women preachers."

If Sir Ernest's optimism can be justified, why is there a movement 39 back to feminine endings in such words as chairwoman, councilwoman and congresswoman? Betty Hudson, of Madison, Conn., is campaigning for the adoption of "selectwoman" as the legal title for a female member of that town's executive body. To have to address a woman as "Selectman," she maintains, "is not only bad grammar and bad biology, but it implies that politics is still, or should be, a man's business." A valid argument, and one that was, predictably, countered by ridicule, the sure-fire weapon for undercutting achievement. When the head of the Federal Maritime Commission, Helen D. Bentley, was named "Man of the Year" by an association of shipping interests, she wisely refused to be drawn into light-hearted debate with interviewers who wanted to make the award's name a humorous issue. Some women, of course, have yet to learn they are invisible. An 8-year-old who visited the American Museum of Natural History with her Brownie scout troop went through the impressive exhibit on pollution and overpopulation called "Can Man Survive?" Asked afterward, "Well, can he?" she answered, "I don't know about him, but we're working on it in Brownies."

Nowhere are women rendered more invisible by language than in pol- 40 itics. The United States Constitution, in describing the qualifications for Representative, Senator and President, refers to each as *he*. No wonder Shirley Chisholm, the first woman since 1888 to make a try for the Presidential nomination of a major party, has found it difficult to be taken seriously.

The observation by Andrew Greeley already quoted—that "man" 41 used "his symbols" to reconstruct "his reality"—was not made in reference to the symbols of language but to the symbolic impact that "nomination of a black man for the Vice-Presidency" would have on race relations in the United States. Did the author assume the generic term "man" would of course be construed to include "woman"? Or did he deliberately use a semantic device to exclude Shirley Chisholm without having to be explicit?

Either way, his words construct a reality in which women are ig- 42 nored. As much as any other factor in our language, the ambiguous meaning of *man* serves to deny women recognition as people. In a recent magazine article, we discussed the similar effect on women of the generic pronoun *he*, which we proposed to replace by a new common gender pronoun *tey*. We were immediately told, by a number of authorities, that we were dabbling in the serious business of linguistics, and the message that reached us from these scholars was loud and clear: It-is-absolutely-impossible-for-anyone-to-introduce-a-new-word-into-the-language-just-because-there-is-a-need-for-it, so-stop-wasting-your-time.

When words are suggested like "herstory" (for history), "sportsone- 43 ship" (for sportsmanship) and "mistresspiece" (for the work of a Virginia Woolf) one suspects a not-too-subtle attempt to make the whole language problem look silly. But unless Alexander Pope, when he wrote "The proper study of mankind is man," meant that women should be relegated to the footnotes (or, as George Orwell might have put it, "All men are equal, but men are more equal than women"), viable new words will surely someday supersede the old.

Without apologies to Freud, the great majority of women do not wish in 44 their hearts that they were men. If having grown up with a language that tells them they are at the same time men and not men raises psychic doubts for women, the doubts are not of their sexual identity but of their human identity. Perhaps the present unrest surfacing in the Women's Movement is part of an evolutionary change in our particular form of life—the one form of all in the animal and plant kingdoms that orders and interprets its reality by symbols. The achievements of the species called man have brought us to the brink of self-destruction. If the species survives into the next century with the expectation of going on, it may only be because we have become part of what Harlow Shapley calls the psychozoic kingdom, where brain overshadows brawn and rationality has replaced superstition.

Searching the roots of Western civilization for a word to call this new 45 species of man and woman, someone might come up with *gen*, as in genesis and generic. With such a word, *man* could be used exclusively for males as *woman* is used for females, for gen would include both sexes. Like the words deer and bison, gen would be both plural and singular. Like progenitor, progeny, and generation, it would convey continuity. *Gen* would express the warmth and generalized sexuality of generous, gentle, and genuine; the specific sexuality of genital and genetic. In the new family of gen, girls and boys would grow to genhood, and to speak of genkind would be to include all the people of the earth.

QUESTIONS ON CONTENT

1. According to the authors, the English language is built upon the assumption that everyone is male. Why do they find that notion harmful?

2. How do the authors define sexist language? In their opinion, are men the only ones guilty of using sexist language?

3. In paragraph 11, the authors assert that "Male and female are not sexist words, but masculine and feminine almost always are." How do they distinguish between *male* and *female* and *masculine* and *feminine*? Miller and Swift offer only one example of male and female words. Can you offer some others? What kinds of examples do they give of masculine and feminine words?

4. What are some of the ways the media works to demean women? What guidelines for the press has one women's group developed?

5. The authors say that religion has produced a "surprising challenge to our male-dominated culture. . . ." In what areas have women come to the forefront of the movement to reexamine the Judeo-Christian traditions? How has the press dealt with these efforts?

QUESTIONS ON RHETORIC

1. What is the figure of speech used in the title of this essay? How does it relate to the authors' argument?

2. The authors begin their essay with two familiar riddles. (Glossary: *Beginnings and Endings*). How do these riddles function to launch the essay? Do you think them effective? Explain.

3. Miller and Swift make liberal use of examples throughout their essay. Choose several of these examples to show how they strengthen the authors' point of view. Do any of them fail to support the authors' argument? Explain.

4. Would you define the tone of this essay as argumentative, angry, or ironic? Use examples of the authors' diction and phrasing to support your answer. Is the tone appropriate to the authors' point and subject? (Glossary: *Diction, Tone*)

5. The word *genkind* does not appear until paragraph 45. Why do you suppose the authors waited until the end of their essay to include it? How does this strategy help to support their argument?

VOCABULARY

riddle (1)	approbation (17)	euphemism (27)
intrepid (8)	surreptitiously (17)	supersede (43)
skewings (9)	invidious (18)	progenitor (45)
nomenclature (9)	lexicographer (18)	progeny (45)
invoking (12)	repudiate (23)	
incongruous (15)		

WRITING TOPICS

1. Casey Miller and Kate Swift published their analysis of sexist language in English in 1972. How much influence have they, as well as others who have dealt with this subject since that time, had on our language? One way to try to assess their impact is to look back at the language used before sexist language became a concern and compare it to today's English. Go to your school library and retrieve from the periodicals collection some issues of *Time* or *Newsweek*, or any other weekly news magazine, published just prior to 1972. Analyze the prose in several articles and compare it to the prose in several recently published articles to see what has changed and what remains the same. Write a report on your findings.

2. Explore the relationship between the language we use and the kind of people we are or would like to be. Can we simply change language and thereby change people's attitudes, or do we need to change people's attitudes first? Can we change people's attitudes without using language? Is there a proper strategy to follow in this regard? Write an essay in which you discuss these important issues, making sure to use examples from your reading of Miller and Swift as well as the other essays in this section.

3. If you own or have access to one or more handbooks of English, summarize the advice the author gives for avoiding sexist language. For example, does the author advise you to avoid using the pronoun *he* unless referring to an antecedent that is clearly male? If the use of *he* is sexist, what advice is given for revision? Write a report on what you find, what you already know, and what you learn.

"I'LL EXPLAIN IT TO YOU": LECTURING AND LISTENING

Deborah Tannen

In 1990 linguist Deborah Tannen of Georgetown University published You Just Don't Understand: Women and Men in Conversation. *The following selection from that best-selling book examines the differing ways that men and women use language in conversing with one another: men, by lecturing, reinforce their independence and establish or test their status; women, by listening, establish rapport and closeness through self-revelation. The result, however, is that men tend to take over conversations by providing information and women become easily bored because the interaction they seek does not come about. Rather than place blame or suggest any drastic remedies to improve communication between the sexes, Tannen believes that "Women and men both can gain by understanding the other's gender style, and by learning to use it on occasion."*

At a reception following the publication of one of my books, I noticed a publicist listening attentively to the producer of a popular radio show. He was telling her how the studio had come to be built where it was, and why he would have preferred another site. What caught my attention was the length of time he was speaking while she was listening. He was delivering a monologue that could only be called a lecture, giving her detailed information about the radio reception at the two sites, the architecture of the station, and so on. I later asked the publicist if she had been interested in the information the producer had given her. "Oh, yes," she answered. But then she thought a moment and said, "Well, maybe he did go on a bit." The next day she told me, "I was thinking about what you asked. I couldn't have cared less about what he was saying. It's just that I'm so used to listening to men go on about things I don't care about, I didn't even realize how bored I was until you made me think about it."

I was chatting with a man I had just met at a party. In our conversation, it emerged that he had been posted in Greece with the RAF during 1944 and 1945. Since I had lived in Greece for several years, I asked him about his experiences: What had Greece been like then? How had the Greek villagers treated the British soldiers? What had it been *like* to be a British soldier in wartime Greece? I also offered information about how Greece had changed, what it is like now. He did not pick up on my

389

remarks about contemporary Greece, and his replies to my questions quickly changed from accounts of his own experiences, which I found riveting, to facts about Greek history, which interested me in principle but in the actual telling left me profoundly bored. The more impersonal his talk became, the more I felt oppressed by it, pinned involuntarily in the listener position.

At a showing of Judy Chicago's jointly created art work *The Dinner Party*, I was struck by a couple standing in front of one of the displays: The man was earnestly explaining to the woman the meaning of symbols in the tapestry before them, pointing as he spoke. I might not have noticed this unremarkable scene, except that *The Dinner Party* was radically feminist in conception, intended to reflect women's experiences and sensibilities. 3

While taking a walk in my neighborhood on an early summer evening at twilight, I stopped to chat with a neighbor who was walking his dogs. As we stood, I noticed that the large expanse of yard in front of which we were standing was aglitter with the intermittent flickering of fireflies. I called attention to the sight, remarking on how magical it looked. "It's like the Fourth of July," I said. He agreed, and then told me he had read that the lights of fireflies are mating signals. He then explained to me details of how these signals work—for example, groups of fireflies fly at different elevations and could be seen to cluster in different parts of the yard. 4

In all these examples, the men had information to impart and they were imparting it. On the surface, there is nothing surprising or strange about that. What is strange is that there are so many situations in which men have factual information requiring lengthy explanations to impart to women, and so few in which women have comparable information to impart to men. 5

The changing times have altered many aspects of relations between women and men. Now it is unlikely, at least in many circles, for a man to say, "I am better than you because I am a man and you are a woman." But women who do not find men making such statements are nonetheless often frustrated in their dealings with them. One situation that frustrates many women is a conversation that has mysteriously turned into a lecture, with the man delivering the lecture to the woman, who has become an appreciative audience. 6

Once again, the alignment in which women and men find themselves arrayed is asymmetrical. The lecturer is framed as superior in status and expertise, cast in the role of teacher, and the listener is cast in the role of student. If women and men took turns giving and receiving lectures, there would be nothing disturbing about it. What is disturbing is the imbalance. Women and men fall into this unequal pattern so often because of the differences in their interactional habits. Since women seek to build rapport, they are inclined to play down their expertise rather than display it. Since men value the position of center stage and the feeling of knowing more, they seek opportunities to gather and disseminate factual information. 7

If men often seem to hold forth because they have the expertise,   8
women are often frustrated and surprised to find that when they have the
expertise, they don't necessarily get the floor.

FIRST ME, THEN ME

I was at a dinner with faculty members from other departments in my   9
university. To my right was a woman. As the dinner began, we introduced ourselves. After we told each other what departments we were in
and what subjects we taught, she asked what my research was about. We
talked about my research for a little while. Then I asked her about her
research and she told me about it. Finally, we discussed the ways that our
research overlapped. Later, as tends to happen at dinners, we branched
out to others at the table. I asked a man across the table from me what
department he was in and what he did. During the next half hour, I learned a
lot about his job, his research, and his background. Shortly before the dinner
ended there was a lull, and he asked me what I did. When I said I was a
linguist, he became excited and told me about a research project he had
conducted that was related to neurolinguistics. He was still telling me about
his research when we all got up to leave the table.

This man and woman were my colleagues in academia. What happens   10
when I talk to people at parties and social events, not fellow researchers?
My experience is that if I mention the kind of work I do to women, they
usually ask me about it. When I tell them about conversational style or
gender differences, they offer their own experiences to support the patterns I describe. This is very pleasant for me. It puts me at center stage
without my having to grab the spotlight myself, and I frequently gather
anecdotes I can use in the future. But when I announce my line of work
to men, many give me a lecture on language—for example, about how
people, especially teenagers, misuse language nowadays. Others challenge me, for example questioning me about my research methods. Many
others change the subject to something they know more about.

Of course not all men respond in this way, but over the years I have   11
encountered many men, and very few women, who do. It is not that
speaking in this way is *the* male way of doing things, but that it is *a* male
way. There are women who adopt such styles, but they are perceived as
speaking like men.

IF YOU'VE GOT IT, FLAUNT IT—OR HIDE IT

I have been observing this constellation in interaction for more than a   12
dozen years. I did not, however, have any understanding of *why* this
happens until fairly recently, when I developed the framework of status
and connection. An experimental study that was pivotal in my thinking

shows that expertise does not ensure women a place at center stage in conversation with men.

Psychologist H. M. Leet-Pellegrini set out to discover whether gender or expertise determined who would behave in what she terms a "dominant" way—for example, by talking more, interrupting, and controlling the topic. She set up pairs of women, pairs of men, and mixed pairs, and asked them to discuss the effects of television violence on children. In some cases, she made one of the partners an expert by providing relevant factual information and time to read and assimilate it before the video-taped discussion. One might expect that the conversationalist who was the expert would talk more, interrupt more, and spend less time supporting the conversational partner who knew less about the subject. But it wasn't so simple. On the average, those who had expertise did talk more, but men experts talked more than women experts. 13

Expertise also had a different effect on women and men with regard to supportive behavior. Leet-Pellegrini expected that the one who did not have expertise would spend more time offering agreement and support to the one who did. This turned out to be true—*except* in cases where a woman was the expert and her nonexpert partner was a man. In this situation, the women experts showed support—saying things like "Yeah" and "That's right"—far *more* than the nonexpert men they were talking to. Observers often rated the male nonexpert as more dominant than the female expert. In other words, the women in this experiment not only didn't wield their expertise as power, but tried to play it down and make up for it through extra assenting behavior. They acted as if their expertise were something to hide. 14

And perhaps it was. When the word *expert* was spoken in these experimental conversations, in all cases but one it was the man in the conversation who used it, saying something like "So, you're the expert." Evidence of the woman's superior knowledge sparked resentment, not respect. 15

Furthermore, when an expert man talked to an uninformed woman, he took a controlling role in structuring the conversation in the beginning *and* the end. But when an expert man talked to an uninformed man, he dominated in the beginning but not always in the end. In other words, having expertise was enough to keep a man in the controlling position if he was talking to a woman, but not if he was talking to a man. Apparently, when a woman surmised that the man she was talking to had more information on the subject than she did, she simply accepted the reactive role. But another man, despite a lack of information, might still give the expert a run for his money and possibly gain the upper hand by the end. 16

Reading these results, I suddenly understood what happens to me when I talk to women and men about language. I am assuming that my acknowledged expertise will mean I am automatically accorded authority in the conversation, and with women that is generally the case. But when 17

I talk to men, revealing that I have acknowledged expertise in this area often invites challenges. I *might* maintain my position if I defend myself successfully against the challenges, but if I don't, I may lose ground.

One interpretation of the Leet-Pellegrini study is that women are getting a bum deal. They don't get credit when it's due. And in a way, this is true. But the reason is not—as it seems to many women—that men are bums who seek to deny women authority. The Leet-Pellegrini study shows that many men are inclined to jockey for status, and challenge the authority of others, when they are talking to men too. If this is so, then challenging a woman's authority as they would challenge a man's could be a sign of respect and equal treatment, rather than lack of respect and discrimination. In cases where this is so, the inequality of the treatment results not simply from the men's behavior alone but from the differences in men's and women's styles: Most women lack experience in defending themselves against challenges, which they misinterpret as personal attacks on their credibility.

Even when talking to men who are happy to see them in positions of status, women may have a hard time getting their due because of differences in men's and women's interactional goals. Just as boys in high school are not inclined to repeat information about popular girls because it doesn't get them what they want, women in conversation are not inclined to display their knowledge because it doesn't get them what they are after. Leet-Pellegrini suggests that the men in this study were playing a game of "Have I won?" while the women were playing a game of "Have I been sufficiently helpful?" I am inclined to put this another way: The game women play is "Do you like me?" whereas the men play "Do you respect me?" If men, in seeking respect, are less liked by women, this is an unsought side effect, as is the effect that women, in seeking to be liked, may lose respect. When a woman has a conversation with a man, her efforts to emphasize their similarities and avoid showing off can easily be interpreted, through the lens of status, as relegating her to a one-down position, making her appear either incompetent or insecure.

A SUBTLE DEFERENCE

Elizabeth Aries, a professor of psychology at Amherst College, set out to show that highly intelligent, highly educated young women are no longer submissive in conversations with male peers. And indeed she found that the college women did talk more than the college men in small groups she set up. But what they said was different. The men tended to set the agenda by offering opinions, suggestions, and information. The women tended to react, offering agreement or disagreement. Furthermore, she found that body language was as different as ever: The men sat with their legs stretched out, while the women gathered themselves in. Noting that research has found that speakers using the open-bodied position are more likely to persuade their listeners, Aries points out that talking more may not ensure that women will be heard.

In another study, Aries found that men in all-male discussion groups   21 spent a lot of time at the beginning finding out "who was best informed about movies, books, current events, politics, and travel" as a means of "sizing up the competition" and negotiating "where they stood in relation to each other." This glimpse of how men talk when there are no women present gives an inkling of why displaying knowledge and expertise is something that men find more worth doing than women. What the women in Aries's study spent time doing was "gaining a closeness through more intimate self-revelation."

It is crucial to bear in mind that both the women and the men in these   22 studies were establishing camaraderie, and both were concerned with their relationships to each other. But different aspects of their relationships were of primary concern: their place in a hierarchical order for the men, and their place in a network of intimate connections for the women. The consequence of these disparate concerns was very different ways of speaking.

Thomas Fox is an English professor who was intrigued by the differ-   23 ences between women and men in his freshman writing classes. What he observed corresponds almost precisely to the experimental findings of Aries and Leet-Pellegrini. Fox's method of teaching writing included having all the students read their essays to each other in class and talk to each other in small groups. He also had them write papers reflecting on the essays and the discussion groups. He alone, as the teacher, read these analytical papers.

To exemplify the two styles he found typical of women and men, Fox   24 chose a woman, Ms. M, and a man, Mr. H. In her speaking as well as her writing, Ms. M. held back what she knew, appearing uninformed and uninterested, because she feared offending her classmates. Mr. H. spoke and wrote with authority and apparent confidence because he was eager to persuade his peers. She did not worry about persuading; he did not worry about offending.

In his analytical paper, the young man described his own behavior in   25 the mixed-gender group discussions as if he were describing the young men in Leet-Pellegrini's and Aries's studies:

> In my sub-group I am the leader. I begin every discussion by stating my opinions as facts. The other two members of the sub-group tend to sit back and agree with me. . . . I need people to agree with me.

Fox comments that Mr. H. reveals "a sense of self, one that acts to change himself and other people, that seems entirely distinct from Ms. M's sense of self, dependent on and related to others."

Calling Ms. M's sense of self "dependent" suggests a negative view   26 of her way of being in the world—and, I think, a view more typical of men. This view reflects the assumption that the alternative to independence is dependence. If this is indeed a male view, it may explain why so many men are cautious about becoming intimately involved with others: It makes sense to avoid humiliating dependence by insisting on independence. But there is another alternative: *inter*dependence.

The main difference between these alternatives is symmetry. Dependence is an asymmetrical involvement: One person needs the other, but not vice versa, so the needy person is one-down. Interdependence is symmetrical: Both parties rely on each other, so neither is one-up or one-down. Moreover, Mr. H's sense of self is also dependent on others. He requires others to listen, agree, and allow him to take the lead by stating his opinions first.

Looked at this way, the woman and man in this group are both dependent on each other. Their differing goals are complementary, although neither understands the reasons for the other's behavior. This would be a fine arrangement, except that their differing goals result in alignments that enhance his authority and undercut hers.

DIFFERENT INTERPRETATIONS—AND MISINTERPRETATIONS

Fox also describes differences in the way male and female students in his classes interpreted a story they read. These differences also reflect assumptions about the interdependence or independence of individuals. Fox's students wrote their responses to "The Birthmark" by Nathaniel Hawthorne. In the story, a woman's husband becomes obsessed with a birthmark on her face. Suffering from her husband's revulsion at the sight of her, the wife becomes obsessed with it too and, in a reversal of her initial impulse, agrees to undergo a treatment he has devised to remove the birthmark—a treatment that succeeds in removing the mark, but kills her in the process.

Ms. M interpreted the wife's complicity as a natural response to the demand of a loved one: The woman went along with her husband's lethal schemes to remove the birthmark because she wanted to please and be appealing to him. Mr. H blamed the woman's insecurity and vanity for her fate, and he blamed her for voluntarily submitting to her husband's authority. Fox points out that he saw her as individually responsible for her actions, just as he saw himself as individually responsible for his own actions. To him, the issue was independence: The weak wife voluntarily took a submissive role. To Ms. M, the issue was interdependence: The woman was inextricably bound up with her husband, so her behavior could not be separated from his.

Fox observes that Mr. H saw the writing of the women in the class as spontaneous—they wrote whatever popped into their heads. Nothing could be farther from Ms. M's experience as she described it: When she knew her peers would see her writing, she censored everything that popped into her head. In contrast, when she was writing something that only her professor would read, she expressed firm and articulate opinions.

There is a striking but paradoxical complementarity to Ms. M's and   32
Mr. H's styles, when they are taken together. He needs someone to listen and agree. She listens and agrees. But in another sense, their dovetailing purposes are at cross-purposes. He misinterprets her agreement, intended in a spirit of connection, as a reflection of status and power: He thinks she is "indecisive" and "insecure." Her reasons for refraining from behaving as he does—firmly stating opinions as facts—have nothing to do with her attitudes toward her knowledge, as he thinks they do, but rather result from her attitudes toward her relationships with her peers.

These experimental studies by Leet-Pellegrini and Aries, and the ob-   33
servations by Fox, all indicate that, typically, men are more comfortable than women in giving information and opinions and speaking in an authoritative way to a group, whereas women are more comfortable than men in supporting others. . . .

LISTENER AS UNDERLING

Clearly men are not always talking and women are not always listening. I   34
have asked men whether they ever find themselves in the position of listening to another man giving them a lecture, and how they feel about it. They tell me that this does happen. They may find themselves talking to someone who presses information on them so insistently that they give in and listen. They say they don't mind too much, however, if the information is interesting. They can store it away for future use, like remembering a joke to tell others later. Factual information is of less interest to women because it is of less use to them. They are unlikely to try to pass on the gift of information, more likely to give the gift of being a good audience.

Men as well as women sometimes find themselves on the receiving   35
end of a lecture they would as soon not hear. But men tell me that it is most likely to happen if the other man is in a position of higher status. They know they have to listen to lectures from fathers and bosses.

That men can find themselves in the position of unwilling listener is   36
attested to by a short opinion piece in which A. R. Gurney bemoans being frequently "cornered by some self-styled expert who harangues me with his considered opinion on an interminable agenda of topics." He claims that this tendency bespeaks a peculiarly American inability to "converse"—that is, engage in a balanced give-and-take—and cites as

support the French observer of American customs Alexis de Tocqueville, who wrote, "An American . . . speaks to you as if he was addressing a meeting." Gurney credits his own appreciation of conversing to his father, who "was a master at eliciting and responding enthusiastically to the views of others, though this resiliency didn't always extend to his children. Indeed, now I think about it, he spoke to us many times as if he were addressing a meeting."

It is not surprising that Gurney's father lectured his children. The act   37
of giving information by definition frames one in a position of higher status, while the act of listening frames one as lower. Children instinctively sense this—as do most men. But when women listen to men, they are not thinking in terms of status. Unfortunately, their attempts to reinforce connections and establish rapport, when interpreted through the lens of status, can be misinterpreted as casting them in a subordinate position—and are likely to be taken that way by many men.

WHAT'S SO FUNNY?

The economy of exchanging jokes for laughter is a parallel one. In her   38
study of college students' discussion groups, Aries found that the students in all-male groups spent a lot of time telling about times they had played jokes on others, and laughing about it. She refers to a study in which Barbara Miller Newman found that high school boys who were not "quick and clever" became the targets of jokes. Practical joking—playing a joke *on* someone—is clearly a matter of being one-up: in the know and in control. It is less obvious, but no less true, that *telling* jokes can also be a way of negotiating status.

Many women (certainly not all) laugh at jokes but do not later re-   39
member them. Since they are not driven to seek and hold center stage in a group, they do not need a store of jokes to whip out for this purpose. A woman I will call Bernice prided herself on her sense of humor. At a cocktail party, she met a man to whom she was drawn because he seemed at first to share this trait. He made many funny remarks, which she spontaneously laughed at. But when she made funny remarks, he seemed not to hear. What had happened to his sense of humor? Though telling jokes and laughing at them are both reflections of a sense of humor, they are very different social activities. Making others laugh gives you a fleeting power over them: As linguist Wallace Chafe points out, at the moment of laughter, a person is temporarily disabled. The man Bernice met was comfortable only when he was making her laugh, not the other way around. When Bernice laughed at his jokes, she thought she was engaging in a symmetrical activity. But he was engaging in an asymmetrical one.

A man told me that sometime around tenth grade he realized that he   40 preferred the company of women to the company of men. He found that his female friends were more supportive and less competitive, whereas his male friends seemed to spend all their time joking. Considering joking an asymmetrical activity makes it clearer why it would fit in with a style he perceived as competitive. . . .

MUTUAL ACCUSATIONS

Considering these dynamics, it is not surprising that many women complain that their partners don't listen to them. But men make the same complaint about women, although less frequently. The accusation "You're not listening" often really means "You don't understand what I said in the way that I meant it," or "I'm not getting the response I wanted." Being listened to can become a metaphor for being understood and being valued. 41

In my earlier work I emphasized that women may get the impression men aren't listening to them even when the men really are. This happens because men have different habitual ways of showing they're listening. As anthropologists Maltz and Borker explain, women are more inclined to ask questions. They also give more listening responses—little words like *mhm, uh-uh,* and *yeah*—sprinkled throughout someone else's talk, providing a running feedback loop. And they respond more positively and enthusiastically, for example by agreeing and laughing. 42

All this behavior is doing the work of listening. It also creates rapport-talk by emphasizing connection and encouraging more talk. The corresponding strategies of men—giving fewer listener responses, making statements rather than asking questions, and challenging rather than agreeing—can be understood as moves in a contest by incipient speakers rather than audience members. 43

Not only do women give more listening signals, according to Maltz and Borker, but the signals they give have different meanings for men and women, consistent with the speaker/audience alignment. Women use "yeah" to mean "I'm with you, I follow," whereas men tend to say "yeah" only when they agree. The opportunity for misunderstanding is clear. When a man is confronted with a women who has been saying "yeah," "yeah," "yeah," and then turns out not to agree, he may conclude that she has been insincere, or that she was agreeing without really listening. When a woman is confronted with a man who does *not* say "yeah"— or much of anything else—she may conclude that *he* hasn't been listening. The men's style is more literally focused on the message level of talk, while the women's is focused on the relationship or metamessage level. 44

To a man who expects a listener to be quietly attentive, a woman giving a stream of feedback and support will seem to be talking too much 45 for a listener. To a woman who expects a listener to be active and enthusiastic in showing interest, attention, and support, a man who listens silently will seem not to be listening at all, but rather to have checked out of the conversation, taken his listening marbles, and gone mentally home.

Because of these patterns, women may get the impression that men aren't listening when they really are. But I have come to understand, more recently, that it is also true that men listen to women less frequently than women listen to men, because the act of listening has different meanings for them. Some men really *don't* want to listen at length because they feel it frames them as subordinate. Many women do want to listen, but they expect it to be reciprocal—I listen to you now; you listen to me later. They become frustrated when they do the listening now and now and now, and later never comes.

MUTUAL DISSATISFACTION

If women are dissatisfied with always being in the listening position, the dissatisfaction may be mutual. That a woman feels she has been assigned the role of silently listening audience does not mean that a man feels he has consigned her to that role—or that he necessarily likes the rigid alignment either.

During the time I was working on this book, I found myself at a book party filled with people I hardly knew. I struck up a conversation with a charming young man who turned out to be a painter. I asked him about his work and, in response to his answer, asked whether there has been a return in contemporary art to figurative painting. In response to my question, he told me a lot about the history of art—so much that when he finished and said, "That was a long answer to your question," I had long since forgotten that I had asked a question, let alone what it was. I had not minded this monologue—I had been interested in it—but I realized, with something of a jolt, that I had just experienced the dynamic that I had been writing about.

I decided to risk offending my congenial new acquaintance in order to learn something about his point of view. This was, after all, a book party, so I might rely on his indulgence if I broke the rules of decorum in the interest of writing a book. I asked whether he often found himself talking at length while someone else listened. He thought for a moment and said yes, he did, because he liked to explore ideas in detail. I asked if it happened equally with women and men. He thought again and said, "No, I have more trouble with men." I asked what he meant by trouble. He said, "Men interrupt. *They* want to explain to *me*."

Finally, having found this young man disarmingly willing to talk about the conversation we had just had and his own style, I asked which he preferred: that a woman listen silently and supportively, or that she offer opinions and ideas of her own. He said he thought he liked it better if she volunteered information, making the interchange more interesting.

When men begin to lecture other men, the listeners are experienced at   51
trying to sidetrack the lecture, or match it, or derail it. In this system, making authoritative pronouncements may be a way to begin an *exchange* of information. But women are not used to responding in that way. They see little choice but to listen attentively and wait for their turn to be allotted to them rather than seizing it for themselves. If this is the case, the man may be as bored and frustrated as the woman when his attempt to begin an exchange of information ends in his giving a lecture. From his point of view, she is passively soaking up information, so she must not have any to speak of. One of the reasons men's talk to women frequently turns into lecturing is *because* women listen attentively and do not interrupt with challenges, sidetracks, or matching information.

In the conversations with male and female colleagues that I recounted   52
at the outset of this chapter, this difference may have been crucial. When I talked to the woman, we each told about our own research in response to the other's encouragement. When I talked to the man, I encouraged him to talk about his work, and he obliged, but he did not encourage me to talk about mine. This may mean that he did not want to hear about it— but it also may not. In her study of college students' discussion groups, Aries found that women who did a lot of talking began to feel uncomfortable; they backed off and frequently drew out quieter members of the group. This is perfectly in keeping with women's desire to keep things balanced, so everyone is on an equal footing. Women expect their conversational partners to encourage them to hold forth. Men who do not typically encourage quieter members to speak up, assume that anyone who has something to say will volunteer it. The men may be equally disappointed in a conversational partner who turns out to have nothing to say.

Similarly, men can be as bored by women's topics as women can be   53
by men's. While I was wishing the former RAFer would tell me about his personal experiences in Greece, he was probably wondering why I was boring him with mine and marveling at my ignorance of the history of a country I had lived in. Perhaps he would have considered our conversation a success if I had challenged or topped his interpretation of Greek history rather than listening dumbly to it. When men, upon hearing the kind of work I do, challenge me about my research methods, they are inviting me to give them information and show them my expertise— something I don't like to do outside of the classroom or lecture hall, but something they themselves would likely be pleased to be provoked to do.

The publicist who listened attentively to information about a radio   54
station explained to me that she wanted to be nice to the manager, to smooth the way for placing her clients on his station. But men who want to ingratiate themselves with women are more likely to try to charm them

by offering interesting information than by listening attentively to whatever information the women have to impart. I recall a luncheon preceding a talk I delivered to a college alumni association. My gracious host kept me entertained before my speech by regaling me with information about computers, which I politely showed interest in, while inwardly screaming from boredom and a sense of being weighed down by irrelevant information that I knew I would never remember. Yet I am sure he thought he was being interesting, and it is likely that at least some male guests would have thought that he was. I do not wish to imply that all women hosts have entertained me in the perfect way. I recall a speaking engagement before which I was taken to lunch by a group of women. They were so attentive to my expertise that they plied me with questions, prompting me to exhaust myself by giving my lecture over lunch before the formal lecture began. In comparison to this, perhaps the man who lectured to me about computers was trying to give me a rest.

The imbalance by which men often find themselves in the role of   55
lecturer, and women often find themselves in the role of audience, is not the creation of only one member of an interaction. It is not something that men do to women. Neither is it something that women culpably "allow" or "ask for." The imbalance is created by the difference between women's and men's habitual styles. . . .

HOPE FOR THE FUTURE

What is the hope for the future? Must we play out our assigned parts to   56
the closing act? Although we tend to fall back on habitual ways of talking, repeating old refrains and familiar lines, habits can be broken. Women and men both can gain by understanding the other gender's style, and by learning to use it on occasion.

Women who find themselves unwillingly cast as the listener should   57
practice propelling themselves out of that position rather than waiting patiently for the lecture to end. Perhaps they need to give up the belief that they must wait for the floor to be handed to them. If they have something to say on a subject, they might push themselves to volunteer it. If they are bored with a subject, they can exercise some influence on the conversation and change the topic to something they would rather discuss.

If women are relieved to learn that they don't always have to listen,   58
there may be some relief for men in learning that they don't always have to have interesting information on the tips of their tongues if they want to impress a woman or entertain her. A journalist once interviewed me for an article about how to strike up conversations. She told me that another expert she had interviewed, a man, had suggested that one should come up with an interesting piece of information. I found this amusing, as it

seemed to typify a man's idea of a good conversationalist, but not a woman's. How much easier men might find the task of conversation if they realized that all they have to do is listen. As a woman who wrote a letter to the editor of *Psychology Today* put it, "When I find a guy who asks, 'How was your day?' and really wants to know, I'm in heaven."

QUESTIONS ON CONTENT

1. What is particularly disturbing for Tannen about what happens in each of the four anecdotes she uses to begin her essay?

2. Tannen writes that the Leet-Pellegrini study was "pivotal" in her thinking. What in particular about that study made it so?

3. Tannen says of Professor Fox's observations that "what he observed corresponds almost precisely to the experimental findings of Aries and Leet-Pellegrini." If this is so, why does Tannen choose to include his findings? Are Fox's observations simply more support for her beliefs? Are there deeper implications in what he found?

4. Having read Tannen's observations and the conclusions she reaches, are you thinking about changing your conversational habits? If so, how? If not, why not?

5. As far as your own observations are concerned, does what Tannen writes about telling jokes seem correct to you? Why, or why not?

6. What conversational strategies do men use when their attempts to lecture other men meet with opposition? Would these same strategies work for women in similar situations? Explain.

QUESTIONS ON RHETORIC

1. Tannen begins her essay with four anecdotes or stories. How effective do you find them as a beginning for her essay? (Glossary: *Beginnings and Endings*) Explain.

2. Tannen has gathered information from several sources for her writing. What are those sources? She seems to like to draw information and conclusions from her experiences. Did you find her experiences more or less helpful or no different from the information and conclusions she drew from published research? Explain.

3. Would you agree that Tannen appears at times to bend over backward to be even-handed and fair, especially toward men? If you agree, why do you think she does this? Does she fear offending her male readers? Does she think there is a possibility she might be incorrect in her analysis?

4. Tannen supplies titles for each of the subsections of her essay. Did you find them helpful to your enjoyment in reading the essay? Were they distracting? Are they a superficial structural device that seem to give more structure to the essay than it actually has?

VOCABULARY

monologue (1)	resentment (15)	harangues (36)
sensibilities (3)	disparate (22)	resiliency (36)
rapport (7)	asymmetrical (27)	incipient (43)
neurolinguistics (9)	revulsion (29)	metamessage (44)
constellation (12)	inextricably (30)	

WRITING TOPICS

1. Write an essay in which you analyze your conversational style. You may want first to record a brief conversation so as to be better able to analyze it and have it available for reference in your paper. Consider in your analysis whether or not what Tannen has to say applies to you.

2. Make a conscious effort to alter your own conversational style. Change from a lecturer to a listener, or vice versa. Try to informally record what transpires. If your new conversational style is noticed, try to assess the new impressions you create. Next, examine your own response to your new conversational style. Are you pleased with it? Finally, write an essay in which you examine the entire experience using as many examples as you can to illustrate the points you make.

TELEVISION INSULTS MEN, TOO

Bernard R. Goldberg

*News correspondent Bernard R. Goldberg has worked with
Dan Rather and the* CBS Evening News *and as a special
correspondent for the CBS program* 48 Hours. *In the
following essay, which was first published in the* New York
Times, *Goldberg uses examples from television shows and
commercials to document what he believes is a high
incidence of male-bashing and the public's tolerance of it.*

It was front page news and it made the TV networks. A mother from   1
Michigan single-handedly convinces some of America's biggest advertisers to cancel their sponsorship of the Fox Broadcasting Company's
"Married . . . With Children" because, as she put it, the show blatantly
exploits women and the family.

The program is about a blue collar family in which the husband is a   2
chauvinist pig and his wife is—excuse the expression—a bimbo.

These are the late 1980's, and making fun of people because of their   3
gender—on TV no less, in front of millions of people—is déclassé. Unless, of course, the gender we're ridiculing is the male gender. Then it's
O.K.

Take "Roseanne." (Please!) It's the season's biggest new hit show,   4
which happens to be about another blue collar family. In this one, the
wife calls her husband and kids names.

"Roseanne" is Roseanne Barr who has made a career saying such cute   5
things as: "You may marry the man of your dreams, ladies, but 15 years
later you are married to a reclining chair that burps." Or to her TV show
son: "You're not stupid. You're just clumsy like your daddy."

The producer of "Roseanne" does not mince words either: "Men are   6
slime. They say they're going to do 50 percent of the work around the
house, but they never do."

I will tell you that the producer is a man, which does not lessen the   7
ugliness of the remark. But because his target is men, it becomes acceptable. No one, to my knowledge, is pulling commercials from "Roseanne."

In matters of gender discrimination, it has become part of the ac-   8
cepted orthodoxy—of many feminists and a lot of the media anyway—
that only women have the right to complain. Men have no such right.
Which helps explain why there have been so many commercials ridiculing men—and getting away with it.

In the past year or so, I have seen a breakfast cereal commercial showing a husband and wife playing tennis. She is perky and he is jerky. 9

She is a regular Martina Navratilova of the suburbs and he is virtually dead (because he wasn't smart enough to eat the right cereal). 10

She doesn't miss a shot. He lets the ball hit him in the head. If he were black, his name would be Stepin Fetchitt. 11

I have seen a commercial for razor blades that shows a woman in an evening gown smacking a man in a tuxedo across the face, suggesting, I suppose, that the male face takes enough punishment to deserve a nice, smooth shave. If he hit her (an absolutely inconceivable notion, if a sponsor is trying to sell a woman something) he would be a batterer. 12

I have seen an airline commercial showing two reporters from competing newspapers. She's strong and smart. He's a nerd. He says to her: I read your story this morning; you scooped me again. She replies to him: I didn't know you could read. 13

I have seen a magazine ad for perfume showing a business woman patting a businessman's behind as they walk down the street. Ms. Magazine, the Journal of American feminism, ran the ad. The publisher told me there was nothing sexist about it. 14

A colleague who writes about advertising and the media says advertisers are afraid to fool around with women's roles. They know, as she puts it, they'll "set off the feminist emergency broadcast system" if they do. So, she concludes, men are fair game. 15

In 1987, Fred Hayward, who is one of the pioneers of the men's rights movement (yes, there is a men's rights movement) studied thousands of TV and print ads and concluded: "If there's a sleazy character in an ad, 100 percent of the ones that we found were male. If there's an incompetent character, 100 percent of them in the ads are male." 16

I once interviewed Garrett Epps, a scholar who has written on these matters, who told me: "The female executive who is driven, who is strong, who lives for her work, that's a very positive symbol in our culture now. The male who has the same traits—that guy is a disaster: He harms everybody around him; he's cold; he's unfeeling; he's hurtful." 17

The crusading mother from Michigan hit on a legitimate issue. No more cheap shots, she seems to have said. And the advertisers listened. No more cheap shots is what a lot of men are saying also. Too bad nobody is listening to *them*. 18

QUESTIONS ON CONTENT

1. Based on the evidence that Goldberg presents, do you think there is a double standard in the portrayal of men and women in television shows and commercials? Why, or why not?

2. What evidence does Goldberg give for his belief that in "matters of gender discrimination, it has become part of the accepted orthodoxy—of many feminists and the media anyway—that only women have a right to complain" (8)? Do you find his evidence convincing? Why, or why not?

3. Why might "advertisers be afraid to fool around with women's roles" (15)?

4. Who was Stepin Fetchitt? How can you find out if you don't know? What is Goldberg's point in referring to him?

QUESTIONS ON RHETORIC

1. What is Goldberg's thesis and where does he state it? (Glossary: *Thesis*)

2. Explain how Goldberg uses examples to support his thesis. (Glossary: *Examples*)

3. What is the relationship between Goldberg's beginning and ending? (Glossary: *Beginnings and Endings*) Has Goldberg used an effective strategy in returning to his beginning? Explain.

4. Are Goldberg's paragraphs developed adequately? Explain.

VOCABULARY

blatantly (1)	batterer (12)	crusading (18)
mince (6)	scooped (13)	

WRITING TOPICS

1. Imagine that Alleen Pace Nilsen and Bernard Goldberg found themselves seated next to each other at dinner and got into a conversation about the way men and women are portrayed in our language and the media. Write what you think their dialogue might be.

2. Do your own informal study of the portrayal of men in television shows and commercials. Goldberg wrote his article in 1989. Does your more recent study reveal any differences with Goldberg's? Is the portrayal of men more or less harsh or simply different than Goldberg claimed? Write an essay in which you compare your study with his.

WRITING ASSIGNMENTS FOR "GENDER AND LANGUAGE"

1. Find twenty-five words in your desk dictionary that have some relation to males and females, and study the words in the way Aleen Nilsen studied her words. (Try to avoid overlapping her examples.) Using Nilsen's article as a model, write a short paper in which you discuss the biases, if any, that you see in the language.

2. Since its beginning, the feminist movement has been surrounded with controversy. One commentator, for example, in an essay in *Time*, said, "The feminist attack on social crimes [sex discrimination, etc.] may be as legitimate as it was inevitable. But the attack on words is only another social crime—one against the means and the hope of communication." Write an essay in which you agree or disagree with this writer's view of women's attempts to change language. Be sure to use examples to support your position.

3. It has been said that the words Americans use to describe old women are more derisive than those describing old men because the words for women represent them as thoroughly repugnant and disgusting. Compile a list of words that you use or that you have heard used to refer to old people. Are the words for women more derogatory and demeaning? Write an essay in which you discuss the words on your list.

4. Write an essay in which you consider one or more of the following potentially sexist words or groups or words in English:

   a. feminine suffixes *-ess* or *-trix*
   b. fellow
   c. old wives' tale
   d. coed
   e. salutations in letters
   f. *Ms.*, *Miss*, and *Mrs.*
   g. *girl* and *gal*

5. Consider the language used to describe the institution of marriage. Write an essay in which you discuss any sexist attitudes that are revealed in the words we use to write and talk about marriage.

6. In an essay, discuss the ways in which sex-biased language has hurt you or others around you. If possible, talk with someone older who was growing up before current attitudes about men and women became popular. How do they handle these affronts? How do you handle these affronts? Do you both perceive them as affronts in the same way?

7. Carefully read the following letter to the editor of the *New York Times*. In it the author, president of a small Manhattan advertising agency, argues against using the word *guys* to address women.

WOMEN AREN'T GUYS
by Nancy Stevens

A young woman, a lawyer, strides into a conference room. Already in attendance, at what looks to be the start of a high-level meeting, are four smartly dressed women in their 20's and 30's. The arriving woman plunks her briefcase down at the head of the polished table and announces, "O.K., guys, let's get started."

On "Kate and Allie," a television show about two women living together with Kate's daughter and Allie's daughter and son, the dialogue often runs to such phrases as, "Hey, you guys, who wants pizza?" All of the people addressed are female, except for Chip, the young son. "Come on, you guys, quit fighting," pleads one of the daughters when there is a tiff between the two women.

Just when we were starting to be aware of the degree to which language affects people's perceptions of women and substitute "people working" for "men working" and "humankind" for "mankind," this "guy" thing happened. Just when people have started becoming aware that a 40-year-old woman shouldn't be called a girl, this "guy" thing has crept in.

Use of "guy" to mean "person" is so insidious that I'll bet most women don't notice they are being called "guys," or, if they do, find it somehow flattering to be one of them.

Sometimes, I find the courage to pipe up when a bunch of us are assembled and are called "guys" by someone of either gender. "We're not guys," I say. Then everyone looks at me funny.

One day, arriving at a business meeting where there were five women and one man, I couldn't resist. "Hello, ladies," I said. Everyone laughed embarrassedly for the blushing man until I added, "and gent." Big sigh of relief. Wouldn't want to call a guy a "gal" now, would we?

Why is it not embarrassing for a woman to be called "guy?" We know why. It's the same logic that says women look sexy and cute in a man's shirt, but did you ever try your silk blouse on your husband and send him to the deli? It's the same mentality that holds that anything male is worthy (and to be aspired toward) and anything female is trivial.

We all sit around responding, without blinking, "black with one sugar, please," when anyone asks, "How do you guys like your coffee?"

What's all that murmuring I hear?

"Come on, lighten up."

"Be a good guy."

"Nobody means anything by it."

Nonsense.

Whatever our different opinions may be about anti-male and anti-female bias in the language, the examples of the man's shirt and the woman's silk blouse in Stevens's letter rings true in our experience. What does it reveal about our perceptions of men and women? Do you agree that this example reveals the same biases that allow even women to use the word *guy* when they refer to women? Write an essay supporting your conclusions.

8. Write an essay in which you provide your own analysis of what goes on in a conversation between a man and a woman or a group of men and women. Do you perceive conversational strategies and counterstrategies that Deborah Tannen does not examine in her essay? Are there aspects of

conversational dynamics that you think deserve more attention than Tannen gives them? For example, does it make any difference how long people have known each other? Does it make any difference what the context or setting of a conversation is? Do the ages of the participants make any difference?

PART IX

Euphemism and Taboos

What do you mean, "did we go moo-moo in our dipe-dipes?"

EUPHEMISM

Neil Postman

In the following essay taken from his book Crazy Talk,
Stupid Talk, *Neil Postman, professor of media ecology at
New York University, defines* euphemism *and explains the
often disapproved process of euphemizing. He believes that
"euphemisms are a means through which a culture may alter
its imagery and by so doing subtly change its style, its
priorities, and its values." There are those people, however,
for whom all euphemisms are bad. Postman argues that many
euphemisms serve worthwhile social purposes.*

A euphemism is commonly defined as an auspicious or exalted term
(like "sanitation engineer") that is used in place of a more down-to-earth
term (like "garbage man"). People who are partial to euphemisms stand
accused of being "phony" or of trying to hide what it is they are talking
about. And there is no doubt that in some situations the accusation is
entirely proper. For example, one of the more detestable euphemisms I
have come across in recent years is the term "Operation Sunshine," which
is the name the U.S. Government gave to some experiments it conducted
with the hydrogen bomb in the South Pacific. It is obvious that the government, in choosing this name, was trying to expunge the hideous imagery that the bomb evokes and in so doing committed, as I see it, an
immoral act. This sort of process—giving pretty names to essentially
ugly realities—is what has given euphemizing such a bad name. And
people like George Orwell have done valuable work for all of us in calling attention to how the process works. But there is another side to euphemizing that is worth mentioning, and a few words here in its defense
will not be amiss.

To begin with, we must keep in mind that things do not have "real"
names, although many people believe that they do. A garbage man is not
"really" a "garbage man," any more than he is really a "sanitation engineer." And a pig is not called a "pig" because it is so dirty, nor a shrimp
a "shrimp" because it is so small. There are things, and then there are the
names of things, and it is considered a fundamental error in all branches
of semantics to assume that a name and a thing are one and the same. It is
true, of course, that a name is usually so firmly associated with the thing
it denotes that it is extremely difficult to separate one from the other.
That is why, for example, advertising is so effective. Perfumes are not
given names like "Bronx Odor," and an automobile will never be called
"The Lumbering Elephant." Shakespeare was only half right in saying
that a rose by any other name would smell as sweet. What we call things

413

affect how we will perceive them. It is not only harder to sell someone a "horse mackerel" sandwich than a "tuna fish" sandwich, but even though they are the "same" thing, we are likely to enjoy the taste of the tuna more than that of the horse mackerel. It would appear that human beings almost naturally come to *identify* names with things, which is one of our more fascinating illusions. But there is some substance to this illusion. For if you change the names of things, you change how people will regard them, and that is as good as changing the nature of the thing itself.

Now, all sorts of scoundrels know this perfectly well and can make us   3
love almost anything by getting us to transfer the charm of a name to whatever worthless thing they are promoting. But at the same time and in the same vein, euphemizing is a perfectly intelligent method of generating new and useful ways of perceiving things. The man who wants us to call him a "sanitation engineer" instead of a "garbage man" is hoping we will treat him with more respect than we presently do. He wants us to see that he is of some importance to our society. His euphemism is laughable only if we think that he is not deserving of such notice or respect. The teacher who prefers us to use the term "culturally different children" instead of "slum children" is euphemizing, all right, but is doing it to encourage us to see aspects of a situation that might otherwise not be attended to.

The point I am making is that there is nothing in the process of euphe-   4
mizing itself that is contemptible. Euphemizing is contemptible when a name makes us see something that is not true or diverts our attention from something that is. The hydrogen bomb kills. There is nothing else that it does. And when you experiment with it, you are trying to find out how widely and well it kills. Therefore, to call such an experiment "Operation Sunshine" is to suggest a purpose for the bomb that simply does not exist. But to call "slum children" "culturally different" is something else. It calls attention, for example, to legitimate reasons why such children might feel alienated from what goes on in school.

I grant that sometimes such euphemizing does not have the intended   5
effect. It is possible for a teacher to use the term "culturally different" but still be controlled by the term "slum children" (which the teacher may believe is their "real" name). "Old people" may be called "senior citizens," and nothing might change. And "lunatic asylums" may still be filthy, primitive prisons though they are called "mental institutions." Nonetheless, euphemizing may be regarded as one of our more important intellectual resources for creating new perspectives on a subject. The *attempt* to rename "old people" "senior citizens" was obviously motivated by a desire to give them a political identity, which they not only warrant but which may yet have important consequences. In fact, the fate of euphemisms is very hard to predict. A new and seemingly silly name may replace an old one (let us say, "chairperson" for "chairman") and for years no one will think or act any differently because of it. And then,

gradually, as people begin to assume that "chairperson" is the "real" and proper name (or "senior citizen" or "tuna fish" or "sanitation engineer"), their attitudes begin to shift, and they will approach things in a slightly different frame of mind. There is a danger, of course, in supposing that a new name can change attitudes quickly or always. There must be some authentic tendency or drift in the culture to lend support to the change, or the name will remain incongruous and may even appear ridiculous. To call a teacher a "facilitator" would be such an example. To eliminate the distinction between "boys" and "girls" by calling them "childpersons" would be another.

But to suppose that such changes never "amount to anything" is to   6 underestimate the power of names. I have been astounded not only by how rapidly the name "blacks" has replaced "Negroes" (a kind of euphemizing in reverse) but also by how significantly perceptions and attitudes have shifted as an accompaniment to the change.

The key idea here is that euphemisms are a means through which a   7 culture may alter its imagery and by so doing subtly change its style, its priorities, and its values. I reject categorically the idea that people who use "earthy" language are speaking more directly or with more authenticity than people who employ euphemisms. Saying that someone is "dead" is not to speak more plainly or honestly than saying he has "passed away." It is, rather, to suggest a different conception of what the event means. To ask where the "shithouse" is, is no more to the point than to ask where the "restroom" is. But in the difference between the two words, there is expressed a vast difference in one's attitude toward privacy and propriety. What I am saying is that the process of euphemizing has no moral content. The moral dimensions are supplied by what the words in question express, what they want us to value and see. A nation that calls experiments with bombs "Operation Sunshine" is very frightening. On the other hand, a people who call "garbage men" "sanitation engineers" can't be all bad.

QUESTIONS ON CONTENT

1. If, as Postman says, "there is nothing in the process of euphemizing itself that is contemptible" (4), why do euphemisms have such a bad name?

2. Postman states, "There are things, and then there are the names of things, and it is considered a fundamental error in all branches of semantics to assume that a name and a thing are one and the same" (2). What does he mean? What happens when people think that a name and a thing are the same?

3. Postman believes that "euphemizing may be regarded as one of our more important intellectual resources for creating new perspectives on a

subject" (5). How can you change people's perception of something by simply changing its name? Give several examples of your own which substantiate Postman's claim.

4. What does Postman mean when he says that the change from "Negroes" to "blacks" is "a kind of euphemizing in reverse" (6)?

5. Why does Postman "reject categorically the idea that people who use 'earthy' language are speaking more directly or with more authenticity than people who employ euphemisms" (7)? Do you agree with him?

QUESTIONS ON RHETORIC

1. What is Postman arguing for in this essay?

2. Postman presents a dictionary definition of *euphemism* in the first sentence of the essay. Why is it appropriate that he begin with a definition of the term? (Glossary: *Beginnings*)

3. What would be lost if Postman hadn't used all the examples that he includes? (Glossary: *Examples*) Are they all functional and necessary? Explain.

4. In what ways has Postman used transitions to make paragraph 2 coherent? (Glossary: *Transitions*)

5. Why are Postman's last two sentences an appropriate conclusion to his essay? (Glossary: *Beginnings and Endings*)

VOCABULARY

auspicious (1)	evokes (1)	illusions (2)
exalted (1)	amiss (1)	contemptible (4)
expunge (1)	semantics (2)	categorically (7)
hideous (1)		

WRITING TOPICS

1. Postman says, "Euphemizing is contemptible when a name makes us see something that is not true or diverts our attention from something that is" (4). Which of the euphemisms listed below do you find contemptible? Why are they contemptible? Why are the others not contemptible?

   pre-owned ("used")
   broadcast journalist ("news reporter")
   Internal Revenue Service ("tax collector")
   nervous wetness ("sweat")
   facial blemishes ("pimples")
   orderly withdrawal ("retreat")
   resources control program ("defoliation")
   health alteration committee ("assassination team")
   convenient terms ("18 percent annual interest")
   queen-size ("large")

Write an essay discussing the uses to which euphemisms can be put. Be sure to include some examples of your own.

2. Several years ago, the editors of *Time* said that "despite its swaggering sexual candor, much contemporary speech still hides behind that traditional enemy of plain talk, the euphemism." Using examples from your own experience or observation, write an essay in which you agree or disagree with the editors of *Time*.

VERBAL TABOO

S. I. Hayakawa and
Alan R. Hayakawa

S. I. Hayakawa, former president of San Francisco State University and United States senator from California, was one of the leading semanticists in this century. In this excerpt from Language in Thought and Culture, *Hayakawa and his son Alan examine the verbal taboo, the phenomenon that occurs in almost all languages when the distinction between language and reality becomes confused.*

In every language, there seem to be certain "unmentionables"—words   1
of such strong affective connotations that they cannot be used in polite discourse. In English, the first of these to come to mind are, of course, words dealing with excretion and sex. We ask waiters and salesclerks where the "lounge" or "rest room" is, although we usually have no intention of lounging or resting. "Powder room" is another euphemism for the same facility, also known as "toilet," which itself is an earlier euphemism. Indeed, it is impossible in polite society to state, without having to resort to baby talk or a medical vocabulary, what a "rest room" is for. (It is "where you wash your hands.")

Words referring to anatomy and sex—and words even vaguely sug-   2
gesting anatomical and sexual matters—have even stronger affective connotations, especially in American and British culture. Polite ladies and gentlemen of the nineteenth century could not bring themselves to say "breast," "leg," or "thigh"—not even of chicken—so the terms "white meat" and "dark meat" were substituted. It was thought inelegant to speak of "going to bed," so "to retire" was used instead. When D. H. Lawrence's first novel, *The White Peacock* (1911) was published, the author was widely criticized for having used the word "stallion," even though its context was innocuous. Taboos and the euphemisms we use as substitutes do change, of course: a novel by Henry James or Edith Wharton uses the phrase "making love" in a way different from the way we use the term now. To Americans at the turn of the century, "making love" meant "wooing" or "courting"—these, in turn, are both words not in current use. Currently, we use "making love" as a more acceptable, romantic alternative to clinical or vulgar expressions for sexual union.

Amusing as these verbal taboos sometimes are, they may also pro-   3
duce serious problems, since they may prevent frank discussion of sexual or physical matters. Finding the nontechnical vocabulary of sex too coarse and shocking, and being unfamiliar with the medical or technical

vocabulary, many people are simply unable to seek or use information about such "sensitive" issues.

When scientists first learned about AIDS, for example, the vague, hesitant vocabulary used to explain how the disease was transmitted confused many people. Gradually, the vocabulary became more specific as newspapers, magazines, and other publications began using a less technical, common vocabulary to convey the critical facts needed by specific groups and audiences at risk for the disease. Nevertheless, some people have objected to, or have been shocked by, the appearance in print of explicit sexual terms designed to ensure that people of all ages know enough about AIDS to help prevent its spread.

Money is another subject about which communication is inhibited. It is acceptable to mention *sums* of money, such as $10,000 or $2.50. But it is considered in bad taste to inquire directly into other people's financial affairs, unless such an inquiry is really necessary in the course of business. When creditors send bills, they almost never mention money, although that is what they are writing about. There are many circumlocutions: "We beg to call your attention to what may be an oversight on your part." "We would appreciate your early attention to this matter." "May we look forward to an early remittance?"

The fear of death carries over, quite understandably in view of the widespread confusion of symbols with things symbolized, into fear of the *words* having to do with death. Many people, therefore, instead of saying someone has "died," substitute such expressions as "passed away," "gone to his reward," "departed," "bought the farm," or "gone west." In Japanese, the word for death, *shi*, happens to have the same pronunciation as the word for the number four. This coincidence results in many linguistically awkward situations, since people avoid "*shi*" in the discussion of numbers and prices, and use "*yon*," a word of different origin, instead.

The stronger verbal taboos have, however, a genuine social value. When we are extremely angry and we feel the need of expressing our anger in violence, the uttering of these forbidden words may provide a relatively harmless verbal substitute for going berserk and smashing furniture; they may act as a kind of safety valve in our moments of crisis.

It is difficult to explain why some words should have such powerful affective connotations while others with the same informative connotations do not. Some of our verbal reticences, especially the religious ones, have the authority of the Bible: "Thou shalt not take the name of the Lord thy God in vain; for the Lord will not hold him guiltless that taketh his name in vain" (Exodus 21:7). "Gee," "gosh almighty," and "gosh darn" are ways to avoid saying "Jesus," "God Almighty," and "God damn." Carrying the biblical injunction one step further, we also avoid taking the name of the devil in vain by means of such expressions as "the deuce," "the dickens," and "Old Nick." It appears that among all the people of the world, among the civilized as well as the primitive, there is a feeling that the names of the gods are too holy, and the names of evil spirits too terrifying, to be invoked lightly.

The primitive confusion of word with thing, of symbol with thing   9
symbolized, manifests itself in some parts of the world in a belief that the name of a person is *part of* that person. To know someone's name, therefore, is to have power over him. Because of this belief, it is customary among some peoples for children to be given at birth a "real name" known only to the parents and never used, as well as a nickname or public name to be called by in society. In this way a child is protected from being put in anyone's power. The story of Rumpelstiltskin is a European illustration of this belief in the power of names.

QUESTIONS ON CONTENT

1. Into what categories do the Hayakawas classify taboo words? Give an example of each subject area.

2. What do the Hayakawas mean when they say that taboo words have "strong affective connotations" (1)? How do affective connotations differ from informative connotations?

3. According to the Hayakawas, what problems result from the existence of verbal taboos?

4. The Hayakawas say that the "stronger verbal taboos have . . . a genuine social value" (7). What is it?

5. What do the Hayakawas mean when they say there is "widespread confusion of symbols with things symbolized" (6)?

6. What is the relationship between taboo words and euphemisms? Provide several examples to illustrate your answer.

QUESTIONS ON RHETORIC

1. Which sentence in paragraph 2 is the topic sentence? How do the Hayakawas support this idea? (Glossary: *Topic Sentence*)

2. How do the Hayakawas make the transition between paragraphs 6 and 7?

3. The authors assume that their readers are familiar with the story of Rumplestiltskin, a children's classic, and therefore do not retell the story to make their point. Is their assumption correct? Do you know the story?

4. In what ways do the Hayakawas' numerous examples function in this essay? (Glossary: *Examples*) Which ones are the most effective for you? Why?

VOCABULARY

affective (1)	frank (3)	injunction (8)
inelegant (2)	circumlocutions (5)	

WRITING TOPICS

1. There is an important distinction between symbols and the things they stand for, that is, their referents. For example, a person should not confuse an actual chair (physical object) with the word *chair* (symbol). Nevertheless, as the Hayakawas observe, there is "widespread confusion of symbols with things symbolized" (3). In this connection, discuss the following episode in which a small child is talking to her mother. "Mommy! I'm scared of *death*. I don't like to hear that word. It frightens me! If only it were called something else, like *looma*." What in your opinion would happen if the word were changed? Can you suggest other examples to support your view?

2. In recent years "concerned citizens" across the country have attempted to remove the *Dictionary of American Slang* as well as certain desk dictionaries from schools and libraries. They have done so to keep their children from being exposed to taboo language. What underlying assumption about the relationship between words and things do such efforts reflect? If these citizens were successful in removing these books, would their children be protected? Why, or why not?

FOUR-LETTER WORDS CAN HURT YOU

Barbara Lawrence

Barbara Lawrence was born in Hanover, New Hampshire, and graduated from Connecticut College. Before becoming a professor of humanities at the State University of New York at Old Westbury, she worked as an editor at McCall's, Redbook, *and the* New Yorker. *In the following essay, published in the* New York Times, *she defines "obscenity" and explains why she finds the obscene language some people use to be "implicity sadistic or denigrating to women."*

Why should any words be called obscene? Don't they all describe natural human functions? Am I trying to tell them, my students demand, that the "strong, earthy, gut-honest"—or, if they are fans of Norman Mailer, the "rich, liberating, existential"—language they use to describe sexual activity isn't preferable to "phony-sounding, middle-class words like 'intercourse' and 'copulate'?" "Cop You Late!" they say with fancy inflections and gagging grimaces. "Now, what is *that* supposed to mean?"

Well, what is it supposed to mean? And why indeed should one group of words describing human functions and human organs be acceptable in ordinary conversations and another, describing presumably the same organs and functions, be tabooed—so much so, in fact, that some of these words still cannot appear in print in many parts of the English-speaking world?

The argument that these taboos exist only because of "sexual hang-ups" (middle-class, middle-age, feminist), or even that they are a result of class oppression (the contempt of the Norman conquerors for the language of their Anglo-Saxon serfs), ignores a much more likely explanation, it seems to me, and that is the sources and functions of the words themselves.

The best known of the tabooed sexual verbs, for example, comes from the German *ficken*, meaning "to strike"; combined, according to Partridge's etymological dictionary *Origins*, with the Latin sexual verb *futuere*; associated in turn with the Latin *fustis*, "a staff or cudgel"; the Celtic *buc*, "a point, hence to pierce"; the Irish *bot*, "the male member"; the Latin *battuere*, "to beat"; the Gaelic *batair*, "a cudgeller"; the Early Irish *bualaim*, "I strike"; and so forth. It is one of what etymologists sometimes call "the sadistic group of words for the man's part in copulation."

The brutality of this word, then, and its equivalents ("screw," "bang," etc.), is not an illusion of the middle class or a crotchet of Women's Liberation. In their origins and imagery these words carry undeniably painful, if not sadistic, implications, the object of which is almost always female. Consider, for example, what a "screw" actually does to the wood it penetrates; what a painful, even mutilating, activity this kind of analogy suggests. "Screw" is particularly interesting in this context, since the noun, according to Partridge, comes from words meaning "groove," "nut," "ditch," "breeding sow," "scrofula" and "swelling," while the verb, besides its explicit imagery, has antecedent associations to "write on," "scratch," "scarify," and so forth—a revealing fusion of a mechanical or painful action with an obviously denigrated object.

Not all obscene words, of course, are as implicitly sadistic or deni-   6
grating to women as these, but all that I know seem to serve a similar purpose: to reduce the human organism (especially the female organism) and human functions (especially sexual and procreative) to their least organic, most mechanical dimension; to substitute a trivializing or deforming resemblance for the complex human reality of what is being described.

Tabooed male descriptives, when they are not openly denigrating to   7
women, often serve to divorce a male organ or function from any significant interaction with the female. Take the word "testes," for example, suggesting "witnesses" (from the Latin *testis*) to the sexual and procreative strengths of the male organ; and the obscene counterpart of this word, which suggests little more than a mechanical shape. Or compare almost any of the "rich," "liberating" sexual verbs, so fashionable today among male writers, with that much-derided Latin word "copulate" ("to bind or join together") or even that Anglo-Saxon phrase (which seems to have had no trouble surviving the Norman Conquest) "make love."

How arrogantly self-involved the tabooed words seem in comparison   8
to either of the other terms, and how contemptuous of the female partner. Understandably so, of course, if she is only a "skirt," a "broad," a "chick," a "pussycat" or a "piece." If she is, in other words, no more than her skirt, or what her skirt conceals; no more than a breeder, or the broadest part of her; no more than a piece of a human being or a "piece of tail."

The most severely tabooed of all the female descriptives, incidentally,   9
are those like a "piece of tail," which suggest (either explicitly or through antecedents) that there is no significant difference between the female channel through which we are all conceived and born and the anal outlet common to both sexes—a distinction that pornographers have always enjoyed obscuring.

This effort to deny women their biological identity, their individu-   10
ality, their humanness, is such an important aspect of obscene language that one can only marvel at how seldom, in an era preoccupied with definitions of obscenity, this fact is brought to our attention. One prob-

lem, of course, is that many of the people in the best position to do this (critics, teachers, writers) are so reluctant today to admit that they are angered or shocked by obscenity. Bored, maybe, unimpressed, aesthetically displeased, but—no matter how brutal or denigrating the material—never angered, never shocked.

And yet how eloquently angered, how piously shocked many of these 11 same people become if denigrating language is used about any minority group other than women; if the obscenities are racial or ethnic, that is, rather than sexual. Words like "coon," "kike," "spic," "wop," after all, deform identity, deny individuality and humanness in almost exactly the same way that sexual vulgarisms and obscenities do.

No one that I know, least of all my students, would fail to question 12 the values of a society whose literature and entertainment rested heavily on racial or ethnic pejoratives. Are the values of a society whose literature and entertainment rest as heavily as ours on sexual pejoratives any less questionable?

QUESTIONS ON CONTENT

1. How does Lawrence explain the existence of taboos? What other explanations does she mention and then dismiss?

2. Why does Lawrence, as a woman, object to obscene language? Could men object to obscene language on the same grounds?

3. Do you agree with Lawrence's argument? Why, or why not? Would it be fair to consider Lawrence's view of obscenity as strictly feminist?

4. In paragraph 4, Lawrence details the origin of "the best known of the tabooed sexual verbs." In what way is this presentation of the word's etymology related to her central argument? How did you respond to this paragraph? Why?

QUESTIONS ON RHETORIC

1. Lawrence begins her essay with a series of questions. What functions do these questions serve? (Glossary: *Beginnings and Endings* and *Rhetorical Questions*)

2. Lawrence consciously avoids using "obscene" words. What, in your opinion, is gained or lost as a result of this strategy? Explain.

3. Comment on the connotations of the words which have been italicized in the following sentence: (Glossary: *Connotation*)

> And yet how *eloquently* angered, how *piously* shocked many of these same people become if denigrating language is used about any minority group other than women. . . .(11)

4. Should paragraphs 11 and 12 have been combined? Why do you feel Lawrence has made separate paragraphs?

5. What is the effect of Lawrence's final question? How would you answer it?

VOCABULARY

preferable (1)   analogy (5)   contemptuous (8)
grimaces (1)   antecedent (5)   pejoratives (12)
oppression (3)   implicitly (6)

WRITING TOPICS

1. Discuss the pros and cons of the proposition that women's use of "liberated" language is self-defeating. Why, in your opinion, do some women make a point of using such language?

2. Do you commonly use sexual obscenities and feel justified in doing so? Or do such words offend you? How would you describe your feelings about obscenities? Defend your feelings to someone who does not share them.

3. Lawrence observes that "some of these words still cannot appear in print in many parts of the English-speaking world" (2)—and books that contain these words, including some dictionaries, are banned from many school libraries and bookstores. What reasons can be given for and against censoring obscene words, or banning publications in which they appear? Does such action really eradicate the problem, or merely force it underground? What is your position? How would you support it?

AIDS: The Linguistic Battlefield

Michael Callen

AIDS, or Acquired Immune Deficiency Syndrome, was first isolated in 1977 and has become a global health crisis. The World Health Organization estimates that 13 million people worldwide may be infected with HIV (the virus believed by most authorities to cause AIDS), and no cure for the presently fatal disease is yet in sight. In this essay, Michael Callen, an AIDS activist, examines the language used to discuss AIDS and those who suffer from it. Because the disease is so threatening, its language is fraught with evasions and taboos; Callen urges us to examine that language carefully and to reform it where necessary as one way of exerting some power over what has been termed a modern plague.

AIDS is the moment-to-moment management of uncertainty. It's like standing in the middle of the New York Stock Exchange at midday, buzzers and lights flashing, everyone yelling, a million opinions. AIDS is about loss of control—of one's bowels, one's bladder, one's life. And so there is often a ferocious drive by those of us with AIDS to exert at least *some* control over it. When I was diagnosed in 1982, I decided that I'd have to pay close attention to the language of AIDS—to keep my wits about me in order to see beyond the obfuscating medical mumbo-jumbo meant to dazzle me into a deadly passivity.

AIDS is a sprawling topic. War is being waged on many fronts. From the beginning of this epidemic, there have been a number of important battles over how we speak about AIDS which have had subtle but profound effects on how we think about—and respond to—AIDS. These linguistic battles have also affected how those of us diagnosed as having AIDS experience our own illness.

In the early seventies, the gay liberation movement won a smashing victory when it forced the American Psychiatric Association to declassify homosexuality as an illness. But with the creation of a new disease called G.R.I.D., or gay-related immune deficiency, as AIDS was first termed, in an instant, those of us whose primary sexual and affectional attraction is to members of our own sex once again became medicalized and pathologized—only now we were considered literally, as opposed to merely morally, contagious.

Soon, gay-related immune deficiency was discovered in nongay people and a new name for this disease had to be found. All factions were poised for a political battle over the new name. Instinctively, those empowered to create and police the definition of AIDS (and those who would be profoundly affected by it) were aware that the new name would affect how the epidemic would be handled by the federal government and the "general" (meaning, generally, the nonhomosexual, non-IV-drug-using, rest-of-you) public.

In the end, a neutral sounding, almost cheerful name was chosen: A.I.D.S. Words can resonate with other words and take on subtle, sympathetic vibrations. AIDS: as in "health and beauty aids" or, to retain some of the sexual connotations of the disease, "marital aids." Or AIDS: as in "aid to the Contras." Or, "now is the time for all good men to come to the aid of their country." "AIDS" sounded like something . . . well, helpful.

My highly trained eye can now spot the letters A-I-D on a page of newsprint at lightning speed. It's amazing how often those three letters appear in headlines: afrAID, mislAID, medicAID, pAID—even bridesmAIDS. Every time I would hear a newscaster say "The president's aide reported today . . . ," I'd be momentarily disoriented by the linkage of "president" and "AIDS."

It's interesting to speculate, by the way, what the public response to AIDS might have been had the name proposed by a group from Boston prevailed: *herpes virus reactivation syndrome*. Prior to AIDS, the American public—general or otherwise—had been barraged by *Time* magazine cover stories about another fearsome, sexually transmitted epidemic: herpes. If those with the power to name the current plague had linked its name to the herpes epidemic, getting the American public to take AIDS seriously might not have been quite so difficult. One important consequence (some would say cause) of the profound immune disturbance we now call *AIDS* is that latent herpes viruses are reactivated, leading to a vicious cycle of immune suppression. Had the name *herpes virus reactivation syndrome*, or *HVRS*, been selected instead of *AIDS*, it might not have taken so long to convince Americans to support research into a disease which, by name at least, everyone was theoretically at risk for. But perhaps because *HVRS*, as an acronym, does not roll tripplingly off the tongue, the more neutral sounding *AIDS* was chosen.

WHAT THE "L" IS GOING ON HERE?

The most momentous semantic battle yet fought in the AIDS war concerned the naming of the so-called AIDS virus. The stakes were high; two nations—France and the United States—were at war over who first identified (and therefore had the right to name) the retrovirus presumed to cause AIDS. Hanging in the balance was a Nobel prize and millions of dollars in patent royalties.

U.S. researcher Dr. Robert Gallo had originally proposed that HTLV-I (human T-cell leukemia virus) was the cause of AIDS. Meanwhile, scientists at the Pasteur Institute isolated a novel retrovirus, which they named *LAV*, to stand for "Lymphadenopathy Associated Virus." The U.S. scoffed at French claims, arrogantly asserting that HTLV-I or HTLV-II must be the cause of AIDS. When it became obvious that neither HTLV-I nor II could possibly be the cause, if for no other reason than because Japan (where HTLV-I and II are endemic) was not in the midst of an AIDS epidemic, the U.S. had to find some way to steal both LAV itself as well as the credit for having discovered it first, while covering over the embarrassing fact that they had proposed the wrong virus as "the cause" of AIDS.[1]   9

What to do? In an election year (1984), it was simply unthinkable that the French could so outshine U.S. medical research. The United States hit upon a brilliant solution. Gallo simply renamed LAV "HTLV-III" and Secretary of Health and Human Services Margaret Heckler staged a preemptive press strike. She declared that another achievement had been added to the long list of U.S. medical breakthroughs: "the probable cause of AIDS has been found—HTLV-III, a variant of a known, human cancer virus . . ."   10

The ploy was certainly ballsy. And looking back, amazingly successful.   11

But what was going on here? The *L* in HTLV-I and II stands for leukemia, since it is proposed that HTLV-I and II account for a particular form of leukemia. Unfortunately for the perpetrators of this massive fraud, it just so happens that leukemia is one of the few diseases which is *not* a complication of AIDS. So, in order to retain the symmetry of nomenclature, Gallo quietly proposed that the *L* in HTLV-III and HTLV-IV now stand for *lymphotropic* instead of *leukemia*.   12

It is now widely acknowledged that HIV is not a member of the HTLV family at all. It is a lentivirus. But the consequences of Gallo's bold attempt at semantic damage control are still with us. The *Index Medicus* listing for AIDS still refers to HTLV-III, not HIV. The legal dispute was eventually settled by the state department; the presidents of the U.S. and France signed an agreement whereby their nations would   13

---

[1]The saga of the competition between U.S. and French AIDS researchers reads like a bad espionage novel. Gallo requested, and the French twice supplied, cultures of LAV. At the time, Gallo claimed that he was not able to grow LAV from these samples. A recent BBC documentary, however, produced evidence of altered documents, suggesting that in fact U.S. researchers had grown LAV from the French cultures. Embarrassingly for Gallo, when he first published on "HTLV-III," he mistakenly provided an electron micrograph photo of "LAV" taken for the French. More damning still, when a DNA-fingerprinting was done on Gallo's HTLV-III and the French's LAV, they were found to be essentially identical.

share credit and royalties, a settlement potentially worth billions. But what was the cost in human lives lost from research delays caused by the willful misclassification of HIV? . . .

WHO HAS THE POWER TO NAME?

The question of who has the power to name is an ongoing turf battle   14
between people with AIDS and those who insist on defining us as victims. I was at the founding of the people with AIDS self-empowerment movement in Denver, Colorado, in 1983. When the California contingent insisted that we make part of our manifesto the demand that we be referred to as "people with AIDS" (or the inevitable acronym "PWAs") instead of "AIDS victims," I must confess that I rolled my eyes heavenward. How California, I thought.

But time has proven them right. Americans, whose ability to think   15
has been desiccated by decades of television and its ten-second sound-bite mentality, think in one-word descriptors. Someone on the TV screen must be labeled: a feminist, a communist, a homosexual, an AIDS victim. The difference between the descriptors *person with AIDS* and *AIDS victim* seems subtle until one watches oneself on reruns on TV. To see oneself on screen and have the words *AIDS victim* magically flash underneath has a very different feel about it than when the description *person with AIDS* appears. Its very cumbersomeness is startling and makes the viewer ask: "Person? Why person? Of course he's a person . . ." In that moment, we achieve a small but important victory. Viewers are forced to be conscious, if only for a moment, that we *are* people first.

The founding statement of the PWA self-empowerment movement   16
(known as the "Denver Principles") is quite eloquent on this point:

> We condemn attempts to label us as "victims," which implies defeat; and we are only occasionally "patients," which implies passivity, helplessness and dependence upon the care of others. We are "people with AIDS."[2]

This statement was further refined in the founding Mission Statement of the National Association of People with AIDS (NAPWA):

> We are people with AIDS and people with AIDS-Related Complex (ARC) who can speak for ourselves to advocate for our own causes and concerns. We are your sons and daughters, your brothers and sisters, your family, friends and lovers. As people now living with AIDS and ARC, we have a unique and essential contribution to make to the dialogue surrounding AIDS and we will actively participate with full and equal credibility to help shape the perception and reality surrounding this disease.

[2]"The Denver Principles," quoted in *Surviving and Thriving with AIDS: Collected Wisdom*, vol. 2, ed. Michael Callen (New York, 1988).

> We do not see ourselves as victims. We will not be victimized. We have
> the right to be treated with respect, dignity, compassion and understanding.
> We have the right to lead fulfilling, productive lives—to live and die with
> dignity and compassion.

In a gratuitous aside in his best-selling AIDS epic, *And the Band*   17
Played On, Randy Shilts attacked the right of people with AIDS to
choose how they wish to be referred to. Completely twisting the em-
powering impulse of people with AIDS to wrest some control of our
lives, Shilts accused us of attempting to minimize the tragedy of AIDS:

> AIDSpeak, a new language forged by public health officials, anxious gay
> politicians, and the burgeoning ranks of "AIDS activists." The linguistic roots
> of AIDSpeak sprouted not so much from the truth as from what was politi-
> cally facile and psychologically reassuring. Semantics was the major denomi-
> nator of AIDSpeak jargon, because the language went to great lengths never
> to offend.
>   A new lexicon was evolving. Under the rules of AIDSpeak, for example,
> AIDS victims could not be called victims. Instead, they were to be called
> People with AIDS, or PWAs, as if contracting this uniquely brutal disease
> was not a victimizing experience. "Promiscuous" became "sexually active,"
> because gay politicians declared "promiscuous" to be "judgmental," a major
> cuss word in AIDSpeak. The most-used circumlocution in AIDSpeak was
> "bodily fluids," an expression that avoided troublesome words like "semen."
>   . . . Thus, the verbiage tended toward the intransitive. AIDSpeak was
> rarely empowered to motivate action; rather, it was most articulately pro-
> nounced when justifying inertia. Nobody meant any harm by this; quite to the
> contrary, AIDSpeak was the tongue designed to make everyone content.
> AIDSpeak was the language of good intentions in the AIDS epidemic;
> AIDSpeak was a language of death.[3]

Shilts notwithstanding, there is now a movement to further emphasize   18
hope. In some quarters *PLWAs* and *PLWArcs* have entered the language:
Persons *Living* with AIDS and Persons *Living* with ARC, respectively.
There is also a new movement to organize all individuals suffering from
conditions related to immune deficiency. Acronym conscious, its leaders
say they are "PISD" (pronounced "pissed"), which stands for "Persons
with Immune System Disorders." . . .

AN EPIDEMIC OF ACRONYMS

There is a separate, specialist language of the AIDS subculture which   19
must be mastered if one wishes to be considered AIDS literate. And this
language contains a great deal of shorthand. To the uninitiated, hearing a

[3]Randy Shilts, *And the Band Played On: The Politics of AIDS* (New York, 1987), pp.
314–15.

conversation among urban gay men is like stumbling into a medical convention and being dazzled and dazed by an explosion of acronyms. Here are just a few one must recognize to be included among the AIDS cognoscenti: Ab+; Ab−; ACTG/ATEU; ARC; ASFV; AZT; CBC; CD_4+; CD8+; CDC; CMV; ddA; ddC; ddI; DFMO; DHEA; DHPG; DNCB; DTC; EBV; ELISA; EPO; FDA; GM-CSF; HBLV; HBV; HIV: HIV-1; HIV-2; HSV-1; HSV-2; HTLV-I, II, III, and IV; IL-1 and IL-2; IND; IVDAs or IVDUs; KS; LAS; LAV; MAI; NIAID; NIH; NK; O/I; PCR; PCP; T_4; TB; TNF; and WBC.

We're in the midst of an epidemic of acronyms. Whatever else AIDS   20
may be, it is itself an acronym. When first introduced, AIDS used to be clearly identified as an acronym because it always appeared with dots: A.I.D.S. Then, consistent with the American tendency towards elision, reduction, and (over)simplification, AIDS rapidly dropped the periods and became a thing in and of itself. In Britain, except for the curious initial capital *A*, AIDS has lost all sense of ever having been an acronym; it is generally referred to as "Aids." (One never sees *syphilis* or *gonorrhea* with an initial capital.)

The acronym epidemic threatens to get out of hand. We even have   21
acronyms within acronyms, as in AIDS-Related Complex—which stands for Acquired Immune Deficiency Syndrome-Related Complex. It verges on an infinite regress. ARC-related symptoms actually translates: Acquired Immune Deficiency Syndrome Related Complex related symptoms. Another redundancy in common usage is *HIV virus*, which translates into "Human Immunodeficiency Virus Virus." I propose that we insist on referring to "the human immunodeficiency virus" or "the HI virus."

Is there anyone who can talk about AIDS and emerge from the battle   22
unscathed? Probably not. We all want to control AIDS somehow, and at times language seems to be our only weapon. But we must not try to master AIDS by crushing its complexities, mysteries, and terrors into convenient labels that roll trippingly and with false authority off the tongue. We must always speak fully and carefully about AIDS, even if that often requires a mouthful—cumbersome constructions full of words strung together by hyphens—to say precisely what we mean. The stakes are simply too high to do otherwise.

QUESTIONS ON CONTENT

1. What connotations come to mind when you see and hear the word AIDS? Does the word sound to you like something that is "helpful" (5)?

2. Do you agree with Callen that the linguistic battles over the language of AIDS can affect how we think about AIDS? Explain.

3. An acronym is a word made from the initials of other words (e.g., AIDS). An initialism is a group of initials that doesn't make a recognizable word (e.g., HTLV). What do the following acronyms or initialisms stand for: AIDS, HTLV, HIV, PISD, PLWA?

4. What was the competition between France and the United States? How was it resolved?

5. Why does Callen disagree with Randy Shilts, the author of *And the Band Played On*? Do you agree with Callen or with Shilts? Explain.

6. Why, according to Callen, is there such an interest in the language related to the AIDS crisis?

QUESTIONS ON RHETORIC

1. Callen's title "AIDS: The Linguistic Battlefield" introduces the metaphor of war (Glossary: *Metaphor*). Does Callen relate the linguistic struggles of the AIDS crisis to warfare again? If so, how, where, and with what effect?

2. What does Callen achieve in his first two paragraphs? (Glossary: *Beginnings*)

3. Examine the passages of quoted material that Callen uses. How has he used the quoted material to support his argument? (Glossary: *Evidence*)

4. How would you describe the tone that Callen has established in his essay? (Glossary: *Tone*)

VOCABULARY

obfuscating (1)	scoffed (9)	desiccated (15)
resonate (5)	preemptive (10)	wrest (17)
barraged (7)	perpetrators (12)	cognoscenti (19)
trippingly (7)	contingent (14)	

WRITING TOPICS

1. Write an essay in which you discuss the attitudes and feelings that you and those your own age have about AIDS. Is the language used to refer to AIDS and its sufferers clear to you? What characterizes the language you and your peers use to discuss the crisis? Is your language sensitive, obscure, realistic, cruel? Do you think that people your age are well informed about AIDS?

2. As Callen argues, some issues, such as AIDS, are so emotionally charged, so vital to one's well being and even one's life that they become language sensitive. Write an essay in which you examine another area of our lives (e.g., cancer, sexually transmitted diseases, nuclear war, child abuse, Alzheimer's disease, rape, homosexuality) where the way in which we use language and the way language is used about us takes on extraordinary importance.

WRITING ASSIGNMENTS FOR "EUPHEMISM AND TABOOS"

1. Linguist Benjamin Lee Whorf has pointed out that "the structure of a given language determines, in part, how the society that speaks it views reality." Explain how our use of euphemisms affects both our behavior and our opinion of our behavior. Consider, for example, the following expressions and the euphemisms for them:

> false teeth ("dental appliance")
> typist ("data processor")
> bombing raid ("limited duration protective reaction strike")
> lie ("inoperative statement")
> rerun ("encore telecast")
> fire ("terminate")
> constipation ("occasional irregularity")

List other euphemisms used by government, journalists, business, and the professions. How may the use of such euphemisms influence behavior?

2. Write an essay in which you respond to the following quote from *Time* magazine: "Like stammers or tears, euphemisms will be created whenever men doubt, or fear, or do not know."

3. In an article called "Public Doublespeak," Terence Moran presented the following list of recommendations given to the faculty of an elementary school in Brooklyn:

FOR PARENT INTERVIEWS AND REPORT CARDS

Harsh Expression (Avoid)	Acceptable Expression (Use)
Does all right if pushed	Accomplishes tasks when interest is stimulated.
Too free with fists	Resorts to physical means of winning his point or attracting attention.
Lies (Dishonest)	Shows difficulty in distinguishing between imaginary and factual material.
Cheats	Needs help in learning to adhere to rules and standards of fair play.
Steals	Needs help in learning to respect the property rights of others.
Noisy	Needs to develop quieter habits of communication.
Lazy	Needs ample supervision in order to work well.
Is a bully	Has qualities of leadership but needs help in learning to use them democratically.
Associates with "gangs"	Seems to feel secure only in group situations; needs to develop sense of independence.
Disliked by other children	Needs help in learning to form lasting friendships.

After reading Neil Postman's essay on euphemisms, write an essay in which you discuss what this list recommends and the possible effects of its use on teachers, students, and parents.

4. Write an essay in which you compare and contrast the analyses of taboo words by the Hayakawas and Lawrence.

5. Write an essay in which you argue that the euphemism, when used honestly, is "a handy verbal tool to avoid making enemies needlessly or shocking friends."

6. People use euphemisms when they want to avoid talking directly about subjects that make them uncomfortable, although what makes people uncomfortable changes. For example, we have been able to mention the words *legs* and *breasts* for quite a while and *venereal disease* for a shorter time, but many people still avoid the words *die* and *death*. Identify some other subjects for which euphemisms are still prevalent, and list several euphemisms for each. Do you use the same euphemisms as your parents? As your grandparents?

7. A fascinating area of language study is the names of places or geographical locations, so-called place names. Place-name studies are concerned, in part, with the history of a place, who settled it, what its geographical features are, and how it got its name. Place names can be controversial, especially if they are themselves, or include, prejudicial terms, intended or unintential (e.g., Dead Irishman Gulch, South Dakota; Maggie's Nipples, Wyoming; Intercourse, Pennsylvania). What should be done about such place-names in your view? Do we need to eradicate these distasteful or taboo words? Can any argument be made to retain such names? Does each case have to be examined separately or is there some basic principle that should be applied? Is the changing of such names censorship? Write an essay expressing your views on this subject.

8. Dr. Joyce Brothers says that the words we consider offensive change from generation to generation. Pay attention to television drama for a week. What do you notice about the language? What words are spoken that would have been considered offensive on television as recently as five years ago? What other "unmentionables," such as homosexuality, menstruation, and venereal disease, are now regular subjects of television advertising and drama? In an essay, discuss your reaction to the changing attitudes reflected in the use of these words and topics.

9. AIDS is an unprecedented disease, one that many people have referred to as a modern plague. Its linguistic aspects, however, have characteristics not unlike those of some other afflictions (for example, cancer, Alzheimer's disease, diabetes, herpes, tuberculosis, muscular dystrophy). Consider the linguistic aspects of one of these diseases, or of a disease of your own choosing, and write a report on what you learn. What similarities, what differences, do you see between what Callen says about the language of AIDS and what you have learned about the language of another disease?

10. It seems that all too often when we go to a doctor about a medical problem, the diagnosis and advice given to deal with it are characterized by two types of language that are equally problematic. That is, we are given either highly technical language filled with numbers and letters and unfamiliar words, or language that is so vague as to be mysterious and more anxiety-producing than informative. If the problem we present to a doctor concerns a disease that is on the cutting edge of our discovery and knowledge, matters are even worse. As Callen has indicated, when he was diagnosed, the language being used related to him and his very survival, and yet he understood very little about what was being said. Where does the responsibility for poor medical communication rest? What can be done by the medical profession to improve doctor-patient communications? What can be done by our teachers and schools to help us better understand the benefits and limitations of medicine, and what can be done by each one of us to understand our bodies better? Write an essay in which you express your views on this subject. Rely on your reading and your own medical experiences wherever possible to support your views.

PART X

Censorship and the First Amendment

I can't think of a word that rhymes with "amend-ment."

"SPEECH CODES" ON THE CAMPUS AND PROBLEMS OF FREE SPEECH

Nat Hentoff

Nat Hentoff, a columnist for the Washington Post *who also writes for such liberal publications as the* Village Voice *and the* Progressive, *has recently published* Free Speech for Me— but Not for Thee: How the American Left and Right Relentlessly Censor Each Other. *Vince Passaro, who reviewed the book, spoke for many people when he wrote: "I admire Nat Hentoff. He performs a vital service to the republic, week in and week out, in his advocacy of First Amendment rights." In the following essay, first published in* Dissent *in 1991, Hentoff reports on the establishment of "Speech Codes" at our colleges and universities that threaten freedom of expression and even thought.*

During three years of reporting on anti–free-speech tendencies in higher education, I've been at more than twenty colleges and universities—from Washington and Lee and Columbia to Mesa State in Colorado and Stanford.

On this voyage of initially reverse expectations—with liberals fiercely advocating censorship of "offensive" speech and conservatives merrily taking the moral high ground as champions of free expression—the most dismaying moment of revelation took place at Stanford.

In the course of a two-year debate on whether Stanford, like many other universities, should have a speech code punishing language that might wound minorities, women, and gays, a letter appeared in the *Stanford Daily*. Signed by the African-American Law Students Association, the Asian-American Law Student Association, and the Jewish Law Students Association, the letter called for a harsh code. It reflected the letter and the spirit of an earlier declaration by Canetta Ivy, a black leader of student government at Stanford during the period of the grand debate. "We don't put as many restrictions on freedom of speech," she said, "as we should."

Reading the letter by this rare ecumenical body of law students (so pressing was the situation that even Jews were allowed in), I thought of twenty, thirty years from now. From so bright a cadre of graduates, from so prestigious a law school would come some of the law professors, civic leaders, college presidents, and even maybe a Supreme Court Justice of

439

the future. And many of them would have learned—like so many other university students in the land—that censorship is okay provided your motives are okay.

The debate at Stanford ended when the president, Donald Kennedy,   5
following the prevailing winds, surrendered his previous position that once you start telling people what they can't say, you will end up telling them what they can't think. Stanford now has a speech code.

This is not to say that these gags on speech—every one of them so   6
overboard and vague that a student can violate a code without knowing he or she has done so—are invariably imposed by student demand. At most colleges, it is the administration that sets up the code. Because there have been racist or sexist or homophobic taunts, anonymous notes or graffiti, the administration feels it must *do something*. The cheapest, quickest way to demonstrate that it cares is to appear to suppress racist, sexist, homophobic speech.

Usually, the leading opposition among the faculty consists of conser-   7
vatives—when there is opposition. An exception at Stanford was law professor Gerald Gunther, arguably the nation's leading authority on constitutional law. But Gunther did not have much support among other faculty members, conservative or liberal.

At the University of Buffalo Law School, which has a code restricting   8
speech, I could find just one faculty member who was against it. A liberal, he spoke only on condition that I not use his name. He did not want to be categorized as a racist.

On another campus, a political science professor for whom I had great   9
respect after meeting and talking with him years ago, has been silent—students told me—on what Justice William Brennan once called "the pall of orthodoxy" that has fallen on his campus.

When I talked to him, the professor said, "It doesn't happen in my   10
class. There's no 'politically correct' orthodoxy here. It may happen in other places at this university, but I don't know about that." He said no more.

One of the myths about the rise of P.C. (politically correct) is that,   11
coming from the left, it is primarily intimidating conservatives on campus. Quite the contrary. At almost every college I've been, conservative students have their own newspaper, usually quite lively and fired by a muckraking glee at exposing "politically correct" follies on campus.

By and large, those most intimidated—not so much by the speech   12
codes themselves but by the Madame Defarge–like spirit behind them—are liberal students and those who can be called politically moderate.

I've talked to many of them, and they no longer get involved in class   13
discussions where their views would go against the grain of P.C. righteousness. Many, for instance, have questions about certain kinds of affirmative action. They are not partisans of Jesse Helms or David Duke, but they wonder whether progeny of middle-class black families should get

scholarship preference. Others have a question about abortion. Most are not pro-life, but they believe that fathers should have a say in whether the fetus should be sent off into eternity.

Jeff Shesol, a recent graduate of Brown and now a Rhodes scholar at   14
Oxford, became nationally known while at Brown because of his comic strip, "Thatch," which, not too kindly, parodied P.C. students. At a forum on free speech at Brown before he left, Shesol said he wished he could tell the new students at Brown to have no fear of speaking freely. But he couldn't tell them that, he said, advising the new students to stay clear of talking critically about affirmative action or abortion, among other things, in public.

At that forum, Shesol told me, he said that those members of the left   15
who regard dissent from their views as racist and sexist should realize that they are discrediting their goals. "They're honorable goals," said Shesol, "and I agree with them. I'm against racism and sexism. But these people's tactics are obscuring the goals. And they've resulted in Brown no longer being an open-minded place." There were hisses from the audience.

Students at New York University Law School have also told me that   16
they censor themselves in class. The kind of chilling atmosphere they describe was exemplified last year as a case assigned for a moot court competition became subject to denunciation when a sizable number of law students said it was too "offensive" and would hurt the feelings of gay and lesbian students. The case concerned a divorced father's attempt to gain custody of his children on the grounds that their mother had become a lesbian. It was against P.C. to represent the father.

Although some of the faculty responded by insisting that you learn to   17
be a lawyer by dealing with all kinds of cases, including those you personally find offensive, other faculty members supported the rebellious students, praising them for their sensitivity. There was little public opposition from the other students to the attempt to suppress the case. A leading dissenter was a member of the conservative Federalist Society.

What is P.C. to white students is not necessarily P.C. to black stu-   18
dents. Most of the latter did not get involved in the N.Y.U. protest, but throughout the country many black students do support speech codes. A vigorous exception was a black Harvard law school student during a debate on whether the law school should start punishing speech. A white student got up and said that the codes are necessary because without them, black students would be driven away from colleges and thereby deprived of the equal opportunity to get an education.

A black student rose and said that the white student had a hell of a   19
nerve to assume that he—in the face of racist speech—would pack up his books and go home. He's been familiar with that kind of speech all his life, and he had never felt the need to run away from it. He'd handled it before and he could again.

The black student then looked at his white colleague and said that it   20
was condescending to say that blacks have to be "protected" from racist
speech. "It is more racist and insulting," he emphasized, "to say that to
me than to call me a nigger."

But that would appear to be a minority view among black students.   21
Most are convinced they do need to be protected from wounding language. On the other hand, a good many black student organizations on
campus do not feel that Jews have to be protected from wounding language.

Though it's not much written about in reports of the language wars on   22
campuses, there is a strong strain of anti-Semitism among some—not all,
by any means—black students. They invite such speakers as Louis Farrakhan, the former Stokely Carmichael (now Kwame Touré), and such
lesser but still burning bushes as Steve Cokely, the Chicago commentator
who has declared that Jewish doctors inject the AIDS virus into black
babies. That distinguished leader was invited to speak at the University of
Michigan.

The black student organization at Columbia University brought to the   23
campus Dr. Khallid Abdul Muhammad. He began his address by saying:
"My leader, my teacher, my guide is the honorable Louis Farrakhan. I
thought that should be said at Columbia Jewniversity."

Many Jewish students have not censored themselves in reacting to this   24
form of political correctness among some blacks. A Columbia student,
Rachel Stoll, wrote a letter to the *Columbia Spectator*: "I have an idea.
As a white Jewish American, I'll just stand in the middle of a circle
comprising . . . Khallid Abdul Muhammad and assorted members of the
Black Students Organization and let them all hurl large stones at me.
From recent events and statements made on this campus, I gather this will
be a good cheap method of making these people feel good."

At UCLA, a black student magazine printed an article indicating there   25
is considerable truth to the *Protocols of the Elders of Zion*.* For months,
the black faculty, when asked their reactions, preferred not to comment.
One of them did say that the black students already considered the black
faculty to be insufficiently militant, and the professors didn't want to
make the gap any wider. Like white liberal faculty members on other
campuses, they want to be liked—or at least not too disliked.

Along with quiet white liberal faculty members, most black pro-   26
fessors have not opposed the speech codes. But unlike the white liberals,
many honestly do believe that minority students have to be insulated from
barbed language. They do not believe—as I have found out in a number

---

Ed. note: A fraudulent "document," purportedly containing the records of plans by
Jewish elders to vanquish Christian civilization. The *Protocols* were published originally in
Russia in 1903 and have been widely circulated as a staple of anti-Semitic propaganda.

of conversations—that an essential part of an education is to learn to demystify language, to strip it of its ability to demonize and stigmatize you. They do not believe that the way to deal with bigoted language is to answer it with more and better language of your own. This seems very elementary to me, but not to the defenders, black and white, of the speech codes.

Consider University of California president David Gardner. He has   27 imposed a speech code on all the campuses in his university system. Students are to be punished—and this is characteristic of the other codes around the country—if they use "fighting words"—derogatory references to "race, sex, sexual orientation, or disability."

The term "fighting words" comes from a 1942 Supreme Court deci-   28 sion, *Chaplinsky* v. *New Hampshire*, which ruled that "fighting words" are not protected by the First Amendment. That decision, however, has been in disuse at the High Court for many years. But it is thriving on college campuses.

In the California code, a word becomes "fighting" if it is directly   29 addressed to "any ordinary person" (presumably, extraordinary people are above all this). These are the kinds of words that are "inherently likely to provoke a violent reaction, *whether or not they actually do*." (Emphasis added).

Moreover, he or she who fires a fighting word at any ordinary person   30 can be reprimanded or dismissed from the university because the perpetrator should "reasonably know" that what he or she has said will interfere with the "victim's ability to pursue effectively his or her education or otherwise participate fully in university programs and activities."

Asked Gary Murikami, chairman of the Gay and Lesbian Association   31 at the University of California, Berkeley: "What does it mean?"

Among those—faculty, law professors, college administrators—who   32 insist such codes are essential to the university's purpose of making *all* students feel at home and thereby able to concentrate on their work, there has been a celebratory resort to the Fourteenth Amendment.

That amendment guarantees "equal protection of the laws" to all, and   33 that means to all students on campus. Accordingly, when the First Amendment rights of those engaging in offensive speech clash with the equality rights of their targets under the Fourteenth Amendment, the First Amendment must give way.

This is the thesis, by the way, of John Powell, legal director of the   34 American Civil Liberties Union, even though that organization has now formally opposed all college speech codes—after a considerable civil war among and within its affiliates.

The battle of the amendments continues, and when harsher codes are   35 called for at some campuses, you can expect the Fourteenth Amendment—which was not intended to censor *speech*—will rise again.

A precedent has been set at, of all places, colleges and universities,   36

that the principle of free speech is merely situational. As college administrators change, so will the extent of free speech on campus. And invariably, permissible speech will become more and more narrowly defined.
Once speech can be limited in such subjective ways, more and more
expression will be included in what is forbidden.

One of the exceedingly few college presidents who speaks out on the   37
consequences of the anti–free-speech movement is Yale University's
Benno Schmidt:

> Freedom of thought must be Yale's central commitment. It is not easy to   38
> embrace. It is, indeed, the effort of a lifetime. . . . Much expression that is
> free may deserve our contempt. We may well be moved to exercise our own
> freedom to counter it or to ignore it. But universities cannot censor or sup-
> press speech, no matter how obnoxious in content, without violating their
> justification for existence. . . .
>
> On some other campuses in this country, values of civility and commu-   39
> nity have been offered by some as paramount values of the university, even to
> the extent of superseding freedom of expression.
>
> Such a view is wrong in principle and, if extended, is disastrous to free-   40
> dom of thought. . . . The chilling effects on speech of the vagueness and
> open-ended nature of many universities' prohibitions . . . are compounded by
> the fact that these codes are typically enforced by faculty and students who
> commonly assert that vague notions of community are more important to the
> academy than freedom of thought and expression. . . .
>
> This is a flabby and uncertain time for freedom in the United States.   41

On the Public Broadcasting System in June, I was part of a Fred   42
Friendly panel at Stanford University in a debate on speech codes versus
freedom of expression. The three black panelists strongly supported the
codes. So did the one Asian-American on the panel. But then so did
Stanford law professor, Thomas Grey, who wrote the Stanford code, and
Stanford president Donald Kennedy, who first opposed and then embraced the code. We have a new ecumenicism of those who would control speech for the greater good. It is hardly a new idea, but the mix of
advocates is rather new.

But there are other voices. In the national board debate at the ACLU   43
on college speech codes, the first speaker—and I think she had a lot to
do with making the final vote against codes unanimous—was Gwen
Thomas.

A black community college administrator from Colorado, she is a   44
fiercely persistent exposer of racial discrimination.

She started by saying, "I have always felt as a minority person that   45
we have to protect the rights of all because if we infringe on the rights of
any persons, we'll be next."

"As for providing a nonintimidating educational environment, our   46
young people have to learn to grow up on college campuses. We have to

teach them how to deal with adversarial situations. They have to learn how to survive offensive speech they find wounding and hurtful."

Gwen Thomas is an educator—an endangered species in higher education.   47

QUESTIONS ON CONTENT

1. What happened at Stanford that so dismayed the author? Why is the example of what happened at Stanford more important than the other examples he provides?

2. What is the meaning of Justice William Brennan's phrase, "the pall of orthodoxy" (9)?

3. What is P.C. or political correctness? Does it exist on your campus? If so, in what form?

4. What reasons does Hentoff give for the lack of opposition to campus speech codes? Are they valid reasons in your view? Explain.

5. What guarantee does the Fourteenth Amendment provide? What happens when the Fourteenth Amendment and the First Amendment collide? Why?

6. Why does Hentoff like what Gwen Thomas had to say about speech codes (paragraphs 43 through 46)?

QUESTIONS ON RHETORIC

1. What is Hentoff's purpose in this essay? (Glossary: *Purpose*) What is the thesis of his essay? (Glossary: *Thesis*) Where is his thesis located?

2. What irony does Hentoff see in the treatment of Jews on campus? (Glossary: *Irony*) Can you cite other instances of irony in this essay? What do you suppose was his intent in using it?

3. Examine the last sentence in each of Hentoff's paragraphs. He often likes to use a short, dramatic sentence in that position. Do you think that this is an effective strategy? Explain.

4. Why has Hentoff italicized "do something" in paragraph 6?

VOCABULARY

dismaying (2)	arguably (7)	moot court (16)
ecumenical (4)	progeny (13)	disuse (28)
cadre (4)	discrediting (15)	situational (36)
homophobic (6)		

WRITING TOPICS

1. Write an essay in which you consider your views on censorship. You may want to consider the following questions before beginning to write.

Is censorship ever justifiable? Should First Amendment rights be limited? What are the dangers of limiting free speech? Haven't we always to a certain degree limited free speech in America?

2. Hentoff's essay raises some interesting questions about higher education: Who establishes policy? What is the principle of academic freedom? Has academic freedom been eroding on college campuses? Is college a time to protect one's cherished beliefs or a time to explore the marketplace of ideas? Should one be afraid to express one's point of view or be allowed to impose it on others? Write an essay in which you draw upon your own observations and experiences to comment on the purposes of higher education with respect to these issues.

NOTES FROM A FREE-SPEECH JUNKIE

Susan Jacoby

*Susan Jacoby broke into reporting when "women's subjects"
were not what they are today. As she put it, "To write about
women was to write about trivia: charity balls, cake sales,
and the like." Times changed, however, and Jacoby has
since written about more meaningful women's issues in*
McCall's, *and in the "Hers" column of the* New York
Times. *Many of her essays have been collected in her book*
The Possible She. *In the following essay, Jacoby takes a
strong stand against feminists who want to censor
pornography and gives her unqualified support to the First
Amendment.*

It is no news that many women are defecting from the ranks of civil   1
libertarians on the issue of obscenity. The conviction of Larry Flynt,
publisher of *Hustler* magazine—before his metamorphosis into a born-
again Christian—was greeted with unabashed feminist approval. Harry
Reems, the unknown actor who was convicted by a Memphis jury for
conspiring to distribute the movie *Deep Throat*, has carried on his legal
battles with almost no support from women who ordinarily regard themselves as supporters of the First Amendment. Feminist writers and scholars have even discussed the possibility of making common cause against
pornography with adversaries of the women's movement—including opponents of the equal rights amendment and "right to life" forces.

All of this is deeply disturbing to a woman writer who believes, as I   2
always have and still do, in an absolute interpretation of the First Amendment. Nothing in Larry Flynt's garbage convinces me that the late Justice
Hugo L. Black was wrong in his opinion that "the federal government is
without any power whatsoever under the Constitution to put any type of
burden on free speech and expression of ideas of any kind (as distinguished from conduct)." Many women I like and respect tell me I am
wrong; I cannot remember having become involved in so many heated
discussions of a public issue since the end of the Vietnam War. A feminist writer described my views as those of a "First Amendment junkie."

Many feminist arguments for controls on pornography carry the im-   3
plicit conviction that porn books, magazines, and movies pose a greater
threat to women than similarly repulsive exercises of free speech pose to
other offended groups. This conviction has, of course, been shared by

447

everyone—regardless of race, creed, or sex—who has ever argued in favor of abridging the First Amendment. It is the argument used by some Jews who have withdrawn their support from the American Civil Liberties Union because it has defended the right of American Nazis to march through a community inhabited by survivors of Hitler's concentration camps.

If feminists want to argue that the protection of the Constitution   4 should not be extended to *any* particularly odious or threatening form of speech, they have a reasonable argument (although I don't agree with it). But it is ridiculous to suggest that the porn shops on 42nd Street are more disgusting to women than a march of neo-Nazis is to survivors of the extermination camps.

The arguments over pornography also blur the vital distinction be-   5 tween expression of ideas and conduct. When I say I believe unreservedly in the First Amendment, someone always comes back at me with the issue of "kiddie porn." But kiddie porn is not a First Amendment issue. It is an issue of the abuse of power—the power adults have over children— and not of obscenity. Parents and promoters have no more right to use their children to make porn movies tħan they do to send them to work in coal mines. The responsible adults should be prosecuted, just as adults who use children for back-breaking farm labor should be prosecuted.

Susan Brownmiller, in *Against Our Will: Men, Women, and Rape*,   6 has described pornography as "the undiluted essence of anti-female propaganda." I think this is a fair description of some types of pornography, especially of the brutish subspecies that equates sex with death and portrays women primarily as objects of violence.

The equation of sex and violence, personified by some glossy rock   7 record album covers as well as by *Hustler*, has fed the illusion that censorship of pornography can be conducted on a more rational basis than other types of censorship. Are all pictures of naked women obscene? Clearly not, says a friend. A Renoir nude is art, she says, and *Hustler* is trash. "Any reasonable person" knows that.

But what about something between art and trash—something, say,   8 along the lines of *Playboy* or *Penthouse* magazines? I asked five women for their reactions to one picture in *Penthouse* and got responses that ranged from "lovely" and "sensuous" to "revolting" and "demeaning." Feminists, like everyone else, seldom have rational reasons for their preferences in erotica. Like members of juries, they tend to disagree when confronted with something that falls short of 100 percent vulgarity.

In any case, feminists will not be the arbiters of good taste if it be-   9 comes easier to harass, prosecute, and convict people on obscenity charges. Most of the people who want to censor girlie magazines are equally opposed to open discussion of issues that are of vital concern to women: rape, abortion, menstruation, contraception, lesbianism—in fact, the entire range of sexual experience from a woman's viewpoint.

Feminist writers and editors and filmmakers have limited financial   10 resources: Confronted by a determined prosecutor, Hugh Hefner will fare better than Susan Brownmiller. Would the Memphis jurors who convicted Harry Reems for his role in *Deep Throat* be inclined to take a more positive view of paintings of the female genitalia done by sensitive feminist artists? *Ms.* magazine has printed color reproductions of some of those art works; *Ms.* is already banned from a number of high school libraries because someone considers it threatening and/or obscene.

Feminists who want to censor what they regard as harmful pornography have essentially the same motivation as other would-be censors: They want to use the power of the state to accomplish what they have been unable to achieve in the marketplace of ideas and images. The impulse to censor places no faith in the possibilities of democratic persuasion.   11

It isn't easy to persuade certain men that they have better uses for $1.95 each month than to spend it on a copy of *Hustler*? Well, then, give the men no choice in the matter.   12

I believe there is also a connection between the impulse toward censorship on the part of people who used to consider themselves civil libertarians and a more general desire to shift responsibility from individuals to institutions. When I saw the movie *Looking for Mr. Goodbar*, I was stunned by its series of visual images equating sex and violence, coupled with what seems to me the mindless message (a distortion of the fine Judith Rossner novel) that casual sex equals death. When I came out of the movie, I was even more shocked to see parents standing in line with children between the ages of ten and fourteen.   13

I simply don't know why a parent would take a child to see such a movie, any more than I understand why people feel they can't turn off a television set their child is watching. Whenever I say that, my friends tell me I don't know how it is because I don't have children. True, but I do have parents. When I was a child, they did turn off the TV. They didn't expect the Federal Communications Commission to do their job for them.   14

I am a First Amendment junkie. You can't OD on the First Amendment, because free speech is its own best antidote.   15

QUESTIONS ON CONTENT

1. Why, according to Jacoby, are so many women who might otherwise support First Amendment rights "defecting from the ranks of civil libertarians on the issue of obscenity" (1)?

2. Does Jacoby find pornography offensive? How do you know?

3. How, according to Jacoby, do the "arguments over pornography blur the vital distinction between expression of ideas and conduct" (5)? Why isn't "kiddie porn" a First Amendment issue as far as Jacoby is concerned?

4. Jacoby writes in paragraph 11: "The impulse to censor places no faith in the possibilities of democratic persuasion." What does she mean? How

would you define democratic persuasion? Do you think it will help resolve the clash between First Amendment rights and offensive expression?

5. According to Jacoby, where does the responsibility for the rejection of pornography rest, with the individual or with our institutions?

QUESTIONS ON RHETORIC

1. How has Jacoby used definition in her essay? (Glossary: *Definition*) How important is it for her argument to provide a definition of pornography? Whose definition does she use? Does she find it a good definition? Explain.

2. In paragraph 9, Jacoby says, "Most of the people who want to censor girlie magazines are equally opposed to open discussion of issues that are of vital concern to women: rape, abortion, menstruation, contraception, lesbianism—in fact, the entire range of sexual experience from a woman's viewpoint" What evidence does she present for this statement? (Glossary: *Evidence*)

3. Comment on Jacoby's title. Where does it come from? What is a free-speech junkie?

4. Comment on Jacoby's last sentence. What does it mean? Is it a fitting conclusion to her essay? (Glossary: *Beginnings and Endings*) Why, or why not?

VOCABULARY

defecting (1)	conviction (3)	arbiters (9)
libertarians (1)	odious (3)	antidote (15)
metamorphosis (1)	brutish (6)	

WRITING TOPICS

1. How do you respond to attempts to limit your First Amendment rights? Do you care? Do they make you angry? Does it matter really? If yes, how so? Is the issue of abridgments to our First Amendment rights simply a theoretical one with few if any practical consequences? Write an essay in which you argue either for or against the idea that the consequences of limitations to our freedom of speech are very serious, indeed. If possible, include specific examples and situations drawn from your experience to support your argument.

2. Is there anything about the way we as Americans express ourselves personally and in the media today that especially upsets you? Do you feel strongly enough to do something about the situation? What? For example, are you in favor of limiting our First Amendment rights with respect to "kiddie porn," violence directed at women in the movies, or attacks on a particular religion or ethnic group? If you are, how would you go about accomplishing your goals in a democratic society? Do you think you could do so in a fair manner? Write an essay in which you examine your own thoughts and feelings on this issue.

WHAT SHOULD BE DONE ABOUT ROCK LYRICS?

Caryl Rivers

A frequent contributor to Saturday Review, Glamour,
McCall's, Boston Magazine, *and the* New York Times
Magazine, *Caryl Rivers is professor of journalism at Boston
University and the author of a number of both nonfiction
books and novels. The following essay was first published in
the* Boston Globe *in 1985. After calling attention to the
explicit violence directed at women in today's rock lyrics and
music videos, Rivers asks her readers, and especially men, to
end their silence and speak out against such violence.*

After a grisly series of murders in California, possibly inspired by the   1
lyrics of a rock song, we are hearing a familiar chorus: don't blame rock
and roll. Kids will be kids. They love to rebel, and the more shocking the
stuff, the better they like it.

There's some truth in this, of course. I loved to watch Elvis shake his   2
torso when I was a teenager, and it was even more fun when Ed Sullivan
wouldn't let the cameras show him below the waist. I snickered at the
forbidden "Rock with Me, Annie" lyrics by a black rhythm and blues
group, which were deliciously naughty. But I am sorry, rock fans, that is
not the same thing as hearing lyrics about how a man is going to force a
woman to perform oral sex on him at gunpoint in a little number called
"Eat Me Alive." It is not in the same league with a song about the de-
lights of slipping into a woman's room while she is sleeping and mur-
dering her, the theme of an AC/DC ballad that allegedly inspired the
California slayer.

Make no mistake, it is not sex we are talking about here, but vio-   3
lence. Violence against women. Most rock songs are not violent—they
are funky, sexy, rebellious, and sometimes witty. Please do not mistake
me for a Mrs. Grundy. If Prince wants to leap about wearing only a
purple jock strap, fine. Let Mick Jagger unzip his fly as he gyrates, if he
wants to. But when either one of them starts garroting, beating, or
sodomizing a woman in their number, that is another story.

I always find myself annoyed when "intellectual" men dismiss vio-   4
lence against women with a yawn, as if it were beneath their dignity to
notice. I wonder if the reaction would be the same if the violence were
directed against someone other than women. How many people would
yawn and say, "Oh, kids will be kids" if a rock group did a nifty little
number called "Lynchin," in which stringing up and stomping on black

people were set to music? Who would chuckle and say, "Oh, just a little adolescent rebellion" if a group of rockers went on MTV dressed as Nazis, desecrating synagogues and beating up Jews to the beat of twanging guitars?

I'll tell you what would happen. Prestigious dailies would thunder on   5
editorial pages; senators would fall over each other to get denunciations into the *Congressional Record*. The president would appoint a commission to clean up the music business.

But violence against women is greeted by silence. It shouldn't be.   6

This does not mean censorship, or book (or record) burning. In a   7
society that protects free expression, we understand a lot of stuff will float up out of the sewer. Usually, we recognize the ugly stuff that advocates violence against any group as the garbage it is, and we consider its purveyors as moral lepers. We hold our nose and tolerate it, but we speak out against the values it proffers.

But images of violence against women are not staying on the fringes   8
of society. No longer are they found only in tattered, paper-covered books or in movie houses where winos snooze and the scent of urine fills the air. They are entering the mainstream at a rapid rate. This is happening at a time when the media, more and more, set the agenda for the public debate. It is a powerful legitimizing force—especially television. Many people regard what they see on TV as the truth; Walter Cronkite once topped a poll as the most trusted man in America.

Now, with the advent of rock videos and all-music channels, rock   9
music has grabbed a big chunk of legitimacy. American teenagers have instant access, in their living rooms, to the messages of rock, on the same vehicle that brought them Sesame Street. Who can blame them if they believe that the images they see are accurate reflections of adult reality, approved by adults? After all, Big Bird used to give them lessons on the same little box. Adults, by their silence, sanction the images. Do we really want our kids to think that rape and violence are what sexuality is all about?

This is not a trivial issue. Violence against women is a major social   10
problem, one that's more than a cerebral issue to me. I teach at Boston University, and one of my most promising young journalism students was raped and murdered. Two others told me of being raped. Recently, one female student was assaulted and beaten so badly she had $5,000 worth of medical bills and permanent damage to her back and eyes.

It's nearly impossible, of course, to make a cause-and-effect link be-   11
tween lyrics and images and acts of violence. But images have a tremendous power to create an atmosphere in which violence against certain people is sanctioned. Nazi propagandists knew that full well when they portrayed Jews as ugly, greedy, and powerful.

The outcry over violence against women, particularly in a sexual con-   12
text, is being legitimized in two ways: by the increasing movement of

these images into the mainstream of the media in TV, films, magazines, albums, videos, and by the silence about it.

Violence, of course, is rampant in the media. But it is usually set in 13 some kind of moral context. It's usually only the bad guys who commit violent acts against the innocent. When the good guys get violent, it's against those who deserve it. Dirty Harry blows away the scum, he doesn't walk up to a toddler and say, "Make my day." The A team does not shoot up suburban shopping malls.

But in some rock songs, it's the "heroes" who commit the acts. The 14 people we are programmed to identify with are the ones being violent, with women on the receiving end. In a society where rape and assaults on women are endemic, this is no small problem, with millions of young boys watching on their TV screens and listening on their Walkmans.

I think something needs to be done. I'd like to see people in the 15 industry respond to the problem. I'd love to see some women rock stars speak out against violence against women. I would like to see disc jockeys refuse air play to records and videos that contain such violence. At the very least, I want to see the end of the silence. I want journalists and parents and critics and performing artists to keep this issue alive in the public forum. I don't want people who are concerned about this issue labeled as bluenoses and bookburners and ignored.

And I wish it wasn't always just women who were speaking out. Men 16 have as large a stake in the quality of our civilization as women do in the long run. Violence is a contagion that infects at random. Let's hear something, please, from the men.

QUESTIONS ON CONTENT

1. What specific problems does Rivers see in today's rock lyrics and music videos? Is she opposed to sexually explicit lyrics? Explain.

2. How has violence against women touched Rivers's own life?

3. In what two ways has violence against women been legitimized, according to Rivers?

4. How does Rivers answer the question her title asks: "What Should Be Done about Rock Lyrics?"

5. Rivers claims that violence against women in the media has been met by silence. Her essay was published in 1985. Has the situation changed since that time? Explain.

QUESTIONS ON RHETORIC

1. What kind of person does Rivers reveal herself to be in this essay? Why do you suppose she wants us to know what her attitudes are? (Glossary: *Attitudes*)

2. How has Rivers used examples to illustrate the points she makes? (Glossary: *Examples*)

3. In paragraph 11, Rivers writes, "It's nearly impossible, of course, to make a cause-and-effect link between lyrics and images and acts of violence." To what extent, however, does she, in fact, try to make that link in the rest of her essay? (Glossary: *Cause and Effect*)

4. Examine Rivers's diction. (Glossary: *Diction*) Cite as many examples as you can of the diction that she uses to characterize the violence in our society and those who promote it.

VOCABULARY

funky (3)	synagogues (4)	cerebral (10)
gyrates (3)	purveyors (7)	endemic (14)
garroting (3)	proffers (7)	forum (15)
sodomizing (3)	sanction (9)	bluenoses (15)
desecrating (4)		

WRITING TOPICS

1. Write a report on research that attempts to prove a cause-and-effect relationship between sexually explicit materials (preferably written materials) that advocate or encourage violence against women and actual acts of such violence. What's probable, what's not? If there is a cause-and-effect link (Rivers doubts it), what can be done about it? If there is no probable link, does that mean that there is no problem? Is it possible that such materials, while not necessarily causing violent acts, send messages that create a mindset or climate in which they are more likely to occur?

2. Write an open letter to all rock musicians encouraging them to exercise restraint in writing and performing lyrics detrimental to the safety and well-being of women.

CURBING THE SEXPLOITATION INDUSTRY

Tipper Gore

Tipper Gore is the cofounder of the Parents' Music Resource Center and the author of Raising PG Kids in an X-Rated Society, *a book about violence and obscenity in music, television, and film. In the following selection from her book, published in 1987, Gore offers a cause-and-effect analysis of violence in music and film to argue for parents' right to screen the music their children listen to. To uphold that right, the author suggested that producers use a labeling system for rock music album covers, similar to the one used for films, to alert parents to objectionable lyrics—a system that many of the larger record companies voluntarily adopted shortly after her book was published. Now that she has risen to even greater national prominence as the wife of Vice-President Albert Gore, Jr., it will be interesting to observe what new ideas she brings to efforts to protect children from the "sexploitation industry."*

I can't even count the times in the last three years, since I began to express my concern about violence and sexuality in rock music, that I have been called a prude, a censor, a music hater, even a book burner. So let me be perfectly clear: I detest censorship. I'm not advocating censorship but rather a candid and vigorous debate about the dangers posed for our children by what I call the "sexploitation industry." 1

We don't need to put a childproof cap on the world, but we do need to remind the nation that children live in it, too, and deserve respect and sensitive treatment. 2

When I launched this campaign in 1985 . . . I went to the source of the problem, sharing my concerns and proposals with the entertainment industry. Many producers were sympathetic. Some cooperated with my efforts. But others have been overtly hostile, accusing me of censorship and suggesting, unfairly, that my motives are political. This resistance and hostility has convinced me of the need for a two-pronged campaign, with equal effort from the entertainment industry and concerned parents. Entertainment producers must take the first step, by labeling sexually explicit material. 3

But the industry cannot be expected to solve the problem on its own. Parents should encourage producers to cooperate and praise them when 4 they do. Producers need to know that parents are aware of the issue and are reading their advisory labels. Above all, they need to know that somebody out there cares, that the community at large is not apathetic about the deep and lasting damage being done to our children.

What's at issue is not the occasional sexy rock lyric. What troubles— indeed, outrages—me is far more vicious: a celebration of the most grue- some violence, coupled with the explicit message that sado-masochism is the essence of sex. We're surrounded by examples—in rock lyrics, on television, at the movies and in rental videos. One major TV network recently aired a preview of a soap opera rape scene during a morning game show.

The newest craze in horror movies is something called the "teen slasher" film, and it typically depicts the killing, torture and sexual muti- lation of women in sickening detail. Several rock groups now simulate sexual torture and murder during live performances. Others titillate youthful audiences with strippers confined in cages on stage and with half-naked dancers, who often act out sex with band members. Sexual brutality has become the common currency of America's youth culture and with it the pervasive degradation of women.

Why is this graphic violence dangerous? It's especially damaging for young children because they lack the moral judgment of adults. Many children are only dimly aware of the consequences of their actions, and, as parents know, they are excellent mimics. They often imitate violence they see on TV, without necessarily understanding what they are doing or what the consequences might be. One 5-year-old boy from Boston re- cently got up from watching a teen-slasher film and stabbed a 2-year-old girl with a butcher knife. He didn't mean to kill her (and luckily he did not). He was just imitating the man in the video.

Nor does the danger end as children grow older. National health offi- cials tell us that children younger than teenagers are apt to react to exces- sive violence with suicide, satanism, drug and alcohol abuse. Even grown- ups are not immune. One series of studies by researchers at the University of Wisconsin found that men exposed to films in which women are beaten, butchered, maimed and raped were significantly desensitized to the violence. Not only did they express less sympathy for the victims, they even approved of lesser penalties in hypothetical rape trials.

Sado-masochistic pornography is a kind of poison. Like most poi- sons, it probably cannot be totally eliminated, but it certainly could be labeled for what it is and be kept away from those who are most vulner- able. The largest record companies have agreed to this—in principle at least. In November 1985, the Recording Industry Association of America adopted my proposal to alert parents by having producers either put warn- ing labels on records with explicitly sexual lyrics or display the lyrics on the outside of the record jackets. Since then, some companies have com- plied in good faith, although others have not complied at all.

College Department
ST. MARTIN'S PRESS
175 Fifth Avenue
New York, N.Y. 10010

Desk Or Examination Copies for

ATTN: MS MICHELE SMALL   ORD#: 17035
NORTHLAND COLLEGE   DATE: 06/07/95

QTY.	NUMBER AND TITLE
1	ESCH6 LANGUAGE AWARENESS -6E
1	ESCH6M -MANUAL FOR LANGUAGE AWARENESS -6E

Your comments on our books help us estimate printing requirements, assist us in preparing revisions, and guide us in shaping future books to your needs. Will you please take a moment to fill out and return this postpaid card?

☐ you may quote me for advertising purposes

I ☐ will adopt   ☐ have adopted   ☐ am seriously considering it

Course title _____ Enrollment _____

Comments _____

_____

_____

_____

_____

_____

_____

_____

_____

Fold, tape, and mail

BUSINESS REPLY MAIL
First Class   Permit No. 1147   New York, N.Y.

Postage will be paid by

College Department
ST. MARTIN'S PRESS, INC.
175 FIFTH AVENUE
NEW YORK, N.Y. 10010

This is where we parents must step in. We must let the industry know   10
we're angry. We must press for uniform voluntary compliance with labeling guidelines. And we must take an active interest at home in what our
children are watching and listening to. After all, we can hardly expect
that the labels or printed lyrics alone will discourage young consumers.

Some parents may want to write to the record companies. Others can   11
give their support to groups like the Parent Teacher Association, which
have endorsed the labeling idea. All of us can use our purchasing power.
We have more power than we think, and we must use it. For the sake of
our children, we simply can't afford to slip back into apathy.

My concern for the health and welfare of children has nothing to do   12
with politics: It is addressed to conservatives and liberals alike. Some
civil libertarians believe it is wrong even to raise these questions—just as
some conservatives believe that the Government should police popular
American culture. I reject both these views. I have no desire to restrain
artists or cast a "chill" over popular culture. But I believe parents have
First Amendment rights, too.

The fate of the family, the dignity of women, the mental health of   13
children—these concerns belong to everyone. We must protect our children with choice, not censorship. Let's start working in our communities
to forge a moral consensus for the 1990's. Children need our help, and
we must summon the courage to examine the culture that shapes their
lives.

QUESTIONS ON CONTENT

1. Does Gore's claim that she "detests censorship" so early in her essay
reassure you or raise doubts? Explain.

2. What is the sexploitation industry that Gore refers to? Does she define
it?

3. Gore writes that two steps must be taken to curb the sexploitation
industry. What are they?

4. Gore describes some actions that parents can take to convey to the
record industry their anger about violence in contemporary music. Which
of these measures do you think would be the most effective? Why?

QUESTIONS ON RHETORIC

1. Why does the author include so many examples of the results of explicit violence in music and films in her essay? What is your reaction to
these examples? (Glossary: *Examples*)

2. At the end of her essay Gore reiterates that the concerns she voices are
not political and that she doesn't wish to censor artists. This is a point she
makes earlier in her essay. How effective is the technique of linking her
beginning and ending in this way? (Glossary: *Beginnings and Endings*)

3. How does the question that Gore uses to begin paragraph 7 help to develop that paragraph?

4. How has Gore organized the evidence for her argument? Make a scratch outline of the essay. (Glossary: *Organization*)

VOCABULARY

prude (1)	sado-masochism (5)	hypothetical (8)
candid (1)	titillate (6)	pornography (9)
explicit (3)	degradation (6)	consensus (13)
apathetic (4)	desensitized (8)	

WRITING TOPICS

1. Do an informal study of your own on what rock listeners themselves think about explicitly sexual and violent lyrics. Do they find them as offensive as their parents do? Do they want to listen to these songs only because other, perhaps, older friends are listening to them? Do they feel they are being manipulated or damaged by the lyrics? Are their attitudes toward people, particularly women, affected by them? Write a report on what you learn from talking to the "consumers" of this music.

2. Should rock and roll stations be allowed to play any music they want to? Many college radio stations, because they are noncommercial, are free to broadcast whatever they choose, limited only by the school's administrative policies. What are your thoughts on this issue? In a short essay, present your argument for or against unrestrained air time for rock music that includes sexually and violently explicit lyrics.

THE WIVES OF BIG BROTHER

Frank Zappa

Frank Zappa is a rock musician well known for his albums
Apostrophe, Chunga's Revenge, Hot Rats, Joe's Garage, *and*
You Are What You Is, *among others. An outspoken critic of
any efforts to interfere with the music industry, Zappa has
strenuously and sometimes stridently opposed the record
labeling proposal put forth by Tipper Gore and the Parents'
Music Resource Center. The following is what Zappa had to
say in testimony before the Senate Commerce Committee
hearing on record labeling in September 1985.*

These are my personal observations and opinions. They are addressed   1
to the PMRC as well as this committee. I speak on behalf of no group or
professional organization.

The PMRC proposal is an ill-conceived piece of nonsense which fails   2
to deliver any real benefits to children, infringes the civil liberties of
people who are not children and promises to keep the courts busy for
years, dealing with the interpretational and enforcemental problems inherent in the proposal's design.

It is my understanding that, in law, First Amendment Issues are de   3
cided with a preference for the least restrictive alternative. In this context,
the PMRC's demands are the equivalent of treating dandruff by decapitation.

No one has forced Mrs. Baker or Mrs. Gore to bring Prince or Sheena   4
Easton into their homes. Thanks to the Constitution, they are free to buy
other forms of music for their children. Apparently they insist on purchasing the works of contemporary recording artists in order to support a
personal illusion of aerobic sophistication. Ladies, please be advised: the
$8.98 purchase price does not entitle you to a kiss on the foot from the
composer or performer in exchange for a spin on the family Victrola.
Taken as a whole, the complete list of PMRC demands reads like an
instruction manual for some sinister kind of "toilet training program" to
house-break all composers and performers because of the lyrics of a few.
Ladies, how dare you?

The ladies' shame must be shared by the bosses at the major labels   5
who, through the RIAA,* chose to bargain away the rights of composers,
performers, and retailers in order to pass H. R. 2911, The Blank Tape
Tax: A private tax, levied by an industry on consumers, for the benefit of

*Ed. note: Recording Industry Association of America.

a select group within that industry. Is this a "consumer issue"? You bet it is. PMRC spokesperson, Kandy Stroud, announced to millions of fascinated viewers on last Friday's ABC Nightline debate that Senator Gore, a man she described as "A friend of the music industry," is co-sponsor of something she referred to as "anti-piracy legislation." Is this the same tax bill with a nicer name?

The major record labels need to have H. R. 2911 whiz through a few   6
committees before anybody smells a rat. One of them is chaired by Senator Thurmond. Is it a coincidence that Mrs. Thurmond is affiliated with the PMRC? I can't say she's a member, because the PMRC has no members. Their secretary told me on the phone last Friday that the PMRC has no members . . . only founders. I asked how many other D. C. wives are non-members of an organization that raises money by mail, has a tax-exempt status, and seems intent on running the Constitution of the United States through the family paper-shredder. I asked her if it was a cult. Finally, she said she couldn't give me an answer and that she had to call their lawyer.

While the wife of the Secretary of Treasury recites "Gonna drive my   7
love inside you . . .", and Senator Gore's wife talks about "Bondage!" and "oral sex at gunpoint," on the CBS Evening News, people in high places work on a tax bill that is so ridiculous, the only way to sneak it through is to keep the public's mind on something else: "Porn Rock."

The PMRC practices a curious double standard with these fervent   8
recitations. Thanks to them, helpless young children all over America get to hear about oral sex at gunpoint on network TV several nights a week. Is there a secret FCC dispensation here? What sort of end justifies THESE means? PTA parents should keep an eye on these ladies if that's their idea of "good taste."

Is the basic issue morality? Is it mental health? Is it an issue at all?   9
The PMRC has created a lot of confusion with improper comparisons between song lyrics, videos, record packaging, radio broadcasting, and live performances. These are all different mediums, and the people who work in them have a right to conduct their business without trade-restraining legislation, whipped up like an instant pudding by The Wives of Big Brother.

Is it proper that the husband of PMRC non-member/founder/person   10
sits on any committee considering business pertaining to the Blank Tape Tax or his wife's lobbying organization? Can any committee thus constituted "find facts" in a fair and unbiased manner? This committee has three. A minor conflict of interest?

The PMRC promotes their program as a harmless type of consumer   11
information service providing "guidelines" which will assist baffled parents in the determination of the "suitability" of records listened to by "very young children." The methods they propose have several unfortunate side effects, not the least of which is the reduction of all American

Music, recorded and live, to the intellectual level of a Saturday morning
cartoon show.

Teenagers with $8.98 in their pocket might go into a record store   12
alone, but "very young children" do not. Usually there is a parent in
attendance. The $8.98 is in the parent's pocket. The parent can always
suggest that the $8.98 be spent on a book.

If the parent is afraid to let the child read a book, perhaps the $8.98   13
can be spent on recordings of instrumental music. Why not bring jazz or
classical music into your home instead of Blackie Lawless or Madonna?
Great music with no words at all is available to anyone with sense enough
to look beyond this week's platinum-selling fashion plate.

Children in the "vulnerable" age bracket have a natural love for mu-   14
sic. If, as a parent, you believe they should be exposed to something
more uplifting than "Sugar Walls," support Music Appreciation programs
in schools. Why haven't you considered your child's need for consumer
information? Music Appreciation costs very little compared to sports ex-
penditures. Your children have a right to know that something besides
pop music exists.

It is unfortunate that the PMRC would rather dispense governmentally   15
sanitized Heavy Metal Music, than something more "uplifting." Is this an
indication of PMRC's personal taste, or just another manifestation of the
low priority this administration has placed on education for The Arts in
America? The answer, of course, is neither. You can't distract people
from thinking about an unfair tax by talking about Music Appreciation.
For that you need sex . . . and lots of it.

Because of the subjective nature of the PMRC ratings, it is impossible   16
to guarantee that some sort of "despised concept" won't sneak through,
tucked away in new slang or the overstressed pronunciation of an otherwise innocent word. If the goal here is total verbal/moral safety, there is
only one way to achieve it: watch no TV, read no books, see no movies,
listen to only instrumental music, or buy no music at all.

The establishment of a rating system, voluntary or otherwise, opens   17
the door to an endless parade of Moral Quality Control Programs based
on "Things Certain Christians Don't Like." What if the next bunch of
Washington Wives demands a large yellow "J" on all material written or
performed by Jews, in order to save helpless children from exposure to
"concealed Zionist doctrine"?

Record ratings are frequently compared to film ratings. Apart from   18
the quantitative difference, there is another that is more important: People
who act in films are hired to "pretend." No matter how the film is rated,
it won't hurt them personally. Since many musicians write and perform
their own material and stand by it as their art (whether you like it or not),
an imposed rating will stigmatize them as individuals. How long before
composers and performers are told to wear a festive little PMRC arm
band with their Scarlet Letter on it?

The PMRC rating system restrains trade in one specific musical field: 19
Rock. No ratings have been requested for Comedy records or Country
Music. Is there anyone in the PMRC who can differentiate infallibly
between Rock and Country Music? Artists in both fields cross stylistic
lines. Some artists include comedy material. If an album is part Rock,
part Country, part Comedy, what sort of label would it get? Shouldn't the
ladies be warning everyone that inside those Country albums with the
American Flags, the big trucks, and the atomic pompadours there lurks a
fascinating variety of songs about sex, violence, alcohol, and the devil,
recorded in a way that lets you hear every word, sung for you by people
who have been to prison and are proud of it.

If enacted, the PMRC program would have the effect of protectionist   20
legislation for the Country Music Industry, providing more security for
cowboys than it does for children. One major retail outlet has already
informed the Capitol Records sales staff that it would not purchase or
display an album with any kind of sticker on it.

Another chain with outlets in shopping malls has been told by the   21
landlord that if it racked "hard-rated albums" they would lose their lease.
That opens up an awful lot of shelf space for somebody. Could it be that
a certain Senatorial husband and wife team from Tennessee sees this as
an "affirmative action program" to benefit the suffering multitudes in
Nashville?

Is the PMRC attempting to save future generations from SEX IT-   22
SELF? The type, the amount, and the timing of sexual information given
to a child should be determined by the parents, not by people who are
involved in a tax scheme cover-up.

The PMRC has concocted a Mythical Beast, and compounds the chi-   23
canery by demanding "consumer guidelines" to keep it from inviting your
children inside its sugar walls. Is the next step the adoption of a "PMRC
National Legal Age For Comprehension of Vaginal Arousal." Many people in this room would gladly support such legislation, but, before they
start drafting their bill, I urge them to consider these facts:

1. There is no conclusive scientific evidence to support the claim that exposure to any form of music will cause the listener to commit a crime or
   damn his soul to hell.
2. Masturbation is not illegal. If it is not illegal to do it, why should it be
   illegal to sing about it?
3. No medical evidence of hairy palms, warts, or blindness has been linked
   to masturbation or vaginal arousal, nor has it been proven that hearing
   references to either topic automatically turns the listener into a social liability.
4. Enforcement of anti-masturbatory legislation could prove costly and time
   consuming.
5. There is not enough prison space to hold all the children who do it.

The PMRC's proposal is most offensive in its "moral tone." It seeks   24 to enforce a set of implied religious values on its victims. Iran has a religious government. Good for them. I like having the capitol of the United States in Washington, DC, in spite of recent efforts to move it to Lynchburg, VA.

Fundamentalism is not a state religion. The PMRC's request for la-   25 bels regarding sexually explicit lyrics, violence, drugs, alcohol, and especially occult content reads like a catalog of phenomena abhorrent to practitioners of that faith. How a person worships is a private matter, and should not be inflicted upon or exploited by others. Understanding the Fundamentalist leanings of this organization, I think it is fair to wonder if their rating system will eventually be extended to inform parents as to whether a musical group has homosexuals in it. Will the PMRC permit musical groups to exist, but only if gay members don't sing, and are not depicted on the album cover?

The PMRC has demanded that record companies "re-evaluate" the   26 contracts of those groups who do things on stage that THEY find offensive. I remind the PMRC that groups are comprised of individuals. If one guy wiggles too much, does the whole band get an "X"? If the group gets dropped from the label as a result of this "re-evaluation" process, do the other guys in the group who weren't wiggling get to sue the guy who wiggled because he ruined their careers? Do the founders of this tax-exempt organization with no members plan to indemnify record companies for any losses incurred from unfavorably decided breach of contract suits, or is there a PMRC secret agent in the Justice Department?

Should individual musicians be rated? If so, who is qualified to deter-   27 mine if the guitar player is an "X", the vocalist is a "D/A" or the drummer is a "V". If the bass player (or his Senator) belongs to a religious group that dances around with poisonous snakes, does he get an "O"? What if he has an earring in one ear, wears an Italian horn around his neck, sings about his astrological sign, practices yoga, reads the Quaballah, or owns a rosary? Will his "occult content" rating go into an old CoIntelPro computer, emerging later as a "fact," to determine if he qualifies for a home-owner loan? Will they tell you this is necessary to protect the folks next door from the possibility of "devil-worship" lyrics creeping through the wall?

What hazards await the unfortunate retailer who accidently sells an   28 "O" rated record to somebody's little Johnny? Nobody in Washington seemed to care when Christian Terrorists bombed abortion clinics in the name of Jesus. Will you care when the "friends of the wives of big brother" blow up the shopping mall?

The PMRC wants ratings to start as of the date of their enactment.   29 That leaves the current crop of "objectionable material" untouched. What will be the status of recordings from that Golden Era to censorship? Do they become collectors' items . . . or will another "fair and unbiased committee" order them destroyed in a public ceremony?

Bad facts make bad law, and people who write bad laws are, in my   30
opinion, more dangerous than songwriters who celebrate sexuality. Freedom of Speech, Freedom of Religious Thought, and the Right to Due
Process for composers, performers and retailers are imperiled if the
PMRC and the major labels consummate this nasty bargain. Are we expected to give up Article One so the big guys can collect an extra dollar
on every blank tape and 10 to 25% on tape recorders? What's going on
here? Do WE get to vote on this tax? There's an awful lot of smoke
pouring out of the legislative machinery used by the PMRC to inflate this
issue. Try not to inhale it. Those responsible for the vandalism should
pay for the damage by voluntarily rating themselves. If they refuse, perhaps the voters could assist in awarding the Congressional "X", the Congressional "D/A", the Congressional "V", and the Congressional "O".
Just like the ladies say: these ratings are necessary to protect our children.
I hope it's not too late to put them where they really belong.

QUESTIONS ON CONTENT

1. What, according to Zappa, is wrong with the PMRC proposal calling
for record labeling?

2. Is Zappa's counterargument, that the PMRC can't be serious about
shielding young people from explicitly sexual and violent lyrics because
their very actions have placed the issue on the network news, a valid one?
Explain.

3. What are the politics of the record labeling issue, as far as Zappa is
concerned? What is the "Blank Tape Tax," the "tax scheme cover-up"?
What is a conflict of interest? What are the conflicts of interest that Zappa
sees in the issue of record labeling?

4. How do you respond to Zappa's argument? Do you think he's right?
Why, or why not?

QUESTIONS ON RHETORIC

1. What analogy does Zappa use in paragraph 3? (Glossary: *Analogy*) Is
the analogy effective? Why, or why not?

2. Zappa engages in some name-calling with respect to the members of
the PMRC. What examples of this can you cite? Does this name-calling
aid his argument or detract from it? Explain.

3. How would you label Zappa's tone in this essay? (Glossary: *Tone*)
How, specifically, does he achieve that tone? (Glossary: *Diction*) Do you
find Zappa funny in any way? Explain.

4. What does Zappa mean by his title? To what does he allude in the
label "Big Brother"? (Glossary: *Allusion*)

VOCABULARY

decapitation (3)   sanitized (15)   pompadours (19)
fervent (8)   stigmatize (18)   chicanery (23)
recitations (8)   festive (18)

WRITING TOPICS

1. Zappa testified before the Senate in 1985. Where does the record labeling controversy stand today? Consult the *Reader's Guide to Periodical Literature* for more recent articles addressing the issue and write a report on the current status of efforts to curb what Tipper Gore has called the "sexploitation industry." Have there been more recent controversies over the lyrics used by rock or rap groups? If so, what are the specific issues? How has the media handled these situations?

2. Write an essay in which you examine the reasoning in Zappa's testimony. For example, are the differences and similarities between record ratings and film ratings significant with respect to the point the PMRC is making about the sexual explicitness and violence in rock lyrics? Is it fair to suggest that the PMRC's proposals would open the door to such policies as labeling with a "J" any records made by Jewish musicians? What other problems do you see in what Zappa has to say?

WRITING ASSIGNMENTS FOR "CENSORSHIP AND THE FIRST AMENDMENT"

1. In a 1991 newspaper article Frank Zappa said about the music censorship movement: "The only thing that is going to stop this movement is if there is the proper use of the educational system. How can you miss your rights if you didn't know you had those rights to begin with? Most kids in high school now don't even know what the Constitution guarantees them." Is Zappa correct? When you were in high school did you know what your constitutional rights were? If you didn't know in high school, do you know now? What does the First Amendment say about your guarantee to freedom of speech? Is it an unlimited right or are there certain restrictions placed on it? How has this constitutional right been challenged in the courts? Do some research in your school library and then write a report of your findings.

2. If you were a public school administrator, what would your policy be concerning students' freedom to express themselves in the school newspaper, yearbook, and other student publications? Can administrators impose restrictions on what can be said? Can parents? Can the taxpayers in a community? What was your high school's policy? What are the policies in the public school systems near your campus? How have the courts ruled in disputed situations? Research the Supreme Court ruling in the Hazelwood East High School censorship case. Try writing as policy statement.

3. Write an essay in which you use information and ideas that you have gleaned elsewhere in *Language Awareness* to shed new light on the censorship question. For example, what have the Hayakawas said about the confusion of the symbol with the thing symbolized that may help you understand the impulse to censor?

4. Millie Davis, director for affiliate and member services for the National Council of Teachers of English, wrote in the September 1992 issue of *The Council Chronicle*: "Challenges against books continued to be reported to the NCTE during the 1991–92 school year. Most challenges objected to one or all of the three S's—sex, swear words, and Satanism—but some also objected to the portrayal of less than uplifting situations in books (i.e., alcohol abuse, cigarette smoking, lack of parental respect). Complaints were filed against the following texts:

"A Rose for Emily" by William Faulkner
Bridge to Terabithia by Katherine Paterson
The Effect of Gamma Rays on Man-in-the-Moon Marigolds by Paul Zindel
The Color Purple by Alice Walker
Grendel by John Gardner
Fallen Angels by Walter Dean Myers
Blubber by Judy Blume
The Catcher in the Rye by J. D. Salinger

I Am the Cheese by Robert Cormier
Starring Sally J. Freedman as Herself by Judy Blume
Run Shelley Run by Gertrude Samuels
ABZ Book by Shel Silverstein
A Wrinkle in Time by Madeleine L'Engle
The Gray King by Susan Cooper
The Dark Is Rising by Susan Cooper
The King Who Rained by Fred Gwynne
"The Lottery" by Shirley Jackson
The Floatplane Notebooks by Clyde Edgerton
The Boy Who Drank Too Much by Shep Greene
Long Live the Queen by Ellen E. White
The *Impressions* series, published by Harcourt Brace Jovanovich"

Choose one of these texts, preferably one that you are familiar with, and review it. What is there in the work that might be construed as objectionable? Write an essay on the pros and cons of the challenge to the text.

5. Does your school newspaper include advertisements for beer and wine? What is your attitude toward such advertising? Write an argument for or against allowing such ads in your newspaper.

6. Write an essay in which you describe your parents' role in guiding and shaping your early childhood attitudes toward what might be termed objectionable materials. Did they monitor your viewing of movies, your purchase of tapes and records, your reading material? Did they explain their actions to you?

7. How has your student government and the administration of your school handled the appearances of invited speakers on campus with respect to protests? Are protests allowed? Have speakers' appearances been canceled or disrupted? Do you have a written school policy about the First Amendment rights of invited speakers? Investigate your school's policies and write a report of your findings.

8. Review Hentoff's article on speech codes on campus. Does your school have a policy against hate speech? What is it? Do you agree with it? Has Hentoff's article changed your thinking about such speech codes? Write an essay explaining your school's policy on hate speech and whether or not you support that policy. If your school does not have such a policy and you think that it should, write an argument in favor of instituting one.

Writing Well:
Five Writers
on Writing

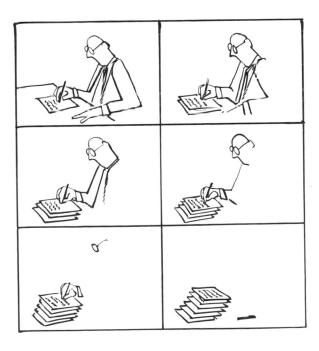

WHAT HAPPENS WHEN PEOPLE WRITE?

Maxine Hairston

Professor of English and writing expert Maxine Hairston provides a useful overview of the writing process and then goes on to focus on the differences between two different kinds of writing—explanatory and exploratory—that we must master and value equally.

Many people who have trouble writing believe that writing is a mysterious process that the average person cannot master. They assume that anyone who writes well does so because of a magic mixture of talent and inspiration, and that people who are not lucky enough to have those gifts can never become writers. Thus they take an "either you have it or you don't" attitude that discourages them before they even start to write.

Like most myths, this one has a grain of truth in it, but only a grain. Admittedly the best writers are people with talent just as the best musicians or athletes or chemists are people with talent. But that qualification does not mean that only talented people can write well any more than it means that only a few gifted people can become good tennis players. Tennis coaches know differently. From experience, they know any reasonably well-coordinated and healthy person can learn to play a fairly good game of tennis if he or she will learn the principles of the game and work at putting them into practice. They help people become tennis players by showing them the strategies that experts use and by giving them criticism and reinforcement as they practice those strategies. In recent years, as we have learned more about the processes of working writers, many teachers have begun to work with their writing students in the same way.

AN OVERVIEW OF THE WRITING PROCESS

How Professional Writers Work

- Most writers don't wait for inspiration. They write whether they feel like it or not. Usually they write on a schedule, putting in regular hours just as they would on a job.
- Professional writers consistently work in the same places with the same tools—pencil, typewriter, or word processor. The physical details of writing are important to them so they take trouble to create a good writing environment for themselves.

471

- Successful writers work constantly at observing what goes on around them and have a system for gathering and storing material. They collect clippings, keep notebooks, or write in journals.
- Even successful writers need deadlines to make them work, just like everyone else.
- Successful writers make plans before they start to write, but they keep their plans flexible, subject to revision.
- Successful writers usually have some audience in mind and stay aware of that audience as they write and revise.
- Most successful writers work rather slowly; four to six double-spaced pages is considered a good day's work.
- Even successful writers often have trouble getting started; they expect it and don't panic.
- Successful writers seldom know precisely what they are going to write before they start, and they plan on discovering at least part of their content as they work. (See section below on explanatory and exploratory writing.)
- Successful writers stop frequently to reread what they've written and consider such rereading an important part of the writing process.
- Successful writers revise as they write and expect to do two or more drafts of anything they write.
- Like ordinary mortals, successful writers often procrastinate and feel guilty about it; unlike less experienced writers, however, most of them have a good sense of how long they can procrastinate and still avoid disaster.

Explanatory and Exploratory Writing

Several variables affect the method and speed with which writers work— how much time they have, how important their task is, how skilled they are, and so on. The most important variable, however, is the kind of writing they are doing. I am going to focus on two major kinds here: *explanatory* and *exploratory*. To put it briefly, although much too simply, explanatory writing *tends* to be about information; exploratory writing *tends* to be about ideas.   4

Explanatory writing can take many forms: a movie review, an explanation of new software, an analysis of historical causes, a report on a recent political development, a biographical sketch. These are just a few possibilities. The distinguishing feature of all these examples and other kinds of explanatory writing is that the writer either knows most of what he or she is going to say before starting to write or knows where to find the material needed to get started. A typical explanatory essay might be on some aspect of global warming for an environmental studies course. The material for such a paper already exists—you're not going to create it or discover it within your subconscious. Your job as a writer is to dig out the material, organize it, and shape it into a clearly written, carefully supported essay. Usually you would know who your readers are for an explanatory essay and, from the beginning, shape it for that audience.   5

Writers usually make plans when they are doing explanatory writing,   6 plans that can range from a page of notes to a full outline. Such plans help them to keep track of their material, put it in some kind of order, and find a pattern for presenting it. For explanatory writing, many writers find that the traditional methods work well; assertion/support, cause and effect, process, compare/contrast, and so on. Much of the writing that students do in college is explanatory, as is much business writing. Many magazine articles and nonfiction books are primarily explanatory writing. It's a crucially important kind of writing, one that we depend on for information and education, one that keeps the machinery of business and government going.

Explanatory writing is not necessarily easy to do nor is it usually formulaic. It takes skill and care to write an accurate, interesting story about the physician who won a Nobel Prize for initiating kidney transplants or an entertaining and informative report on how the movie *Dick Tracy* was made. But the process for explanatory writing is manageable. You identify the task, decide what the purpose and who the audience are, map out a plan for finding and organizing information, then divide the writing itself into doable chunks and start working. Progress may be painful, and you may have to draft and revise several times to clarify points or get the tone just right, but with persistence, you can do it.

Exploratory writing may also take many forms: a reflective personal essay, a profile of a homeless family, an argument in support of funding for multimillion dollar science projects, or a speculative essay about the future of the women's movement. These are only a few possibilities. What distinguishes these examples and exploratory writing in general is that the writer has only a partially formed idea of what he or she is going to write before starting. A typical piece of exploratory writing might be a speculative essay on why movies about the Mafia appeal so much to the American public. You might hit on the idea of writing such a piece after you have seen several mob movies—*Goodfellas, Miller's Crossing*, and *Godfather III*—but not really know what you would say or who your audience would be. The material for such a paper doesn't exist; you would have to begin by reading, talking to people, and by drawing on the ideas and insights you've gleaned from different sources to reach your own point of view. And you would certainly expect some of your most important ideas—your own conclusions—to come to you as you wrote.

Because you don't know ahead of time exactly what you're going to say in exploratory writing, it's hard to make a detailed plan or outline; however, you can and should take copious notes as you prepare to write. You might be able to put down a tentative thesis sentence, for example, "Americans moviegoers are drawn to movies about the Mafia and mob violence because they appeal to a streak of lawlessness that has always been strong in the American character." Such a sentence could be an anchor to get you started writing, but as a main idea, it could change or even disappear as the paper developed.

Many papers you write in college will be exploratory papers, for example, an interpretive paper in a literature course, an essay on the future of an ethnic community for a cultural anthropology course, or an argumentative paper for a government course proposing changes in our election laws. Many magazine articles and books are also exploratory, for example, an article on the roots of violence in American cities or an autobiographical account of being tagged a "slow learner" early in one's school career. Both in and out of college, exploratory writing is as important as explanatory writing because it is the springboard and testing ground for new ideas. 10

Exploratory writing isn't necessarily harder to do than explanatory writing, but it is harder to plan because it resists any systematic approach. That makes it appeal to some writers, particularly those who have a reflective or speculative turn of mind. They like the freedom of being able just to write to see what is going to develop. But although exploratory writers start out with more freedom, eventually they too have to discipline themselves to organize their writing into clear, readable form. They also have to realize that exploratory writing usually takes longer and requires more drafts. 11

When you're doing exploratory writing, anticipate that your process will be messy. You have to tolerate uncertainty longer because ideas keep coming as you write and it's not always clear what you're going to do with them and how—or if—you can fit them into your paper. Exploratory writing is also hard to organize—sometimes you'll have to outline *after* you've written your first draft in order to get the paper under control. Finally, you also have to have confidence in your own instincts; now that you are focusing on ideas and reflections more than on facts, you have to believe that you have something worth writing about and that other people are interested in reading it. 12

Of course, not all writing can be easily classified as either explanatory or exploratory; sometimes you'll be working with information and ideas in the same paper and move from presenting facts to reflecting about their implications. For example, in an economics course you might report on how much Japan has invested in the United States economy over the last decade and where those investments have been made; then you could speculate about the long-range impact on American business. If you were writing a case study of a teenage mother for a social work class, you would use mostly explanatory writing to document the young woman's background, schooling, and important facts about her present situation; then you could go to exploratory writing to suggest how her options for the future can be improved. 13

In general, readers respond best to writing that thoughtfully connects facts to reflections, explanations to explorations. So don't hesitate to mix the two kinds of writing if it makes your paper stronger and more interesting. At this point, you might ask "Why do these distinctions matter to me?" I think there are several reasons. 14

First, it helps to realize that there isn't *a* writing process—there are 15
writing *processes*, and some work better than others in specific situations.
Although by temperament and habit you may be the "just give me the
facts, ma'am," kind of person who prefers to do explanatory writing, you
also need to become proficient at exploratory writing in order to write the
speculative, reflective papers that are necessary when you have to write
about long-range goals or speculate about philosophical issues. If, on the
other hand, by temperament you'd rather ignore outlines and prefer to
spin theories instead of report on facts, you also need to become proficient at explanatory writing. In almost any profession, you're going to
have to write reports, summarize data, or present results of research.

Second, you'll become a more proficient and relaxed writer if you 16
develop the habit of analyzing before you start, whether you are going to
be doing primarily explanatory or exploratory writing. Once you decide,
you can consciously switch into certain writing patterns and write more
efficiently. For instance, when you're writing reports, case studies, research papers, or analyses, take the time to rough out an outline and
make a careful list of the main points you need to make. Schedule time
for research and checking facts; details are going to be important. Review
some of the routine but useful patterns you could use to develop your
paper: cause and effect, definition, process, narration, and so forth. They
can work well when you have a fairly clear idea of your purpose and
what you're going to say.

If you're starting on a less clearly defined, more open-ended paper— 17
for example, a reflective essay about Picasso's portrayal of women for an
art history course—allow yourself to be less organized for a while. Be
willing to start without knowing where you're going. Look at some paintings to get your ideas flowing, talk to some other students, and then just
start writing, confident that you'll find your content and your direction.
Don't worry if you can't get the first paragraph right—it will come later.
Your first goal with exploratory writing should be to generate a fairly
complete first draft in order to give yourself something to work with.
Remember to give yourself plenty of time to revise. You'll need it.

Finally, resist the idea that one kind of writing is better than another. 18
It's not. Sometimes there's a tendency, particularly in liberal arts classes,
to believe that people who do theoretical or reflective writing are superior; that exploratory writing is loftier and more admirable than writing
in which people present facts and argue for concrete causes. That's not
really the case. Imaginative, thoughtful writing about theories and opinions is important and interesting, but informative, factual writing is also
critically important, and people who can do it well are invaluable. Anyone who hopes to be an effective, confident writer should cultivate the
habits that enable him or her to do both kinds of writing well.

QUESTIONS FOR STUDY AND DISCUSSION

1. What erroneous belief about writing does Hairston concern herself with in her first two paragraphs? In what ways is a writing teacher like a tennis coach? Does this analogy help you as a writer? (Glossary: *Analogy*)

2. Review the list of items that Hairston provides to explain how professional writers work (3). What points did you already know? What points in the list surprised you? Why do you suppose Hairston provides this list?

3. What is the difference between explanatory and exploratory writing (4)? How has Hairston used examples to illustrate each type of writing? (Glossary: *Example*) How does she answer the question: "How do these distinctions matter to me?"

4. How has Hairston used transitions to connect the ideas in paragraphs 15 and 16? (Glossary: *Transitions*)

5. According to Hairston, is outlining more useful in explanatory or exploratory writing? Why?

6. Is Hairston's essay explanatory, exploratory, or a combination of both types of writing?

FIVE PRINCIPLES FOR GETTING GOOD IDEAS

Jack Rawlins

*One of the most troublesome aspects of learning to write well
is getting good ideas. Good ideas are not simply picked up
and tacked on to a piece of writing. They are the by-products
of an active, indeed interactive, mind that is engaged in the
world, continuously connecting and responding to it. In the
following essay, taken from his book* The Writer's Way, *Jack
Rawlins discusses five principles for getting good ideas that
you can build into your thinking and that will help you
become a more creative and interesting writer.*

Brains that get good ideas follow five principles:

1

> Don't begin with a topic.
> Think all the time.
> To get something out, put something in.
> Go from little, concrete things to big, abstract things.
> Connect.

We'll talk about each in turn.

DON'T BEGIN WITH A TOPIC

Essays rarely begin with subject matter alone. Why would a person say
out of the blue, "I think I'll write about linoleum, or the national debt"?
Nor are the kernels of essays always "good ideas"—they often aren't
ideas at all, in the sense of whole assertions. Thinking begins in lots of
ways:

2

> With a question: "Is there any real difference between the Republicans and
> the Democrats anymore?" "Why is Ralph so mad at me?"
> With a problem: "I'm always behind in my work." "Violent crimes against
> women are on the increase."
> With a purpose: "I want to tell people about what's really going on in this
> class." "I want to let people know about alternatives to traditional medi-
> cine."
> With a thesis: "There are cheaper, healthier alternatives to regular grocery
> stores." "Old people are the victims of silent injustice in our culture."
> With a feeling: anger, frustration, surprise.

> With a sensation or image: a smell, a glimpse of a bird in flight, an eye-catching TV ad.

What shall we call that thing an essay begins with—the seed, the spark, the inspiration, the sense of "gotcha"? I'll call it a prompt.

THINK ALL THE TIME

If you have a sense of humor, you know that the surest way to prevent   3
yourself from being funny is to have someone (even yourself) demand that you be funny *now*. Comedians have always bemoaned the fact that people introduce them to friends by saying, "This is Milton. He's a riot. Be funny, Milton." Thinking's the same way. Being put on the spot is the surest way of preventing the creative juices from flowing.

So don't expect to discover a good prompt by sitting down for a   4
scheduled half-hour of profundity. Minds that think well think all the time. One prolific student wrote that she goes through the world "looking for *writable* things" and is thought weird by her friends because she scribbles notes to herself at parties.

Thinking all the time sounds like work, but it isn't. Your mind works   5
all the time whether you want it to or not, the same way your body moves all the time. Any yogi will tell you that it takes years of practice to learn to turn the mind *off*, even for a minute or two. And it's physiologically impossible for your brain to get tired, which is why you can study or write all day, go to bed, and find your mind still racing while your body cries for rest. So I'm really not asking your brain to do anything new; I'm just asking you to *listen* to it.

TO GET SOMETHING OUT, PUT SOMETHING IN

One popular, poisonous image for thinking is the light bulb flashing on   6
over someone's head—the notion that ideas spring from within us, caused by nothing. To become good thinkers, we have to replace that image with another; think of ideas as billiard balls set in motion when something collides with them. Ideas are *re*actions—we have them in response to other things.

A thinker thinks as life passes through him and does what I call "talk-   7
ing back to the world." Many of us separate our input and output modes; we are either putting information into our brains or asking our brains to produce thoughts, but we don't do both at the same time. I call such people data sponges. But the best time to try to get things out is when things are going in. Let them bounce off you and strike sparks. People do this naturally until they've been taught to be passive; try reading a book to a three-year-old, and listen to her react to everything she hears and

sees, or take her to a movie and watch her struggle not to talk back to the screen.

Are you a data sponge? To find out, answer the following questions.   8

Do you find yourself mentally talking back to the newspaper when you read it?

Do you write in the margins of books you read?

Are at least 25 percent of the notes you take during course reading or lectures your own thoughts, questions, doubts, and reactions?

As you meet up with life's outrages, do you find yourself complaining to imaginary audiences?

After a movie, do you feel like you're going to burst until you find someone to talk about it?

When you listen to a speaker or a teacher, do you find yourself itching to get to the question-and-answer period?

If you said yes to these questions, you're not a sponge. If you said no, you're going to have to practice your reacting skills.

GO FROM LITTLE, CONCRETE THINGS
TO BIG, ABSTRACT THINGS

This principle is a logical consequence of the one before. Since ideas   9
come best in reaction to life's incoming billiard balls, the best thinking follows a predictable course: from little, concrete bits of experience to large, abstract implications. You see an ad on TV and start thinking about it, and it leads you to speculations on American consumerism, media manipulation, and the marketing of women's bodies. You overhear a snippet of conversation between a parent and child at the grocery store and start thinking about it, and it leads you to speculations on American child-rearing practices, the powerlessness of children, parental brainwashing, and antiyouth bigotry.

Here's what going from little particulars to big issues is like. I was   10
sitting doing nothing one day when my eyes fell on a box of Girl Scout cookies. The box had on it a picture of a girl and the slogan, "I'm not like anyone else." I reacted. I thought, "Gosh, that sounds lonely." And I valued the reaction enough to notice it and think about it. It led me to a big issue: How does Americans' love of individuality affect their ability to be members of a culture? And I formulated a thesis: Americans love their individuality so much that they'll cut themselves off from everything and everyone to get it. Being unlike everyone else is a curse, because it means you're separated from other human beings by your differentness. I was raised a proud individualist, and I've only recently realized that the reward for being unique is loneliness.

I went from little things to big issues when I drew essays out of   11

Sally's life.[1] When she mentioned that she couldn't drink too heavily in high school because it would affect her shot-putting, I instantly saw the abstract issue illustrated by her experience: People who have things they love dare not practice self-destructive behavior, because they'll destroy what they love in the process. So alcoholism or drug abuse is neither a crime nor a disease nor a moral failure in the individual; it's a symptom of a social failure, the failure of our society to offer the alcoholic or drug addict a life too precious to risk destroying.

Beginning writers want to start with large abstractions, in the mistaken belief that the bigger the topic is, the more there is to say about it. It doesn't work out that way. Usually the first sentence of the essay tells whether the writer knows this or not. Essays on friendship that begin "Friendship is one of the most important things in life" are doomed, because the writer doesn't know it. Essays that begin "Mary was my best friend in high school" will thrive, because the writer does know it.   12

CONNECT

Those who think well make connections between things. An essay begins when two previously unrelated bits in the brain meet and discover a connection. Usually a new stimulus hitches up with an old bit stored long ago in the memory; the incoming billiard ball hits an old one that's just lying there, and they fly off together.   13

It's hard to learn the connecting skill if you don't have it already. Here's what it feels like inside. One day I was sitting in an English Department faculty meeting, and we were discussing an administrative change. A colleague said, "We couldn't do that until we were sure our people would be protected." I thought momentarily, "I wonder how he knows who 'his people' are?" Months later I was vacationing in a small mountain town and picked up the local newspaper. On the front page was an article about the firing of a group of non-union construction workers. The boss had asked the union for workers, but none were available, so he trained out-of-work mill workers. Later the union rep showed up, announced that union workers were now available, and insisted that the others be fired. Something clicked, and I had an essay. My colleague's attitude and the union rep's were the same: I'll watch out for "my people," and everyone else can watch out for himself. I wanted to talk about why people think that way and how they learn to rise above it.   14

How did I make that connection? Incredible as it sounds, and unbeknownst to me, I must have been checking everything that came into my brain against the faculty-meeting remark for a possible connection. Or perhaps I had opened a file in my mind labeled "people who think in   15

[1]Sally is a student discussed earlier in Rawlins's text.

terms of those who belong and those who don't" and dumped anything related in there as it came along.

I just read a great essay by Arthur Miller connecting the current   16
prayer-in-school political debate with his memories of saying the Pledge of Allegiance in elementary school. What brought the two things together? Miller must have checked prayer in schools against everything in his memory relating to state-mandated loyalty and come up with recollections of third grade. That sounds exhausting, but we all know that when something clicks in memory, we haven't "worked" at all—in fact, the way to bring the connection that's on the tip of the tongue to the surface is to forget about it and let the subconscious do its work unwatched.

The more unlike two things are and the less obvious the connection   17
between them is, the fresher and more stimulating the connection is when
you make it. Finding a connection between mountain climbers and sky-divers is merely okay; finding a connection between inflation rates and the incidence of breast cancer will make the world open its eyes. This is the Head Principle. Mr. Head was an aviation engineer who got interested in downhill skiing. Apparently no one had ever connected aircraft technology and skiing before; Mr. Head took a few runs down the hill and realized that he could make a better ski if he simply made it according to the principles and with the materials used in making airplane wings. He invented the Head ski, the first metal ski, and made millions of dollars. He then did the same thing in tennis, by inventing the Prince racket. Apparently aircraft engineers didn't play tennis either.

The Head Principle says you can't predict what will connect with   18
what. So you can't tell yourself what information to seek. You can only take in experience and information voraciously and stir it all up together. If I had been formally researching stupid faculty remarks, I'd never have thought to read up on northern Californian construction workers. If you're writing about Charles Dickens and you read only about Charles Dickens, you're just guaranteeing you won't make any connections except those other Dickens scholars have already made. Instead, go read *Psychology Today*, read Nixon's memoirs, see a movie, watch a documentary on insect societies, or visit a mortuary. As you talk back to all of it, keep asking yourself, "What is this like? When have I thought things like this before? When was the last time I reacted like this?" When I read about the construction workers, I reacted, and I remembered that I'd had a conversation with myself like that one before sometime. Perhaps that's the key to connecting.

It's easy to block ideas from coming by practicing the exact opposite   19
of our idea-getting principles. Just set aside a time for idea-getting, cut yourself off from the outside world by locking yourself in a stimulus-free study room, and muse on a cosmic abstraction. If you're doing any of that, your idea-getting regimen needs overhauling.

QUESTIONS FOR STUDY AND DISCUSSION

1. Rawlins advises against beginning your writing by thinking about a topic. What's wrong with thinking about a topic? How does he suggest you begin?

2. What is a "data sponge," according to Rawlins? Are you a data sponge? How do you know? What does Rawlins suggest you do if you are a data sponge?

3. What is the point of the story Rawlins tell about his faculty meeting and the piece he read in the newspaper about the firing of a group of non-union construction workers?

4. What, according to Rawlins, is the Head Principle (17)?

5. Can you recall any writing experiences you have had when you have gone from "little particulars to big issues"? Why is it not a good idea to begin with abstraction and move to particulars?

6. What part(s) of the advice Rawlins gives do you think will be most helpful to you in your writing? Explain.

WRITING FOR AN AUDIENCE

Linda Flower

Linda Flower is an associate professor of English at Carnegie-Mellon University, where she directed the Business Communication program for a number of years. Her widely recognized research on the composing process resulted in the textbook Problem-Solving Strategies for Writing. *In the following selection taken from that text, Flower discusses the importance of defining your audience of readers before you start writing.*

The goal of the writer is to create a momentary common ground between the reader and the writer. You want the reader to share your knowledge and your attitude toward that knowledge. Even if the reader eventually disagrees, you want him or her to be able for the moment to *see things as you see them*. A good piece of writing closes the gap between you and the reader.

ANALYZE YOUR AUDIENCE

The first step in closing that gap is to gauge the distance between the two of you. Imagine, for example, that you are a student writing your parents, who have always lived in New York City, about a wilderness survival expedition you want to go on over spring break. Sometimes obvious differences such as age or background will be important, but the critical differences for writers usually fall into three areas: the reader's *knowledge* about the topic; his or her *attitude* toward it, and his or her personal or professional *needs*. Because these differences often exist, good writers do more than simply express their meaning; they pinpoint the critical differences between themselves and their reader and design their writing to reduce those differences. Let us look at these three areas in more detail.

KNOWLEDGE This is usually the easiest difference to handle. What does your reader need to know? What are the main ideas you hope to teach? Does your reader have enough background knowledge to really understand you? If not, what would he or she have to learn?

ATTITUDES When we say a person has knowledge, we usually refer to his conscious awareness of explicit facts and clearly defined concepts. This kind of knowledge can be easily written down or told to someone else. However, much of what we "know" is not held in this formal,

483

explicit way. Instead it is held as an attitude or image—as a loose cluster of associations. For instance, my image of lakes includes associations many people would have, including fishing, water skiing, stalled outboards, and lots of kids catching night crawlers with flashlights. However, the most salient or powerful parts of my image, which strongly color my whole attitude toward lakes, are thoughts of cloudy skies, long rainy days, and feeling generally cold and damp. By contrast, one of my best friends has a very different cluster of associations: to him a lake means sun, swimming, sailing, and happily sitting on the end of a dock. Needless to say, our differing images cause us to react quite differently to a proposal that we visit a lake. Likewise, one reason people often find it difficult to discuss religion and politics is that terms such as "capitalism" conjure up radically different images.

As you can see, a reader's image of a subject is often the source of   5
attitudes and feelings that are unexpected and, at times, impervious to mere facts. A simple statement that seems quite persuasive to you, such as "Lake Wampago would be a great place to locate the new music camp," could have little impact on your reader if he or she simply doesn't visualize a lake as a "great place." In fact, many people accept uncritically any statement that fits in with their own attitudes—and reject, just as uncritically, anything that does not.

Whether your purpose is to persuade or simply to present your per-   6
spective, it helps to know the image and attitudes that your reader already holds. The more these differ from your own, the more you will have to do to make him or her *see* what you mean.

NEEDS   When writers discover a large gap between their own knowl-   7
edge and attitudes and those of the reader, they usually try to change the reader in some way. Needs, however, are different. When you analyze a reader's needs, it is so that you, the writer, can adapt to him. If you ask a friend majoring in biology how to keep your fish tank from clouding, you don't want to hear a textbook recitation on the life processes of algae. You expect the friend to adapt his or her knowledge and tell you exactly how to solve your problem.

The ability to adapt your knowledge to the needs of the reader is often   8
crucial to your success as a writer. This is especially true in writing done on a job. For example, as producer of a public affairs program for a television station, 80 percent of your time may be taken up planning the details of new shows, contacting guests, and scheduling the taping sessions. But when you write a program proposal to the station director, your job is to show how the program will fit into the cost guidelines, the FCC requirements for relevance, and the overall programming plan for the station. When you write that report your role in the organization changes from producer to proposal writer. Why? Because your reader needs that information in order to make a decision. He may be *interested* in your scheduling problems and the specific content of the shows, but he

reads your report because of his own needs as station director of that organization. He has to act.

In college, where the reader is also a teacher, the reader's needs are a   9
little less concrete but just as important. Most papers are assigned as a way to teach something. So the real purpose of a paper may be for you to make connections between two historical periods, to discover for yourself the principle behind a laboratory experiment, or to develop and support your own interpretation of a novel. A good college paper doesn't just rehash the facts; it demonstrates what your reader, as a teacher, needs to know—that you are learning the thinking skills his or her course is trying to teach.

Effective writers are not simply expressing what they know, like a   10
student madly filling up an examination bluebook. Instead they are *using* their knowledge: reorganizing, maybe even rethinking their ideas to meet the demands of an assignment or the needs of their reader.

QUESTIONS FOR STUDY AND DISCUSSION

1. What, for Flower, should be the goal of the writer?

2. What does Flower mean by the "distance" between the writer and the reader? How, according to Flower, do writers close the gap between themselves and their readers?

3. What does Flower see as the three critical differences between writers and readers? Why do you suppose she devotes so little attention to "knowledge" and so much more to both "attitude" and "needs"?

4. What is the difference between "knowledge" and "attitude"? Why is it important to know the difference?

5. Why is it so important for writers to adapt their knowledge to their readers' needs? How do you determine what your reader's needs are? Explain.

6. What, according to Flower, does a good college paper do? What does she mean when she says that effective writers do not simply express what they know, they *use* their knowledge?

7. Flower wrote this selection for college students. How well did she assess your knowledge, attitude, and needs about the subject of a writer's audience?

SIMPLICITY

William Zinsser

The following essay is taken from William Zinsser's On
Writing Well: An Informal Guide to Writing Nonfiction. *In it
Zinsser, a longtime writer, editor, critic, and teacher of
writing, advises and demonstrates that self-discipline and
hard work are necessary to achieve clear, simple prose. No
matter what your experience as a writer has been, you will
find Zinsser's observations sound and his advice practical.*

Clutter is the disease of American writing. We are a society strangling   1
in unnecessary words, circular constructions, pompous frills and meaningless jargon.

Who can understand the viscous language of everyday American   2
commerce and enterprise: the business letter, the interoffice memo, the
corporation report, the notice from the bank explaining its latest "simplified" statement? What member of an insurance or medical plan can
decipher the brochure that describes what the costs and benefits are?
What father or mother can put together a child's toy—on Christmas Eve
or any other eve—from the instructions on the box? Our national tendency is to inflate and thereby sound important. The airline pilot who
announces that he is presently anticipating experiencing considerable precipitation wouldn't dream of saying that it may rain. The sentence is too
simple—there must be something wrong with it.

But the secret of good writing is to strip every sentence to its cleanest   3
components. Every word that serves no function, every long word that
could be a short word, every adverb that carries the same meaning that's
already in the verb, every passive construction that leaves the reader unsure of who is doing what—these are the thousand and one adulterants
that weaken the strength of a sentence. And they usually occur, ironically, in proportion to education and rank.

During the late 1960s the president of a major university wrote a letter   4
to mollify the alumni after a spell of campus unrest. "You are probably
aware," he began, "that we have been experiencing very considerable
potentially explosive expressions of dissatisfaction on issues only partially related." He meant that the students had been hassling them about
different things. I was far more upset by the president's English than by
the students' potentially explosive expressions of dissatisfaction. I would
have preferred the presidential approach taken by Franklin D. Roosevelt
when he tried to convert into English his own government's memos, such
as this blackout order of 1942:

Such preparations shall be made as will completely obscure all Federal buildings and non-Federal buildings occupied by the Federal government during an air raid for any period of time from visibility by reason of internal or external illumination.

"Tell them," Roosevelt said, "that in buildings where they have to keep the work going to put something across the windows."   5

Simplify, simplify. Thoreau said it, as we are so often reminded, and no American writer more consistently practiced what he preached. Open *Walden* to any page and you will find a man saying in a plain and orderly way what is on his mind: 6

> I went to the woods because I wished to live deliberately, to front only the essential facts of life, and see if I could not learn what it had to teach, and not, when I came to die, discover that I had not lived. I did not wish to live what was not life, living is so dear; nor did I wish to practice resignation, unless it was quite necessary. I wanted to live deep and suck out all the marrow of life, to live so sturdily and Spartan-like as to put to rout all that was not life, to cut a broad swath and shave close, to drive life into a corner, and reduce it to its lowest terms, and, if it proved to be mean, why then to get the whole and genuine meanness of it, and publish its meanness to the world; or if it were sublime, to know it by experience, and be able to give a true account of it.

How can the rest of us achieve such enviable freedom from clutter? The answer is to clear our heads of clutter. Clear thinking becomes clear writing; one can't exist without the other. It's impossible for a muddy thinker to write good English. You may get away with it for a paragraph or two, but soon the reader will be lost, and there's no sin so grave, for the reader will not easily be lured back.   7

Who is this elusive creature, the reader? The reader is someone with an attention span of about sixty seconds—a person assailed by forces competing for the minutes that might otherwise be spent on a magazine or a book. At one time these forces weren't so numerous or so possessive: newspapers, radio, spouse, home, children. Today they also include a "home entertainment center" (TV, VCR, video camera, tapes and CDs), pets, a fitness program, a lawn and a garden and all the gadgets that have been bought to keep them spruce, and that most potent of competitors, sleep. The person snoozing in a chair, holding a magazine or a book, is a person who was being given too much unnecessary trouble by the writer.   8

It won't do to say that the reader is too dumb or too lazy to keep pace with the train of thought. If the reader is lost, it's usually because the writer hasn't been careful enough. The carelessness can take any number of forms. Perhaps a sentence is so excessively cluttered that the reader, hacking through the verbiage, simply doesn't know what it means. Perhaps a sentence has been so shoddily constructed that the reader could read it in any of several ways. Perhaps the writer has switched pronouns in midsentence, or has switched tenses, so the reader loses track of who   9 is talking or when the action took place. Perhaps Sentence B is not a logical sequel to Sentence A—the writer, in whose head the connection is clear, hasn't bothered to provide the missing link. Perhaps the writer has used an important word incorrectly by not taking the trouble to look it up. The writer may think that "sanguine" and "sanguinary" mean the same thing, but the difference is a bloody big one. The reader can only infer (speaking of big differences) what the writer is trying to imply.

Faced with such obstacles, readers are at first remarkably tenacious. 10 They blame themselves—they obviously missed something, and they go back over the mystifying sentence, or over the whole paragraph, piecing it out like an ancient rune, making guesses and moving on. But they won't do this for long. The writer is making them work too hard, and they will look for one who is better at the craft.

Writers must therefore constantly ask: What am I trying to say? Sur- 11 prisingly often they don't know. Then they must look at what they have written and ask: Have I said it? Is it clear to someone encountering the subject for the first time? If it's not, that's because some fuzz has worked its way into the machinery. The clear writer is someone clearheaded enough to see this stuff for what it is: fuzz.

I don't mean that some people are born clearheaded and are therefore 12 natural writers, whereas others are naturally fuzzy and will never write well. Thinking clearly is a conscious act that writers must force upon themselves, just as if they were embarking on any other project that requires logic: adding up a laundry list or doing an algebra problem. Good writing doesn't come naturally, though most people obviously think it does. The professional writer is constantly being bearded by strangers who say they'd like to "try a little writing sometime"—meaning when they retire from their real profession, like insurance or real estate. Or they say, "I could write a book about that." I doubt it.

Writing is hard work. A clear sentence is no accident. Very few sen- 13 tences come out right the first time, or even the third time. Remember this as a consolation in moments of despair. If you find that writing is hard, it's because it *is* hard. It's one of the hardest things that people do.

QUESTIONS FOR STUDY AND DISCUSSION

1. What is the relationship that Zinsser sees between thinking and writing?

2. What is clutter? How does Zinsser think that we can free ourselves of clutter?

3. What assumptions does Zinsser make about readers? According to Zinsser, what responsibilities do writers have to readers?

4. What questions should the writer constantly ask? Why are these questions so important?

5. What does Zinsser mean by "simplicity"? Would you agree with him that "our national tendency is to inflate and thereby sound important" (2)? Why, or why not?

6. Zinsser uses short sentences (seven or fewer words) effectively in his essay. Locate several examples of short sentences, and explain the function of each within its paragraph.

7. The following two pages show a passage from the final manuscript for this essay. Carefully study the manuscript, and then discuss the ways in which Zinsser has been able to eliminate clutter.

5 --

is too dumb or too lazy to keep pace with the ~~writer's~~ train
of thought. My sympathies are ~~entirely~~ with him. ~~He's not so dumb.~~ (If the reader is lost, it is generally because the
writer ~~of the article~~ has not been careful enough to keep
him on the ~~proper~~ path.

This carelessness can take any number of ~~different~~ forms.
Perhaps a sentence is so excessively ~~long and~~ cluttered that
the reader, hacking his way through ~~all~~ the verbiage, simply
doesn't know what it ~~the writer~~ means. Perhaps a sentence has
been so shoddily constructed that the reader could read it in
any of several ~~two or three different~~ ways. ~~He thinks he knows what the writer is trying to say, but he's not sure.~~ Perhaps the
writer has switched pronouns in mid-sentence, or ~~perhaps he~~
has switched tenses, so the reader loses track of who is
talking ~~to whom,~~ or ~~exactly~~ when the action took place. Perhaps Sentence B is not a logical sequel to Sentence A -- the
writer, in whose head the connection is ~~perfectly~~ clear, has
not bothered to provide ~~given enough thought to providing~~ the missing link. Perhaps the writer has used an important word incorrectly by not
taking the trouble to look it up ~~and make sure.~~ He may think
that "sanguine" and "sanguinary" mean the same thing, but
~~I can assure you that~~ (the difference is a bloody big one, ~~to the reader.~~ The reader ~~He~~ can only ~~try to~~ infer ~~what~~ (speaking of big differences) what the writer is trying to imply.

Faced with these ~~such a variety of~~ obstacles, the reader
is at first a remarkably tenacious bird. He ~~tends to~~ blames
himself. ~~He~~ obviously missed something, ~~he thinks,~~ and he goes
back over the mystifying sentence, or over the whole paragraph,

6 --

piecing it out like an ancient rune, making guesses and moving

on. But he won't do this for long. ~~He will soon run out of~~

~~patience.~~ (The writer is making him work too hard ~~— harder~~

~~than he should have to work —~~ and the reader will look for

~~a writer~~ **one** who is better at his craft.

The writer must therefore constantly ask himself: What am

I trying to say? ~~in this sentence?~~ (Surprisingly often, he

doesn't know.) ~~And~~ Then he must look at what he has ~~just~~

written and ask: Have I said it? Is it clear to someone

~~who is coming upon~~ **encountering** the subject for the first time? If it's

not, ~~clear,~~ it is because some fuzz has worked its way into the

machinery. The clear writer is a person ~~who is~~ clear-headed

enough to see this stuff for what it is: fuzz.

I don't mean ~~to suggest~~ that some people are born

clear-headed and are therefore natural writers, whereas

others ~~other people~~ are naturally fuzzy and will ~~therefore~~ never write

well. Thinking clearly is ~~an entirely~~ a conscious act that the

writer must **force** ~~keep forcing~~ upon himself, just as if he were

embarking ~~starting out~~ on any other ~~kind of~~ project that **requires** ~~calls for~~ logic:

adding up a laundry list or doing an algebra problem ~~or playing~~

~~chess.~~ Good writing doesn't ~~just~~ come naturally, though most

people obviously think **it does.** ~~it's as easy as walking.~~ The professional

NOTES ON PUNCTUATION

Lewis Thomas

Lewis Thomas has had a distinguished career as a physician, administrator, researcher, teacher, and writer. Thomas began his writing career in 1971 with a series of essays for the New England Journal of Medicine; *many of these have been collected in* The Lives of a Cell: Notes of a Biology Watcher, The Medusa and the Snail: More Notes of a Biology Watcher, Late Night Thoughts on Listening to Mahler's Ninth Symphony, *and* The Fragile Species: Notes of an Earth Watcher. *"Notes on Punctuation" is taken from* The Medusa and the Snail. *In this selection Thomas demonstrates the value, meaning, and practical usefulness of various punctuation marks.*

There are no precise rules about punctuation (Fowler lays out some general advice (as best he can under the complex circumstances of English prose (he points out, for example, that we possess only four stops (the comma, the semicolon, the colon and the period (the question mark and exclamation point are not, strictly speaking, stops; they are indicators of tone (oddly enough, the Greeks employed the semicolon for their question mark (it produces a strange sensation to read a Greek sentence which is a straightforward question: Why weepest thou; (instead of Why weepest thou? (and, of course, there are parentheses (which are surely a kind of punctuation making this whole matter much more complicated by having to count up the left-handed parentheses in order to be sure of closing with the right number (but if the parentheses were left out, with nothing to work with but the stops, we would have considerably more flexibility in the deploying of layers of meaning than if we tried to separate all the clauses by physical barriers (and in the latter case, while we might have more precision and exactitude for our meaning, we would lose the essential flavor of language, which is its wonderful ambiguity)))))))))))).

The commas are the most useful and usable of all the stops. It is highly important to put them in place as you go along. If you try to come back after doing a paragraph and stick them in the various spots that tempt you you will discover that they tend to swarm like minnows into all sorts of crevices whose existence you hadn't realized and before you know it the whole long sentence becomes immobilized and lashed up squirming in commas. Better to use them sparingly, and with affection, precisely when the need for each one arises, nicely, by itself.

I have grown fond of semicolons in recent years. The semicolon tells you that there is still some question about the preceding full sentence;

1

2

3

something needs to be added; it reminds you sometimes of the Greek usage. It is almost always a greater pleasure to come across a semicolon than a period. The period tells you that that is that; if you didn't get all the meaning you wanted or expected, anyway you got all the writer intended to parcel out and now you have to move along. But with a semicolon there you get a pleasant little feeling of expectancy; there is more to come; read on; it will get clearer.

Colons are a lot less attractive, for several reasons: firstly, they give   4
you the feeling of being rather ordered around, or at least having your nose pointed in a direction you might not be inclined to take if left to yourself, and, secondly, you suspect you're in for one of those sentences that will be labeling the points to be made: firstly, secondly and so forth, with the implication that you haven't sense enough to keep track of a sequence of notions without having them numbered. Also, many writers use this system loosely and incompletely, starting out with number one and number two as though counting off on their fingers but then going on and on without the succession of labels you've been led to expect, leaving you floundering about searching for the ninethly or seventeenthly that ought to be there but isn't.

Exclamation points are the most irritating of all. Look! they say, look   5
at what I just said! How amazing is my thought! It is like being forced to watch someone else's small child jumping up and down crazily in the center of the living room shouting to attract attention. If a sentence really has something of importance to say, something quite remarkable, it doesn't need a mark to point it out. And if it is really, after all, a banal sentence needing more zing, the exclamation point simply emphasizes its banality!

Quotation marks should be used honestly and sparingly, when there is   6
a genuine quotation at hand, and it is necessary to be very rigorous about the words enclosed by the marks. If something is to be quoted, the *exact* words must be used. If part of it must be left out because of space limitations, it is good manners to insert three dots to indicate the omission, but it is unethical to do this if it means connecting two thoughts which the original author did not intend to have tied together. Above all, quotation marks should not be used for ideas that you'd like to disown, things in the air so to speak. Nor should they be put in place around clichés; if you want to use a cliché you must take full responsibility for it yourself and not try to fob it off on anon., or on society. The most objectionable misuse of quotation marks, but one which illustrates the dangers of misuse in ordinary prose, is seen in advertising, especially in advertisements for small restaurants, for example "just around the corner," or "a good place to eat." No single, identifiable, citable person ever really said, for the record, "just around the corner," much less "a good place to eat," least likely of all for restaurants of the type that use this type of prose.

The dash is a handy device, informal and essentially playful, telling   7 you that you're about to take off on a different tack but still in some way connected with the present course—only you have to remember that the dash is there, and either put a second dash at the end of the notion to let the reader know that he's back on course, or else end the sentence, as here, with a period.

The greatest danger in punctuation is for poetry. Here it is necessary to be as economical and parsimonious with commas and periods as with the words themselves, and any marks that seem to carry their own subtle meanings, like dashes and little rows of periods, even semicolons and question marks, should be left out altogether rather than inserted to clog up the thing with ambiguity. A single exclamation point in a poem, no matter what else the poem has to say, is enough to destroy the whole work. 8

The things I like best in T. S. Eliot's poetry, especially in the *Four Quartets*, are the semicolons. You cannot hear them, but they are there, laying out the connections between the images and the ideas. Sometimes you get a glimpse of a semicolon coming, a few lines farther on, and it is like climbing a steep path through woods and seeing a wooden bench just at a bend in the road ahead, a place where you can expect to sit for a moment, catching your breath. 9

Commas can't do this sort of thing; they can only tell you how the different parts of a complicated thought are to be fitted together, but you can't sit, not even take a breath, just because of a comma. 10

QUESTIONS FOR STUDY AND DISCUSSION

1. What point does Thomas make about punctuation in his opening paragraph? How does he continue to develop this point throughout his essay?

2. Point out the four similes that Thomas uses in this essay. What is being compared in each? Why is each comparison appropriate? Why do you suppose Thomas chose to use figurative language in an essay on punctuation? (Glossary: *Figures of Speech*)

3. In paragraph 5, Thomas personifies exclamation points. What other examples of personification can you find in the essay? Why is this figure of speech particularly useful for Thomas's purposes? (Glossary: *Figures of Speech*)

4. In the course of explaining its function, Thomas actually uses each mark of punctuation. This is an interesting example of illustration, of "showing" while explaining. When did you become aware of what he was doing? Did this strategy help you to understand and appreciate the uses of punctuation?

5. What is Thomas's attitude toward writing? toward punctuation? What in his diction reveals his attitude? (Glossary: *Diction*)

WRITING ASSIGNMENTS FOR "WRITING WELL: FIVE WRITERS ON WRITING"

1. Write a brief interpretation of the Jeff Danziger cartoon that begins this section of the text. What point does the cartoon make about the writer? about the writing itself?

2. In his essay, Jack Rawlins gives his five principles for getting good ideas. Write an explanation of the way you get ideas. Do some of your principles for getting ideas overlap his? Do you think your method of getting ideas is unique to you and the way you write or might they might be helpful to someone else as well?

3. How well do you know yourself as a writer? Write an essay in which you describe the process you normally follow in writing a composition. Do you begin by brainstorming for ideas? Do you do a lot of thinking before you write or do you simply start writing, hoping that ideas will come to you as you write? How many drafts does it usually take before you have a composition that satisfies you? What part of the process gives you the most difficulty? What part of the process comes easiest for you?

4. Each of the essays in this section is concerned with the importance of writing well, of using language effectively. Write an essay in which you discuss the common themes that are emphasized in two or more of the essays.

5. Write an essay in which you discuss the proposition that honesty, while it does not guarantee good writing, is a prerequisite of good writing.

6. Philosopher Ludwig Wittgenstein once said, "The limits of my language are the limits of my world." What do you think he meant? Write an essay in which you support Wittgenstein's generalization with carefully selected examples from your own experience.

7. In order to write well, a writer has to identify his or her audience. Choose a topic close to your heart, such as the benefits of living away from home or how well your diet is going. Write an essay designed for reading by your best friend. Now write an essay on the same subject to be read by your instructor. How does your voice differ from essay to essay? Which voice comes more easily? Why?

8. We are often told that writing is an important means of communication. But the more writing we do, the more we realize that writing is important in other ways as well. Write an essay in which you discuss the particular reasons why you value writing.

9. Some of our most pressing social issues depend for their solutions upon a clear statement of the problem and the precise definition of critical terms. For example, the increasing number of people kept alive by machines has brought worldwide attention to the legal and medical defini-

tions of the word *death*. Debates continue about the meanings of other controversial words, such as *morality, minority* (ethnic), *alcoholism, life* (as in the abortion issue), *pornography, kidnapping, drugs, censorship, remedial, insanity, monopoly* (business), *literacy, censorship,* and *political correctness*. Select one of these words, and write an essay in which you discuss the problems associated with the term, and its definition.

RHETORICAL TABLE OF CONTENTS

The essays in *Language Awareness* are arranged in eleven sections according to their subjects. The following alternate table of contents, which is certainly not exhaustive, suggests some of the rhetorical strategies that the essays exemplify.

ANALOGY

Lance Morrow, "If Slang Is Not a Sin"	135
Robert MacNeil, "English Belongs to Everybody"	140
Martin Luther King, Jr., "I Have a Dream"	192
Frank Zappa, "The Wives of Big Brother"	459
Lewis Thomas, "Notes on Punctuation"	492

ARGUMENT AND PERSUASION

S. I. Hayakawa and Alan R. Hayakawa, "Giving Things Names"	39
George Orwell, "Politics and the English Language"	70
Dorothy Z. Seymour, "Black Children, Black Speech"	122
Rachel L. Jones, "What's Wrong with Black English"	131
Lance Morrow, "If Slang Is Not a Sin"	135
Robert MacNeil, "English Belongs to Everybody"	140
Thomas Jefferson, "The Declaration of Independence"	176
Elizabeth Cady Stanton, "Declaration of Sentiments and Resolutions"	181
Abraham Lincoln, "The Gettysburg Address"	186
John F. Kennedy, "Inaugural Address"	188
Martin Luther King, Jr., "I Have a Dream"	192
William Jefferson Clinton, "Inaugural Address"	197
Gloria Steinem, "Sex, Lies, and Advertising"	217
Barbara Ehrenreich, "Drawing the Line"	327
Bernard R. Goldberg, "Television Insults Men, Too"	404
Nat Hentoff, "'Speech Codes' on the Campus and Problems of Free Speech"	439
Caryl Rivers, "What Should Be Done about Rock Lyrics?"	451
Tipper Gore, "Curbing the Sexploitation Industry"	455
Frank Zappa, "The Wives of Big Brother"	459

CAUSE AND EFFECT ANALYSIS

George Orwell, "Politics and the English Language"	70
Dorothy Z. Seymour, "Black Children, Black Speech"	122
Neil Postman, "Now . . . This"	205

Consumers Union, "It's Natural! It's Organic! Or Is It?"   268
Itabari Njeri, "What's in a Name?"   345
Deborah Tannen, "'I'll Explain It to You': Lecturing and
  Listening"   389
Frank Zappa, "The Wives of Big Brother"   459

COMPARISON AND CONTRAST

Newman P. Birk and Genevieve B. Birk, "Selection, Slanting,
  and Charged Language"   47
Paul Roberts, "A Brief History of English"   89
David Crystal, "The Prescriptive Tradition"   101
Dorothy Z. Seymour, "Black Children, Black Speech"   122
Roberto Santiago, "Black *and* Latino"   342
Amy Tan, "The Language of Discretion"   352
Deborah Tannen, "'I'll Explain It to You': Lecturing and
  Listening"   389
Bernard R. Goldberg, "Television Insults Men, Too"   404
Maxine Hairston, "What Happens When People Write?"   471

DEFINITION

Victoria Fromkin and Robert Rodman, "What Is Language?"   25
Newman P. Birk and Genevieve B. Birk, "Selection, Slanting,
  and Charged Language"   47
William Lutz, "The World of Doublespeak"   59
Lance Morrow, "If Slang Is Not a Sin"   135
Consumers Union, "It's Natural! It's Organic! Or Is It?"   268
S. I. Hayakawa and Alan R. Hayakawa, "Words with Built-in
  Judgments"   298
Gloria Naylor, "The Meanings of a Word"   305
Rosalie Maggio, "A Guide to Nondiscriminatory Language"   309
Roberto Santiago, "Black *and* Latino"   342
Itabari Njeri, "What's in a Name?"   345
Neil Postman, "Euphemism"   413
Barbara Lawrence, "Four-Letter Words Can Hurt You"   422
Michael Callen, "AIDS: The Linguistic Battlefield"   426
William Zinsser, "Simplicity"   486

DESCRIPTION

Paul Roberts, "A Brief History of English"   89
Bill Bryson, "Order out of Chaos"   108
Dorothy Z. Seymour, "Black Children, Black Speech"   122
Ron Rosenbaum, "The Hard Sell"   257

DIVISION AND CLASSIFICATION

William Lutz, "The World of Doublespeak"   59
Donna Woolfolk Cross, "Propaganda: How Not to Be
  Bamboozled"   149

Jib Fowles, "Advertising's Fifteen Basic Appeals"   **231**
Rosalie Maggio, "A Guide to Nondiscriminatory Language"   **309**
Alleen Pace Nilsen, "Sexism in English: A 1990s Update"   **365**
S. I. Hayakawa and Alan R. Hayakawa, "Verbal Taboo"   **418**

EXAMPLE AND ILLUSTRATION

Peter Farb, "The Story of Human Language"   **17**
S. I. Hayakawa and Alan R. Hayakawa, "Giving Things
    Names"   **39**
Newman P. Birk and Genevieve B. Birk, "Selection, Slanting,
    and Charged Language"   **47**
William Lutz, "The World of Doublespeak"   **59**
David Crystal, "The Prescriptive Tradition"   **101**
Bill Bryson, "Order Out of Chaos"   **108**
Rachel L. Jones, "What's Wrong with Black English"   **131**
Lance Morrow, "If Slang Is Not a Sin"   **135**
Gloria Steinem, "Sex, Lies, and Advertising"   **217**
Jib Fowles, "Advertising's Fifteen Basic Appeals"   **231**
Jeffrey Schrank, "The Language of Advertising Claims"   **249**
Consumers Union, "It's Natural! It's Organic! Or Is It?"   **268**
Gordon Allport, "The Language of Prejudice"   **287**
Gloria Naylor, "The Meanings of a Word"   **305**
Rosalie Maggio, "A Guide to Nondiscriminatory Language"   **309**
Alleen Pace Nilsen, "Sexism in English: A 1990s Update"   **365**
Casey Miller and Kate Swift, "One Small Step for Genkind"   **377**
Deborah Tannen, "'I'll Explain It to You': Lecturing and
    Listening"   **389**
Neil Postman, "Euphemism"   **413**
S. I. Hayakawa and Alan R. Hayakawa, "Verbal Taboo"   **418**
William Zinsser, "Simplicity"   **486**

NARRATION

Malcom X, "Coming to an Awareness of Language"   **9**
Helen Keller, "The Day Language Came into My Life"   **13**
Paul Roberts, "A Brief History of English"   **89**
Peggy Noonan, "Speech! Speech!"   **160**
Gloria Naylor, "The Meanings of a Word"   **305**
Edite Cunha, "Talking in the New Land"   **331**
Amy Tan, "The Language of Discretion"   **352**

PROCESS ANALYSIS

Peggy Noonan, "Speech! Speech!"   **160**
Gordon Allport, "The Language of Prejudice"   **287**
Maxine Hairston, "What Happens When People Write?"   **471**
Jack Rawlins, "Five Principles for Getting Good Ideas"   **477**
Linda Flower, "Writing for an Audience"   **483**

GLOSSARY OF RHETORICAL TERMS

Abstract   See *Concrete/Abstract*.

Allusion   An allusion is a passing reference to a familiar person, place, or thing drawn from history, the Bible, mythology, or literature. An allusion is an economical way for a writer to capture the essence of an idea, atmosphere, emotion, or historical era, as in "The scandal was his Watergate," or "He saw himself as a modern Job," or "Everyone there held those truths to be self-evident." An allusion should be familiar to the reader, for if it is not, it will add nothing to the meaning.

Analogy   Analogy is a special form of comparison in which the writer explains something complex or unfamiliar by comparing it to something familiar: "A transmission line is simply a pipeline for electricity. In the case of a water pipeline, more water will flow through the pipe as water pressure increases. The same is true of a transmission line for electricity." When a subject is unobservable, complex, or abstract—when it is so generally unfamiliar that readers may have trouble understanding it—analogy is particularly useful.

Argument   Argument is one of the four basic types of prose. (Narration, description, and exposition are the other three.) To argue is to attempt to convince a reader to agree with a point of view, to make a given decision, or to pursue a particular course of action. Logical argument is based upon reasonable explanations and appeals to the reader's intelligence. See also *Persuasion, Logical Fallacies, Deduction,* and *Induction.*

Attitude   A writer's attitude reflects his or her opinion of a subject. For example, a writer can think very positively or very negatively about a subject. In most cases the writer's attitude falls somewhere between these two extremes. See also *Tone*.

Audience   An audience is the intended readership for a piece of writing. For example, the readers of a national weekly news magazine come from all walks of life and have diverse opinions, attitudes, and educational experiences. In contrast, the readership for an organic chemistry journal is made up of people whose interests and educations are quite similar. The essays in this book are intended for general readers, intelligent people who may lack specific information about the subjects being discussed.

Beginnings and Endings   A *beginning* is that sentence, group of sentences, or section that introduces the essay. Good beginnings usually identify the thesis or controlling idea, attempt to interest the reader, and establish a tone. Some effective ways in which writers begin essays include (1) telling an anecdote that illustrates the thesis, (2) providing a controversial statement or opinion that engages the reader's interest, (3) presenting startling statistics or facts, (4) defining a term that is central to the discussion that follows, (5) asking thought-provoking questions, (6) providing a quotation that illustrates the thesis, (7) referring to a current event that helps to establish the thesis, or (8) showing the significance of the subject or stressing its importance to the reader.

An *ending* is that sentence or group of sentences that brings an essay to closure. Good endings are purposeful and well planned. Endings satisfy readers when they are the natural outgrowths of the essays themselves and give the readers a sense of finality or completion. Good essays do not simply stop; they conclude.

Cause and Effect Analysis   Cause and effect analysis is one of the types of exposition. (Process analysis, definition, division and classification, and comparison and contrast are the others.) Cause and effect analysis answers the question *why*. It explains the reasons for an occurrence or the consequences of an action. Whenever a question asks *why*, answering it will require discovering a *cause* or series of causes for a particular *effect*; whenever a question asks *what if*, its answer will point out the effect or effects that can result from a particular cause.

Classification   See *Division and Classification*.

Cliché   A cliché is an expression that has become ineffective through overuse. Expressions such as *quick as a flash, dry as dust, jump for joy*, and *slow as molasses* are all clichés. Writers normally avoid such trite expressions and seek instead to express themselves in fresh and forceful language. See also *Figures of Speech*.

Coherence   Coherence is a quality of good writing that results when all sentences, paragraphs, and longer divisions of an essay are naturally connected. Coherent writing is achieved through (1) a logical sequence of ideas (arranged in chronological order, spatial order, order of importance, or some other appropriate order), (2) the thoughtful repetition of key words and ideas, (3) a pace suitable for your topic and your reader, and (4) the use of transitional words and expressions. Coherence should not be confused with unity. See also *Unity* and *Transitions*.

Colloquial Expressions   A colloquial expression is characteristic of or appropriate to spoken language or to writing that seeks its effect. Colloquial expressions are informal, as *chem, gym, come up with, be at loose ends, won't*, and *photo* illustrate. Thus, colloquial expressions are acceptable in formal writing only if they are used purposefully.

Comparison and Contrast   Comparison and contrast make up one of the types of exposition. (Process analysis, definition, division and classification, and cause and effect analysis are the others.) In comparison and contrast, the writer points out the similarities and differences between two or more subjects in the same class or category. The function of any comparison and contrast is to clarify—to reach some conclusion about the items being compared and contrasted. An effective comparison and contrast will not dwell on obvious similarities or differences; it will tell readers something significant that they may not already know.

Conclusions   See *Beginnings and Endings*.

Concrete/Abstract   A concrete word names a specific object, person, place, or action that can be directly perceived by the senses: *car, bread, building, book, John F. Kennedy, Chicago*, or *hiking*. An abstract word, in contrast, refers to general qualities, conditions, ideas, actions, or relationships which cannot be directly perceived by the senses: *bravery, dedication, excellence, anxiety, stress, thinking,* or *hatred.*

Although writers must use both concrete and abstract language, good writers avoid too many abstract words. Instead, they rely on concrete words to define and illustrate abstractions. Because concrete words affect the senses, they are easily comprehended by a reader.

Connotation/Denotation   Both connotation and denotation refer to the meanings of words. Denotation is the dictionary meaning of a word, the literal meaning. Connotation, on the other hand, is the implied or suggested meaning of a word. For example, the denotation of *lamb* is "a young sheep." The connotations of lamb are numerous: *gentle, docile, weak, peaceful, blessed, sacrificial, blood, spring, frisky, pure, innocent,* and so on. Good writers are sensitive to both the denotations and the connotations of words and use these meanings to advantage in their writing.

Deduction   Deduction is the process of reasoning from stated premises to a conclusion that follows necessarily. This form of reasoning moves from the general to the specific. See also *Syllogism.*

Definition   Definition is one of the types of exposition. (Process analysis, division and classification, comparison and contrast, and cause and effect analysis are the others.) Definition is a statement of the meaning of a word. A definition may be either brief or extended, part of an essay or an entire essay itself.

Denotation   See *Connotation/Denotation.*

Description   Description is one of the four basic types of prose. (Narration, exposition, and argument are the other three.) Description tells how a person, place, or thing is perceived by the five senses. Objective description reports these sensory qualities factually, whereas subjective description gives the writer's interpretation of them.

Diction   Diction refers to a writer's choice and use of words. Good diction is precise and appropriate—the words mean exactly what the writer intends, and the words are well suited to the writer's subject, intended audience, and purpose in writing. The word-conscious writer knows that there are differences among *aged, old,* and *elderly; blue, navy,* and *azure;* and *disturbed, angry,* and *irritated.* Furthermore, this writer knows in which situation to use each word. See also *Connotation/Denotation.*

Division and Classification   Division and classification make up one of the types of exposition. (Process analysis, definition, comparison and contrast, and cause and effect analysis are the others.) Division involves breaking down a single large unit into smaller subunits, or separating a group of items into discrete categories. Classification, on the other hand, involves arranging or sorting people, places, or things into categories according to their differing characteristics, thus making them more manageable for the writer and more understandable for the reader. Division, then, takes apart, while classification groups together. Although the two processes can operate separately, most often they work hand in hand.

Endings   See *Beginnings and Endings.*

Essay   An essay is a relatively short piece of nonfiction in which the writer attempts to make one or more closely related points. A good essay is purposeful, informative, and well organized.

Evidence   Evidence is the data on which a judgment or argument is based or by which proof or probability is established. Evidence usually takes the form of statistics, facts, names, examples or illustrations, and opinions of authorities.

Examples Examples illustrate a larger idea or represent something of which they are a part. An example is a basic means of developing or clarifying an idea. Furthermore, examples enable writers to show and not simply to tell readers what they mean. The terms *example* and *illustration* are sometimes used interchangeably. An example may be anything from a statistic to a story; it may be stated in a few words or go on for several pages. What is required of an example is that it be closely *relevant* to the idea or generalization it is meant to illustrate. To be most effective, an example should be *representative*. The story it tells or the fact it presents should be typical of many others that readers are sure to be familiar with.

Exposition Exposition is one of the four basic types of prose. (Narration, description, and argument are the other three.) The purpose of exposition is to clarify, explain, and inform. The methods of exposition are process analysis, definition, division and classification, comparison and contrast, and cause and effect analysis. For a detailed discussion of each of these methods of exposition, see the appropriate entries in this glossary.

Fallacy See *Logical Fallacies*.

Figures of Speech Figures of speech are brief, imaginative comparisons which highlight the similarities between things that are basically dissimilar. They make writing vivid and interesting and therefore more memorable. The most common figures of speech are:

Simile: An implicit comparison introduced by *like* or *as*. "The fighter's hands were like stone."

Metaphor: An implied comparison which uses one thing as the equivalent of another. "All the world's a stage."

Personification: A special kind of simile or metaphor in which human traits are assigned to an inanimate object. "The engine coughed and then stopped."

Idiom An idiom is a word or phrase that is used habitually with a particular meaning in a language. The meaning of an idiom is not always readily apparent to nonnative speakers of that language. For example, *catch cold, hold a job, make up your mind*, and *give them a hand* are all idioms in English.

Illustration See *Examples*.

Induction Induction is the process of reasoning to a conclusion about all members of a class through an examination of only a few members of the class. This form of reasoning moves from a set of specific examples to a general statement or principle. As long as the evidence is accurate, pertinent, complete, and sufficient to represent the assertion, the conclusion of the inductive argument can be regarded as valid; if, however, you can spot inaccuracies in the evidence or point to contrary evidence, you have good reason to doubt the assertion as it stands. Inductive reasoning is the most common of argumentative structures. See also *Deduction*.

Introductions See *Beginnings and Endings*.

Irony The use of words to suggest something different from their literal meaning. A writer can use irony to establish a special relationship with the reader and to add an extra dimension or twist to the meaning.

Jargon See *Technical Language*.

Logical Fallacies   A logical fallacy is an error in reasoning that renders an argument invalid. Some of the more common logical fallacies are:

Oversimplification: The tendency to provide simple solutions to complex problems. "The reason we have inflation today is that OPEC has unreasonably raised the price of oil."

Non sequitur ("It does not follow"): An inference or conclusion that does not follow from established premises or evidence. "It was the best movie I saw this year, and it should get an Academy Award."

Post hoc, ergo propter hoc ("After this, therefore because of this"): Confusing chance or coincidence with causation. Because one event comes after another one, it does not necessarily mean that the first event caused the second. "I won't say I caught cold at the hockey game, but I certainly didn't have it before I went there."

Begging the question: Assuming in a premise that which needs to be proven. "If American autoworkers built a better product, foreign auto sales would not be so high."

False analogy: Making a misleading analogy between logically unconnected ideas. "He was a brilliant basketball player; therefore, there's no question in my mind that he will be a fine coach."

Either/or thinking: The tendency to see an issue as having only two sides. "Used car salesmen are either honest or crooked."

Logical Reasoning   See *Deduction* and *Induction*.

Metaphor   See *Figures of Speech*.

Narration   One of the four basic types of prose. (Description, exposition, and argument are the other three.) To narrate is to tell a story, to tell what happened. While narration is most often used in fiction, it is also important in nonfiction, either by itself or in conjunction with other types of prose. A good narrative essay has four essential features. The first is *context*: the writer makes clear when the action happened, where it happened, and to whom. The second is *point of view*: the writer establishes and maintains a consistent relationship to the action, either as a participant or as a reporter simply looking on. The third is *selection of detail*: the writer carefully chooses what to include, focusing on those actions and details that are most important to the story while merely mentioning or actually eliminating others. The fourth is *organization*: the writer organizes the events of the narrative into an appropriate sequence, often a strict chronology with a clear beginning, middle, and end.

Objective/Subjective   Objective writing is factual and impersonal, whereas subjective writing, sometimes called impressionistic, relies heavily on personal interpretation.

Organization   In writing, organization is the thoughtful arrangement and presentation of one's points or ideas. Narration is often organized chronologically. Exposition may be organized from simplest to most complex or from most familiar to least familiar. Argument may be organized from least important to most important. There is no single correct pattern of organization for a given piece of writing, but good writers are careful to discover an order of presentation suitable for their subject, their audience, and their purpose.

Paradox   A paradox is a seemingly contradictory statement that may nonetheless be true. For example, *we little know what we have until we lose it* is a paradoxical statement.

Paragraph The paragraph, the single most important unit of thought in an essay, is a series of closely related sentences. These sentences adequately develop the central or controlling idea of the paragraph. This central or controlling idea, usually stated in a topic sentence, is necessarily related to the purpose of the whole composition. A well-written paragraph has several distinguishing characteristics: a clearly stated or implied topic sentence, adequate development, unity, coherence, and an appropriate organizational strategy.

Personification See *Figures of Speech*.

Persuasion Persuasion, or persuasive argument, is an attempt to convince readers to agree with a point of view, to make a given decision, or to pursue a particular course of action. Persuasion heavily appeals to the emotions whereas logical argument does not. See *Argument, Induction*, and *Deduction*.

Point of View Point of view refers to the grammatical person of the speaker in an essay. For example, a first-person point of view uses the pronoun *I* and is commonly found in autobiography and the personal essay; a third-person point of view uses the pronouns *he, she*, or *it* and is commonly found in objective writing.

Process Analysis Process analysis is a type of exposition. (Definition, division and classification, comparison and contrast, and cause and effect analysis are others.) Process analysis answers the question *how* and explains how something works or gives step-by-step directions for doing something.

Purpose Purpose is what the writer wants to accomplish in a particular piece of writing. Purposeful writing seeks to *relate* or *tell* (narration), to *describe* (description), to *explain* (process analysis, definition, division and classification, comparison and contrast, and cause and effect analysis), or to *convince* (argument).

Rhetorical Questions A rhetorical question is asked but requires no answer from the reader. "When will nuclear proliferation end?" is such a question. Writers use rhetorical questions to introduce topics they plan to discuss or to emphasize important points.

Simile See *Figures of Speech*.

Slang Slang is the unconventional, very informal language of particular subgroups in our culture. Slang, such as *zonk, coke, split, rap, cop*, and *stoned*, is acceptable in formal writing only if it is used purposefully.

Specific/General General words name groups or classes of objects, qualities, or actions. Specific words, on the other hand, name individual objects, qualities, or actions within a class or group. To some extent the terms *general* and *specific* are relative. For example, *dessert* is a class of things. *Pie*, however, is more specific than *dessert* but more general than *pecan pie* or *chocolate cream pie*.

Good writing judiciously balances the general with the specific. Writing with too many general words is likely to be dull and lifeless. General words do not create vivid responses in the reader's mind as concrete specific words can. On the other hand, writing that relies exclusively on specific words may lack focus and direction, the control that more general statements provide.

Style Style is the individual manner in which a writer expresses his or her ideas. Style is created by the author's particular selection of words, construction of sentences, and arrangement of ideas.

Subjective See *Objective/Subjective*.

Syllogism   A syllogism is an argument that utilizes deductive reasoning and consists of a major premise, a minor premise, and a conclusion. For example,
All trees that lose leaves are deciduous. (major premise)
Maple trees lose their leaves. (minor premise)
Therefore, maple trees are deciduous. (conclusion)
See also *Deduction*.

Symbol   A symbol is a person, place, or thing that represents something beyond itself. For example, the eagle is a symbol of America, and the bear, a symbol of Russia.

Syntax   Syntax refers to the way in which words are arranged to form phrases, clauses, and sentences as well as to the grammatical relationship among the words themselves.

Technical Language   Technical language is the special vocabulary of a trade or profession. Writers who use technical language do so with an awareness of their audiences. If the audience is a group of peers, technical language may be used freely. If the audience is a more general one, technical language should be used sparingly and carefully so as not to sacrifice clarity. Technical language that is used only to impress, hide the truth, or cover insecurities is termed *jargon* and is not condoned. See *Diction*.

Thesis   A thesis is a statement of the main idea of an essay. Also known as the controlling idea, a thesis may sometimes be implied rather than stated directly.

Tone   Tone is the manner in which a writer relates to an audience, the "tone of voice" used to address readers. Tone may be described as friendly, serious, distant, angry, cheerful, bitter, cynical, enthusiastic, morbid, resentful, warm, playful, and so forth. A particular tone results from a writer's diction, sentence structure, purpose, and attitude toward the subject. See also *Attitude*.

Topic Sentence   The topic sentence states the central idea of a paragraph and thus limits and controls the subject of the paragraph. Although the topic sentence normally appears at the beginning of the paragraph, it may appear at any other point, particularly if the writer is trying to create a special effect. Also see *Paragraph*.

Transitions   Transitions are words or phrases that link sentences, paragraphs, and larger units of a composition in order to achieve coherence. These devices include parallelism, pronoun references, conjunctions, and the repetition of key ideas, as well as the many unconventional transitional expressions such as *moreover, on the other hand, in addition, in contrast*, and *therefore*. Also see *Coherence*.

Unity   Unity is achieved in an essay when all the words, sentences, and paragraphs contribute to its thesis. The elements of a unified essay do not distract the reader. Instead, they all harmoniously support a single idea or purpose.

TOPICS FOR
RESEARCH PAPERS

The following is a list of suggested research-paper topics. Because each topic is broad, you will need to limit and focus the subject you choose for your paper.

1. the language of college catalogues
2. how children learn language
3. the differences between the language of men and the language of women
4. the history of English
5. stereotyping in the language of cartoons
6. the values conveyed by song lyrics
7. the language of political propaganda
8. names and naming: people, places, or things
9. advertising and children
10. the language of the funeral industry: death, dying, or burial
11. insults, taunts, and jeers
12. language and violence
13. advertising jingles and slogans
14. curses and obscenities
15. censorship
16. Bowdler and bowdlerization
17. the Sapir-Whorf hypothesis
18. college slang on your campus
19. sports jargon
20. language games (such as pig Latin, rhyming slang, and "op" languages)
21. the language of menus
22. prescription vs. description in language study
23. public doublespeak
24. nonverbal communication
25. medical jargon: the language of doctors, dentists, and nurses
26. the English-only movement
27. gender bias in the media
28. problems of translation
29. problems in learning a second language
30. words in English borrowed from other languages
31. social or regional dialect variations
32. the language of legal documents (such as insurance policies, sales agreements, and leases)
33. language in women's magazines and in men's magazines
34. body language and advertising
35. the jargon of a subculture
36. how a dictionary is made

37. advertising techniques today and fifty years ago
38. English as a world language
39. contemporary propaganda
40. defining good writing
41. African-American slang
42. the language of news reporting
43. gay slang
44. nicknames
45. etymologies
46. slips of the tongue and other bloopers
47. contemporary euphemisms
48. prejudice and language
49. parody
50. verbal taboos in America
51. a sampling and analysis of vogue words
52. how language began
53. standard vs. nonstandard English
54. bilingualism
55. sign language
56. animal communication
57. medical jargon
58. the history of (and precursors to) rap
59. differing interpretations of the right to freedom of speech

ACKNOWLEDGMENTS (*continued from page iv*)

Crystal, David. From "The Prescriptive Tradition." In *The Cambridge Encyclopedia of Language* by David Crystal. Reprinted by permission of Cambridge University Press.

Cunha, Edite. "Talking in the New Land." By Edite Cunha in *The New England Monthly*, August 1990. Reprinted by permission of the author.

Ehrenreich, Barbara. "Drawing the Line." By Barbara Ehrenreich in *Mother Jones Magazine*, 1989. Copyright © 1989 by the Foundation for National Progress. Reprinted by permission.

Farb, Peter. "The Story of Human Language." From *Word Play: What Happens When People Talk* by Peter Farb. Copyright © 1973 by Peter Farb. Reprinted by permission of Alfred A. Knopf, Inc.

Flower, Linda. "Writing for an Audience." Excerpt from *Problem-Solving Strategies for Writing*, Fourth Edition, by Linda Flower, copyright © 1993 by Harcourt Brace & Company, reprinted by permission of the publisher.

Fowles, Jib. "Advertising's Fifteen Basic Appeals." By Jib Fowles. Reprinted from *Etc.* Volume 39 Number 3 by permission of the International Society for General Semantics.

Fromkin, Victoria, and Robert Rodman. "What Is Language? From *An Introduction to Language*, Fourth Edition, by Victoria A. Fromkin and Robert Rodman, copyright © 1988 by Holt, Rinehart and Winston, Inc., reprinted by permission of the publisher.

Goldberg, Bernard R. "Television Insults Men, Too." By Bernard R. Goldberg in the *New York Times*, March 14, 1989. Copyright © 1989 by The New York Times Company. Reprinted by permission.

Gore, Tipper. "Curbing the Sexploitation Industry." By Tipper Gore in the *New York Times*, March 14, 1988. Copyright © 1988 by The New York Times Company. Reprinted by permission.

Hairston, Maxine. "What Happens When People Write?" Reprinted from *Successful Writing*, Third Edition, by Maxine C. Hairston, by permission of W. W. Norton & Company, Inc., Copyright © 1992, 1986, 1981 by Maxine C. Hairston.

Hayakawa, S. I., and Alan R. Hayakawa. "Verbal Taboo," "Words with Built-in Judgments," and "Giving Things Names." Excerpts from *Language in Thought and Action*, Fifth Edition, by S. I. Hayakawa and Alan R. Hayakawa, copyright © 1990 by Harcourt Brace & Company, reprinted by permission of the publisher.

Hentoff, Nat. "'Speech Codes' on the Campus and Problems of Free Speech." By Nat Hentoff in *Dissent*, Fall 1991. Reprinted by permission of the author.

Hunt-Wesson, Inc. Ad. Reprinted by permission of Hunt-Wesson, Inc.

Jacoby, Susan. "Notes from a Free-Speech Junkie." By Susan Jacoby in the *New York Times*, January 26, 1978. Copyright © 1980 by Susan Jacoby. Reprinted by permission of Georges Borchardt, Inc. for the author.

Jones, Rachel L. "What's Wrong with Black English." Reprinted by permission of the author.

King, Martin Luther, Jr. "I Have a Dream." By Martin Luther King, Jr. Copyright © 1963 by Martin Luther King, Jr., copyright renewed 1991 by Coretta Scott King.

Lawrence, Barbara. "Four-Letter Words Can Hurt You." By Barbara Lawrence in the *New York Times*, October 27, 1973. Copyright © 1973 by The New York Times Company. Reprinted by permission.

Lutz, William. "The World of Doublespeak." By William Lutz in Christopher Ricks and Leonard Michaels, *State of the Language*, 1990 ed., pages 254–264. Copyright © 1989 The Regents of the University of California. Reprinted by permission.

MacNeil, Robert. "English Belongs to Everybody." From *Wordstruck* by Robert MacNeil. Copyright © 1989 by Neely Productions, Ltd. Used by permission of Viking Penguin, a division of Penguin Books USA Inc.

Maggio, Rosalie. "A Guide to Nondiscriminatory Language." Reprinted from *The Dictionary of Bias-Free Usage: Guide to Nondiscriminatory Language* by Rosalie Maggio. Copyright © 1991 by Rosalie Maggio. Published by The Oryx Press. Used by permission of Rosalie Maggio and The Oryx Press.

Malcolm X. "Coming to an Awareness of Language." From *The Autobiography of Malcolm X* by Malcolm X with Alex Haley. Copyright © 1964 by Alex Haley and Malcolm X. Copyright © 1965 by Alex Haley and Betty Shabazz. Reprinted by permission of Random House, Inc.

Miller, Casey, and Kate Swift. "One Small Step for Genkind." By Casey Miller and Kate Swift in the *New York Times*, April 16, 1972. Copyright © 1972 by Casey Miller and Kate Swift. Reprinted by permission of the authors.

Morrow, Lance, "If Slang Is Not a Sin." By Lance Morrow in *Time*, Novermber 1982. Copyright © 1982 Time Inc. Reprinted by permission.

Mutual of America. Ad. Reprinted by permission of Mutual of America.

Naylor, Gloria. "The Meanings of a Word." By Gloria Naylor. Copyright © 1986 by Gloria Naylor. Reprinted by permission of Sterling Lord Literistic, Inc.

Nilsen, Alleen Pace. "Sexism in English: A 1990s Update." From "Sexism in English: A Feminist View" by Alleen Pace Nilsen from the book *Female Studies VI: Closer to the Ground: Women's Classes, Criticism, Programs—1972*, eds., Nancy Hoffman, Cynthia Secor, Adrian Tinsley. Copyright © 1972 by Nancy Hoffman, Cynthia Secor, Adrian Tinsley. Updated for this text by the author. Reprinted with permission of Alleen Pace Nilsen.

Njeri, Itabari. "What's in a Name?" From *Every Good-bye Ain't Gone* by Itabari Njeri. Copyright © 1990 by Itabari Njeri. Reprinted by permission of Time Books, a Division of Random House, Inc.

Noonan, Peggy. "Speech! Speech!" From *What I Saw at the Revolution* by Peggy Noonan. Copyright © 1989 by Peggy Noonan. Reprinted by permission of Random House, Inc.

Orwell, George. "Politics and the English Language." By George Orwell, copyright 1946 by Sonia Brownell Orwell and renewed 1974 by Sonia Orwell, reprinted from his volume *Shooting an Elephant and Other Essays* by permission of Harcourt Brace & Company and the estate of the late Sonia Brownell Orwell and Martin Secker & Warburg Ltd.

Postman, Neil. From "Euphemism." In *Crazy Talk, Stupid Talk* by Neil Postman. Copyright © 1976 by Neil Postman. Reprinted by permission of the author.

Postman, Neil. "Now . . . This." From *Amusing Ourselves to Death* by Neil Postman. Copyright © 1985 by Neil Postman. Used by permission of Viking Penguin, a division of Penguin Books USA Inc.

Rawlins, Jack. "Five Principles for Getting Good Ideas." From *The Writer's Way*, Second Edition. Copyright © 1992 by Houghton Mifflin Company. Used by permission.

Rivers, Caryl. "What Should Be Done about Rock Lyrics?" By Caryl Rivers in the *Boston Globe*, September 15, 1985. Reprinted by permission of the author.

Roberts, Paul. "A Brief History of English." From *Understanding English* by Paul Roberts. Copyright © 1958 by Paul Roberts. Reprinted by permission of HarperCollins Publishers.